The Psychology of Language

The Psychology of Language

PAUL WHITNEY

Washington State University

HOUGHTON MIFFLIN COMPANY
Boston   New York

For Marion Marchand and Chelsea Nicole,
my bookends

Sponsoring Editor: David C. Lee
Senior Associate Editor: Jane Knetzger
Senior Project Editor: Christina M. Horn
Senior Production/Design Coordinator: Carol Merrigan
Senior Manufacturing Coordinator: Sally Culler
Marketing Manager: Pamela Laskey

Cover design: Harold Burch, Harold Burch Design, New York.
Cover image: Harold Burch, Harold Burch Design, New York.

Photo and text credits begin on page A-35.

Copyright © 1998 by Houghton Mifflin Company. All rights reserved.

No part of this work may be reproduced or transmitted in any form or by any means, electronic or mechanical, including photocopying and recording, or by any information storage or retrieval system without the prior written permission of Houghton Mifflin Company unless such copying is expressly permitted by federal copyright law. Address inquiries to College Permissions, Houghton Mifflin Company, 222 Berkeley Street, Boston MA 02116-3764.

Printed in the U.S.A.

Library of Congress Catalog Number: 97-72560

ISBN: 0-395-75750-9

1 2 3 4 5 6 7 8 9-QF-01 00 99 98 97

BRIEF CONTENTS

CONTENTS

UNIT THREE   *Language and the Brain* 301

PREFACE

While I was teaching an introductory psychology class for the honors program at my university, I encountered a bright student who seemed awfully jaded for one so young. I recall his definition of academia: "A place where very intelligent people take intrinsically interesting information and make it as boring as they possibly can." Though few students would be willing to state this opinion so baldly, at least in class, I suspect that many would agree with the sentiment expressed. From the other side, I frequently hear professors comment on the downward spiral of textbooks, as authors struggle to engage students' interest by watering down the content. Indeed, both sides of this debate can offer examples in support of their gloom. My own view, however, is that each side misunderstands the other. "Boring" typically means "I don't understand enough about this to see why it is interesting." And "uninterested" often refers to students who have been given a lot of "facts" without the context to relate them to anything they can understand. Bridging this gulf is something that skilled teachers do well; but it is a difficult chore, and one in which textbook authors should serve as a partner to both the teacher and the student.

I wrote this book because of my own feeling that no existing text on psycholinguistics was adequately bridging the gulf between instructors and students. In addition, a growing number of psychology departments offer upper-level undergraduate surveys and graduate seminars in psycholinguistics, and I have heard instructors at several of these institutions express frustration over their inability to find a text that strikes the appropriate balance between depth of coverage and clarity of explanation.

My overarching goal in writing *The Psychology of Language* was to place the study of language within the contexts of the cognitive, social, and biological processes that make language the remarkably useful tool that it is. When the study of language is placed in these contexts, it is easier to see not only *what* psycholinguists study but also *why* we study these things. Moreover, I wanted to communicate not just what is unique about language but also how our language system must constantly and smoothly interact with perception, memory, and reasoning within a brain that has powerful, but limited, processing capacities. Seeing how all the processes work together gives me a sense of wonder, which, I believe, is one of the most important outcomes of education and investigation. This book is an attempt to help others get at least some of the same sense of wonder.

That's the big picture. But to have some hope of accomplishing my main goal, I also had to have subgoals. That is, I had to have some specific objectives in mind for the book as a whole. I think of these objectives as falling into two categories, corresponding to the time-honored distinction between declarative and procedural knowledge. In other words, there are both *facts* and *skills* that I believe students should possess after studying psycholinguistics. Following are the factual objectives I want students to achieve:

- *Understand the universal characteristics of all languages.* Specifically, students should be able to describe both the rule-based nature of language and the semantic aspect of language. This ability, in turn, requires that students understand how to distinguish between language and communication, and, in order to appreciate different approaches to rules and representations, that they have some familiarity with the distinction between symbolic and connectionist models.

- *Place language in its cognitive context.* In particular, students should be able to discuss how language processes interact with perceptual, memory, and reasoning abilities.

- *Place language in its biological context.* That is, students should be able to describe different views of the biological factors at work both in the origin of language in our species and in the acquisition of language by individuals. Students should also understand the key role that cognitive processing models play in determining how language functions are localized in the brain.

- *Place language in its social context.* Specifically, students should be able to describe how language shapes, and is shaped by, social interaction and cultural forces.

These are the skills objectives I want students to achieve:

- *Use empirical evidence to defend or refute an argument about the nature of language processing.* I find that students need practice at distinguishing among opinions, logical arguments, and empirical evidence. Moreover, I think it is important that students develop the habit of evaluating a hypothesis by looking at the weight of evidence on both sides. I have tried to foster that habit by organizing each of the chapters in *The Psychology of Language* around a hypothesis to be evaluated.

- *Apply ideas from basic research to come up with potential problem solutions.* At several points throughout the text, I comment on how basic research has led to practical applications. In addition, the book contains several special features, discussed below, that are designed to generate insights into the research process—especially in terms of its importance to answering questions, both basic and applied.

To help students master these objectives, I have organized the topics in the book into three units, each building logically on the prior one. The major purpose of Unit One, "Language and Its Functions," is to raise the major questions that are addressed in the rest of the book and thereby provide the necessary background for understanding psychological models of language processing. This unit is composed of four chapters. The first chapter begins . . . at the beginning. Specifically, it addresses, in evolutionary terms, the issue of what language is, how it developed in our species, and whether it is a uniquely human ability. The second chapter follows this discussion with an overview of linguistics, detailing how linguistics research has influenced the idea that language is not only uniquely human but also a special mental ability that operates differently from the rest of our cognitive functions. The third chapter provides balance to the question of the "specialness" of language by providing an overview of the major components of our cognitive system with which language processes must interact. And the fourth chapter builds on the issue of how cognition and language are related by addressing the directions of influence between thought and language. Going beyond the traditional question of "Can our language influence the way we think?" this chapter addresses new research in both cognitive and social psychology that shows just how interdependent language, memory, and reasoning are.

Unit Two, "Models of Language Processing," presents processing models of the mental activities that underlie language. Along the way, I consider, and reconsider, the evidence regarding whether particular language processes operate relatively autonomously or whether they depend heavily on general cognitive mechanisms. I focus on spoken and visual word recognition in Chapters 5 and 6, sentence processing in Chapter 7, and the processing of connected discourse in Chapter 8. Then, in Chapter 9, I explore language production in the contexts of conversations and writing. A unique feature of the presentation across these chapters is that they show how the ambiguity of language (including ambiguity over whether an utterance is intended figuratively or literally) runs as a central theme through psycholinguistics research. The same chapters also illustrate how research on individual differences in language processing can be useful in terms of both practical applications *and* the testing of general theories.

Unit Three, "Language and the Brain," uses the general conclusions from the first two units as a guide to exploring the biological basis of language. Specifically, Chapters 10 and 11 address the question raised in the very first chapter: *Just how "special" is language as a human ability?* I explore this question by assessing, on the basis of both normative and atypical language development, how much of our language ability is "built in." Along the way, I compare the developmental courses of signed and spoken languages, discuss second-language acquisition, and consider what we can learn from language disturbances associated with particular developmental disorders. Finally, in Chapter 12, I examine the implications of the material covered in Units One and Two for the question of how language processes are localized in the brain. This chapter includes an up-to-date discussion of the research on both brain lesions and neuro-imaging techniques of language functions. Such research is revolutionizing our understanding of the relationship between the brain and language, and challenging a model of brain-language relationships that has been accepted since the turn of the century.

To effectively build on the key themes throughout the book, I conclude each of the three units with a reprise that reviews the major questions and answers that run through the unit as a whole. And as noted earlier, each chapter contains special features designed to help students master the course objectives:

- Chapter outlines encourage students to follow the connections among the different topics in each chapter.

- Activity boxes allow students not only to try out adaptations of classic experiments but also to observe important phenomena in action.

- Each chapter is organized around a hypothesis that students can evaluate as the material is read and then can reevaluate in a conclusion section that ties together different threads of evidence relevant to the hypothesis.

- Each chapter ends with a list of key terms (defined in the glossary), a series of review questions, and suggestions regarding projects and thought experiments in a special "On Further Reflection . . ." section.

An ancillary consisting of an instructor's manual and test bank is available to accompany the text. The manual provides demonstration ideas and discussion topics; it also identifies useful websites for students to explore. The test bank contains more than 400 multiple-choice and essay questions. In addition, both students and instructors can make use of Houghton Mifflin's psychology website, which they can locate by going first to http://www.hmco.com and then to the College Division Psychology page. This website provides access to useful and innovative teaching and learning resources that complement and support the text.

My hope is that both instructors and students will find this package of resources to be a useful partner in the teaching and learning process. In fact, I welcome input from anyone who uses this book, whether to tell me what worked well or to tell me what didn't. Readers can reach me via e-mail at pwhitney@mail.wsu.edu.

In closing, I must note that a great many people helped make this text possible. Everyone at Houghton Mifflin has been a pleasure to work with, but I have particularly benefited from the skills and insights of my editor, Jane Knetzger. A number of my colleagues and students at Washington State University have also helped me in many ways, from reading drafts and proofs to keeping my research program going despite the lack of attention I was able to give it while writing this book. I thank you all. In addition, my efforts were improved by several very fine outside reviewers who provided thorough and conscientious feedback on each draft of each chapter. My sincere thanks go to the following:

Thomas Allaway, Algoma University College

Susan Garnsey, University of Illinois

Gail M. Gottfried, Occidental College

Kenneth D. Kallio, State University of New York at Geneseo

Kerry Kilborn, University of Glasgow

Susan D. Lima, University of Wisconsin at Milwaukee

William R. Smith, California State University at Fullerton

Aimée Surprenant, Purdue University

Rolf A. Zwaan, Florida State University

Finally, I thank my family for their support during this extraordinarily time-consuming project. My wife, Diana, has not only a keen editorial eye but also a very sustaining faith in the value of doing one's best to teach clearly and effectively.

Paul Whitney

UNIT ONE

Language and Its Functions

CHAPTER 1

The Nature of Language

*I*f people who talk to themselves are "crazy," then we're all crazy. No one uses language exclusively as a tool for communicating thoughts to other people. We talk to ourselves to work out problems. We talk to ourselves to rehearse things we want to remember. In fact, language is so intimately bound up with *what it means to be human* that understanding language is a large part of understanding people—how our minds operate, how we learn and develop, and how we make the decisions that shape our lives and determine world events. To clarify this point, let's examine the following hypothesis: *Whereas all organisms pass on information to other members of their species, only humans use language.*

You may find the first part of this hypothesis questionable. What about bacteria? Do they pass on information to other bacteria? Yes, but only in the sense that they pass on their genetic code when they reproduce. This is a limited kind of "communication": Only information that can be encoded into genetic instructions can be passed on.

It is the second part of the hypothesis that many people undoubtedly find even more questionable. Is language really unique to humans? After all, many organisms can communicate that they are hurt, or feel threatened, or are receptive to a mate. Is this all that different from humans' use of language? Consider the animals that use a vocal system to communicate a very specific idea. Vervet monkeys, for example, tell other members of their group when a leopard is present by giving a distinctive "leopard call." And when a python or an eagle is approaching, they use different calls (Seyfarth, Cheney & Marler, 1980).

To determine whether a particular form of animal communication is fundamentally different from human language, we have to consider what language really is. Certainly, each specific human language is a system for communication, but human languages have more in common than that general goal. For example, all languages have words that serve as symbols for objects. But words, by themselves, may not seem that different from the different calls used by vervet monkeys to signal different predators. Another very important common feature of all human languages is that they have systems of rules for combining words into sentences. It is not obvious that any other animal communicates with such a rule-governed system. However, before we decide that language is a uniquely human ability, we have to take a closer look at the features of language, and at whether these features are shared by other forms of communication.

Two areas of inquiry are especially useful for helping us to define language and its place among human (and nonhuman) abilities. First, we will consider what is known about how language originated as humans evolved. Second, we will compare language with other forms of animal communication. Third, having examined this evidence, we will be ready to evaluate the hypothesis stated above, and then to explore the methods by which language use can be studied as a part of the broader field of psychology. Finally, we will investigate different ways of approaching the study of language that are relevant to psychology.

Language Origins, Human Origins

An Overview of Human Evolution

There is much uncertainty about both the evolution of humans and the development of language within our species. However, the broad outlines of human origins are fairly clear. An overview of human evolution is depicted in Figure 1.1. The time course of human evolution—that is, the period since our lineage separated from other primate lines—encompasses approximately seven million years.* In the last four million years, several hominid species emerged and coexisted, but only our species, *homo sapiens,* exists today. As shown in the figure, anatomically modern humans first appeared about 150,000 years ago (Stringer & Andrews, 1988). Virtually all of what we would call technological advancement has occurred in only the last 40,000 years. Thus, modern humans—in particular technologically advanced modern humans—are a very recent occurrence in historical terms.

These basic facts present us with an interesting puzzle. Why do we see a such a sudden change in the genus *homo*? How did we become the technological and cultural species that we are over such a short span of time? A possible resolution to this puzzle is that language developed quite recently in human evolution. Indeed, its emergence rather late in evolution would help explain why the behavior of modern humans seems so different from our ancestors and other primates. Language could have allowed for efficiency in communication that, in turn, could have increased cooperation among members of a group. The connection between language evolution and the rather sudden appearance of technological progress, though only speculative at present, is certainly plausible. Richard Leakey (1994), a foremost authority on the fossil record of human evolution, put it this way:

> There is no question that the evolution of spoken language as we know it was a defining point in human prehistory. Perhaps it was *the* defining point. Equipped with language, humans were able to create new kinds of worlds in nature: the world of introspective consciousness and the world we manufacture and share with others, which we call "culture." *(p. 119)*

Language made culture possible, and it may also have revolutionized thought. As we will examine in detail later in this chapter, language is a system that allows for an abstract and flexible means of representing facts about the world and, hence, may account for our ability to entertain hypothetical notions. These thinking skills, coupled with the communicative power of language, may have given our species quite a competitive edge.

One thread of evidence for late evolution of a sophisticated version of spoken language comes from a comparative analysis of vocal tracts. According to Lieberman (1991), the vocal apparatus in modern humans is specially adapted for language (see

---

* A common misconception about the theory of evolution is that it states that humans evolved from apes. Actually, neither Charles Darwin nor any reputable modern biologist made any such claim. What Darwin said is that apes and humans have a common ancestor, a claim well-supported by fossil and genetic evidence (e.g., Leakey, 1994).

FIGURE 1.1   **A Brief History of Human Evolution**

Creatures similar to modern humans began to appear almost four million years ago, but anatomically modern humans appeared only recently. The skulls of several key hominid species are shown here to illustrate changes in the cranium during human evolution. Note especially how the skull becomes more rounded to accommodate larger areas on the side and front of the brain.

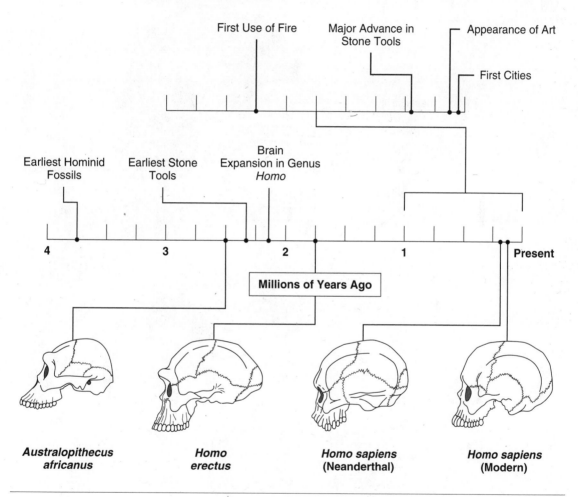

Australopithecus africanus · *Homo erectus* · *Homo sapiens (Neanderthal)* · *Homo sapiens (Modern)*

Figure 1.2). Modern humans have a short rounded tongue, and our larynx, or voice box, is lower in the throat than that of any other species. This particular arrangement allows us to produce a wide variety of speech sounds. However, it comes with a considerable cost. Did you ever wonder why so many of us have mouths so crowded with teeth that we need to have our wisdom teeth surgically removed? This circumstance is not a devious plot perpetrated by greedy oral surgeons. Our mouths really are crowded, and the reason seems to be that the vocal tract was radically redesigned

FIGURE 1.2   **Human and Chimpanzee Vocal Tracts**

Shown here is the air passage of a chimpanzee compared with that of a human. The shorter jaw, the rounded tongue, and the lower larynx position in the human are adaptations for speech, but these adaptations have disadvantages as well.

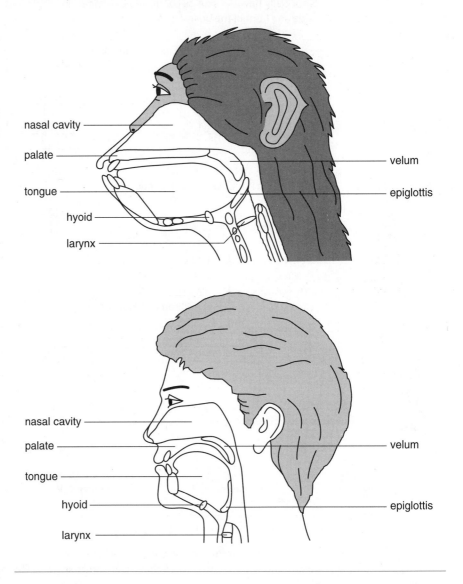

by evolutionary trends that favored speech. The downside of these trends is that our jaws have shortened, thereby crowding our teeth. In addition, humans are at greater risk of choking than are other animals. The positioning of our larynx is such that food is much more likely to fall into it and block the air passage to our lungs.

Lieberman (1991) has used fossil data to make reasonable guesses about the vocal tract of Neanderthals. There is considerable doubt as to whether even that relatively modern hominid could produce the wide variety of speech sounds found in today's spoken languages (but see Deacon, 1992, for an opposing view). Of course, Lieberman's conclusions about the human vocal tract refer to refinements of our capacity for speech. But there is much more to language than being able to produce a variety of sounds. Other aspects of our language ability may have developed gradually over a longer period of time as the brain size of modern hominids increased. Thus, although the articulate speech we see in modern humans may be a very recent development, it is quite possible that language as a whole developed over millions of years. Opinions among those interested in language origins are quite divided on this issue.

Theories of Language Evolution: Continuity or Discontinuity?

There are several different disciplines that study language. **Anthropologists** are interested in, among other things, the role of language in early human evolution. And when anthropologists devise theories of language evolution, they look to at least two other disciplines for evidence: Scientists who study the biology and behavior of primates, **primatologists,** contribute information about communication and thinking in our closest existing animal relatives; and **linguists** study the nature of language, focusing, for example, on the rules governing the organization of words into sentences. Indeed, without a linguistic description of the nature of language in general, it is difficult even to speculate about how language might have evolved.

In general, theorists who rely more on evidence from primatology tend to take a **continuity view** of language evolution. That is, these theorists believe language evolved gradually from the system of gestures and calls of the ancestors of modern humans (Hockett, 1978; Hewes, 1973; Cartmill, 1990). Many continuity theorists further assume that we should be able to see at least some elements of language ability in other existing primates whose early ancestors we share (King, 1994). In contrast, theorists who place more emphasis on linguistic evidence for the complexity of language tend to construct evolutionary theories that claim **discontinuity.** In other words, these theorists see language as a late-developing ability that is very different from the gestures and calls of our hominid ancestors (Bickerton, 1990; Burling, 1993; Davidson & Noble, 1993; Noble & Davidson, 1991). The discontinuity view does not maintain that language suddenly sprang out of nowhere; it acknowledges that important evolutionary changes in communication or thinking abilities may have taken place over the millennia. However, according to this view, the final "recent" changes produced an ability, language, that is qualitatively different from communication in other primates, either living or extinct.

You should think of discontinuity and continuity theories as existing along a continuum rather than as being completely separate categories. In other words, there is room for middle ground between the two extreme positions. For example, Lieberman (1991) is something of a continuity theorist in that he believes many important elements of language developed before the human capacity for articulate speech, and he sees considerable continuity between existing primate communication systems and language in humans. However, Lieberman also believes that the relatively late evolutionary changes to the vocal tract were critical for the development of the complex spoken language ability seen only in modern humans.

We do not have enough evidence right now to conclusively answer the difficult questions surrounding the evolution of language. Nevertheless, an understanding of the basic ideas behind continuity and discontinuity theories of language evolution is important—for two reasons. First, despite the differences between the two positions, they share some commonalities. And when two views differ so sharply, it is useful to see what facts they agree on. Second, the two positions lead to very different ideas regarding the purpose of language and the relationship between language and thought.

In terms of the middle ground between the two views, both continuity and discontinuity theorists can agree with Leakey that the development of language was a critical event in human evolution. It made possible both social cooperation and styles of thinking that profoundly affected our species' ability to manage the environment so that we could not only survive but flourish. Thus, the two camps agree not only on the importance of language but also on the close connection between language and thought.

Of course, we want to be able to say more than just that language and thought are closely intertwined. Any common-sense view claiming that language is used to express thought suggests that language and thought are related. But what's even more interesting, and more complex, is to be able to specify exactly how language and thought are related. That is the central issue of the rest of this book—an issue closely tied to our second reason for keeping the continuity-discontinuity distinction in mind. Indeed, these two views are often associated with very different ideas about exactly how language and thought are related.

Some psychologists have argued that our language, memory, and reasoning abilities are just different expressions of a powerful general capacity for forming concepts and manipulating information (e.g., Piaget, 1974). Others have argued that we possess numerous very different kinds of mental abilities and that each operates in its own way (e.g. Fodor, 1983; Piattelli-Palmarini, 1994). The latter theorists believe that language is one of several modules within our mental system. A **module** is a specialized system for performing a certain kind of mental task.

The question of whether language functions as a separate module is connected with the continuity-discontinuity issue. Most continuity theorists do not see a sharp division between communication and thinking abilities in humans or other primates (e.g., King, 1994). Accordingly, continuity theorists are less likely than discontinuity theorists to view language as a separate module. From a continuity point of view, language came about gradually as mental abilities changed, and these changes made possible increasingly sophisticated communication. Discontinuity theorists, on the other hand, see a sharp division between language and other primate communication and a sharp division between language and the rest of our mental abilities (e.g., Bickerton, 1990).

Keep in mind, however, that there are positions at each extreme as well as a large middle ground between continuity and discontinuity. So, taking a discontinuity approach does not necessarily mean that one thinks the mind is organized into modules, of which language is a single example. However, the most extreme discontinuity perspectives certainly lend themselves to this modular view of the mind (e.g., Chomsky, 1988; Fodor, 1983; Piattelli-Palmarini, 1989, 1994).

Unfortunately, it is very difficult to test the continuity and discontinuity views. As there are no living examples of Neanderthals or *Homo erectus* around, their language capacities cannot be directly assessed. Accordingly, some scientists have turned to a more indirect comparative approach in order to get evidence relevant to the continuity-discontinuity debate. If this approach reveals substantial approximations of language in other animals, then the continuity position would be supported.

Comparing Human and Nonhuman Communication

Pictures and descriptions of animal communication, including well-publicized examples of apes apparently communicating their thoughts and feelings to their human trainers, capture the public imagination as few other topics in language do. However, many scientists who study language have been much less willing than the popular media to accept claims of a close correspondence between the communication abilities of humans and those of nonhuman animals. Exaggerated claims in magazine articles and on television have helped fuel debates over "animal language" studies that have generated a good deal of heat but little light. Before we review the evidence on animal communication and its relevance to studies of language, then, it is worth considering the limitations inherent in such comparative studies of human and nonhuman communication.

Perhaps the most serious impediment to an objective analysis of studies of animal communication is that arguments over whether or not animals are using language sometimes spill over into the issue of the intrinsic value of other species. Note, however, that the "value" of a species should not be judged by its similarity to us. The logical extension of this idea would hardly be a boon to the environmental movement.

A less inflammatory, but still serious, impediment to getting useful information out of animal communication research is based on an incorrect assumption about evolutionary theory. Some researchers have argued that logic dictates that a continuity view must be correct (e.g., Cartmill, 1990; Miles, 1983). Their reasoning goes like this: (1) A capacity for language must have evolved through natural selection;* (2) natural selection produces gradual changes in preexisting structures; therefore, (3) a unique human ability for language would contradict evolutionary principles. For example, Miles (1983) claimed:

> Unless one takes a creationist view, human language evolved from earlier hominoid communication systems, which in turn share origins with ape communication in the hominoid systems of the Miocene. A comparison of the relative language capabilities of apes and humans will . . . help us understand human origins. *(pp. 44–45)*

This line of reasoning fails to recognize two important truths about evolution. First, given that extinction is a fact of life on earth, our closest *living* relatives may not be all

---

* Recall that natural selection is one of the most important processes in evolutionary theory. The idea is that organisms within a species vary somewhat in their characteristics. Many of these differences have no effect on survival. For example, whether you have brown eyes or blue eyes doesn't matter much in terms of your survival. However, other characteristics give individuals an adaptive advantage. With such characteristics they are better able to survive and can produce more offspring who themselves survive to reproduce. Over time, the greater reproduction rate of the members with the adaptive characteristics increases the overall prevalence of those characteristics in the species.

that close. Many branches of a family tree, including species that show the intermediate stages in the development of some trait, may be extinct. Therefore, a characteristic that changed gradually over time may still be unique among *living* species. You might object to this argument that we may not be all that similar to other primates if you have heard the widely circulated statistic that humans and chimpanzees share 99 percent of their DNA. In actuality, however, this kind of genetic similarity does not mean that we are 99 percent similar to chimps in physical form or in abilities. Even a small difference between two genes can make a big difference to an organism. As Pinker (1994) put it, it is a bit like changing a single letter in a word. Even a small change can completely alter the word's meaning.

Second, both the fossil record and observations of evolution in action (e.g., Gould & Eldredge, 1977; Mayr, 1991) suggest that some changes in a species happen relatively fast. The point is that evolution does not always involve a simple string of slow, gradual changes. Therefore, if we do find language-like ability in nonhuman animals, a continuity view of language evolution would be supported. However, if we fail to find much evidence for continuity, it does *not* follow that humans are the "highest" form of life on some scale of perfection, that evolutionary theory is wrong, or that continuity theories of language evolution are wrong. Rather, there may simply be no living species close enough to us to reveal the continuous nature of language evolution.

From this discussion, it would appear that what we stand to gain from a comparison between human language and nonhuman communication is pretty modest. However, aside from serving as a sort of testing ground for the continuity view of language evolution, a comparative analysis can help us determine what the important characteristics of language are. In fact, it is misleading to think of language as a simple trait, though we often phrase our questions on the basis of this assumption. How did language evolve? Do other animals possess language? As the next section makes clear, we must take the complex nature of language into account if we hope to answer these questions.

Universal Characteristics of Language

In a very influential comparison of animal communication and language, Hockett (1959, 1960, 1961) proposed several universal characteristics of the languages used by humans and looked for the same characteristics among animal communication systems. The number of universals that he considered important to language varied from seven to sixteen in the different presentations of his view. Here we will concern ourselves with the six linguistic universals that have received the most attention. The first four of these six universals deal with the nature of the elements that make up a language.

- **Semanticity.** Language signals are symbols that convey meaning. In linguistic terms, the symbols of language have semantic content, such that language signals are associated with things in the world. If I say the word "dog," you know that I am talking about the furry thing that barks, slurps noisily, and wags its tail.

- **Arbitrariness.** Language signals are arbitrary in that there is no resemblance between the signal and the thing the signal represents. "Dog" is a label for a furry creature, but the word "dog" does not look like the creature. The arbitrariness of the words makes language very different from communicating with pictures, which actually resemble the objects they represent.

- **Discreteness.** Language signals are distinct, or discrete; they do not vary continuously. Consider the following nonlanguage example. Raising my hand to show that I agree with you and keeping my hand down otherwise would be a discrete communication signal; raising my hand higher the more I agree with you would be a continuous communication signal. As noted, language is based on discrete symbols. Thus, for instance, I don't say "dog" in a high-pitched voice to mean a little dog, and use deeper and deeper pitches to mean bigger and bigger dogs. Rather, I use the discrete signal "dog" and combine it with another discrete signal, such as "huge," if I want you to know the size.

- **Duality of Patterning.** The patterns in language signals occur on two levels. On one level are the symbols we have already discussed—namely, symbols that are meaningful, discrete, and arbitrary. On the other level are smaller units that make up the meaningful symbols. The smaller units do not have meaning of their own. By itself the /d/ sound does not convey meaning. But combine that with other sounds, as in "dog," and you have a meaningful symbol. In spoken languages, the basic sound units, such as the /d/ sound, are called **phonemes.** Phonemes are combined to make up meaningful units called **morphemes.** Note that a morpheme does not necessarily correspond exactly to a word, though a word can be a morpheme. For example, the word *untie* consists of two morphemes: *un + tie.* The prefix *un* consists of two phonemes that, when combined, are meaningful in that they indicate the *un*doing of the morpheme that follows. Of course, we cannot throw together just any set of phonemes and expect to be understood. On the contrary, any given language has a set of rules that specifies permissible sound combinations. These rules are known as the **phonology** of the language.

The last two universals are features of language use.

- **Productivity.** Humans' use of language is very creative. Although words and sentences are made up of relatively few basic elements, these elements can be combined in many novel ways. We can even invent new words; try looking up *microchip* in a 1940s dictionary! More fundamentally, most of what we say and comprehend consists of utterances that are original. We don't make the same stereotypic statements over and over in the same situations. (Conversations between parents and teenagers may seem an exception to the principle of productivity, however.) What's remarkable is that, despite the nonrepetitive nature of most utterances, comprehension is usually quite easy. I'd bet that in the history of the world no human, until now, has ever said: "My dog grew tired of soiling his own yard, so he took up pole vaulting, much to the dismay of the neighbor." Yet even though this sentence is new, you probably had a complete picture of the idea I had in mind about a half-second after reading the word *neighbor.* Once again, it is important to note that we cannot haphazardly put just any words together to make a sentence. In addition to its phonological rules for putting phonemes together to make morphemes, any given language has a set of grammatical rules, or a **syntax,** that specifies how sentences can be constructed.

- **Displacement.** By using language, we can communicate about things that are physically and temporally displaced. That is, we can talk about things that are not physically present, and we can talk about past and future rather than just the present. As the "pole-vaulting dog" sentence shows, we can talk about things that do not even exist. This last feature is one that implies an important connection between language and the rest of our cognitive system. Language cannot show displacement unless we have some type of memory system that preserves information from our past.

Dancing Bees, Talking Monkeys, and Language Universals

When honeybees find a source of nectar they return to the hive and accurately signal the location of the nectar with an intricate set of movements (von Frisch, 1974) that have been likened to a dance (see Figure 1.3). And as I noted earlier, vervet monkeys display a highly effective vocal communication system. If a vervet gives the call to indicate the presence of an eagle, the other vervets look up in the sky. If it gives the call to signify a python, the other vervets look down. These two examples of animal communication are very different, but both are efficient and serve their species well. How similar is each communication system to language?

Obviously, monkeys and humans are closer to each other, in an evolutionary sense, than either species is to insects. For that reason, a continuity view implies that we might

| FIGURE 1.3 | The Dance of the Bee |

The movements of the honeybee tell other workers where to find a food source. The angle of the dance indicates the direction of the food source relative to the position of the sun and the hive. This figure was used in the lecture given by von Frisch upon his receipt of the Nobel prize.

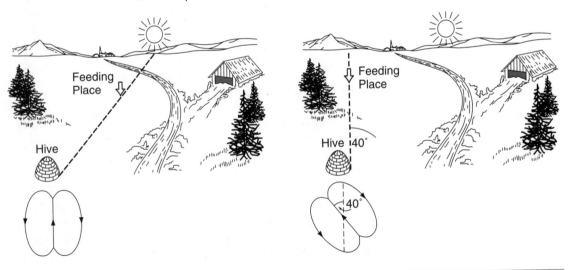

expect stronger similarities between monkey communication and language than between bee communication and language. The most obvious comparison seems to bear this out. The mode of communication for the bees is movement, whereas both humans and monkeys use a vocal mode. However, this conclusion is misleading inasmuch as some humans use sign languages, which are also based on movement. As you will see in Chapter 11, the sign languages used for communication in the deaf community are true languages in every respect. Indeed, the six language universals noted above are seen in both signed and spoken languages. Thus, mode of communication is not a good basis for comparing animal communication and language. Instead, we will examine our two representatives of animal communication for indications that they possess language universals. Before reading further, make the comparison yourself. Decide the degree to which you think bee and vervet monkey communication entails each of the six universals, and then check your views against the ones presented below.

Semanticity. When Hockett (1960) considered the semanticity of animal communication, he defined semanticity as any associative relationship between the sign (i.e., the symbol or language signal) and the thing being represented (i.e., the referent). By this simple definition, both the bee's dance and the monkey's calls have semanticity. In more recent discussions of the semantic character of language, however, researchers have referred to semanticity in terms of symbols being associated with internal concepts that represent objects and actions in the world (e.g., Bickerton, 1990). By this more stringent definition, few would credit the bee with having an internal representation of flowers that is called up in memory when another bee waggles a location. In contrast, studies of the mental abilities of primates have convinced many researchers that monkeys do have mental representations of concepts that meet the more stringent definition of semanticity (e.g., Premack, 1983).

Arbitrariness. It is clear that the bee's dance is not an arbitrary symbol. For example, the angle of the dance is used to directly show the angle of the food source relative to the sun and the hive. In contrast, the vervet monkey's call seems more comparable to language utterances in terms of arbitrariness. The call made by the monkeys is not imitative of the predator being signaled.

Although vervet monkeys' calls are arbitrary in Hockett's sense of the term, there is an important difference concerning the source of arbitrariness in animal calls versus human language. In language, the arbitrary symbols that we use vary across cultures. Even words that are *intended* to resemble the referent—namely, onomatopoetic words like "bow-wow"—are quite arbitrary (Brown, 1958). For example, as Pinker (1994) observed:

> Onomatopoeia . . . is almost as conventional as any other word sound. In English, pigs go 'oink'; in Japanese they go 'boo-boo.' *(p. 152)*

What this example shows is that the symbols in language are not just arbitrarily related to their referent; they are also based on conventions that vary across cultures. Vervet monkeys' calls, by contrast, are mostly determined by the monkeys' genetic inheritance. Different groups of vervets do not arbitrarily settle on different predator signals (Burling, 1993).

Discreteness.   The fact that bees waggle a circular movement for "near" and a figure eight for "far" provides evidence for discreteness in their communication. Other aspects of the dance seem less discrete, however. For example, the speed of the circular movement indicates the quantity of food at the source. Although this signal is somewhat arbitrary (there is no reason that faster has to mean more food), it is definitely not discrete. The monkey calls, however, *are* discrete, so we have another case in which a feature of vervet communication is similar to human language.

Duality of Patterning.   This feature is possible only in a discrete system because duality of patterning means that each discrete symbol can be broken down into component parts. So, we have to disqualify the bees on this criterion. However, there is no solid evidence that the vervet monkey's call, or any other natural system of animal communication, shows duality of patterning. Here, too, we see an important difference between human and animal communication systems. As Pullyblank (1989) suggested, duality of patterning, such as the phoneme-morpheme distinction in spoken language, is critical to having a language system that is easy to acquire and easy to comprehend. The reason is that duality of patterning allows for a communication system with infinite capacity for new utterances to be constructed from a finite, even relatively small, number of basic elements.

Productivity.   Of course, duality of patterning is only part of the story behind the remarkable flexibility of language. Another explanation for language's infinite capacity for constructing new utterances is that language has syntax. Is there a similarly open-ended productivity in animal communication? Bees' dances do show a limited kind of productivity in that a worker bee can signal a location that has never been signaled before. However, this productivity is related to the continuous nature of the bees' dances, rather than to a syntax that governs the combination of discrete signals. Monkeys, in contrast, have a discrete system with no means of productivity. Their calls have semantic content, but they cannot be recombined in novel ways. Indeed, the huge gulf in productivity between language and animal calls (and gestures) is one of the main reasons that some theorists doubt whether language evolved from animal call systems (e.g., Bickerton, 1990; Burling, 1993).

Displacement.   Bees do display a kind of displacement in their communication. Some time elapses between a worker bee's discovery of a field of flowers and the bee's arrival at the hive with the good news. Thus, the bee is communicating the location of objects that are not physically present at the time of the communication. Of course, bees don't sit around the hive planning their next excursion or "talking" about their glory days when they found that great field of buttercups. In short, bees show only a very limited type of displacement. Vervet monkeys' calls, by contrast, show no displacement at all. Each of their calls is made in the presence of a specific predator.

What can we conclude from this exercise in comparisons? Human language and communication by nonhuman primates do appear to have some features in common, but it is not clear that communication among monkeys is dramatically closer to language than is the communication of a very distant species—the honeybees. In fact, the differences in productivity and displacement among the three systems illustrate an important general point—namely, that the two animal communication systems serve very specific purposes. For example, the vervet monkeys' signaling system is not inferior to language because it lacks displacement. If anything, the fact that this system does *not* show displacement is a good design feature. Displacement in signaling about predators would be the monkey equivalent of falsely yelling "Fire!" in a movie theater. The point is that monkey calls serve a specific purpose, and this purpose is quite different from that served by the language ability of humans.

An analogy may help reinforce this point. Let's compare a machine with a very specific purpose—say, a can opener—with a general-purpose machine like a computer. After all, both are mechanical devices that make certain jobs easier, both run on electricity, and so on. However, we would not expect to see the design features that give computers generality of purpose (e.g., the ability to store and manipulate information) in a can opener, nor would we expect a computer to have the sharp blades of a can opener. Likewise, natural animal communication systems have evolved to serve specific functions—and this fact sets them apart from language, which somehow evolved as a system that has tremendous flexibility and generality.

This brings us back to the issue of continuity versus discontinuity. The degree of correspondence between primate communication systems and language does not obviously favor a continuity view. But maybe we have looked for continuity in the wrong place. Consider the following hypothetical scenario. Evolution endowed a group of early humans with general mental abilities that gave them a large memory capacity and a high level of skill at forming and manipulating mental representations of events and objects in the world. These intelligent ancestors were then able to invent language. In turn, language gave them even greater advantages, and they increased in population, gradually spreading out over the world. According to this scenario, language is just a particularly complex expression of our general mental abilities. It is not a separate mental module. What are the implications of this scenario? If language were just an invention by our most clever ancestors, and if existing nonhuman primates have mental abilities that are fairly close to ours, then it might be possible to teach language to our primate relatives. If another primate species could learn language, then this would provide some support for a continuity view.

Attempts to Teach Language to Nonhumans

Throughout the years, many attempts have been made to determine whether primates other than humans could be taught a language. In the earliest studies, people attempted to teach spoken language to chimpanzees (e.g., Kellogg & Kellogg, 1933). However, as we have already seen, the human vocal tract is uniquely adapted for articulate speech, so it is not surprising that attempts to teach spoken language to chimps met with virtually no success.

More recently, two other techniques have been used to test whether a language could be taught to another species. Some researchers have attempted to teach a scaled-down version of American Sign Language (ASL) to chimps or gorillas. Others have invented an "artificial language" in which symbols, such as arbitrary plastic tokens, are used to stand for concepts.

Using each type of training technique, some researchers have made remarkable claims for the ability of other species to approximate language use. In one of the better-known projects, a chimp named Washoe was trained in ASL from a very early

(continued on page 18)

ACTIVITY 1.1   The Token Game

This is a game in which you have to determine the proper combinations for a set of arbitrary symbols. In the first practice phase, I'll show you some symbols along with pictures of real objects, to help you figure out what the symbols mean.

Practice Phase 1:

Now, in this second practice phase I'll show you some correct combinations of the symbols.

Practice Phase 2:

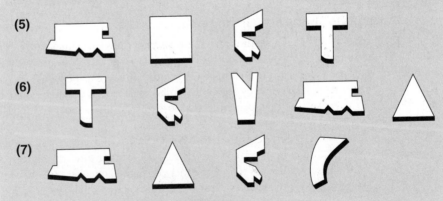

Activity 1.1 *continued*

Test Phase:

Here is the set of symbols you can work with:

(a) (b) (c) (d)

(e) (f) (g)

From among this set, which symbol or combination of symbols would you place in each blank? (Remember, each blank can have one <u>or more</u> symbols in it.)

(1)   _____

(2)   _____

(3)   _____   _____

Answers appear at the end of the chapter. What would you guess that this symbol means:

?

How about this symbol   ?

age (Gardner & Gardner, 1969, 1975). According to the Gardners, Washoe acquired a vocabulary of several hundred signs and displayed the rudiments of syntax by putting signs together with some regularity of ordering. In addition, Washoe reportedly displayed productivity in language by coining new words. Upon seeing a swan, Washoe is said to have signed "water-bird." Similar claims were made for a gorilla named Koko, who also was schooled in sign language (Patterson, 1978).

Among the researchers who have used artificial systems invented for animal language training, claims have been more mixed. For example, Premack (1971) taught a chimp named Sarah to name objects by choosing plastic tokens that represented the objects. Then he trained Sarah to string symbols together in standard ways to produce sentences. Initially, Premack felt that Sarah was able to display at least the beginnings of syntactic ability. With continued investigation, however, he came to doubt that Sarah was learning a language at all, although he continued to be impressed with her ability to mentally represent concepts (Premack, 1983). To understand some of the reasons behind Premack's skepticism, try Activity 1.1 (pages 16–17).

Sarah had a lot more practice at mastering the token "language" in Activity 1.1 than you did, but you had several other advantages over Sarah. For one, you knew that this was a simulation of language acquisition, so you probably guessed that the symbols were words and that the order of the words mattered. You may also have realized that some tokens were nouns and others were not. Although Sarah learned to use combinations of symbols to get rewards, there was no evidence that she was doing more than associating tokens with objects and understanding that putting some tokens together could result in a reward. There was also no evidence that Sarah understood that the tokens fell into different categories of types or that certain orders were permissible and others were not. In short, Sarah did not acquire syntax.

In contrast to the conclusions Premack drew from his studies based on an artificial language, Savage-Rumbaugh and colleagues have argued that the pygmy chimpanzee, or bonobo, is capable of closely approximating the language ability of a young child (Savage-Rumbaugh et al., 1986; Savage-Rumbaugh et al., 1993). The most famous subject from this lab, Kanzi, apparently acquired proficiency in communicating by watching his mother's (mostly unsuccessful) training. Kanzi's communication system is based on pressing keys on a portable keypad that features arbitrary symbols representing different concepts. Kanzi possesses a considerable vocabulary and is said to sometimes use word order to express sentence meaning. For example, *Kanzi tickle Sue* would mean Kanzi wants to do the tickling, while *Sue tickle Kanzi* would mean Kanzi wants to be tickled.

Do these examples demonstrate the rudiments of a syntax-governed language, or can the data on primate language training be interpreted in other ways? We should always maintain a healthy, objective skepticism in science, but it is especially important to take a skeptical attitude when scientific investigations seek to prove something that we really *want* to believe. Even the subjects who have been among the fastest learners in this research, such as Kanzi, require an enormous investment of time and energy to train, and they learn much more slowly than humans learn language. Some critics charge that, for these reasons, investigators are particularly prone to interpret often subjective data in ways that support the continuity view, even if such interpretations are not warranted by the data (Umiker-Sebeok & Sebeok, 1981).

Nonhuman Language: A Closer Look at the Data

Let's first consider the efforts to teach ASL to chimps and gorillas. Terrace and colleagues (Terrace, 1979; Terrace, Petitto, Sanders, and Bever, 1980) attempted to teach ASL to a chimp they dubbed Nim Chimpsky, after the famous linguist Noam Chomsky. They found, however, that Nim's communications bore little resemblance to the language abilities of his namesake. As in other projects involving signing among chimps, Nim acquired a fairly extensive vocabulary and strung together two-word "sentences" that often followed a predictable word order. For example, when Nim asked for something with the sign for *more,* the *more* sign was used in the first position 85 percent of the time, as in *more drink* or *more banana.* However, when the project ended and Terrace looked back at his data, he came to suspect that it was not a language-like ability that Nim had displayed (see Figure 1.4).

Even though Nim's vocabulary increased as he was trained, the length of his utterances showed little development over time. The average "sentence" length remained around 1.5 signs. In addition, Nim's longer utterances were not novel or

---

FIGURE 1.4   **Ape Language?**

Nim Chimpsky interacts with his teacher and signs *me hug cat.* Although Nim is communicating, Terrace came to doubt that signing behavior by Nim should be considered an example of language. The cat seems to be communicating something here, too!

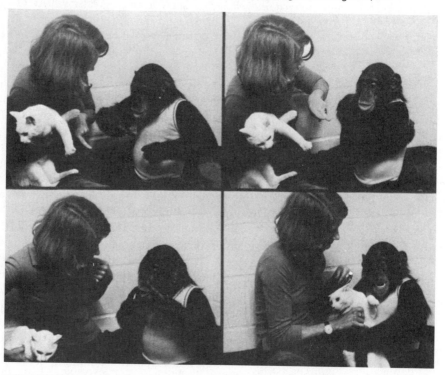

sentence-like. They were characterized by repetition. Nim's longest utterance was "give orange me give eat orange me eat orange give me eat orange give me you." When Terrace closely watched the tapes of Nim's signing, he observed that what was originally taken to be spontaneous and syntactically organized utterances could be explained as imitations of the teachers in order to get specific rewards (Terrace, 1983). Other animal language researchers criticized the teaching methods used in the Nim project and claimed that Nim's limitations were not representative of the abilities of other language-trained chimps (e.g., Gardner, 1981). However, when Terrace and colleagues examined films of the training of chimps or gorillas in other studies, they saw the same problem that they themselves had experienced: The experimenters failed to distinguish between language utterances and the imitation of signs (Terrace et al., 1980; Seidenberg & Petitto, 1979).

A number of other criticisms have been leveled against studies supporting the claim that chimps can learn language (Wallman, 1992). For instance, fluent users of ASL have noted that it takes a very generous interpretation of the chimps' use of signs mixed with pointing and other natural gestures to come up with vocabulary estimates in the hundreds. And because the trainers possess language, it is all too easy for them to extrapolate beyond the chimps' behavior. When Washoe signed "water-bird," was this a novel label for a swan? Or did Washoe merely give a sign for water and a sign for bird, thus separately naming each object?

Kanzi, probably the most accomplished chimp communicator of those studied, uses his board about 95 percent of the time to make requests. In contrast, children who are acquiring language show a much greater variety of types of utterances. The implication is that Kanzi is mainly imitating trainers to get rewards (Pinker, 1994). Like the utterances of other trained chimps, Kanzi's are usually only one or two symbols long, and although he displays some use of word order to make meaningful distinctions, the evidence for syntax is scant (cf. Bickerton, 1990).

Nevertheless, the conceptual abilities of our primate relatives are more impressive than many researchers would have suspected before the language training studies began. These primates can learn to associate numerous arbitrary symbols with their referents, and they can learn to communicate with humans to get rewards. However, communication is not necessarily language. The consensus among those who study language is that chimp-human communication is quite discontinuous with language communication among humans. In short, the data on teaching language to other animals do not provide support for the hypothetical scenario that language is an invention made possible by the general cognitive abilities of our ancestors.

To summarize our discussion so far: We have too little data right now to conclusively determine how language came about in our species; neither a continuity nor a discontinuity view can be rejected on the basis of current evidence. At the same time, however, there is little evidence that language is simply an invention. It appears to be a basic part of the mental system that comes with our biological inheritance. Thus another fundamental question about language is raised: How is our ability for language related to our other mental abilities?

This question of how language operates in the context of the rest of our mental processes is a key concern of the field known as **psycholinguistics.** Although the study of language is one of the oldest topics in psychology, psycholinguistics is viewed today as a branch of one of the newest subfields of psychology—**cognitive psychology.** And as cognitive psychology is the study of how people take in, store, and retrieve information, language is one of many abilities studied by cognitive psychologists.

As we will see, there are major differences of opinion in the field of psycholinguistics over whether the principles by which language operates are very different from the principles by which the rest of our cognitive system operates. We touched on this point earlier, when I noted that strongly discontinuous views of language evolution tend to be associated with the modular view that language is a separate system with its own unique operating principles. Of course, if there *is* a language module, it must exchange information with our memory system (and other basic cognitive systems). In the view of other theorists, language is so much a part of the rest of our cognitive system that it would be misleading to consider it a separate module. This is known as the **interactive view** of language (Carpenter, Miyake & Just, 1994; McClelland & Elman, 1986). Let's take a brief overview of some specific questions about language and cognition that I will attempt to answer in the course of this book.

A Look Ahead: The Study of Psycholinguistics

Let's say that you are running late for your Psychology of Language class. In your haste to get into the classroom, you burst in more noisily than you intended. Everyone stops and looks at you as you head for a seat. Your usually benevolent professor, in the middle of a wonderful example at the time of your interruption, says in an irritated tone of voice, "Could you please close the door behind you?" You immediately understand what is meant, and you go back, embarrassed, and close the door.

Because we so automatically produce and comprehend language in situations like this, the complexity of language processes is not obvious. But think for a moment about everything you had to do to respond appropriately to the professor's "question," which was really a command. One step was to get the meaning of each individual word in mind. For now, you can think of this process as analogous to very quickly looking up each word in a mental dictionary. However, you cannot understand the professor's statement by stringing together each word's definition to get the sentence meaning. After all, many words are ambiguous. If you look up *behind* in your mental dictionary you know that it could mean "in back of" or it could mean your "rear end." Right away we have a paradox. The meaning of the word *behind* contributes to the meaning of the whole sentence, and yet the sentence itself helps determine the meaning of the individual word. We understand sentences by understanding words, yet *at the same time* we understand words by understanding the sentence in which the words appear. How can we do both at the same time?

The word meaning/sentence meaning paradox is only part of the problem of comprehension. Note that if you take the literal meaning of the professor's question, the appropriate response is *not* to go over and close the door. Rather, it would be to truthfully answer whether you are capable of closing the door. I doubt, however, that many people would respond to the professor's statement by saying "Yes, I am perfectly capable of closing the door" but then fail to close the door. Our knowledge of social situations tells us to respond to the implication of the professor's statement, not to its literal meaning.

Just how, in less than a second, did you solve the word meaning/sentence meaning paradox *and* consult enough of your background knowledge of the world to realize that there was an unstated implication to which you should make a particular response? Clearly, there is a great deal of mental work to be done in comprehending language, and there is just as much involved in producing language. That we accomplish most of this work with so little apparent effort is a genuine intellectual puzzle. Indeed, most researchers who study language do so because language presents such an intriguing and complex puzzle. Many of us engage in the study of language as basic research—that is, as the pursuit of knowledge for its own sake. We do this not just because the work is intellectually exciting (it is intellectually maddening just as often) but also because basic principles that are uncovered allow for applications of research to "real world" issues.

A clear example of the importance of basic research for dealing with applied issues can be seen in the critical issue of literacy. Even in American society, where the level of basic literacy is relatively high, there are thousands of children and adults who have tremendous difficulty with reading (Kozol, 1985). Rates of functional literacy, the ability to read and write well enough to meet the increasingly technical demands of the workplace, are a continuing concern (Anderson, Hiebert, Scott & Wilkinson, 1985), with approximately 10 percent of adults encountering literacy-related problems at work (Barton, 1994). Globally, the problem is even more acute. Widespread illiteracy is a major impediment to economic development and the elimination of poverty in many countries (World Bank, 1988).

Of course, there are many different reasons for widespread illiteracy, some economic, some political; but a substantial part of the problem can be addressed through scientific research on reading. One of the best ways to create innovative programs for teaching literacy skills is to use basic research on reading as a guide. An interesting example of this strategy was reported recently by McCormick (1994), who designed a special reading program for a severely disabled reader. Despite two and a half years of reading instruction, the boy, Peter, was able to recognize only four words. McCormick's program was grounded in basic research on word recognition, including some of the models of word recognition that I will discuss in Chapter 6. After three and half years under this program, Peter was able to read and comprehend text at the seventh-grade level.

I do not mean to imply that McCormick's technique, or any other system designed to help poor readers, is *the* cure for reading disability. One thing that should become clear as you study language comprehension is that many different factors are involved in this complex process. One of the implications of the complexity of reading is that there are many different kinds of reading problems and many different ways of addressing them. Still, because the public, and some educators, are "hooked on panaceas," each new reading tool that gets marketed tends to be touted as *the* answer to reading problems.

As a more subtle example of the relationship between basic research and applied issues, consider the main question that we will address throughout this text: How does the operation of language processes relate to the rest of cognition? The usual assumption about the general relationship between language and thinking is that we use language to express our thoughts. However, some researchers have also asked whether language can affect our thinking. A particularly strong version of this hypothesis was advocated by Benjamin Lee Whorf, who claimed that we are able to think only in terms of concepts that represent distinctions in our language. In other words, Whorf claimed that our language places strong boundaries on the way we think. This view is known as **linguistic determinism.**

As we will see in later chapters, existing evidence does not support a strong version of linguistic determinism. But what about a weaker version of the hypothesis? Can our language make it easier to think along certain lines? Can the wording of a problem affect our thinking and decision making? These questions are actively being addressed by research today (Hunt & Agnoli, 1991; Hardin & Banaji, 1993). They also have applied implications. Consider, for example, the ongoing debate in our society over whether it is appropriate to use male pronouns to refer to both sexes and whether terms like *mankind* and *chairman* should be replaced. Does this way of speaking reinforce sex-role stereotypes, or is it merely a harmless tradition? As I discuss later in some detail, our ability to answer this question depends in part on our having a basic understanding of the thought-language relationship.

Although there is much to be gained from studying how language works, the processes involved are deceptively complex, and they are difficult to study. Accordingly, there are several ways to study language. In the next section, I present the different levels on which language can be studied and relate these levels to the way the overall book is organized.

Levels of Analysis and the Plan Behind This Book

Scientists study many different complex systems in nature, and all sciences break complex problems up into subparts in order to make it easier to study them. There are many different ways to divide up the problem of understanding a complex system, but a particularly useful way of doing so was developed by David Marr (1982). Although Marr was interested in the visual system, his general approach is applicable to the study of cognition in general and language in particular. Marr said that, when trying to explain any system that processes information, we can divide the things we need to know into three interdependent **levels of analysis:** the **computational level,** the **representational level,** and the **implementational level.** As Table 1.1 shows, we can think of each level of analysis as a different set of questions to be asked whenever we are interested in how something works.

Before we apply the different levels of analysis to language, let's take a simplified look at what might be involved in explaining the visual system. First, at the computational level, we could ask what kinds of problems vision solves for us. One obvious answer is that vision allows us to locate objects in space. In other words, one thing the visual system has to be able to "compute" is depth. Second, at the representational level, we could answer questions about how the computational tasks are accomplished as a set of steps. Specifically, we could consider the **algorithms,** or step-by-step procedures, used to get depth information. One such algorithm might involve taking note of visual cues. For example, if object A partially blocks your view of object B, then object A must

TABLE 1.1	Questions Posed at Each Level of Analysis of an Information-Processing System

Level of Analysis		
Computational	*Representational*	*Implementational*
What is the goal of processing? What is the nature of the input and output? What rules describe the input-output relations?	How is the input information represented? How is the information used to produce the output?	How can the processes at the representational level be performed physically?

be closer to you. Finally, at the implementational level, we could answer questions about how the processes described at the representational level can be accomplished physically. So, in the case of vision, we might try to determine which brain areas are used to process visual cues for depth.

Levels of Analysis Applied to Language

Imagine that a friend of yours has witnessed a robbery and then describes the whole affair to you. At that point, you could describe it to someone else with reasonable accuracy. Even from this simple scenario, then, it is clear that, at a computational level, language helps us solve the problem of exchanging information. We produce words and sentences that capture our thoughts, and someone else decodes those utterances to get the meaning.

The details of the computational analysis of language come from linguistics. Indeed, the aim of linguistics is to provide a description of language input and to determine what kinds of rules describe the relationship between the physical form of spoken or written language and its meaning. The most influential modern linguist, Noam Chomsky, believes that the key to understanding language is to understand the syntactic rules for specifying how words can be put together to make utterances.

Consider this simple example. If your friend says, "The robber took Bill as a hostage," the meaning is quite different from that of another sentence with the same words, "Bill took the robber as a hostage." This is related to the word meaning/sentence meaning paradox we encountered earlier. In this case, the structure of the sentence as well as the words contribute to the meaning. Thus, at the computational level, we might ask what abstract rules seem to govern the way sentences are constructed. Chomsky (1965) clarified this idea by stating that linguists study *competence* as opposed to *performance*. What we derive from such an analysis, however, is *not* a theory of how people actually use language. For example, from a computational point of view we can say that sentences in English generally follow a subject-verb-object rule—but this rule is only the starting point for psychological theories of language at the representational level.

What psychologists who study language want to explain is exactly what happens between input and output *in the mind of the language user.* For example, although speakers of English know that sentences in this language follow a subject-verb-object rule, they do not determine a sentence's meaning by retrieving this rule from memory and then matching up the words in the sentence with the rule. Rather, they appear to make use of the ordering of the words and the meaning of the concepts all at the same time. Indeed, there may be several different algorithms for how to use both word meanings and syntactic rules to understand a sentence. Thus, even though people may behave as though they are following a particular rule, we cannot necessarily conclude that the syntactic rule exists as an explicit rule in their minds. To test how people actually understand sentences, we have to measure aspects of their behavior, such as the time it takes them to understand a sentence or the errors in interpretation that people make. (Research that takes precisely this approach is described in Chapter 7.)

Note that the representational level addresses the abstract mental steps we use in language performance. Accordingly, representational theories are theories about the mind, not the brain. Without saying anything at all about the brain, we could propose, and test, a theory maintaining that people use syntactic rules before they try to determine the meaning of a sentence. Alternatively, however, we could ask where certain kinds of mental processes take place in the brain. This question is posed at the implementational level. Just as the computational level provides the basis to begin theorizing at the representational level, representational theories can be used to guide research at the implementational level.

Let's say that our study of language at the computational and representational levels has convinced us that we have two sets of language processes. One set of processes performs the task of syntactic analysis, such as determining which words in the sentence are nouns and which are verbs. Another set of processes is used to "look up" the meanings of the words in a mental dictionary. This idea suggests that at the implementational level, in the brain, we should find two different language areas—one for understanding word meanings and one for determining syntax. It further suggests that we should see two different kinds of language problems associated with brain damage. We will examine this issue more closely in the context of **aphasias,** language disorders caused by damage to the brain.

A major goal of psycholinguistics, and of this book, is to explore the nature of language by making use of the computational, representational, and implementational levels of analysis. It is important that you understand how each of these levels contributes to an overall understanding of language. Thus, before you read any further, please check your understanding of the concept of levels of analysis by doing Activity 1.2.

A machine such as a cash register could use any of several algorithms to perform addition. To keep things simple, let's consider only two. The first algorithm could be based on fact retrieval. All the totals of each possible pair of prices that the store uses are stored in a kind of memory. Thus, if the clerk types in $2 and $4, the machine retrieves the total from a system of stored totals in memory and then displays the answer. The other algorithm could be based on counting. That is, if the cash register has stored information about the sequence of numbers, it could start with the largest

ACTIVITY 1.2   **A Review of the Levels of Analysis**

Let's say that you see a clerk at a cash register and decide that you want to understand how the cash register works. The point of this activity is that what is meant by "how the cash register works" depends on the level of analysis that you use.

I'll get you started by providing a computational level of analysis. You see the clerk type in numbers, hit a button, and then get a total. So, the input to the cash register is a set of individual prices and the output is a total price. The cash register must be applying the rules of addition to the input in order to produce the output. But to apply these rules, what must the cash register be able to do? It must be able to store numbers, and it must have some procedure for adding them up. Like a linguistic analysis of sentences, this computational analysis of the cash register gives us some guidance in asking and answering questions at the two other levels. The most basic question we would want to answer at the other levels of analysis is, How does the cash register actually perform the addition?

Think about what it would mean to answer this question. What steps would any machine (including the one in your head) use to perform addition? Try to come up with at least one possible algorithm for adding 2 + 3. If you are testing whether the cash register you saw is using a certain algorithm, at what level of analysis are you working? Alternatively, if you are asking how the mechanical parts of the cash register are actually performing the algorithm, at what level of analysis are you working?

number and count up in increments equaling the smallest number. So, in our example, the machine would start with $4 and count up by $2, yielding the answer $6.

We could even do an experiment to see which algorithm the cash register is using. If the clerk types in two prices that the store has never used before and the machine is unable to provide a total, then it must be using the fact-retrieval algorithm. But if it comes up with the correct answer, then it is adding by counting. Determining which algorithm is being used by the machine involves a representational-level answer to the question of how the cash register works.

No matter which algorithm for addition is used by the cash register, the algorithm has to be performed by physical machine components. And if we determine how the machine physically performs the algorithm, we are working at the implementational level. How do the circuits in the machine actually allow it to perform the addition process? Note that the representational and implementational levels are separate in the sense that any given representational system could be implemented in a variety of different physical systems. For example, either of our two addition algorithms could be implemented in a human brain or in a computing machine.

Also note that we can answer many representational questions without knowing how a given algorithm is implemented. For example, we could test which algorithm the cash register used to perform addition without even knowing which physical components were used to make the cash register. The same is true of *human* information processing. For example, we know that a counting algorithm is used by children just beginning to learn their math facts, because the time it takes them to solve a math problem is determined by the amount of counting required in the problem (e.g., Ashcraft, 1992). Thus, for example, 6 + 4 takes longer to solve than 6 + 2, because in both cases the kids start with 6 and count up. In the case of 6 + 2, they have to do only half the counting. Later, children have the facts stored in memory and do not need to count. What then predicts the time they will take to solve a problem is how often they have worked the problem in the past. The lesson here is that cognitive psychology can answer questions about how mental processes work—that is, what mental algorithms are performed—without answering the question of how the brain is performing the algorithm. Likewise, psycholinguists can answer questions about the mental steps involved in language use without knowing how those mental steps are performed in the brain.

Of course, a *complete* understanding of any complex system involves using and integrating information at all three levels of analysis. Scientists do not yet have a complete understanding of language; but, as you will discover, the last few decades have revealed a great deal about the functions of language, the processes used to perform those functions, and the way the brain goes about accomplishing those processes.

The Organization of This Text

As a final review of the different levels of analysis, take a look back at the Table of Contents for this book. You will notice that the three units in the text reflect the theme of using three levels of analysis to explore the relationship between language and the rest of our cognitive processes.

Unit One, which began with this first chapter, lays the groundwork. In Chapter 2, we survey a computational analysis of language by considering an overview of linguistics. This overview sets the stage for many of the mysteries of language that we will explore in the rest of the book. Of course, we have already seen that language performance is closely associated with other mental processes. Next, to put the upcoming representational analysis of language in perspective, Chapter 3 provides a representational analysis of our general cognitive system. Then, in Chapter 4, we examine the language-thought relationship in more detail.

Unit Two provides a representational analysis of language. In Chapters 5 and 6, we examine the mental processes involved in language by focusing on auditory and visual word recognition. Then, in Chapters 7 through 9, we study language processes of increasing complexity, ending with an analysis of the processes that take place during conversation.

Unit Three, which is based on an implementational analysis of language, focuses on brain-language relationships and the related question of the degree to which language is built in genetically. In Chapter 10, we explore how language is implemented in the brain as children acquire language. In Chapter 11, we examine special cases of language acquisition, such as sign language and second-language acquisition. And finally, in Chapter 12, we look at research on brain damage and at studies using new techniques for brain imaging to see how language processes are physically implemented. My hope is that, by the end of this text, you will have an appreciation of both the special nature of language and the unique mysteries it presents to psychology, as well as an understanding of the interdependence between language processes and the ways that we plan, decide, and act in our daily lives.

CONCLUSIONS

Is Language a Uniquely Human Ability?

The validity of the hypothesis that language is uniquely human depends on how language is defined. Certainly we have seen that there are good reasons to avoid using the terms *language* and *communication* interchangeably. And with respect to at least some of its characteristics, we have seen that language appears to be a unique form of communication, unparalleled among nonhuman species. Language does not make us inherently superior in some qualitative sense, but it does make us different.

Our brief survey of approaches to language evolution serves as a useful background to the question of how language abilities are related to mental processes more generally. Recall, however, that proponents of the interactive view do not necessarily claim that language evolution must have been continuous. After all, it is possible that language *and* other mental abilities followed a discontinuous evolutionary path. Therefore, our best hope for determining whether a modular or an interactive position is correct—or, more likely, for uncovering the truth in each position—lies in research that explores how language operates and how its operation fits into the general scheme of our cognitive system. In turn, an understanding of language and our general cognitive system requires information at the computational, representational, and implementational levels of analysis.

CHAPTER REVIEW

Checking Your Understanding

Key Terms

algorithms (23)
anthropologists (7)
aphasias (25)
arbitrariness (10)
cognitive psychology (21)
computational level (23)
continuity view (7)
discontinuity view (7)
discreteness (11)

displacement (12)
duality of patterning (11)
implementational level (23)
interactive view (21)
levels of analysis (23)
linguistic determinism (23)
linguists (7)
module (8)
morphemes (11)

phonemes (11)
phonology (11)
primatologists (7)
productivity (11)

psycholinguistics (20)
representational level (23)
semanticity (10)
syntax (12)

Review Questions

1. Why is the development of spoken language considered such a critical event in human evolution?

2. What evidence suggests that spoken language as we now know it was a recent development in evolution, occurring less than 100,000 years ago? What evidence suggests that at least some aspects of language developed over the last few million years?

3. Do the studies of attempts to teach language to other primates support a continuity view of language evolution? Why or why not?

4. We can summarize the analysis of language in this chapter by saying that language is symbolic and rule-governed. Which of Hockett's six features show that language is symbolic? Which show that language is rule-governed?

5. Distinguish between the modular and interactive views of the relationship between language and other cognitive processes.

6. Some scientists believe that human memory is like a computer in that both are general-purpose problem-solving systems and both encode, store, and retrieve information. Is this comparison based on a computational, representational, or implementational level of analysis? If you specified just one level of analysis in answer to that question, discuss whether computers and human memory can be compared at the other two levels.

On Further Reflection . . .

1. Find a magazine article or TV program about an animal communication system that was not discussed in this chapter. (Numerous articles have been written about communication among dolphins, for example.) Try to analyze the animal communication system in terms of Hockett's features of language. Which features are present, and which are absent?

2. Try Activity 1.1 on some friends who are not taking this class. Tell one group that it is a logic game requiring that they figure out the rules behind putting the patterns of symbols together. Tell the other group that they should figure out which words are tied to each symbol and how sentences can be formed on the basis of those words. What differences in strategies are used by these two groups? Do they differ in terms of what they think the symbols mean at the end?

    When Premack (1979) trained students to learn the token language in the same way that Sarah did, he found that they could perform correctly but that they had no idea the strings of symbols were sentences. Note that Premack's "sentences" were formed vertically, lessening the chances that the students would see the game as a language simulation. What does this outcome suggest about whether or not Sarah's performance was an example of language?

3. Most college libraries carry several journals that publish applied research in the areas of linguistics and psycholinguistics. Two

examples are the *Journal of Applied Psychol-inguistics* and *Reading Research Quarterly*. Skim through recent issues of these and other applied journals to see what kinds of research are being conducted. Now, select one article and examine the review of prior research that led up to the study. How much of the research that led up to the applied study appears to be basic research?

Answers to Activity 1.1: The Token Game

The identities of the seven symbols you had to work with are as follows:

a. apple   d. yellow   f. red
b. no/not   e. is   g. banana
c. color of

Therefore, you could form the following sentences:

1. Yellow *is not* red.

2. Apple is *red.*

3. Red *is* color of *apple,* or Red *is not* color of *banana.*

CHAPTER 2

What Language Users Must Know

*t*he nature of language has been debated throughout virtually all of recorded human history. If you read what ancient philosophers had to say about language, you find that the debates have a familiar ring to them. For example, in *Cratylus,* one of Plato's dialogs (cited in Harris and Taylor, 1989), Cratylus suggests that names have an inherent correctness to them, whereas Hermogenes claims that there is an arbitrary relation between the name for a thing and the thing itself. Thus, one of the earliest recorded linguistic debates in Western literature is over an issue we reviewed in the last chapter: the arbitrariness of language.

Plato, like many other thinkers throughout history, wrestled with questions about the nature of language and its origins. Is language a logical system handed down from the gods, or is it an arbitrary form invented by people? Many centuries after Plato, Humboldt (1836) considered the question of the nature of language, asserting that, "since the natural disposition to language is universal in man, and everyone must possess the key to understanding all languages, it follows automatically that the form of all languages must be essentially the same, and always achieve the universal purpose" (p. 215).

There are two key ideas in this quote from Humboldt: first, that language is an integral part of human nature, and, second, that there are universal aspects of language that serve as the foundation for all languages, despite the obvious differences among languages. Both of these claims are consistent with the view in modern linguistics that evolution has endowed humans with a unique biological capacity for language.

However, it is time to get much more specific. When we say that there is an inherited human capacity for language, what does this entail? Recall from the last chapter that there are several different kinds of knowledge that language users must possess. As we explore the major contributions of linguistics to a computational analysis of language, keep the following hypothesis in mind: *Language is founded on a set of innate ideas.* Many linguists believe the knowledge that language users must have is so subtle and so extensive that at least some of that knowledge must be part of our genetic inheritance. Of course, to evaluate this **nativist hypothesis,** we have to be clear about what is meant by the *innate ideas* that language is *founded on.*

The concept of innate ideas may strike you as rather strange. We usually think of ideas, or knowledge, as something we can consciously mull over, and perhaps something we can describe. If I say, "What are your ideas on that new movie?" you can bring thoughts to mind and describe them. However, much of our knowledge is not of the explicit sort that can be articulated. This latter type of knowledge is known as **tacit knowledge.** Although we use tacit knowledge frequently, the knowledge itself is often difficult to describe and we are not consciously aware of using it.

One of the main lessons from modern linguistics is that a great deal of tacit knowledge is required to allow us to use language. This is easy to see in children. Draw a silly-looking bird on a piece of paper and tell a four-year-old, "This is a wug." Draw another silly-looking bird next to the first and say, "Here is another. Now there are two . . ."; then pause and look at the child. The child will respond happily with "wugs!" (Berko, 1958). The child seems to know that you form a plural noun by adding

-s, but can the child describe the rule? Not a chance! The child's understanding of the rule is tacit.

Keep in mind that, even if you are an adult, most of the knowledge that we use to produce and comprehend language is tacit knowledge. Consider the following two sentences and decide which one is grammatical, even if meaningless:

(1) Colorless green ideas sleep furiously.

(2) Sleep colorless furiously ideas green.

Even though both sentences are nonsense sentences, it is obvious that sentence (1) seems to follow language rules, whereas sentence (2) does not. Even if you cannot tell someone why sentence (1) seems better, you have the strong feeling that it is better. You have internalized the rules of English and you use these to judge the sentences. However, the conscious experience of this process is typically one of just feeling that the sentence seems acceptable or unacceptable.

Most linguists believe that we are born with some of this tacit knowledge—or, at least, that we are specially equipped biologically to acquire tacit knowledge from our language experience. However, exactly what tacit knowledge is required for language and how much of it is innate are matters of considerable debate.

Overview: Two Linguistic Problems

From the outset, we can dismiss an extreme version of the nativist hypothesis. It is *not* the case that children inherit a particular language from their parents. Children born to French-speaking parents *learn* French because that is what they hear. They are not born with a knowledge of the French language. The question remains, though, whether children learn to speak a particular language relatively quickly because they have certain kinds of knowledge built in that assists in the language-acquisition process. We tackle this question more completely in Chapters 10 and 11, but for now, I want you to see why many linguists feel that a computational analysis of language leads to the idea that there must be a biological basis for language acquisition.

First, consult Table 2.1 for a review of the kinds of information that language users seem to possess. Several of these forms of knowledge can be described, at least partially, in terms of rules. For example, you already encountered the morphological rule that -s is added to the end of a noun to make it plural. But you should not confuse this idea of grammatical rules with the idea of proscriptive rules. Linguists try to specify the rules and other knowledge that characterize language as people actually speak it or write it. They do not try to specify the "right" way to speak or write.

What is it about the ways that people use language that has convinced linguists that we need to have these various types of knowledge? Two mysteries about language suggest that language use requires a great deal of special knowledge. The first mystery is the "Problem of Productivity." Recall that one of the main contrasts between language and animal communication is the amount of novelty shown in human language. Language behavior is characterized by an extreme degree of novelty even though our brains have a finite capacity for storing and manipulating information. Moreover, each of us has a finite vocabulary, yet we can produce and understand an

TABLE 2.1	Forms of Knowledge Required for Language Use
Phonology	The sound pattern of language, including basic elements (phonemes) and the rules for their combination.
Morphology	The structure of words and rules for building words out of pieces (morphemes).
Syntax	The structure of sentences and rules for building sentences out of words.
Semantics	Meaning at the level of words, phrases, and sentences.
Pragmatics	Rules for how literal meaning can be changed by social context.

infinite variety of utterances. How languages can generate an infinite capacity for expression out of a finite system of sounds (or gestures) within a limited-capacity brain is the "Problem of Productivity."

The second mystery that suggests we have several different kinds of linguistic knowledge is the "Problem of Meaning." The essence of this mystery is the question of how we take arbitrary symbols and somehow combine them to describe states of affairs in the world. There is an often-told story that illustrates the "Problem of Meaning." Though not literally true, the story illustrates the nature of real problems that researchers in *artificial intelligence* (AI) encountered when they tried to get computers to simulate language comprehension (Searle, 1980; Gardner, 1985). According to the story, early researchers in AI were trying to program a computer so that an English sentence could be input and they would get back the equivalent sentence in Russian. The researchers' scheme was to store a set of dictionary-style definitions for each word in the English vocabulary of the computer and then key each concept in the definition to an equivalent term in Russian.

After months of labor, the researchers finished the programming of the computer and gathered around excitely for a test of the new system. Naturally, for such a momentous occasion, they did not want history to record that the first "language-comprehending computer" translated something silly like "Come here! I need you!" Instead, they gave the computer something profound to think about: "The spirit is willing, but the flesh is weak." For a few anxious moments, switches switched and lights flickered, and then the translation was printed out. The computer, to the researchers' dismay, came up with the Russian equivalent of "The vodka is fine, but the meat is tasteless."

The problem with understanding the semantics of language is that we cannot discern the meaning of a sentence in the simple fashion described in the story. There is more to understanding the meaning of an utterance than "looking up" each word in a mental dictionary and then stringing the meanings together. For one thing, it is not enough to store word meanings in a mental dictionary because the meanings of words have to refer to things in the world, not just to other words. In addition, there is the paradox that I mentioned in the previous chapter: Word meanings determine sentence meaning, *and* the meaning of a sentence as a whole determines the meaning of individual words. We get very different ideas about what is meant by *ball* in each of these sentences:

(3) The child rolled the ball along the beach.

(4) The batter swatted the ball over the fence.

(5) Cinderella longed to attend the ball with her sisters.

Sentences (3) and (4) require a very different interpretation of *ball* than does sentence (5). However, it is also true that different kinds of balls are implied in sentence (3) and sentence (4). As these sentences illustrate, we need to be able to describe not only the nature of word meanings but also how meanings are combined. To complicate matters, we sometimes expect someone to respond to *pragmatic implications* rather than to the literal meaning of a statement. If you say to someone, "Could you please close the door behind you," you do not expect them to tell you whether they are capable of closing the door. In fact, your question is not really a question at all but, rather, a request. People must have knowledge of social interactions and the nature of requests, which are examples of pragmatic knowledge, to understand when we should respond to the literal meaning of an utterance, and when an utterance means something quite different from its literal meaning.

In the remainder of this chapter, we will explore how linguists describe phonological, morphological, and syntactic knowledge in order to understand the productivity of language. We will also see how linguists describe semantic and pragmatic knowledge to account for meaning in language.

Phonology and Productivity

Leaving aside, for now, the issue of gestural languages such as American Sign Language (ASL), note that all spoken languages have infinite productivity even though they are based on a limited set of basic speech sounds—phonemes. By using rules for combining these basic sounds, we get everything from the preschooler's "Milk all gone" to Shakespeare's "To be or not to be" monologue.

English has forty phonemes, slightly above average for the world's languages. Some languages get by with only about a dozen phonemes. Because written letters do not have a precise one-to-one correspondence with language sounds, we cannot use the written alphabet to describe speech sounds. Instead, we turn to phonetic alphabets. The one most commonly used is the *International Phonetic Alphabet* (IPA), part of which is shown in Table 2.2. As you explore the nature of speech sounds and how they are made, it will be very helpful if you have some familiarity with the IPA. So, before reading further, try Activity 2.1.

Language Sounds and How We Make Them

Our main question is how we get the communicative power of spoken language out of a relatively small set of phonemes. To answer this question, we first have to know what speech sounds are really like. To make any speech sound, we modify a stream of air as it passes from the lungs through the mouth (see Figure 2.1). To illustrate how this works, we'll look at how you modify the air stream in order to produce a /t/ sound.

| TABLE 2.2 | A Sample of the International Phonetic Alphabet |

Consonants

Phonetic Symbol	As In	Phonetic Symbol	As In
p	pit	l	lip
b	buy	č	chew
m	my	ǰ	jump
f	free	š	shake
v	vat	ž	treasure
θ	thick	r	ripe
ð	the	y	yet
t	tick	w	witch
d	die	k	kin
n	not	g	girl
s	sun	ŋ	thing
z	zoo	h	hot

Vowels

i	meet	U	book
I	it	o	open
e	great	ɔ	taught
ɛ	met	a	hot
æ	at	ay	eye
ə	cut	aw	house
u	booze	oy	boy

Let's say that you are on a photographic expedition. You come over a ridge, look down toward a river, and yell to your companion, "Tigers!" As you release air from your lungs, the first point at which the air stream can be modified is the larynx. The larynx has bands of stretchy tissue, called vocal folds (or "cords"), that can be tensed to vibrate or kept relaxed so that they do not vibrate. In the case of the /t/ sound, the folds are relaxed so that there is no **voicing**—that is, no sound produced by the vocal folds. Therefore, we say that the /t/ sound is voiceless. From the larynx, the air stream moves up into the mouth, where you move the tip of your tongue up until it touches the alveolar ridge (position 4 in Figure 2.1). With your tongue in this position, you briefly block the air stream and then abruptly release air by moving your tongue back down. With this intricately coordinated activity, you just produced the phoneme that we call /t/.

Actually, it is not quite accurate to say you produced the /t/ phoneme. In a physical sense, *there is no such thing as a phoneme*. What I mean is that there are variations in the way the same phonemes are produced by different speakers and in different words. Physically, there is not just one /t/ sound. A phoneme is really a category of different sounds that speakers of a given language *perceive* to be the same sound.

ACTIVITY 2.1   Cracking the Code: Phonological Transcription

Use Table 2.2 to transcribe each of these sentences into the phonetic alphabet:

1. The quick red fox jumped over the lazy brown dog.
2. Harry Houdini was a famous magician.
3. Never cough around a funny physician.
4. (*Phonetic spelling of your name*) is a famous phonetician.

Let's return to the /t/ sound that we traced through the vocal tract. The /t/ at the beginning of "Tigers!" is *aspirated*. That means the sound is accompanied by a puff of air. Say "tiger" with your palm close to your lips and you will feel a burst of air upon saying that particular /t/. Now say "stripe." Notice that now the /t/ was *unaspirated*. There was no puff of air accompanying that /t/. There are at least seven different pronunciations of /t/. These variants are not unique to /t/; every phoneme has variants. The technical term for each variant is **allophone**. So, each phoneme is a category that contains different allophones.*

Distinctions Among Consonants.   Of course, the different allophones of a particular phoneme are produced in a generally similar fashion. That's why they are classified as a part of the same phoneme. What makes one phoneme different from another has to do with relatively bigger differences in how the sounds are produced. Consonant phonemes vary in terms of voicing and two other features: **point of articulation** and **manner of articulation.** For example, the phonemes /d/ and /t/ have the same point of articulation, at the alveolar ridge, as well as the same manner of articulation. That is, both are made by blocking and then releasing air. The only difference between these two types of sounds is in voicing. Place your fingers on your larynx as you say /t/ and /d/. Only for /d/ will you feel a vibration at the beginning of the sound.

As Figure 2.1 shows, there are six different points of articulation. There are also six different manners of articulation. If you are reading this in a library or other public place right now, you might want to move someplace private. The only way to get a feel for the different manners of articulation is to make the sounds out loud. The six manners of articulation are as follows:

- **Stops.** Stops are the manner of articulation for /t/, /d/, and several other sounds that are produced by blocking and then releasing the air stream.

- **Fricatives.** To produce fricatives you create a narrow passage at some point in the vocal tract so that sound is produced as air is forced through the narrow passage. For example, make an /f/. You did that by creating a narrow passage with your lips and then pushing air through that passage.

---

* Consistent with standard linguistic notation, I'll use parallel lines (//) for phonemes and brackets ([ ]) for allophones.

| FIGURE 2.1 | **Points of Articulation** |

There are six positions in the mouth where the air stream is altered to produce speech sounds—namely, the (1) bilabial, (2) labiodental, (3) interdental, (4) alveolar, (5) palatal, and (6) velar positions.

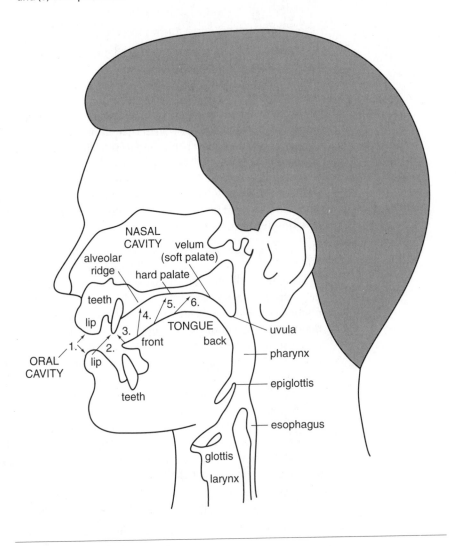

- **Affricates.** These are sounds produced by a stop and then a fricative in rapid succession. For example, pronounce /d/, then /ž/—separately at first, then more and more rapidly. If you say them fast enough they lose their distinct sounds and become /ǰ/, which is an affricate.

- **Nasals.** Locate the velum in Figure 2.1. This is the soft back part of the roof of your mouth. When the velum is lowered, air can pass through the nasal cavity. Depending on where your tongue is at the time that air is passed through the nasal cavity, different nasals are produced. Repeat /ŋ/ several times in succession and then try it again with your nose closed off. You'll be able to tell that the nasal cavity is involved in this sound.

- **Liquids.** This term refers to two sounds that are similar in many respects: /l/ and /r/. They are produced with only a slight obstruction of the air flow in the mouth.

- **Glides.** The glides /y/ and /w/ are also known as *semivowels* because they sometimes act as vowels. These sounds are produced with virtually no obstruction of the air flow through the mouth.

All the consonant sounds of English are shown in Table 2.3, classified according to point and manner of articulation and voicing. You'll notice that many cells of this table are not filled in. However, all the cells would be filled in if we included sounds that are used in other languages. Indeed, there are a number of possible sound distinctions that we do not recognize as separate phonemes in English but that are recognized as such in other languages. For example, to a native English speaker the initial sound of *seat* and *salt* are the same. But the sounds are physically different, and they are two different phonemes in Arabic. Likewise, the two liquids, /l/ and /r/, are distinctly different to us but not to a speaker of Japanese.

Distinctions Among Vowels.   The production of vowels is different from the production of consonants in that we don't have the distinctive sets of features for vowels that we do for consonants. Vowels are distinguished by the placement of the tongue on two continuous dimensions: high to low, and front to back (see Figure 2.2). Compare the /i/ sound (as in *each*) with /æ/ as in *at*. For /i/ the tongue is almost touching the hard palate, whereas for /æ/ the tongue is nearly resting on the bottom of the mouth. Notice,

TABLE 2.3		Consonants Arranged by Point and Manner of Articulation and Voicing					
		Labial		**Dental**			
Manner	*Point*	*Bilabial*	*Labiodental*	*Interdental*	*Alveolar*	*Palatal*	*Velar*
Stop	Voiceless	P			t		k
	Voiced	b			d		g
Fricative	Voiceless		f	θ	s	š	
	Voiced		v	ð	z	ž	
Affricate	Voiceless					č	
	Voiced					ǰ	
Nasal		m			n		ŋ
Liquid					l	r	
Glide						y	w

FIGURE 2.2	**Vowel Sounds**

The differences among vowel sounds are produced by differences in the position of the tongue. When you say [i], your tongue is forward and almost touching the roof of your mouth. When you say [a], which the doctor asks you to do when checking your throat, the tongue is low and toward the back of your mouth.

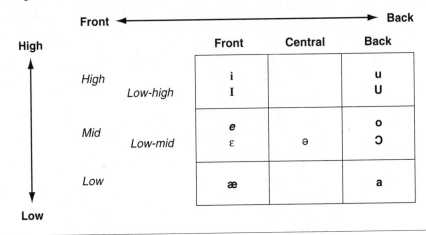

Front ⟵—————————⟶ Back

		Front	Central	Back
High	High	i		u
	Low-high	I		U
Mid	Mid	e		o
	Low-mid	ε	ə	ɔ
Low	Low	æ		a

too, that for both /i/ and /æ/, your tongue stays pretty far forward in your mouth. Now say /u/ (as in f*u*ll) and /a/ (as in h*o*t). For these two sounds, the tongue varies in height but stays more to the rear of your mouth. Obviously, these different sounds can blend in to one another depending on small differences in the placement of the tongue. As we will see in Chapter 5, the apparent distinctiveness of these sounds has as much to do with our psychology as with the physical characteristics of the sounds.

Phonological Rules

Now that you are familiar with the basics of how speech sounds are produced, you can examine the underlying rules that govern how the sounds are combined. There are two kinds of phonological rules: sequence constraints and pronunciation variations.

Sequence Constraints. Pronounce each pair of letter strings shown below. Which one could *not* be a word?

bnuke

bluke

Neither of these strings form English words, but you could probably tell very quickly that *bluke* could be a word whereas *bnuke* could not. The phonological rules of English do not allow the /bn/ combination. Because neither of the letter strings is a word, you could not have made this decision by finding one of the letter strings stored in your memory as a word. Your decision must have been made using your tacit knowledge of

ACTIVITY 2.2   An Amateur Linguist Discovers a Phonological Rule

This activity is based on an example provided by Callary (1985), who noted that English allows only nine consonant sounds to precede /r/ at the beginning of a word:

[p b t d k g f θ š]

These sounds fall into two groups based on manner of articulation. Use Table 2.3 on page 39 to determine which two groups of sounds can precede /r/.

You found, I'm sure, that one of the categories is the fricatives. However, not all the fricatives are permissible. What is different about the fricative that is not permitted? Now try to phrase what you have found to be a rule about the initial sounds that can precede /r/. Compare your rule with the one stated in the text.

sequences of sounds. Apparently, people are able to use this tacit knowledge very quickly and easily.

The rules for combining phonemes place considerable limitations on possible words in our language. For example, if the rules allowed any combination of one, two, or three consonants at the beginning of a word, there would be over 12,000 different ways to begin an English word with a consonant. However, the phonological rules of English actually allow fewer than 60 of these possible combinations (Callary, 1985). Not only are the phonological rules quite restrictive, they are also quite subtle. To get a feel for what phonological rules are like, try Activity 2.2 before you read any further.

If you worked carefully through Activity 2.2, you arrived at a rule that seems arbitrary, to say the least. A formal statement of the rule is this: *At the beginning of an English word, /r/ can be preceded by a stop or a voiceless fricative, as long as the fricative is not alveolar.* This rule is a mouthful, if not a brainful. Yet, as the *bnuke* versus *bluke* example showed, your tacit knowledge of phonology somehow allows you to use information about sequences of sounds in words to make decisions very rapidly. Given the amount of *conscious* thought required to deduce this rule, it seems very remarkable that you can quickly and easily make *unconscious* use of such subtle knowledge. But not all of the sequence constraints, or other phonological rules, seem so arbitrary. As you will see below, some rules actually make pronunciation easier.

Pronunciation Variations. I noted earlier that each phoneme is really a family of different sounds. Part of our phonological knowledge includes rules for systematic variation in the way that phonemes are pronounced depending on the context. For example, read the following sentence out loud:

I made stewed tiger before a battle.

You just produced three /t/ sounds, each one differently.

The unaspirated [t], as in "stewed," is used when /t/ is followed by a vowel, but the /t/ is not in the initial position of the word. The aspirated [t] of "tiger" is the /t/ we use at the beginning of the word when a vowel follows. When you said "battle" you produced yet another allophone of /t/. The tip of your tongue touched the alveolar ridge (as is usual for /t/), but then you dropped the sides of your tongue. This action produced a [t] that is indistinguishable from [d] in many dialects of English. We use this [t] between a stressed (emphasized) vowel and an unstressed vowel. For example, we use the [d]-sounding [t] in "Betty" but not in "Betsy."

Not only do people obey these rules regularly and unconsciously, but the rules themselves can be quite general. For example, the rule that says that we aspirate the consonant before a vowel at the beginning of a word applies not just to /t/ but also to /p/ and /k/. In fact, speech that alters the usual shifts between allophones often sounds artificial or comically stiff. I recall preparing for a speech contest in seventh grade and being told by my speech instructor to go around saying "better-butter" with aspirated [t] sounds. In other words, I was saying the [t] the same way that you would for "tiger." However, no amount of "aspiration practice" got me to pronounce all my /t/ sounds with aspiration, and I would have sounded silly if I had.

Whereas some of these pronunciation rules seem arbitrary, others make rapid speech easier. For example, the [t] in *button* is a nasal [t] allophone. When we release the [t] we also drop the velum so that the [t] and the following [n] are both released nasally. The nasal [t] makes it easier to produce the next sound when that sound has a nasal point of articulation. This process of altering a sound to make it more like an adjacent sound is known as **assimilation.** Assimilation is found in all languages and dialects; it is a normal part of language. Some people (like my old speech teacher) think that these shifts are examples of sloppy pronunciation, when in fact they reflect systematic and rule-governed aspects of phonology.

Morphology and Productivity

In Chapter 1, I introduced you to the idea of a morpheme, the smallest unit of language that carries meaning. A common-sense way to describe our morphological knowledge is as a mental dictionary that lists the words we know along with all the existing variations on those words. However, this simple view of people's knowledge of morphology is incomplete. As we just saw in the case of phonology, our morphological knowledge involves a tacit understanding of abstract rules. The reason that linguists describe at least part of our morphological knowledge in terms of abstract rules is that our use of words is characterized by productivity.

To account for the productivity of people's use of words, linguists think of our **lexicon,** the technical name given to our knowledge of words, as consisting of both listings of morphemes and the rules for combining morphemes. The different types of morphemes and rules are defined in Table 2.4. The morphemes themselves can be thought of as listings of entries in a kind of mental dictionary. I'll have more to say about what the entries consist of, and how they are organized, later in this chapter and in subsequent chapters. For now, however, our main focus is on the morphological rules because they help account for the productivity of language.

Inflectional Rules

Inflectional rules describe the procedures for adding morphemes to a word such that the usage of the word is changed but the basic meaning is not altered. For example, the

TABLE 2.4	**Components of the Lexicon**	
Free morphemes	These are morphemes that can stand alone as words (e.g., *help*).	
Bound morphemes	These are the morphemes that must be combined with another morpheme (e.g., the suffix *-ful*, as in *helpful*).	
Inflectional rules	Rules for changing the form of a word to fit the word's role in a sentence (e.g., adding *-ed* to show past tense).	
Derivational rules	Rules for combining morphemes so that the meaning or grammatical category is changed (e.g., *help* + *er* yields *helper*, which makes a noun out of a verb).	

rule that says you add *-s* to a word in order to form a plural is an example of a more general rule:

> *Rule 1:* N → Nstem (Ninfl). (A noun consists of a noun stem and an optional noun inflection.)

As languages go, English is not very productive in its inflectional morphology. English nouns come in two forms—singular and plural—and the verbs come in four forms. With the verb *lick*, for example, you can say, "I *lick* the ice cream, he *licks* the ice cream, she *licked* the ice cream, and they *are licking* the ice cream," but then you run out of forms of *lick*. Compare this to Spanish, with its approximately 50 forms for each verb, or to classic Greek in which each verb has 350 forms (Pinker, 1994).

The important point here is that when people use inflections they are following rules, not just memorizing new word forms. One way we can see this is by reference to languages in which inflections do not just involve the addition of a particular morpheme but, instead, follow a rule for reduplicating a part of a word (Anderson, 1988; Marantz, 1982). In the English sentence "The great loves of his life were his many works of art," both *love* and *work* are used as nouns, and their plurals follow the regular rule of adding *-s*. In Samoan, by contrast, the singular form of *love* is *alofa* and the plural is *alolofa*. Based on the same abstract rule, *galue* (work) is singular and *galulue* is plural.

Even in English, with its poverty of inflections, it is clear that the use of inflections follows rules. As children acquire English, they often apply valid rules to specific cases that happen to be exceptions to the rule (Brown, 1973). A colleague of mine once reported that her preschooler ran into the house one day and said: "Billy taked my bike!" To her knowledge, no one had ever used "taked" around this child. He was simply applying a rule that he had learned.

Derivational Rules

Unlike the inflectional rules of English, its derivational rules are positively prolific. Derivational rules allow us not only to add morphemes that change word classes but also to combine words into compounds. So, for example, we have a very general derivational rule that says we can create new noun stems by compounding existing noun stems:

Rule 2: Nstem → Nstem Nstem

Examples of the application of this rule include compound nouns such as *toothpaste*, *bug-eater* (often applied to obnoxious younger siblings), and *great-grandmother* (a compound of a compound). Other derivational rules allow us to add a morpheme that changes the word class of the stem. For example, an adjective can be created from a verb by adding an adjective suffix:

Rule 3: Adjstem → Vstem Adjsuff (as in: teachable → teach + able)

Now, let's return to the central issue of this chapter and ask what the study of morphology implies for the nativist hypothesis. Is there any reason to think that morphological knowledge has an innate basis? The consensus among linguists is that the answer is "yes," but we must qualify this answer carefully.

Specific morphological rules and specific morpheme stems are *not* genetically programmed. The specifics of morphology vary too much among languages for the rules themselves to be genetically programmed. In addition, it is clear that many morphological rules are accidents of history. For example, the English suffix *-hood* comes from the Old English *had*, which meant "state" or "rank." The Old English word was a noun stem that stood alone. With frequent usage of *had* behind a variety of other nouns, it evolved into our modern suffix *-hood*.

Such historical changes in syntax and morphology are common in all languages. In fact, the morphology of any given language is always changing. Again, consider the *-hood* example. That suffix has now also become a free morpheme in some dialects of English; in fact, it is quite prevalent in rap music. A more general example of this type of productivity in morphology comes from a recent study by Sproat (1992), who kept track of the number of distinct words used in Associated Press news stories from February to December 1988. The total came to about 300,000 distinct word forms! On just the last day of the study, Sproat noted the use of 35 forms that had not appeared on any of the previous days. These uses were not simply the result of authors dusting off obscure words they had found in a thesaurus. Rather, many of the forms that appeared were new words or novel variations on old forms.

So, it is clear that if there are any innate aspects of morphology, they must exist at a more general and abstract level. Pinker (1990) offered a cogent example of how an abstract innate principle might work in morphology. The idea is that our tacit knowledge of language has a **uniqueness principle** that is innately built in. This principle concerns the tacit knowledge that tells the language user that, for example, there can be only one past-tense form of a verb. Such a principle could greatly assist our acquisition of morphology. As I mentioned earlier, children often misapply morphological rules to irregular forms. "Billy taked my bike" is a classic example. As children learn more language, they come to realize that particular verbs have irregular forms. The uniqueness principle would make it easy to delete incorrect forms (such as *taked* and *goed*) from the lexicon as soon as the irregular forms are learned.

Whether innate ideas like the uniqueness principle are really needed to explain language acquisition is a question that we will address in Chapter 10. For now, it is enough that you see that a restricted version of the nativist hypothesis is at least plausible, based on our survey of morphology.

Syntax and Productivity

As we have seen, people show productivity by combining sounds and by combining morphemes. However, the real power of language as a communication tool comes from our ability to use syntactic rules to combine words into sentences. For example, any theory positing syntactic rules must be able to account for **iteration.** Iteration allows us, at least in principle, to generate sentences of infinite length, inasmuch as we can always add another phrase to the end of a given sentence. So, each of these sentences is a legal utterance in English:

(6) The student likes the professor.

(7) The student likes the professor who tells interesting stories.

(8) The student likes the professor who tells interesting stories in her afternoon class.

Iteration is not the only way that sentences can be made infinitely longer. Languages also show **recursion,** whereby phrases can be embedded inside a simple sentence. So, we could expand on sentence (6) from the inside out:

(9) The student who often falls asleep in classes likes the professor.

(10) The student who often falls asleep in classes held in the afternoons likes the professor.

With limitless time and patience you could continue adding phrases inside sentence (10) without violating the grammatical rules for forming sentences in English. At some point, of course, the sentence would become very difficult to understand, thus violating the *proscriptive* rules passed on by English teachers. Yet no matter how many embeddings you added, the sentence would not violate *grammatical* rules.

What makes this high degree of productivity possible? I have implied that it is based on underlying rules, but you might wonder whether such rules are really necessary to explain syntax. Before we look for the underlying rules of syntax, let's consider an alternative idea.

A Finite-State View of Syntax

Once upon a time, both linguists and psychologists hoped that syntax could be explained in relatively simple terms. As suggested by the quote from Humboldt, traditional linguistics was concerned with language as a mental event and with the search for universals across languages. In the 1930s, however, a major shift occurred in the focus of linguistics, owing largely to the influential ideas of Bloomfield (1933).

Bloomfield put linguistics on the same path that psychology was beginning to take at the time, with a focus on observable behavior and an avoidance of theories that invoked the concept of mental processes. Bloomfield called this approach *mechanism.* He stated that linguists should be mechanists and that "the mechanist believes that *mental images, feelings,* and the like are merely popular terms for various bodily movements" (p. 142). Similarly, many psychologists of this era were convinced that a scientific psychology was possible only if psychology turned to *behaviorism,* whereby objective stimuli and overt behaviors were studied without reference to mental processes. From the 1930s through the 1950s, the notions of mechanism and behaviorism dominated linguistics and psychology, at least in the United States.

The preeminent behaviorist during this time was B. F. Skinner. Among his many interests was the question of how language is learned and how it is produced. To address this question, Skinner had to propose how words are put together to make sentences. There wasn't a lot of linguistic work being done on the issue of syntax at the time, but the studies that had been conducted (e.g., Hockett, 1954; Shannon & Weaver, 1949) suggested that the productivity of language might be based on a simple system known as a **finite-state grammar** (FSG). An FSG consists of transitions between a series of states or elements. Each state, which is a word or word category, leads to the next state. Likewise, Skinner's explanation for language productivity was based on a kind of FSG (Skinner, 1957).

According to this view, sentences, like other complex behaviors, are chains of responses that we have learned to produce in particular situations. Skinner believed that an objective stimulus in the environment elicited the first word in a sentence, the first word served as the stimulus for the second word, and so on. An example of this simple kind of FSG is shown in Figure 2.3.

Is this kind of grammar a reasonable way to think of the problem of productivity? Certainly, the sample FSG in Figure 2.3 can generate several English sentences, such as "The tired boy tasted defeat" and "A lucky girl saw treats." Moreover, if we added a feedback loop from s3 to s2, the FSG would have the power to generate infinitely long sentences. For example, an FSG with such a feedback loop would allow the sentence "The lucky lucky . . . boy tasted treats," with "lucky" repeated for emphasis as many times as the speaker desires.

However, our sample FSG works only because we have organized the possible word choices for each state by grammatical category. Therefore, we can express a more

---

FIGURE 2.3   **A Simple Finite-State Grammar**

In principle, we could produce a sentence by making a series of transitions between an initial state (s0) and a final state (s5). At each state, one or more words are available for production.

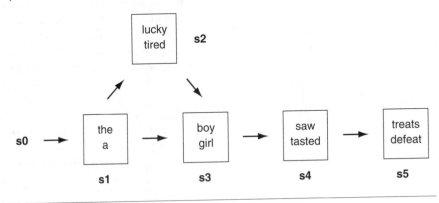

FIGURE 2.4   A General Finite-State Grammar

This more general finite-state grammar is based on transitions between different grammatical categories of words. In many cases, it can explain why a particular sentence is considered grammatical or ungrammatical. However, this grammar cannot explain recursion.

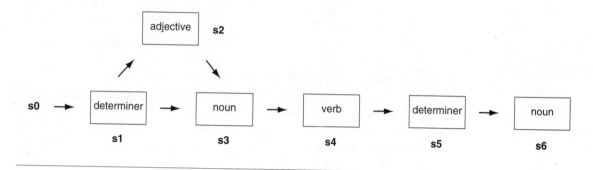

general FSG by using grammatical categories such as those shown in Figure 2.4. This FSG could be used to generate the example sentence given earlier: "The student likes the professor." If a child were learning a language based on this kind of grammar, the main thing to be learned would be associations among pairs of words.

To be a good candidate for the means behind real language production, though, the FSG must be able to show productivity in the form of iteration and recursion. Could we get this kind of grammar to show iteration? What if we added an optional conjunction state to the end of the sequence in Figure 2.4, with an arrow pointing back to the beginning? Because the conjunction state would allow for generation of the words *and, but,* and *or,* we could now add new elements to the end of each sentence.

But what about recursion? It is here that we find the FSG's Achilles' heel. In a series of early papers, including a review of Skinner's (1957) book *Verbal Behavior,* Noam Chomsky (e.g., Chomsky, 1957, 1959) showed that an FSG is unable to account for recursion in language.* The problem is that FSGs are a very amnesic form of grammar. They have no way of "remembering" anything except the last word produced. This is a problem for FSGs because dependencies between words in a sentence can extend over many words. Look back at the example of recursion shown in sentence (10). Why is the verb *likes* rather than *like?* The subject, *student,* is singular, so the main verb has to be *likes* rather than *like.* In other words, the subject and the verb have to agree in number. However, these two words are not adjacent in the sentence. According to the FSG, the word *afternoons,* which precedes the main verb, is supposed to be the word that elicits *likes,* but this word is useless for telling us whether *like* or *likes* should be chosen.

---

* Chomsky covers much more than a refutation of FSGs in his review of *Verbal Behavior* (Chomsky, 1959). Indeed, the precision of Chomsky's arguments make his review well worth reading. However, many feel that the article has the tone of a personal attack, which, unfortunately, seems to be a tradition in linguistics.

You may be experiencing either of two reactions to the demise of FSGs. One reaction is to try to rescue FSGs by saying that, instead of having each word elicit the next word, we could have each preceding context elicit the next word. So, in a four-word sentence, the fourth word would be controlled by the previous *three* words. Sorry, but this system cannot work either. George Miller, the person most responsible for bringing Chomsky's ideas into psychology, noted that dependencies between words can potentially extend over fourteen words or more (Miller, 1962; Miller & Chomsky, 1963). Here's an example from a hypothetical soap opera plot:

> (11) Jason, who was married to Amanda while dating Karen, and who only pretended to be dying of a rare terminal illness in order to play on the sympathies of the Wilson twins, has now dedicated his life to helping others.

In FSG terms, the proper form of the thirty-third element, *has* or *have*, depends on the nature of the first element, Jason. Even in more ordinary sentences that do not describe television shows, approximately one billion associative links among specific word combinations would have to be acquired for this kind of FSG system to work. Even if a child learned these associations at the ridiculously high rate of one association per second, it would take thirty years for the child to learn a language!

The other reaction you may have to the failing of FSGs would be to say, "So what?" The question of whether FSGs can accommodate recursion may seem pretty esoteric. What you should keep in mind, though, is that in the late 1950s the dominant approach to psychology in the United States was radical behaviorism, with all its disdain for mentalistic concepts like memory. It was in this context that Chomsky showed that behavioristic principles cannot account for a basic feature of language productivity. Because language is so obviously fundamental to human behavior, behaviorism's failure to adequately deal with language caught the attention of many psychologists, thus contributing to the development of the field of cognitive psychology in general and psycholinguistics in particular. This issue is discussed further in Chapter 3; but as you will see in the next section of the present chapter, Chomsky's ideas did not just change psychology, they revolutionized linguistics and greatly changed the relationship between linguistics and psychology.

Chomsky's Theories of Grammar

It is one thing to criticize someone else's ideas, but a much more difficult matter to point the way toward better alternatives. And, indeed, it was clear even from his review of Skinner's book that Chomsky had more in mind than demolishing a behavioral view of language. As Chomsky noted at the end of the review:

> The fact that all normal children acquire essentially comparable grammars of great complexity with remarkable rapidity suggests that human beings are somehow specially designed to do this, with data-handling or "hypothesis-formulating" ability of unknown origin. *(p. 57)*

Over time, Chomsky made good on the promise implied in this quote. In particular, he developed specific and influential ideas of grammar (e.g., Chomsky, 1957, 1965, 1980). What made his ideas so revolutionary is that he changed the very kinds of questions that linguists tried to investigate. In the 1950s, most linguists were following

Bloomfield's lead. They were trying to describe the features of samples of language stimuli, and they were avoiding any discussion of the language users' knowledge. Chomsky's vision of the job of linguistics was much more ambitious. Chomsky believed that linguists should describe not language **performance** but language **competence**. In other words, the job of linguists is to describe the nature of the tacit knowledge that allows people to use language.

Ultimately, Chomsky would like to describe the tacit knowledge of grammar that underlies *all* languages. That is, Chomsky seeks to reveal the **Universal Grammar (UG)**. Of course, to do this, he would have to examine and compare particular languages so to determine what kind of grammatical system makes them work. There are several kinds of grammatical knowledge that could be described, but Chomsky's main concern is to describe the universal aspects of syntactic knowledge.

Chomsky's ambitious goal raises a very important question: How would linguists know whether they have come up with the "right" grammar for describing the nature of a particular language, let alone the universal grammar as the basis of all languages? Chomsky has proposed that linguists should try to develop a theory of grammar that fulfills two goals:

- First, a theory of grammar should have **descriptive adequacy** (Chomsky, 1982). There are two criteria for descriptive adequacy. A descriptively adequate grammar should specify (1) what utterances are acceptable and not acceptable in the language, and (2) how different utterances are related to each other. For example, the grammar should explain why "John drove the car" is acceptable but "Drove the car John" is not. It should also explain how two different sentences, such as "John drove the car" and "The car was driven by John," can have the same meaning. Note that Chomsky is saying we can determine how sentences are related, or whether a sentence is acceptable, simply in terms of the intuitions available to the typical speaker of the language.

- Second, a theory of grammar should have **explanatory adequacy** (Chomsky, 1965, 1982). In other words, the grammar should be learnable by children. Linguists might be able to come up with several different grammatical theories that are all descriptively adequate. But in this case, we would prefer a theory that also explains how the grammar can be acquired based on innate knowledge and language experience.

To better understand the development of Chomsky's ideas, let's begin with the basic framework that he developed in order to meet the goal of a descriptively adequate grammar. Then we will look at the changes he made to his theory in order to meet the goal of a linguistic theory with explanatory adequacy.

Describing Language Competence. One failure of FSGs was that they did not account for dependencies between words that are quite distant in a sentence. Chomsky felt that this shortcoming was part of a larger problem that was not addressed by other theories in linguistics: In short, sentences seem to consist not just of words but of phrases. He proposed that a major aspect of the tacit knowledge that people have about language can be depicted as a set of formal rules for creating sentences out of groups of words. These rules are called **phrase structure rules**. The notation for depicting these rules is similar to the notation we used for depicting morphological rules. Here are some examples of basic phrase structure rules (including "translations" of each into English):

Rule 4: S→ NP VP (A sentence is composed of a noun phrase and a verb phrase.)

Rule 5: NP→ (DET)(ADJ) N (A noun phrase is composed of an optional determiner, an optional adjective, and a noun.)

Rule 6: VP→ V (NP) (ADV) (A verb phrase is composed of a verb, an optional noun phrase, and an optional adverb.)

These and other phrase structure rules provide a skeleton for the relationships among words in a sentence. Now, instead of thinking of sentences as a chain of words, we can see them as a set of hierarchical relationships. This concept becomes even clearer if we express a sentence as a phrase structure tree. For example, the sentence "The student likes the professor" can be expressed as the tree diagram shown in Figure 2.5.

Phrase structure rules help us understand why we can judge sentences as grammatical even if they do not have meaning. The sentence "Colorless green ideas sleep furiously" was devised by Chomsky to illustrate the point that we can think of syntax as distinct from meaning. The sentence is meaningless, but it seems syntactically correct because it follows *Rule 6* above. Scramble the word order, and the sentence no longer follows the rule.

I hope that at this point you are ready to raise a serious objection. What about productivity? So far, phrase structure rules do not seem to be any better than FSGs at

---

FIGURE 2.5   **A Phrase Structure Tree Diagram**

A tree diagram is a useful way to express the phrase groupings that make up a sentence.

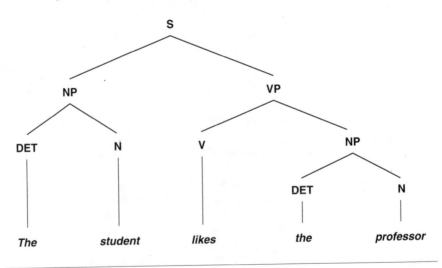

capturing the productivity of language. Can phrase structure rules express the recursiveness of language? Unlike FSGs, phrase structure rules can represent recursiveness. To do so, phrase structure rules must allow for rewriting sentence constituents like this:

Rule 7: NP→ (DET)(ADJ) N (S)

If you compare *Rule 4* and *Rule 7,* you see that the sentence element, S, can occur on both sides of the arrow. This allows us to embed one sentence inside another. Consider the following complex, but grammatical, sentence:

(12)   The rat that the cat killed ate the cheese.

To see how this sentence is made possible by *Rule 7,* we first have to break it down into the separate sentences from which it is constructed:

(13)   The rat ate the cheese.

(14)   The cat killed the rat.

According to *Rule 7,* we can use recursion to embed sentence (14) inside sentence (13). We simply rewrite the NP of sentence (13) as

NP→ [The rat] [the cat killed the rat]

If we use this new construction as a single noun phrase, then we are a short step from using *Rule 4* to create the compound sentence (12). However, notice that we don't just plug in the new NP like this:

(15)   *The rat the cat killed the rat* ate the cheese.

Instead, we apply a **transformation** to the phrase structure in order to produce sentence (12), the correct version of the embedding. Transformations are syntactic rules for moving, deleting, or adding elements within a phrase structure. In our current example, two transformations are used to produce sentence (12) from sentence (15): The second occurrence of *the rat* is deleted and the word *that* is inserted before the embedded sentence.*

Many children's nursery rhymes seem to be enjoyable precisely because they involve the repeated application of rules like the ones we have been using here. However, it is important to note that phrase structure rules and transformations help us to explain much more than "word games" or even recursion. In particular, Chomsky (1965) used the concept of transformation to explain how two sentences can be phrased differently and yet have similar meanings. Consider this sentence:

(16)   Jack put the car in the garage.

Figure 2.6 shows the phrase structure tree for this sentence. All the necessary pieces seem to be in place. This sentence follows *Rule 4* as well as another general rule:

Rule 8: VP→ V NP PP

---

* You might have noted that insertion of the word *that* in this example is an optional transformation. Sentence (12) would also be grammatical, though slightly harder to understand, if it read, "The rat the cat killed ate the cheese." The other transformation, deletion of the second occurrence of the initial NP, is not optional.

The term *PP* refers to a prepositional phrase. Note that for the specific verb *put,* the NP and the PP do not seem to be optional. That is, the verb *put* requires both a noun that represents the object, the thing that is put, and a place for it to be put, which is expressed by the PP. We would not say "Jack put the car"; nor would we say "Jack put in the garage." Regarding each of the latter two sentences, we have the strong sense that a necessary element is missing.

Now, however, we run into a problem. The following sentence seems just fine:

(17)   The car was put in the garage.

Where is the missing NP for the verb *put?* Actually the thing being put is not missing at all. It's there in the sentence, but it has been moved into a new position as the subject of the sentence rather than the object of *put.* What causes the problem is that sentence (17) is in the passive voice, as opposed to the active voice, which is used in sentence (16). To handle the problem of the "missing" object, Chomsky explained that there are really two phrase structures for a given sentence. In the **deep structure,** all the elements appear in their expected places based on the general phrase structure rules. However, the transformations that are allowed by the grammar of a language can move some elements to different places in the **surface structure.** A depiction of the deep and surface structures for sentence (17) appears in Figure 2.7.

The deep structure expresses the relationships among the sentence elements, so two sentences with different surface forms can express the same underlying relationships among elements. Another reason for the proposed distinction between surface

| FIGURE 2.6 | A Phrase Structure Tree with a Prepositional Phrase |

This tree diagram shows the phrase structure for a sentence that follows the rule VP→ V NP PP.

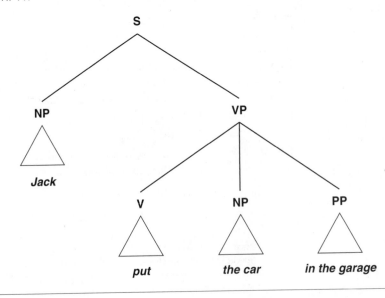

FIGURE 2.7	**Surface Structure and Deep Structure**

Shown here is a comparison of two phrase structures for the passive sentence *The car was put in the garage.* The surface structure captures the relationships between sentence elements as they are directly expressed by the sentence. (A "trace" shows that the NP that serves as the object for *put* has been placed elsewhere.) And the deep structure captures the relationships between sentence elements in terms of the general phrase structure rules, independent of whether the sentence is in the active or passive voice.

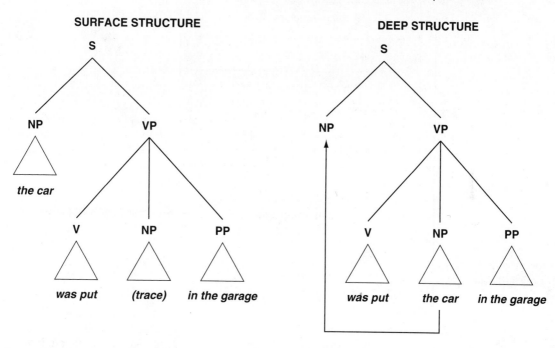

structure and deep structure is that sometimes one surface structure can be mapped onto two different deep structures, as in the ambiguous sentence "Flying planes can be dangerous." This sentence could mean that the act of flying a plane is dangerous, or it could mean that planes that are flying around are dangerous to people on the ground. Each of these intended meanings is associated with a different deep structure.

Note, however, that the deep structure is not the same thing as *meaning*. According to Chomsky, the deep structure is an aspect of the syntactic component of grammar, which is independent of the semantic component of grammar. However, it *is* the deep structure that gets interpreted by the semantic component. An outline of the whole scheme that Chomsky (1965) had in mind is shown in Figure 2.8.

The "base" of the syntax consists of phrase structure rules, the lexicon, and rules for inserting words into phrase structures. So, the function of the base is to generate a deep structure. The deep structure is based on a particular phrase structure tree into which appropriate words have been plugged. The deep structure plays a pivotal role in

| FIGURE 2.8 | Chomsky's (1965) Transformational Grammar |

Phrase structure rules and lexical knowledge are used to generate a deep structure, which is semantically interpreted by a separate component of the grammar. Transformations operate on the deep structure to produce the surface structure.

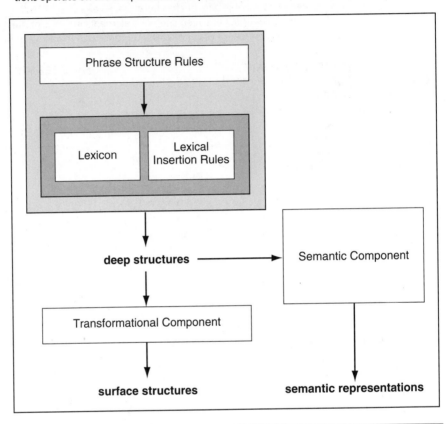

this version of Chomsky's theory. It serves as the input to the semantic component, which produces a meaningful interpretation of a sentence. In addition, the deep structure serves as input to the transformational component, which produces the surface structure. During language production the surface structure is submitted to the phonological component of grammar (not shown in the diagram).

Thus, different elements—syntax, the base, the transformational system, and the deep and surface structures they generate—all serve the purpose of relating meaning and sound. According to Chomsky, the productivity of language is completely due to this syntactic system. It is easy to see why Chomsky concentrated his efforts on understanding syntax but left more general notions about semantic and phonological components relatively vague.

At this stage of his work, Chomsky (1965) proposed many different kinds of transformations. In addition to the movement transformation, which accounts for passive and active voice, there are transformations specific to formation of commands, generation of particular questions from a statement, and negation—to name just three examples. Indeed, Chomsky's theory of transformational grammar (TG) led to some of the first experimental studies in psycholinguistics as researchers tried to test the psychological reality of the transformations he had proposed (e.g., Blumenthal & Boakes, 1967; Miller, 1962). In the next chapter we'll explore the impact of these studies on the field of psychology. For now, however, remember that Chomsky is interested in competence rather than performance, so psychological tests of whether these transformations actually take place in our minds have not been of great interest to him in testing his theory. Nevertheless, Chomsky has continued to revise the theory. One reason is that, although the 1965 version of TG was descriptively appealing, it has problems as an explanatory theory. We turn now to revisions of Chomsky's original theory that were motivated by explanatory concerns.

Toward an Explanatory Theory.   In brief, the problem with Chomsky's (1965) transformational grammar is that it is difficult to see how so many different and specific kinds of transformations could be part of our genetic endowment for language. Could children learn all these transformations based simply on their language experience? Probably not, given that language is acquired so quickly and easily.

Concerns about explanatory adequacy have led Chomsky (1982, 1986) to a new view, the **principles and parameters theory.** Chomsky's latest theory is known more

---

| FIGURE 2.9 | An Outline of Chomsky's (1982) Principles and Parameters Theory |

The d-structure and s-structure are similar to the earlier concepts of deep and surface structure except that it is the s-structure that is related to the PF (phonetic form, or sound information) and the LF (logical form, or meaning information). This theory posits only one kind of transformation: movement of an element in a phrase structure.

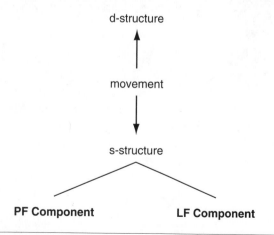

technically as **government and binding theory,** but "principles and parameters" seems the more apt title, for reasons that I will make clear shortly. A sketch of how Chomsky now views grammar is depicted in Figure 2.9 (page 55).

As in the previous version of Chomsky's theory, syntax is considered a bridge between sound and meaning. Chomsky believes that the syntactic component does its work autonomously; for this reason, he says, we can study syntactic processes without knowing how sound perception and semantic interpretation are performed. Syntactic processes generate the phonetic form (PF) and logical form (LF), which connect, respectively, with our knowledge of speech sounds and our knowledge of meaning.

The most important change from the earlier TG theory is that the principles and parameters theory posits only a single generic transformation: move-α, which means "move some element." The reason that Chomsky has been able to propose one type of transformation rather than many types is that in his new theory the rules of language are stated in much more general terms. This change is easiest to see in terms of the modifications that Chomsky has made to phrase structure rules. Chomsky has replaced rules about NPs and VPs with more abstract rules that refer to sentence elements in general, much as we use a variable like *X* in algebra to stand for any number.

The change in Chomsky's theory came from the observation that all phrases in all languages share certain characteristics. We can grasp the validity of this observation by comparing two phrases, as in Figure 2.10.

Even though one of the phrases in the figure is an NP and the other is a VP, the two phrases have identical structures. First, each has a subject (also known as a *specifier*) that is the doer—the causal agent—in the phrase. In our example, *linguists* is the

| FIGURE 2.10 | **X-Bar Phrase Analysis** |

Even though one of these two phrases is a VP and the other is an NP, the structure of each phrase is the same. In particular, each has a subphrase—that is, a V-bar or an N-bar. In turn, each subphrase has a *head*, which is the noun or verb that determines what type of phrase it is, and the head is followed by a *role player* (in these examples, an NP or a PP).

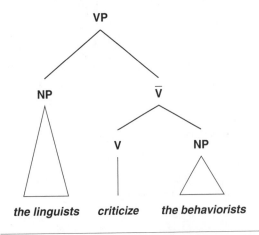
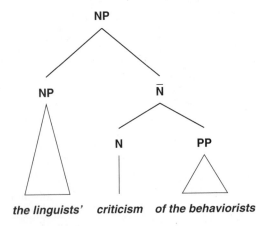

subject of both phrases. Second, each phrase also has a subphrase, the V-bar in the VP and the N-bar in the NP. The V-bar and the N-bar subphrases each have a **head,** a word that determines what kind of phrase it is, as well as **role players** that go along with the head. The verb *criticizes* is the head of the V-bar and the noun *criticism* is the head of the N-bar.*

Because the design of phrases is so general, it is not necessary to describe phrase structure rules with specific elements like NP or N-bar. Instead of NP, we can use the term *X-phrase* to cover all types of phrases. So, for example, we can say:

Rule 9: XP → (SPEC) $\overline{X}$ YP (A phrase is composed of an optional specifier, or subject, and an X-bar plus any number of modifiers.)

Rule 10: $\overline{X}$ → X Rps (An X-bar is composed of a head and role players.)

Now for the interesting part. Remember our hypothesis at the beginning of the chapter, that language is founded on innate knowledge. Now we can be more specific about what that innate knowledge might be like. English is an example of a head-first language. The head of an X-bar always occurs before the role players. So, if you meet a friend coming out of the art museum, she might tell you that a new "picture is hanging on the wall." Here *picture* is the subject, *is hanging* is the head, and *on the wall* is a role player. As Cook (1988) has pointed out, in Japanese this phrase would be

(18) *E wa kabe ni kakatte imasu* (picture wall on is hanging).

Not only does the verb come after the role player, but the role player itself, *ni* (on), which is the head of the PP, comes at the end of the PP. So, in Japanese, a PP is really a *post*positional phrase, not a *pre*positional phrase. Japanese is a head-last language. Thus, although languages vary in terms of whether they are head-first or head-last, each language is consistently one or the other across all phrase types. Chomsky uses the term **head-parameter** to refer to the issue of whether a language is head-first or head-last. The idea of the head-parameter is that when you are an infant acquiring a language, you have innate knowledge that says you must use your language experience to determine whether your language is head-first or head-last. Once you hear enough language to set this parameter, you know tacitly where all heads will be in all phrases. Which particular setting is used in your language is learned, but knowing to look for that distinction is part of the innate foundation for language.

Yet, obviously, to use your language you must know much more than just how to set the head-parameter. Chomsky has identified a number of other linguistic universals that represent parameters to be set during language acquisition. The specific parameters are not as important for our study of language as is the general notion of parameter setting. According to Chomsky, the innate knowledge that serves as the foundation for language can be represented as parameters to be set during language acquisition.

To review: Some of the basic ideas behind the principles and parameters theory are similar to Chomsky's earlier theory of transformational grammar. Syntactic

---

* If the V-bar and N-bar jargon seems arbitrary and difficult to remember, here's a mnemonic for you. Neighborhood bars always have a head—usually the bartender—who gives the bar its personality, its own particular ambiance. Just as some people hang around in bars that reflect the character of the head, words hang around in N-bars and V-bars that take on the character of the head. After all, what makes a V-bar a V-bar is that the head is a verb.

knowledge is still viewed as a separate component of grammar that bridges sound and meaning. There remain two types of phrase structures in the theory (now called d-structure and s-structure). And a movement transformation is still used to move elements inside phrase structures. However, to avoid postulating many different kinds of transformations, Chomsky has developed much more abstract and general kinds of syntactic rules in the principles and parameters theory.

Not all linguists agree that Chomsky's new approach addresses all the relevant concerns about transformational grammar. In fact, some have made a radical departure from transformational grammar in developing alternative theories of syntactic knowledge.

Lexicalist Grammars: No Transformations Required

A common trend in recent alternatives to Chomsky's transformational theories has been to eliminate the idea of transformations altogether. According to these theories (e.g., Bresnan, 1978; Fillmore, 1971), the role that transformations play in Chomsky's work is actually performed by knowledge that is part of the lexicon.

The groundwork for this idea was laid in Fillmore's (1968, 1971) theory of **case role grammar**. According to this view, our lexical knowledge includes information about the roles that we expect to have filled based on the verb in the sentence. As an example, let's consider the following two sentences from Fillmore:

(19) The key opened the door.

(20) The janitor opened the door with a key.

From a purely syntactic view, the word *key* plays a different role in each sentence; certainly, it would appear in quite different places in a phrase structure diagram. But Fillmore noted that this distinction is misleading. The relationship between *key, door,* and *open* is exactly the same in both sentences. That is, the key is the instrument being used to open the door. According to the theory of case role grammar, the information stored for a given verb includes what roles should be filled when a sentence uses that verb. Some examples of roles stored in our lexical knowledge include the roles of instrument (thing used to perform the action), agent (doer of the action), and location (place at which the action is performed). Fillmore regarded the cases as universal and probably innate.

A related approach has been taken by Bresnan (1978) in the more recent theory of **lexical functionalist grammar (LFG)**. Like Chomsky, Bresnan accounts for the productivity of language with phrase structure rules. And as with TG, these rules and lexical knowledge generate a structure that contains all the information needed for semantic interpretation. In LFG, this structure is called the *functional structure.* Thus, the functional structure is generated from syntactic knowledge that is analogous to the syntactic base in TG. In contrast to TG, however, no transformations between a deep and surface structure are required to understand how different sentences can have the same underlying meaning. Let's take a close look at LFG to see how it eliminates the transformations proposed in Chomsky's TG.

Recall that one reason Chomsky proposed transformations between deep and surface structures was to explain the relationship between active and passive sentences. In LFG, Bresnan suggests that the necessary information regarding this relationship is part of our lexicon. The idea is similar to Fillmore's case role notion: Lexical entries include information about the grammatical relations that can be expected when we encounter particular words. Consider the following pair of sentences:

(21)   Jack gave the dog a bone.

(22)   A bone was given to the dog by Jack.

When we read sentence (21), we find *gave* in the lexicon. The entry shows that it is the past tense of *give*. Thus we are led to the following entry in the lexicon:

give: GIVE [SUBJ] [OBJ] [to-OBJ]

This entry tells us that *give* requires a subject (the giver), an object (the thing given), and an object of the preposition *to* (the recipient).

When we read sentence (22) and encounter *given*, the lexical entry includes

given: GIVE [SUBJ] [to-OBJ] [by-OBJ]

This entry tells us that there must be a subject, an object of *to*, and an object of *by*. We understand the structure of each of these sentences as well as the fact that they have the same meaning because of the information in our lexicon. No transformations required.

In comparison to Chomsky's theories, lexicalist theories like LFG tend to maintain a less firm boundary between syntactic knowledge and semantic knowledge. As we will soon see in more detail, the issue of whether syntactic knowledge is as autonomous and distinguishable from semantic knowledge as Chomsky has claimed is hotly contested in both linguistics and psychology. Before we begin to discuss how these types of knowledge interact, or even whether they *are* different forms of knowledge, we need to see how semantic knowledge has been conceptualized by linguists. This brings us to the second of our central mysteries of language.

The Problem of Meaning

So far, we have considered important aspects of the knowledge that humans must have to use language, but little has been said about meaning. As an illustration of some of the issues we will have to address, let's project ahead a few years. You almost finished college but were lured away before graduating to take a position in the private sector. You arrive for work one day and your boss says, "I'm afraid that you have to go over and clear out your desk."

Under most circumstances you would interpret the boss's sentence to mean that you have been fired. In fact, the boss could have communicated the same idea by saying, "You're fired" or "You have been selected to assist the company in its downsizing by becoming a nonemployee." The relationship among the latter two statements is one of **synonymy,** or equivalence of meaning. Note, however, that these are very different utterances. They have different phrase structures and almost no words in common. Therefore, in contrast to our previous example about the active and passive versions of a sentence, the synonymy of these utterances does not result from syntactic transformations of the same deep structure. There is something else going on here.

There is another curiosity to consider as well. Imagine a different scenario in which you know you were being considered for a big promotion (because of your recent college graduation), which would involve a move to the much-valued corner office on the top floor. When you come in, your smiling boss says, "I'm afraid that you have to go over and clear out your desk." In this context, the utterance is clearly a joke and you are going to move your things to a new office. Now, the meaning of the utterance is completely different because of the context, and the instruction to "clear out your desk" no longer communicates the same idea as "You're fired."

These alternative scenarios illustrate that the study of meaning is no simple matter. Two sentences composed of completely different words can mean the same thing. The implication is that understanding meaning depends on our knowledge of semantics, which is not reducible to syntactic knowledge. Moreover, the same sentence, uttered in two different contexts, can take on two very different meanings. As discussed earlier in the chapter, we often need our knowledge of pragmatics to place the correct interpretation on a sentence spoken in context.

In this section, I'll sketch the basics of several different views of meaning and compare these views in terms of several issues of particular relevance to psycholinguistics. Our main focus will be on semantic knowledge, but we will try to get a sense of pragmatics as well. Specifically, we will consider how each view of meaning addresses four important questions:

- When we say that a particular word such as "desk" has a meaning, of what does that meaning consist? This question concerns the issue of **lexical semantics,** or word meanings.

- When we say that an utterance such as "clear out your desk" has meaning, how do we combine the word meanings to get the meaning of the whole utterance? Here we are dealing with the issue of **compositional semantics,** or the meanings of phrases and sentences.

- To what extent does our knowledge of meaning depend on innate ideas? In this context, we will consider the nativist question for semantics just as we did for other types of knowledge.

- What is the relationship between our knowledge of meaning and our knowledge of syntactic structure?

An Overview of Ideas of Meaning

No existing view of meaning provides a completely satisfactory answer to the four questions posed above. Nevertheless, a number of key ideas proposed in philosophy and linguistics have helped psychologists study meaning in language. An influential view of meaning developed within philosophy is known as the theory of **truth-conditional semantics** (e.g., Montague, 1974). This theory explains meaning as a relationship between symbols and a model of objects in the world. Truth-conditional semantics is known as an "objectivist" view because it doesn't concern itself with how people actually mentally represent objects. Instead, it regards meaning as an abstract concept related to objective situations and entities.

The other two views that we will consider grew out of linguistics. Both see meaning as a mental phenomenon rather than as a formal relationship between symbols and objects in the world. One of these views is Jackendoff's (1992) theory of **conceptual semantics,** which tries to flesh out the semantic component of Chomsky's theory by explaining semantic knowledge in terms of mental concepts and rules for combining them.

The other view is the recent development in linguistics known as the theory of **cognitive grammar** (Fauconnier, 1985; Lakoff, 1987b; Langacker, 1977, 1991). The central idea of this theory is that the rules of language can be reduced to relationships between semantic and phonological knowledge without reliance on a separate syntactic level of knowledge. According to Langacker, for example, a rich semantic system that stores information about roles of individual lexical items can interact directly with phonological information. Thus, the theory of cognitive grammar claims that there is no real dividing line between our knowledge of meaning and our knowledge of language structure. Of course, this notion is heresy to those in the Chomskyan tradition. Let's take a closer look at how each of these views answers the four questions that I posed above.

Truth-Conditional Semantics

The theory of truth-conditional semantics has been more concerned with the meaning of expressions than with the meaning of individual words. To keep things simple, let's just assume that words have commonly agreed-upon meanings (akin to dictionary definitions). But how do we go from word meanings to the meaning of an expression? The truth-conditional view answers this question by building on an insight by the nineteenth-century philosopher Gottlob Frege (1879). Frege noted that there is a distinction between the **reference** of an expression and the **sense** of an expression. The reference of an expression is the thing it stands for. The sense of an expression corresponds to the traditional idea of meaning as a combination of the meanings of words.

To use Frege's classic example: The expressions *the morning star* and *the evening star* have the same reference, the planet Venus. However, the sense of *the morning star* is of a bright light in the sky that is visible in the morning, whereas the sense of *the evening star* is of a bright light visible in the evening. Now consider this more topical example, in which the reference of both of the following expressions is Michael Jordan:

> *the greatest basketball player in the NBA*

> *the athlete who earns the most from endorsements*

The reference is the same, but the sense of these two expressions is quite different. Note that in the year 2010, although the sense of each of these expressions will be the same as it is today, the reference of each expression will no doubt have changed.

How, then, do we arrive at the meanings of sentences?

Returning to the scenario in which you were canned from your job (synonymy strikes again) , let's say you went to the local watering hole to drown your sorrows and overheard the following conversation:

"Hey, did you hear that Jack dumped Martha?"

"No, you're wrong, Martha dumped Jack."

There are two key assertions in this conversation that will show us how truth-conditional semantics works:

(23) Jack dumped Martha.

(24)   Martha dumped Jack.

These two assertions contain exactly the same lexical items, and the items mean the same thing in each assertion. Nevertheless, the meaning of each assertion is quite different. Recall that when I said one of the features of language is arbitrariness, I was speaking of lexical semantics. Accordingly, Martha could start calling herself "Glorph," or Jack could refer to himself with an unpronounceable symbol (which would be a good reason for Martha to dump him). In any case, single words like *Martha* or *dumped* cannot be true or false. However, compositional semantics is not arbitrary in the same way. A statement such as *Martha dumped Jack, can* be true or false, and we refer to such a statement as a **proposition**. In short, a proposition is a relationship between concepts that, in principle, can be true or false. A fairly standard notation for describing propositions specifies, first, the relation followed by the agent (or doer) and, then, the patient (or recipient of the action). Thus, sentence (24) could be expressed as:

dumped (Martha, Jack)

The sense of this sentence is the proposition that is expressed. We arrive at the sense of the expression by combining the word meanings in the way specified by the relevant syntactic rules. For example, we use the syntactic rule S→ NP VP to assign *Martha* the role of the agent because she appears as the initial NP. And we know that *dumped* is the relational term because it is the head of the VP.

The reference of a sentence is its truth value (i.e., its truth or falsity) in different possible models of the world (Kripke, 1963). For example, in some possible worlds, Martha has dumped Jack; in others, Jack has dumped Martha; in still others, they are still together or have never met. Two sentences are synonymous if they are true in terms of the same conditions, the same set of possible worlds. For any world in which sentence (24) is true, the following statement is also true:

(25)   Martha broke up with Jack.

The truth-conditional approach also provides a useful way to think about the semantic relationship known as **antonymy,** in which expressions have opposite meanings. Sentences (23) and (24) have this relationship inasmuch as any world in which one of these sentences is true precludes the possibility that the other statement could be true.

Next, consider the following sentence:

(26)   Martha and Jack are no longer a couple.

Clearly, this sentence is related to, but not synonymous with, sentence (24). The similarity of meaning can be traced to the overlap in the possible worlds in which both sentences would be true. In fact, for any world in which sentence (24) is true, sentence (26) is also true. However, Jack and Martha could stop being a couple for a lot of reasons, so sentence (26) could be true even if sentence (24) were not also true. In terms of truth-conditional semantics, then, sentence (26) is an **entailment** of, or logical inference from, sentence (24).

Therefore, according to the truth-conditional view, semantics is a matter of truth conditions, and pragmatics is a matter of other factors that affect meaning but are not captured by truth conditions (Gazdar, 1979). For example, you have to have some knowledge about people and their social relationships to know that "clear out your desk" could be a joke rather than an expression that means you are fired. Likewise, it is your knowledge of implications in social situations, not your analysis of truth conditions, that tells you that "could you pass the salt?" is really a request. Without such social and conversational knowledge, you would derive the wrong sense of many things that are said.

In summary, truth-conditional semantics defines meaning in terms of a logical relationship between an utterance and the states of affairs in possible worlds. The idea that compositional semantics depends on truth conditions is compatible with Chomskyan linguistics in that semantic analysis of a sentence depends on prior syntactic analysis. Without a syntactic analysis of a sentence as a guide, you cannot construct the meaning of an utterance.

Keep in mind that the theory of truth-conditional semantics does not claim that people actually consider possible worlds when determining the meaning of a sentence. Rather, truth-conditional semantics is meant to be a formal, logical way of considering what meaning is and how different sentences are related in meaning. It also allows us to explain certain basic types of meaningful relationships between statements such as synonymy, antonymy, and entailment.

Of course, the truth-conditional view also leaves a lot of things unexplained. For example, it does not take a strong stand on the question of whether there is an innate basis to semantics, nor has it clearly addressed the issues surrounding lexical semantics. In contrast, both the nativist hypothesis and lexical semantics have been addressed by the views of meaning that have grown out of linguistics.

Conceptual Semantics

Unlike the truth-conditional view, Jackendoff's theory of conceptual semantics regards meaning as a relationship between language symbols and mental concepts. In other words, meaning is not a formal, logical relationship between symbols and the world; rather, meaning is in the mind of the language user. The term Jackendoff uses to refer to the mental representation of a sentence is *conceptual structure*. From his standpoint, the central problem of meaning is one of mapping between a syntactic structure and a conceptual structure. A schematic of how Jackendoff envisions this process is shown in Figure 2.11.

We'll first consider Jackendoff's (1992) approach to lexical semantics. In his view, conceptual structures are built up, in part, from our stored concepts about the world. These concepts are used not only in language processing but in other forms of cognition as well. For example, whether we see a dog or we hear the word "dog," the same concept is brought to mind. Like most linguists before him, Jackendoff argues that concepts are composed of sets of features. This idea is known as the principle of **lexical decomposition.** So, our concept of *robin* might consist of features like *animate, lays eggs, sings,* and *red-breasted.* We know that a robin is a bird, which is a *thing.* And just knowing what kind of concept we are dealing with—a *thing*, as opposed to a *person,* an *action*, an *event*, or a *place*—tells us a lot about what roles a particular concept can enter into.

Jackendoff assumes, as do many other theorists, that some kinds of features serve as a basis for comparison across all kinds of concepts. These features are so basic that

FIGURE 2.11   **Jackendoff's (1992) View of the Language System**

Like Chomsky, Jackendoff sees syntax as a mapping process between phonology and semantics. According to this view, semantic analysis produces a conceptual structure that can be related to our general knowledge of the world, including a mental image of what was described in an utterance.

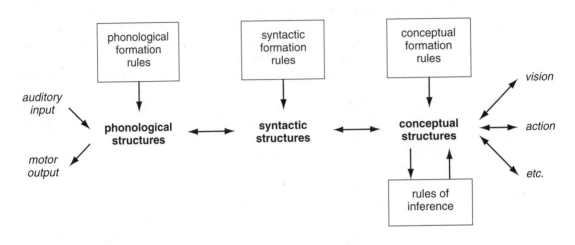

they are considered **semantic primitives.** As suggested earlier, one example of a semantic primitive may be whether an object is animate or inanimate. Innate knowledge may cause us to look for such features when learning about a concept. However, Jackendoff does not claim that all the features we use to define concepts are based on innately guided primitives. For example, a feature like *red-breasted* would not be innate.

Lexical decomposition is, however, only part of the story of lexical semantics. According to Jackendoff, our knowledge of concepts also includes images of objects and knowledge of how to perform actions. So, part of the meaning of *robin* has to do with our knowledge of how to form an image of a robin. Thus, if asked whether a certain bird looks like a robin, we could answer based on inspecting an image of a robin.

Now, let's consider how word meanings are combined. Jackendoff's view of compositional semantics depends on several different types of knowledge. One type involves *conceptual formation rules,* which we use to map semantic combinations onto simpler paraphrases that are part of our conceptual structures. For example, the expression "two times" can be converted to the term "twice." The *rules of inference* referred to in Figure 2.11 represent another type of semantic information. These rules allow for connections between a set of conceptual structures and other information that such concepts logically imply. So, in our sad little story of Martha and Jack, if Martha took off her engagement ring, placed it on the table, and said "Good-bye, Jack!" we would infer that "good-bye" means the engagement is off. Thus, the rules of inference include pragmatic knowledge.

Although conceptual formation rules and rules of inference are helpful to understanding meaning, the *correspondence rules* are what lie at the heart of compositional semantics in Jackendoff's theory. These are rules that relate syntactic structures to conceptual structures. The idea here is very similar to the proposal in truth-conditional semantics that a syntactic structure is used to guide semantic interpretation. The correspondence rules are applied to deep structures or surface structures in order to fit the semantic concepts into the proper roles specified in a sentence. Thus, like truth-conditional semantics, conceptual semantics maintains the central idea of Chomsky's transformational grammar: An autonomous syntactic module works prior to, and is uninfluenced by, the development of a semantic interpretation.

Jackendoff's view of compositional semantics differs from the theory of truth-conditional semantics in that he believes the essence of meaning is a mental representation of the sentence. As an example, consider this sentence:

(27)   Martha placed the ring on the table.

The product of mapping between the concepts in sentence (27) and its phrase structure is a conceptual structure that Jackendoff would depict as shown in Figure 2.12. This conceptual structure, in turn, would give us access to knowledge of how such a scene would appear visually or of how to act out such a scene.

Cognitive Grammar

There are important differences between the way semantics and pragmatics are treated in cognitive grammar and the way they are treated in conceptual semantics and truth-conditional semantics. Nevertheless, there is some common ground as well. Like the conceptual semantics view, the theory of cognitive grammar (Lakoff, 1987b; Langacker, 1987) explains meaning in terms of mental representation. In addition, a central idea in cognitive grammar is that we interpret language in terms of mental models. A **mental model** is an internal representation of a situation in the world. This notion is similar to Jackendoff's proposal that semantic processes give us access to visual and motor knowledge. It is also similar to the idea of a *possible world* in truth-conditional semantics, except that a mental model is a representation of a particular possible world in the mind of the language user. As we will see in later chapters, the general idea of mental models has proven quite useful in psycholinguistic theories of comprehension (e.g., Glenberg, Kruly & Langston, 1994; Johnson-Laird, 1983).

Unlike conceptual semantics, however, cognitive grammar proposes that mental models, or what Lakoff (1987b) called *idealized cognitive models* (ICMs), are the fundamental basis of both lexical and compositional semantics. Take a "simple" term like *weekend*. A true understanding of this word requires a model in which a calendar is divided into seven-day weeks, with five days designating a *work week* and the last two days designating a *weekend*. Thus, what at first seems a simple concept, which should have an easy definition, is really defined in terms of the ICM of a particular calendar system.

To understand word or sentence meaning in reference to an idealized cognitive model, we need to understand how ICMs are constructed. Lakoff and other

FIGURE 2.12	**Conceptual Semantics**

According to Jackendoff's (1992) theory, semantic analysis involves the building of a conceptual structure. This structure is built through the use of correspondence rules and the syntactic structure to determine each concept's role in the sentence. In this case, the verb *put* categorizes the sentence as an "event" that requires three elements, or "arguments" as they are known technically. The arguments required are a subject, an object, and a place. The phrase structure and the correspondence rules determine which part of the sentence is used for each argument.

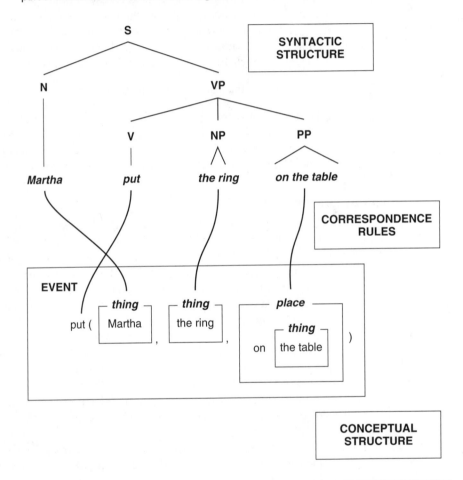

proponents of cognitive grammar (e.g., Lakoff, 1987b; Langacker, 1987) have proposed two kinds of building blocks for ICMs: basic-level concepts and image schemas.

Basic-level concepts reflect the level of abstraction that we use most readily in classifying and interacting with things in the world (Rosch et al., 1976). For example, you would typically say "I sat in the *chair* and typed for hours" rather than "I sat in the *piece of furniture* and typed for hours." Actually, basic-level concepts are intermediate in their level of generality. Most objects and activities can be classified as existing at one of three different levels: a very specific, subordinate level (e.g., *swivel chair*), the basic level (e.g., *chair*), or a more general, superordinate level (e.g., *furniture*). One characteristic of the basic level is that it is the most general level at which you can form a mental image of the category. It is hard to image *furniture* in general, but you can easily image a generic *chair*.

The second type of building blocks for our ICMs is the **image schema,** a very simple kind of model that represents fundamental aspects of our interaction with objects in the world. For example, we have a CONTAINER image schema that is the generalized idea that entities have an inside and an outside and can hold other entities inside. Some other common examples are the PATH image schema, which is a simple model of an entity moving in a particular direction, and the PART-WHOLE image schema, which represents the general idea that many objects are composed of separable parts. Thus, the models that we use to interpret words and sentences are built up from basic concepts and from generic image schemas.

Consider what is meant by the word *over* in the sentence *I flew over the city.* The meaning of *over* in this sense is represented by the simple model shown on the left side of Figure 2.13. The PATH image schema is a basic building block of this model. There are, of course, variations on the meaning of *over,* and those variations can be explained in terms of differences in the underlying model. Another sense of *over* is used in the sentence *Martha's relationship with Jack is over.* This sense of *over* is depicted on the right side of Figure 2.13. The relationship between this sense of *over* and the model is a metaphoric one in that the "distance" in the model represents a PATH through time rather than space, and the landmark is defined by the beginning and ending of something in time.

Though quite simple, models such as the ones shown in the figure can be combined with other models to capture the meaning of sentences. Recall that in the

---

FIGURE 2.13   **Two Idealized Cognitive Models for Different Meanings of *Over***

Model A depicts the meaning of *over* in an utterance where something (TR) takes a path (dotted line) above and across a landmark (LM). Model B depicts the meaning of *over* in an utterance where something is on the other side of a boundary.

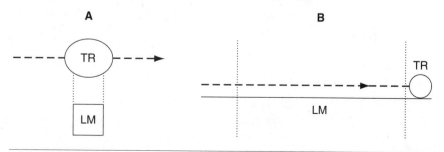

final scene of the Martha and Jack tragedy, Martha puts the engagement ring on the table and leaves. Let's look at how cognitive grammar would view the meaning of

(28)   The ring is on the table.

The words *ring* and *table* are associated with basic-level concepts, which can be understood directly in terms of the corresponding mental images. And the word *on* can be understood in terms of a model that combines three image schemas: ABOVE, CONTACT, SUPPORT. So, to understand sentence (28) you could create a model in which one entity is above, in contact with, and supported by the other entity. According to the other views we have examined, the entities *ring* and *table* would be assigned their proper roles based on a prior syntactic analysis of the sentence structure. However, in cognitive grammar, syntactic relations are understood in terms of the same kinds of image schemas that are used to explain semantic knowledge.

Let's say that we have a model of what a sentence is and that this model is based on the PART-WHOLE and LINK schemas. These schemas, in turn, tell us that a sentence is something made of parts and that these parts are linked by relationships. In our example above, the model of a sentence with *on* specifies that the first entity mentioned is the supported object and the entity mentioned after *on* is the supporting object.

Of course, in the context of our sad little story, the ICM that depicts the ring on the table does not, by itself, capture what the sentence means in terms of Martha and Jack's relationship. The pragmatics of the social situation, which are essential to the meaning of the sentence in context, would be structured by the model of *over* on the right side of Figure 2.13. The relationship is over, and the model of leaving the ring on the table would mark the boundary that the relationship has moved past. The central point of this example is that syntactic relations, word meanings, sentence meanings, and pragmatic knowledge are, in the cognitive grammar view, built out of the same basic materials. Thus, they do not represent fundamentally different kinds of knowledge.

What is unique about cognitive grammar is that all the knowledge brought to bear in language processing is the same type of knowledge used in other aspects of cognition. Accordingly, theorists working from the cognitive grammar view are suspicious of the idea that language is a special mental faculty that operates differently from the rest of our mental processes. Langacker (1987) commented:

> Even if the blueprints for language are wired genetically into the human organism, their elaboration into a fully specified system during language acquisition, and their implementation in everyday use, are clearly dependent on experiential factors and inextricably bound up with psychological phenomena that are not specifically linguistic in character. Thus we have no valid reason to anticipate a sharp dichotomy between linguistic ability and other aspects of cognitive processing. *(pp. 12–13)*

In short, cognitive grammar places the study of language firmly and inextricably within the general study of cognitive processes. It follows that this view takes a much less nativist position than most of the other views that we have examined. A summary

TABLE 2.5	Summary of Different Views of the Problem of Meaning			
	Lexical Semantics	Compositional Semantics	Innate Aspects?	Modularity of Syntax?
Truth-Conditional Semantics	not specified	mapping to a possible world	not specified	yes
Conceptual Semantics	semantic decomposition & mental images	conceptual structure guided by syntactic structure	semantic primitives	yes
Cognitive Grammar	basic level concepts & image schemas	idealized cognitive models	little or none	no

of the stances taken by cognitive grammar and these other views regarding the problem of meaning is provided in Table 2.5.

CONCLUSIONS

What a Language User Needs to Know

We have surveyed many different linguistic perspectives concerning the types of knowledge that people must have in order for language to be productive and meaningful. Ultimately, however, the purpose of this chapter has been to raise questions rather than to answer them. Remember that psychologists who are interested in language take linguistic analyses as a starting point. More precisely, the psychological study of language that we will explore throughout this book uses linguistics as a computational analysis of the tasks that have to be performed in language comprehension and production. Unlike linguistics, psycholinguistics aims to determine how these jobs are done at both a representational (mental processing) level and an implementational (neural) level.

Linguistic analyses have shown that it is the rule-governed nature of language that makes sense of the problem of productivity. Indeed, we get a system of communication with infinite expressive power out of a finite system of sounds and symbols because there are rules, common to users of a given language, that permit novel but comprehensible combinations of sounds and symbols. And despite the complexity and subtlety of the rules, people master them with little or no direct instruction. Such observations have led many linguists to support the nativist hypothesis that we are born with an extensive body of knowledge that guides language acquisition (e.g., Halle, 1990).

Perhaps the most important topic in language productivity is syntactic knowledge, particularly as it pertains to the tree-like structure of the phrases that make up sentences. Our computational analysis has led us to the central question of whether we rely on abstract rules for parsing sentences into phrases and whether these rules are part of an autonomous syntactic module.

Regarding the issue of meaning, we saw that most linguists believe that the meaning of words is based on concepts that can be decomposed into features. At the same time, however, it is evident that the meaning of a sentence depends in a complex way on word meanings and our knowledge of the relationships between different parts of a sentence. Clearly, then, representational theories of language must address more than just the question of the nature of concepts. Indeed, we need to determine how concepts are combined into sentence meanings and how we relate utterances to states of affairs in the world.

From a somewhat broader perspective, it is clear that a great deal of knowledge is required to be a competent language user. The extent of the knowledge we use to produce and understand language raises many questions about how the different aspects of our knowledge are coordinated with such apparent ease. Although almost everyone would agree that some aspects of our ability to use so many kinds of information at once are innate, the relative balance of innate and learned factors in language is a key issue for psychology to address.

Perhaps the broadest question raised in our survey of linguistics is one concerning the relationship between language and the rest of our cognitive system. Exploring this issue is the overarching goal of the rest of this book. However, before we can proceed on that journey, we need to get an overview of the cognitive system.

C H A P T E R   R E V I E W

Checking Your Understanding

Key Terms

affricates (38)

allophone (37)

antonymy (62)

assimilation (42)

basic-level concepts (66)

case role grammar (58)

cognitive grammar (61)

competence (49)

compositional semantics (60)

conceptual semantics (60)

deep structure (52)

descriptive adequacy (49)

entailment (62)

explanatory adequacy (49)

finite-state grammar (FSG) (46)

fricatives (37)

glides (39)

government and binding theory (56)

head (57)

head-parameter (57)

image schema (67)

iteration (45)

lexical decomposition (63)

lexical functionalist grammar (LFG) (58)

lexical semantics (60)

lexicon (42)

liquids (39)

manner of articulation (37)

mental model (65)
nasals (39)
nativist hypothesis (32)
performance (49)
phrase structure rules (49)
point of articulation (37)
principles and parameters theory (55)
proposition (62)
recursion (45)
reference (61)
role players (57)

semantic primitives (64)
sense (61)
stops (37)
surface structure (52)
synonymy (59)
tacit knowledge (32)
transformation (51)
truth-conditional semantics (60)
uniqueness principle (44)
Universal Grammar (UG) (49)
voicing (36)

Review Questions

1. If you ask typists where a particular letter is on a keyboard, they will often have to make finger movements to answer your question. Is knowing how to type a form of tacit knowledge? What is the relation between tacit knowledge and innate knowledge?

2. In what sense does phonology show productivity? What about morphology? Or syntax? Why do many linguists feel that the most important kind of knowledge for explaining the productivity of language is syntactic knowledge?

3. Can two different allophones in one language be different phonemes in another language? Provide an example.

4. Why do linguists believe that the lexicon must consist of more than just a listing of the words in our language?

5. How many morphemes are there in each of these words: *hotter, heater, weather*? You know that the same free morpheme sometimes has different meanings (e.g., "catch a *ball*" versus "attend a *ball*"). Do bound morphemes (e.g., *-er*) also show this kind of ambiguity?

6. How do we know that language is not based on a finite-state grammar? Why is this fact so damaging to Skinner's view of language?

7. What is the relationship between phrase-structure rules and transformational rules? Think about the differences in language phenomena that each type of rule is used to explain.

8. Use Chomsky's criteria for evaluating a grammar to explain why he moved from the transformational grammar he proposed in 1965 to the newer "principles and parameters theory." How do the ideas used in lexical-functional grammar overcome some of the concerns about Chomsky's earlier theory?

9. Why are many linguists, including Chomsky, interested in discovering features that are universal across all languages?

10. Draw a phrase structure tree for the sentence "Bill crossed the line."

11. Compare the three views of meaning that we considered in terms of how they would explain the meaning of "Bill crossed the line." Would each of these views recognize the difference between a literal interpretation of the sentence and a metaphoric one (such as "Bill did something he shouldn't have done.")?

12. Of all the aspects of linguistic knowledge that we have studied, for which is there the strongest evidence of an innate basis to language? For which is the evidence weakest?

On Further Reflection . . .

1. Because inflectional and derivational rules look a lot like phrase structure rules, it is reasonable to ask whether there is really any difference between morphology and syntax. Why not just keep extending a phrase structure tree down to the components of individual words, and consider the rules used to generate the whole tree as one kind of knowledge? This approach may seem reasonable at first, but in actuality there are a number of differences between syntactic and morphological rules. These differences have convinced most linguists that morphology and syntax are two different types of tacit knowledge (e.g., Chomsky, 1970; Jackendoff, 1975; Anderson, 1988).

   I have already hinted at a few differences between morphological and syntactic rules. Which kind of rule allows lots of exceptions? Which kind of rule can change the grammatical category of a word?

   Are there any other differences between syntactic rules and morphological rules? Recall that, syntactically, English is a head-first language. However, we can also think of the "headness" of morphology (cf. Pinker, 1994). Consider compound nouns like *toothbrush* or *Superman*. Does one of the two nouns serve as a head? Is a toothbrush a kind of tooth or a kind of brush? When we add an adjective suffix to the end of a verb stem (e.g., *teach* + *able*), do we get an adjective or a verb? From these observations would you say that English is a head-first language in terms of syntax *and* morphology?

2. Judging by how often newspaper headlines provide unintended humor, writing unambiguous headlines must be pretty hard. Here are a few prize examples noted by Richard Lederer (1987):

   PROSTITUTES APPEAL TO POPE

   COLLEGIANS ARE TURNING TO VEGETABLES

   COMPLAINTS ABOUT NBA REFEREES TURNING UGLY

   The humor comes from a semantic "model" for each sentence that is different from the one the writer (presumably) intended. Why are headlines especially prone to this problem?

   Using the examples given above, or other examples you find in the newspaper, try to determine whether the ambiguity comes from a purely semantic confusion or whether it arises because there are two different possible phrase structures for the headline. Would the different views of semantics explain these ambiguities in different ways?

CHAPTER 3

Language in Relation to Other Cognitive Processes

*A*s I noted in Chapter 1, psycholinguistics is generally viewed as a branch of cognitive psychology. Cognitive psychologists, including those who specialize in the study of language, try to understand how the *mind* works. Note that I said *mind*, not *brain*. The field of cognitive psychology focuses primarily on a representational level of analysis of how people come to understand their world and how their knowledge allows them to make decisions, perform actions, and solve problems.

Of course, the levels of analysis are not completely independent. Clearly, information can and should be integrated among levels. With regard to language, we saw in the last chapter that linguistics is a computational analysis of language that focuses on competence rather than performance. Psycholinguists often use the issues raised by linguists to develop theories of language performance.

What about the relationship between the representational level and the implementational level? As you will see, theories of mental processes can be formulated and tested without reference to how these processes are implemented in the brain. Nevertheless, cognitive theories of language and other mental processes are being used with increasing regularity to understand the workings of the brain. Thus, a major trend in the study of cognition generally, and language specifically, is the integration of the representational and implementational levels.

Before these themes are developed throughout the rest of the book, we need to address a very basic and important question: Can a psychological analysis of language be separated from an analysis of general cognition? To see why we need to address this question, try to solve the following verbal puzzle before you read any further:

> A stranger comes up to you and shows you a photograph. The stranger points to a person in the photograph and says, "Brothers and sisters have I none, that man's father is my father's son." *Who is the person in the photograph?*

There are two general ways you could solve this puzzle. If you heard the puzzle before and were given the answer, you might recognize the puzzle and remember the answer. If you never heard the puzzle before, you have to try to use your reasoning abilities to figure out the correct answer (there *is* a single correct answer, but we'll get to that later). Either way, when you try to solve this puzzle, the abilities that allow you to read and comprehend the sentences of the puzzle must work closely with your memory or reasoning abilities in order to arrive at a solution. If our use of language is based on a mental ability that is separate from other cognitive abilities like memory and reasoning, then, at the very least, we have to acknowledge that our language faculty must work closely with our other abilities. On the other hand, we could argue that we have general abilities for processing information, and that those general abilities are used across tasks involving language, memory, and reasoning. An extreme version of this view suggests that language is inseparable from the rest of cognition.

In order to get a better sense of the relationship between language and our other cognitive abilities, we need to survey how psychologists conceive of our mental processes, with a particular emphasis on those processes most closely associated with our language abilities. As we survey this information, keep in mind, and evaluate, the following hypothesis: *Language processes can be studied at least somewhat independently of our other mental abilities.*

First, we will take a look at how this hypothesis has been viewed throughout the history of psychology. Although considerations of language go back to the earliest days of experimental psychology, it was a relatively recent merging of issues in linguistics and psychology that helped spur the development of the field of cognitive psychology. This helped put the study of language on the front burner among issues to be addressed by psychology.

After taking a historical look at language and cognition, we will explore what is currently known about the cognitive abilities that are most closely tied to our language abilities. Finally, we will consider two very different proposals for how the representational theories of cognitive psychology can be integrated with the study of the brain. These two proposals have very different implications for the relationship between language and our other cognitive abilities. Along the way, I'll use the "brothers and sisters" puzzle to illustrate some of the processes to be discussed. You might want to reconsider your answer before moving on, though. There is a more than 70 percent chance that you came up with an incorrect answer.

A Historical View of Language and Cognition

Whereas philosophical treatments of psychological issues have a very long history, laboratory research in psychology began late in the last century. Wilhelm Wundt is credited with establishing the first psychology laboratory in Germany in 1879. Wundt is best known for his technique of training people to monitor and report on their own mental processes, a technique known as **introspection**. This technique made sense in light of Wundt's belief that the proper topic of scientific psychology was the study of immediate conscious experience. Thus, much of Wundt's research was concerned with issues of conscious perception and mental imagery. Nevertheless, Wundt used a variety of techniques in his laboratory and wrote widely on several topics related to language, especially speech production (see Blumenthal, 1970).

A notable aspect of Wundt's work on speech production is his notion that we begin with a whole thought, which we then translate into speech. So, although speech must be produced on a word-by-word basis, the thought we want to express already exists. Thus, Wundt made a clear distinction between thought and language.

It is also clear from Wundt's writings (e.g., Wundt, 1907) that he was skeptical about whether language could be studied through experimentation. However, at about the same time as Wundt was considering speech production, Huey (1908) and Thorndike (1917) were making some progress in the study of reading, though these researchers were also impressed by the complexity of language phenomena. For example, Thorndike criticized the generally held belief that reading could be explained as "a simple compounding of habits" whereby words gave rise to their sound and meaning, which were then easily combined into the total thought. According to Thorndike himself, people's answers to comprehension questions showed that

reading is a very elaborate procedure, involving a weighing of each of many elements in a sentence, their organization in the proper relations to one another, the selection of certain of their connotations and the rejection of others, and the cooperation of many forces to determine final response. In fact, we shall find that the act of answering simple questions about a simple paragraph . . . includes all the features characteristic of typical reasonings. *(p. 323)*

In Thorndike's study, answers to questions about a paragraph revealed that readers not only use context to get the meaning of words, they also actively engage in complex reasoning about the causes of events. Thus, Thorndike made the case that reading even a brief passage engages sophisticated mental processes rather than a simple set of associations established through practice.

The Beginnings of Psycholinguistics

Despite the early warnings about the complexity of language, the view that language and other seemingly complex human behaviors could be explained in simple associative terms prevailed through the first half of this century. Since the time of Aristotle, people have thought of knowledge in terms of associations among concepts. However, the behaviorists, who dominated American psychology until the late 1950s, believed that a scientific psychology must be founded on the study of a different kind of association, that between a stimulus (S) and a response (R). When Pavlov (1927) showed that a dog could be conditioned to salivate to a sound by pairing the ringing of a bell with food, all the elements of this learning episode were objective and easily studied. What the animal learns is an S-R association—an association between stimuli presented close together in time.

B. F. Skinner, in his studies of operant conditioning, dethroned the S by focusing on the association between a response and its consequences (e.g., Skinner, 1938). For example, to get food, rats will press a lever at different rates, depending on how often their lever pressing is rewarded. The beauty of this approach is its objectivity. All the constructs are clearly defined and can be measured objectively. However, as you already know, Skinner's (1957) attempt to apply conditioning principles to language was not widely accepted. Not only was the finite-state grammar at the heart of Skinner's approach unable to account for productivity, but observations of language acquisition did not support the idea that language was acquired through reinforcement of specific speech patterns (Brown, 1958; Chomsky, 1959). Indeed, Chomsky pointed out that Skinner was not so much explaining language phenomena as relabeling them with terms from the literature on conditioning.

With Skinner's approach to the study of language devastated by Chomsky's critique, psychologists began to consider other ways of thinking about language behavior. The logical place to begin was to test whether the ideas of grammar that Chomsky was developing (Chomsky, 1957, 1965) could serve as a model of the mental processes that took place in language. Thus began a period of unprecedented alliance between linguistic theories and psychological theory testing. This alliance resulted in a major change of assumptions about the relationship between language and our other abilities. In Skinner's view, language was simply another expression of our general learning abilities. By taking Chomsky's view of language as a hypothesis to be tested, psychologists made two important assumptions that were contrary to Skinner's view: (1) that language can be studied as a unique mental faculty with its own special operating principles, and (2) that the explanation for language need not be based solely on observable stimuli and responses.

The first assumption follows from the fact that Chomsky's theory was a theory of language, not of cognition in general. And the second assumption is necessary because if we take Chomsky's theory seriously as a psychological model, our explanation for language behavior is based on mental processes that cannot be observed directly. This raises an important question. How can we objectively test for the existence of mental processes that are not directly observable?

George Miller and his students (e.g., Clifton, Kurtz & Jenkins, 1965; Miller, 1962) reasoned that if people's comprehension of language included the syntactic processes outlined in Chomsky's theory, then it should be possible to use Chomsky's theory to predict whether a particular sentence will be easy or hard to understand. The idea was that, in comprehension, people first determine the surface structure of the sentence and then use transformations to map the surface structure onto the deep structure. If so, then the more transformations that are needed, the longer it should take to comprehend the sentence. This set of assumptions was known as the **derivational theory of complexity** (DTC). To test the theory, you need two sentences that, according to Chomsky's transformational grammar, differ in the number of transformations. Then, you measure how long it takes people to understand each sentence. For example, you could have a computer start timing the point at which a sentence is flashed on the screen and measure the time until the reader presses a button to indicate that he or she is ready to answer a question about the sentence.

Consider the following two sentences:

(1) Noam Chomsky is in France.

(2) Noam Chomsky is not in France.

According to Chomsky's transformational grammar, sentence (2) involves an extra transformation because it uses negation. In support of the DTC, sentences with negation generally do take longer to comprehend. So far, so good. Of course, you might object that sentence (2) is longer and that the sentences differ in meaning, not just number of syntactic transformations. Now consider these two sentences:

(3) The rat was killed by the cat.

(4) The rat was killed.

According to transformational grammar, sentence (4) involves an extra transformation to delete the expected prepositional phrase. So, in this case, the DTC makes the prediction that the shorter sentence is actually more difficult to process. However, people do not take longer to comprehend a sentence like (4) in comparison to a sentence like (3). Numerous such studies of sentence-comprehension times have failed to support the DTC (for a review, see Fodor, Bever & Garrett, 1974).

Cognitive Psychology Comes of Age

With the fall of the DTC, psychologists interested in language began to doubt that Chomsky's transformational grammar could be used to create a plausible theory of sentence comprehension. The effort was not a failure, however. Although the DTC was not a good theory of language comprehension, the studies did prove that it was possible to test theories about mental processes. Thus, whereas the assumption that language is a special mental faculty apart from our other mental abilities began to weaken, the assumption that mental processes could be studied experimentally was strengthened.

At the same time, but on a different research front, many psychologists who studied human learning became convinced that theories of mental processes were needed to explain behavior. Indeed, the 1960s saw the end of behaviorism's dominance and the rise of cognitive psychology. Moreover, the trend in research on human learning and memory was now to view the memory system as intimately bound up with language processes. Let's take a look at how this view of the connection between memory and language developed.

By the 1950s, behaviorists were running into difficulty on their own "home turf": the study of learning. When behaviorally trained researchers studied human learning, they naturally adopted an S-R approach; specifically, they tried to simplify the study of human learning by removing the effects of prior learning. One method they used was to examine **paired associate learning** of nonsense syllables. So, for example, a research participant might have been asked, first, to study a list of pairs of items like BAC-FOD, JAT-TUP, and so on; and then, later, upon being given the first member of each pair, to supply the second member. Lots of variations on this procedure can be used to study learning. Researchers can examine how the time between learning and test affects performance. They can look at whether the first or second member of each pair serves as the better cue. They can look at the effect of lists learned earlier on later acquisition of paired associates. All these factors and more were investigated.

Over time, however, it became clear that researchers in this area had a real problem: The research participants kept doing all sorts of creative things that contaminated attempts to establish basic learning principles (see Lachman, Lachman & Butterfield, 1979). When participants studied a pair of nonsense syllables, they would often use a strategy to help them remember the pair. For example, they might have made the nonsense syllables more meaningful by thinking of "BAC-FOD" as short for "backward-forward." When researchers used words as stimuli, and when they used tasks other than paired associate learning, it became even more evident that many of the important influences on learning were active strategies initiated by the learner. For example, Bousfield (1953) found that if participants were given a list of randomly ordered words to recall, they tended to recall the words in clusters of semantic categories. Clearly, then, many of the strategies that people use are based on their knowledge of words and word meanings.

What at first seemed to be nuisance factors, the strategies and background knowledge of the learner, gradually became the object of study. Thus, the investigators became more focused on issues of memory, having acknowledged that learning involves storage of information in the mind of the learner. More and more attention was given to the old idea that there are two kinds of memory: short-term memory (STM) and long-term memory (LTM) (cf., James, 1890).

A major landmark in the transition from a behavioral to a cognitive approach was George Miller's (1956) paper entitled "The Magical Number Seven, Plus or Minus Two: Some Limits on Our Capacity for Processing Information." What Miller meant by the "magical number" was the remarkable consistency across experiments that examined short-term retention of information: No matter whether the stimuli are digits, syllables, or words, people can hold around seven pieces of information in STM. Furthermore, this rather rigid limitation on immediate recall is defined not in terms of seven

ACTIVITY 3.1   Short-Term Memory Span

Test three or four friends or family members individually using the stimuli below. Make sure each "participant" is someone whose phone number you know. Read the numbers in each set at the rate of about one digit per second. Then, at the end of each set, look up at the person as a signal that he or she should write down the digits in order.

(1) 9 4 3 6

(2) 1 7 5 9 8

(3) 2 4 7 3 1 6

(4) 5 7 9 1 2 7 4

(5) 4 5 8 2 1 7 2 3

(6) 5 8 6 4 7 2 1 9 4

(7) 9 7 4 5 7 6 8 2 6 1

(8) For this last set, in the same tone and at the same pace, pretend to read off digits but make them the person's phone number followed by 7-3-6.

Almost no one will be able to write set (7) correctly, but everyone should get set (8), even though the two sets have the same number of items. What does this tell you about the fixed capacity of STM?

stimulus items but, rather, in terms of seven "chunks" of information. A chunk is a unit that the learner creates based on background knowledge. To see this process in action, try Activity 3.1.

Miller (1956) suggested that there is a fundamental limitation on our ability to process information. He further suggested that to explain the behavior of people in learning tasks, we have to be willing to study the strategies and procedures the learners use to work around the limitations on their ability to process information. In other words, to explain objective data about behavior in learning experiments, we must think not just in terms of the stimuli and responses in the experiment; we must think in terms of the processes going on *in the mind of the learner*.

At about the same time, great strides were being reported in the development of computers. Many psychologists noted the similarities between computers and people as two examples of general-purpose problem-solving devices. Both computers and people seem to be able to solve many kinds of problems because they can input, store, and retrieve information. In addition, the distinction between computer hardware (the physical machine) and software (the set of instructions that allows the machine to perform a task) is analogous to the distinction between brain and mind. This analogy gave psychologists a formal way of thinking about, and talking about, processes that were not directly observable. For many experimental psychologists, the view that humans are limited-capacity information processors replaced the view that behavior could be understood in terms of S-R connections.

Psychology and Linguistics Drift Apart

By the late 1960s, enough research on the nature of human information processing had been conducted that Atkinson and Shiffrin (1968; Shiffrin & Atkinson, 1969) could propose a model of human memory that summarized the existing research and stimulated new research for several years to come. Because Atkinson and Shiffrin believe that human memory consists of three storage systems and a set of control processes that help move information among these storage systems, their model is usually referred to as a **multistore model** of memory. A diagram of this model is shown in Figure 3.1.

According to this view of processing, information, whether a visual stimulus or a spoken word, is first held in a very brief sensory format before being further analyzed, as demonstrated by the vision studies of Sperling (1960) and, later, by the auditory studies of Darwin, Turvey, and Crowder (1972). Of all the information registered, only a subset receives our attention and is transferred to other parts of the memory system.

According to the multistore model, information that we attend to and recognize is transferred to the **short-term store (STS)**.* This is where information resides when we consciously manipulate information, as when we rehearse a phone number that we just looked up so that we'll remember it long enough to complete our dialing. Atkinson and Shiffrin believed that the STS was distinguished from more permanent memory, the **long-term store (LTS)**, not only by the strict limits on STS (about seven chunks) but also by the way that information is coded. They believed that the short-term store was characterized by the coding of information in terms of speech. Thus, according to the model, when a word was visually presented to a participant in a memory experiment, the visual record of the word was converted to the speech sound of the word so that the person could hold it in the STS. One reason we might convert information to speech sounds is to rehearse the information by silently repeating the word to ourselves. In contrast to the STS, according to Atkinson and Shiffrin, the LTS makes use of various kinds of codes—especially semantic codes. Thus, in this early model of memory we see concepts relating to language—phonology and semantics—being intertwined with those relating to the rest of the cognitive system.

The LTS is also the repository for all the information that we hold more or less permanently. In the terms of the multistore model, when we retrieve some information, what we have done is copy the information from the LTS into the STS. So, if I ask you the name of your first-grade teacher and that name "comes to mind," you have copied the name from the LTS to the STS. Moreover, unless you rehearse the name, it will decay quickly from the STS. In these terms, then, what we usually think of as forgetting is really a sort of retrieval block that prevents the transfer of information from the LTS to the STS.

Let's pause here and take stock. Something quite dramatic happened in the history of psychology in the 1950s and 1960s. Many psychologists who studied human behavior began this period committed to explanations of behavior based on the

---

* Students are often confused about the distinction between short-term store (STS) and short-term memory (STM). When we speak of short-term memory, we are talking about tasks that require us to hold information for brief periods of time. Short-term store, on the other hand, is a theoretical construct. In using the term STS, Atkinson and Shiffrin were saying that STM tasks are performed by a separate memory system, the STS.

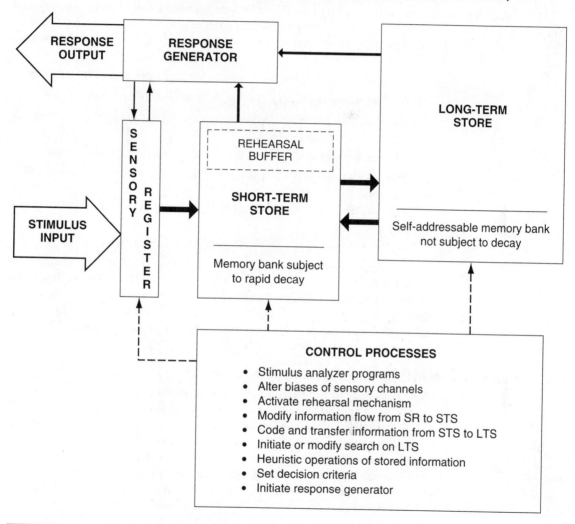

FIGURE 3.1 **The Multistore Model**

Solid lines show the pathways of information transmission. Dashed lines show where control processes (such as rehearsal) have their effects. The short-term store was believed to be a very limited-capacity buffer for working with information consciously.

RESPONSE OUTPUT

RESPONSE GENERATOR

LONG-TERM STORE

SENSORY REGISTER

STIMULUS INPUT

REHEARSAL BUFFER

SHORT-TERM STORE

Memory bank subject to rapid decay

Self-addressable memory bank not subject to decay

CONTROL PROCESSES
- Stimulus analyzer programs
- Alter biases of sensory channels
- Activate rehearsal mechanism
- Modify information flow from SR to STS
- Code and transfer information from STS to LTS
- Initiate or modify search on LTS
- Heuristic operations of stored information
- Set decision criteria
- Initiate response generator

acquisition of S-R connections, but they ended the period trying to flesh out the details of how information moved through the memory system. As we have seen, numerous separate influences came together to bring about this change, but the influence of computer science is particularly evident in the flowchart-style model depicted in Figure 3.1. Many psychologists viewed this model not just as a way of summarizing the results of memory experiments but as a description of our generic information-processing system. In short, they believed that our multistore memory system allows us to perform many different tasks, including linguistic ones—much as the basic capabilities of a computer permit it to represent, hold, and manipulate information and to solve many different kinds of problems. In any case, the idea that language should be studied as a separate mental faculty was not widely accepted among cognitive psychologists in the 1970s.

The consensus that language processes are very closely tied to memory and thinking processes was strengthened by a series of groundbreaking studies by Bransford and Franks (1971; Bransford, Barclay & Franks, 1972). In one study, people read either sentence (5a) or (6a):

(5a) Three turtles rested beside a floating log, and a fish swam beneath them.

(6a) Three turtles rested on a floating log, and a fish swam beneath them.

The participants who had read sentence (5a) were later asked if they had read this sentence:

(5b) Three turtles rested beside a floating log, and a fish swam beneath it.

Most of the people who had read sentence (5a) knew that (5b) was not the sentence they had studied.

Meanwhile, those who had read sentence (6a) were asked if they had read this sentence:

(6b) Three turtles rested on a floating log, and a fish swam beneath it.

These participants tended to accept sentence (6b) as the one they had actually read. Note that, unlike sentences (5a) and (5b), sentences (6a) and (6b) describe exactly the same scene. That is, (6a) logically implies (6b) because if the fish swam under the log, it also swam under the turtles. These data were interpreted as suggesting that comprehending sentences is a constructive process that uses general knowledge about the world, not just knowledge specific to language processing.

Current Trends in Psycholinguistics: A Reintegration

Clearly, psycholinguistics changed radically between the 1960s and the 1970s. Initially, linguistic theory played a major role in guiding psycholinguistics research, and there was a great deal of interest in syntactic processing. In addition, psycholinguistics contributed extensively to the decline of behaviorism and the rise of cognitive psychology. However, by the 1970s, psychologists interested in language were either studying the early perceptual aspects of language, such as word recognition (e.g., Marslen-Wilson, 1973), or concentrating on the semantic aspects of memory and language. Tanenhaus (1988) has described this period in the study of language as "psycholinguistics without linguistics." During this time, psychologists showed little interest in testing linguistic theories of syntax as potential psychological models.

More recently, the trend has been to put more linguistics back into psycholinguistics. One reason that psychology and linguistics have become less isolated from one another is that linguistics has changed. For example, as we saw in Chapter 2, Chomsky moved away from his original transformational grammar and proposed a theory with clear implications for language processing and language acquisition. Indeed, Chomsky's ideas are consistent with the view that language is a module that is distinct from other cognitive activities. In addition, the newer theories by Jackendoff (1992), Bresnan (1981), and Lakoff (1987a) are easier to integrate into psychological theory than was the original theory of transformational grammar. These changes have helped to reignite psychology's interest in syntactic processing (e.g., Frazier & Rayner, 1982; Taraban & McClelland, 1988), and psychology, in turn, has influenced linguistic theory. There is now a great deal of interest in how syntactic and semantic processes interact during language comprehension (e.g., Mitchell, 1994a).

Overall, the history of the interaction between linguistics and psychology reflects the shifting tides of opinion about the hypothesis that we are focusing on in this chapter. During those periods in which psychologists have supported a more modular view of language, linguistics has played a major role in psychological theory. But when the consensus has tended more toward the unity of language and other aspects of cognition, there has been less linguistics in psycholinguistics. Today, most psycholinguists take a middle ground on this issue: They recognize that some aspects of language processing may be unique to language, but that memory and other cognitive processes also play a large role in language. However, as is often said in politics, "The devil is in the details." A middle-ground position regarding the relationship between language and cognition does not tell us much unless we are more specific about how particular language processes affect, and are affected by, other cognitive processes. Before we can be more specific, however, we need some background on the current view of the cognitive processes most connected to language.

Memory, Language, and Reasoning: Beyond the Multistore Model

You have waited long enough. When the stranger pointed to someone in a photograph and said, "That man's father is my father's son," to whom was he pointing? Based on a recent study by Casey (1993) that used this old puzzle, there's a good chance you said that the person in the photograph is the stranger himself. In Casey's research, 77 percent of his subjects gave that *incorrect* answer. The person in the photograph has to be the *son of the stranger* who is talking to you. Consider the key sentence:

That man's father is *my father's son.*

Let's take the last part of the sentence (in italics) and paraphrase it. Assume that I am the stranger talking to you. If I am an only child ("brothers and sisters have I none"), then "my father's son" can only be me. So, the key sentence can be restated as

That man's father is me.

So, I am the father of the man in the photograph. The man in the photograph is my son.

People find this problem very difficult, not because it requires great deductive reasoning powers but, rather, because *the wording of the problem taxes our memory system.* Of course, if you had heard the problem before, you might have remembered the answer, even if you could not explain why it is correct. As I will discuss shortly, this means of solving the problem—by recalling the answer—requires a different process than if the problem is reasoned out. Note, however, that some aspects of both processes are connected with language processing.

In terms of relating language, memory, and reasoning together, the general framework of Atkinson and Shiffrin's multistore model remains important as a way of describing the "architecture" of the cognitive system. However, some of the specific

ACTIVITY 3.2   Working Memory and Verbal Reasoning

For this activity you need to work with a classmate or friend as a partner. One of you will be the experimenter and the other will be the participant. The experimenter should make a series of flash cards that present verbal reasoning problems in which the participant decides whether a sentence accurately describes a target below the sentence. For example, the participant might be asked to decide whether the following statement is a true description of the target below it:

A is preceded by B

[B-A]

The experimenter should make up twenty-four problems like this—half true, as in this example, and half false. A couple of extra problems should be included for practice. In addition, the experimenter should vary the wording of the problems according to whether active or passive voice is used and whether the statement is in the affirmative or the negative, as in the following examples:

B is followed by A

[B-A] (true)

A is not followed by B

[A-B] (false)

A precedes B

[A-B] (true)

claims of the model have been refuted by ongoing research on human memory (e.g., Atkinson, 1993). The specifics of this research need not concern us as background for our study of language. However, two important trends in responses to the multi-store model will prove helpful to our understanding of some of the research on language.

One trend concerns the increasing differentiation of the STS, such that it is now usually viewed as a **working memory** (WM) system with several parts of its own (e.g., Baddeley, 1992; Schneider, 1993). You can think of the WM system as a kind of cognitive workbench where limited amounts of information can be manipulated. It is this system's limitations that account for the difficulties people have with the "brothers and sisters" puzzle.

The other trend in memory research since the proposal of the multistore model concerns the recognition that there may be different systems, or at least very different types of information, constituting the LTS (e.g., Tulving, 1985). I will outline each of these trends in turn.

From the STS to a Working-Memory System

In the original proposal of the multistore model, one of the distinguishing characteristics of the short-term store was that it worked only with phonological codes. This idea was soon refuted by evidence that the STS also works with both semantic codes

Activity 3.2 *continued*

When the experimenter has completed the flash cards, they should be shuffled thoroughly and divided into four sets of six problems each. Now the demonstration is ready. First, the experimenter should let the participant work through the two practice problems. Then, for the real test, the experimenter should time, in seconds, how long it takes the participant to do a set of six problems in a row. Also, the experimenter should keep track of errors during a set. For the first set of six problems, the experimenter should specify two random digits for the participant to hold in memory while the verbal reasoning task is performed. At the end of this set (rather than during the set, while the problems are being solved), the participant should be asked to report the two digits. For the second set, the participant should perform the task with no digits to hold in memory. For the third set, the experimenter should give the participant six random digits to be held in memory *and* to be repeated out loud rapidly as the verbal problems are being solved. Finally, for the fourth set, the participant should simply repeat "the-the-the" out loud at a rapid pace while solving the problems.

   Compare the time needed for completion of each set (and the number of errors) across the four different conditions. How did memory load affect performance? Of course, on later trials the person also had more practice at performing the task. How could practice have influenced your results?

(Shulman, 1972) and visual codes (Kroll, 1972; Shepard & Metzler, 1971) in short-term memory tasks. Still, however, one could argue that the STS is a passive storage buffer that holds about seven chunks of information, regardless of the type of code used to represent the information.

   This simple, passive view of short-term memory came under attack in a classic series of studies by Alan Baddeley and his colleagues (Baddeley & Hitch, 1974; Baddeley & Lieberman, 1980; Salame & Baddeley, 1982). These researchers reasoned that if the short-term store is simply a passive storage buffer with about seven "slots" for holding chunks of information, then any activity that takes up some of the storage slots should interfere with storing new information in a second short-term memory task. However, as you'll see in Activity 3.2, the situation is not that simple.

   When Baddeley did experiments similar to Activity 3.2, he found that a two-digit load was not detrimental to the verbal reasoning task, even though two "slots" are equal to almost a third of someone's short-term memory capacity. However, Baddeley found that a six-digit load had a sizable effect. Was this effect due to the verbal interference involved in the participant's effort to rehearse six digits while also comprehending something verbal? This is the question addressed by the **articulatory suppression task,** which involves repeating the same word over and over. Even though this task is very simple, it interferes with the verbal reasoning task, but not as much as the six-digit load. Baddeley's conclusion: The six-digit load interferes with verbal reasoning both because it affects phonological processes and because it is a general drain on attentional capacity.

In other research, Baddeley and his colleagues looked at the effects of different short-term memory loads on the performance of concurrent verbal tasks and tasks that require holding visual-spatial information in short-term memory. An example of a visual-spatial STM task is shown in Figure 3.2. What Baddeley found is that both modality-specific and modality-general effects arise when a person performs two short-term memory tasks at the same time. *Modality-specific interference* is the term applied to a situation in which two verbal tasks or two visual-spatial tasks interfere with each other, whereas *modality-general interference* refers to a situation in which tasks from different modalities, such as a visual-spatial task and a verbal task, interfere with each other.

To account for both modality-specific and modality-general interference effects, as well as a number of other phenomena in the psychology of memory, Baddeley (1986, 1992) proposed that short-term memory tasks are handled by a complex working-memory system, as depicted in Figure 3.3. Many of the functions that Atkinson and Shiffrin (1968) called control processes are handled by the **central executive.** You can think of the central executive as the connection between the memory system and a pool of attentional resources that are divided up among the different mental tasks being performed at a given time. Short-term memory is limited because this pool of attention is limited. What the central executive does, then, is to allocate attention to either of two different short-term buffers: the **phonological loop,** which holds speech-based information, and the **visual-spatial sketch pad,** which holds mental images of visual and spatial information. For example, you would use your visual-spatial sketch pad when you perform the task in Figure 3.2.

Unless you direct attention to the information in the buffers, that information decays very quickly. So, for example, if you have to hold some piece of information in the phonological loop and also do additional attention-demanding activities, the

---

| FIGURE 3.2 | **A Visual-Spatial STM Task** |

Close your eyes and form a mental image of this picture. In your mind's eye, scan the image starting from the asterisk and moving in the direction of the arrow. When you come to a corner, say "yes" if the corner is at the top or bottom of the figure; otherwise, say "no." *(Adapted from Brooks, 1968.)*

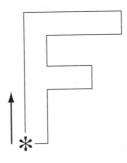

| FIGURE 3.3 | Baddeley's (1986) Model of Working Memory |

The central executive distributes a limited pool of attention to two STM buffers, one for phonological (speech-based) information, and one for visual-spatial information.

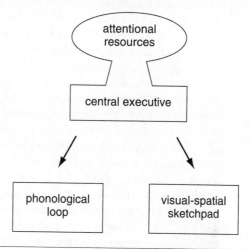

information stored in your phonological loop will be lost within a couple of seconds. However, because the two buffers in Baddeley's model are two different memory structures, there is less interference between verbal and visual-spatial tasks than between two tasks that need the same buffer.

Baddeley's model can be used to help explain why the "brothers and sisters" puzzle is so hard. People seem to have particular difficulty with the double possessive in the key sentence of this puzzle. They have to hold the possessive "that man's father" in working memory while also determining the referent for the next possessive "my father's son." In other words, the complex syntax of the sentence places high demands on WM. Most people lose track of some of the information they need; they stop short of the idea that the stranger is saying "That man's father is me" and come up with "That man is me." The problem is not just with the "size" of the phonological loop but also with the attentional resources needed both to hold the parts of the sentence in WM *and* to work though the tortuous syntax.

Many other reasoning problems also depend on an interaction between language processes and WM. For example, Johnson-Laird (1983) has studied how people solve **syllogisms,** which are reasoning problems in which you must decide whether a conclusion follows validly from two premises. For example, do the following conclusions follow logically from their premises?

1. Some A are B.

   All B are C.

   Therefore, some A are C.

2. All A are B.

Some B are C.

Therefore, some A are C.

The first syllogism is valid, but the second is not. Johnson-Laird's research suggests that one way people solve syllogisms is to first use their language abilities to convert the premises into a mental model that represents the situation. (This conclusion is similar to the idea of idealized cognitive models in Lakoff's [1987a] semantics study.) Then, they compare the conclusion to the mental model. This mental model could be a visual-spatial representation similar to the ones depicted in Figure 3.4.

People often have difficulty with syllogisms because of the limitations of their WM. Typically, they can hold just one of the models of a premise in their visual-spatial sketch pad. As Figure 3.4 implies, however, there can be several possible models for a particular premise. In short, people may not be able to hold several different models of premises in WM and compare each to the conclusion. Instead, because of their WM limitations, people tend to reason from a single concrete model, which can lead to incorrect decisions.

The important point to bear in mind here is that our working-memory system plays a central role in many cognitive processes, including those involved in language and reasoning. As our mental workspace, WM is the point at which language-based information, imagery, and knowledge stored in LTM are integrated. However, given the attentional limitations on how much information we can work with at a given time, WM is also a place where critical information may be lost.

From the LTS to Memory Systems

Let's turn now to a discussion of memory as you usually think of it: in terms of recalling something you have experienced. In a very real sense, it is our long-term memory that makes us who we are. LTM is not just a repository of "facts" such as "The solution to the 'brothers and sisters' puzzle is 'his son.'" Indeed, the LTM system stores information about *all* our experiences, about the events in our lives that shape our outlook, opinions, and feelings. In their model of memory, Atkinson and Shiffrin (1968) recognized that a complete model of the LTS would have to specify the nature of three memory processes: encoding, storage, and retrieval. In other words, it would have to

---

FIGURE 3.4   **Two Mental Models of "Some A are B"**

People sometimes think that the statement "Some A are B" has to correspond to the model on the left. However, the model on the right is another valid way to represent this premise. Syllogisms are especially difficult when people have to keep track of more than one possible model of each premise.

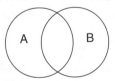

explain how information gets into LTM, how information is organized and represented when we have stored it, and how we retrieve the information for use in working memory. One major development in memory research since the publication of the multistore model is the recognition that these three processes may differ depending on the type of information that is being processed (e.g., Richardson-Klavehn & Bjork, 1988; Tulving, 1985).

There is some debate over whether we should think of LTM as having several distinct memory systems or whether there is one LTM system with different processes used for different types of information (see Roediger & Craik, 1989). The consensus, however, is that the LTM system is a good deal more complex than anyone, including Atkinson and Shiffrin, realized in the 1960s.

In terms of the types of information in LTM, perhaps the most widely accepted distinction is that between knowing facts (declarative knowledge) and knowing how to perform some action (procedural knowledge). For example, let's assume that you rode your new twelve-speed mountain bike to your friend's house to show it off. Your friend says, "That's a great bike. Where did you get it?" Your knowledge that you bought the bike at E-Z Ed's Sport Shop is an example of **declarative memory.** Declarative memory includes all sorts of factual knowledge of things you did or experienced. It also includes your general factual knowledge about the world. So, knowing that a bicycle is a human-propelled two-wheeled vehicle is also part of your declarative memory. The memory for declarative knowledge of personally experienced events is known as **episodic memory.** And the memory for declarative knowledge of general concepts about the world is known as **semantic memory.** Thus, semantic memory includes the knowledge of concepts, which, as we saw in the last chapter, is absolutely fundamental to language.

Both forms of declarative memory can be distinguished from **procedural memory.** For example, think about your knowledge of *how* to ride a bicycle. That is not factual knowledge. We cannot tell people how to ride a bicycle and then expect them to jump on and know how to ride. Procedural memory is different from knowing facts. It is memory for how to perform an action. We might be able to describe the procedures with words, but that is not the same thing as having the knowledge.

In the rest of this section we will survey what is known about encoding, storage, and retrieval of declarative and procedural memory, beginning with semantic declarative knowledge because this type of information is especially important to psycholinguistics.

Semantic Memory. In Chapter 2 we saw that there is considerable disagreement among linguists about how to conceive of semantic knowledge. As you might guess, psychologists have not settled on a single theory that explains how semantic information is stored and used. However, most of the theories of semantic memory currently used in psychology are based on the general idea that this kind of memory can be represented as a network of interconnected concepts (see Figure 3.5). When you see a particular object, or hear or see a word that signifies an object, relevant concepts are activated in the network. For example, if you hear the statement "A robin is a bird," you can verify that it is true based on the intersection of activation that spreads out from the *robin* node of the network and the *bird* node of the network.

FIGURE 3.5	A Semantic Network of Concepts

Psychologists often depict semantic memory as a network in which concept nodes are linked together. The links are labeled here to show that some links are based on category membership and that others define the properties of a concept.

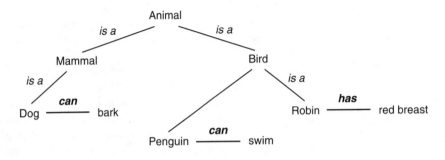

You can think of *spreading activation* as being analogous to actual physiological processes in the brain. The idea is that nodes, like areas of the brain, are connected, and that activating one node spreads activation just as a set of nerve cells in the brain can activate other areas with which they are connected. As appealing as this analogy may be, however, it is important to remember that semantic memory models do not describe actual physiological processes in the brain. Spreading activation is a representational construct that describes people's behavior in a number of different memory experiments.

The spreading of activation among related concepts in semantic memory is an **automatic** rather than **controlled process.** An automatic process is one that occurs without conscious control and without taking up much in the way of our attentional resources (Schneider & Shiffrin, 1977). For example, the automatic nature of **semantic priming** has been demonstrated in numerous experiments in which the semantic relationship between one stimulus affects a person's response to a subsequent stimulus (e.g., Masson, 1995; Meyer & Schvaneveldt, 1971; Neely, 1977). Let's say that I ask you to decide as quickly as possible whether strings of letters form a word. This is known as a **lexical decision task.** So, if I present *dog* the answer is "yes," and if I present *plik* the answer is "no."

To get precise measurements of your lexical decision time, I could flash the test stimuli on a computer screen and measure the time between the onset of the word and the moment at which you press a button to signal word or nonword. What's interesting is that if I precede a test stimulus with a related word, your response time (RT) is faster than if the stimulus is not preceded by a related word. For example, if I show you *bird* and then *robin*, your RT to *robin* is faster than if I show you *xxxx* and then *robin*. This effect can be explained in terms of spreading activation. When you see *bird*, activation spreads to *robin* so that the concept of a robin is already activated before you see the word. That head start on activating *robin* makes your lexical decision faster.

FIGURE 3.6   An Example of Automatic Semantic Priming

Shown here are results from an experiment by Neely (1977) in which participants expected a lexical decision target that followed a category name to be a member of that category. The horizontal axis shows the length of time the category name was presented before the target word appeared. As it turns out, performance was facilitated (in comparison to a control condition) when the trial conformed to expectations, whereas performance was inhibited when the trial went against expectations. Unlike the facilitation effects, which occurred rapidly, inhibition took time to build up.

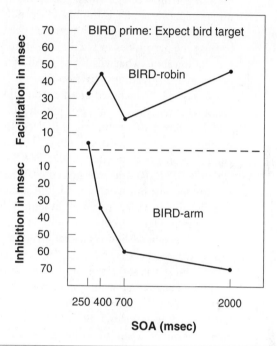

How do we know that semantic priming is an automatic effect rather than a conscious strategy? A remarkably clear demonstration of the automatic nature of semantic priming can be found in results obtained by Neely (1977). In this series of experiments, the participants performed a lexical decision task similar to the one I described above. The first stimulus of each trial was a prompt that could be a word or a row of X's. The second stimulus was a string of letters that could be a word or a nonword. Two important variables that Neely manipulated were (1) the relationship between the first and second stimuli, and (2) the time interval between the first and second stimuli. Take a look at Figure 3.6, which shows a portion of Neely's results. In this particular experiment, people were told that when *BIRD* was presented the second stimulus would probably be a type of bird. The vertical axis shows how much faster (facilitation) or slower (inhibition) people responded in comparison to a control condition—namely, *XXXXX* as the first stimulus. The horizontal axis shows the time interval between the display of the first stimulus and that of the second stimulus—a time interval known as the **stimulus onset asynchrony** (**SOA**). The longer the SOA, the more time the person has to activate information based on the first stimulus before the second stimulus appears. (Note that the display of the second stimulus is the point at which the experimenter begins to measure the person's RT.)

There are two important things to notice in Figure 3.6. First, if the first and second stimuli on a trial are related, RT is facilitated, even when the prime word is processed for only 250 milliseconds (msec) before the target word appears. If the two stimuli are unrelated, however, RT is inhibited. Second, in contrast to facilitation, it takes about 500 milliseconds for this inhibition to appear. The conclusion: Inhibition takes longer because the person has to see the first stimulus long enough to develop a conscious expectation about what will follow. Facilitation occurs more quickly because it is based on automatic spreading activation.

Neely (1977) included another condition in his experiments to further test the idea that spreading activation is automatic. In this condition, the participants were told that when the first stimulus is *BODY PART*, they should expect a part of a building to appear as the second stimulus. Think about what should happen under this condition on a trial in which *BODY PART*—*door* is presented compared to a trial in which *BODY PART*—*heart* is presented. When *door* is the stimulus, the trial conforms to expectations; but when *heart* is the stimulus, the two stimuli are connected by a preexisting association in semantic memory. Neely's results for these two types of trials are shown in Figure 3.7.

As shown in the figure, facilitation occurs on *BODY PART*—*door* trials, but it takes time to develop because it is based on a conscious expectation. The data for the *BODY PART*—*heart* trials are the most interesting. If the SOA is brief enough, we see facilitation based on the automatic spreading activation from *BODY PART* to *heart* in semantic memory. However, when a person is given enough time to think about the conscious expectation that *BODY PART* should be followed by a part of a building, the presentation of a stimulus that goes against the expectation, even *heart*, results in inhibition.

These data support the general idea that knowledge in semantic memory is stored in a network of connected concepts, which are retrieved through a process of automatic spreading of activation. Semantic priming effects are an observable consequence of the activation process. Contrived situations like those in Neely's experiments help us to study semantic priming in the laboratory, but the process itself seems to be a ubiquitous part of everyday life. Because the process works so automatically, we may not notice how important it is—unless it leads us astray. We have all had the embarrassing experience of saying something we were thinking but did not intend to say. As we will explore in some detail in a later chapter, such "slips of the tongue" may sometimes be due to an automatic effect of semantic priming on our word choices. In his book *Anguished English*, Lederer (1979, p. 108) offers a wealth of such slips. Here are a couple of examples:

This movie is not for the screamish.

I ate in a restaurant where the food was abdominal.

| FIGURE 3.7 | **More Priming Results from Neely (1977)** |

Neely also presented a condition in which participants expected a category shift. For example, when the prime was BODY, people expected to see a part of a building as the target word. According to Neely's results, the effects of expectation are not seen unless the person has about 500 milliseconds to process the prime. In contrast, automatic spreading activation effects appear very quickly.

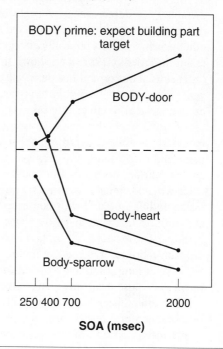

Although these word choices are probably not what the speaker intended, it is easy to see why the inappropriate words were activated by the other ideas being communicated.

Of course, there have to be limits on the spreading activation process or everything we know would get activated by any stimulus. The activation must spread out with decreasing strength and decay quickly unless the information is placed in working memory and rehearsed. In fact, because the activation process is quite limited, only information that is strongly linked in memory is automatically primed.

One way to see the limits on activation is to observe the range of information that is primed when a category name is presented. Look back at Figure 3.5. Note that the members of a category vary in their distance from the category name. For example, *penguin* is more distant from *bird* than is *robin*. This is a way of representing the finding that not all members of a category are equally representative. In other words, some category members are more semantically distant than others (Rosch & Mervis, 1975; Smith, Shoben & Rips, 1974). Thus, category membership is not all-or-none; rather, there are degrees of membership in categories. Let's say that someone from another culture is just beginning to learn English and she wants to know what a "bird" is. Would you show her a robin and a sparrow or a penguin and a chicken? If she wanted to know what "furniture" means, would you show her a chair and a sofa or a television and a rug? The gradations that we recognize in category membership are known as differences in **typicality.**

In terms of the network shown in Figure 3.5, the distance between concepts is a metaphor for differences in strength of association. So, less typical instances of a category are not as strongly connected to the category as more typical instances. In other words, there is a **typicality effect** on classification. Numerous studies (reviewed in Smith & Medin, 1981) have shown that people reliably verify the truth of category statements about typical instances (e.g., "A robin is a bird") more quickly than they verify category statements about atypical instances (e.g. "A chicken is a bird"). How can we explain this effect in terms of spreading activation?

A useful metaphor for what is going on in sentence verification with category members involves the assumption that activation spreads out from both the category name and the instance. For example, if you are asked to verify whether a dog is an animal, activation spreads from both "dog" and "animal," and when the activation from each node intersects, you respond "yes" (cf., Collins & Loftus, 1975). Less typical instances are associated with slower verification times because it takes longer for the activation to intersect, given the longer semantic distance. This is a nice metaphor because it is concrete and easy to understand. Keep in mind though, that typicality is probably more accurately thought of in terms of differences in strength of association. So, it takes longer for the retrieval of information about less typical instances in memory because the connections to the category name are weaker.

Now, think back to the issue involving the range of spreading activation and the phenomenon of semantic priming. What would you expect to happen in an experiment like Neely's (1977) if you varied the typicality of the targets that followed category names as priming stimuli? After the prime *BIRD* was presented, would the amount of automatic facilitation of responding to *penguin* be the same as that to *robin*? No, you would find that responses to *robin* are facilitated to a greater extent. A number of studies are consistent with this hypothesis (e.g., Lorch, 1982; Whitney & Kellas, 1984). What these studies suggest is that activation spreads out automatically, but with rapidly decreasing strength.

Another example of the limits on spreading activation comes from studies of "mediated priming." We expect that *lion* will prime *tiger* and that *tiger* will prime *stripes,* whereas mediated priming would be found if *lion* primed *stripes.* This effect has been observed (Balota & Lorch, 1986; McNamara, 1992), but it is weak and easily disrupted. That is probably a good thing, as people might be more prone to forming irrelevant associations during comprehension.

The ideas that we have explored here—that semantic information is stored in a network of concepts and that retrieval of this information occurs through a limited spreading activation process—have been quite influential in cognition generally and psycholinguistics in particular. However, for some kinds of questions about storage and retrieval of semantic information, network models seem to be on the wrong scale. After all, when trying to use our knowledge to interpret something, we often seem to retrieve more than just a few isolated concepts. Indeed, in many such instances we seem to bring a whole package of information to bear. To see what I mean, read the following excerpt from a story about a prison escape that was used in a study by Anderson, Reynolds, Schallert, and Goetz (1977):

> Rocky slowly got up from the mat, planning his escape. He hesitated a moment and thought. Things were not going well. What bothered him most was being held, especially since the charges against him had been weak. He considered his present situation. The lock that held him was strong but he thought he could break it. He knew, however, that his timing would have to be perfect.

This passage seems clear and perfectly interpretable as a prison story. Now, however, think of it as a description of a wrestling match, and reread it carefully. As a wrestling story, it makes sense too, but notice how the interpretation of almost every sentence is different from before. Each way of thinking about the excerpt makes sense because the events described fit into a whole set of related ideas that we have about each topic domain—wrestling and prisons. We seem to retrieve a set of ideas that is integrated together and to use it as a framework for interpreting the whole story. The term for such an integrated set of ideas is a **schema**. In the study just described (Anderson et al., 1977), the researchers found that most people, if not told in advance what the passage was about, interpreted it as a prison-escape story. However, physical education majors, who are more likely to retrieve a schema for a sport like wrestling, naturally interpreted the story as a wrestling match.

The idea that a whole package of information is used to facilitate comprehension predates network models of semantic memory. For example, Sir Frederick Bartlett (1932) published detailed results of studies in which English participants were asked to remember a Native American folktale. Lacking the appropriate background knowledge to make sense of the story, the people seemed to remember details that fit their preexisting knowledge; they even added details that were not in the story, but that reflected their own understanding of the world. Bartlett (1932) concluded that we interpret new information by assimilating it into a schema, a set of related ideas from our background knowledge.

There are several different ways to formalize the concept of a schema. One approach that has been used in AI simulations of story comprehension is to build scripts for common activities into the knowledge base. Thus, for example, if you are reading a story that mentions going to a restaurant, you would retrieve a generic script for restaurants (see Figure 3.8). This script contains variables that either are filled by the story or are filled with default items from memory. Your memory for the story is based on the generic script as it is fleshed out by the details of the particular story. In this case, you would expect to hear something about a waiter in the story because "waiter" is a variable in the script. There is also a variable for paying the check. Even if paying the check is not mentioned in the story, this act may be part of your memory for the story because it is in the script.

I will have much more to say about schema theory as an explanation of understanding when I discuss discourse comprehension in a later section. But for now, think about how schema theory's proposal that a large set of integrated concepts are used

FIGURE 3.8   **A Mental Script for Eating at a Restaurant**

These four scenes, and the actions associated with each of them, serve as expectations that can guide both our actions *and* our comprehension of descriptions of actions that take place in a restaurant. Indeed, knowledge of stereotypic social situations is a major point of intersection for language processes and general cognitive processes.

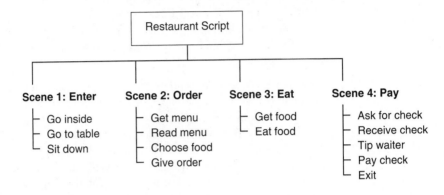

together contrasts with the limited knowledge retrieval described in network models based on spreading activation. Is there any way to reconcile these two views of semantic memory storage and retrieval? One possibility is suggested by the idea that schema-based processing is a special case of spreading activation in which some parts of the network are so strongly linked together that they get activated as a single unit (Abbott, Black & Smith, 1985). According to this perspective, our processing can be more or less schema driven depending upon the circumstances (Whitney, Budd, Bramucci & Crane, 1995).

Now, think back to the study by Bransford and Franks (1971) that I discussed in the historical overview of psycholinguistics. These researchers demonstrated that what people remember after reading a sentence is a depiction of the scene described rather than the surface form of the sentence itself. What this study, and more recent research on semantic memory, suggests is that we use general knowledge of concepts not only to understand word meanings but also to build a model of the situation described in a sentence. Often, it is the model, not the linguistic form of the sentence, that we remember later. Thus, both our memory and language processes depend upon the same store of general knowledge that we call semantic memory. We may be able to separate some aspects of language from the study of memory, but the two sets of processes certainly come together in semantic memory.

Episodic Memory.   If someone asks you tomorrow what the answer is to the "brothers and sisters" puzzle, you will not reason out the answer; rather, you'll just recall it from LTM. This outcome begs a question that I did not address earlier, when I talked about the retrieval of semantic concepts. How does information get stored in LTM in the first place? Or, in the language of information processing, how is new information encoded? This question is fundamental not only to cognitive psychology in general but also to psycholinguistics in particular.

One reason that understanding knowledge acquisition is important to psycholinguistics goes back to the debate over whether language is a separate module. According to some linguists and psycholinguists, much of the semantic knowledge that makes language possible is innate (e.g., Fodor, 1980; Piattelli-Palmarini, 1989). However, our memory for personal experiences cannot be innate. So, the adherents of a very strong modularity position say that acquiring language must be completely different from learning other kinds of information. A less radical position is that some linguistic universals are built in and that we use these innate features to learn the specifics of our particular language. A way to test this latter view is to determine what aspects of language appear to be acquired through a means different from our usual way of acquiring information.

Another reason that psycholinguists need to know how episodic memory works is that the goal behind much of language behavior is to instruct or to be instructed. Any college textbook or lecture is a prime example of the intersection between language and memory. From both a theoretical and an applied perspective, we need to know about how people learn in order to understand how particular language experiences promote (or inhibit!) learning.

So, how is declarative knowledge encoded in the first place? Think about the relatively simple case of people studying a list of words in a memory experiment. Each person is told to study the list for a few minutes in preparation for a recall test. According to the multistore model, the words would be encoded into a verbal format for rehearsal in the STS. The more rehearsal any given word received, the greater its likelihood of transfer to the LTS.

This view of how information becomes part of LTM predicts that your performance in intentional learning, when you deliberately try to store information in memory, should exceed performance in incidental learning, when you are not aware that you will be asked to remember some information you processed. This idea seems reasonable, but it is wrong.

The following study demonstrates why. Hyde and Jenkins (1969) gave people one of two tasks to perform. They either wrote down the number of letters in each word (thus focusing attention on the surface characteristics of the stimulus) or rated the pleasantness of each word (thus focusing attention on the meaning of the stimulus). Later, on a surprise recall test, the group that processed the words for meaning remembered many more of the words than the group that focused on the surface characteristics (68 percent vs. 39 percent). Even though the learning by the semantic group was incidental, the performance of these people was virtually identical to that of another group who were told that they would be asked to recall the words (68 percent vs. 69 percent).

Based on a body of research that challenged the view that intentional rehearsal was the main factor facilitating LTM storage, Craik and Lockhart (1972) proposed the **levels of processing theory**. According to this view, encoding information for LTM storage seems to happen as a natural by-product of attending to a stimulus, but the level at which we analyze the stimulus affects our ability to remember it later. Craik and Lockhart believed that semantic encoding was the deepest level because it led to the best recall.

Soon, however, it became apparent that memory does not depend only on the level of processing used at encoding. Memory also depends on the degree of elaboration at a given level of processing. Elaboration is the process of forming connections between one set of concepts and another. How this process affects memory was illustrated in an experiment by Stein and Bransford (1979). The participants read sentences and later were shown the same sentences with a word missing. The memory task was to supply the missing word. The sentences came in three different versions: (1) a simple factual statement such as *The fat man read the sign,* (2) the same simple statement but with an irrelevant elaboration such as *The fat man read the sign that was on the grass,* and (3) the same simple statement plus a relevant elaboration such as *The fat man read the sign warning about the thin ice.* Later, when the participants were presented with the simple sentences and asked to supply the critical adjective (e.g., The _____ man read the sign), their performance varied by sentence version, as shown in Figure 3.9.

Note, however, that elaborations were helpful to memory only if they decreased the arbitrary nature of the relationship between the sentence elements. Memory was worse for sentences with arbitrary elaborations than for simple sentences. In other words, memory for sentences improved when all the parts were connected in a meaningful fashion.

Clearly, nonarbitrary elaborations can help memory. But why? What is the mechanism by which elaborations increase memory performance? To answer that question

---

| FIGURE 3.9 | Stein and Bransford's (1979) Study of Sentence Memory |

In this study, people read sentences in which the main idea was stated in a simple form, sentences in which a relevant elaboration made the statement more meaningful, and sentences in which an irrelevant elaboration just gave more detail. The results indicated that memory for key words in the sentences was best when the sentence contained a relevant elaboration.

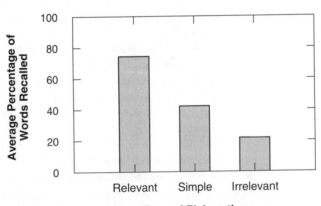

we first have to look at the reasons for memory failure. Why do we forget things? Traditionally, there are two theories of forgetting: **decay theory** and **interference theory.** According to decay theory, information that is not used simply fades from memory over time. According to interference theory, forgetting is not a loss of information from memory but a failure to retrieve information. It has long been accepted that information decays rapidly from short-term memory when attention is withdrawn; however, decay theory has been less influential in accounting for forgetting from long-term memory. Much of our forgetting from LTM occurs when some items in memory interfere with our ability to retrieve other items.

Interference is quite easy to demonstrate. For example, let's say you have one group of participants learn word list A and then word list B, followed by a test of memory for list B. If you compare this group's performance with that of a group who learns just list B and then is tested on list B, you find that the first group confuses the items on list A with those on list B and performs more poorly. You have probably noticed a similar phenomenon that occurs when someone's name is on the "tip of your tongue" but you can't quite recall it. In such instances, another name sometimes comes to mind—a name that you continue retrieving though you know it is incorrect.

Now, back to the question of elaboration. If much of forgetting is retrieval failure due to interference, why would elaboration help memory? A simple explanation is that elaboration may help memory because elaborated facts have more connections to other information. Thus, even if one route to retrieving the information is blocked, another may be accessible. Let's say I walk up to the local tennis courts and I see the face of someone familiar and he waves and says, "Hi Paul! How about a game of tennis?" The man's face is not too distinctive and I can't quite recall his name, but, thankfully, I notice that he is wearing burnt-orange tennis shorts and immediately his name comes to mind: "Sure Ralph, I'll play you." I am saved by having extra information—that Ralph wears odd-colored shorts—stored with Ralph's name in my memory.

So, elaborative processing can sometimes mean that there are more potential cues to help us retrieve a piece of information. That is not the whole story, however, because having more connections to some concept in memory can also interfere with the retrieval process. I'll use an example that is quite relevant to psycholinguistics because it involves memory for sentences. Suppose that you ask a group of people to study these four sentences until they can recite without error which people are in which places:

- The lawyer is in the bank.

- The teacher is in the park.

- The doctor is in the church.

- The doctor is in the park.

Next, after the study phase, you give your participants a speeded recognition test. You present test sentences such as "The doctor is in the park" or "The teacher is in the bank" and ask the participants to say, as quickly as possible, whether each statement is true or false. You consistently find that people are fastest at verifying sentence 1 and slowest at verifying sentence 4, and that their response times to sentences 2 and 3 fall in between

FIGURE 3.10	A Network of Propositions

The person-location pairings in the earlier example can be depicted as a network of propositions that capture the meaning of the sentences that were memorized.

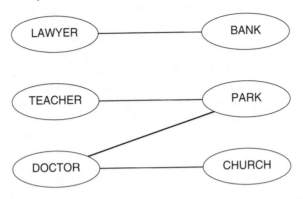

the response times to the other sentences. There is a very systematic trend here, so what's going on?

According to Anderson (1983a, 1995b) the facts that people learn in this kind of experiment are represented in network structures like the semantic memory networks I discussed earlier. In fact, Anderson sees no distinction between the two kinds of information except that, in the case of episodic knowledge, we still have access to where and when we learned the information. A network representation for the four sentences in the above example is shown in Figure 3.10.

If you match the elements of the network representation with the sentences, you can easily see the difference between sentence 1 and sentence 4—namely, that there are more pathways off the concepts involved in sentence 4. This type of elaboration does not help retrieval, though. Instead we get a **fan effect**. That is, response times involved in verifying whether a particular fact was studied become slower with the greater number of pathways off the concepts. Anderson (1983a) explained fan effects by reference to a limited-capacity spreading activation mechanism, whereby the activation of any given concept fans out over all the pathways off the concept. Moreover, there is a limited amount of activation at any concept, so the more links that fan out from a concept, the less activation travels down any particular link. Therefore, the intersection of activation that results in a "yes" response is weaker, resulting in a slower response.

Now we have a big problem. Despite considerable evidence that elaboration helps memory, fan effects reflect interference in the retrieval of elaborated concepts. So, if it *is* true that elaboration can produce interference, what does this fact imply about experts in some knowledge domain, who presumably have a richly interconnected network of facts that they have learned? The implication is that experts should get slower and slower at retrieving information about their area of knowledge as they learn more and more. And yet this is not what we see when we study experts. They are fast and efficient at retrieving information from their knowledge domain (Ericsson & Smith, 1991).

There may be several reasons why experts do not suffer from fan effects when retrieving information from their knowledge domain. Indeed, the paradox is at least partly resolved in a study by Reder and Ross (1983), who had participants learn a set of thematically related facts such as these:

Jim bought a ticket for a 10 A.M. trip.

Jim heard the conductor yell, "All aboard."

Jim arrived at Grand Central Station.

When asked to verify a statement about the theme, such as *Jim took a train trip*, individuals were *faster* in proportion to the number of facts they studied. Represented as a single model, the three statements above can be retrieved together, without a weakening of activation, through a fanning out across three different links. This seems to be what happens in experts, who not only have more facts in memory but also have facts more highly organized into groups. Thus, the key to our question about elaboration aiding memory seems to be the formation of a schema-like structure in the semantic network. If separate propositions can be integrated into a single mental model of a situation, then a fan effect does not occur, and may even be reversed (e.g., Radvansky, Zacks & Hasher, 1996).

To summarize what we have examined about episodic memory so far: At least some aspects of the encoding, storage, and retrieval of episodic declarative knowledge is not fundamentally different from knowledge in semantic memory. We can think of information as being represented in a network of propositions that are retrieved through a spreading activation process. Thus, when we read and remember sentences, the information from the sentences is being stored as an integrated network of propositions. One key to successful retrieval is to have a set of elaborated connections that form a coherent unit so that any particular cue from the environment that activates one part of the network can result in retrieval of the whole set of relevant concepts.

Obviously, having cues available at the time of retrieval that are strongly associated with a particular memory is important to avoiding interference. And, indeed, a major factor in our ability to remember information is the similarity between the encoding context and the retrieval context. The idea that memorability depends on the overlap between the conditions at encoding and the conditions at retrieval is known as the **encoding specificity principle** (Tulving, 1983; Tulving & Thomson, 1971).

A classic example of encoding specificity was reported by Thomson and Tulving (1970). Participants studied a list of words to be recalled later. Paired with some of these words were "cue words." For example, people might have studied the target word *COLD* without a cue, with a strong associate as in *hot-COLD*, or with a weak associate as in *wind-COLD*. Later, the high- or low-associate cues were presented when the participants tried to remember the target words. The researchers found that when the participants were given the low-associate cue at retrieval (e.g., *wind-?*), it helped them retrieve the target word only if the low associate was present at encoding. Furthermore, if the participants had studied a pairing like *wind-COLD*, the word hot did not help cue memory for the word *COLD*. The high associates were effective cues when they were present at study *and* when the target word was studied without a cue. Why would *hot*-? be a cue for *COLD* when *COLD* was studied in isolation? You should be able to explain this result in terms of spreading activation at encoding.

The encoding specificity principle is quite general. Almost any aspect of the environment that is similar at encoding and retrieval can have some effect. For example, people remember information better if they retrieve it in the same room in which they studied it (Smith, Glenberg & Bjork, 1978). And memory is generally better if people are in the same physiological state (e.g., sober or intoxicated) at both encoding and retrieval (Parker, Birnbaum & Nobel, 1976).*

The aspect of encoding specificity that is perhaps most important for our study of language is that memory depends on the overlap between the processes used at encoding and the processes used at retrieval. This aspect is known as **transfer-appro-priate processing** (Bransford, Franks, Morris & Stein, 1979). As we have seen, the results of many studies suggest that elaborate semantic processing often helps memory. However, according to the principle of transfer-appropriate processing, we have to qualify this general conclusion based on how memory is tested. For example, Morris, Bransford, and Franks (1977) had individuals perform different orienting tasks on a set of target words. These tasks forced the participants to focus either on the phonological properties of the words or on the semantic properties of the words. Later, the participants were given incidental recognition memory tasks. The findings were similar to those of other studies reviewed here: Semantic processing led to better memory performance if the recognition task required people to distinguish between target words and foils (words that had not been studied) that were different in meaning. However, if the recognition task required that participants pick out words that rhymed with words that had been studied, then the group that performed phonological analysis of the words at encoding did better than the group engaged in semantic processing.

In short, the kind of processing that leads to better memory depends on how memory is tested. As you will see later in the book, this idea has become very influential in the study of memory for stories and other forms of discourse. What people seem to remember from reading a passage depends both on the types of language processes that received the most attention during reading and the way their memory for the passage is tested. These data are further evidence that language and memory processes are closely intertwined, particularly at the level of semantics.

Note, however, that the close relationship between memory and the semantics of language does not invalidate the hypothesis that language processes can be at least partly separated from other cognitive processes. Think about this issue from a Chomskyan point of view. What is the most unique and productive aspect of language? It is our syntactic processing ability, right? Thus, from the Chomskyan perspective, we might argue that for language to be useful as a communication tool, the semantic products of language must be shared with the rest of our cognitive system, even if syntactic processes are quite special to language. One way that we will address this issue,

---

* Although people may remember more if they are intoxicated at both encoding and retrieval than if they are sober at either encoding or retrieval, I hasten to add that the best memory performance occurs when people are sober at both encoding and retrieval.

later in the text, is to see whether the learning of syntactic rules is different from other kinds of learning. Perhaps the point is best stated as follows: People must learn many skills, and language is one of those skills. Does learning the skill of comprehending and producing language differ from learning other kinds of skills? To answer this question we must know something about the knowledge that underlies skill learning: procedural knowledge.

Procedural Knowledge.   Attempts to understand our knowledge of how to perform actions have a long history. Almost a hundred years ago, Bryan and Harter (1899) studied people who were learning to use Morse code on a telegraph key. They said that people learning such skills pass through distinct phases in the learning process. Later, this idea of stages of skill acquisition was elaborated by Fitts and Posner (1967), who said that people work through three stages of skill acquisition as they move from slow, deliberately controlled actions to fast, automatic performance. This three-stage theory has been further elaborated by Anderson (1983a, 1995b). According to Anderson, the three stages of skill acquisition are as follows.

- During the **cognitive stage,** you establish a declarative encoding of an action. So, when you were learning to drive a standard shift car, you first encoded a set of facts about how to perform each step. You probably said to yourself, "O.K., I check to see that I'm in first gear, then I slowly release the clutch as I depress the gas pedal." At that point, of course, the car probably lurched forward and stalled.

- During the **associative stage,** you strengthen the connections among the different elements of the skill. Recall that as you practiced the skill of starting off in first gear, you got better and better at smoothly coordinating the clutch and the accelerator. In short, the different skill elements were becoming more strongly associated in memory.

- During the **autonomous stage,** you gradually increase your ability to perform the skill automatically and rapidly. After driving a standard shift car for a while, you are now able to pull away from a traffic light while talking to a friend— without being consciously aware that you have shifted the gears.

If someone tried to talk to you about an irrelevant topic when you were in the cognitive stage of learning how to drive a standard shift car, you probably would have told that person to shut up because you couldn't concentrate. What happened between the first and third stages that so dramatically changed your performance? According to Anderson's (1983a) theory, what happened is that you changed how you performed the actions. Specifically, you converted the declarative propositions about the skill into a set of production rules. Production rules are to procedural knowledge what propositional networks are to declarative knowledge: They are the stuff of which mental representations are made.

Production rules can be described in terms of condition-action statements. For our driving example, the production rule for starting forward would be this:

if goal is [go forward], then [release clutch and depress gas pedal].

Although I've written this production rule out as a declarative "if . . . then" statement, the statement is really just a description of a conditional-action procedure. When you have converted your knowledge of driving to a set of production rules, you don't say to yourself, "If I want to go forward, then I should depress the gas pedal and let up on the clutch." Rather, your stored production rules match their conditionals (the "if" portions of the rules) with the contents of working memory. When information that is active in working memory matches a conditional (as when you are thinking of going forward), the corresponding production rule automatically "fires." (In other words, the "then" portion of the rule is executed.) Of course, early in skill learning, you may be developing many separate procedures. So "release clutch" and "depress gas pedal" would be independent procedures that you awkwardly try to coordinate. With practice, these are "compiled" into one smooth procedure.

Systems of production rules can serve as general descriptions of the "machinery" behind all mental processes; they are not just physical actions as in the driving example. For instance, as you saw in the last chapter, linguists have devised verbal descriptions of grammatical rules. However, psycholinguists do not believe that you must retrieve these declarative rules from memory in order to produce or comprehend language. Instead, you obey grammatical rules that are represented as conditional-action procedures that guide mental processes, just as other such pairs can be used to guide physical movements. Perhaps it is because grammatical rules are represented as procedural knowledge that they are so hard to describe in declarative terms.

Are the procedures used in language processing, particularly those involved in syntactic analysis, acquired or used differently from other types of cognitive procedures? We will consider this fundamental question from a number of different perspectives throughout the text. One means of addressing the question will make use of information that integrates representational and implementational levels of analysis; that is, we will explore data on how language is implemented in the brain to see how language and other cognitive processes are related. Accordingly, in this final section of the chapter, we will examine two broad, cutting-edge debates that involve the integration of cognitive and brain sciences.

How Should the Study of the Brain Influence the Study of the Mind?

The two debates that concern us here are at the heart of the issue of how best to characterize the mental architecture that allows for language, memory, perception, and our other cognitive abilities. The first debate involves the degree to which our cognitive models of mental processing should resemble processes that take place at the neural level of the brain. The second debate is one that is somewhat familiar to you already. As discussed in the previous two chapters, there is disagreement over whether the language-thought relationship should be considered interactive or modular. Actually, the debate over modularity extends *beyond* the language-thought connection, in that it concerns how the general mental architecture should be characterized and how studies of cognitive and brain processes can be integrated.

Neural Processes and Cognitive Models: The Connectionist Debate

Our discussion of mental processes thus far has been framed in terms of a symbolic architecture. That is, we have viewed mental processes as a series of steps, or procedures, in which mental symbols are stored and manipulated. Over the last decade or so, however, a new approach to modeling cognitive processes has developed (McClelland & Rumelhart, 1986c). This approach, known as **connectionism**, assumes that our cognitive models, like the brain itself, should be based on the principle of **parallel distributed processing** (**PDP**). The "parallel" part of PDP refers to the idea that many activities are going on simultaneously. The "distributed" part means that an information-processing system can be composed of an interconnected set of units that do not individually store information. Instead, information is stored in patterns of activity among the units.

The units that compose the brain are, of course, neurons. Each neuron is a pretty dull creature. It can fire or not fire, but it does not, by itself, know anything. However, neurons are very richly interconnected. When you learn to recognize a stimulus, what happens in your brain is that you recreate a particular pattern of activity among some subset of your brain's neurons. Thus, the knowledge that you have about a specific stimulus is stored as a distributed pattern of activation among neurons.

Likewise, we can build models of cognitive processes based on simple units that are analogous to neurons. As an example, let's start with a simple model that illustrates parallel processing. Take a look at the stimulus in Figure 3.11, and try to identify it.

With only a little difficulty, you probably came to the conclusion that the word is *RED*. How were you able to do so, even though some features of the stimulus are missing? A model developed by McClelland and Rumelhart (1981) is one way to explain this result (see Figure 3.12). Their model is based on connections among units at three levels. Words are identified by their letters, and letters are identified by their features. However, there is parallel activation among the connections at all three levels until one word "wins out" by getting the most activation. Your knowledge about what features make up a given letter, and what letters make up a certain word, is represented in terms of positive (excitatory) connections between units. Also represented is your knowledge about what features or letters do not go together. For example, because the letter R is present in the stimulus shown in Figure 3.11, the word KEY is ruled out as a possible identification of the stimulus. In other words, there is a negative (inhibitory) connection between these letters. So, even if the letter E is present, thereby giving KEY some activation, the inhibition from R helps to counteract this effect.

The model in Figure 3.12 is not a fully PDP model, however, because each node in the network stands for something, such as a particular letter or word. In short, the

---

FIGURE 3.11   **Can You Read This Word?**

Although many of its visual features are missing, this word can easily be recognized. Connectionist models are well suited to describing how we can recognize patterns even when we are lacking some information. *(From Johnson-Laird, 1988.)*

| FIGURE 3.12 | A Connectionist Model of Word Recognition |

Illustrated here are three layers of units involved in McClelland and Rumelhart's (1981) model of word recognition. Arrows show excitatory connections, and lines with rounded points show inhibitory connections.

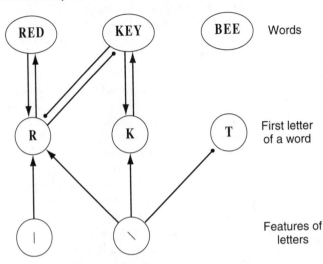

model is parallel but not distributed. We can convert it to a fully PDP model by portraying each of the three levels as one layer of a distributed representational system (Seidenberg & McClelland, 1989). The idea of a distributed representation for the letter level is depicted in Figure 3.13. Bear in mind that each node in the network is just a simple processing unit that is either on or off. A given letter is signaled when positive and negative connections from lower (or higher) levels create a stable pattern of activation across the letter level. Now, with a similar network for each level, as well as appropriate connections between levels, the model is both parallel and distributed.

One of the attractions of PDP models, like the word recognition system I just described, is that such models are at least somewhat consistent with what we know about neural processing. Of course, there is much we do not know about how either individual neurons or collections of neurons function. And even when compared with what we do know, PDP models are only a simple approximation of neural processes (cf., Norman, 1986). Nevertheless, PDP models have already provided new insights about how information is encoded and how learning takes place (e.g., Farah, 1994; Hinton, 1992). In fact, one of the main differences between symbolic and PDP systems is that the latter are much more likely to specify how the skill or behavior being modeled is acquired. The reason is that PDP models have a very natural way of accounting for the learning process in terms of using feedback about performance to alter the connections between nodes.

FIGURE 3.13	A PDP Representation for Letters

Each layer of McClelland and Rumelhart's word recognition model can be depicted as a set of linked nodes. The nodes themselves do not represent information. Instead, it is the pattern of activity across the network that signals a particular letter. The arrows show which nodes must be active in order for a certain letter to be signaled.

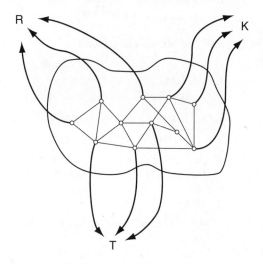

For example, we could study learning using a PDP version of McClelland and Rumelhart's (1981) word recognition model. We present certain stimuli to the model over and over. With each stimulus presentation, the connection strengths between nodes are adjusted so that, over time, the model more quickly and easily settles into the particular pattern of activation that signals a certain stimulus. Applying this kind of strategy, McClelland and Rumelhart (1986b) used a PDP network to model learning of the past tenses of various verbs.

Have PDP models won the day, and are symbolic models on their way out? No, connectionism is one useful way to represent mental processes; but it has its weaknesses, too. Even the renewed interest in learning (as opposed to just memory and performance) that connectionism has swept into cognitive psychology has caused some problems for PDP models. For example, in a PDP model, new learning involves changing the strengths of connections. However, as a PDP network learns to recognize a new pattern, the changes in the connections can make it hard for the model to recognize previously learned patterns (McCloskey & Cohen, 1989). Of course, some interference is also found in human learning, but the problem is often much more severe in PDP networks.

Perhaps more important for psycholinguistics, critiques of connectionist models have pointed out that PDP models have been most successful in explaining the early perceptual processes involved in recognizing visual or auditory patterns (Norman,

1986; Johnson-Laird, 1988). To explain more complex behaviors, like figuring out who is in the photograph in the "brothers and sisters" puzzle, different PDP networks apparently have to be acting as subprocessors to do different parts of the overall task. In this context, it is not clear whether the connectionist architecture will have distinct advantages over other kinds of models. At any rate, the idea of separate subprocessors for different language tasks is taken a step further by the modular view of cognition and language, as we will see in the next section.

Brain, Mind, and the Modularity Debate

Caplan (1992) described the case of a patient, B.D., who had damage to a portion of the left hemisphere of his brain. After his brain damage, B.D. had no trouble reading a sentence like (7), but he was confused by a sentence like (8):

(7) Jackie weighed the meat.

(8) Jackie weighed Reggie.

Upon reading sentence (8), B.D. would have no idea which person was weighed. Note that sentence (8) is reversible, in that "Reggie weighed Jackie" is also sensible. However, because meat cannot weigh a person, sentence (7) is not reversible. In other words, even a person who has trouble with syntax can figure out sentence (7) just on the basis of semantics. But there is no purely semantic way to determine who does the weighing in sentence (8).

The case of B.D. illustrates a very general phenomenon in the study of brain damage and cognitive functioning. It is quite common for brain lesions to have very specific effects, apparently sparing some abilities but leaving other abilities devastated (Kosslyn & Koenig, 1992). The specificity of the effects of brain lesions is hard to reconcile with the view that the brain is like one big connectionist network, such that the same set of units are performing each and every cognitive job. Instead, it seems that the brain is composed of a set of functionally distinct subsystems that are dedicated to particular kinds of activities. One or more of these subsystems can be disturbed and still leave other subsystems relatively intact. For example, based on B.D.'s case, we might assume that there are distinct syntactic and semantic subprocessors within the overall language processor. As we have seen, B.D.'s brain damage appears to have selectively disturbed his syntactic subprocessor.

The general notion that different subprocessors are associated with different brain areas is not controversial. What is controversial is the identity of the various subsystems and the question of whether they communicate in a modular or interactive fashion. One of the most influential thinkers on the modular side of this debate has been Jerry Fodor, whose 1983 book, *The Modularity of Mind,* laid out an explicit proposal for how to connect cognitive science and neuroscience. A schematic of what Fodor had in mind is shown in Figure 3.14. Two aspects of Fodor's view are particularly relevant to our study of language. First, he considers language to be an input system rather than part of the central systems. Second, he argues that the input systems have a modular architecture. Let's look at each of these points in turn.

According to Fodor (1983), the central systems include much of what we have covered in this chapter—activities like attention and memory that cut across different knowledge domains. Fodor argued that, because of their generality, central processing

FIGURE 3.14	A Modular View of the Mind

Fodor (1983) divides the cognitive system into transducers (sensory organs), which convert physical stimulation into neural signals; input systems, which include the brain pathways for processing sensory information and language; and central systems like memory. It is the input systems that are composed of modules.

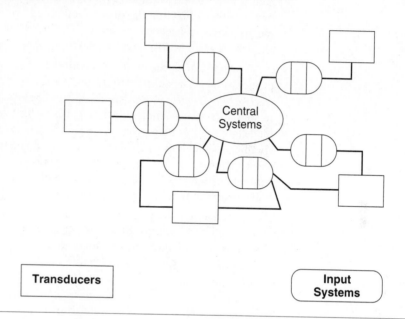

Transducers

Input Systems

activities cannot be localized in terms of specific brain regions. Indeed, he claimed that the neuropsychology of central processes is not something we can determine. Contrary to Fodor's idea, many neuropsychologists believe that the brain activities that underlie central processes can be studied and understood (e.g., Shallice, 1991). Fodor's claims about the nature of the input systems are perhaps more interesting, however. He said that the input systems are composed of modules. According to Fodor:

- A module is **domain specific.** Each input system works with particular kinds of information from whatever sensory system(s) is (are) feeding it information. The input system then works with codes that are special to that sensory system. After processing the information, the input system makes the information available to the central systems. For example, both the visual input system and the language input system get information from the eyes, but only the language system recodes that information into a phonological representation.

- Each module is **informationally encapsulated.** A module receives information from earlier modules and gives information to later modules, but the processing is strictly data driven, or "bottom-up." The operation of a given module cannot be affected by the operation of modules later in the processing stream.

Thus, this view does not allow for knowledge-driven, or "top-down," effects on a module. No module can give partial results to a higher level and in turn receive information about activities from later modules or from the central systems. For example, if the language system has a syntactic module that gives its analysis of an utterance over to the semantic module, then we cannot use semantic information to tell us how to syntactically parse a sentence. You'll recall from Chapter 2 that this idea of an autonomous syntactic module is a major issue for linguistic theories (cf., Jackendoff, 1992; Langacker, 1991), and we will see it again when we discuss psycholinguistic theories of sentence processing.

- A module displays **localization of function.** In other words, each module is implemented in a particular brain region. It was this idea that made modularity attractive to many neuroscientists. If modules are localized to particular brain regions, then understanding the neural wiring for language, for example, is made more simple because we can expect the effects of brain lesions to affect specific modules in predictable ways. However, Fodor might be wrong. If, instead, regions of the brain are dedicated to particular kinds of processes but the communication among them is interactive, then understanding cognition-brain associations becomes much more complex (e.g., Farah, 1994).

As a simple example of the implications of Fodor's ideas about localization of function, consider the syntactic processing of sentences. If there is a syntactic module that functions autonomously, then damage to that brain area should affect syntactic processing in a pretty specific way. What if, instead, syntactic processing is accomplished through the interaction of several different brain areas with each other, and with semantic information, all at the same time? In this case, it would be much harder to predict or interpret the effects of damage to any particular region of the brain.

Certainly some of the relevant evidence for testing interactive and modular theories comes from neuropsychology. Other evidence has been provided by studies at the representational level. Thus, the debate over modular versus interactive views of the cognitive system is a good example of how different levels of analysis are important to the study of language. The study of the mental processes used in language does not *depend* upon the study of the brain, but both the representational and implementational levels benefit from integration, where integration is possible.

CONCLUSIONS

The Independence of Language

Opinions about the relationship between language and other cognitive abilities have shifted like tides during the history of psychology and linguistics. One of the few points of agreement between behavioral approaches to psychology (e.g., Skinner, 1957) and some of the early information-processing views of cognition (Atkinson & Shiffrin, 1968) was a deemphasis on the independence of language and other human capacities. In contrast, Chomsky's view, that the productive aspects of language proceed from a special language-specific ability, influenced many psychologists. Even though Chomsky's transformational grammar was not an adequate psychological model, his general notion that language processes are special and independent remains influential today.

Everyone can agree, however, that there must be some links between language and other mental abilities. As we have seen, the necessity for points of contact between language and cognition is most evident when we consider language and memory. Language tasks, like other mental tasks, are constrained by our limited-capacity working memory. And our semantic memory system plays the key role of providing the information critical to determining meaning during language performance. As we have also seen, there are links between language and episodic memory. What we remember later, once we have comprehended some utterance, is a function both of the way we elaborate upon the information and of the relationship between the encoding context and the retrieval context. Finally, there are links between language and other mental abilities in the context of language acquisition. Indeed, at least some of what we learn may consist of mental procedures that are acquired in the same way that we learn other skills.

As researchers have tried to understand the details of how language and memory work together, they have integrated both the representational and the implementational levels of analysis. One approach to this integration has taken the form of connectionist models, which are cognitive models that try to be consistent with how the brain works on a neural level. Another approach to integrating the different levels is modularity. The modular view attempts to uncover the distinct processing systems that perform specific mental tasks. Thus, it strongly supports the idea that, although language processes make information available for memory and reasoning, the language system has its own special parts that work independently from the rest of cognition. Whether this modular view is correct, or, conversely, whether the language system consists of a number of processors that interact almost constantly with the rest of our cognitive system, is a major issue to be decided in upcoming chapters.

CHAPTER REVIEW

Checking Your Understanding

Key Terms

articulatory suppression task (85)
associative stage (103)
automatic process (90)
autonomous stage (103)
central executive (86)
cognitive stage (103)
connectionism (105)
controlled process (90)
decay theory (99)
declarative memory (89)
derivational theory of complexity (DTC) (77)

domain specific (109)
encoding specificity principle (101)
episodic memory (89)
fan effect (100)
informationally encapsulated (109)
interference theory (99)
introspection (75)
levels of processing theory (97)
lexical decision task (90)
localization of function (110)
long-term store (LTS) (80)

multistore model (80)

paired associate learning (78)

parallel distributed processing (PDP) (105)

phonological loop (86)

procedural memory (89)

schema (95)

semantic memory (89)

semantic priming (90)

short-term store (STS) (80)

stimulus onset asynchrony (92)

syllogisms (87)

transfer-appropriate processing (102)

typicality (94)

typicality effect (94)

visual-spatial sketch pad (86)

working memory (WM) (84)

Review Questions

1. Contrast Wundt's view of language and its relation to our other abilities with Skinner's view of this issue.

2. What developments outside of linguistics helped bring about the formation of the field of cognitive psychology?

3. In the 1970s, cognitive psychologists moved away from incorporating linguistic theory into explanations of language. Why? More recently, why has there been a resurgence of interest in integrating linguistics and psychology?

4. How would you describe the relationship between general cognition and language from the viewpoint of Atkinson and Shiffrin's (1968) multistore model?

5. How would you describe the relationship between general cognition and language from the viewpoint of Baddeley's model of working memory?

6. What data indicate that the spread of activation in a semantic network is an automatic process?

7. Studies of sentence memory (e.g., Bransford & Franks, 1971) suggest that people's memory for a sentence includes logical inferences they can make from the sentence. How would you explain these data using schema theory?

8. Under what circumstances does elaboration help memory? When can elaboration hurt memory?

9. Is it possible for people to follow a rule when performing some task (such as producing a sentence) without thinking of the rule consciously? In terms of the psychological aspects of sentence production, how would "following a rule" be different in a production system model versus a PDP model?

10. Why is testing for top-down processes a key to deciding between modular and interactive views of language?

On Further Reflection . . .

1. Bousfield's (1953) classic experiment on clustering is easy to reproduce. In my own classes, for example, I often read off a list of items like these—except that I read them in random order:

eggs	cat	flower	football
butter	dog	tree	soccer
milk	snake	bush	wrestling

Then, after distracting the students with another activity for a few minutes, I ask them to recall all the words from the list that they can, in any order. Even though I read the items in random order, when students try to recall the items a few minutes later they tend to cluster many of the items by category. And when they leave out an item, it is often one of the more unusual members of the category (like *snake* in the "pet" category). What is most interesting is that some students notice they have clustered the items only after I mention clustering. And a few students cluster the items in terms of scenes. So, they might remember *cat, milk,* and *bush* together because they pictured a cat drinking milk under a bush when the items were read.

Think about the principles we covered in this chapter and how they are illustrated by these clustering results. You should be able to use at least the following concepts to explain typical clustering results: spreading activation, automatic processes, encoding specificity, typicality, and schema. If so much of our knowledge base is brought to bear in remembering a brief list of words, what does this suggest about how extensively we use our knowledge base in understanding lengthy stories?

2. As I noted in this chapter, some of the specific claims of the derivational theory of complexity were not supported by research on comprehension times. However, the general idea that the more complex the structure of a sentence, the more difficult it is to comprehend is still very important. To see why, think about how difficult it is to comprehend sentences with multiple embeddings. Remember, through recursion we can continue embedding more and more clauses inside a sentence. So, *Wanda went to the store* can be expanded to *Wanda, the woman who lives next door, went to the store.*

Embed a few more clauses in the latter sentence. At what point does the sentence become nearly impossible to understand? Think about why this comprehension problem happens, given Baddeley's model of working memory. Start with the assumption that we must hold a sentence in working memory while language comprehension processes work on the sentence.

CHAPTER 4

Theories of the Language-Thought Relationship

*C*urare is a powerful drug used by some South American Indians to make poisoned arrows for hunting. The drug causes complete paralysis of the skeletal muscles, including the muscles used in breathing. In 1947, an experiment ·was conducted in which Scott Smith was injected with more than twice the amount of curare needed to induce paralysis. After ten minutes, he was unable to move his jaw or speak. After twenty minutes, he could not use the muscles of his eyelids to open his eyes. After thirty minutes, he could no longer breathe on his own, and he was placed on a respirator to keep him alive.

The point of this experiment was to test the usefulness of curare as a general anesthetic for surgery. At the time, no one knew whether curare blocked pain sensations. Smith was a physician who voluntarily underwent the procedure, which resulted in no ill effects once the drug wore off. He found that curare did not stop pain or other sensations. In fact, he was alert the entire time, performed mental arithmetic, and could remember the conversations of those who monitored him.

Smith's experiment was not designed as a test of the relationship between language and thought. Nevertheless, the experiment is a classic in the history of psycholinguistics because the results refuted a once-popular theory of the relationship between language and thought. John Watson (1925), the ground-breaking behaviorist, believed that what we call thinking is just silent, subvocal speech. Consistent with Watson's idea, Jacobson (1932) placed electrodes near the vocal folds of people as they performed a learning task and found that the people made minute muscle movements during the task.

Another way of stating Watson's view is that he believed that speech *is* thought. As you have seen in the last two chapters, Watson's view is quite different from the modern view that speech is only part of language and that language and other mental abilities are separable. Smith's experiment refuted Watson's view, because even though Smith could produce no articulatory movements at all, his thinking was unaffected.

Unlike Watson, the Russian developmental psychologist Lev Vygotsky (1934) believed that speech and thought have different genetic roots, and that they initially develop independently in the infant. However, Vygotsky also believed that Watson was somewhat on the right track in pointing the way toward the idea that there is a link between inner speech and thought. According to Vygotsky, the thought development and language development of children intersect as they begin to use the "voice inside their head" while thinking. It is somewhat later that speech begins to take on the social communication function that we normally associate with it. Thus, Vygotsky's general position was that thought and language were separable, but closely related, mental abilities.

Of course, the idea that we can make a distinction between language and thought predates modern psycholinguistics. The traditional view of the relationship between language and thought, going back at least to Aristotle, is that language is a tool that functions to communicate thoughts. Hence, according to Aristotle, if language is to serve as a useful tool for communication, the different categories of elements in language must reflect the categories used in thinking. Some researchers in linguistics and psychology, notably Chomsky and Fodor, have taken Aristotle's idea a step further by arguing that language functions as a mental organ separate from the rest of cognition. That is, the language system exchanges information with the general cognitive system in order to serve its function of communicating thoughts, but the operating principles of the language system are unique and not shared by the rest of the cognitive system.

Another hypothesis about the language-thought relationship, very different from either the behaviorist or the traditional view, has received some interest in linguistics and psychology at various times—namely, that *language has a strong influence on the way we think*. This controversial hypothesis is the one that we will examine in the present chapter. It has been espoused to varying degrees by many people from different backgrounds:

> Thus we may conclude that the mental development of the individual, and his way of forming concepts, depend to a high degree upon language. This makes us realize to what extent the same language means the same mentality. *(Einstein, 1954, p. 336)*

> I find it gratuitous to assume that a Hopi who knows only the Hopi language ... has the same notions, often supposed to be intuitions, of time and space that we have, and that are generally assumed to be universal. In particular, he has no general notion or intuition of TIME as a smooth-flowing continuum in which everything in the universe proceeds at an equal rate, out of a future, through a present, into a past. *(Whorf, 1956, p. 57)*

> Without words we should scarcely be able to form categories at all.... [S]ome labels, such as "blind man," are exceedingly salient and powerful. They tend to prevent alternative classification, or even cross-classification. Ethnic labels are often of this type. ... These symbols act like shrieking sirens, deafening us to all finer discriminations that we might otherwise perceive. *(Allport, 1954, pp. 178–179)*

Although the general idea that language affects thought is about as old as the more widely accepted traditional view of Aristotle, you'll notice that each of these quotes was from the 1950s. The first half of this century was the period in which the general idea that language guides thought received the most attention. That the quotes above are from such a diverse group—respectively, a physicist, an insurance adjuster who did linguistics as a sideline, and a prominent social psychologist—is an indication of the idea's pervasiveness during this period. However, during the second half of this century, the same idea—that language guides thought—nearly died out, at least in psychology and linguistics. Part of the reason for its decline was the rise of Chomsky's influence and his emphasis on linguistic universals as opposed to cross-linguistic differences. However, as you will see in the next section, the idea that language guides thought also lost favor because it was not supported in direct tests of a strong version of the hypothesis.

It may seem, then, that this chapter should be a very short one, and that I have spoiled the plot in terms of the hypothesis to be evaluated. Fear not. Recently, there has been a resurgence of interest in at least some aspects of the general idea that language guides thought, along with some empirical demonstrations that psychologists and linguists may have dismissed the idea prematurely. First, we'll consider an influential version of the hypothesis and explore why it was rejected. Then, we'll examine some alternative conceptions of the ways that language may guide thought, and try to extract the general lessons that this research area holds regarding the relationship between language and the rest of the cognitive system.

The Sapir-Whorf Hypothesis

In one sense, the question of whether language affects thought is a trivial one, with an obvious answer. We use language to persuade, command, and cajole others. And, clearly, what we say to people can affect their behavior. "Stop or I'll shoot!" had better affect their behavior. In these cases, however, we can say that it is the thought (or threat) behind the message that controls what the person thinks and does. Language is just the means for delivery of the information. Our interest here is in the idea that the nature of the language we use is related to how we think, or perhaps even how we are capable of thinking. The best-known, and most controversial, proponent of this idea was Benjamin Lee Whorf. Whorf provided a number of examples that he felt showed the influence of how differences among languages lead to differences in characteristic ways of thinking. His work was influenced by Edward Sapir, under whom he had studied. Thus, Whorf's claim about the ways that language influences thought is known as the **Sapir-Whorf hypothesis.**

The Sapir-Whorf hypothesis actually consists of two parts. One part is known as the principle of **linguistic relativity.** This principle is expressed in the quote by Whorf that I presented above. The idea is that lexical and syntactic differences between languages are mirrored by nonlinguistic cognitive differences. For example, a culture that has different words for two related objects will tend to think about the two objects differently, whereas a culture with only one term for both objects will treat them more similarly. In short, the principle of linguistic relativity holds that there are cultural differences in cognition that are correlated with linguistic differences between cultures.

One possible source of linguistic relativity is that cross-cultural differences in patterns of thought could cause the differences that exist among languages. That, however, is not what Whorf believed. What he did believe pertains to the second part of the Sapir-Whorf hypothesis, known as the principle of **linguistic determinism.** The principle of linguistic determinism maintains that people in various cultures think differently *because of differences in their languages.* The hypothesis that we are evaluating in this chapter is one way of stating this principle.

What evidence led Whorf to argue for linguistic relativity and linguistic determinism? To understand Whorf's views, you will find it helpful to know a little about his background. Whorf was certainly not a traditional academic linguist. He was trained as a chemical engineer at MIT and had a long career working for a fire insurance company. His analysis of Native American languages began as a hobby, but he later studied under Edward Sapir at Yale University. Whorf's interest in the relationship between language and thought was clearly based on his fascination with the languages of Native Americans and how the world views of their various cultures differed from those of the majority. Thus, most of the evidence he mounted focused on cross-cultural comparisons.

Whorf's mentor, Sapir, was a prominent linguist and an expert on Native American languages. Sapir himself was careful in his use of linguistic and anthropological research methods, whereas Whorf, though clearly a bright and original thinker, was methodologically somewhat sloppy (see Longacre, 1956). In being less objective and precise in his analysis of language samples from other cultures than he needed to be, Whorf opened himself up to much criticism, which in turn may have contributed to the almost wholesale, and perhaps premature, rejection of his ideas.

Whorf offered many examples of linguistic and cognitive variation, but two of them will suffice to illustrate the nature both of his evidence and of the criticism of his work. To make the point that there is no single "most natural" way to classify things in the world, Whorf noted that the language of the Hopi Indians has one word for everything that flies but is not a bird. If you find this category rather bizarre, you may be led to assume that Hopi language, or Hopi cognition, is primitive. However, Whorf claimed that an Eskimo would find it just as bizarre to have only one word for all forms of snow, when there are actually many different kinds of snow and an Eskimo must recognize these distinctions in order to survive.

Whorf's point, that we should not be ethnocentric and assume our language cuts the world up in the only logical way, is valid. Many linguists before and after Whorf have documented that supposedly primitive cultures have languages that are just as intricate, complex, and powerful as the languages of "civilized" Europe (e.g., Boas, 1938). Unfortunately, however, Whorf's "Eskimo example" is based on a linguistic myth that reoccurs periodically in the media, becoming increasingly exaggerated with each retelling. You may have heard or read that Eskimos have many different words for snow, whereas English has only one word. This cultural difference would be a good example of linguistic relativity if the verbal distinctions in question were associated with differences between Eskimos and non-Eskimos in recognizing different types of snow. In actuality, however, this "fact" about Eskimo words for snow, which almost everybody seems to have heard, is untrue. Boas (1911) mentioned that an Eskimo group he studied had four different root words for snow. Then Whorf elaborated on Boas's observation and said that there were seven Eskimo words for snow. And the last time I saw a reference to the Eskimo snow-words story, it was in a *New York Times* article that put the figure in the hundreds!

Besides the exaggeration, there are other fundamental flaws in this Eskimo story. For one, there is no single homogenous group of "Eskimo people." The various indigenous peoples of the Arctic—the Inuit, the Aleut, and the Yupiks, to name a few—rightly object to being considered a single group called Eskimo. These groups speak different languages, and not all of the languages spoken in the Arctic even belong to the same "Eskimo-Aleut" language family (e.g., Collins, 1990). So, it makes no sense to say how many words for snow Eskimos have; it only makes sense to talk about the number of words within a particular language.

In addition, it is not accurate to say that English has only one word for snow. Other words include *powder* and *hardpack*. And if you ski, you probably know even more words for snow. It is quite common for different groups in the same culture to vary in terms of how many words they use for things. For example, most people probably think there are only one or two kinds of memory. However, as you saw in the last chapter, cognitive psychologists talk about many different kinds of memory. It is the same within any domain of expertise. Experts make many distinctions, both verbally and in practice, that novices do not recognize.

A less famous, but more important, example from Whorf's writings involves the Hopi concept of time. As the earlier quote illustrates, Whorf's analysis of the language of the Hopi led him to believe that their conception of time is fundamentally different from that of Western cultures. He believed that the Hopi think in terms of events rather than units of time, and that these events occur, and sometimes reoccur in long cycles, because they are "prepared for" by other events. Whorf further claimed that this alternate way of thinking is reinforced and sustained by the Hopi language, which he said lacks verb tenses. Instead of expressing past, present, or future with the tense of a verb, he said, the Hopi use a special class of words to express ideas like *announcing*, *preparing*, and *persistence*, which are important to the Hopi view of the world.

One can certainly imagine that, in the absence of words or grammatical forms to express units of time or tense, habitual ways of thinking about time would be very different. This is a provocative idea, and it is indeed a bit mind-boggling to conceive of a culture that takes such a different view of time. We must ask, however, were Whorf's observations accurate? As it turns out, subsequent analyses of the Hopi language and culture have revealed that Whorf's observations were seriously flawed (e.g., Hill, 1988; Malotki, 1983). The Hopi language *does* make use of verb tenses, and it *does* have words for different units of time.

Nevertheless, it is true that there are fundamental differences among languages. For example, Sapir's claim that some Native American languages lack a distinction between nouns and verbs has withstood later scrutiny (Hill, 1988). To see whether the Sapir-Whorf hypothesis has any validity, we need to look at empirical studies of whether the real linguistic differences that exist between cultures are accompanied by differences in cognition.

In addition, it is important to bear in mind that linguistic determinism does not apply solely to cross-language comparisons. In fact, given Whorf's fascination with Native American languages, it is ironic that one of the most compelling examples of linguistic determinism that he offered was not cross-cultural. The central idea behind many of Whorf's claims was that the important influence of language on thought does not come from advertising slogans or jargon or other special linguistic attempts to manipulate ideas. Instead, Whorf claimed, our everyday language habits guide our thoughts at an unconscious level. Whorf (1956) said he first noticed this phenomenon in the course of investigating the causes of fires:

> But in due course it became evident that not only a physical situation . . . but the meaning of that situation to people, was sometimes a factor, through the behavior of the people, in the start of the fire. And this factor of meaning was clearest when it was a LINGUISTIC MEANING, residing in the name or the linguistic description commonly applied to the situation. Thus, around a storage of what are called "gasoline drums," behavior will tend to a certain type, that is, great care will be exercised; while around storage of what are called "empty gasoline drums," it will tend to be different—careless, with little

suppression of smoking or of tossing cigarette stubs about. Yet the "empty" drums are perhaps the more dangerous, since they contain explosive vapor. (p. 135)

If the usual meaning of *empty* causes you to ignore the threat of explosive gasoline vapor, then linguistic determinism can get you killed. Of course, this anecdote does not prove that it was the label *empty* that caused some workers to be careless, as opposed to ignorance of the danger of the residual vapor left in a container. As with cross-language comparisons, what we need are controlled studies of the possible effects of language on cognition. Let's take a look at evidence from both cross-cultural and within-language studies that directly test the Sapir-Whorf hypothesis.

Cultural Variations in Thought and Language

Is it possible to go beyond cataloging apparent differences among languages and world views of various cultures and get conclusive experimental evidence regarding how language is related to thought? Most psychologists have approached this question by trying to test the most radical version of the Sapir-Whorf hypothesis, strong linguistic determinism, because it makes the clearest predictions. The specific tasks that have been used to test linguistic determinism have spanned perception, memory, and reasoning. Across most of these studies, the issue has been whether the cognitive system can use distinctions that are not coded by the person's language. However, as you will see, some studies have attempted to test a weaker version of the hypothesis: the idea that our habitual ways of thinking are influenced by our language, but not completely determined by it.

Color Terms and Color Processing

Initially, much of the research on the Sapir-Whorf hypothesis focused on color terms because the number of different color terms varies widely across languages. For example, the color names in classical Greek did not distinguish between blue and black. Does that mean that someone who spoke only classical Greek would have trouble distinguishing blue and black perceptually? A few early studies showed that the colors easiest to describe and remember varied by language (e.g., Landar, Ervin & Horowitz, 1960; Stefflre, Castillo Vales, & Morley, 1966). But do these studies provide conclusive evidence for a strong version of linguistic determinism?

Actually, the use of color names to test Whorf's ideas is more complicated than it appears to be. Across different cultures, there is a surprising regularity in which colors are given distinct names. For instance, Berlin and Kay (1969) found that there are eleven specific colors from which all languages get their basic color names. Most interesting was their discovery that languages follow a hierarchy in assigning names to particular colors. There are a few languages that have only two color terms; invariably these correspond to black and white. In any language that has three color terms, the names always correspond to black, white, and red. And in languages that have additional basic color terms, these terms are added in the order of the following groupings: yellow-blue-green, then brown, then purple-pink-orange-gray. Thus, any language with five basic color names will have words corresponding to white, black, red, and two colors from the yellow-blue-green grouping.

In contrast to Whorf's ideas, these data suggest that there are universal, physiologically based principles behind color naming. Moreover, the notion that color names determine color perception received a serious blow in a classic study by Eleanor R. Heider (1972).* Heider studied the Dani tribe in New Guinea, who use only two color terms. First she presented colored chips; then, a short time later, she asked each person to try to recognize which of two chips was presented previously. The chips were either a focal color (e.g., the shade that people judge to be the most typical red) or a nonfocal color (e.g., still red, but an off-shade). Even though the Dani have only two color names, they not only recognized focal colors better than nonfocal colors, just as we do, but also could distinguish between colors that were not represented by different words in their language.

The research by Heider (1972) and by Berlin and Kay (1969), along with questions about the accuracy of the linguistic anecdotes offered by Whorf, led to the general impression that, to the extent that linguistic determinism was testable, it had been conclusively refuted (e.g., Brown, 1976; Clark & Clark, 1977). More recently, however, several investigators have claimed that reports of the death of linguistic determinism have been greatly exaggerated (e.g., Hunt & Agnoli, 1991). These authors point out that Heider's data were not the crucial test of linguistic determinism that many have taken them to be. Rather, what data like Heider's show is that the *strongest* version of linguistic determinism is not supported: People can distinguish between hues that are not given separate words in their language. So, now we know that the ability to perceive color is relatively independent of the color-naming practices of a language. But what about a less extreme version of the hypothesis: Do naming practices influence how easily we can distinguish or remember colors? Before you read about the research that has attempted to answer this question, try Activity 4.1, during which you may induce for yourself a linguistic principle that is important to the Sapir-Whorf hypothesis.

At the heart of the principle illustrated in Activity 4.1 is the concept of **codability.** Codability refers to how easily a concept can be described in a language. It makes sense that our most frequently used words are the most highly codable; we can say or write them easily with short words.

Codability also comes into play in considerations of how easy or difficult it is to describe a particular color. For example, if asked to describe the color of a stop sign, you'd probably just say "red" because a focal shade of red is used on stop signs. But what about the color of a fox? You'd probably describe that shade as a "brownish-red." These two shades of red, the one for the sign and the one for the fox, differ in terms of their codability.

Consistent with a weaker version of the Sapir-Whorf hypothesis is the fact that more easily coded colors are better remembered (Lucy, 1992; Lucy & Shweder, 1979; Lucy & Wertsch, 1987). In addition, comparative judgments among colors may be affected by color-naming practices. For example, Kay and Kempton (1984) conducted

---

* Heider is the same person cited in Chapter 3 for her ground-breaking work on typicality and categorization, the seeds of which you can see in her work on color names. Her research on typicality was published under her maiden name, Rosch.

ACTIVITY 4.1   Word Length and Word Frequency

Listed below are twenty words chosen at random from the Thorndike and Lorge (1944) norms of frequency of occurrence in the English language. Beside each word is a number indicating how many times the word was used in a million-word sample of written English. Plot the number of letters in each word against its frequency. (Note: For very high-frequency words, the Thorndike-Lorge norms specify only that the frequency is greater than 100.) Is there a relationship between word length and word frequency?

hunter	46	midway	7
rag	28	feud	6
devastate	5	chair	100+
hay	46	fault	50
technique	6	unarmed	7
intake	1	car	100+
revolt	22	oversee	1
ambush	·5	save	100+
igneous	1	result	100+
win	100+	misadventure	1

A systematic study of this relationship was conducted by Zipf (1935), who examined samples of Latin, Chinese, and English. In all three languages he found that there was a tendency for the most frequent words to be shorter words. This tendency is known as **Zipf's law.** The data you plotted show the same general relationship. Of course, I could have cheated and "fixed" the data. So, I'd suggest that you get samples of your own from Thorndike and Lorge (1944) or from Kucera and Francis (1967) and plot them as well. If you know a little statistics, you can calculate correlations on each sample; see if you find the negative correlations predicted by Zipf's law. If you are really industrious, do a little research and figure out why the correlations are generally stronger when you use the logarithm of frequency rather than raw frequency values.

a study in which they created color chips representing several different points along the color continuum from green to blue. On each trial, they presented three color chips from among which the person had to pick the "odd one out." That is, participants had to choose which two chips were most similar in color and which one stood out as different from those two.

Two sets of participants were involved in this experiment: English speakers and speakers of Tarahumara, a Mexican-Indian language that does not have separate terms for blue and green. Kay and Kempton created some trials in which most English speakers would label Chip A as a shade of green and Chip B as a shade of blue, even though the two chips were relatively close in color. That is, they were close in terms of the wavelength of light they reflected. Chip C was a focal example of green, but it was actually farther away in wavelength from Chip A than was Chip B.

If people are judging such stimuli based on physical characteristics alone, then they should pick the two chips that are most similar in terms of wavelength of light reflected (i.e., Chips A and B). The Tarahumara speakers did just that. However, the English speakers were affected by their color-naming practices: They selected as more similar the two chips that would both be labeled "green," even though these chips were farther apart in wavelength of reflected light. Thus, the English speakers evaluated the colors more in terms of the categories into which they were easily coded, whereas the Tarahumara speakers evaluated the colors more in terms of their continuous physical dimensions.

In sum, the research on the effects of color terms on color processing has not supported the strongest version of the Sapir-Whorf hypothesis, which would predict that people cannot perceive a color distinction unless that distinction is represented by different terms in their language. On the other hand, there *is* support for a weaker version of linguistic determinism. The ease with which a particular hue can be described in a language does appear to influence memory for, and comparative judgments about, color.

Language, Culture, and Higher Cognitive Processes

In retrospect, it seems a little odd that color processing became such a lightning rod for criticism of linguistic determinism. Intuitively, we would expect language habits to have their greatest influence over more complex and controlled cognitive processes that are likely to vary by culture. In contrast, color processing is relatively simple and automatic, and is based largely on biological factors that are unlikely to vary by culture.

A processing domain that depends more on specific learning experiences than does color perception would seem a better testing ground for linguistic determinism. As we saw in the last chapter, human cognition depends on a large set of different kinds of complex processes, so there are many possible candidates for domains within which we might see linguistic determinism. Let's now examine two general domains that give a relatively clear picture of the status of linguistic determinism.

Counting and Arithmetic. Analogous to the cultural variations in number of color terms, it is possible to identify cultures that have a very limited set of words for counting. For example, there are cultures whose languages have number terms corresponding only to *one*, *two*, and *many* (Greenberg, 1978). Obviously, this cultural feature places limitations both on counting and on comparing the numbers of items in different sets (Hunt & Agnoli, 1991).

Language can have subtle effects on arithmetic as well. Take a moment to examine Table 4.1, which shows the names for numbers 1 to 20 in five languages. Note how the number names are more regular in Chinese, Japanese, and Korean than in English or, especially, French. For example, in English, the word *eleven* does not tell you that the number is one more than ten, but in Chinese, and in languages that are based on the Chinese system, the name for the number eleven is literally *ten-one*. For this reason, children who speak such languages have an easier time learning to count into the teens than do their English-speaking counterparts (Miller & Stigler, 1987).

A series of studies by Irene T. Miura and her colleagues (Miura, 1987; Miura et al., 1993; Miura & Okamoto, 1989) suggest that the effects of language differences in

TABLE 4.1	The Names for Numbers 1 to 20 in Five Languages				
Number	English	French	Chinese	Japanese	Korean
1	one	une	yi	ichi	il
2	two	deux	er	ni	ee
3	three	trois	san	san	sam
4	four	quatre	si	shi	sah
5	five	cinq	wu	go	oh
6	six	six	liu	roku	yook
7	seven	sept	qi	shichi	chil
8	eight	huit	ba	hachi	pal
9	nine	neuf	jui	kyu	goo
10	ten	dix	shi	juu	shib
11	eleven	onze	shi-yi	juu-ichi	shib-il
12	twelve	douze	shi-er	juu-ni	shib-ee
13	thirteen	treize	shi-san	juu-san	shib-sam
14	fourteen	quatorze	shi-si	juu-shi	shib-sah
15	fifteen	quinze	shi-wu	juu-go	shib-oh
16	sixteen	seize	shi-liu	juu-roku	shib-yook
17	seventeen	dix-sept	shi-qi	juu-shichi	shib-chil
18	eighteen	dix-huit	shi-ba	juu-hachi	shib-pal
19	nineteen	dix-neuf	shi-jui	juu-kyu	shib-goo
20	twenty	vingt	er-shi	ni-juu	ee-shib

regularity of number names may extend beyond learning to count. As shown in Figure 4.1, Japanese and Korean first-graders, who speak languages based on the Chinese naming system, have largely mastered the concept of place value. Thus, these children, in comparison to their French- or English-speaking counterparts, are much more likely to understand that in the number "23" there are two tens and three ones. This understanding is important because place value is fundamental to the study of arithmetic in general.

Of course, there are many possible ways to explain why children from Japan and Korea tend to outperform U.S. and European children in math. One obvious example has to do with differences in teaching practices and degree of emphasis on education across these different cultures (see Sternberg & Ben-Zeev, 1996). However, the data from Miura and her colleagues (1993) suggest that part of the reason for the better performance of Asian children may be the "head start" they get in understanding number concepts due to the language that they speak. Because performance differences begin to emerge in early kindergarten, these researchers argue that differences in teaching style across the cultures could not have had a chance to exert much of an effect.

Reasoning and Judgment.   One of the most intriguing—and controversial—claims regarding linguistic determinism came from Bloom (1981), who argued that Chinese and English speakers differ in their ability to use **counterfactual reasoning.** Counter-

---

FIGURE 4.1   **Children's Understanding of Place Value**

Miura and her colleagues (1993) examined the mean performance, by country, on a set of five problems that tested first-grade children's understanding of place value in numbers. The children in those countries with the most regular system for number names showed the earliest mastery of place value.

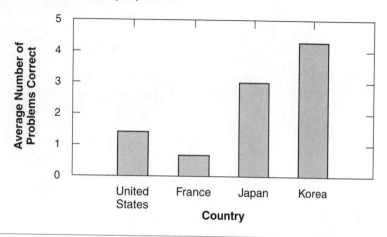

---

factual reasoning refers to the ability to think hypothetically about a situation that is contrary to fact. Bloom became interested in cultural differences in counterfactual reasoning while doing research in Hong Kong on political thinking:

> I happened to ask Chinese-speaking subjects questions of the form, "If the Hong Kong government were to pass a law requiring that all citizens born outside of Hong Kong make weekly reports of their activities to the police, how would you react?"; or "If the Hong Kong government had passed such a law how would you have reacted?" Rather unexpectedly and consistently, subjects responded "But the government hasn't"; "It can't"; or "It won't." (Bloom, 1981, p. 13)

Bloom suggested that, compared to English speakers, the Chinese speakers were less inclined to consider counterfactual ideas because their language does not mark counterfactuals differently from other conditional statements. Note that in English, there is a clear distinction between the following two forms:

(1) If John had missed the meeting, then he wouldn't have been elected treasurer.

(2) If John missed the meeting, then he wasn't elected treasurer.

We would use sentence (1) if John had gone to the meeting and going to the meeting was what got him elected. In contrast, sentence (2) applies to a situation in which John may have missed the meeting. So sentence (1) deals with a counterfactual: John did go to the meeting, but the sentence expresses what would have happened if he had not gone.

Bloom said that because Chinese lacks an explicit form for marking counterfactuals as in sentence (1), Chinese speakers are less likely to think in counterfactual terms. He reported experiments in which he found that Chinese speakers had difficulty drawing conclusions in counterfactual situations. If accurate, Bloom's conclusions have important implications for cross-cultural communication. His work suggests that misunderstandings can arise, even in cases of apparently accurate translation, because of differences between languages in terms of whether certain thinking patterns are coded.

Bloom's conclusions have been challenged, however, by Au (1983, 1992) and Liu (1985). Arguing that the passages used by Bloom were not well expressed in Chinese, these investigators found that with different materials the Chinese speakers performed better on tests of counterfactual thinking than Bloom had claimed. It is important to bear in mind, however, that the question is not whether Chinese speakers are capable of reasoning counterfactually but, rather, whether they do so less readily or less efficiently than speakers of English or other European languages (Bloom, 1984; Hunt & Agnoli, 1991). Of course, when dealing with a reasoning problem that has been translated into two different languages, researchers may have difficulty establishing that the two versions of the problem are equivalently well presented.

This problem was largely avoided in a classic study of social judgment conducted by Hoffman, Lau, and Johnson (1986). They were interested in determining how the codability of a personality description influences the impression that is formed after a person reads about someone. In this study, Chinese-English bilinguals were asked to read descriptions of people and to form impressions about each person. One of the critical manipulations in the experiment was whether the description of the person matched a stereotype that possessed a single brief label. For example, in English, an *artistic* person is often viewed as someone who not only produces art but also is intense, moody, and unconventional. In Chinese, there is no single personality descriptor that encompasses this collection of traits. On the other hand, there is no English term referring to someone who is worldly, reserved, socially skillful, and devoted to family. In Chinese, all these traits are captured by the term *shì gù.*

The other critical manipulation in the study was whether the personality descriptions were presented in Chinese or in English. The participants studied the descriptions in one language or the other; then they wrote their impression of what the person was like and responded to questions that asked them to make inferences about each person's character and behavior. The investigators found that the ready availability of a general term that fit the personality description led to a stereotyped impression of the person described. Thus, when reading in English, the participants tended to form an impression of the artistic person that included a trait like *unreliable*, which, though not mentioned in the description, is consistent with the stereotype of the "artistic temperament." When the same story was read in Chinese, the participants did not elaborate on the description with other stereotypic traits. Analogous results were obtained for the *shì gù* stereotype: The participants elaborated on the description when reading in Chinese, but they stuck closer to what was actually said when the description was read in English.

Hoffman and associates' (1986) data show that we are most likely to judge people in terms of a category, or a stereotype, if the person appears to fit a category that is easily coded in our language. Once again, the evidence supports not a strong version of linguistic determinism but, rather, a weaker version maintaining that the information that is most easily expressed by our language has an important effect on our cognitive processes.

It is most interesting that Hoffman and associates were able to demonstrate this effect in bilinguals. The implication is that the bilinguals' thought processes were affected by language not just in a general way but also, more specifically, by which language they happened to be using at the time. This empirical observation dovetails nicely with anecdotal reports by many bilinguals who feel as though they think differently depending on which language they are using (e.g., Wierzbicka, 1985).

In summary, when we get beyond the hypothesis that language fully determines thought, and instead consider the hypothesis that language influences thought, the existing body of cross-cultural research provides some support for Whorf's ideas. However, in most cross-cultural research, the two groups being compared will inevitably differ across many factors. Thus, even in Miura's relatively well-controlled studies of number concepts, it is difficult to be sure how much of the effect is due purely to language and how much is due to other cultural factors. In short, it is difficult in cross-cultural research to discern whether we have supported linguistic relativity and found that there are parallel differences in language and thought across cultures, or whether we have found support for linguistic determinism and showed that language differences cause cognitive differences between cultures (e.g., Au, 1992; Hardin & Banaji, 1993). Therefore, as a complement to the cross-cultural research, we also need to examine whether we can find evidence for linguistic determinism by looking at language-thought relationships within a particular language and culture.

Within-Language Studies of Linguistic Determinism

If you think back to the "empty gasoline drum" example from Whorf (1956), you can get an idea of how data relevant to linguistic determinism can be found within a single language. In Whorf's example, the use of the word *empty* may have influenced people's actions in an unintended way. Thus, the question becomes "Do the forms of expression in a language, rather than just the intended ideas behind utterances, affect how we think?" Once again, there are a number of different domains within which this question could be posed. We will focus on three areas that are often mentioned as especially relevant to the Sapir-Whorf hypothesis: the effects of language on visual memory, the effects of language on reasoning, and, the effects of language on social inferences.

Language and Visual Memory

One of the early discoveries made by researchers investigating human memory was that recall of a picture could be affected by the verbal label for the picture (e.g., Bartlett, 1932; Carmichael, Hogan & Walter, 1932). In some respects, the logic of these studies was similar to that of the experiments on color names and memory for colors. In each case, the question was whether access to a verbal label can alter visual perception or visual memory.

| FIGURE 4.2 | **Bartlett's Visual Memory Research** |

At the top is one of the original pictures that Bartlett showed to the participants in his study. At the bottom is an example of how a participant drew the picture from memory in response to two different verbal labels.

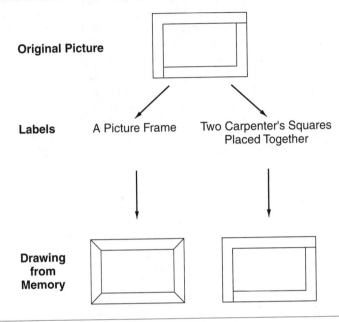

Original Picture

Labels   A Picture Frame   Two Carpenter's Squares Placed Together

Drawing from Memory

In one part of Bartlett's (1932) study, for example, participants were presented pictures like those shown in Figure 4.2 and, later, were asked to draw them from memory. As the bottom half of the figure shows, there were variations among the drawings that the people produced, depending on how they first verbally labeled each picture. Similar data were obtained by Carmichael, Hogan, and Walter (1932) when they randomly assigned either of two labels to simple, vague line drawings: Recall of the drawings was distorted in the direction of the verbal label that had been assigned.

More recently, researchers have expressed considerable interest in the ways that verbal stimuli can distort more complex forms of visual memory. For example, Loftus and Palmer (1974) found that people's estimates of how fast two cars were going in a filmed traffic accident varied according to how they were asked to estimate the speed. One group was asked, "How fast were the cars going when they *hit?*" Another group was asked, "How fast were the cars going when they *smashed* into each other?" Speed estimates were higher when the *smashed* form of the question was used. It is also possible to insert specific presupposed information into a question about an accident or crime scene. In this case, later memory for the scene may include information from the leading question, even if that information is inaccurate (Loftus, Miller & Burns, 1978). For example, regarding the filmed traffic accident, I could pose a straightforward question: "Did you see any blood?" Alternatively, I could say: "When you saw the broken glass, did you also see any blood?" If asked the second form of the question, you are more likely to later report that you saw broken glass, even if there was no broken glass in the film.

Neither the classic visual memory studies by Bartlett (1932) and Carmichael and associates (1932) nor the studies of eyewitness testimony by Loftus were designed specifically as tests of linguistic determinism. Nevertheless, because they reveal verbal effects on visual memory, the results of these studies have been taken as support for linguistic determinism (e.g., Hardin & Banaji, 1993). But is this a proper interpretation of the data? Consider the findings obtained by Bartlett (1932) and Carmichael and associates (1932). If the way the picture is encoded is what is altered by the verbal label, or if the visual memory for the picture is what is changed when the verbal label is given, then we would have evidence for a kind of linguistic determinism. However, it is also possible that memory for the details of the picture was lost over time, yet the verbal label was well remembered. At the time of the recall test, perhaps the participants drew what they assumed they had seen based on their memory for the label. If so, the outcome would not be a case of the verbal label determining memory for the visual stimulus; rather, it would represent a kind of guessing strategy based on remembering language instead of the picture. At the very least, the data might point to a confusion between a visual memory and a separate verbal memory. In that event, the distorted responses would reflect uncertainty about what was seen rather than a true effect of the label on the visual memory itself.

We can raise a similar question about the relevance of much of Loftus's data to linguistic determinism. There is an ongoing debate over whether leading questions distort eyewitness accounts because they change the original memory or because the misinformation sometimes present in such questions is stored as a separate, but related, memory that causes confusion as the person tries to recall the event (McCloskey & Zaragoza, 1985; Weingardt, Loftus & Lindsay, 1995; Zaragoza & Lane, 1994). In addition, the distorting effects of misinformation may not be unique to language. For example, in cases where people form a vivid visual image of a childhood event that they think may have happened, later attempts to recall the event may include inaccurate, imagined details (e.g., Garry, Manning, Loftus & Sherman, 1996). Thus, when we try to remember an event, it seems that various related memories can influence what we report. Moreover, it may not matter whether the information and misinformation come from language, vision, or visual imagery.

It seems a stretch to say that the confusion caused by separate but related memories formed from visual and verbal stimulation is an example of linguistic determinism. Yet one of the findings from Loftus's research does seem to be in the spirit of Whorf's ideas.

Loftus and Zanni (1975) asked whether the type of article used in a question can influence what people report after an accident. People were asked several questions, including one of these:

(3) Did you see a broken headlight?

(4) Did you see the broken headlight?

ACTIVITY 4.2   A Matter of Life and Death

There are no right or wrong answers to the following problems. Simply consider each one carefully, and decide which choice you would make to deal with the crisis in question.

1. The government is preparing for the outbreak of an unusual disease, which you know will kill 600 people if nothing is done to fight the disease. Two alternative programs have been proposed. If program A is adopted, 200 people will be saved. If program B is adopted, there is a one-third probability that all 600 people will be saved and a two-thirds probability that no people will be saved. Which program would you adopt?

2. A ship hits a mine out in the middle of the ocean and 600 passengers on board will die if action is not taken immediately. There are two options. If option A is adopted, 400 passengers will die. If option B is adopted, there is a one-third probability that no passengers will die and a two-thirds probability that no passengers will be saved. Which option would you choose?

In reality, the traffic accident film that they showed did not feature a broken headlight, but asking the question with the definite article *the,* as in sentence (4), significantly increased people's tendency to report that they had seen a broken headlight.

This effect is more unambiguously linguistic than others we have considered here; but we can still ask: What is being affected: memory for the accident or the response that people make when they are uncertain of their memory? Perhaps the place to look for linguistic determinism is not in memory distortions but in the kinds of decisions we make under conditions of uncertainty—that is, when there is no clearly "right" answer. Can we find more pure evidence that the linguistic format in which information is conveyed affects cognition, apart from the content of the information itself? We will turn to studies of language and reasoning to answer this question. Before reading on, however, try Activity 4.2.

Language, Reasoning, and Problem Solving

The two problems in Activity 4.2 are worded differently, but they are logically equivalent. If 200 lives are saved, that means 400 lives are lost. Go back now and rephrase the disease problem so that it is stated in terms of lives lost rather than lives saved, as was done in the ship problem. You can see that the outcomes are the same, regardless of which way the problem is stated.

In short, even when the "gain" and "loss" versions of a problem are logically equivalent, people tend to make different choices depending on whether the problem is stated in terms of lives saved or lives lost. Another way of putting it is that the wording of a problem tends to affect people's choices even when differences in the wording do not change the logic of the problem. This tendency is known as a **framing effect.** Tversky and Kahneman (1981) found that when the disease problem was stated in terms of lives saved, 72 percent of the research participants chose program A. That is, they played it safe. When the same problem was stated in terms of lives lost, the preferences reversed: 78 percent chose program B and took a risk. A variety of studies have shown that, in general, people tend to avoid risks when the problem is stated in terms of gains and to take risks when the same problem is stated in terms of losses (e.g., Jou, Shanteau & Harris, 1996; Kahneman & Tversky, 1979; Redelmeier & Tversky, 1992).

This phenomenon is similar in some ways to Whorf's "empty gasoline drum" example, in that the use of a particular term—in this case, *loss* or *gain*—seems to block at least some consideration of the implications of our actions. However, we are not complete prisoners to the linguistic manipulations of problems. Jou and associates (1996) showed that if the wording of a problem causes people to compare and interrelate the options, the framing effect disappears. For example, they modified the disease problem by stating that an effective dose of medicine could be given to one person, thereby saving that person, or a dose could be divided between two people, but each would risk having too low a dose. Faced with this more concrete scenario, people's choices were not influenced by whether the problem was phrased in terms of losses or gains. Thus, framing shows evidence of a weak form of linguistic determinism, but one that can be overcome.

Another way to approach the study of the language-thought relationship is to examine whether verbalizing one's thoughts during problem solving is beneficial or harmful. Overall, the data suggest that verbalization can have either effect, depending on the nature of the problem. Research by Schooler, Ohlsson and Brooks (1993) has helped to clarify some of the conditions in which language helps or hurts reasoning and problem solving. On the one hand, they noted, several studies show that verbalizing thoughts during problem solving can be beneficial (Ahlum-Heath & di Vesta, 1986; Gagne & Smith, 1962) or neutral (Ericsson & Simon, 1984) compared to a nonverbalizing condition. On the other hand, Schooler and associates themselves demonstrated that verbalizing thoughts can be detrimental to performance on **insight problems.** An insight problem is one in which a person arrives at a solution quite suddenly—that is, all at once, rather than by getting closer and closer to the solution in a step-by-step fashion. Figure 4.3 gives an example of an insight problem used in the study by Schooler and associates.

In insight problems, the solution often comes to people when they entirely shift the way they are approaching the problem. So, verbalization of thoughts may interfere with insight problems because attention shifts to the thoughts that are verbally reportable when in fact it is the nonreportable thoughts that are important to the solution. This idea has two implications for the relationship between language and thought. First, the data on insight and verbalization are consistent with the view that thought and language are separable. Second, these data provide converging evidence for the conclusion we drew from other reasoning and problem-solving research: that language can limit the thoughts we engage in, thereby inhibiting performance.

Language and Social Inference

Clearly, one of the most important ways that we use language is in our relationships with other people. As we saw in Chapter 1, language conferred an adaptive advantage to the early hominids from whom we evolved, and a large part of that advantage was

FIGURE 4.3	An Example of an Insight Problem

This square pen holds nine pigs. Put in two more square enclosures that would leave each pig in a pen by itself. The solution appears at the end of the chapter.

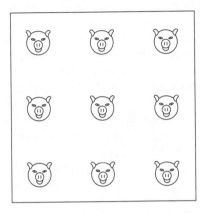

that language allows for a great deal of cooperation and information exchange among group members. Another possible effect of language, however, is that it may sometimes reinforce our perception that some people belong to a different group than we do, or that one particular group is superior to another. This idea is at the heart of Allport's quote at the beginning of the chapter. Was he right? Do some labels blind (or "deafen") us in our relations with other people?

This question has been of considerable interest recently in the debate over whether sexist language has a negative impact on how women are viewed and treated (e.g., Cameron, 1990; Lakoff, 1975). If you read the newspaper editorials on this issue, you find that some people think overzealous feminists are making the English language more cumbersome and less expressive by insisting on the use of *human beings* for *mankind* or *postal carrier* for *mailman*. Others argue that changing sexist language is a necessary first step toward changing sexist minds. Unfortunately, the current research base does not tell us definitively how much discrimination and biased thinking can be traced directly to sexist language. Much of the existing research does suggest, however, that sexist language may influence our thinking in subtle ways.

Several studies have examined the effects of using masculine terms to refer to people in general (e.g., Gastil, 1990; Khosroshahi, 1989). For example, in a sentence like "When someone has a fever of 101 degrees, he needs to see a doctor," the pronoun *he* is not meant to refer only to males. The intent is to refer to anyone, male or female—but that does not mean people always interpret such references in a neutral way. In a study by Khosroshahi (1989), for example, participants were asked to read a paragraph, the content of which was gender-neutral. In one version, masculine pronouns were used in reference to people in general; in other versions, the generic references were replaced with gender-neutral terms such as *he or she* or *they*. When the participants drew pictures to represent what was said in the paragraph, those who had read the version with the generic use of masculine pronouns were more likely to draw pictures that contained only males. Analogous results have been reported by Ng (1990) and by Cole, Hill, and Dayley (1983).

More disturbing was a study by Briere and Lanktree (1983). They had students read either the 1972 version of the American Psychological Association's statement of ethical principles or a revised version of the same statement. The original version included sentences like these:

> The psychologist believes in the dignity and worth of the individual human be-ing. He is committed to increasing man's understanding of himself and others.

The revised version that these researchers tested had been rephrased to remove sexist use of masculine pronouns and nouns as generic references. Later, each group of students was asked to rate the attractiveness of psychology as a profession for males and for females. The students who had seen the original sexist wording of the ethical principles rated psychology as a less attractive profession for women.

Although Briere and Lanktree's (1983) data provide some support for linguistic determinism, they do not allow us to conclude that women's actual career choices are affected by sexist language. The societal impact of biased language is a difficult hypothesis to test, and one not likely to be settled by a few psycholinguistic experiments. Indeed, given that emotions often run high on the issue of sexist language's impact, it may be worthwhile for us to pause here and take stock of what is, and isn't, at stake when that impact is considered from a psycholinguistic point of view. Whether women (or others in our society) suffer discrimination is not at issue in a psycholinguistics context. Nor is the question of whether knowledge of another person's gender affects how we interact with that person. Such effects are well documented (e.g., Martell, Lane & Emrich, 1996; Ridgeway & Smith-Lovin, 1996). However, even people who agree on these points may see the issue of sexist language quite differently. For example, on the Internet, I recently came across a debate in which someone suggested that focusing on minor issues like sexist language actually detracts from more important battles against sexism and discrimination. Complaints about the use of the term *manmade* in the North American Free Trade Agreement were cited by this person as an example of too much interest in minor issues. Other people responded that changing such language makes what is written more accurate (given that an enormous amount of *manmade* products are made by women), and that discussing such changes can raise awareness of more serious issues of discrimination.

My point here is that considerations of sexist language spill over into broad societal questions that, though important, are not easily addressed by simple studies of masculine pronouns and one-time ratings of the attractiveness of a profession. However, what the field of psycholinguistics *can* contribute to this debate, and related ones, is a greater understanding of the way that language and cognition are interlinked. Such an understanding would tell us more about the kinds of effects on thinking that language may, in principle, generate. This seems to me a more important goal for psycholinguistics than isolated demonstrations of potential Whorfian effects.

From the data thus far reviewed in this chapter, it is clear that our thinking is not limited to the terms or forms of expression in our language. On the other hand, it seems likely that the specific language forms that we use can have subtle effects on our thinking. One mechanism for these effects has been explored by McConnell and Fazio (1996; see also McConnell & Gavanski, 1994). These researchers tested the effects of the use of masculine versus gender-neutral occupational titles (e.g., *chairman* versus *chairperson* of a board of directors) on the interpretation of the characteristics of a person described in a passage. They found that people were more likely to rate the person as high on masculine characteristics if the masculine occupational title was used. Because this effect increased with repeated exposure to a masculine job title, McConnell and Fazio (1996) argued that the automatic priming effects of masculine terms are different from those of neutral terms. The implication is that sexist terms activated in the lexicon may automatically spread activation to more masculine concepts in semantic memory. In turn, this process may sometimes provide the context within which people experience social perceptions and make social judgments.

Another line of research that exemplifies the interdependence of language and thought is concerned with how the use of language helps us maintain our beliefs and biases in the face of contradictory evidence (e.g., Karpinski & von Hippel, 1996; Maass, Salvi, Arcuri & Semin, 1989; Martijn, Van der Pligt & Spears, 1996; Semin & Fiedler, 1992). According to the **linguistic category model** (Semin & Fiedler, 1992), the same behavior can be described linguistically at four different levels of abstraction (see Table 4.2). Yet the implications of each level differ. The more abstract the level of description, the more likely the statement will lead to inferences about the person who performed the act.

Maass and others (Maass, Milesi, Zabbini & Stahlberg, 1995; Maass, Salvi, Arcuri & Semin, 1989; Martijn, Van der Pligt & Spears, 1996) have shown that people often use these different levels of description in a biased fashion. For example, in the 1989 study conducted by Maass and associates, members of two different teams in a horse racing competition were shown pictures of people engaging in either desirable (e.g., helping) or undesirable (e.g., littering) behavior. If the person in a given picture was said to be from the same team as the person describing the picture, the descriptions of desirable behavior were at a higher level of abstraction, and the descriptions of

TABLE 4.2	Levels of Description in the Linguistic Category Model	
	Level	**Example**
	1. *Action verb* Describes a specific, observable behavior.	Marilyn kissed Wingate.
	2. *Interpretive verb* Describes a general class of behaviors.	Marilyn harassed Wingate.
	3. *State verb* Describes an enduring state that goes beyond a specific behavior.	Marilyn desired Wingate.
	4. *Trait description* Refers to an abstract personal trait that reflects the person's disposition.	Marilyn acted impulsively with Wingate.

undesirable behavior were at a lower level of abstraction. The opposite trend was observed when the person in the picture was supposedly from the other racing team.

Maass and associates (1989) referred to this effect as a **linguistic intergroup bias (LIB)**. That is, positive behaviors by a member of one's own group tend to be described in a way that suggests that the member has positive qualities, whereas the same behavior by a member of a different group is described in a way that refers only to the behavior, not to the person who performed it. The reverse is true for undesirable behaviors.

What are the implications of the LIB for the relationship between language and thought? On the one hand, the LIB seems to demonstrate the classic view that our beliefs and our thoughts determine the language that we use. We feel more positively about our friends than about our competitors, so we describe the behavior of each group accordingly. On the other hand, the LIB can be viewed in terms of a group's attempt to use linguistic determinism to maintain its cohesion. In other words, we use language to keep our own group together by maintaining a negative view of unfavored groups.

We need not choose between these two views of the LIB. If there is an interdependent relationship between language and thought, then both views may be correct. Consistent with this idea, recent evidence suggests that the LIB is both a reflection of our opinions and a linguistic device for maintaining them. Karpinski and Von Hippel (1996) and Maass and associates (1995) have extended the LIB to the study of personal expectations about other people's behavior. Their evidence suggests that many people describe the unexpectedly positive behavior of enemies at a low level of abstraction. This allows people to maintain their opinions, and biases, in the face of contradictory evidence. So, if you dislike Jack and yet you saw him picking up cans along a highway, you might say, "I saw Jack picking up cans" rather than "I saw Jack being a helpful citizen."

This finding is an interesting and disturbing twist on the Sapir-Whorf hypothesis. It suggests that we are able to manipulate our own use of language in a way that moderates how much of an impact new information can have on our prejudices.

CONCLUSIONS

The Interdependence of Thought and Language

Let's review by reconsidering the quotes from Einstein, Whorf, and Allport that I provided earlier. The statements from both Einstein and Whorf reflect strong versions of linguistic relativity as well as linguistic determinism. In particular, Whorf's tendency to make rather extreme claims for linguistic determinism set several psychologists to the task of demonstrating that we can think in terms that are not represented linguistically. Few, if any, psycholinguists today would support the strongest version of linguistic determinism. But that doesn't mean we should throw out the deterministic baby with the Whorfian bathwater.

Now consider Allport's statement. The first part of his quote is another example of an overstated position on determinism. Contrary to Allport's statement, it is possible to form and use concepts apart from language. If you think back to Chapter 1, you may recognize that this possibility is one of the conclusions Premack drew from his attempts to teach a language to nonhuman primates. However, the general idea embodied in the rest of Allport's statement—that particular terms in our language can influence how we think—has received a good deal of support. We have seen evidence for this influence in such diverse domains as social inference, problem solving, reasoning, and arithmetic processing.

In the final analysis, the relationship between thought and language is not a simple one. Perhaps that's why it has often been misrepresented. We know for certain that thought and language are not the same thing, and that many of the thoughts we are capable of are not completely determined by our language. Beyond that, the data suggest that language and thought are interdependent. This interdependence is often very useful to us. Our ability to use language to transmit our thoughts to others has been crucial to the survival of our species. In addition, we often use processes like verbal rehearsal to aid memory or problem solving. It is important to remember, though, that the interdependence of language and thought can also be a liability. As we saw throughout this chapter, our thoughts are not determined by our language, but they may be constrained by our language.

CHAPTER REVIEW

Checking Your Understanding

Key Terms

codability (121)
counterfactual reasoning (124)
framing effect (130)
insight problems (131)
linguistic category model (134)

linguistic determinism (117)
linguistic intergroup bias (LIB) (135)
linguistic relativity (117)
Sapir-Whorf hypothesis (117)
Zipf's law (122)

Review Questions

1. Is linguistic relativity possible without linguistic determinism? Is the reverse possible?

2. Explain how Chomsky's approach to linguistics might have decreased interest in the Sapir-Whorf hypothesis.

3. What evidence suggests that color naming is based largely on universal, biologically determined aspects of color perception?

4. Distinguish between a weak and a strong version of linguistic determinism. What version (or versions) of linguistic determinism is (are) refuted by Heider's data?

5. Is Miura's research on cross-cultural differences in the development of arithmetic skill an example of linguistic relativity or of linguistic determinism? Explain.

6. Why is the concept of codability important in research on cross-cultural differences in reasoning?

7. Explain the data on memory distortions in eyewitness testimony from both a Whorfian perspective and a non-Whorfian perspective.

8. Give some original examples of how framing is used in advertising. As a start, con-

sider how sausage is advertised in the market: as "25 percent fat" or "75 percent fat-free"?

9. Some related words in our language differ in terms of whether they are connected to a straightforward definition or an entire schema. For example, think about the difference between "Do you see that woman over at the counter?" and "Do you see that blonde over at the counter?" How might such differences in lexical-conceptual connections play a role in stereotyping?

On Further Reflection . . .

1. Try scanning some newspaper and magazine articles for examples of the linguistic intergroup bias. One good place to find such examples is in articles that report the comments from two feuding governments on the same issue. You can either use a current event or dig back into the past. For example, during the Tiananmen Square incident in China in 1989, when the Chinese government stopped pro-democracy rallies, how did that government's descriptions of the behavior of the protesters differ from the descriptions given by Western news agencies and Western governments? Another place to look is in old newspapers that describe incidents from the Cold War in the 1950s and 1960s between the United States and the Soviet Union.

2. Try out the following classic puzzle on several people:

A boy goes out with his father to see a movie. At an intersection near the hospital, another driver runs a stop sign, crashing into the passenger side of the car, where the boy is seated. The father scoops up the boy, who is seriously injured, and runs into the hospital. A surgeon is summoned who, upon seeing the boy, declares, "I can't operate on this boy. He's my son!" How can this be?

Many people have trouble with this puzzle because they assume that the surgeon is a man. Now try out the puzzle on a few other people, substituting *mother* in place of *father* in the story. Now it doesn't seem a puzzle at all. Consider the bias that makes this problem difficult: Does it reflect the influence of language on thoughts, or is it an effect of thoughts, in the form of prior beliefs, on language interpretation?

FIGURE 4.4   **Solution to the "Pigs in a Pen" Insight Problem**

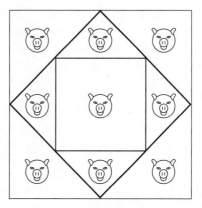

What Must the Psychology of Language Explain?

A typical dictionary definition of *language* is that it's a system of symbols used for communication. That makes it sound like language is a straightforward process of taking an idea, representing it with symbols that someone else understands, and then transmitting those symbols. What could be simpler?

As you now know, the simplicity of language is more apparent than real. When you take a closer look at what must be going on in order for humans to use language, the process seems anything but simple. That's why I have taken four chapters to define what language is, and what it is not. Along the way, several related questions about the nature of language were answered. Is language different from other forms of animal communication? Is it based on knowledge that we are born with? Can we study language separately from other mental abilities? What's the direction of influence between language and thought? The answers are yes(!); probably to some degree; yes, to an extent; and mutual.

Each of these questions deals in some way with the relationship between language and the rest of our cognitive system. We have seen plenty of evidence that language and thought are conceptually separable but functionally very intertwined. Along with other primates, we can think without language; but for us language is a tool of thought, not just a tool of communication. As just one example, think back to how ideas about short-term memory have changed over time. No longer do we consider short-term memory to be a simple buffer holding about seven chunks; rather, we think of it as a two-buffer system in which one buffer deals with language-based information (the phonological loop) and the other buffer deals with nonlinguistic information (the visual-spatial sketch pad). Both of these buffers are tied into a system for allocating attention. Thus, even within this one part of the cognitive system we see evidence both for the separateness of language and for its close ties with the rest of cognition.

The idea that language has a special status among our cognitive processes has two intellectual parents, at least for the growth of the idea in psychology. The special nature of language comes both from anthropological studies of human evolution and from linguistics. The most influential proponent of the idea has been Chomsky. His work helped convince many psychologists that understanding language involves internalizing sets of rules. We saw examples of these rules at the phonological, morphological, and syntactic levels. Because these rules are quite subtle, and because they do not seem to be directly taught during language acquisition, many experts believe that we use innate knowledge of language to acquire the rules from our language environment.

However, investigators working from a connectionist framework are less comfortable with the traditional "rules-in-the-head" approach. Models developed by these investigators show how systems of interconnected units can behave as though they are following a rule, without explicit representation of the rule anywhere in the system. These researchers may still believe that language processing depends on special networks of information dedicated to language. However, connectionist models tend to illustrate how strongly language processes may interact with other kinds of cognitive processes. This arrangement may allow language to influence, as well as to be influenced by, thought. To better understand the interdependency of language and other mental abilities, we need to look in detail at how language works, and at the points of contact between the inner workings of language and the rest of the cognitive system. That is our task in the rest of this book.

Models of Language Processing

CHAPTER 5

The Recognition of Spoken Words

*I*n virtually every science-fiction movie in which people interact with computers, the computers flawlessly recognize human speech. But until quite recently, anything resembling this kind of computer capability was for science fiction only. While in graduate school in the 1980s, I heard a lot of bluster from some people in AI who claimed that computer speech recognition systems that performed as well as people in recognizing speech were "just around the corner." Well, it has been a long, hard corner to turn. In fact, although millions and millions of dollars have been spent on research into the development of computerized speech recognition systems over the last four decades, it has only been in recent years that we've seen widespread practical application of such systems (Rabiner & Juang, 1993).

In previous chapters, we have seen that language is a very complex phenomenon. But when we think of the complexity of language, syntactic rules and semantic decomposition come to mind, not the "simple" process of word recognition. After all, by age four, children are experts at recognizing speech. Why would the initial step in spoken language understanding—recognizing the words—be so hard for a computer to perform? It isn't just that the task is complex. Computers can perform some very complex tasks. The best chess-playing programs can defeat, at least occasionally, the very best grandmaster chess players. And chess seems more complex than word recognition. In addition, visual scanners have been developed that allow for computer input of words or numbers. What, then, is so much tougher about recognizing spoken words? The present chapter examines how people perform auditory word recognition, so by the end of the chapter you should have a good idea of how to answer this question.

For now, I'll hint at what lies ahead, by noting the general problem that makes automated speech recognition such a difficult problem. In general, automated systems have performed well when all they have to do is recognize a few words from a particular speaker. Where such systems failed in the past was in trying to recognize many different words produced by many different speakers (Markowitz, 1995). Thus, what makes automated speech recognition difficult is the variability of speech signals. Recently, by applying what has been learned from basic research on the nature of speech, and on how humans recognize speech, AI researchers have produced some impressive speech recognition devices. These newer systems can, for example, allow general-purpose input with acceptable accuracy (Juang, Perdue & Thompson, 1995). The pace of such advances is impressive. The accuracy rate for recognition of a thousand-word vocabulary produced by different speakers went from 40 percent in the mid-1980s to 97 percent by the mid-1990s (Rudnicky, Hauptmann & Lee, 1994).

Clearly, speech recognition systems are now advancing rapidly, and they continue to improve as more basic research is integrated into product development (e.g., Cole, Yan & Bailey, 1996; Yan, Fanty & Cole, 1997). However, the best speech recognition system is still the one in the human brain. So, we come back to the question of why humans can recognize speech so easily, when AI research shows that speech recognition is an inherently difficult problem. Many investigators in the area of speech processing believe that the answer to this question lies in our biology. That is, in addition to the ability to hear and process sounds, we may have a special system dedicated specifically to the processing of speech sounds. In the language of modularity, this hypothesis can be stated as follows: *Speech has its own input system, which is different from the input system for other auditory stimuli.*

To put the same idea more succinctly: Speech is special. Special, in this case, means that once the brain receives an auditory signal from the ears, that signal is processed differently depending on whether it comes from speech or from another kind of auditory stimulus. Keep this hypothesis in mind throughout the chapter, and evaluate it based on the evidence. By the end of the chapter you should be able to decide whether speech really is special in this sense.

In considering spoken word recognition, we will explore four topics: (1) the nature of the physical stimulus, (2) the component parts, or features, that are used to recognize the stimulus, (3) the word-level variables that make recognition easier or harder, and (4) the role of context in word recognition. The fourth topic, the role of context, is especially important for testing the hypothesis that speech is special. The more evidence we find for the role of context in word recognition, the more difficulty we will have in using a strictly modular, "speech is special" view to account for the data. Finally, at the end of the chapter, we will examine two formal models of word recognition in speech to see how they try to accommodate the data that we've reviewed.

The Nature of the Speech Signal

Toss a stone into a calm pool of water and you will see a wave ripple out from the point of the stone's entry into the water. When you make a sound, a very similar process occurs, except that you are making waves through air. To understand how the nature of sound waves has implications for word recognition, let's start with the simplest kind of sound, which consists of a wave of a particular **frequency** and **amplitude.** Frequency refers to the number of times the wave cycles from peak to peak each second. Thus, frequency is measured in cycles per second, or **Hertz (Hz).** The higher the frequency, the more high-pitched the sound seems. Amplitude refers to the height of the wave. The higher the amplitude, the louder the sound. Figure 5.1 shows a graph of three such waves.

Typically, the sounds we hear or produce consist of several frequencies at once. As we saw in Chapter 2, different physical properties of sounds are produced as we modify a stream of air when it passes through the vocal folds, mouth, and lips. We can get a picture of the acoustic properties of an utterance with a device called a **speech spectrograph** (see Figure 5.2). The visual record produced by this device is known as a **speech spectrogram.** A speech spectrogram shows the frequencies of sounds that are produced over time. Frequency is on the vertical axis and time is on the horizontal axis. An example of a speech spectrogram is shown in Figure 5.3. As you can see from the figure, the /ga/ and /ka/ sounds are distinguished mainly by the presence or absence of frequencies in the 2000–2500 Hz range.

The dark bands that you can see in spectrograms are called **formants.** Formants show the frequencies at which the acoustic energy is concentrated in an utterance. The darker the band, the more intense the sounds of a given frequency. As shown in Figure 5.4, the lowest frequency formant is designated F1 (first formant), the next lowest is

FIGURE 5.1   Sound Waves

Each of these three waves represents a simple tone. Wave A and Wave C are equally loud because they have the same height, or amplitude. Wave B sounds louder than the other two waves because of its higher amplitude. Waves A and B have the same pitch because they take the same amount of time to go through a complete cycle. Wave C is associated with a lower-pitched tone because it takes a longer amount of time to complete a cycle. The number of cycles per second is known as the frequency of a wave.

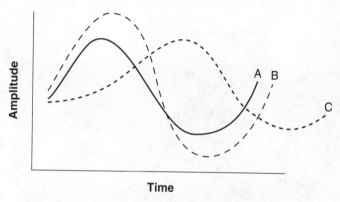

F2, and the next lowest after that is F3. The figure shows spectrograms for the pronunciation of "a yacht" and "a watt." These are similar-sounding utterances, so we would expect both similarities and differences in their spectrograms. Indeed, you can see that F1 is strongly similar across the spectrograms, but the shape of F2 is different.

As you can also see from the figure, some formants do not change much in frequency over time. These are known as **steady-state formants**. Other formants do undergo changes over time. Such changes are known as **formant transitions**. Thus, in the spectrograms in Figure 5.4, the sounds differ mostly in the transition in the second formant (F2). In summary, then, the differences among the speech sounds that we hear are based on differences in the frequencies at which the formants occur as well as on differences in the shape of the formants.

What Makes Speech Processing a Difficult Problem?

So far, what I have described suggests that each speech sound is associated with a unique, distinguishing pattern. If so, then speech recognition should be a simple matter of detecting which pattern is present at a given time. Then, the patterns could be assembled into words. However, speech recognition is definitely *not* that simple. Three major problems complicate attempts to extract information from a stream of speech. These problems are at the heart of the obstacles that have slowed the development of automated speech recognition systems. Indeed, what is remarkable about speech recognition by humans is that these problems cause us much less trouble than would be expected. The three problems are as follows:

| FIGURE 5.2 | A Speech Spectrograph |

This version of a speech spectrograph was built by Bell Laboratories in the 1940s. A sound was analyzed into its component frequencies by a bank of filters, and lights connected to the filters were used to make a running record of the sound on a phosphorescent belt that was run past the lights. In this figure, the speech signal is shown as light bands on a dark background. More typically, the two are reversed so that the speech signal appears as dark bands on a white background.

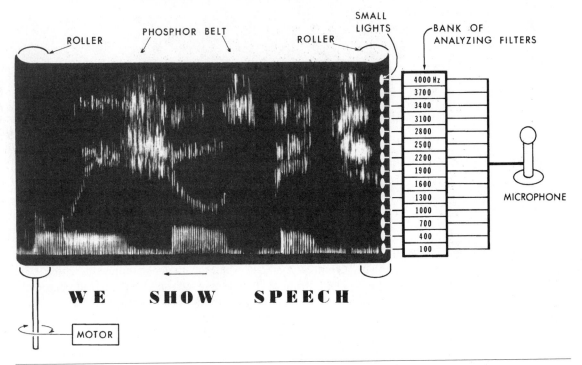

- The **lack of invariance problem.** The acoustic signal for a given segment of speech varies depending on the context in which it is produced. Figure 5.5 shows that even the first 200 milliseconds (msec) of "bet" and "bee" look quite different even though they both start with the same consonant. In contrast, the spectrograms for "bet" and "debt" look very similar, even though they begin with different consonant sounds. Typically, when we look at the spectrogram for a spoken word, it is not possible to isolate one phoneme from another. The reason is that we do not produce one phoneme after another. Instead, speech is based on **coarticulation,** or the production of phonemes in parallel. You can actually observe coarticulation in action. Go to a mirror and observe your mouth as you say "cola can." Notice how your lips and jaw are in a different configuration at the very beginning of each of the two words, even though the words start with the same phoneme. That's because the production of the initial consonant and the following vowel actually overlap in time. This coarticulation makes speech production fast and efficient, but it also rules out the possibility that speech is identified in a simple phoneme-by-phoneme fashion over time.

FIGURE 5.3	**Spectrograms for Two Consonant Sounds**

Two consonants are represented by these spectrograms: /ga/ and /ka/. The dark bands show which frequencies are produced at the greatest intensities over time.

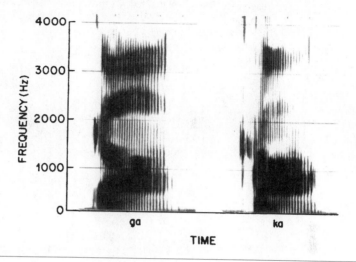

FIGURE 5.4	**Physical Differences in Speech Sounds**

The two phrases represented here differ in only one feature: the point of articulation of the consonant glides /j/ and /w/. This difference is clearly recognizable from the spectrograms.

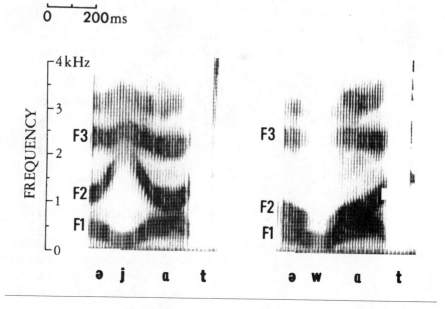

| **FIGURE 5.5** | **The Lack of Invariance Problem** |

By scanning down the left and right columns in this figure, you can see that the physical sound pattern changes dramatically even though the same initial phoneme is used in each case. The vowel that follows the initial consonant alters the way the overall sound is produced.

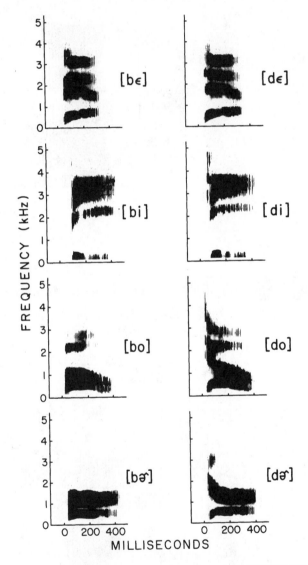

- The **problem of speaker variability.** Because of differences among people in the size and shape of their vocal tracts, no two speakers are exactly alike in their production of a particular sound. As an example, consider the two spectrograms in Figure 5.6. Here, the "same" /ga/ sound is physically different depending on whether it is spoken by a male or a female. There are also sizable differences in the way that a particular sound looks on a spectrogram when it is produced by the same person on different occasions. Even producing a sound with a smile or without a smile can affect the formant frequency pattern considerably. Thus, a major question for speech recognition researchers is how to pick out what is consistent across contexts in the midst of all this variation.

- The **segmentation problem**. Typically, speakers do not leave clear breaks between words. And because speech is not naturally broken into easy-to-identify word units (see Figure 5.7), the process of dividing a speech signal into its component words—a process known as segmentation—is part of the speech recognition process. Segmenting speech is normally something you are able to do effortlessly. However, you become aware of the lack of physical segmentation between words when you hear someone speaking an unfamiliar foreign language. It may then seem to you that the person speaking talks unusually fast, because you don't hear breaks between words. In reality, the person probably talks no faster than you do.

| FIGURE 5.6 | Variability in Production of the Same Speech Sound |

These two spectrograms look different, even though the same /ga/ sound was produced in each case—once by a male speaker (a) and once by a female speaker (b). The two utterances are recognized as being the same, despite the differences in their acoustic patterns.

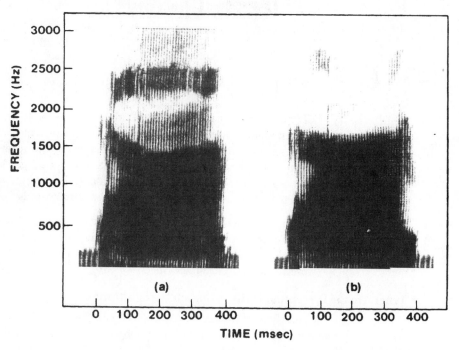

| FIGURE 5.7 | **The Segmentation Problem** |

The top spectrogram shows a sentence being spoken with a deliberate pause between each word. The bottom spectrogram shows the same sentence being spoken normally. In the latter case, there is no clear break between words, so the hearer has the problem of dividing the stream of speech into its component words.

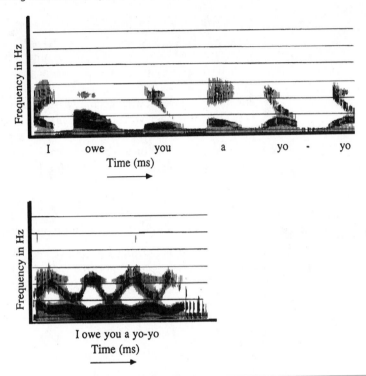

The problem that a lack of segmentation presents for automatic speech recognition systems, and seemingly should present to us as listeners, is well summarized in a classic description by Hockett (1955). Imagine that a row of raw but colored Easter eggs is moving toward you on a conveyor belt. Before the eggs get to you they are run through a wringer that squishes the eggs. Hockett likened the speech stream to the mess on the other side of the wringer and he said that you, as a listener, are like

> an inspector whose task is to examine the passing mess and decide, on the basis of the broken and unbroken yolks, the variously spread-out albumen, and the variously colored bits of shell, the nature of the flow of eggs which previously arrived at the wringer. *(p. 210)*

What Are the Perceptual Units in Speech Recognition?

The point behind Hockett's colorful anecdote is that speech recognition is a remarkable ability because it is so much simpler for us than it should be, given the nature of the problem. What do we focus on to recognize words when the stream of speech going by seems so messy? In the visual domain, most writing systems separate words by spaces, and despite variations in writing style, letters do appear to contain distinctive collections of features. In speech, identifying any invariant features that listeners could use to recognize particular sounds has proven very difficult. However, some progress has been made in mapping the relationship between the acoustic properties of speech and the recognition of words.

One of the most important advances that helped us to understand how speech recognition works was technological in nature. Ideally, scientists want to be able to establish control over a situation in order to manipulate each aspect of it. Such manipulation allows us to determine what causes a phenomenon. Specifically, given the complexity of the speech signal, the more control we have over precisely what a listener hears, the better we can determine what aspects of the signal are used in recognition. Beginning in the mid-1940s, researchers at Haskins Laboratories began trying to develop a machine that would allow the blind to "read" (Cooper, 1950; Cooper, Liberman & Borst, 1951). They intended to invent a device that would scan words on a page and convert the words to an automatic speech signal. They assumed—incorrectly, as we now know—that the machine would only have to sequentially turn each letter into its associated sound. Unfortunately, as they tried to put the sounds together at a rate that would approximate speech, their machine produced only an unintelligible jumble (see Liberman, 1982). The problem, they realized, was that their assumptions about the simplicity of speech were unfounded.

Out of this applied research "failure" came two important developments. First, the researchers learned that they needed to know more about speech and how it was understood. The applications they were interested in were not possible without more knowledge from basic research on the nature of speech recognition. Second, based on their work with converting print patterns to sound, the Haskins group invented a speech synthesizer (Cooper et al., 1952). With this machine they could input a visual pattern of formants and receive the corresponding sound as output. In short, the speech synthesizer has allowed researchers to precisely manipulate the physical characteristics of the sound that a listener receives in order to determine how the sound characteristics affect what the listener perceives.

One of the first things researchers learned when they started to use synthesized speech was that there is more going on in recognition than "meets the ear." To see what I mean, take a look at Figure 5.8. Imagine sixteen different sounds that have the same F1 as well as the same steady-state region of F2, but that differ in the F2 transition. With a device for producing synthesized speech, we could keep everything else constant and see how perception changes when we vary the F2 transition in any of the ways shown in the figure. We know that the F2 transition is important because when F2 is shaped as shown by the +9 position we hear the sound as /ga/, but when F2 is shaped as shown by the –6 position we hear the sound as /ba/.

Shortly, we'll examine what happens when F2 is produced at the intermediate positions shown in Figure 5.8. First, however, let's consider some other manipulations of the signal. What happens if we chop off the steady states and produce just one of the possible sets of formant transitions—say, the F1 transition in the figure and the F2 shown by the –6 position? Simple logic would dictate that we should hear the first part

FIGURE 5.8   **Manipulation of Synthetic Speech Sounds**

Here is a schematic drawing of how formants can be manipulated in synthetic speech. In this example, F1 is held constant and the initial portion of F2 can be produced in any of sixteen ways. As the F2 transition changes from the –6 position to the +9 position, the sound shifts from /ba/ to /ga/.

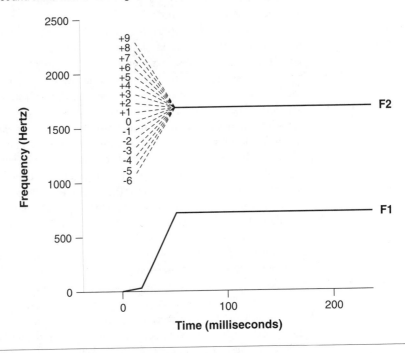

of the sound—in this case, /b/. But simple logic would be wrong. Remember that speech production involves coarticulation. So, even though it is the formant transitions that differ between /ga/ and /ba/, what is produced by the transitions alone does not sound like a speech consonant; instead, it sounds like a "chirp" (Studdert-Kennedy, 1976). On the other hand, if we produce a sound based only on the steady state, we *do* hear the expected vowel sound. For example, if the two steady states shown in Figure 5.8 are produced by a speech synthesizer, what we hear sounds like the vowel /a/ (Delattre, Liberman, Cooper & Gerstman, 1952).

So, does that mean that vowel perception is relatively simple, with steady-state information providing a stable feature that is always used to identify vowels? Of course not! As we've seen, nothing about speech is that simple. However, assume for a minute that the frequency of the F1 and F2 steady states is *the* information we need to recognize a vowel. Let's say we present consonant-vowel-consonant (CVC) sequences like /bib/, /bæb/, and /bab/ to people in a random order and ask them to identify which CVC they heard. The spectrogram for each CVC consists of an initial formant transition, a steady state, and a final formant transition. Obviously, people are good at identifying which CVC was presented when we give them all the acoustic information. But what would happen if we took out the steady-state portion of the signal? If the steady states are the cue to vowel discrimination, then people should not be able to tell one C-V from another. Yet, as long as we keep the same time interval between the formant transitions, we could remove the steady-state frequencies and people *would* still be able to tell the syllables apart (Jenkins, Strange & Edman, 1983). Even if we leave out the very information that seems to cue vowel identity—namely, the steady-state frequencies—people can still identify the vowel sound as long as there is the right time gap between the first and last formant transition! What this tells us is that we can use different kinds of information to distinguish vowels, depending on the speech context. For example, Strange (1989) showed that we can use three types of information to identify vowel sounds: (1) the frequencies of the steady states in the formants, (2) the time interval between transitions that show vowel duration, and (3) the formant transitions into and out of the steady states. Thus, at least part of the information we use to recognize vowels is dynamic. That is, we are sensitive to the point at which a signal is changing, and not changing, over time (Tuller, Case, Mingzhou & Kelso, 1994).

Now let's consider some of the basic facts known about the perception of consonants. Take a look back at Figure 5.8. Remember that when the F2 transition is in the +9 position we hear /ga/ and when it is in the –6 position we hear /ba/. What should happen if we present the sounds at each of the intermediate positions shown in the figure and ask people what sounds they hear? The natural assumption is that their perceptions will reflect the continuous nature of the changes in the speech signal. That is, as we move from the +9 position to the 0 position, it should become less and less likely that people will identify the sound as /ga/. As we go from the 0 position to the –6 position, it should become more and more likely that the speech sound is identified as /ba/. This potential result is illustrated in the left panel of Figure 5.9. What *really* happens in such experiments is shown in the right panel of the figure (e.g., Liberman, Harris, Hoffman & Griffith, 1957; Repp, 1984). Identification data such as these suggest that consonants are perceived by categories. The sharp shift in perception of a speech sound, despite the continuous variation in the nature of the signal, is known as **categorical perception.**

Does Categorical Perception Imply a Speech Module?

The phenomenon of categorical perception suggests that speech really is something quite special. If I play a nonspeech signal, such as a pure tone, and vary the frequency in a set of ordered steps similar in magnitude to the changes in categorical perception experiments, you'd hear each transition as a small change in the sound. You wouldn't divide a whole set of small tone changes into two separate categories. In the case of speech, however, the sets of stimuli do seem to be divided into two discrete categories.

A reasonable objection to the idea of categorical perception, at least as I have outlined it so far, is that the data on identification of speech sounds may not reflect what we can actually hear. Maybe we categorize the speech sounds because we have two preexisting categories available to us, but we still *hear* the differences in sounds within each category. A test of this idea is to contrast identification data, like those shown in Figure 5.9, with data on *discrimination* of speech sounds. A discrimination test is one in which we present a pair of test sounds that are either the same or slightly different. Then we present a comparison sound, at which point the participants must

FIGURE 5.9	**Continuous Versus Categorical Perception**

If the sixteen sounds illustrated in Figure 5.8 are played in a random order, how do people classify each sound? Here, the left panel indicates what we would expect if perception shifted continuously with changes in the acoustic signal. The right panel shows typical results actually obtained in identification studies: People's identifications of speech sounds jump from one speech category to the other.

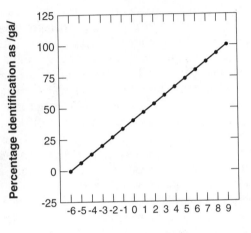
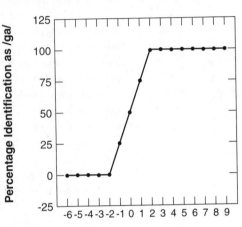

Formant Transition   Formant Transition

choose which of the two test sounds matches the comparison sound. If the two test sounds are the same, then the participants must guess which one we have arbitrarily selected as the correct answer. In other words, when the test sounds are the same, the participants' discrimination performance should be about 50 percent correct because they are guessing which alternative is correct. But to the extent that the two test sounds can be distinguished, so that the correct answer is not arbitrary, the participants' performance should rise above the 50 percent level.

The question of interest in categorical perception is whether people can discriminate between two different sounds that are identified as members of the same category. To illustrate the typical results on a test of discrimination of speech sounds, let's consider two sounds that are different in terms of only one basic feature of production: /ba/ and /pa/. The initial phonemes of both these sounds are stop consonants, but they differ in that the consonant in /ba/ is voiced, whereas the consonant in /pa/ is voiceless. What this means, as you'll recall from Chapter 2, is that the /pa/ sound, but not the /ba/ sound, involves a delay between the puff of air as the /p/ is released and the point at which the vocal folds begin to vibrate. The time difference between the release of the stop consonant and the vibration of the vocal folds is known as **voice-onset-time (VOT)**. A typical-sounding /ba/ has a VOT of 0 msec (which means that the release and the voicing are simultaneous), whereas a typical-sounding /pa/ has a VOT of about 45 msec.

What happens to discrimination performance if we use a speech synthesizer to create sounds that vary in VOT from 0 msec to 45 msec in increments of 5 msec?

Performance is what we'd expect if categorical perception reflects what we can hear rather than just a categorization effect (Liberman, Harris, Hoffman & Griffith, 1957). That is, people perform at about chance level when trying to discriminate between sounds within the same phonemic category. However, a VOT difference of the same size *is* easily discriminated if the two sounds cross the boundary between categories (e.g., Eimas, 1985). To summarize: Discrimination performance corresponds to identification performance.

The Motor Theory of Speech Perception. Data on categorical perception pose a strong challenge to the idea that speech perception works like other forms of auditory processing. The correspondence between identification and discrimination suggests that we hear speech based not only on its physical form but also on preexisting speech categories. One way to interpret the categorical perception of speech is to say that speech is processed by a special system *dedicated to speech* rather than by the more inclusive system that processes auditory signals in general. This idea is the basis for the **motor theory** of speech perception (e.g., Liberman, Cooper, Shankweiler & Studdert-Kennedy, 1967). According to the motor theory, we have a speech processing system that analyzes speech sounds based on how the sounds are produced.

In its original version, the motor theory claimed that the listener uses tacit (unconscious) knowledge of how to produce a sound in order to covertly recreate the gestures that produced the sound. However, it soon became clear that this version of the motor theory could not be correct. For example, if people covertly recreate speech gestures in order to understand speech, then loss of the ability to speak should also disrupt speech perception. Yet speech perception remains intact even in those people who, as a result of diseases or accidents, are unable to articulate speech sounds (MacNeilage, Rootes & Chase, 1967). Accordingly, Liberman and Mattingly (1985) have revised the motor theory. Perception and production are still associated, according to these researchers, but not at the level of physical gestures. They claim that we perceive phonetic segments in terms of the motor commands in the brain that direct the movement of the muscles used in speech. Thus, the updated motor theory claims that invariance in speech recognition is a function of the mental commands used to produce speech, not of the physical movements that produce speech.

How does this theory explain the phenomenon of categorical perception? Liberman and Mattingly (1985) believe that a special speech module is used to map the acoustic signal onto the motor commands that produce each phonetic segment. Thus, we perceive sounds like /ba/ and /pa/ categorically, because what we hear when we process speech is based not just on the physical sound but also on the motor signal that the brain would use to produce that sound. Further, according to the motor theory, the speech module that associates sounds with motor codes is innate and uniquely human.

One of the most striking indications that we may have a speech recognition module that operates separately from other auditory processes has been revealed by a phenomenon known as **duplex perception**. In a duplex perception experiment, a listener is given two different auditory signals, one to each ear. Simultaneously, the listener hears both a speech sound and a nonspeech sound from the same auditory stimulation (Mann, Madden, Russell & Liberman, 1981; Liberman, 1982). The duplex perception technique is illustrated in the bottom panel of Figure 5.10. As you can see,

FIGURE 5.10 **Integration of Speech Sounds**

Typically, studies using synthetic speech stimuli present information to both ears simultaneously (top). However, in duplex perception situations (bottom), separate information is presented to each ear. Even with this duplex presentation, listeners can automatically integrate the information across each ear and hear a normal speech sound.

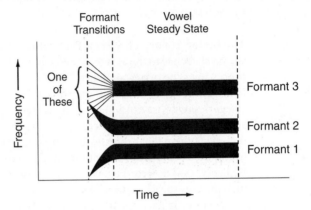

[da] to [ga]
Normal (Binaural) Presentation

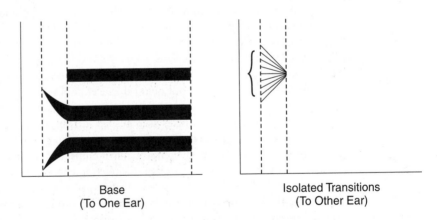

Duplex-Producing (Dichotic) Presentation

part of the signal is presented to one ear and the rest is presented to the other ear. Listeners perceive the sound as /da/ or /ga/ depending on which F3 transition is used. In addition, they hear a nonspeech "chirp" sound, which is presented at the same time as the /da/ or /ga/. This is the chirp we would expect people to hear if they were presented with the formant transition only. Note that the top panel of the figure shows various possible stimuli for the typical categorical perception experiment in which the same information is presented to *both* ears. Here, too, depending on the F3 transition that is used, the listener hears either /da/ or /ga/.

According to the motor theory, people in the duplex situation get two completely different perceptions out of the same speech stimulus because the speech module is creating a normal speech perception out of all the information present in both ears, while the separate auditory processing system is giving accurate information about the nonspeech nature of the sound heard in one ear.

The motor theory has generated a great deal of interest because it can account for the stability of our perception of speech, despite both coarticulation and the lack of invariance. In essence, the theory holds that we perceive speech so easily, notwithstanding the messiness of the signal, because we have built-in knowledge of how sounds are produced. In short, we are able to associate the physical speech signal with the abstract motor commands with which our brain is already equipped.

Although the motor theory accounts for several aspects of speech perception, a number of researchers have expressed skepticism that the data require us to accept the existence of a speech module that is separate from other types of auditory processing. (See Remez, 1994, for a discussion of both sides.) These challenges to the motor theory center on its interpretation of categorical perception.

Because the motor theory explains categorical perception in terms of people's use of information about how sounds are articulated, one way to test the theory is to see if categorical perception can also be found in animals that do not use speech but have human-like auditory systems. If these animals show evidence of categorical perception in recognizing speech sounds, then it seems logical to conclude that speech recognition can be accomplished through normal auditory channels without recourse to a special speech module.

Several such experiments have been conducted by Kuhl (1981, 1987) and others (e.g., Miller, 1978). For example, Kuhl (1981) tested auditory discrimination in the chinchilla, a type of small rodent. The presentation of one sound, such as /ba/, signaled the test animals to escape over a barrier to the other side of the cage in order to avoid a shock. A sound at the other end of a VOT continuum, such as /pa/, signaled the animals to stay put and receive a reward. Once the animals learned this much, the central question was how they would react to sounds in between the two ends of the continuum. The researchers could tell how the animals perceived the sound by observing whether they escaped to the other side of the cage or stayed put. Interestingly, the chinchillas categorized the sounds in the same way that humans do. They showed the same sharp boundary in their identification of the sounds as we saw in the human experiments on categorical perception. Contrary to the claims of the motor theory, then, categorical perception need not result from the ability to produce speech sounds.

The Fuzzy Logic Model of Speech Perception. Of course, Kuhl's (1981) data do not rule out the possibility that the motor commands play a role in *human* speech perception. A more direct challenge to the motor theory has come from researchers who have claimed that categorical perception does not imply that we have a special module for processing speech (e.g., Massaro, 1987; Werker, 1991). Specifically, the most influential challenge to the motor theory's "speech is special" assumption is Massaro's

(1979, 1987, 1994) **fuzzy logic model of perception (FLMP)**. According to this model, categorical perception, as well as many other speech perception phenomena, can be understood as a problem of classifying the features that are present in an acoustic pattern. A key assumption of the FLMP is that categorization in speech processing is based on the same kinds of categorization processes that we use in other perceptual situations.

The concepts that people use to categorize all sorts of objects have fuzzy boundaries. For example, we respond "yes" to both "Is a robin a bird?" and "Is a penguin a bird?" But we are significantly faster at responding if the question is about a robin. As we saw in Chapter 3, the reason is that a robin better fits our notion of the prototypical bird. We are slower at classifying a penguin because it is not as representative of the "bird" category. Thus, a category has fuzzy boundaries in the sense that we consider some things to be strong members of the category, other things to be weak members of the category, and still other things to be nonmembers of the category.

According to the FLMP, the same type of category judgment is taking place when we process speech sounds. Although the exact physical form of a particular syllable, such as /ba/, differs across contexts and speakers, there is enough resemblance to classify the different instances as members of the same /ba/ category. Massaro (1987) proposed that this categorization process takes place in three stages:

- *Evaluation.* First, the features of the acoustic signal are analyzed. The auditory system processes each syllable according to the formant transitions and steady states, the VOTs, and probably other basic features yet to be discovered.

- *Integration.* Second, the features of a given acoustic signal are compared with the features of prototypes that are stored in memory. (Prototypes consist of the features that are characteristic of each of the syllables that we can recognize.) In other words, we match the features of a given acoustic signal with the features of the prototypes, and we attempt to determine which prototype best integrates the features of the signal.

- *Decision.* Third, the sound is classified as the pattern that best fits the features of the stimulus that was presented to us.

Thus, according to the FLMP, we analyze speech in the same way that we analyze other auditory signals. The apparent categorical nature of speech perception comes from our ability to classify the pattern very quickly and automatically. Massaro (1987; Massaro & Cohen, 1983) tested this model by replicating the classic category perception experiments. But instead of measuring just identification and discrimination, he also collected reaction times (RTs) on the stimulus classification judgments. In other words, he measured not only whether the person called the stimulus a /ba/ or a /pa/ but also how long it took the person to make the decision. What he found was that, within a given category, RTs increased as the stimulus was moved farther from an ideal /ba/ or /pa/ sound. This result suggests that we classify sounds into categories in the same way that we classify other stimuli—that is, based on the matching of features to prototypes. The lower the resemblance to the prototype, the longer the classification takes. The motor theory, in contrast, cannot easily account for these RT differences within a syllable category.

FIGURE 5.11   ### The Fuzzy Logic Model of Perception

According to Massaro (1987), speech is recognized in a series of three stages. In the first stage, sound and sight (vocal movements) of speech are analyzed in terms of the auditory features (af) and visual features (vf) that are present. In the second stage, the feature information is integrated so that the decision process in the third stage can make use of the overall evidence (E) to classify the speech sound.

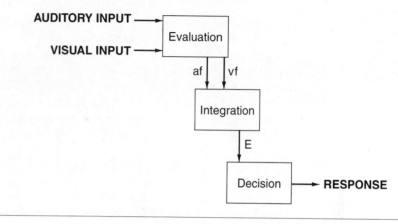

Massaro's FLMP is summarized in Figure 5.11. You'll note that the model actually includes the analysis of both auditory and visual features. To see why visual features are included in the model, try Activity 5.1.

Related to Activity 5.1 is another speech phenomenon that has been studied in the laboratory. It is called the **McGurk effect,** after one of its discoverers (McGurk & MacDonald, 1976). The McGurk effect occurs when a person's perception of a speech sound is influenced by the *sight* of a different sound being produced. For example, if you see a speaker produce /ga/ but simultaneously hear the sound /ba/, you perceive the sound as /da/. The perceived sound is a kind of "best-fitting" compromise between what you saw and the sound pattern that reached your ears.

Think about what these visual effects on speech perception suggest from the standpoint of the motor theory and the FLMP. According to the motor theory, the McGurk effect demonstrates that motor patterns are relevant to speech perception. And according to the FLMP, visual and auditory information are first analyzed separately and then integrated to produce speech perception. That's why the depiction of the FLMP (in Figure 5.11) shows separate "channels" for auditory and visual input analysis.

It is clear that neither the motor theory nor the FLMP completely answers the question of what units are used in auditory word recognition. In the process of speech perception, we seem to almost effortlessly overcome the problems posed by speaker variability, segmentation, and the lack of invariance. Indeed, there is growing consensus that as listeners we can make use of the way formants do and do not change over time, and that we can use different features in different contexts to discriminate speech

ACTIVITY 5.1   The Integration of Sight and Sound

Preparation for this activity entails some pretty agreeable homework: Rent a movie. Pick one that you have not seen before. Make sure it has lots of dialogue and close-ups of people as they speak. Once the movie is under way, turn down the volume until you can just barely tell what the characters are saying. Now, alternate between trying to follow the dialogue with your eyes open (i.e., watching the characters) and trying to follow it with your eyes closed. If you don't notice a difference, turn down the sound a bit further.

If you keep at it, you will find a volume level at which you can tell what is being said only if you are able to see the characters speaking. You might have noticed before that people who wear glasses will sometimes say that they can hear better with their glasses on while watching television. Although this statement sounds anomalous, it actually makes good sense. People can integrate the sound and the sight of someone speaking in order to recognize speech.

A related phenomenon sometimes occurs when you watch a foreign film that has been dubbed into English. Even if the film is expertly dubbed, the voices sound strange and often appear to be mistimed with the vocal movements of the speakers. You may notice, though, that if the original language in the film uses a word that is similar to the English equivalent, the word sounds normal and seems to correspond exactly to the vocal movements. Yet this latter effect is, in all likelihood, partly illusory. What really happens? Normally, there is a correspondence between the vocal movements of the speaker and the sound that is heard. However, when the sight and sound fail to correspond, the speech seems strange and stilted. As you experienced by listening to dialogue with your eyes closed, speech perception often involves an effort to integrate visual and auditory information. When a word in a dubbed film has a pronunciation similar to that of its English counterpart, the integration process is able to work such that the film and the dialogue suddenly "snap together" in time.

sounds from one another. Nevertheless, much remains to be discovered about the features used in speech recognition.

Although the two theories we have focused on in this section are incomplete in their explanation of these processes, it is quite useful to contrast the basic approaches taken by the motor theory and the FLMP because they differ so greatly regarding the principal question underlying this chapter: Is speech special? The motor theory answer says "yes" and the FLMP says "no." (Recall that the FLMP stresses how speech recognition depends on the same sort of auditory and general cognitive mechanisms that are used outside the speech domain.) Yet there has not been (and probably cannot be) a single definitive test of the two theories. These theories will rise or fall based on the weight of evidence across several different research problems. The evidence on language acquisition that we will examine later in the book has implications for the general approaches taken by the motor theory and the FLMP. For now, though, we can contrast the two different approaches embodied in these theories by taking a look at the factors that affect word recognition.

Although both the motor theory and the FLMP address the processing of basic speech sounds rather than whole words, the two theories have different implications for word recognition. The motor theory predicts a modular, bottom-up approach to word recognition, whereas the FLMP is congruent with the idea that the context in which a word occurs can affect some aspects of word recognition. In the next section, we explore the factors that influence word recognition, including the issue of whether context exerts an influence on auditory word recognition.

From the Speech Signal to Word Recognition

The lesson from the previous section is that there is no simple set of features that allow us to recognize a word on a phoneme-by-phoneme basis. Instead, we seem to be able to use a variety of different cues for identifying and segmenting words in a stream of speech. We turn now to a discussion of the major variables that affect how easily a particular word can be recognized.

Why Some Words Are Recognized More Easily Than Others

A number of factors affect how quickly and easily we can identify spoken words, but the variable that has received the most attention in the study of word recognition is *frequency of occurrence*. Across several different methods for determining the efficiency of word recognition, researchers have found that high-frequency words are processed more easily than low-frequency words (Luce, 1986; Savin, 1963). In one study, for example, Savin (1963) presented both high- and low-frequency words amid noise and found that people were better at identifying the high-frequency words. Clearly, then, one major phenomenon that any model of word recognition must account for is that word recognition is easier for high-frequency words.

Savin (1963) also found that lexical similarity influences word recognition. In the case of most words, there are at least a few other words that sound similar and, as such, are considered to be in the same "phonological neighborhood." In Savin's (1963) experiment, when participants made an error in identifying a target word, they usually said a word that was phonetically similar to the target. This outcome is an example of one type of **neighborhood effect,** whereby the recognition of a particular word is affected by the number of similar words in the lexicon. Is it therefore true that when we identify a word, similar words in the lexicon (i.e., words from the same neighborhood) are also processed to some degree?

In a study by Pisoni, Nusbaum, Luce, and Slowiaczek (1985), the effect of *auditory neighborhood size* was examined, with word frequency held constant. Auditory neighborhood size was defined as the number of words that differed from the target word by only one phoneme. The researchers found that words with numerous phonetically similar neighbors are identified more slowly than words without many neighbors. This result suggests that similar-sounding words may compete with each other for activation during recognition.

Further evidence for competition among words during speech processing comes from a series of studies by McQueen and colleagues (McQueen, Norris & Cutler, 1994;

Norris, McQueen & Cutler, 1995). Participants were asked to pick out real words contained within nonsense words. For example, the real word [mɛs] (i.e., *mess*) occurs within both the nonsense word [dəmɛs] and the nonsense word [nəmɛs]. Note, however, that the nonsense word [dəmɛs] also has the same beginning as the real words *domestic* and *domesticate*. McQueen and associates (1994) predicted that the activation of words like *domestic* and *domesticate* would compete with the activation of *mess*, making it harder to detect [mɛs] as a word inside [dəmɛs]. As they expected, possible "competitors" did make it more difficult to spot real words inside the nonsense words.

Finally, it is important to note that two variables we have been discussing, word frequency and neighborhood size, have joint effects on word recognition. What affects the recognition time of a word is not just the frequency of the word itself but also the frequencies of its phonological neighbors (Cutler, 1995; Luce, Pisoni & Goldinger, 1990). If a particular word has a high frequency, and it has only low-frequency neighbors, then the neighbors provide little competition for selection during word recognition. In this case, the word is recognized very quickly. However, if the word is a low-frequency word, and it has several high-frequency neighbors, then the neighbors will compete with the word, slowing down the selection process (Lively, Pisoni & Goldinger, 1994).

Although there is still much to be learned about neighborhood effects, the data suggest an important finding: that several alternatives for the identification of a word may be considered in the fraction of a second that it takes us to ascertain what word we have heard. The extent to which the possible alternatives compete is determined by the word frequencies of the alternatives. As we will see shortly, these ideas play a key role in evaluating models of word recognition and in deciding whether word recognition is modular or interactive.

Context Effects in Word Recognition

Most of the time, we do not have to recognize words in isolation. Instead, they occur as components of sentences, which in turn establish contexts. On the one hand, such contexts might make word recognition *easier* by helping us identify a particular word. On the other hand, given that there are no clear breaks between most spoken words in a sentence, sentence contexts might make word recognition *harder* by adding to the segmentation problem. Which view is correct? Do sentence contexts make word recognition easier or harder? To help answer these questions for yourself, try Activity 5.2.

When Marslen-Wilson and Welsh (1978) performed an experiment similar to Activity 5.2, they found that people often corrected words that had speech errors—*as long as the speech errors occurred in a predictable context*. Note that the sentences in the activity provide a context in which a particular word can be expected. The researchers created each of the speech errors in these sentences by changing the initial phoneme of the expected word. Interestingly, when the task is to detect speech errors rather than to shadow speech, people are faster at detecting errors that occur in predictable contexts (Cole & Jakimik, 1978).

These studies, and a number of others, show that context can influence speech recognition. For example, when words are presented in a noisy environment, people are good at identifying words that are part of meaningful sentences, but they perform

ACTIVITY 5.2   Context and Speech Recognition

This activity is based on studies by Cole and Jakimik (1978) and Marslen-Wilson and Welsh (1978). Practice reading each of the following sentences; then record them on tape. Some of the sentences have errors (shown in italics). Be sure to pronounce these errors in as natural a fashion as possible.

1. She wanted a mink coat to go with the Rolls-Royce her husband had left her.
2. Mrs. Jones was pleased to see that the broom swept the floor very well.
3. He wore a gold *ling* on the little finger of his left hand.
4. The student flew home for Christmas on a *blane* loaded with other people.
5. The janitor cleaned the hallway with a mop that was old and worn.
6. His knife *tut* the bread neatly, and then he buttered the slices.
7. The fans applauded as the boxer punched his opponent.
8. The girl chased her dog through the field, but could not catch it.
9. The tourist drove all over the city in the *gar* she had rented for the week.
10. The children glued the pictures to the paper with the *baste* the teacher gave them.

Now have a friend or two try to "shadow" the sentences as they are played on the tape. That is, ask them to repeat every word in the sentences out loud as soon as possible after hearing it. Along the way, note whether they "correct" any of the "mistakes" that you initially recorded on tape.

less well at identifying isolated words or words in nonsense sentences (e.g., Bronkhorst, Bosman & Smoorenburg, 1993; Miller, Heise & Lichten, 1951; Pollack & Pickett, 1964). Sentence contexts also allow listeners to identify the last word in a sentence, even if only part of the word is actually presented (Tyler & Wessels, 1983).

So, there is considerable evidence that contexts can aid word recognition. But why do the beneficial effects of context prevail over the segmentation problem that sentence contexts may potentially cause? One explanation is that we are able to use the **prosody** of speech to help us identify and understand words. Prosody refers to the variations in stress, loudness, pitch, and duration that occur among the sounds made by speakers. For example, the syllables that speakers stress can be used in segmenting speech (Liberman & Prince, 1977). Have someone read each of the following sentences out loud while you listen carefully:

(1) The reporter, who was doing a feature on drug busts, stood outside a white house.

(2) The reporter, who wanted to see the president, stood outside the White House.

In the phrase *white house*, speakers normally put stress on the noun *house*. However, in the compound noun *White House*, speakers usually stress *White*. This difference in stress tells the listener how to organize the speech sounds into words.

A number of studies have shown that variations in speaking rate help determine how we categorize syllables and recognize words (e.g., Miller, 1987; Sommers, Nygaard & Pisoni, 1992). For example, Sommers and associates (1992) presented lists of words mixed with noise and asked people to identify the words. They found that people were better at identifying the words when they were all spoken at the same rate than when the rate of speech varied from word to word. This result suggests that rate information is not just stripped away as irrelevant variation. Rather, variation is just one of the many cues that we can use in word recognition.

We also appear to use the characteristics of individual speakers to help with speech recognition (e.g., Mullennix & Pisoni, 1990; Nygaard, Sommers & Pisoni, 1994). As we saw earlier, different speakers produce different acoustic patterns for the same speech sounds. Until recently, the typical view was that listeners ignore this variability and focus on what does not vary across speakers. That may not be the whole story, however. For example, Nygaard and associates (1994) had participants try to recognize words mixed with noise, but in this experiment the participants had previously been exposed to the voices of some of the speakers. As it turns out, the participants were better able to identify the words amid noise when they were spoken by a familiar voice. A possible explanation is that aspects of the voices of specific talkers may be represented in memory and used to facilitate word recognition (Nygaard & Pisoni, 1995).*

The overall pattern of data on the effects of context shows that several different kinds of contextual familiarity can help with word recognition. Both familiarity with the semantic content of a sentence and familiarity with the particular speech characteristics of the speaker can help us recognize words. However, there are two possible explanations for the beneficial effects of context. One is that people may use context to bolster the analysis of the speech signal. In the most controversial case, context—specifically, knowledge of the content of what has been said previously—may have a top-down effect on the early stages of analysis of a word. Alternatively, perhaps speech analysis itself does not change with context. That is, in situations where we are not sure of what we have heard (e.g., in noisy environments), maybe speech analysis leaves us with some candidate words that *might* have been spoken. Then, the role of context would be to help us make an educated guess as to which of the possible words was *really* spoken. A related idea is used in Massaro's FLMP model to explain context effects. According to this model, context influences recognition of speech at the integration stage, but there are no top-down effects on the evaluation stage, in which the features of the speech signal are processed.

In short, the question is not whether context can be used to help us process speech; clearly, it can. Rather, the question is whether context influences the bottom-up

---

* The power of this effect is evident to anyone who has become the stepparent of a small child. Some years ago, I became the stepfather of a four-year-old girl. For the first few weeks, I frequently had to ask her mother what the little girl had just said. Soon, however, her speech sounded perfectly articulate to me, even though it remained somewhat unclear to strangers for a while longer. Fortunately, most young children give us *lots* of practice at understanding their speech!

analysis of the speech signal, or whether it simply helps us make a guess when the bottom-up analysis leaves us uncertain. Let's look at some more data on this issue.

One of the most interesting examples of a context effect in speech processing is the powerful auditory illusion known as the **phonemic restoration effect.** In instances of phonemic restoration, participants report that they hear a phoneme that has been deleted from a sample of speech. For example, Warren (1970; Warren & Warren, 1970) presented spoken sentences such as this:

> *The state governors met with their respective legislatures convening in the capital city.*

However, among Warren's stimuli, one of the phonemes, such as the final phoneme in *legislatures,* was actually deleted from the speech stream and replaced with a cough. The interesting finding was that people reported hearing the phoneme even though it was not present. Furthermore, when told that a sound was missing, most participants could not accurately state what had been deleted.

Warren's demonstration of phonemic restoration is remarkable because it suggests that top-down processing based on context can be powerful enough to make us "hear" a sound for which there is no bottom-up evidence. This idea has been qualified somewhat by later research, however. Samuel (1981) looked at performance on two kinds of trials: (1) Either a burst of noise *was added to* the speech signal to coincide with a phoneme or (2), as in Warren's original study, the noise *replaced* a phoneme. If context helps the speech processing system "create" the missing sound, then the noise-added trials and the phoneme-replaced trials would sound the same. However, that is not what Samuel found. What he did find is that a relevant sentence context made it *easier* for participants to determine whether the noise was added to the phoneme or replaced the phoneme. This result suggests that, whereas sentence context influences people's responses, context may not influence the way that speech information is initially processed. If information from the sentence context can directly affect the processing of the bottom-up speech information, then a relevant sentence context should have made it more difficult for listeners to tell whether the noise was added to or replaced a phoneme.

A series of experiments by Connine (1987; Connine & Clifton, 1987) suggest that there are some top-down effects in word recognition, but that they are of a limited nature only. Connine and Clifton (1987) reasoned that if word recognition were completely bottom-up, then whether a spoken string was a word or nonword should not affect how it is analyzed. And, conversely, if there is some top-down processing, then the activation from possible words might lead people to perceive an ambiguous stimulus as a word. Connine and Clifton used a categorical perception design and varied the VOT of the stimulus. For example, with a 10-msec VOT, one of the utterances sounded clearly like the nonword *dype.* But when the VOT was increased to 40 msec, the utterance sounded clearly like the word *type.* The interesting question here was how the utterance would be identified when an intermediate value for the VOT was used, such as 15 or 30 msec. Both in terms of what they called the stimulus and in terms of how quickly they identified the stimulus, people were biased toward identifying the utterances as words at the intermediate VOTs. This result suggests that having an item represented in the lexicon may provide top-down activation that influences analysis of utterances that are somewhat ambiguous.

Connine (1987) performed a similar study in which she used sentences to bias interpretation toward one word or another. For example, she manipulated the VOT of the initial phoneme so that she could present utterances that were in between clear cases of *tent* and *dent*. She presented the test words in the context of sentences such as "She drives the car with the _____." In this second study, however, Connine did not obtain evidence for top-down processing. The contexts did not increase the likelihood that people would identify the test word as the alternative that was consistent with the sentence. Thus, across the two experiments, Connine's data support only a very restricted form of top-down processing.

Bear in mind that neither Connine's (1987) data nor Samuel's (1981) rule out the possibility that context can influence the bottom-up analysis of spoken words. It could be that simple sentence contexts are too weak to show top-down effects. For that matter, different results might be obtained in the context of a passage about a topic that is familiar to the listener. We will confront this issue again in the next chapter, where strength of context is shown to be an important factor in testing for top-down effects on visual word recognition.

There is evidence for other kinds of context effects as well. For example, because of coarticulation, the ending phoneme of one word can influence our perception of the initial phoneme of the next word (Mann & Repp, 1981). Let's say that someone is presented with a word in which the initial phoneme is ambiguous, halfway between /t/ and /k/, and that the rest of the word is *-apes*. If the ambiguous word is *preceded* by the /s/ sound, the participant hears the ambiguous word as *capes*. But if the ambiguous word is preceded by the /š/ sound, the person hears the word as *tapes*. So, if the first word is *Christmas* the person hears the phrase as *Christmas capes*, whereas if the first word is *foolish* the person hears the phrase as *foolish tapes*.

Elman and McClelland (1988) wondered if the same coarticulation effects would be obtained if the /s/ and /š/ sounds were deleted so that the subject heard the "words" *Christma-* or *fooli-* before the ambiguous word. Even though the final sounds apparently responsible for the coarticulation effects were missing, people perceived the ambiguous word as if it were preceded by *Christmas* or *foolish*. According to Elman and McClelland (1988), when a word is activated in a person's lexicon, it provides top-down information that influences even the early stages of acoustic analysis.

In summary, although it is clear that context influences our responses in word recognition experiments, there is mixed evidence regarding which aspects of word recognition can be altered by context. As we will see in the next section, different theorists have very different views on this matter.

Models of Spoken Word Recognition

Over the past couple of decades, researchers have proposed a number of different models to explain and organize the data on word recognition. Several of these models have addressed both spoken word recognition and the recognition of visually presented words, a topic we will explore in the next chapter. Our job here is not to survey all, or even most, of these models. Instead, this section will guide us through a couple of influential models that have focused on issues that are unique to spoken language. The goal is to illustrate the basic strategies that researchers in this area have used to explain the phenomena they discovered while studying word recognition. We will concentrate on how the models try to elucidate the most basic aspects of word recognition. Clearly, any reasonable model of word recognition must be able to account for the effects of word frequency. Further, it must address the issue of how neighbors of a given word in the lexicon also come into play in word recognition. Finally, a good model of word recognition must provide a means for explaining data that suggest that context may influence some aspects of the word recognition process.

The Cohort Model

The cohort model, proposed by Marslen-Wilson (1984), was one of the first to address the problems of word recognition that are specific to speech. In particular, the speech signal for a particular word unfolds over time in a way that is not true for visual word recognition. Marslen-Wilson suggested that we handle spoken word recognition by using the initial phoneme to activate the set of all words in the lexicon that have the same phoneme. Then, as more information is received, we narrow the set down. The set of activated words is called a *cohort*. So, the problem of word recognition becomes one of eliminating items from the cohort until only one item is left. This process is illustrated in Figure 5.12.

The initial activation of a cohort is based only on bottom-up information—the initial sound in the word. However, items can be eliminated from the cohort due to

---

FIGURE 5.12   **The Cohort Model of Word Recognition**

This model is concerned with spoken word recognition, so sounds are depicted as being input sequentially over time. Based on the initial sound, a set of possible words (the first cohort, C1) is activated. Items are then deleted from the set as more sounds are input.

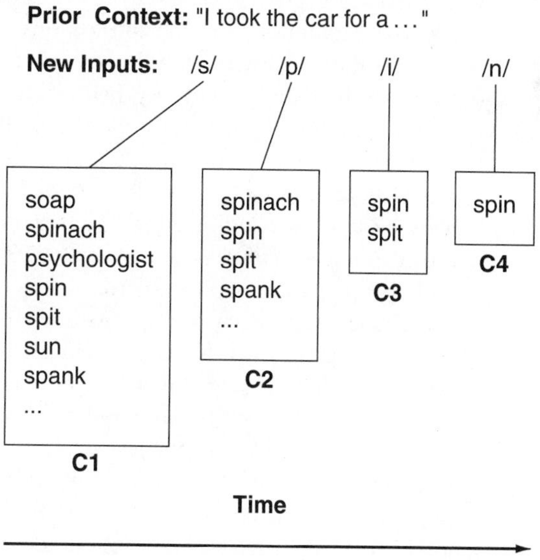

Prior Context: "I took the car for a ..."

New Inputs: /s/   /p/   /i/   /n/

soap spinach psychologist spin spit sun spank ...	spinach spin spit spank ...	spin spit	spin
C1	C2	C3	C4

Time

inconsistency with the context as well as inconsistency with new phonemic information that is present. For example, in the cohort illustrated in Figure 5.12, we might eliminate *spit* from contention even before the third phoneme is processed because of its implausibility as a completion for the sentence. Thus, the model allows for context effects, but only after the initial cohort is activated.

A major change in more recent versions of the cohort model (Marslen-Wilson, 1987, 1990) is the added assumption that activation among items in the cohort varies so that entries are not just "in or out." This assumption allows the model to more easily account for frequency effects; in other words, an entry in the cohort can now be judged against competitors, with higher-frequency words getting more activation from the same evidence than lower-frequency words. The new assumption also allows a means for accounting for *lexical similarity effects*, whereby a whole neighborhood of words is activated but higher-frequency words get more activation. Lexical similarity effects are consistent with the finding that we are slower at recognizing low-frequency words with high-frequency neighbors because the competitors are harder to eliminate (e.g., Lively, Pisoni & Goldinger, 1994).

Thus, according to the more recent version of the cohort model, recognition speed and accuracy depend on how easily we can sort out the competing word candidates. The general idea that items in the lexicon compete with each other for selection as the correct identification is also important in several other models of word recognition, including some we will examine in the next chapter.

The TRACE Model

The TRACE model, developed by McClelland and Elman (1986), is a speech recognition model similar to the interactive model of visual word recognition that we examined in Chapter 3 (McClelland & Rumelhart, 1981). Like the earlier model, TRACE is based on a connectionist system. There are connections among units at three levels: features, phonemes, and words. As shown in Figure 5.13, the connections within a level are inhibitory and the connections between levels are facilitory. The TRACE model is thus consistent with the idea of competition among units in the lexicon. In other words, at any given time, the units within a level are competing for activation. As an example, let's say that the activation of a set of features gives activation to a set of phonemes, which in turn activates some possible words. The more one word is activated, the more other possible words are inhibited. In addition, the connections between levels are bidirectional. That is, once a word starts to become somewhat activated, more activation goes down to its features and phonemes, thus aiding the bottom-up processing of the word.

Higher-frequency words are assumed to have higher baseline levels of activation, so high-frequency words reach a critical activation threshold for recognition more quickly than low-frequency words. Note that the TRACE model can also accommodate lexical similarity effects because multiple features, phonemes, and word neighbors are activated in parallel, with the less relevant ones being inhibited as more evidence is received. What most distinguishes this model from the cohort model, and several other models, is the degree to which TRACE is interactive. Indeed, TRACE is a highly interactive model that accounts for context effects in terms of top-down effects on the activation of features. Thus, TRACE maintains that you recognize "dog" relatively quickly after hearing "The woman got a leash and went for a walk with the . . ." because

| FIGURE 5.13 | The TRACE Model of Word Recognition |

TRACE is a connectionist model of spoken word recognition. It assumes the existence of both bottom-up and top-down sources of activation (depicted as arrows). Activation patterns change dynamically over time as the utterance (auditory input) unfolds. Inhibitory connections within a level allow for a particular word to win the competition for activation over time.

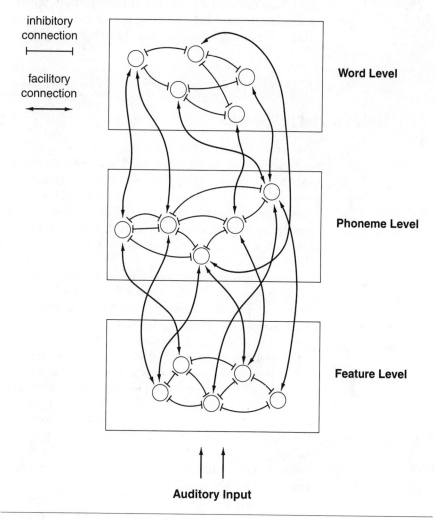

the features and phonemes for "dog" are already more activated than usual due to the context. Thus, unlike the cohort model, TRACE allows for context effects at the earliest stages of word recognition.

The TRACE model seems to provide a reasonable way to account for the principal phenomena in speech recognition. However, this model has weaknesses as well. For one, it assumes a feature level of processing without spelling out what features are at work. (As we have seen, the basic feature units of speech recognition have been very hard to pin down.) Also unclear is whether word recognition is really as highly interactive as the model claims, or whether such a high degree of interactivity would work in real lexicons, which are much larger than the small lexicons that have been used in computer simulation tests of TRACE. However, if TRACE is on the right track and it turns out that word recognition *is* a highly interactive process, then the hypothesis that we have considered in this chapter will have to be rejected. It would be premature to draw that conclusion now, but there is enough evidence for coming to some other firm conclusions about the recognition of spoken language.

C O N C L U S I O N S

How Special Is Speech?

The central issue in speech recognition is that the "same" segment of speech is actually quite variable across different speech situations. As researchers tried to understand speech recognition, they typically relied on an important assumption: There must be a simple set of features that are constant amid all the variability in a given utterance. According to this assumption, people must somehow discard what is variable and process whatever is constant. However, it has proven very difficult for speech researchers to determine what is physically constant about the "same" sound across different contexts.

As we saw in research on vowel perception, listeners may work around this problem by using different cues in different speech contexts. To perceive consonants or syllables, people combine several different acoustic cues and even some visual cues. According to the motor theory, this process involves a special system dedicated specifically to speech. In particular, the motor theory claims that phenomena like categorical perception show that the speech recognition system does not operate on the same principles as general auditory processing. Other evidence, however, suggests that categorical perception need not imply a special module. Moreover, although we still do not know the details of how phonemes or syllables are processed, the overall data increasingly suggest that the standard assumption—that we find what is constant about a speech sound and ignore the variability—is wrong. Indeed, a key to human speech perception may be that we *make use of* the variability in the speech signal rather than discarding or ignoring it. Prosody plays a role in this process, particularly in terms of the way we use intonation to help us segment speech.

Thus, humans solve the problem of speech perception by using a variety of kinds of information to make sense out of the messy stream of speech that Hockett likened to broken eggs on a conveyor belt. Yet, though we make what should be the very difficult job of speech recognition seem easy, there is no conclusive evidence that we do so by means of a special speech module that is distinct from other auditory and cognitive abilities.

Although there remains much disagreement about the precise way in which we recognize spoken words, different models of word recognition have converged on one central idea: that it is useful to view word recognition in speech as a process in which some units in the lexicon become more activated than other similar units. This competitive activation and selection process is affected by a word's frequency, by the number of similar words in the lexicon, and, to some extent, by context.

We began this chapter by considering why it took so long to create reliable automated speech recognition systems, and what this fact implies for a modular view of speech processing. From the perspective of a person trying to develop such systems, the speech stream is a variable, confusing mess. Yet humans perform the process of speech recognition quite automatically, efficiently, and quickly. Whether or not speech perception is special, in the sense implied by the modularity view, it is irrefutably remarkable.

CHAPTER REVIEW

Checking Your Understanding

Key Terms

amplitude (142)
categorical perception (151)
coarticulation (144)
duplex perception (153)
formant transition (143)
formants (142)
frequency (142)
fuzzy logic model of perception (FLMP) (156)
Hertz (Hz) (142)
lack of invariance problem (144)
McGurk effect (157)

motor theory (153)
neighborhood effect (159)
phonemic restoration effect (163)
problem of speaker variability (146)
prosody (161)
segmentation problem (147)
speech spectrogram (142)
speech spectrograph (142)
steady-state formant (143)
voice-onset-time (VOT) (152)

Review Questions

1. What is the relationship between coarticulation and lack of invariance?

2. How did the development of the speech synthesizer, and with it the ability to manipulate an acoustic signal, influence speech recognition research? Discuss two discoveries that were made possible by the use of synthetic speech in research.

3. Explain how the problems of lack of invariance, speaker variability, and segmentation have greatly complicated the development of automated speech recognition systems.

4. Almost everybody thinks that, when they hear people conversing in a foreign lan-

guage that they don't understand, the people are talking especially fast. Explain why this impression may have little to do with speaking-rate differences across languages.

5. Contrast the interpretations of categorical perception by the motor theory and the FLMP.

6. How does the motor theory explain duplex perception? Could this phenomenon be explained by the FLMP?

7. What findings make the best case for top-down effects in speech recognition?

8. If you were someone who believes that word recognition depends mainly on

bottom-up processes, how would you explain each of the phenomena that you discussed in question 7?

9. What are the implications of the research on prosody for the question of whether "speech is special"?

On Further Reflection . . .

1. As we saw earlier, both the motor theory and the FLMP maintain that visual information can play a role in speech perception. What are the implications of each of these theories for lip reading? Would either view predict that lip reading can be a relatively accurate way to perceive language? How would a person's level of language experience affect the accuracy of his or her lip reading? Check your ideas on these questions against studies of lip reading. There are a number of informative books and articles on the subject. A good place to start is *Hearing by Eye: The Psychology of Lip Reading*, by Dodd and Campbell (1987).

10. What phenomena have convinced many researchers that entries in the lexicon compete for activation?

2. Go back and review the experiment by Kay and Kempton (1984) that was discussed in Chapter 4. How was this experiment on color names and color perception similar to Connine and Clifton's (1987) study of people's tendency to perceive a somewhat ambiguous auditory stimulus as a word rather than as a nonword? Is evidence for linguistic determinism provided by Connine and Clifton's study? Does the answer to this last question depend on whether speech is processed by a separate module?

CHAPTER 6

Visual Word Recognition

What is the most important invention in human history? Leaving aside the TV remote control, which seems crucial only on weekend afternoons, is our most important invention the wheel? How about the bow and arrow? There is no definitive answer to this question, but a strong candidate for our most important invention has to be written language. Written language allows for a level of cultural transmission and preservation of knowledge that is synonymous with our notion of progress.

The fact that our species acquired written language by invention, rather than by the evolutionary processes that gave us speech, has some important implications. For one thing, it is at least plausible that we might have a special module for processing speech, although, as we saw in the last chapter, the case for this idea is unproved. However, since written language is a human invention, no one claims that we have a special input system for visual word recognition. Thus, when we study visual word recognition we are definitely observing an interaction between general processes, such as visual feature analysis, and processes that are specific to language, such as activation of the lexicon.

Another implication of the invented nature of written language is that there are very different systems for writing, and not all of these may involve the same kinds of interactions between the visual system and the lexicon. Therefore, as we study visual word recognition it is important that we examine the process across different cultures and writing systems. Finally, the invented nature of written language may help explain an irony: The relative difficulties of recognizing auditory and visual patterns are reversed for machines and people. As we saw in the last chapter, spoken word recognition is problematic for automated systems but easy for people (at least those with normal hearing and brain functioning). In contrast, automated scanners of visual input have been more easy to develop, but there are millions of people who, though able to learn other skills, have severe problems with visual word recognition. Thus, in this chapter we will also explore whether the basic research on visual word recognition can help us explain **dyslexia,** especially *developmental dyslexia.* Children with developmental dyslexia have great difficulty learning to read despite normal intelligence and normal visual acuity.*

Of course, most people who get an adequate education learn to read fluently and perform similarly on tests of visual and spoken word recognition. This outcome makes sense: Once the physical pattern analysis has been performed, the basic job of word recognition is similar in both domains. That is, whether the pattern is visual or auditory, it is matched with information in the lexicon. For example, one way to accomplish lexical access from vision is to connect the visual stimulus with the sound of the word. And, indeed, we learn spoken word recognition before we start to learn visual word recognition. Thus, the sound-meaning links are already established.

---

* In Chapter 12, I will discuss another form of dyslexia known as *acquired dyslexia,* which refers to the loss of reading ability due to brain damage. In the remainder of the present chapter, however, I will use the term *dyslexia* to refer only to developmental dyslexia.

The foregoing seems a reasonable view of visual word recognition, but is it correct? Consider the following hypothesis, which is consistent with this view: *Among skilled readers, word recognition is largely a matter of bottom-up visual analysis that is used to activate the sound-based (phonemic) representation of the word.* You should evaluate this hypothesis against the data that will be reviewed throughout the chapter. Note that the hypothesis predicts that we get access to the meaning of a word through the sound of the word. Also note that the hypothesis, though it refers to skilled readers, has implications for dyslexia. In particular, it implies that dyslexia may have more than one cause. For example, some dyslexics may have a problem with the visual analysis of words, such that their difficulty lies completely outside the language processing system. Others, though able to form a good visual representation of a word, may have difficulty mapping between the visual form of a word and its phonemic representation. And still other dyslexics may have reading problems for different reasons.

To understand what goes wrong in dyslexia, we first need to see what goes right in skilled visual word recognition. To do this we will follow the same general outline as in the previous chapter, on auditory word recognition. We will look at the nature of the visual stimulus, the components of the words that are used in recognition, the variables that affect visual word recognition, and the ways that models of visual word recognition account for the data we have examined. Then we will return to the issue of dyslexia and see what specific predictions about this disorder can be generated and tested based on the models of visual word recognition.

The Nature of the Stimulus

The folks who invented written language were pretty clever.* The fundamental unit of language on which they based their system was the word. Even those humans whose particular writing system does not codify higher units like sentence structure or paragraph boundaries can get by pretty well. However, it really makes things tough if we can't tell what the words are or where words begin and end.

There are three ways that we can symbolize words in writing. We can use a unique symbol for each word or morpheme, in what is known as a **logographic system.** We can represent syllables with arbitrary symbols, in what is known as a **syllabic system.** Or we can approximate the phonemes of a language with symbols, in what is called an **alphabetic system.** A comparison of these systems is shown in Figure 6.1.

The closest thing we have to a logographic system still in use is the writing system for Chinese. Because Chinese is a **tonal language,** in which changing the rise and fall in the pitch of a vowel sound can alter meaning, it would be difficult to create a workable set of arbitrary symbols for each sound in Chinese. At the same time, Chinese writing does not have a "picture" to symbolize each word. Rather, it uses abstract

---

*I should note, however, that writing's apparent beginnings about 5,500 years ago were fairly humble. Among the writing samples discovered so far, the earliest consist of records of financial transactions and the media hype of public-relations advisers for kings.

FIGURE 6.1   **A Sampler of Visible Speech**

There are many different ways to make a visual record of spoken language. In the top line, the beginning of Lincoln's Gettysburg Address is represented as an acoustic waveform, which is a picture of the sound waves. The second line represents Lincoln's words as a phonetic transcription. In the third and fourth lines, the sound pattern is represented in two different alphabets, English and Russian, respectively. The fifth line shows the speech transcribed into a Japanese syllabic system. The last two lines, which transcribe the sounds with symbols from Chinese and from late Egyptian hieroglyphics, show that even in writing systems designed to directly signify words with symbols, it is possible to represent speech sounds.

fɔr s k   ɔr æ n d s ɛ v n j i r z ɔ g o

four score and seven years ago

фор скор энд сэвэн йирз эго

フォアー　スコア　アンド　セブン　イヤーズ、アゴー

佛爾斯國爾恩得色文伊爾斯阿鈞

symbols to represent morphemes that can be combined to form words. Thus, the Chinese use about 4,500 characters to represent the approximately 40,000 words in common use (Taylor, 1981). However, Chinese writing is far from a pure logography. In fact, the vast majority of Chinese characters are a combination of morphemic and phonetic components, so the writing system includes cues to pronunciation (DeFrancis, 1989).

One of the Japanese writing systems, kana, is an example of a syllabic system. What this means is that it has not just syllables but also symbols to represent combinations of sounds rather than individual phonemes. Unlike English, in which there are perhaps 1,000 different syllable combinations, Japanese uses only about 100 unique syllables. Thus, it is practical to use a symbol to represent each syllable in Japanese.

For English and most other nontonal languages, it makes more sense to have an alphabet in which written symbols (letters) are used to approximate the phonemes of the language. No language has a perfect one-to-one correspondence between phonemes and letters. In fact, alphabetic languages vary widely in terms of how close that correspondence is. Some languages, including Finnish, Spanish, and Serbo-Croatian, have a relatively **shallow orthography,** in which the phoneme-letter correspondence is quite close. What about English? Given the infamous difficulties that people have in learning to spell words in English, you may infer that English has a fairly **deep orthography.** Indeed, there is a less direct spelling-to-sound correspondence in English than in Spanish and many other languages. Thus, in English the same letter is often used to signify different sounds in different contexts.

Although it might seem preferable for languages to have a shallow orthography, there is a tradeoff at work here. Written languages with deeper orthographies, such as English, are more likely to spell morphologically related words in the same way to indicate their related meaning. For example, the form *sign-* is pronounced differently in *signing* and *signal.* Clearly, however, *signing* and *signal* are related in meaning, as is represented by the consistent spelling of the root, *sign-,* in each word.

It would be a mistake, though, to assume that English orthography is an optimal compromise between representations of phonemic and morphological structures. After all, many of the rules of English spelling were set during a time when pronunciations were changing. In addition, English has been influenced by spelling rules from two very different language families (Germanic and Romance). Therefore, if you used to complain to your teachers that English spelling rules are both arbitrary and exception-ridden, you had a good point.

What surveys of different writing systems have made clear is that there's no one "best" way to go from a spoken language to a visual pattern. Each writing system is an attempt to reflect the spoken language as well as possible, but tradeoffs and simplifications are inevitable. Thus, in reading, we should not expect that associating a printed symbol with a language sound will be simple and direct. As we examine the processes behind word recognition, the question of how extensively humans rely on spelling-to-sound translation will be a major focus. Because most of the research has been done on word recognition in English, we will concentrate on studies of word recognition in this language. However, bear in mind that some theories of word recognition may predict processing differences among languages that vary in the nature of their writing systems.

ACTIVITY 6.1   **Recognizing Symbols Based on Their Component Features**

Time yourself as you try to find all instances of the letter *C* in each of the following two lines:

(1)   GQSJCGQRPRCDBCRCPDGGPQCRCD

(2)   XCLNZCFNVAKZVXCLNLKWYZXCLK

Now, find all instances of the letter *S* in each of these two lines:

(3)   MZSTYLKVSHWLVZSTXNXWFKYSF

(4)   PQCPSGOCSRQPDJSDQRBJRPSGQB

Finally, go back and see if you got all the instances of the target letter in each line. Were you slower or more error-prone at finding the letter in one line or the other in each search?

What Components of Written Words Are Used to Recognize Them?

In asking what component parts of words are used in recognition, we are making the important assumption that visual analysis involves breaking up a stimulus pattern into its component parts. But why make this assumption at all? Let's say that the retina of your eye has transmitted a reasonably accurate image of a word to your brain. If you stored **templates** (i.e., whole-word visual patterns) in memory, then you could match up a visual image from your retina with a stored visual representation. The problem with the template idea, however, is that you are just too flexible in your pattern recognition for the system to work this way. Like most people, you recognize words visually despite considerable variability in the way words are written. Otherwise, how could teachers grade handwritten essay exams produced under time pressure? For that matter, if you were matching templates, how could YoU REad styles that you have never practiced before?

Your flexibility in word recognition comes from recognizing symbols based on their component features. To get a feel for this process in action, try Activity 6.1.

The Analysis of Visual Features

As Kinney, Marsetta, and Showman (1966) demonstrated in their study, you probably found it harder to search for a specific letter when it was hidden among letters with similar features. For instance, finding a *C* was more difficult in line (1) than in line (2). Indeed, people seem to identify letters based on the collection of lines and curves that compose them. Across the wide variety of styles of print and handwriting, enough of the features are preserved that the letters can be identified.

An early model of how the letter recognition process might work was devised by Selfridge (1959). This *Pandemonium* model is shown in Figure 6.2. The basic idea behind Pandemonium is that the job of recognizing a letter is performed by cortical

FIGURE 6.2 The Pandemonium Model of Letter Recognition

Cortical signal processors, represented by the "demons" shown here, analyze a pattern in terms of its component features. The pattern is identified in terms of which demon yells the loudest. In other words, the particular letter detector that best matches the actual features has the highest level of activation.

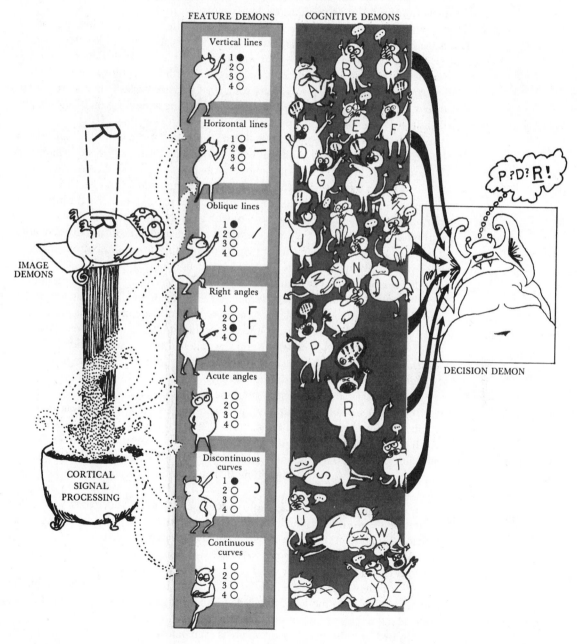

signal processors—or "demons," in the language of the model—at several different levels. A letter pattern is first registered by image demons. Then, feature demons, which represent different possible letter features, monitor the image and send a signal to the next level if their specific features are present. At the next level, each cognitive demon represents a letter. These demons send increasingly louder signals as more and more of their particular features are detected at the feature level. A decision is reached when one of the cognitive demons clearly "out-shouts" the others.

How does this model explain the results from letter search tasks like the one you performed in Activity 6.1? Note that when you were searching for the letter *C*, one of the features you were trying to find was a curve at the top of the letter. When you scanned through line (1) and came to the letter *S*, both the cognitive demon for an *S* and the cognitive demon for a *C* were somewhat signaled because they share the feature of a curve at the top. It was this "noise" of having several letters being signaled that slowed down your search process.

You might recognize that the Pandemonium model shown in the figure is an intellectual ancestor of the model of word recognition proposed by McClelland and Rumelhart (1981) that you learned about in Chapter 3.

Two major differences between the Pandemonium model and McClelland and Rumelhart's interactive activation model are of concern to us here. First, the interactive activation model considers recognition of whole words as well as individual letters, so it proposes that several letters are processed at once. Second, the interactive activation model proposes that recognition depends on both top-down and bottom-up processes, whereas Pandemonium is a purely bottom-up model.

One reason that McClelland and Rumelhart chose their approach over the simpler view espoused in Pandemonium is that there is strong evidence that we do not recognize words on a letter-by-letter basis. In support of this conclusion is a phenomenon known as the **word superiority effect.** As early as 1886, Cattell reported that when words or letters were flashed very briefly, people had an easier time identifying the words. This counterintuitive result went largely unnoticed until it was replicated and extended by Reicher (1969) and Wheeler (1970).

On a typical trial, participants saw either a letter (*D*), a nonword (*ORWD*), or a word (*WORD*) presented very briefly. Then a meaningless visual pattern was presented to shut off visual processing of the stimulus. The participants were then asked to say which of two letters had been in the stimulus (*D* or *K*). Over a large number of trials with different letters, words, and nonwords, people were typically about 10 percent more accurate in the word condition than in either the nonword *or the single-letter condition.*

If you think about it, this result is quite remarkable. Participants were more accurate in the word condition even though, in a sense, they had to process four times as many stimuli as in the single-letter condition. Apparently, words are not perceived on a letter-by-letter basis; if they were, the word superiority effect would not be possible. Therefore, a model of word recognition cannot simply involve a Pandemonium-like system that identifies a word one letter at a time. On the other hand, the interactive activation model of McClelland and Rumelhart (1981) does provide an explanation of the word superiority effect. Recall that in their model, word candidates are activated by bottom-up feature analysis even before all the letters are completely identified. Then, top-down activation (and inhibition) from the word candidates can assist the letter-processing level. According to the interactive activation model, it is this top-down influence that leads to the word superiority effect.

How Many Routes to the Lexicon?

Note that the interactive activation model of McClelland and Rumelhart (1981) contradicts our hypothesis for this chapter in two ways. First, as I noted, they believe that processing is not just bottom-up. In addition, their model suggests that there is a **direct route** from the visual word form to the lexicon—in other words, that we process letters in parallel and learn to associate particular letter sequences with their lexical entries. In contrast to this view, the hypothesis I laid out in the introduction to this chapter claims that readers use an **assembled route** to go from a visual word form to the lexicon. According to this hypothesis, we process letters or letter clusters (perhaps syllables) in parallel, associate these units with their corresponding speech sounds, and then put these sounds together (assemble them) in order to identify the word.

Which view is correct? Do we go directly from the written word to the lexicon, or do we use spelling-to-sound correspondence as a "go between"? Most researchers in this area think that *both* views are correct. The idea that we can use both a direct and an assembled route to the lexicon is known as the **dual-route model** of reading (Coltheart, 1978; Coltheart, Curtis, Atkins & Haller, 1993; Humphreys & Evett, 1985).

Some of the evidence consistent with the dual-route view comes from studies of word recognition in different languages. For example, researchers have compared languages that differ in orthographic depth in order to determine if one route or another is predominant in a given language. Given what you have learned so far, would an assembled route be more common in languages with a shallow orthography or in those with a deep orthography?*

Frost, Katz, and Bentin (1987) examined evidence for direct and assembled word recognition routes in three languages: Hebrew, English, and Serbo-Croatian. Hebrew has a very deep orthography because only the consonants are represented by letters. In Hebrew texts, vowels can be indicated by small marks added to consonants, but most of the time these vowel marks are omitted. Thus, most adults who read Hebrew are accustomed to reading print that lacks vowel indicators altogether. English, as we have seen, has a moderately deep orthography, whereas Serbo-Croatian has a very shallow orthography with nearly a one-to-one correspondence between letters and phonemes.

Frost and associates (1987) had speakers of each language name target words as quickly as possible; they also varied whether the target was semantically primed by a relevant category name or was unprimed. They reasoned that, according to the dual-route view, the size of semantic priming effects on naming a word should vary with orthographic depth. The basis for this prediction is illustrated in Figure 6.3. To put it simply, if someone is using a direct route to the lexicon, the pronunciation of a

---

* If you figured out that languages with a shallow orthography are better equipped to make use of an assembled route, in which people use the letters to determine the phonology of a word in order to access its meaning, then you are tracking pretty well. If not, then try rereading the earlier section on orthographic depth.

| FIGURE 6.3 | **A Dual-Route View of Lexical Access** |

We can get access to the meaning of a printed word directly from visual processing, or the visual analysis can give rise to the sound of the word (prelexical speech code), which leads us to the meaning. We can also process the sound of the word *after* we access its meaning (postlexical speech code). Because word recognition happens so fast, it has been difficult for researchers to determine whether the speech code was prelexical or postlexical. *(From Just & Carpenter, 1987.)*

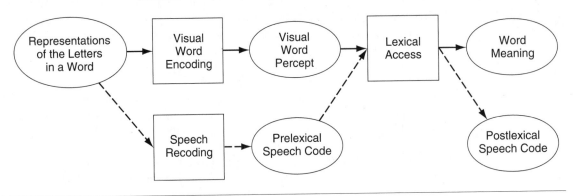

word will not be available until *after* lexical access. And if someone is using the assembled route, the pronunciation of a word is available *before* its meaning has been activated in the lexicon.

Frost and associates (1987) found that naming times were faster after a category prime in both Hebrew and English, but that in Serbo-Croatian there was no effect of semantic priming on word naming. The strongest priming effects were obtained in Hebrew, where having a lexical item activated before it appeared significantly improved naming times. The implication is that the phonological form of a word is not usually available in Hebrew before the word is visually identified. But in Serbo-Croatian, with its shallow orthography, the phonological characteristics of a word may be available from the visual form before meaning is accessed, so prior semantic activation does not improve naming. These data suggest that readers of Hebrew rely mainly on a direct route, readers of Serbo-Croatian rely mainly on an assembled route, and readers of English fall somewhere in between.

If English is in between Hebrew and Serbo-Croatian in terms of orthographic depth, can we get evidence that readers of English use both direct and assembled routes in word recognition? To get a feel for the role that phonological processes may play in word recognition, try Activity 6.2.

Activity 6.2 is based on studies by Van Orden (1987; Van Orden, Pennington & Stone, 1990) and Jared and Seidenberg (1991). Van Orden's experiments showed that people make more errors in rejecting targets that do not belong to a category if the target is a homophone of a member of the category. For example, we are likely to be more error-prone, or at least slower, on a category judgment task in which we must respond "no" to a trial like *food-meet* in comparison to a trial like *food-melt*. The confusion arises because we should respond "yes" to *food-meat* but "no" to *food-meet*. This finding suggests that phonological information is used in getting access to word

ACTIVITY 6.2   The Role of Phonological Processing in Word Recognition

For this activity, you will need at least a couple of volunteers to help you. First, get two stacks of ten index cards. Write each word from List A on one set of cards and each word from List B on the other set of cards.

List A	List B
1. prince	prince
2. noun	none
3. seller	seller
4. prophet	prophet
5. flex	flee
6. fowl	fowl
7. trod	towed
8. whack	wail
9. pigeon	pigeon
10. knife	night

The volunteers' task is to go through a stack of cards (half of them will do List A, the other half will do List B) and to say for each item whether it is a living thing. They should proceed as quickly as possible while still being accurate. Make note of any items that seem to take longer or on which a volunteer makes an error.

You will notice that the lists are the same except for cards 2, 5, 7, 8, and 10—the cards to which the person should respond "no." There is nothing special about these items in List A, but in List B the words for the nonliving items are homonyms of living things (nun, flea, toad, whale, and knight). What conclusion will you draw if your volunteers have a harder time with List B?

meanings. In the case of a trial like *food-meet*, the visual information that tells us to respond "no" conflicts with phonological information that tells us to respond "yes." Meanwhile, a study by Jared and Seidenberg (1991) showed that this homophone effect occurs mainly for low-frequency words. Words that occur very frequently in English show little evidence of causing confusion based on a sound similar to that of a real category member. Taken together, the two sets of studies suggest that the meaning of low-frequency words is accessed via an assembled phonological route and the meaning of high-frequency words is accessed via the direct visual route.

Most researchers who study visual word recognition accept the basic idea behind the dual-route model—namely, that there is a role for direct connections of visual information to the lexicon *as well as* a role for phonological information. Not everyone, however, thinks that these roles represent two separate routes to the lexicon. For example, Seidenberg and McClelland (1989), who developed a fully connectionist version of McClelland and Rumelhart's (1981) word recognition model, claim that a layer of phonological units participates in the interactive activation processes involved in recognizing words.

Although there is some consensus that both visual-lexical connections and visual-phonology connections participate in word recognition, it is less clear what units below the word level are involved in the recognition process. We have seen that letters are processed in parallel, but is it also the case that letters are "chunked" into familiar groupings of morphemes or syllables?

Sublexical Processing

Although it is clear that we do not recognize words by processing each letter in turn, it does not necessarily follow that we process words as wholes without breaking them up perceptually into smaller units. For example, we sometimes break up new words into parts as part of a conscious strategy to figure out what they mean. Consider the word *sublexical* in the heading for this section. You may never have encountered that word before. Nevertheless, if you recognize that *lexical* is similar to *lexicon* and you know that the prefix *sub-* means "below," then you can determine that the word *sublexical* refers to units of processing below, or more simple than, the whole-word level.

Our question here, however, is not whether we can process words in this way if we try but whether we automatically divide words into parts as we recognize them. A number of investigators have claimed that we do use sublexical groupings to process words (e.g., Feldman & Andjelkovic, 1992; Rapp, 1992; Spoehr & Smith, 1973; Taft & Forster, 1975, 1976). The most straightforward case to consider is the processing of compound words, such as *daydream*. When we recognize this word, do we also recognize that it has two separate parts, *day* and *dream?* Taft and Forster (1976) had people perform a lexical decision task on letter strings that were either compound words, like *daydream*, or compound nonwords, like *dustworth* or *mowdflisk*.

Interestingly, people took longer to recognize a compound with real words in it, like *dustworth*, as a nonword than to recognize another compound composed of two pronounceable nonwords, like *mowdflisk*, as a nonword. This finding suggests that the participants were momentarily confused about what response to make, word or nonword, because they had recognized the actual words in stimuli like *dustworth*.

At this point we might argue that such compounds are a special case, and that the results might apply only to compounds. If we do break up noncompound words to recognize them, what groupings within a word would we use? One idea is that we might use morphemic boundaries. It is common for a root word, like *mount*, to take several possible forms by the addition of prefixes or suffixes, as in *dismount, mounted,* and *mounting*. Accordingly, Taft and Forster (1975) suggested that we might recognize morphemically complex words in a lexical decision task by first locating the root word in the lexicon and then searching through a list of variations on the root word. Consistent with this claim, they found that people had difficulty classifying strings like *juvenate* as nonwords. It was as if some part of the lexicon represented the word *rejuvenate* as re + *juvenate*, even though the English language actually has no such word as *juvenate*. Of course, English does have related words from the same Latin root word—*juvenile*, for example.

There is a problem here, though. What about a word like *repertoire*? Here the *re* is not a prefix at all. How do we know when to strip off *re-* as a prefix and when not to?

Taft and Forster (1975) argued that we are able to work around these problems because the lexicon uses an index of terms based on shared root words, but all words are represented as wholes in the lexicon itself. Thus, the index helps us locate words based on root forms, but because the entries in the lexicon are whole words, we know that *repertoire* is a word whereas *pertoire* is not.

Other evidence for morphemic effects in word recognition comes from priming studies. For example, Stanners, Neiser, Hernon, and Hall (1979) gave people a list of words to make lexical decisions about in sequence. Specifically, they tested what would happen to the time participants took to decide that a root word, like *jump*, is a word when it was preceded by a lexical decision about either the same word or a variation of it, such as *jumped*.

Not surprisingly, Stanners and associates (1979) found that the lexical decision time for a word like *jump* was faster if the person had already made a recent lexical decision about that word. A less obvious result was that a lexical decision about *jump* was equally facilitated if the person had recently made a lexical decision about *jumped*. This finding suggests that people accessed the root word *jump* when they processed *jumped*.

It is not just because *jump* and *jumped* share letters that such priming effects were achieved. For example, all of the letters in *select* are also found in *selective*, but there is not much priming of *select* by *selective* (Stanners, Neiser, Hernon, & Hall, 1979). Note that the suffix *-ive* changes *select* from a verb to an adjective. As it turns out, morphemic priming is reduced when the more complex word is from a different grammatical category than the root word (Balota, 1994). In addition, Lima (1987) found that seeing the word *dishonest* facilitated a lexical decision about *honest*, but *arson* did not facilitate *son*. Drews and Zwitserlood (1995) reported similar priming effects in Dutch and German.

One interpretation of these priming data is that readers are sensitive to morphemic boundaries within words. However, Seidenberg (1987) has argued that these effects do not reflect a morphemic level of processing (see also Jared & Seidenberg, 1990; Seidenberg & McClelland, 1989). Instead, what looks like morphological priming may just be the overlap between word forms and word meanings. Thus, *dishonest* may facilitate recognition of *honest* because the similarity in visual forms is accompanied by a relationship between the meanings of the two words. However, *arson* does not prime *son* because the similarity in their visual forms is not accompanied by a connection between the meanings of the words. Thus, the priming effects need not be due to the breaking up of words into their constituent morphemes.

However, more recent data using a segment shifting task rather than a priming task favor the idea that readers are sensitive to morpheme boundaries within words (e.g., Feldman, 1994; Feldman, Frost & Pnini, 1995). In the segment shifting task, a person is shown a word along with an indication of a segment of that word that is to be added to another word. For example, the person might be shown:

HARD*EN*

BRIGHT

In this case, the person has to respond with "BRIGHTEN" as quickly as possible. Note that the *-EN* segment is a morpheme in the word *HARDEN*. We could, instead, have the person perform the segment shifting task using this stimulus:

GARD*EN*

BRIGHT

The response the person has to make is the same, but this time the *-EN* segment that is shifted is not a separate morpheme in the word from which it is taken. Feldman and associates (1995) showed that people perform the shift more quickly when the segment is a morpheme than when it is not. The implication is that readers can more easily break up words at morpheme boundaries than at points that are not morpheme boundaries. Given that this phenomenon does not depend on semantic overlap in the same way that lexical decision priming does, the segment shift data run counter to Seidenberg's claim that there is no morphemic level in word recognition.

So, there is evidence that part of the process of word recognition involves breaking morphologically complex words into the individual morphemes that make up the word. In fact, this conclusion is supported in studies of both visual and auditory word recognition (cf., Feldman, Frost & Pnini, 1995; Marslen-Wilson, Tyler, Waksler & Older, 1994). We can take the idea of breaking up words into their parts a step further and ask whether people might also break up words into syllables. For example, in order to recognize the word *vodka*, do we break it up into *vod + ka*? Just as we saw in the literature on morpheme effects (e.g., Feldman, Frost & Pnini, 1995), this question has been a contentious one, with some investigators arguing strongly that we do make use of component syllables (e.g., Spoehr & Smith, 1973) and others claiming that we do not divide words into syllables (e.g., Jared & Seidenberg, 1990).

A very clever set of experiments that tested this question was reported by Prinzmetal, Treiman, and Rho (1986). Their task was very simple. On each trial, a person was shown a target letter; then a word that contained the target letter was flashed on a screen. The word was printed in two different colors, and the person had to report which color the target letter was printed in. For example, a given trial might work this way (I'll use CAPITALS to indicate one color and *italics* to indicate another color):

target letter: d

word: VO*dka*

Prinzmetal and associates (1986) reasoned that if people were processing by syllables, then they might be inclined to make errors on trials like the one above in which the color division is not consistent with the syllable boundary. That is, people might mistakenly say that the target letter, d, was the same color as the VO- because of the natural tendency to group items by syllable. This phenomenon is called an **illusory conjunction** because people experience a visual illusion in which a particular feature— in this case, color—is perceptually attached to the wrong pattern. Prinzmetal and associates compared the number of illusory conjunctions on trials in which the colors were divided consistently (e.g., VOD*ka*) and inconsistently (VO*dka*) with a syllable boundary. What they discovered is that the illusory conjunction errors were much more common on trials in which the color boundary was inconsistent with the syllable boundary. This finding suggests that syllable boundaries serve as natural perceptual groupings in visual word recognition.

However, as in the studies on morpheme effects (e.g., Feldman, Frost & Pnini, 1995), Seidenberg (1987) questioned whether people divide words up into sublexical units (see also Jared & Seidenberg, 1990). Specifically, Seidenberg (1987) noted that pairs of letters differ a great deal in terms of how often they occur together. That is, letter pairs differ in **bigram frequency**. Take a word like *vodka*. Of the letter pairs—*vo, od, dk,* and *ka*—the least common, by far, is *dk*. Seidenberg suggested that the apparent syllable effects on illusory conjunctions are actually due to parts of a word in which bigram frequency is low. Let's consider how this possibility would affect processing in an interactive word recognition system like the McClelland and Rumelhart (1981) model we examined earlier. In particular, note that frequent letter combinations activate word candidates with the same letter combinations. Top-down processing from the word candidates thus increases the activation to those letter combinations. So, some letter combinations, often forming syllable or morpheme groups, will get more activation than others along the way toward recognition of the word. It follows that a conjunction error in a stimulus like VO*dka* may have come from greater top-down activation from the word level to the *od* bigram than to the *dk* bigram.

An important difference between the explanation given by Prinzmetal and associates (1986) and the explanation given by Seidenberg (1987) concerns the role of top-down processing in word recognition. Prinzmetal and associates claimed that dividing words by syllable is part of the bottom-up processing of the word, whereas Seidenberg claimed that the apparent syllable effects are the result of top-down activation from words back to the letter level of processing.

More recent evidence suggests that the bottom-up explanation may be correct. Rapp (1992) replicated the Prinzmetal and associates (1986) study, but controlled for bigram frequency across the syllable boundaries. Rapp's data do not rule out the possibility that top-down activation can have some effect, but they do support the idea that dividing complex words into syllables may be part of the bottom-up processing of these words. To be fair to approaches like Seidenberg's (1987, 1995), however, I should acknowledge that connectionist representations of word processing, which do not use sublexical units beyond the letter or phoneme level, are relatively new and developing rapidly. It remains to be seen whether they can be modified to account for the full range of data on sublexical processing.

Of course, word recognition time depends on much more than just the number of morphemes or syllables in a word. Some words take longer to recognize than others, even if neither set of words has to be broken into smaller units. It is to the issue of word-level variables that we now turn.

Variables That Influence Visual Word Recognition

Some words can be identified even if flashed on a screen for only 50 milliseconds. Other words may require hundreds of milliseconds of processing for us to identify them. It is through understanding what factors influence these large differences in word recognition speed that we can formulate models of the word recognition process. As with spoken word recognition, we will examine visual word recognition in terms of the effects of three variables: frequency, neighborhood size, and context.

Frequency Effects

Not surprisingly, in the visual modality as in the auditory modality, the higher the general frequency of usage of a word, the more quickly the word is recognized. For example, high-frequency words can be named more rapidly than low-frequency words

(Balota & Chumbly, 1984), and lexical decisions about high-frequency words tend to be faster (e.g., Forster, 1976).

Evidence in support of the dual-route view suggests that the direct route is more important for high-frequency words and the assembled route is more important for low-frequency words. This distinction has been demonstrated by the lack of phonologically based confusions in category judgments for high-frequency targets (Jared & Seidenberg, 1991). Indeed, there is a general pattern of evidence suggesting that, for high-frequency words, it matters little to naming or lexical decision times whether the words follow standard phonological rules. However, low-frequency words that follow regular spelling-to-sound-correspondence rules are recognized more quickly than phonologically irregular words (e.g., Seidenberg, Waters, Barnes & Tanenhaus, 1984). For example, because *stop* and *says* are high-frequency words, the recognition times for both are about equal, even though *says* is not "spelled like it sounds." On the other hand, *plump* and *caste* are both low-frequency words, but *plump* is recognized more rapidly because its spelling follows the usual phonological rules.

One way to understand these results is to imagine that the direct route and the indirect assembled route are like two horses racing to the finish line of recognizing the word. The direct route is fast enough for high-frequency words that it wins the race consistently, so we see little evidence of the assembled route in the recognition of such words. But with lower-frequency words, the direct route is not so fast and the assembled route will sometimes "win the race." In short, word identification will be based on the assembled route whenever phonological regularity is the main factor affecting the speed of the process (Coltheart, Curtis, Atkins & Haller, 1993).

Neighborhood Effects

As we saw in the discussion of spoken word recognition, another important factor in recognition time is the influence of lexical similarity, or the *neighborhood effect*. In the case of visual word recognition, we can measure the size of a particular word's neighborhood by determining how many other words can be formed by changing only one letter of the word (e.g., Coltheart, Davelaar, Jonasson & Besner, 1977). For example, two neighbors of the word *kind* are *king* and *find*.

Imagine a study in which we contrast naming or lexical decision times for words from small and large neighborhoods; what kind of effect would we expect neighborhood size to have? On the one hand, if we recognize words by "searching" through the lexicon to match a given word with the right entry in the lexicon, then having a large neighborhood would be expected to cause interference and slow down the word recognition process. On the other hand, if there is an interactive activation process, as McClelland & Rumelhart (1981) claim in their model, then having a large neighborhood would be expected to facilitate word recognition. In other words, top-down activation from multiple, similar-word candidates would presumably speed the activation of the correct features at the feature and letter levels.

As it turns out, a series of experiments by Andrews (1989, 1992) has shown that, in the case of low-frequency words, recognition is *faster* if the words are from large neighborhoods. This finding is very problematic for any model proposing that we perform some kind of item-by-item search of the lexicon. However, Andrews's (1992) results are also problematic for the simple interactive activation view of McClelland

and Rumelhart (1981) because they show *no effect* of neighborhood size in the case of high-frequency words. A simple way to conceptualize Andrews's results is to suppose that high-frequency words are identified so efficiently by direct bottom-up processing of the stimulus that there is little time (or need) for top-down processes to have an influence. However, for lower-frequency words, identification may not be complete before top-down activation from multiple word candidates begins to boost activation of the appropriate features and letters.

A series of studies by Grainger and colleagues (e.g., Grainger & Jacobs, 1996; Grainger & Segui, 1990; Segui & Grainger, 1990) has demonstrated a different kind of neighborhood effect. If a word has a neighbor that is higher in frequency than the actual target word, the neighbor can cause interference with lexical decisions. Thus, what matters may be not just neighborhood size, which was the variable investigated by Andrews (1992), but also the frequency of the words in a neighborhood. In the case of Grainger's studies, what seems to happen is that an incorrect word from the neighborhood of the target word gets highly activated on the basis of only a little bottom-up evidence. The incorrect neighbor then begins to inhibit its neighbors, including, temporarily, the correct target word. More bottom-up analysis is then required to overcome this interference.

For our purposes here, the important point is this: The effects obtained by Andrews (1992), Grainger and Segui (1990), and Segui and Grainger (1990) suggest that not all word recognition processes are bottom-up. Word recognition is affected by more than just what visual features are present, and by more than just the frequency with which a particular collection of features has been processed. In short, neighborhood effects, whether positive or negative, suggest that activation of multiple related entries in the lexicon has a top-down effect on the processing of a particular word.

You should note, however, that the status of these kinds of neighborhood effects is controversial. There is still much to learn about the conditions in which neighbors can facilitate or interfere with responding in word recognition tasks. For example, Forster and Shen (1996) recently questioned the importance of neighborhood effects because they observed effects of neighborhood size on lexical decisions but not on the time needed to categorize a word as animal or nonanimal. As the literature on neighborhood effects grows and we find out more about how activated neighbors influence recognition of particular words, we should get a better idea of how the various processes at the feature, sublexical, and lexical levels all interact, particularly with regard to whether there is top-down activation that influences the analysis of visual features or phonological forms (Grainger & Jacobs, 1996).

Because one of the major dimensions of difference among models of word recognition is the degree of top-down processing, it is of interest to see what other examples of top-down processing in word recognition can be found. An intriguing example of such effects was obtained recently by Kellas, Ferraro, and Simpson (1988), who studied speed of word recognition for **homographs,** or words with multiple meanings. For instance, consider the distinct meanings of the word *bat.* In one context it refers to something used to strike a ball, whereas in another it is a flying mammal. The key result from the study by Kellas and associates was that homographs were recognized more rapidly than nonhomographs. This was true even when the two sets of words were equated in terms of familiarity. Apparently, the multiple meanings of a word like *bat*, or the multiple entries for *bat* in the lexicon, provide top-down activation that speeds the bottom-up analysis of the word. This idea is similar to the notion of facilitation based on having a large neighborhood of similar words in the lexicon, except that, among homographs, the different meanings are associated with the same orthographic pattern.

Context Effects

The data from Kellas and associates (1988) seem to indicate that word meaning can influence word recognition. But this should not be the case if word recognition is a strictly bottom-up affair. Something about such reasoning may seem odd, however. The point of word recognition is usually to get the meaning of a word. How, then, can what we are after, meaning, affect the earlier stages of a process designed to give us access to a word's meaning? This question is one of the main issues dividing theorists in the areas of both visual and auditory word recognition.

Some theorists have argued that recognition normally depends only on the bottom-up processing of a stimulus. Other theorists have argued that expectations or associations based on preceding information can affect word recognition from the top down. In Chapter 3, we saw a kind of context effect on visual word recognition through Neely's (1977) research on semantic priming. This research suggested that when we are making a lexical decision about a target word, our decision is faster if the target is preceded by a semantically associated word, such as a category name. What may be happening is that concepts in our semantic network, when activated, activate not just other concepts but also the information used to recognize the corresponding word. So, the features we need to recognize the word "dog" may already be somewhat activated when we hear the word "animal." This makes subsequent recognition of the word "dog" easier than usual. However, a different interpretation of context effects is that context does not affect the analysis of visual features but merely influences a later stage, such as our decision about whether we have identified the right word.

One approach to the question of how context affects word recognition is to see if there are context effects in the natural reading of text. If, for example, context affects only our decision to say "yes" or "no" in lexical decision experiments, then it seems likely that context does not affect the bottom-up flow of information. To understand the data on context effects in reading, we must first explore the nature of eye movements that we make as we read.

Some people have the impression that their eyes move smoothly over a line of text, constantly taking in new information. However, if you have watched someone's eyes while that person reads, you know that reading actually consists of quick eye movements followed by noticeable pauses during which the eyes do not move. The movements are called **saccades** and the pauses are called **fixations.** How long we spend fixating on a particular word depends on several factors. Unless the text is unusually difficult, a typical college student will read at a rate of around 200 words per minute. That works out to about 3 or 4 words encoded every second. So, on average, each word is fixated for about 300 milliseconds (msec). As noted earlier, however, we can recognize most words in isolation even when they are presented as briefly as 50 msec. The implication is that we are doing more than recognizing a word during a 300-msec fixation. Indeed, one of the most interesting discoveries about reading made in this

FIGURE 6.4	Eye Fixation Patterns in Reading

The locations and durations of the eye fixations of a typical college student are indicated in this figure. Note that the upper row of numbers shows where and in what order the fixations occurred, whereas the lower row of numbers shows the duration of each fixation in milliseconds. People fixate on almost every word in a passage, but the duration of fixations varies greatly depending on the nature of the words.

```
    1       2    3    4     5      6        7       8     9      1      2
  1566    267  400   83   267    617      767     450   450    400    616
Flywheels are  one  of  the  oldest mechanical devices known to  man. Every internal-

    3       5    4    6     7      8                9       10     11          12        13
  517     684  250  317   617   1116             367      467    483         450        383
combustion engine contains a  small flywheel  that converts the jerky motion of the pistons into the

   14     15   16   17          18   19   20   21
  284    383  317  283         533   50  366  566
smooth flow of energy  that powers the drive shaft.
```

century is how closely linked the fixations and saccades are to virtually all of the mental processes that take place in reading (Dodge, 1900; Just & Carpenter, 1980; McConkie & Rayner, 1975; Tinker, 1939).

Clearly, with regard to reading, it is far too simplistic to think of the visual system as just a pathway into the language system; the degree of coordination between vision and understanding in reading is a marvel. In fact, saying that an average fixation lasts for 300 msec is a little misleading, because fixations vary a great deal above and below that average depending on the characteristics of the word itself, the sentence that the word is in, and even the text that the word is in. To see what I mean, examine Figure 6.4. It shows the fixation locations and durations of a typical college student for a few lines of a passage. (To see how this type of data is collected, turn to Figure 6.5.) Note that we tend to fixate on almost every content word, though our eyes sometimes skip over simple function words such as *that* or *to*. As Figure 6.4 also clearly demonstrates, the amount of time that we spend on a given word varies a great deal. The length of this student's fixations ranged from 50 milliseconds to more than 1.5 seconds. Thus, the longest fixation may be more than thirty times greater than the shortest!

How could we use data on fixation times to see if there are top-down effects on word recognition? Consider the following two sentences used in a study by Zola (1984; see also McConkie & Zola, 1981):

(1) Movie theaters must have buttered popcorn to serve their patrons.

(2) Movie theaters must have adequate popcorn to serve their patrons.

If earlier words can act as semantic primes to speed word recognition from the top down, then we would expect the fixation time on the word *popcorn* to be briefer in sentence (1) because of the strong association between *buttered* and *popcorn*. However, there was little evidence in Zola's study that people use this type of top-down information in reading. Fixation durations were only about 15 msec faster in the predictable condition, such as sentence (1), than in the unpredictable condition, such as sentence (2).

| FIGURE 6.5 | Recording Eye Movements During Reading |

Shown here is a reader viewing text printed on a computer screen. A video camera feeds information to the computer so that the reader's eye fixations can be recorded automatically.

Zola's (1984) results suggested that lexical access proceeds with little help from previously activated information. Somewhat larger effects were obtained by Stanovich and West (1979, 1983), who, after presenting a sentence up to the final word, asked participants to name the final word or to make a lexical decision about the final word. However, the generally accepted conclusion from these early studies was that context has only a modest effect on lexical access in normal reading.

In contrast to studies that have examined word association effects, more recent studies have obtained much larger context effects on word recognition by looking at how lexical access is affected by the main idea of a sentence or passage (e.g., Hess, Foss & Carroll, 1995; Morris, 1994). In one such study, conducted by Morris (1994), readers' fixation times were recorded for several different kinds of sentences. Consider the following examples:

(3) The friend talked as the person trimmed the mustache after lunch.

(4) The friend talked to the barber and trimmed the mustache after lunch.

(5) The friend talked as the barber trimmed the mustache after lunch.

Morris was interested in the amount of time it would take readers to process the word *mustache* in each of these sentences. Sentence (3) is the control sentence because, although *mustache* makes sense in this context, there is little in the sentence that would be expected to prime the concept of *mustache* before the word is presented. Sentence (4) is similar to the stimuli in the associative priming studies of Stanovich and West (1983) noted above, so we might expect the occurrence of the words *barber* and *trimmed* to slightly prime *mustache*. As expected, Morris found that the reading time for the target word in sentence (4) was only slightly faster than in the control sentence. In fact, the difference was not statistically reliable. In contrast, the reading time for the target word was significantly faster in priming sentences like sentence (5), in which the idea behind the sentence was related to the target word. In other words, lexical access of *mustache* was significantly speeded by the idea of a barber who is trimming something. Note that sentence (4), which showed little priming, also has the terms "barber" and "trimmed" but the message behind the sentence did not prime "mustache."

Morris's (1994) data—along with the similar results found by Hess and associates (1995), who used the main idea of a paragraph to prime the naming of the last word in the passage—indicate that lexical access depends not just on bottom-up processes acting on the visual stimulus but also on the semantic activation that has already taken place as a sentence is being read. Somehow, readers use sentence information to understand words, even while using the words in a sentence to determine the sentence meaning. We will examine this process more closely in Chapter 7, when we see how ambiguous words (like the homographs used in Kellas's research) are processed in sentence contexts. For now, however, keep in mind that studies of visual word recognition in context suggest that models of word recognition must allow for top-down processes as well as bottom-up processes.

Models of Visual Word Recognition

The point of proposing a model of a particular psychological process is to provide a coherent explanation for existing data, and to do so in a way that leads to new testable predictions. As new data are collected, a model is either abandoned or altered to fit the new information. For example, in the previous chapter we saw how the cohort model has evolved along with our growing knowledge of speech recognition.

As with speech recognition, many different models of visual word recognition have been proposed, and there is no need for us to explore all, or even most, of these models. Instead, my aim is to present three different models that were chosen specifically because they provide an overview of the different strategies that theorists have used to account for the basic phenomena we have discussed—notably, frequency, neighborhood, and context effects. In addition, to give you a feel for how models can be extended and subjected to further testing, I will explore whether the lessons gained from developing models of word recognition have implications for understanding deficient rather than normal word recognition.

The Logogen Model

An influential early model of word recognition was the logogen model proposed by Morton (1964, 1969, 1982). This model is illustrated in Figure 6.6. Like several models of visual word recognition, the logogen model has been extended to spoken word

FIGURE 6.6　The Logogen Model of Word Recognition

Word detectors, or logogens, monitor evidence from the stimulus as well as from the context. Recognition occurs when the evidence for a particular word exceeds a threshold of activation.

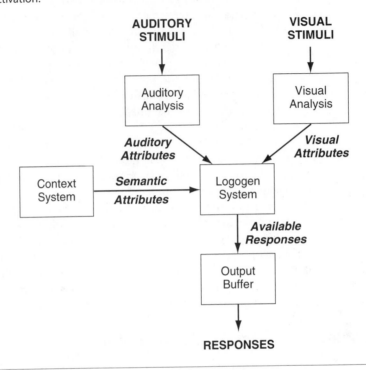

recognition. So, we examine it here as a general model of word recognition. The term **logogen** refers to an entry in the lexicon. (*Logos* is Greek for "word.") Logogens are like the demons in the Pandemonium model that we examined earlier, except that each logogen corresponds to a word. A specific logogen monitors the visual or auditory input, and it becomes activated when orthographic, phonological, syntactic, or semantic information in the input matches the information that identifies the logogen. A particular word is recognized when a logogen is sufficiently activated to reach a threshold for recognition.

The logogen model accounts for frequency effects in terms of different resting levels of activation. As a simple illustration of this idea, let's say that a logogen has to cross a threshold of 10 units of activation for the corresponding word to be recognized. As the features of a word match the features that designate a particular logogen, that logogen gets more units of activation. In these terms, high-frequency words would be recognized more quickly than low-frequency words because they start with a higher baseline activation level. So, the word *love* might start with 5 units before we see any word at all, whereas the word *loathe* (which is less frequent than love, fortunately) might start with only 2 units of activation. Consequently, it would take less evidence before the logogen for *love* is sufficiently activated for recognition.

Can the logogen model handle lexical similarity effects? Clearly, this model would suggest that several word candidates can be activated at once. However, because each logogen is activated independently based on the evidence, one logogen cannot facilitate or inhibit the activation of other logogens. This situation makes it difficult for the logogen model to account for lexical similarity effects.

Can the logogen model handle the data on context effects? According to this model, context, such as semantic information that precedes the word we are recognizing, increases activation of a logogen in the same way that actual auditory or visual input increases activation. In this way, the model accounts for the evidence that sentence contexts can speed up word recognition. Note, however, that context adds activation, but it does not influence the visual or auditory analysis of the word itself. Thus, the logogen model allows for only a limited form of interaction among different units in word recognition. That is, it suggests that there can be top-down effects on word recognition, but that the early stages of visual (or auditory) analysis are completely bottom-up.

Overall, the logogen model accounts for only some of the data on word recognition that we have examined. However, keep in mind that this model was not intended to account for such phenomena as neighborhood effects, inasmuch as it was proposed before many things we now know about word recognition were discovered. In fact, attempts to refine the logogen model as additional evidence was being discovered helped lead to many of the newer models of word recognition. For example, in the version of the model depicted in Figure 6.6, the visual route to the logogen system is not mediated by phonological information. To account for the more recent data that support a dual-route view, we would need to add a route that goes from visual analysis to phonological attributes. Thus, the logogen model could be altered to describe a dual-route view of recognition (see also Coltheart, Curtis, Atkins & Haller, 1993).

The Autonomous Search Model

The major competitor to the logogen model in early cognitive research on word recognition was Forster's (1976, 1979) autonomous search model. Whereas the central idea of the logogen model is that word representations can become activated in parallel, the central idea of the autonomous search model is that the lexicon is organized like a list that we search through in order to match the sensory input with the right lexical entry. The latter model is depicted in Figure 6.7. Like the logogen model, it was originally a visual recognition model but, in a newer version, has been applied to speech as well (Bradley & Forster, 1987).

To understand Forster's autonomous search model, think of the lexicon as a huge library and each word you know as a book in the library. If you want to find a particular book, you don't just go searching through the library; you check a catalog system that tells you where the book is located. As you know, a catalog system usually lets you find a book by author, title, or subject. According to the autonomous search model, then, the master lexicon is like the shelves of a library and the access files are like a catalog system with several different attributes that can point you to the location of the desired item. For example, in the version of Forster's model shown here, orthographic or

| FIGURE 6.7 | **The Autonomous Search Model of Word Recognition** |

Based on the input, different access files (designated here as letters) can be searched in order of frequency. Following location of the word that fits the input, a pointer leads to access of the semantic characteristics of the word in the master lexicon.

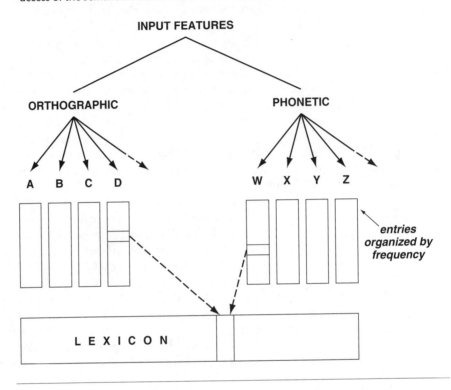

phonological input can be used to consult the access files, each of which has pointers to specific locations in the master lexicon.

When a word is presented, the letters are analyzed and this information is used to select one of the access files to be searched. A serial (i.e., entry-by-entry) search is then made through that access file. (Note that higher-frequency items are listed first in the access files, so high-frequency words are identified more rapidly than low-frequency words.) After the word is located in the access file and found in the master lexicon, a check is made to be sure the match is accurate for all the orthographic properties of the word. This checking procedure helps prevent us from mistaking nonwords for words (e.g., *pleazure* for *pleasure*).

In its original version, the autonomous search model did not have a very natural way to account for either lexical similarity effects or context effects. But if word recognition is based on a search that is dictated completely by bottom-up processing of the word, how can phonological or visual neighbors, or sentence contexts, influence word recognition? They cannot. So, the autonomous search model has been changed to be more consistent with the data. For example, Becker (1979) proposed a *verification model* similar to the autonomous search model, except it maintained that semantic context could generate a list of likely words to be used and that this likely candidate list could be used to narrow down the search. Recent versions of the autonomous search model (Forster, 1987, 1989) have become more similar to activation models in that several access bins can be searched at once and there is variation in the activity level of the items in the lexicon. However, the model has retained the idea that the lexicon functions autonomously. For example, Forster (1990) continues to maintain that context affects our decision processes in a lexical decision task without affecting the process of lexical access itself.

A Connectionist Model

A strategy for explaining word recognition that is different from the approaches taken in the logogen model and the autonomous search model is to depict the lexicon as an interactive network of connections among different layers of processing. We first saw this general approach in McClelland and Rumelhart's (1981) model of word recognition. As I noted earlier in the present chapter, that model is limited to a visual route to word recognition. An updated model of the same general type was presented by Seidenberg and McClelland (1989; Seidenberg, 1995). Their model is shown in Figure 6.8.

As in other connectionist models, information, such as our concept of what the word *make* means, takes the form of activating a particular set of units in the appropriate layer. Instead of depicting two different routes to getting access to meaning, Seidenberg and McClelland's model proposes two different layers of units, orthographic and phonological, that connect with each other and with a layer of units that represent concepts. The patterns of activation in these layers, and of the activation that has resulted from prior context, all determine what gets activated at the meaning layer. According to this connectionist model, word frequency affects word recognition because the more often a particular set of units are activated together, the more the pathways that result in that pattern are strengthened.

Likewise, at least some neighborhood effects make sense within Seidenberg and McClelland's model. Visual (and phonological) neighbors are words that are represented by similar patterns in the orthographic and phonological layers. Therefore, one pattern of activation (representing a particular word) has to win out over other similar patterns of activation. Interference would result if the competing pattern were higher in frequency than the correct pattern (cf., Grainger & Jacobs, 1996). On the other hand, if the word to be recognized has a lot of neighbors that are not higher in frequency, then the similarity in their patterns of activation could help the network settle on the correct pattern more quickly, as with the facilitation effects found by Andrews (1992). Thus, neighborhood effects are a natural feature of a connectionist model like Seidenberg and McClelland's (1989). However, whether models of word recognition continue to develop along these lines will depend, in part, on how the controversies over neighborhood effects are resolved (cf., Forster & Shen, 1996).

Another contrast between this connectionist model and the two other models we examined earlier is the highly interactive nature of the connectionist model. Because it posits extensive top-down as well as bottom-up connections, it predicts that context

| FIGURE 6.8 | An Interactive Model with Phonological Processing |

The model depicted here is an extension of the interactive activation model of McClelland and Rumelhart (1981). Separate sets of phonological and orthographic units interact with each other and with meaning units during lexical processing. The unlabeled ovals represent sets of "hidden units" that allow for all the units of one type to be connected to all the units of another type. So, for example, all the orthographic units and all the phonemic units are connected through the hidden units between these two levels.

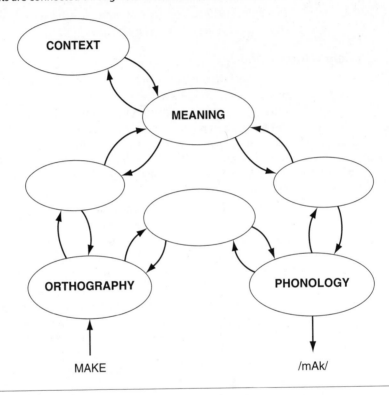

can, at least potentially, affect all aspects of word recognition, including early visual processing. However, Seidenberg and McClelland (1989) have not concentrated on context effects in their model, so we must wait and see how they will deal with the ever-changing literature on top-down effects.

In the meantime, their model has generated a great deal of debate over whether it can adequately capture many of the effects reported in the word recognition literature (Balota, 1994; Besner, Twilley, McCann & Seergobin, 1990). As I mentioned earlier, such an interactive view predicts that the apparent division of words into syllables during recognition is actually the result of bigram frequency. However, Rapp (1992) has claimed that there may be more to sublexical processing than bigram frequency. In any case, a number of variations on the general idea behind Seidenberg and McClelland's model have been proposed, and these may yet account even more effectively for some of the data on word recognition (e.g., Grainger & Jacobs, 1996; Norris, 1994).

As Forster (1989) noted, none of the existing models of word recognition is going to turn out to be *the one true model*. Therefore, it is important that we determine which general approaches proposed in the various models seem to be most promising. One thing each of these models illustrates is that a great deal of intricate processing takes place in visual word recognition. Moreover, that processing depends on both visual and phonemic connections to word meaning. The complexity of the processes described by the models examined here implies that if we turn from the study of skilled word recognition to the study of disturbances in word recognition, we should expect to find more than just a single cause for all failures to recognize words. The machinery for visual word recognition is simply too complex to expect that it will break down in only one way.

Dyslexia and Word Recognition

Before we examine the implications of models of skilled word recognition for dyslexia, we need to survey what is known about this disorder. It is important to keep in mind that if you were told "You have dyslexia," this is quite different from being given a medical diagnosis like "You have pneumonia." Pneumonia is a well-understood disease with a generally accepted course of treatment. Dyslexia, in contrast, is a label for a set of conditions of which the cause—or causes—are still being investigated.

Terms like *dyslexia* or *specific reading disability* are applied when there is no obvious cause for someone's inability to master reading. So, if general intellectual impairment, poor vision, and lack of either opportunity or motivation to learn to read are ruled out, then dyslexia is diagnosed by default. According to the Diagnostic and Statistical Manual (DSM-IV) of the American Psychiatric Association (1994), approximately 4 percent of school-aged children in the United States fall within the diagnostic criteria for specific reading disability. A similar figure was obtained in a large-scale study of the incidence of dyslexia among British schoolchildren (Yule, Rutter, Berger & Thompson, 1974).

Because of its prevalence, and because failures to learn to read can have devastating consequences for self-esteem, personal satisfaction, and employability, dyslexia has received a good deal of attention in the popular media. A view commonly promoted in the media holds that dyslexia is a subtle problem of visual processing. In other words, it has often been claimed that although dyslexics may test normally on standard tests of visual acuity, their visual information "gets turned around." You may have heard that dyslexia is indicated if a child frequently reverses letters in his or her writing and that this letter reversal reflects a visual processing problem.

It is clear that dyslexics have a particularly hard time with visual word recognition. Take a look at Figure 6.9, which shows the eye movement pattern of a typical dyslexic reader. If you compare this pattern with the one illustrated in Figure 6.4, you can see that dyslexic readers tend to fixate much longer on each word and experience many more regressive fixations in which they return to a word already read.

As noted earlier in the chapter, eye fixations in reading reflect a combination of many different visual and cognitive processes (Just & Carpenter, 1987). Therefore, we

| FIGURE 6.9 | Eye Movements by a Dyslexic Reader |

Compared to a normal reader, a dyslexic reader fixates much longer on each word and tends to backtrack to earlier words much more often.

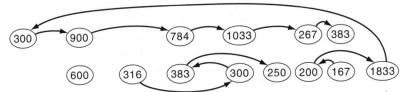

In appearance the surface of Mars is more like rocky

volcanic deserts on the earth than it is like the highly cratered surface

of the moon, yet Mars, once visualized as being largely a world of gently

rolling dunes, seems to possess little sand.

cannot assume that readers with abnormal eye movement patterns are having problems because of their eye movements, and we cannot assume that their visual system is functioning abnormally. In fact, the eye movement pattern shown in Figure 6.9 is abnormal only compared to that of a skilled reader. If you compared the eye movements of, say, a twelve-year-old dyslexic reading at a second-grade level with the eye movements of a second-grader reading at an age-appropriate level, you'd find that their eye movements are quite similar (Hyona & Olson, 1995). Nevertheless, people with dyslexia have found it very difficult to recognize words automatically and efficiently. The question is, Why?

As we have seen, one of the main insights derived from studies of skilled word recognition is that for high-frequency words readers can go directly from print to meaning, but for less familiar words the connection to meaning is mediated by phonological processing. Regardless of whether we think of this phenomenon in terms of two different routes or in terms of two different sets of nodes in an interactive network, the fact remains that phonology plays a role in recognizing at least some words. It makes sense, then, to ask, How do frequency and phonological regularity affect a dyslexic's ability to recognize words?

A pattern associated with many dyslexics was observed in a case study of an adolescent boy, J.M. (Snowling, Hulme & Goulandris, 1994). At the time of the study, J.M. was reading approximately five years below the expected level for his age. Despite the rather severe nature of his reading disability, his word recognition problems were pretty specific. His reading of very high-frequency words was relatively normal, regardless of whether they were phonologically regular or irregular. But J.M. performed very poorly when reading words that are less frequent. Even compared to younger children reading at his level, J.M. was impaired in his reading of less frequent but phonologically regular words.

These data, combined with a host of similar findings (e.g., Mann, 1993; Perfetti, 1992; Shankweiler & Crain, 1986), suggest that many dyslexics have trouble with the assembled, phonological route in word recognition. In particular, they have difficulties with the sublexical processing that allows a more skilled reader to go from a printed word to a phonemic representation of the word to the meaning of the word. Because their bottom-up processing is so inefficient, dyslexic readers often make greater use of context than skilled readers do; thus, dyslexics guess at words based on context, rather than sounding out the words. Stanovich (1986, 1988) has called this tendency **interactive compensatory processing**. In short, poor readers use top-down processing to compensate for their inefficient bottom-up processing.

This "phonological" form of dyslexia may be characteristic of as many as 60 percent of dyslexics (Boder, 1973). However, there are other dyslexics who perform relatively well in their reading of phonologically regular words but have great difficulties with irregular words (e.g., Boder, 1973; Castles & Coltheart, 1993). These "surface dyslexics" have to sound out words laboriously, like beginning readers, because some problem with visual perception or visual memory has prevented them from developing good bottom-up visual processing. In addition, there are "mixed dyslexics" who experience both visual and phonemic processing problems (e.g., Seidenberg & Manis, 1994).

In summary, as the data on skilled reading suggest, dyslexia does not represent just one kind of problem (e.g., Rayner, Pollatsek & Bilsky, 1995; Vellutino, 1979). Nevertheless, severe difficulties in learning to read are most often associated with language-related problems rather than a purely visual defect. Indeed, letter reversals are not a particularly reliable diagnostic sign for dyslexia (Olson, 1994). Knowing this, how should we recommend that dyslexia be treated? First, it is important to realize that there can be no single "one size fits all" treatment for dyslexia. For many dyslexics, though, a key seems to be intensive training in spelling-to-sound correspondence in addition to other forms of reading instruction (Olson, 1994; Wise & Olson, 1992). Even with a great deal of such training, however, some dyslexics will not reach normal levels of reading achievement (Just & Carpenter, 1987). Nevertheless, as you have seen several times already in this course, people are remarkably flexible and adaptable information processors. Many individuals with dyslexia do eventually find ways to work around their processing problems and achieve the highest levels of academic and professional success.

CONCLUSIONS

Toward a Consensus on Word Recognition

Let's look back at the "common sense" view that I introduced at the beginning of this chapter. Given that people already have links established between word sounds and word meanings before learning to read, it's possible that we learn visual word recognition by learning to sound out printed words. Indeed, support for this idea is provided by studies indicating that phonemic information is especially important for reading less frequent words.

Reading, though, is not just a simple matter of mapping visual words onto word sounds. For one thing, reliance on visual or phonemic information depends in part on the orthographic regularity of the writing system in question. In English, for example, frequent words may be recognized without recourse to a phonemic route. Moreover, skilled readers definitely do not sound out words letter-by-letter, but they do appear to break up words at morphemic or syllable boundaries in order to process them. Exactly how these actions are accomplished is not known, but the different models of word recognition that have been proposed do converge on some important ideas. If you look at what the different models have in common, at least in their latest versions, two facts become clear. First, there is consensus that both orthographic and phonological information can play a role in recognizing words—a conclusion that receives further support from studies of different types of dyslexia. In other words, it is possible for a particular dyslexic person to experience a disturbance in only one of these pathways to meaning. Second, there is growing evidence that multiple word candidates become activated during recognition, and that some type of selection mechanism acts on the activated entries. On the one hand, it may be that top-down activation from the meaning level facilitates orthographic or phonological processing, thus helping a particular word meaning to win out over other possibilities. On the other hand, lexical items like logogens may be activated in parallel, with inhibitory connections between one possibility and others. In any case, the idea that multiple word candidates compete for activation is a promising one (McQueen, Cutler, Briscoe & Norris, 1995). Indeed, as we will see in the next chapter, this idea has been important in explaining some of the data on sentence-level language comprehension.

Finally, in considering the models discussed for both auditory and visual word recognition, we have seen that context can affect the time it takes to respond to a word. In neither this chapter nor the previous one on speech recognition, did we resolve the issue of whether word recognition is based on an autonomous system. However, both the work by Massaro (1989) on units of speech recognition and the success of interactive models of word recognition present a strong challenge to the idea that word recognition processes are special in the sense of being handled by a module that is separate from other cognitive processes. Of course, not all the evidence is in, so we will deal with this question again in the next several chapters.

CHAPTER   REVIEW

Checking Your Understanding

Key Terms

alphabetic system (173)
assembled route (179)
bigram frequency (185)
deep orthography (175)
direct route (179)
dual-route model (179)
dyslexia (172)
fixations (188)
homographs (187)
illusory conjunction (184)

interactive compensatory processing (199)
logogen (192)
logographic system (173)
neighborhood effect (186)
saccades (188)
shallow orthography (175)
syllabic system (173)
templates (176)
tonal language (173)
word superiority effect (178)

Review Questions

1. Why are feature models of word recognition preferred over template models?

2. Why wouldn't you expect a tonal language, like Chinese, to use an alphabetic system of writing?

3. Describe how McClelland and Rumelhart's (1981) interactive activation model explains the word superiority effect.

4. Explain how the dual-route model of reading has been tested by researchers who have contrasted word recognition processes in written languages that vary in orthographic depth.

5. What data suggest that we divide words up into syllable or morpheme units in order to recognize them?

6. What research finding or phenomenon described in the chapter makes the best case that there are top-down effects on visual word recognition?

7. Contrast the logogen model, the autonomous search model, and the interactive model of Seidenberg and McClelland (1989) in terms of their accounts of (a) frequency effects, (b) neighborhood effects, and (c) whatever finding of top-down processing you chose for question 6.

8. What pattern of performance suggests that many dyslexics may have trouble with a phonemic route to word recognition?

On Further Reflection . . .

In the figure below, two dimensions are shown. One depicts an autonomous versus interactive continuum. As we have discussed, autonomous word recognition models assume that context cannot affect the early stages of word recognition, whereas interactive models assume that context can affect all aspects of word recognition. Of course, models vary in terms of how much interaction they permit. Likewise, there is a dimension representing the question of whether word recognition is explained as a search process or as an activation process. Indicate where the cohort model, the TRACE model, and each of the three models discussed in this chapter would fall along these dimensions. (If you need a hint to get started, put Forster's autonomous search model in the upper-right quadrant.) Justify your choices.

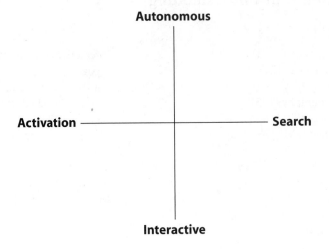

CHAPTER 7

Sentence Processing

e will know that the phenomenon of language comprehension is completely explained when we thoroughly understand how people can make sense of the sports page. After a recent baseball game, I came across this rather typical sentence in a local newspaper's sports section:

(1) Once again, the starting pitching was solid, but the bullpen blew a save opportunity.

If you know a little about baseball, this sentence probably seems very simple. However, when you consider all the mental processes involved, comprehending this sentence is really quite a feat. As you saw in the last chapter, the perceptual processes that allow you to recognize the words in a sentence are very intricate. Yet these perceptual processes are just the beginning. You must also use your syntactic and semantic knowledge to determine what each word means in context and how to combine the meanings. Clearly, part of the semantic information you need is knowledge specific to baseball. For example, if you know nothing about baseball, it is unlikely that *bullpen* is in your lexicon. Moreover, you must make use of the pragmatic knowledge that this sentence's meaning is figurative rather than literal. Even if you know that the bullpen is a set of pitchers who relieve the starters, the sentence does not make sense literally because the whole bullpen did not come in and pitch. Rather, the term *bullpen* is being used to stand for the person who did come in and pitch. Thus, comprehending even a "simple" sentence involves several different kinds of information.

We studied the "early" perceptual processes in comprehension in the last chapter, so now we move on to ask how syntactic, semantic, and pragmatic information is coordinated while we interpret a sentence. There are two very different views of how knowledge is used during sentence comprehension. One group of psycholinguists (e.g., Frazier, 1989; Swinney, 1979), consistent with linguistic theory in the tradition of Chomsky (1981b), believe that initial lexical access and the initial syntactic parsing of a sentence are autonomous. These researchers claim that prior semantic information in the sentence or relevant background knowledge do not influence the modules that perform the "early" processes of lexical and syntactic analysis. Other researchers (e.g., Taraban & McClelland, 1988; Trueswell, Tanenhaus & Garnsey, 1994), consistent with recent linguistic challenges to Chomsky's approach (e.g., Langacker, 1988), maintain that semantic information can be used to guide lexical access and syntactic analysis. These researchers see the communication between processors at the lexical, syntactic, and semantic levels as being highly interactive. The distinction between the modular and interactive positions can be understood as differences in the information flow illustrated in Figure 7.1.

An analogous issue emerges when we ask how semantic and pragmatic factors are coordinated during sentence processing. For example, when a person reads a sentence with metaphoric content like the baseball example I used earlier, it could be that the sentence must be processed literally before pragmatic knowledge comes into play. Alternatively, it could be that pragmatic factors come into play early in semantic analysis, in which case we'd conclude that metaphoric understanding can occur alongside literal comprehension (Gibbs, 1994; Glucksberg, 1991).

In the remainder of this chapter, you'll examine evidence on the question of how different forms of knowledge are used during sentence comprehension. I would like

FIGURE 7.1   **An Overview of Sentence Processing**

The job of processing a sentence can be broken up into lexical, syntactic, and semantic subprocesses. As each word is analyzed, these subprocessors produce a semantic representation, illustrated here as a proposition, and a syntactic representation, illustrated as a phrase structure tree. If the flow of information is only bottom-up, then this system is modular. If, instead, the semantic subprocessor can influence syntactic and lexical processes (denoted by dashed lines), then the system is interactive.

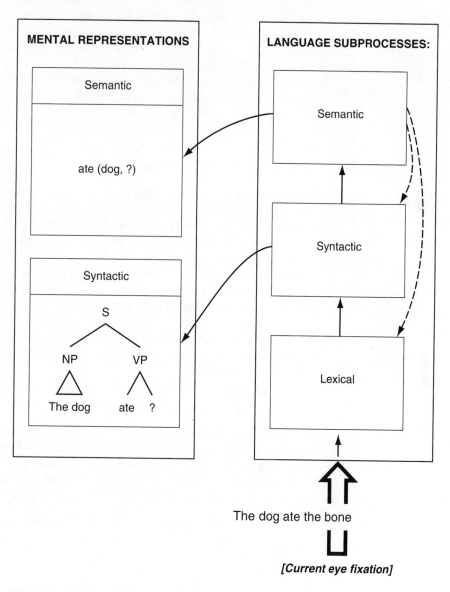

you to view the evidence as a test of the following general hypothesis: *Sentence comprehension occurs in a series of stages from lexical access to pragmatic analysis, with each earlier stage working autonomously from information at the later stages.* There are three possible outcomes associated with this hypothesis: (1) The hypothesis could be correct, such that each stage is found to be distinct and independent; (2) the hypothesis could be completely false, such that semantic and pragmatic information is found to be available for use at each stage; or (3) the hypothesis could be partially correct. For example, lexical access and syntactic parsing might be functioning autonomously, or nearly so, whereas semantic and pragmatic analysis may be completely interactive.

As you might expect, it is quite a scientific challenge to determine how all these different kinds of knowledge are used during sentence comprehension. Comprehension usually takes place relatively quickly, and the processes that people use are generally quite automatic. How can we obtain systematic data that reveal the nature of these intricate mental events? First we'll take up the question of how sentence processing can be studied, and then we'll review the data relevant to the issue of modular versus interactive processing.

How Can We Study Sentence Processing?

One relatively simple method we could try as a way of getting insight into how people comprehend sentences is to examine the products of the comprehension process. That is, what people remember about a sentence can potentially tell us about the processes used to comprehend the sentence. As you'll recall from Chapter 3, some of the early research in cognitive psychology showed that people seldom recall sentences verbatim (Bransford & Franks, 1972). Instead, they tend to recall the situation described by the sentence. This finding suggests that at some point in the comprehension process considerable knowledge about the world is available. To study the interaction between linguistic processes and general knowledge, Fillenbaum (1974) asked people to read a series of sentences and paraphrase them. Specifically, they read a sentence, wrote a paraphrase, and then went on to the next sentence at their own pace. Some of these sentences were anomalous:

(2) Get a move on or you will catch the bus.

(3) John dressed and had a bath.

Fillenbaum found that anomalous sentences were often paraphrased as though a more reasonable statement had been made. For example, people often paraphrased sentence (3) as "John had a bath and then got dressed." Many people did not notice that they had changed the meaning of the sentences. They thought that their paraphrases said the same thing as the originals, but more clearly. As Fillenbaum wrote:

> It was as though people focus not on the linguistic messages per se, but on the information they embody or appear to convey, considering and assimilating this information in relation to their preexisting knowledge of the ways of the world. *(p. 578)*

So, Fillenbaum's data might be taken to suggest that semantic or pragmatic knowledge is predominant in comprehension. But is this a fair interpretation? Perhaps people first fully analyze each sentence syntactically, but when their syntactic analysis leads to an anomalous interpretation they use world knowledge to "fix" the sentence. If comprehension processes take place rapidly and automatically, then the ultimate interpretation we place on the sentence may not clearly reflect all the processing that was performed on the sentence. Therefore, to really understand sentence processing, we need to be able to measure what's going on *as it happens.*

To study sentence comprehension as it happens, we have to answer another question: Does understanding happen all at once, or does sentence comprehension unfold gradually over time? This is an interesting question because there is a kind of mismatch between what we need to do to understand a sentence and the way we receive language. Whether in spoken or written form, language is received on a word-by-word basis (though in reading we can backtrack to earlier parts of a sentence). However, as linguistic analyses of syntax make clear, a sentence is not just a chain of words. Indeed, the syntactic roles and meanings of specific words often depend on the content of other words and phrases that are quite distant.

One way around this paradox would be to process sentences the way a linguist does. That is, we could wait until we have received the whole sentence before trying to analyze how the parts relate to each other syntactically and semantically. The problem with this approach, however, is the burden it would place on our working-memory (WM) system. Given the limitations on holding and maintaining information in WM, we'd be running a high risk of losing critical information. Besides, in situations involving spoken language, the speaker usually keeps plowing ahead. So, if you held a whole sentence in WM and then started to analyze it, you'd probably miss the next sentence.

Instead of trying to hold an entire sentence in WM before beginning to interpret it, people seem to utilize a strategy of **immediacy of interpretation.** That is, we try to interpret each word as completely as possible as soon as the word is received. When a word is received, we don't just identify what the word is; we also try to determine the word's syntactic and semantic role in the sentence. Two techniques have proven especially useful in revealing the degree of immediacy of interpretation in comprehension: semantic priming and eye fixation durations. We have touched on both of these techniques in previous chapters. Here, we will take our analysis one step further, into a discussion of the ways that semantic and syntactic processes work during sentence comprehension.

In order for priming effects or fixation durations to tell psycholinguists something about the nature of sentence processing, performance must be measured under carefully controlled conditions. In particular, to distinguish between modular and interactive sentence processing, psycholinguists often measure priming or fixation durations as people comprehend sentences that are, at least temporarily, ambiguous. For example, consider the processing of a sentence like this one:

(4) For several weeks after the exterminator's visit they did not find a single bug in the apartment.

This sentence contains a **lexical ambiguity.** That is, it contains a word with more than one meaning—a word whose meaning must be determined from the context. When you read sentence (4), you naturally thought of bug as meaning "insect" rather than "a secret listening device that the CIA might use." It is possible that the latter "spy" meaning was intended, but given the use of *exterminator* in the sentence, you were probably aware only of the "insect" meaning of *bug*. However, as you know by now, just because you were conscious of only one meaning of *bug*, you cannot assume that the other meaning was never activated in the lexicon. By looking at what aspects of the meaning of *bug* are primed immediately after you encounter that word in the sentence, you can get an idea of how semantic interpretation occurs during sentence processing. According to a modular view of lexical processing, you would access multiple meanings of *bug* when you see or hear the word, and only after that initial access of multiple meanings would you use context to narrow down the activation to the appropriate meaning. Alternatively, an interactive view would predict that contexts that strongly bias interpretation toward one particular meaning would allow you to activate only the contextually appropriate meaning.

Next, consider the following pair of sentences:

(5) The student warned about the failing grade dropped the class.

(6) The student who was warned about the failing grade dropped the class.

Both of these sentences are grammatical. But in sentence (5), unlike sentence (6), you were faced with a **syntactic ambiguity** when you encountered the word *warned*. At that point in the sentence you could build either of two different types of phrase structures. The word *warned* could be the start of the main verb phrase (VP) for the sentence, or it could be part of a relative clause. Of course, it is pretty typical that the first verb we come to will be the main verb for the sentence. Accordingly, in sentence (5) people naturally take *warned* to be the main verb until they come to *dropped*, which is the actual main verb. If you were to compare the durations of readers' fixations on the verb *dropped* in sentences (5) and (6), you'd find that the fixation time is much longer in sentence (5) (Just & Carpenter, 1992). The extra time spent on *dropped* in that sentence is necessary because people have to backtrack and try another syntactic analysis when it becomes clear that "warned" is not the main verb.

A sentence that initially leads to an incorrect interpretation or parsing, like sentence (5), is called a **garden-path sentence.** In sentence (6), the optional, but helpful, *who* signals that the upcoming verb is part of a relative clause, so we are not "led down the garden path" by sentence (6). As this example shows, eye fixations can tell us about the syntactic parsing that occurs during the process of sentence comprehension. It also demonstrates that immediacy of interpretation is our normal operating strategy, though it can sometimes lead us astray in garden-path sentences.

Of course, it is sometimes impossible to immediately integrate a word into the ongoing interpretation of a sentence. Consider the following example:

(7) Kate knew that when it wanted to go outside, the dog scratched at the door.

A complete interpretation of *it* in sentence (7) must await a term that refers back to *it*—in this case, *dog*. Indeed, immediacy of interpretation means that we usually integrate a word *as fully as we can*, but we do not always perform complete syntactic analysis and semantic integration of each word before we move to the next word. The key question we will address in connection with syntactic ambiguity is whether, as a modular view suggests, we make an initial commitment to the parsing of a phrase before we make use of any semantic or pragmatic information.

Before we review the data on how people resolve lexical and syntactic ambiguities, however, we should consider an objection to this whole research approach. If our

ACTIVITY 7.1   **On the Problem of Prolific Polysemy**

Words that have more than one meaning are **polysemous.** To get an idea of just how common polysemy is, take a paragraph out of a newspaper or magazine article and determine what percentage of the words used have more than one *completely distinct* meaning. (For example, *nut* can refer to the seed of a tree, a crazed person, or a device designed to hold a bolt tight.) Now, ask a couple of friends or family members to see how many polysemous words they can find in the paragraph. They might find some that you missed. This activity is harder than it seems because, in context, we are usually aware of only one meaning of a word, even if it has multiple meanings. When I tried this activity myself, I found that polysemous words made up approximately 25 percent of each of the two paragraphs I examined.

efforts are focused on the processing of ambiguous sentences, don't we risk coming up with results that are artificial because of the use of strange or unrepresentative stimulus materials? To some extent, we have to be concerned about this general issue in *all* laboratory research, both within and outside of psycholinguistics. In order to isolate causes and effects, scientists typically set up laboratory conditions that are different from real-world conditions. Then, later, when they have a handle on the potential causes of a phenomenon, they try to confirm the laboratory principles in more naturalistic settings.

There is another response to the objection that research on ambiguity does not tell us about "normal" sentence processing: Ambiguity is much more common in language than most people realize. As you have seen, one form of ambiguity is lexical ambiguity. To see how common it is, try Activity 7.1.

Ambiguity and the Question of Modularity

As I noted above, the reason that many of the studies of sentence processing make use of one form of ambiguity or another is because the major views of sentence processing clash most sharply when ambiguity is considered. On the one hand, a strictly modular view assumes that separate processors analyze lexical, syntactic, and semantic information, and that semantic information cannot influence our initial lexical or syntactic analysis even if a word or a syntactic structure is ambiguous. On the other hand, an interactive view sees the resolution of both lexical and syntactic ambiguity as being a matter of constraints based on simultaneous consideration of lexical, syntactic, and semantic information. Let's examine the evidence on how each of the two types of ambiguity is resolved.

Lexical Ambiguity

To study how people handle lexical ambiguity, Swinney (1979; Onifer & Swinney, 1981) used stimuli like sentence (4) above. Participants listened to these sentences through headphones, and either immediately upon auditory presentation of the ambiguous word or after a brief delay, a target word was visually presented for lexical decision. In a sentence with the word *bug*, for example, the expected result was more facilitation of the lexical decision to a word like *insect* than to an unrelated control word such as *custom*. (Control words were matched to target words for length and frequency.) And as expected, Swinney's experiments found evidence that *insect* was immediately primed upon presentation of the word *bug*.

The interesting question to consider is whether another meaning of *bug* was also primed by the sentence, even if only briefly. Consistent with the modular view, Swinney found that when the target appeared immediately after the ambiguous word, multiple meanings were activated (see also Seidenberg, Tanenhaus, Leiman & Bienkowski, 1982). For example, immediately after presentation of the word *bug* in sentence (4), not only a lexical decision for "insect" would be facilitated, but so would a lexical decision for *spy* compared to the control word *tan*. Apparently, both the "insect" meaning and the "spy" meaning of *bug* were accessed, even though only one of the meanings is appropriate to the context. When activation was tested as little as a few hundred milliseconds after the ambiguous word, only the appropriate meaning was activated.

These data offered strong support for a modular view that sees initial lexical access as independent of context. Subsequently, when the word meanings were integrated into the overall message of the sentence, only the appropriate meaning was preserved. However, other studies have obtained evidence that initial lexical access of ambiguous words can be dependent on the context. At least two factors determine whether evidence for multiple or selective lexical access is obtained: meaning dominance and strength of context (Simpson, 1994).

Meaning dominance refers to the relative frequency of each meaning of an ambiguous word. Often, two meanings of a word are not equally probable. For example, if we examined a large sample of language utterances and writings, we'd find that people most often use the word *bank* to refer to a financial institution, but it can also mean the side of a river. In this case we call the money-related meaning "dominant" and the river-related meaning "subordinate." In contrast, the word *pitcher* can refer to a container for liquid, or it can refer to someone who throws a ball to a batter. Neither of these two meanings is used a great deal more than the other, so we describe this ambiguous word as "equibiased."

The other important factor, strength of context, should come as no surprise. In Chapter 4, we reviewed the evidence on top-down effects in word recognition and found that whether we see evidence for such effects depends on whether the context strongly suggests a particular word. Similarly, whether we find evidence for selective or multiple access of an ambiguous word depends on how strongly the sentence suggests a particular meaning of the word.

These two factors, meaning dominance and strength of context, jointly influence lexical access in sentence contexts. For example, both Simpson (1981; Simpson & Kreuger, 1991) and Tabossi (1988; Tabossi & Zardon, 1993) have found that selective access is most likely in cases where a strong context suggests the dominant meaning of the ambiguous word. For example, if we test for activation immediately after a person hears *bank*, the most likely result is that only the money-related meaning of bank will be primed in sentence (8) but both meanings will be momentarily active in sentence (9):

TABLE 7.1	Examples of Equibiased and Nonequibiased Sentences (Duffy, Morris & Rayner, 1988)

	Equibiased
Ambiguous Before	Because it was kept on the back of a high shelf, the *pitcher* (whiskey) was often forgotten.
Ambiguous After	Of course the *pitcher* (whiskey) was often forgotten because it was kept on the back of a high shelf.
	Nonequibiased
Ambiguous Before	When she finally served it to her guests, the *port* (soup) was a great success.
Ambiguous After	Last night the *port* (soup) was a great success when she finally served it to her guests.

Note: In each of these example sentences, the ambiguous target word is italicized, whereas the corresponding control word is enclosed in parentheses.

(8) I opened a checking account at the bank.

(9) The fisherman waited by the bank.

In sentence (8), only the money-related meaning of *bank* makes sense, and this meaning is the dominant one. In sentence (9), the context suggests the subordinate meaning of *bank*, but the dominant meaning is still a viable interpretation. Given weaker contextual support for the subordinate meaning, activation of multiple meanings is followed by selection of the most probable meaning.

Studies of readers' eye movements provide further support for the idea that context and meaning dominance affect lexical access. For example, Duffy, Morris, and Rayner (1988) measured word-by-word reading times for sentences containing a lexical ambiguity as well as for corresponding control sentences. There were two important variables in their study: (1) whether the ambiguous word was equibiased or nonequibiased, and (2) whether the clause that resolved the ambiguity came before or after the ambiguous word. Examples of the sentences they used are shown in Table 7.1. Note that in the nonequibiased condition, it was always the subordinate meaning that was intended.

Before we look at the results of this study, it is important that you understand the logic behind using reading time to study processing of ambiguous words. In short, readers should take more time to select the appropriate meaning in a condition where the initial lexical access of an ambiguous word activates two or more meanings than in a condition where only one meaning has been activated. In the study by Duffy and associates (1988), therefore, multiple access of meanings was expected to show up as longer reading times for ambiguous words in comparison to the unambiguous control words. The relevant reading times are shown in Figure 7.2. Take a look at the figure and try to determine what the pattern of results says about the modularity-interactive debate.

When information that resolves the ambiguity was encountered *before* the ambiguous word occurred, only the nonequibiased words showed a longer reading time. Remember, it was the subordinate meaning that was intended in this case, so the results

<table>
<tr><td>**FIGURE 7.2**</td><td>**Results of a Study Involving Equibiased and Nonequibiased Sentences (Duffy, Morris & Rayner, 1988)**</td></tr>
</table>

When the clause that resolved an ambiguous word came *before* the ambiguity, readers were slowed (compared to a control sentence) only in the nonequibiased condition. This finding makes sense because the less frequent meaning was the one intended. In contrast, when the clause necessary to resolve the ambiguity came *after* the ambiguous word, readers were slowed by ambiguities that were equibiased (i.e., had two meanings of equal frequency). Apparently, keeping track of both meanings required extra processing time.

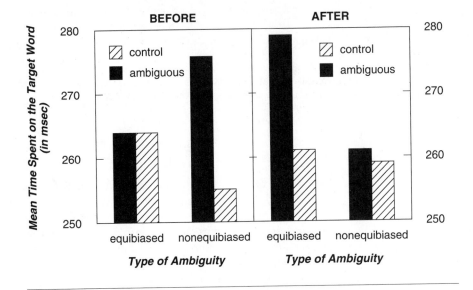

are consistent with those of priming studies showing that multiple access is often obtained when subordinate meanings are intended. In contrast, the equibiased ambiguous words were read just like unambiguous words in these contexts. Apparently, the prior sentence context allowed the subjects to selectively access one meaning of the equibiased ambiguous words.

The pattern was just the opposite when the resolving sentence context came *after* the ambiguous word. The equibiased ambiguous words were read more slowly than the unambiguous control words. This finding suggests that lexical access takes longer when two equally probable meanings must be activated and either could be integrated into the sentence. However, the nonequibiased ambiguous words were read like unambiguous words, presumably because the dominant meaning was selected and integrated very quickly. If so, the reader would have been expected to have a problem when the later context showed that it was the subordinate meaning that was actually intended. Consistent with this interpretation, when Duffy and associates (1988) examined reading times for the region in which the ambiguity was resolved, they found that this region of the text was read more slowly when the earlier ambiguous word was nonequibiased.

The overall pattern of priming and reading-time results is most consistent with the idea that a variety of sources of evidence are monitored to help us resolve lexical ambiguity. Contextual support, in the form of concepts activated by the earlier parts of the sentence, serves as evidence for a particular meaning. However, the most dominant meaning is the easiest to access, so it needs less contextual evidence in order for us to settle on the dominant meaning. It is only when the contextual evidence strongly constrains which meaning is correct that context can influence the initial semantic processing of a word. Otherwise, initial lexical access is context-independent. Thus, the data do not support the strongest versions of either the modularity view or the interactive view. Prior semantic processing can influence lexical access, but there are limits to these top-down effects. The bottom-up flow of information has priority.

Syntactic Ambiguity

Although the data we just reviewed do not provide unambiguous support for the modular view of sentence processing (and here the pun on *unambiguous* is intended!), we may still find evidence for modularity of syntactic parsing. Indeed, Rayner and colleagues (Frazier & Rayner, 1982, 1987; Rayner, Carlson & Frazier, 1983) have argued that, during comprehension, people commit to a particular syntactic parsing of an ambiguous sentence and that this process is unaffected by semantic processing until comprehension of the sentence falters. But the question remains: When a sentence is syntactically ambiguous, on what basis do we commit to parsing the sentence in a particular way?

Parsing Strategies.   According to Frazier (1987), our initial attempt to parse a sentence follows a single general principle: Use the simplest, easiest-to-construct phrase structure tree possible. Frazier and colleagues (Frazier, 1987; Rayner, Carlson & Frazier, 1983) have studied the strategies that people use to keep their initial syntactic parsing as simple as possible. One such strategy is to minimize cognitive effort through **late closure**. Late closure refers to the process of trying to attach new parts of a sentence to the phrase or clause that is currently being processed. I can demonstrate late closure with sentence (10):

(10) Martin had a date with the sister of the teacher who was named in the newspaper last week.

Who was it whose name appeared in the newspaper last week—the *sister* or the *teacher*? If you determined that it was the teacher whom the newspaper named, then you followed the strategy of late closure. You attached the relative clause *who was named in the newspaper* to *the teacher* because it was the most recently processed noun phrase. Attaching the relative clause to the nonadjacent noun phrase, *the sister*, would probably require more time and working-memory capacity.

Another strategy that Frazier (1987) claims we use to minimize the cognitive load of syntactic parsing is **minimal attachment**. Minimal attachment refers to the process of trying to attach new clauses in a way that is both syntactically legal *and* apt to result in the fewest nodes in the phrase structure tree. Figure 7.3 shows two possible phrase structures for sentence (11):

(11) The spy saw the cop with binoculars but the cop didn't see him.

| FIGURE 7.3 | The Minimal Attachment Strategy |

Two possible phrase structure trees for the same sentence are shown. Panel A shows the parsing that occurs when minimal attachment of the PP *with binoculars* is used, whereas Panel B demonstrates nonminimal attachment. The difference is that an extra node is required to capture the meaning that it is the cop who has the binoculars (Panel B). According to Frazier (1987), our initial parsing of this sentence follows minimal attachment because it is the simpler way to parse the sentence.

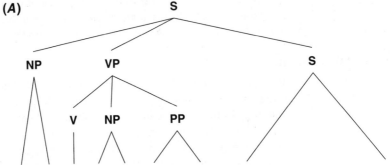

(A)

The spy saw the cop with binoculars but the cop didn't see him.

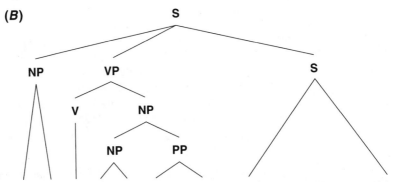

(B)

The spy saw the cop with binoculars but the cop didn't see him.

If the sentence is parsed so that minimal attachment is followed, then it is the spy who has the binoculars. Alternatively, it could be the cop who has the binoculars; but, as you can see from the figure, this phrase structure requires an extra node. Because creating a phrase structure with more nodes is thought to require access to more syntactic rules (Frazier & Fodor, 1978), nonminimal attachment may be more effortful.

Remember, the justification for both the minimal attachment and the late closure strategies is that they minimize the cognitive effort required for syntactic parsing. So, you shouldn't think of these two strategies as two options, as in "Should I parse by minimal attachment or by late closure?" Rather, minimal attachment and late closure simply follow from the general tendency to construct as simple a phrase structure tree as possible.

Now that these two general parsing strategies have been explained, we can review the evidence on whether late closure and minimal attachment serve as general operating principles of an autonomous syntactic module.

Evidence on the Late Closure Strategy. Frazier and Rayner (1982) monitored eye movement patterns and found evidence consistent with a late closure strategy in sentences like (12) and (13):

(12) Since Jay always jogs a mile seems like a short distance to him.

(13) Since Jay always jogs a mile this seems like a short distance to him.

As you could probably tell just from reading these sentences to yourself, the participants in Rayner and Frazier's study spent much more time on the region after the word *jogs* in sentence (12) than in sentence (13). Sentence (13) is easy to parse using a late closure strategy because the NP *a mile* is correctly attached as the object of the verb *jogs*. However, sentence (12) is a garden-path sentence because readers initially assume that *a mile* is the object of *jogs*. Then, when they come to the word *seems*, it is clear that the NP *a mile* is not the object of the verb.

One objection to this study is that sentence (12) is a kind of "trick sentence," in that it would be much easier to read if there was a comma after *jogs*. People reading this sentence may seem to be using a late closure strategy because they are thrown off by the missing punctuation. However, a comma is not required by English grammar in sentences like (12), and such sentences do occur in natural discourse. Other data reveal, though, that we should probably think of the late closure strategy as an optional parsing strategy that is more or less prevalent depending on the language. As we saw in sentence (10), English speakers have a tendency to attach relative clauses to the most recently processed NP. In contrast, Cuetos and Mitchell (1988; Mitchell, 1994b) found that Spanish speakers showed a strong tendency to attach the clause to the earlier NP. For example, if sentence (10) were read in Spanish by a native speaker, he or she would likely assume that *the sister* was the one named in the newspaper.

Data that confirm the use of late closure as a general parsing strategy, such as the eye movement results of Frazier and Rayner (1982), seem to support the idea that syntactic analysis is performed in a modular fashion without influence from semantic or other nonsyntactic factors. On the other hand, if late closure is an optional strategy, followed only in some languages or in some contexts, then it may be only one of several strategies available to an interactive system.

Evidence on the Minimal Attachment Strategy. Compare the following sentence to the similar version presented earlier as sentence (11):

(14) The spy saw the cop with the revolver but the cop didn't see him.

If we followed minimal attachment to parse sentence (14), we'd end up with the anomalous idea that a spy has used a gun in order to look at a policeman. According to Rayner, Carlson, and Frazier (1983), in dealing with a sentence like (14), our syntactic module initially uses minimal attachment to parse the sentence in the same way that it parses sentence (11). However, we monitor the outcome of semantic integration processes, so that in sentence (14), when we arrive at the anomalous interpretation, we go back and reparse the sentence syntactically. This modular view of initial syntactic parsing predicts that comprehension of sentences that require nonminimal attachment should take longer than sentences in which minimal attachment leads to the correct syntactic structure. When Rayner and associates (1983) monitored readers' eye movements in sentences like (11) and (14), the results supported their prediction.

More recent data, however, suggest that factors other than the minimal attachment strategy may account for Rayner and associates' (1983) results. For example, Taraban and McClelland (1988) suggested that semantic expectations were responsible for readers' behavior in the earlier study. In particular, they argued that a semantic context like "*The spy saw . . .*" creates an expectation that the sentence will describe what instrument the spy used. It was this expectation, they said, rather than the syntactic strategy of minimal attachment, that may have led participants to be momentarily confused by presentation of a noun like *revolver* that could not have served as the instrument used by the spy.

To make their case, Taraban and McClelland (1988) contrasted performance on the sentences used by Rayner and associates with sentences like these:

(15) The couple admired the house with a friend but knew that it was over-priced.

(16) The couple admired the house with a garden but knew that it was over-priced.

In these sentences, the semantic context leads the reader to expect that some information about the house will be given. Therefore, even though sentence (16) requires nonminimal attachment in order to be sensible, Taraban and McClellend (1988) believed that it would be processed more easily than sentence (15), which follows minimal attachment but violates semantic expectations. Results for the critical region of each type of sentence are shown in Figure 7.4.

In Taraban and McClelland's (1988) study, it seems that the semantic content of the sentence, not the general principle of minimal attachment, determined how a new phrase is initially attached to the syntactic structure. The results of this study do not rule out minimal attachment as a parsing strategy, but they do indicate that even initial syntactic parsing may be affected by nonsyntactic factors.

A number of other investigators have also obtained evidence that semantics can influence the initial parsing of a sentence (e.g., MacDonald, 1993; Tabossi, Spivey-Knowlton, McRae & Tanenhaus, 1994; Trueswell, Tanenhaus & Garnsey 1994). Consider the following sentences used by Trueswell and associates (1994):

(17) The defendant examined by the lawyer turned out to be unreliable.

(18) The defendant that was examined by the lawyer turned out to be unreliable.

(19) The evidence examined by the lawyer turned out to be unreliable.

(20) The evidence that was examined by the lawyer turned out to be unreliable.

Sentences (17) and (19) begin with an NP V structure, which we can usually expect to represent an agent (NP) and the action of that agent (V). For sentence (17), it is not

FIGURE 7.4	**Semantics Can Override Minimal Attachment**

Panel A shows reading-time results that are consistent with the minimal attachment principle. When the semantic content of a sentence requires nonminimal attachment, as in sentence (14), reading time is slowed in comparison to a condition where minimal attachment leads to the correct semantic interpretation. Panel B shows the results that occur when semantics biases the reader toward nonminimal attachment, as in sentences (15) and (16). In this case, the sentence that conforms to minimal attachment, but goes against semantic expectations, is read more slowly.

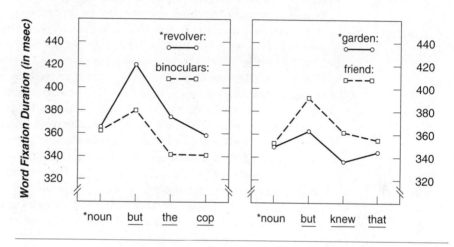

clear that this interpretation is incorrect until we come to *by the lawyer*. So, initially, we might expect people reading sentence (17) to think that the defendant is examining something. In sentence (18), the correct parsing is unambiguous because the phrase *that was examined* tells us that the defendant is being examined. From a purely syntactic standpoint, sentence (19) would be considered just as ambiguous as sentence (17); however, semantics tells us that this NP V structure cannot be an agent-action combination. Evidence is inanimate, so evidence cannot examine something; it must *be* examined. In actuality, then, sentences (19) and (20) are equally unambiguous.

In which of these sentences would people show a delay in reading the phrase *by the lawyer?* This is the question Trueswell and associates (1994) hoped to answer. Their results demonstrated that *by the lawyer* was read equally quickly in sentences (18) through (20). In contrast, sentence (17) exhibited a garden-path effect. Participants took more than 100 msec longer to read the phrase *by the lawyer* in this sentence, apparently because they assumed that it was the defendant who was doing the examining. They did not have this problem in sentence (19) because a semantic factor, the fact that the initial noun is inanimate, ruled out the usual syntactic parsing of the NP V structure.

Trueswell and associates (1994) and MacDonald (1993) have proposed an "evidence-based" model of syntactic ambiguity resolution that is strikingly similar to current notions regarding the resolution of lexical ambiguity. In cases of lexical ambiguity, different word meanings can become activated in parallel, but their strength of activation depends on how frequently they are used. Similarly, the evidence-based approach to syntactic ambiguity holds that different syntactic structures are activated, such that the strength of activation of each structure depends on how frequently it occurs. For example, when we come to a NP V combination at the beginning of a sentence, the agent-action syntactic structure will usually be the one most strongly activated. However, as with lexical ambiguity, baseline frequency of use is not all that is important. If the specific semantic context is strongly constraining, as when a sentence contains an inanimate noun that cannot be the agent for a particular action, then some syntactic structures may be ruled out very early during syntactic analysis.

Although it now seems clear that nonsyntactic information can be used quite quickly to guide syntactic analysis, the data do not rule out some versions of modularity (cf., Frazier, 1989; Mitchell, 1994b). For example, it is plausible that a syntactic module generates syntactic possibilities without any influence from semantics, but semantics can then be used within a couple of hundred milliseconds to assess the validity of the syntactic analysis (Altmann & Steedman, 1988). This interpretation is sometimes known as the "syntax proposes and semantics disposes" view. If purely syntactic considerations always propose possible syntactic structures, which are subsequently pared down by semantic considerations, then the processing system still displays a modular organization. However, the earlier that nonsyntactic information can be used in parsing, the harder it becomes to separate the modular and interactive views (cf., Mitchell, 1989). In short, we seem to be moving beyond the original question of whether sentence processing is strictly modular or completely interactive.

Beyond the Modularity Debate: New Evidence

Scientists are not the only ones who dig through confusion in search of facts. Journalists and other investigators, too, have had a lot of practice in the last few decades trying to discover how far up the chain of leadership a particular governmental scandal went. When some governmental official is suspected of having engaged in a cover-up, the question becomes, "What did he know and when did he know it?"* Psycholinguists have begun to pose the same kind of question about each subprocessor in our language system. For example, recent research on the syntactic parsing system asks what kind of information can it use and when can it use this information. The "when" in this question refers to both "how early in the time course of sentence processing" and "under what conditions." As you could probably tell from the evidence already reviewed, most of the data on these issues come from research on the processing of written language. Very recently, however, intriguing new evidence has come from studies of spoken language.

Of course, the reason that most researchers of sentence processing have concentrated their efforts on written language is that written language seems easier to study, particularly because word-by-word reading times can be precisely measured. However, Tanenhaus and his colleagues (Tanenhaus, Spivey-Knowlton, Eberhard & Sedivy,

---

* I avoid using male pronouns reflexively when what I really mean is people in general. However, in this case a man's shoe fits, so he'll have to wear it.

1995) have developed a new method for studying the processes involved in spoken language processing. In their methodology, eye movements are monitored as people listen to sentences that instruct them to move or touch objects in a visual display.

To see how this method works, let's examine their data on whether people can use a visual context to influence the initial syntactic parsing of a spoken sentence (Eberhard, Spivey-Knowlton, Sedivy & Tanenhaus, 1995; Tanenhaus, Spivey-Knowlton, Eberhard & Sedivy, 1995). Presented in isolation, sentence (21) is ambiguous whereas sentence (22) is not:

(21) Put the saltshaker on the envelope in the bowl.

(22) Put the saltshaker that's on the envelope in the bowl.

According the principle of minimal attachment, when we hear sentence (21) we initially assume that the PP *on the envelope* refers to where the saltshaker should be placed. But what if this sentence is spoken in the context of the visual display depicted in Figure 7.5? Perhaps in this context, we could use the visual information to immediately determine that *on the envelope* identifies which saltshaker is to be moved rather than where the saltshaker is to be placed.

The question of interest here is whether we can use the visual information very rapidly so that we do not initially parse the sentence as though the phrase *on the envelope* refers to the goal of movement. The typical pattern of eye movements in this experiment is shown in Figure 7.6. As listeners heard "the saltshaker on the envelope," they often looked at both saltshakers, which makes sense because they needed the word *envelope* to clarify which saltshaker was being talked about. What's important is that the participants rarely looked at the envelope on the right (a possible, but incorrect, goal). Instead, they looked at the bowl shortly after hearing the word *bowl*. In short, the participants were integrating the visual information and the spoken words so

---

FIGURE 7.5   **A Visual Context for Sentence (21)**

In this study, the investigators were interested in determining whether people could use a visual context to guide their parsing of ambiguous sentences.

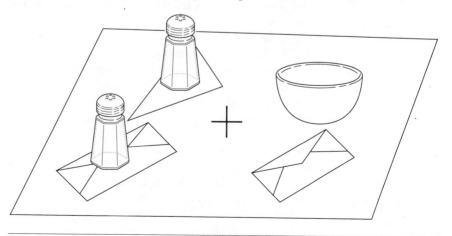

| FIGURE 7.6 | A Test of Visual and Verbal Integration in Parsing |

Shown here are the eye positions of participants as they hear two sentences being spoken—one ambiguous, the other unambiguous. If minimal attachment was used to parse the ambiguous sentence, then the participants should have looked at the envelope on the right.

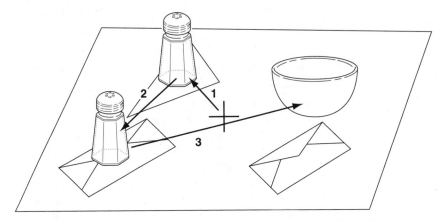

Ambiguous: Put the saltshaker on the **1** envelope **2** in the bowl. **3**
Unambiguous: Put the saltshaker that's **1** on the envelope **2** in the bowl. **3**

rapidly that they were not misled, by minimal attachment parsing, into considering the envelope as a goal.

These data suggest that nonsyntactic information—in this case, visual information from the environment—can affect the initial parsing of spoken sentences. But how do we know that the eye-tracking data are sensitive to initial parsing strategies? Take a look at the display shown in Figure 7.7. Here, you don't need the words *on the envelope* to clarify which object is to be moved. In this case, people who hear the ambiguous sentence apparently do initially parse the sentence so that *envelope* refers to the goal of the movement. This goal shows up as an eye movement that shifts over to the envelope on the right (see Figure 7.8).

The data from Tanenhaus and associates' (1995) study are not consistent with the view that our syntactic processor makes an initial commitment to attaching a phrase structure *only* on the basis of grammatical principles. Indeed, relevant visual information, when available, can be used to guide syntactic commitments. It may still be true that several possible syntactic structures are generated in all contexts and that we select one on the basis of the visual information. However, there is a larger issue here than whether any version of a modular syntactic parser can account for the data. What is remarkable to contemplate is the amount of information that we are able to rapidly coordinate during sentence processing. Using the experimental materials reviewed in this section, researchers have found that people can integrate a visual display, an auditory signal, and general syntactic and semantic information to select the referent for a word as rapidly as *50 msec before the word has finished on the tape* (Eberhard, Spivey-Knowlton, Sedivy & Tanenhaus, 1995).

| FIGURE 7.7 | **An Alternate Visual Display for Sentence (21)** |

Because there is only one saltshaker, subjects do not have to hear the words *on the envelope* in order to know what object to move.

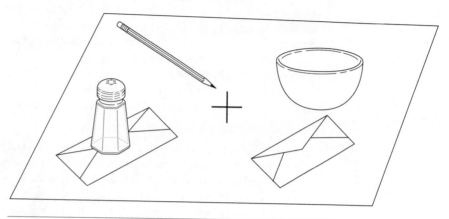

Overall, the data from studies of parsing in both written and spoken contexts confirm that immediacy of processing is the general rule in our language system. Whenever possible, we try to integrate each word into the developing mental representation of what is described in the sentence. This process very much depends on the bottom-up processing of each word. That is, lexical analysis leads to syntactic analysis,

| FIGURE 7.8 | **Another Test of Visual and Verbal Integration in Parsing** |

In this visual context, as we can see from eye movement 2, the ambiguous sentence is parsed in such a way that *on the envelope* is initially taken to be the goal of the movement.

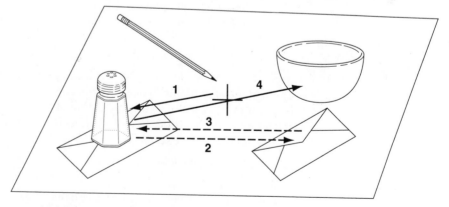

Ambiguous: Put the saltshaker on the **1** envelope **2** in the bowl. **3 4**
Unambiguous: Put the saltshaker that's **1** on the envelope in the bowl. **4**

which in turn leads to semantic analysis. However, the processing is not exclusively bottom-up. When prior sentence information or visual context permits, we can use context to help guide our lexical, syntactic, and semantic processing.

As one final illustration of the flexibility that this type of processing system allows, we'll consider some additional information, unique to spoken language, that may facilitate parsing. Specifically, we are able to use speakers' intonations and pauses, the *prosody* of speech, to divide speech into clauses. Although in many cases speakers are too variable in their stresses and pauses for us to rely strongly on prosody, there do seem to be some reliable prosodic cues to parsing (e.g., Ferreira, Anes & Horine, 1996). For a demonstration of one such cue, read sentence (22) aloud—the first time with no distinct pauses, and the second time with a clear pause where the asterisk occurs:

(22) After Bill left (*) Tamara returned home.

Without the pause, the sentence leads to a garden-path effect because *Tamara* is taken to be part of a verb phrase. With the pause, however, the sentence is easily parsed. Thus, we can add prosody to the list of cues that we use to direct sentence comprehension processes. Although psycholinguists do not yet know the time course of the integration of all the different kinds of information that affect lexical access and parsing, it is clear that sentence processing is guided by multiple kinds of information. In the next section, we will explore this general scheme of language processing in connection with the semantic and pragmatic information needed to understand sentences that are not intended to be taken literally.

Beyond Literal Meaning

As the philosopher J. L. Austin (1962) once reminded those of us interested in language, sentences do more than describe some state of affairs in the world, or even in possible worlds. An utterance, he said, is often a kind of act that produces a particular result. We should keep this observation in mind, as many of the most notable sentences in history are important for the act they represented. Consider sentence (23), for example:

(23) No Freeman shall be taken, or imprisoned, or be disseised of his Freehold, or Liberties, or free Customs, or be outlawed, or exiled, or any otherwise destroyed; *nor will we pass upon him, nor condemn,* but by lawful judgment of his Peers, or by the Law of the Land.

This sentence, from the *Magna Carta,* which was produced in 1215, established the principle that the accused should not be condemned without a fair trial. It is part of a proclamation that has served as the foundation of the concept of individual liberty throughout much of the world. In one sense, its meaning is the same as that of the following simple descriptive sentence:

(24) In England, people accused of a crime have the right to a trial.

In another sense, however, the two sentences are very different. In Austin's terms, sentences (22) and (23) have the same **locutionary meaning,** or meaning in the ordinary sense. How they differ is that sentence (23) has an **illocutionary force** that sentence (24) does not have. Producing this historical sentence involved not just a description but an *action,* the action of promising a trial for the accused.

The same distinction can be made between the following two sentences:

(25) I now pronounce you husband and wife.

(26) So, you two are married.

Sentence (25) is an example of what is commonly known as a **speech act.** A speech act is a sentence with illocutionary force. In this case, sentence (25) produces the action of joining two people in marriage. Sentence (26) has no such illocutionary force. As Searle (1975) pointed out, many statements with illocutionary force perform their action, be it a promise, demand, or request, through an **indirect speech act.** In an indirect speech act, an action is implied rather than directly stated. For example, the sentence used in Chapter 1 to show the need for pragmatics—"Could you please close the door behind you?"—is an indirect speech act. Indeed, we often issue a command only indirectly by asking a question—a question that we do not expect to be answered based on the literal interpretation.

Indirect speech acts are only one of numerous examples of utterances in which the comprehender is expected to go beyond a literal interpretation for the sentence. Once again, consider one of the most celebrated single sentences in Western history, the closing sentence in Abraham Lincoln's address at the dedication of the Gettysburg National Cemetery during the American Civil War:

> It is rather for us to be here dedicated to the great task remaining before us—that from these honored dead we take increased devotion to that cause for which they gave the last full measure of devotion; that we here highly resolve that these dead shall not have died in vain; that this nation, under God, shall have a new birth of freedom; and that government of the people, by the people, for the people, shall not perish from the earth.

Clearly, this is a speech act in which the listeners were asked to rededicate themselves to a cause, and to act on that dedication. The force of this speech act had to be powerful indeed, because what Lincoln was asking for was willingness to risk one's life for the cause. An important tool that Lincoln used to stir the necessary emotion and to acknowledge the seriousness of the situation was the tool of metaphor. For example, he noted that this was the occasion of a "new birth of freedom" and that there existed a risk that truly democratic government could "perish from the earth." Clearly, both freedom and democracy are abstract concepts, not living things that can give birth or perish in the literal sense of these terms. Though a literal interpretation of Lincoln's words would be nonsense, his words were received as both true and very effectively phrased.

In brief, both indirect speech acts and metaphors require something other than literal interpretation.* And as we have seen, the comprehension of sentences is complex enough even when the meaning intended is based on a literal interpretation. How,

---

* Of course, there are several other types of utterances that require a nonliteral interpretation, such as idiom (e.g., "The captured spy spilled the beans") and sarcasm (e.g., "Don't you just love people who use two spaces to park their car?"). Here, however, we will concentrate on indirect speech acts and metaphor because these forms of figurative language have generated particular interest among linguists and psycholinguists.

then, can we explain understanding when the intended force or meaning of a sentence is nonliteral? One response that some people have given to this question is that we can safely avoid, or at least put off, trying to answer it. For example, Bréal (1900) relegated the study of nonliteral speech in general, and metaphor in particular, to the category of "mere stylistic devices" with little importance to the study of language.

Although few psycholinguists today would suggest that figurative language need not be studied as part of the field, there is no doubt that literal interpretation has been the predominant focus of investigation. Increasingly, however, the view that figurative language can be disregarded has lost favor as linguists and psycholinguists have realized the important role that figurative language plays in communication (Katz & Mio, 1996). For example, in his seminal paper "Why Metaphors Are Necessary and Not Just Nice," Ortony (1975) argued persuasively that metaphor is an essential part of communication and has great educational value. In addition, several investigators have noted that figurative language is neither rare nor confined to particular genres such as poetry. For example, in their study of political commentaries and debates on television, Graesser, Long, and Mio (1989) found a unique metaphor for every twenty-five words. And Fainsilber and Ortony (1987) and Williams-Whitney, Mio, and Whitney (1992) discovered that people frequently generate novel metaphors when they are trying to express ideas that are hard to convey directly, as when describing complex emotions. Indeed, these attempts at quantifying the use of figurative language probably underestimate its frequency, particularly when we include indirect speech acts that are used to make requests (Gibbs, 1994).

Clearly, figurative language is an important phenomenon for psycholinguistics to explain. In trying to explain how we comprehend figurative language, two very different theories have been proposed. I will outline each of these views and then consider which view seems best supported by the available evidence.

The Three-Stage View

According to the three-stage view (e.g., Clark & Lucy, 1975; Searle, 1975), we understand figurative sentences by following these steps:

1. Determine the literal interpretation of the sentence.

2. Determine whether the literal interpretation is sensible in the context of the utterance.

3. If the literal interpretation is not fully understandable in context, then infer a nonliteral interpretation.

The essence of the three-stage view, then, is that figurative language is understood through a set of processes that operate only after we check the literal meaning. This view makes a strong distinction between semantic knowledge, which is used in the first stage, and pragmatic knowledge, which is used in the next two stages.

Ideas on how we accomplish stages 2 and 3 have drawn heavily from the work of Grice (1975). According to Grice, people are able to have conversations because they implicitly agree to cooperate and follow the same maxims, or rules. Grice's four conversational maxims are shown in Table 7.2.

When someone appears to violate one of these maxims, the receiver of the message assumes there must be a reason and tries to make sense of the violation by trying to

TABLE 7.2	Grice's Conversational Maxims
Maxim of Quantity	Speakers should say as much as needed to be informative, without saying more than is necessary.
Maxim of Quality	Speakers should say only what they know is true.
Maxim of Relation	Speakers should make each utterance relevant to the context and to what has been said previously.
Maxim of Manner	Speakers should avoid ambiguity by being clear and to the point.

infer a nonliteral interpretation. For example, an indirect speech act such as the one we previously considered—"Could you please close the door behind you?"—appears to be a violation of the maxim of relation because the *literal* meaning of this question has little relevance when you've just entered a room. Because the literal meaning cannot be what is intended, you realize that you must place a different interpretation on the sentence.

As another example, imagine that you are walking down the street and you run into your friend Alf, who always thought his ears were too big. You see immediately that Alf has had cosmetic surgery on his ears, and you see that the surgery was performed poorly. Alf recognizes the look of shock on your face and then utters the following sentence:

(27) My surgeon was a butcher.

The traditional view of how you understand this metaphoric statement begins with the idea that it is a comparison. The subject, or **topic,** of the metaphor (in this case, *surgeon*) is compared to the **vehicle** (in this case, *a butcher*). The basis on which you infer a similarity between the topic and the vehicle is known as the **ground.**

When Alf utters sentence (27), you determine the literal interpretation of the sentence (stage 1); but you recognize that it is very unlikely that a surgeon would also be a butcher, so the utterance appears to violate the maxim of quality identified in Table 7.2 (stage 2). You are sure Alf is still trying to cooperate in the conversation, so he must have another intent behind sentence (27). Thus, you infer that a figurative meaning is intended; specifically, you use your knowledge of the situation to infer that the statement is a comment on the skill of Alf's surgeon (stage 3).

A reasonable question to ask from the perspective of the three-stage view is why speakers, or writers, would violate any of Grice's conversational maxims in the first place. If processing nonliteral sentences requires extra stages, why not always use literal sentences to express meaning? In the case of indirect speech acts, one reason we might use the nonliteral form is that it is especially polite (Bach & Harnish, 1979; Searle, 1975). And in the case of metaphor, there may be several advantages to figurative as opposed to literal expressions. In comparison to their literal counterparts, metaphoric expressions tend to be less wordy and more vivid (Ortony, 1975). Metaphoric expressions also tend to be more memorable and to better communicate feelings (Reyna, 1996).

Given the usefulness of figurative language, it is plausible that people might sometimes violate conversational maxims to make a point, even though extra processing is thus required on the part of the receiver of the message. However, the usefulness of figurative language does not confirm the three-stage view. Indeed, several investigators have challenged the idea that literal meanings must be determined before figurative interpretation can take place (e.g., Gibbs, 1994).

The Single-Stage View

According to the single-stage view, literal and figurative interpretive processes are closely intertwined such that interpretation of figurative language need not await determination of the literal meaning (Gibbs, 1981, 1994; Glucksberg & Keysar, 1990). Some researchers who take a single-stage view (e.g., Glucksberg & Keysar, 1990) believe that we should think of figurative constructs not as a special kind of *linguistic* entity but, rather, as an important part of our general conceptual knowledge. I hinted at this general approach in Chapter 2 in my discussion of the cognitive grammar view of semantics (e.g., Lakoff, 1987b). Recall that, according to Lakoff (1987b; Lakoff & Johnson, 1980), we often interpret literal meaning in terms of metaphoric extensions of cognitive models. The example I used in the earlier chapter was the interpretation of *over* in the sentence *Martha's relationship with Jack is over*. The general meaning of *over* involves a PATH schema, which in turn typically refers to an object moving through space. However, in the sentence about Martha's relationship, the PATH is metaphoric because it is time- rather than distance-related.

As Lakoff and Johnson (1980) pointed out, many sentences that seem quite literal have a metaphor as their basis for interpretation. For example, the metaphoric concept TIME IS MONEY is the basis for comprehending each of the following sentences:

(28) How did you spend your time this summer?

(29) This invention will save you hours.

(30) I don't have enough time to spare for that.

If figurative concepts are involved in the comprehension of supposedly literal sentences, then it is hard to imagine that figurative interpretation occurs as a stage that follows literal interpretation. Moreover, the single-stage view suggests that there is no clear dividing line between literal and figurative sentences. Although some sentences seem strongly literal or strongly figurative, there are sentences between the extremes that vary in terms of how figurative they seem (Cacciari & Glucksberg, 1994; Gibbs, 1984). To further complicate matters, a particular sentence could be clearly literal or figurative depending on the context. Consider the following example:

(31) The sheep followed their leader over a cliff.

In the context of a passage about sheep grazing on a highland pasture, this is a very literal sentence. But the same sentence would be just as sensible, though clearly metaphoric, at the end of a passage about a group of people blindly following a poor investment adviser and thereby losing all their money. At the very least, we must acknowledge that it is difficult to specify exactly what characteristics constitute literal versus figurative sentences.

Given that there is no firm boundary between what is figurative and what is literal, it is also difficult to see how people are able to perform figurative processing only after completing their literal processing. If figurative processing is not performed in a separate stage after literal processing, then how is it performed? One recent proposal concerning the comprehension of metaphorical sentences is that such sentences are understood as **class inclusion assertions** (Glucksberg & Keysar, 1990). In other words, this view treats metaphors as statements of category membership.

Understanding metaphors as class inclusion assertions is quite different from treating metaphors as violations of Grice's conversational maxims. Take sentence (31) as an example. The basis for a metaphorical reading of this sentence is the idea that "Ignorant investors are sheep." In a completely literal sense this is not true, of course, because sheep don't make investments (though they do make deposits. Sorry, I couldn't resist that pun). However, the sentence also represents a class inclusion statement inasmuch as the term *sheep* is being used to represent a category—namely, things that blindly follow leaders. So the metaphor is understood as "Ignorant investors are a member of the category of things that blindly follow a leader." The metaphorical version makes the point in fewer words, but more vividly and more memorably as well.

Evidence on the Nature of Figurative Comprehension

Psycholinguistic studies of how people comprehend figurative language have centered on two related questions:

- Does determination of a figurative interpretation require more time and mental effort than determination of the literal meaning?

- Do we use a different set of cognitive and linguistic processes in comprehending figurative as opposed to literal sentences?

If the three-stage view is correct, we would expect a "yes" answer to both of these questions. However, if the single-stage view is correct, both questions would be answered "no."

The most straightforward way to address the first question is to measure how long it takes people to comprehend figurative and literal expressions of the same idea. In a study by Gibbs (1979), participants read direct requests (e.g., *Please leave the window closed*) or indirect requests (e.g., *Must you open the window?*). After reading a request, the participants had to judge whether a target sentence was an accurate paraphrase of the request.

When the direct and indirect requests were read in isolation (i.e., without any preceding context), indirect requests were processed more slowly than direct requests. By itself, this outcome supports the three-stage view, inasmuch as the participants needed some extra, time-consuming process in order to understand the indirect requests. However, Gibbs (1979) also found that when the requests came at the end of a paragraph that provided an appropriate context, indirect requests were processed as easily as direct requests. If, as the three-stage view claims, a figurative interpretation can be accomplished only after a literal interpretation has been made, then literal interpretations should be made more quickly regardless of context.

Studies of the comprehension of metaphor reveal a similar pattern of data (see Hoffman & Kemper, 1987; Shinjo & Myers, 1987). For example, Ortony, Schallert,

Reynolds, and Antos (1978), who used context-dependent metaphors similar to the one in sentence (31), found that metaphoric or literal interpretations of the same sentence were equally easy to construct, as long as the sentences occurred in appropriate contexts.

Further support for the single-stage view over the three-stage view has been obtained in other studies in which metaphorical meanings were generated at the same time as literal meanings, even without special contexts (Connine & Blasko, 1993; Gildea & Glucksberg, 1983). For example, Connine and Blasko (1993) employed the same cross-modal priming paradigm that has been used to study processing of lexical ambiguity. In their experiment, participants heard simple metaphoric sentences such as *Indecision is a whirlpool*. As the sentence was completed, the participants made lexical decisions to words related to its literal meaning (e.g., *water*), to its metaphorical meaning (e.g., *confusion*), or to a control word. The results indicated that both the literal and metaphoric meanings were accessed simultaneously.

The pattern of data across these different studies clearly shows that figurative comprehension is not just an extra stage tacked onto the end of other sentence processes. Now, consider the second question we posed about figurative language: Does it require a different set of cognitive and linguistic processes than literal language? The data reviewed so far do not answer this question conclusively. It could be that literal and figurative processing involve different processes that occur in parallel, *or* it could be that literal and figurative interpretations occur together because the same processes produce each kind of interpretation. As research is still a long way from producing a complete picture of the processes involved in literal and figurative comprehension, I will not attempt a complete answer to this question. Nevertheless, growing evidence suggests that there is considerable overlap in the ways that both kinds of sentences are processed.

Recall that, according to Glucksberg and Keysar (1990), understanding metaphors is an instance of the general cognitive process of class inclusion. In other words, they argued that we process metaphors in the same way as we perform other types of classifications. Thus, the class inclusion view of metaphor interpretation makes a strong claim that metaphorical and literal processing are not fundamentally different. Much research is still needed for a full evaluation of this view. However, relevant data were reported by Tourangeau and Rips (1991), who compared the features that participants listed for particular concepts in isolation with the features that they listed as important to the interpretations of metaphors involving the same concepts. Here is one of the metaphors that Tourangeau and Rips used in their study:

(32) The eagle is a lion among birds.

Some of the features that participants listed as important to understanding this metaphor were also listed as characteristic of both the topic, *eagle*, and the vehicle, *lion*. The feature *is a predator* is an example of the features in this category. However, other features that were conveyed by the metaphor as a whole were listed as characteristic of only the topic or only the vehicle. For example, the participants listed the feature *is a symbol* as characteristic of the topic but not of the vehicle when these concepts were judged in isolation. Most interestingly, some features were **emergent features:** They were important to the metaphor, but they were not listed as features of either the topic or the vehicle. The feature *is respected* is an example of an emergent feature for sentence (32).*

Of course, the finding that features common to the topic and vehicle help us understand metaphors is quite consistent with the class inclusion view. Yet the importance of emergent features may seem problematic for this view. On the other hand, emergent features are also found when we combine concepts in literal expressions (e.g., Medin & Shoben, 1988). For example, in the sentence "Barb was worried about her empty store because the Christmas season was under way," *empty store* conveys the idea of "losing money." However, by itself, neither *empty* nor *store* conveys this notion of "losing money." It is possible, then, that the phenomenon of emergent features is related to the same conceptual combination processes in both literal and figurative language (Cacciari & Glucksberg, 1994).

In a critique of the class inclusion view, Gibbs (1992a) pointed out that, although many metaphors may be processed as class inclusion statements, this possibility is unlikely to be the whole story behind metaphor comprehension. Indeed, Gibbs (1992a) argued that another key issue in the relation between figurative and literal language comprehension is whether metaphorical concepts affect literal comprehension. Gibbs, like Lakoff (1987b), believes that much of our background knowledge is organized around metaphorical concepts. If so, the three-stage view is not only incorrect but, in a sense, backwards as well. In other words, instead of a scenario in which figurative processing depends upon first finding a literal interpretation, it may be that literal comprehension often depends upon metaphoric processing. Accordingly, Gibbs's central point is that conceptual metaphors guide, or structure, the way we think and how we interpret all sorts of sentences. To understand one of the reasons why Gibbs believes that metaphor structures thinking, try Activity 7.2.

In the next chapter of this book, we turn to the issue of how a connected set of sentences—that is, discourse—is comprehended. However, before we conclude the present chapter on sentence comprehension, it is worth noting that there is support for Gibbs's notion of the organizing role of metaphor in comprehension when people read paragraphs. For example, Allbritton, McKoon, and Gerrig (1995) asked participants to read a series of passages, each one having two versions. In one version, the ideas were based on a metaphor; in the other version, the same ideas were described without the metaphorical connection. So, for example, in a passage about the problem of crime, one version made use of a *Crime is a disease* metaphor. This version included sentences such as "The sources of crime were diagnosed" and "The officials desperately sought a cure." In contrast, the nonmetaphoric version used sentences such as "The sources of crime were studied" and "The officials desperately sought a solution." Allbritton and associates (1995) were interested in determining whether one idea from

---

* Another example of an emergent feature comes from an earlier study by Tourangeau and Sternberg (1982). The statement "Men are wolves" is not intended to mean that men eat meat, though meat eating is a feature of both men and wolves. Rather, what this sentence typically conveys is that men are competitive with other men, though competition with one's own kind is *not* characteristic of wolves.

ACTIVITY 7.2   The Role of Conceptual Metaphors in Interpretation

This activity is based on research reported by Gibbs (1992b). Ask several different people to describe the mental images that arise when they hear one of the following sentences:

A. Some marriages are iceboxes.

B. We felt trapped in our relationship.

C. Some marriages lack affection.

You will need to tape-record these descriptions—but be sure to get permission from each participant before doing so. Finally, play back the tape and determine which sets of descriptions of mental images have the most in common.

When Gibbs examined people's responses to these sentences, he found very similar descriptions of the mental images associated with sentences A and B. Participants reported "seeing" a couple in an enclosure, unable to get out. For sentence C, the responses were more varied, but they included no mention of the couple being trapped in an enclosure. Gibbs (1992b) suggested that the responses to sentences A and B were similar (i.e., consistent) because these sentences are based on the same conceptual metaphor: *Relationships are containers*.

the paragraph could prime recognition of another idea. They found that the connections among the sentences in the passage were stronger (i.e., the sentences primed each other more strongly) in the version containing a metaphor. This result suggests that metaphors play an important role in organizing ideas in memory. It also supports the contention that literal comprehension and figurative comprehension are quite interactive.

CONCLUSIONS

The Interrelations Among Language Processes

It is interesting to note how the issue of ambiguity runs through virtually all the research we have reviewed in this chapter. Even in the studies of figurative comprehension, we can view the problem as one of resolving ambiguity over whether a sentence is intended literally or figuratively. In fact, the issue of conceptual metaphors as a basis for literal comprehension brings us full circle to the first major topic of this chapter: lexical ambiguity. Recall that some words may become polysemous through metaphorical extension (Sweetser, 1991). In sentence (1), at the beginning of the chapter, the word *bullpen* referred to a relief pitcher in a baseball game. Of course, *bullpen* can also refer to an enclosure for bulls. The two meanings are very different, referring in one case to a baseball player and in the other to a physical structure. Nevertheless, the meanings seem related. From the name of an enclosure for bulls, it is a short step to the name of the enclosure where relief pitchers warm up. Then, it is another short step to the name for the *group* of pitchers who are warming up, and, finally, a third short step to the name for a particular pitcher in a particular game.

As we have seen, then, the issue of ambiguity runs consistently throughout this chapter; but bear in mind that resolving different kinds of ambiguity requires different forms of knowledge. The general conception of the components of language processing outlined at the beginning of the chapter (see Figure 7.1) seems to be a reasonable way to view the different jobs we must accomplish in order to comprehend sentences. For instance, we can distinguish lexical processes from syntax, and we can distinguish purely syntactic influences on sentence analysis from semantic considerations that guide interpretation. Although the distinction between semantics and pragmatics has become fuzzier for researchers in the field, the two can, in principle, be considered different kinds of knowledge.

The key point of this chapter is that the mental mechanisms that accomplish all these different processes are in close communication with one another. The hypothesis I introduced at the beginning of the chapter has not received strong support because, with sufficient context, even "early" lexical and syntactic processes have been shown to receive some guidance from "later" semantic processes. Although the data do not completely refute the possibility that some processes are accomplished in a modular fashion, if modules exist, the time in which they process information without higher-level input must be quite brief. The data we have reviewed *are* consistent with the idea of a predominance of bottom-up processing unless the context is strong, but it appears that not all bottom-up processing is literal. Indeed, literal and figurative interpretation can take place in parallel.

Given the interrelatedness of various language processes, a reasonable (if tentative) conclusion is that the strong modular view needs revision. In short, language seems to involve different "subprocessors" that perform lexical analysis, syntactic parsing, and so on. These subprocessors work mostly with bottom-up information, but not exclusively. In other words, sentence comprehension is also sensitive to context. In the next couple of chapters, we'll extend this notion by looking at how context affects more global aspects of the comprehension and production of language.

CHAPTER REVIEW

Checking Your Understanding

Key Terms

class inclusion assertions (227)
emergent features (228)
garden-path sentence (208)
ground (225)
illocutionary force (222)

immediacy of interpretation (207)
indirect speech act (223)
late closure (213)
lexical ambiguity (207)
locutionary meaning (222)

minimal attachment (213)
polysemous (209)
speech act (223)

syntactic ambiguity (208)
topic (225)
vehicle (225)

Review Questions

1. What experimental evidence supports the principle of immediacy of interpretation?

2. What evidence suggests that initial lexical access is unaffected by semantic context? What evidence supports the idea that lexical access is performed in an interactive fashion?

3. Why are garden-path sentences often used to study how people perform syntactic parsing?

4. What evidence supports the hypothesis that people use late closure and minimal attachment strategies to parse sentences?

5. What evidence supports the hypothesis that even "early" syntactic parsing can be guided by nonsyntactic information?

6. Generate examples of sentences that have illocutionary force. Here's a hint: Think of the sentences you might hear in the context of legal or governmental proceedings, sports, and ceremonies. Note that most of

these speech acts are direct rather than indirect. Can you describe some of the differences between direct and indirect speech acts?

7. People usually follow Grice's maxims in conversation, but not always. For each maxim, describe how its use would be affected if the context of conversation was salary negotiations between management and labor. What if the context is a discussion between a teenager and her parents about plans for Friday night?

8. Generate examples of sentences that could be true both literally and metaphorically. Why are such sentences a problem for the three-stage view of figurative language processing?

9. What experimental evidence shows that figurative language is not always interpreted literally before a figurative interpretation is made?

On Further Reflection . . .

1. Osgood (1971) came up with perhaps the best example of the problem of ambiguity in sentence processing:

   Light lights lightly light light lights.

   This is a grammatical sentence with a sensible meaning. See if you can come up with a more natural sounding paraphrase. As you try to find a paraphrase, how are you making use of lexical information? And in what way is syntactic information involved in your understanding of Osgood's sentence? For example, how do you know whether to treat a particular word in the sentence as a

   noun, verb, adjective, or adverb? Does world knowledge or partial comprehension of the sentence come into play while you are paraphrasing particular words? Osgood's paraphrase for the sentence can be found at the bottom of the page,* but give this exercise a try before you read further.

2. Conceptual metaphors are an important part of the language of scientific explanation. In chemistry classes, for example, instructors often use a model of the solar system to introduce students to the idea of

---

* Here is Osgood's (1971) paraphrase of the sentence quoted earlier: *Pale flames gently illuminate airy lanterns.*

atomic structure. In other words, particles orbiting the nucleus are compared to planets going around the sun. Some instructors now feel, however, that this model leads to an incorrect conception, so they speak instead of a "cloud" surrounding the nucleus of the atom.

My point is that conceptual metaphors can clarify or obscure depending on how they are interpreted. What conceptual metaphors are used in the psychology of language? Are network models of semantics based on a conceptual metaphor? How is the computer used as a metaphor? What are the strengths and weaknesses of using the computer as a metaphor for human information processing?

CHAPTER 8

Understanding and Remembering Discourse

A central issue in psycholinguistic research, and a central theme of this book, is the relationship between language processes and other cognitive mechanisms. A noted psycholinguist, Morton Ann Gernsbacher, expressed the issue this way:

> Language can be viewed as a specialized skill involving language-specific processes and language-specific mechanisms. Another position views language (both comprehension and production) as drawing on many general cognitive processes and mechanisms. . . . I have adopted the view that *many of the processes and mechanisms involved in language are general cognitive processes and mechanisms.* (Gernsbacher, 1990, p. 1; emphasis added)

The italicized passage from the above quote is the hypothesis to be evaluated in this chapter. The focus will be on how people understand, and what they remember from, **discourse.** Discourse is defined as a set of sentences that are related to one another in a meaningful way.

Discourse is a very appropriate context in which to investigate the hypothesis that comprehension depends on general cognitive mechanisms because, unlike single words, or even single sentences, discourse typically provides or suggests an extensive background for processing the information that is provided. Thus, comprehension of discourse is a good context in which to observe whether general world knowledge and other general aspects of cognition penetrate and influence more language-specific mechanisms.

Of course, to appreciate the context that discourse provides, we have to connect ideas from different sentences together. How we make these connections, and whether the connections are based mainly on text-based information or on information from general knowledge, has been a subject of considerable debate. It will be easier to grasp the issues in this debate if you first do Activity 8.1.

Forming Connections in Discourse: Local and Global Coherence

The first passage in Activity 8.1 was adapted from a study by Bransford and Johnson (1972). They found that if they presented this passage without an appropriate title, it was very difficult to remember. However, when the title "Washing Clothes" was provided, people could understand and remember the passage quite easily. An important point to be gleaned from the experience of reading this passage is that the **coherence** of discourse cannot always be derived from the text itself. A coherent text is one in which we can establish what relations exist among the sentences. And part of what makes a set of sentences coherent is that we can map them onto a theme, or main idea, such as the schema for washing clothes in the passage used by Bransford and Johnson (1972).

However, the second passage in Activity 8.1 demonstrates that knowing the theme of a passage is not always sufficient for coherence. We must also be able to understand how adjacent sentences in the text relate to one another. In the passage about the medical resident, we know the theme, but the discourse does not seem coherent

ACTIVITY 8.1   Meaningful Discourse

Do your best to get the meaning of each passage below.

Passage A: A Procedure

The procedure is actually quite simple. First you arrange things into different groups depending on their makeup. Of course, one pile may be sufficient depending on how much there is to do. If you have to go somewhere else due to lack of facilities, that is the next step; otherwise you are pretty well set. It is better to do too few things at once than too many. Remember, mistakes can be expensive. At first the whole procedure will seem quite complicated. Soon, however, it will become just another fact of life.

Passage B: A Medical Resident Arrives for Work

Angie rushed through the doors of the old brick building. She almost ran straight into a shadow gazer talking grim-faced with a blade. With a quick apology, she brushed past them and headed for the pup rounds. She had to know if things were zero delta with yesterday's first hit. After all, what looked like a soapbox derby had turned into a bounceback. No matter what had happened overnight, the past twenty-four hours would make a great story to tell her father, the rear admiral, next time she went home to see him.

You probably found that neither of these passages seemed very meaningful to you. Yet the passages are not gibberish. With some additional information each one is quite comprehensible. For example, try reading Passage A over again, but this time remember that its real title is "Washing Clothes." This title gives you a framework—a schema—for understanding the passage so that all the sentences "fall into place." Clearly, however, there is more to sensible discourse than having an overall schema for understanding it. In Passage B, the text does not seem meaningful even though the title provides a schema to use while you are reading. What you need to know to make Passage B more meaningful is discussed in the chapter.

because of the unfamiliar medical jargon that is used. Because the referents used in many of the sentences are hard to understand, we cannot link the sentences together into a coherent set of ideas. Here is the same passage, except that the medical jargon has been replaced with more commonly understood synonyms (which are now italicized):

Angie rushed through the doors of the old brick building. She almost ran straight into a *radiologist* talking grim-faced with a *surgeon*. With a quick apology, she brushed past them and headed for the *briefing on how the patients* *fared overnight.* She had to know if things were *unchanged* with yesterday's first *patient.* After all, what looked like a *patient going downhill fast* had turned into *an unexpected recovery.* No matter what had happened overnight, the past twenty-four hours would make a great story to tell her father, the *proctologist,* next time she went home to see him.*

Stripped of its jargon, the "Medical Resident" passage is coherent and easily understood. For example, in the first version that you read, you were probably puzzled by these two sentences:

(1) She almost ran straight into a shadow gazer talking grim-faced with a blade.

(2) With a quick apology, she brushed past them and headed for the pup rounds.

Even if you were able to come up with a creative interpretation of sentence (1), you were probably confused by the pronoun *them* in sentence (2). Could *them* refer to the *shadow gazer* and the *blade?* In the jargonless version, relating these two sentences was easy. It seems obvious that *them* refers to the *radiologist* and the *surgeon.* In fact, the jargonless passage would seem coherent even if I did not provide a title. Understanding the theme of the passage would be a by-product of relating the individual sentences to each other.

What seems clear from considering the "Washing Clothes" passage and the two versions of the "Medical Resident" passage is that we can speak of coherence on two levels. In one sense, a passage seems coherent when we can understand the relationship between adjacent pairs of sentences. We'll call this **local coherence.** In another sense, a passage seems coherent when we can relate all the sentences to a theme. We'll call this **global coherence.**

One of the major issues in research on discourse comprehension concerns the role of general knowledge in helping us establish both global and local coherence. As you may recall from Chapter 3, several early studies of memory for text suggested that general knowledge is used to drive the process of understanding text. For example, Bartlett (1932) found that his British participants recalled a Native American folktale in a very distorted fashion. In particular, the participants seemed to fit the story into a schema based on their own experiences. Likewise, Bransford and Johnson (1972) noted that people needed a schema in order to understand and remember the "Washing Clothes" passage. According to the **constructivist view** advocated by Bransford and Johnson (1972), understanding discourse entails a good deal of top-down processing, because information is included in our memory for discourse that comes from our knowledge base rather than from the text itself.

However, there is another tradition within psycholinguistics whose adherents argue that people do not normally construct an elaborated model of a text but, instead, stick closely to what the text actually says (e.g., Haviland & Clark, 1974; McKoon & Ratcliff, 1992). These investigators assert that evidence for elaborate, constructive

---

* My source for the medical jargon in Activity 8.1 was an entertaining book by Tom Fahey (1990) entitled *The Joys of Jargon.*

processing of text comes from the use of "weird" texts that must be read abnormally, and from inferences about how people *comprehend* text that are based on data concerning *memory* for text. They point out that reconstructions or additions that appear in memory for text may not reflect how people understood the text initially (e.g., Alba & Hasher, 1983). I'll refer to this tradition as the **minimalist view** because it claims that elaboration beyond the text is minimal, at least in most circumstances.

According to the minimalist view, people *can* elaborate on a text as a special strategy, but most of the time people concentrate on what is stated directly. However, if local coherence breaks down, people will make an inference to connect the ideas. For example, the minimalist view would predict that a person reading this pair of sentences is unlikely to infer that Mary used a spoon:

(3) Mary poured some coffee and sat down to drink it.

(4) She stirred her coffee absent-mindedly and thought about Rex.

Although you could infer that Mary probably used a spoon to stir the coffee, there is no need to infer an instrument in this pair of sentences, so adherents of the minimalist view (e.g., McKoon and Ratcliff, 1992) would say that you are unlikely to do so. However, local coherence breaks down in the following pair of sentences unless you infer that the spoon is the instrument used for stirring the coffee:

(5) Mary poured some coffee and absent-mindedly stirred it.

(6) She failed to realize that the spoon had been licked by the dog.

In short, the minimalist view would predict that an inference about the instrument used to stir the coffee would be made when sentences (5) and (6) are read, but not when sentences (3) and (4) are read. However, if you imagine a scene of someone stirring coffee, you probably picture that person using a teaspoon. So, if comprehension is highly constructive, you might think that the instrument for the action should be inferred in sentences (3) and (4). Thus, two very different stories can be told about how local and global coherence connections are determined during discourse comprehension. Those psycholinguists more inclined to view comprehension as a specialized skill (e.g., Haviland & Clark, 1974; McKoon & Ratcliff, 1992; Reinhart, 1980) suggest that people focus on establishing local coherence and rely, whenever possible, on information directly stated in the text to form connections between text elements. In contrast, those investigators more inclined to view language comprehension as dependent on general cognitive mechanisms (e.g., Garrod & Sanford, 1994; Gernsbacher, 1990; Hobbs, 1979) believe that general world knowledge and other cognitive mechanisms come into play when people are determining coherence in ordinary discourse. Of course, even from a constructivist point of view, there have to be some limits on inferences. It doesn't seem reasonable to propose that all possible inferences are made when discourse is being processed, because someone could go off on a long chain of associations and never really get back to the text. So, you should think of the two views, minimalist and constructivist, as different points on a continuum representing how extensively knowledge is used to make inferences. Note, however, that neither view occupies an extreme end of the continuum. In other words, neither view proposes that no inferences are made or that all possible inferences are made.

Our goal in the rest of this chapter is to examine evidence concerning the extent to which background information is used to establish coherence and to use this evidence to evaluate the minimalist and constructivist views. We'll begin by looking at how people establish local coherence relations and then move on to a discussion of the information that is used to establish global coherence.

Establishing Local Coherence

If discourse is processed primarily by language-specific mechanisms, then coherence should be signaled by the physical properties of a text. Are there physical cues in discourse that allow us to make connections between sentences? Indeed, there are many such cues. They are known as **cohesion devices**. Table 8.1 gives several examples. In most of these devices, there is an **anaphor** and an **antecedent**. An anaphor is a term that gets its meaning from another expression, typically one that precedes it in the text. The term to which the anaphor refers is known as the antecedent. Establishing cohesion by using an anaphor is known as **anaphoric reference**. We will focus on how people process two forms of anaphoric reference: noun phrases used as lexical anaphors and pronouns used as coreferential anaphors. In particular, what we need to know is how people understand anaphoric devices, and whether these kinds of explicit text devices are sufficient to explain local coherence.

Noun Phrase Anaphors. The foundation for understanding how people process anaphoric referents was laid in a series of studies by Clark and Haviland (1977; Haviland & Clark, 1974). Building on Grice's (1975) maxim of relation (see Table 7.5),

TABLE 8.1	Types of Cohesion Devices
Type	**Description**
Lexical	Either a word is repeated or a close synonym is used. (For example, "There was only one *adult* in the room. The *grownup* felt isolated.")
Substitution	One word is replaced with another that is not a synonym. (For example, "Jean was the only *adult* in the room. She hoped another *one* would show up.")
Ellipsis	Reference to an earlier word is understood in the absence of an explicit term. (For example, "Jean was the only *adult* in the room. She hoped another would show up.")
Coreference	A pronoun (or a demonstrative such as *that*) is used to refer to an earlier term. (For example, "*Jean* was the only adult in the room. *She* hoped another one would show up.")
Conjunction	Conjunctions such as *and* or *because* are used to link parts of discourse. (For example, "Jean was often the only adult supervising the children, *because* no one else cared." Note that the conjunction creates a causal link to the proposition that Jean is the only adult present.)

Clark and Haviland noted that most sentences contain both **given information,** which the speaker or writer assumes the other person already knows, and **new information,** which the speaker or writer believes is unknown to the other person. To understand any particular sentence in a piece of discourse, we follow a **given/new strategy:** We locate the antecedent for the given information and attach the new information to the antecedent.

The given/new strategy is exemplified by sentences (7a) and (8):

(7a) Herb unpacked some beer.

(8)   The beer was warm.

In sentence (8), the use of the definite article *the* signals that *the beer* is given information. So, to connect the new information, *was warm,* to the appropriate discourse concept, we need to locate the antecedent for *the beer* in sentence (8). In this case, not much of a search is required because we can directly match *the beer* to its antecedent in sentence (7a). Presto! We have coherence. The beer that Herb unpacked is the same beer that got warm.

Faced with such a simple example, we may find it hard to imagine that people actually have to search for the correct antecedent. So let's consider a slightly more complex example:

(7b) Herb unpacked some picnic supplies.

(8)   The beer was warm.

Like the earlier version of this pair of sentences, sentences (7b) and (8) seem coherent, yet we cannot find the antecedent for *the beer* by directly matching this concept to the same concept in sentence (7b). According to Haviland and Clark (1974), when we fail to find an antecedent we make the appropriate connection through a **bridging inference.** In such instances, the text requires us to supply some information from memory that allows us to connect the appropriate parts of the discourse. In sentences (7b) and (8), the critical piece of information that must be supplied by the bridging inference is that beer is sometimes included among picnic supplies. Thus, we make the inference that the warm beer was one of the picnic supplies that Herb unpacked.

Are these claims by Clark and Haviland just a reasonable story, or do they constitute a testable hypothesis? In their 1974 study Haviland and Clark noted that a condition involving bridging inferences should take extra time compared to a condition in which the antecedent could be found in the prior sentence. Consistent with their hypothesis, sentence (8) was read more slowly after sentence (7b) than after sentence (7a).

More direct evidence that people make bridging inferences comes from a series of studies by Singer and colleagues (e.g., Singer, Halldorson, Lear & Andrusiak, 1992). In the following pair of sentences, a critical piece of knowledge—the fact that water extinguishes fire—is needed if the pair is to be coherent:

(9a)   Murray poured water on the fire.

(10a) The fire went out.

When people read a pair of sentences like these, they can more quickly verify the truth of the bridging facts, such as *water extinguishes fire,* after relevant discourse than after control sentences. Corresponding control sentences for (9a) and (10a) would be as follows:

(9b)   Murray drank a glass of water.

(10b) He watched the fire go out.

Although conditions involving bridging inferences can take extra time compared to conditions in which the connections are explicit, it is remarkable how fast and automatic the process of resolving anaphors really is. This phenomenon was clearly demonstrated in a study of lexical anaphoric reference reported by Dell, McKoon, and Ratcliff (1983). In their study, participants read paragraphs one word at a time. A new word appeared every 250 milliseconds. Along the way, at unpredictable intervals, a target word would appear and the participants had to say whether the target word had occurred in the paragraph. For example, one of Dell and associates' paragraphs started this way:

A burglar surveyed the garage set back from the street. Several milk bottles
    were piled at the curb. The banker and her husband were on vacation.

Then the paragraph ended with one of these two sentences:

(11) The criminal slipped away from the streetlamp.

(12) A cat slipped away from the streetlamp.

If the target word *burglar* was presented immediately after *criminal* or *cat*, the participants were faster at saying "yes, *burglar* was in the paragraph" when processing sentence (11) than when processing sentence (12). This result suggests that within a few hundred milliseconds after seeing the anaphor, *criminal*, the participants had activated its antecedent, *burglar*. Moreover, the participants were not just activating the antecedent; indeed, they were also faster at recognizing that *garage* had been presented if queried during sentence (11) as opposed to sentence (12). The implication is that people retrieve the proposition in which the antecedent occurred in order to connect the anaphor and its antecedent. Other words in the paragraph that were not closely tied to the antecedent, such as *bottle*, were not recognized more quickly after the anaphoric reference.

The data from Dell and associates (1983), and similar results from Gernsbacher (1989), show that we are able to form specific links between anaphors and antecedents quickly and easily. If this type of processing is automatic and is based only on bottom-up information, we might conclude that anaphoric reference is handled by a language-specific module in the sense used by Fodor (1983). However, not all the data on anaphoric reference fit with the simple view outlined so far. In a series of studies, Garrod and Sanford (1982, 1983, 1994) obtained evidence that anaphoric reference can be made quite easily, even if it must be based on a considerable amount of general world knowledge. Consider the following pairs of sentences:

(13a) Simon took his car to the city.

(14)   The car kept overheating.

(13b) Simon drove to the city.

(14)   The car kept overheating.

In sentence (13a) there is a directly matching antecedent for the anaphor in sentence (14), whereas in sentence (13b) there is no such matching antecedent. According to Haviland and Clark (1974), connecting sentences (13b) and (14) should require a time-consuming bridging inference: *The car* is the vehicle that Simon used to drive into the city. But the data do not support this prediction. Garrod and Sanford (1982) found that in sentences like these, the lack of a directly matching antecedent did *not* result in extra time spent on processing the definite noun phrase.

By way of explanation, Garrod and Sanford (1994; Sanford & Garrod, 1981) suggest that when resolving anaphoric reference, we are mapping concepts not in a text-based representation but, rather, in a model of the situation described by the sentences. Thus, in processing sentence (13b) we create a model, or scenario, in our minds that includes Simon driving a car. Sentence (14) does not require a time-consuming bridging inference, then, because we associate *the car* in that sentence with our representation of the car implied by the first sentence.

Clearly, Garrod and Sanford's approach to explaining anaphoric reference is based on the idea that discourse processing is very dependent on general knowledge. That is, finding an antecedent is based on matching the anaphor with a concept in our mental model of what a text describes. Further support for this general idea can be found in studies by O'Brien and colleagues (O'Brien, 1987; O'Brien, Albrecht, Hakala & Rizzella, 1995). They found evidence for a **distance effect** in finding antecedents. That is, it often takes us longer to find the antecedent for an anaphor the farther back in a text the antecedent appeared. However, in cases where concepts are rated as very important to a model of the situation described in the discourse, the distance from the anaphor does not increase the time it takes to make the connection.

In summary, it seems that we resolve noun phrase anaphors by finding the antecedent in a model of the main ideas in the discourse. In turn, this model seems to involve at least some constructive interpretation, rather than a strict representation of the text itself. We now turn to a discussion of anaphoric reference involving pronouns, also called **pronominal reference**, to see if that area of investigation can shed additional light on our key question: To what extent do we use general knowledge to establish local coherence?

Pronominal Reference.   Writers and speakers make extensive use of pronouns. Accordingly, one of the most common tasks we face in comprehension is determining what a particular pronoun refers to. Given what we know about noun phrase anaphors, pronouns, too, should trigger a search for an antecedent. As it turns out, however, we cannot match a pronoun to its antecedent based on semantic similarity as we could when matching up *burglar* and *criminal* in the example from Dell and associates' (1983) research. So, how *do* we match pronouns and antecedents?

One basis for matching pronouns and antecedents is syntactic. For example, pronouns have to agree with their antecedents in gender and number. So, if the pronoun is *he*, we know that the antecedent has to be male. Likewise, the pronoun *they* must be matched with a plural noun. Indeed, studies (Corbett & Chang 1983; Just & Carpenter, 1987) show that people have little trouble matching pronouns and their referents in a pair of sentences like these:

(15) Alan and Patricia left the party.

(16) They left when she began to feel ill.

Nevertheless, there is a distance effect for making these connections: The more separated the pronoun and the referent are in the text, the longer the resolution process takes (e.g., Chang, 1980; Ehrlich & Rayner, 1983). This result suggests that a kind of search process for the correct referent is taking place.

Of course, as useful as syntactic cues are for assigning pronouns to referents, there are many instances in which such linguistic factors are not sufficient. As we saw in the case of noun phrase anaphors, the prominence of a concept in the text affects our ability to link it with an anaphor. In discourse, those concepts that are featured most prominently are known as foregrounded concepts (Chafe, 1976). Speakers and writers foreground certain concepts to keep them in the focus of attention. **Foregrounding** can be accomplished by mentioning a concept repeatedly or by mentioning it first. In particular, the first character mentioned in a passage tends to be the one referred to most often in subsequent text. For example, we have no trouble resolving this pronominal reference, even though it is syntactically ambiguous:

(17) Gina ate the dessert that her sister, Anna, made.

(18) Afterwards, she had some coffee.

Even though both *Anna* and *Gina* agree in gender and number with the pronoun *she*, we easily connect the pronominal reference to *Gina* because *Gina* is foregrounded in sentence (17) in that it is the first proper noun used (Corbett & Chang, 1983; Gernsbacher, 1989).

In addition to syntax and foregrounding, we sometimes use general-knowledge factors to resolve a pronominal reference (Sanford & Garrod, 1981). Note how our interpretation of the pronoun *he* changes based on the overall implication of each of these sentences:

(19) Anthony lent money to Paul because he needed it.

(20) James lent money to Paul because he was generous.

Although the effects of focus and syntactic cues are constant in each of these sentences, we connect *he* with *Paul* in sentence (19) but we connect *he* with *James* in sentence (20). A number of studies have shown that we take general knowledge about objects, actions, and causal relationships into account when assigning pronouns to referents (e.g., Garrod, Freudenthal & Boyle, 1994; Stevenson & Vitkovitch, 1986).

The finding that we take general knowledge into account when resolving pronominal reference helps clarify how we comprehend some types of discourse, but it does not rule out the hypothesis that local coherence depends mainly on language-specific mechanisms. It could be that the initial assignment of pronouns to referents is based on language-specific factors, and that we then revise that initial assignment, if needed.

Recent studies by McKoon and colleagues (Greene, Gerrig, McKoon & Ratcliff, 1994; McKoon, Gerrig & Greene, 1996) shed light on the question of whether initial pronoun assignment is based solely on cues that are physically present in the discourse. These investigators examined the processing of texts with "unheralded pronouns." These are pronouns without a definite referent in the immediate context. As an example, imagine a story in which Roger has broken up with his long-time girlfriend and moved in with Gail. The ex-girlfriend is quite upset and has been trying to win back Roger's affections. Now the scene shifts to Roger and Gail's discussion about a party that includes a lot of Roger's old friends. Gail decides to stay home because she is not feeling well. Roger goes to the party and returns quite a bit later than expected. Gail, visibly distressed, says, "Tell me the truth. Was *she* there?"

The referent for *she* is obviously Roger's ex-girlfriend, and people understand this reference even though there is nothing in the text itself that signals it. McKoon and associates (1996) showed that, in stories like these, in which the two main characters come together at the end, information from the introductory part of the narrative is automatically retrieved from memory. In the above example, this would include the concept of Roger's ex-girlfriend. The information that is retrieved from memory is used to establish the referent of the unheralded pronoun and to maintain the coherence of the discourse.

McKoon and colleagues' interpretation of their data is a minimalist one. They claim that local coherence is based on links between text-based information and those concepts from memory that are quickly and automatically activated by the text. Although they believe that comprehension is made possible by information retrieved from memory, McKoon and associates (1996; McKoon & Ratcliff, 1992) explicitly reject the constructivist view that comprehension depends on the building of an elaborated mental model that guides text interpretation.

Thus, according to the minimalist view, general memory retrieval processes are essential to coherence, but readers or listeners do not stray far from the concepts mentioned in the discourse. Meanwhile, other investigators (e.g., Garrod & Sanford, 1994; Graesser, Singer & Trabasso, 1994) have argued that the minimalist view does not go far enough in connecting comprehension with general cognitive processes and world knowledge. For example, the data on unheralded pronouns could alternatively be interpreted as suggesting that a concept like "Roger's ex-girlfriend" plays a prominent role in the mental model of the situation described in the text. If coherence depends on relating the text to such a model, then it could be the model itself that allows some unheralded pronouns to be understood easily. To help distinguish between the minimalist and constructivist positions, let's consider research on whether people elaborate their text representations based on general knowledge.

Elaborative Inferences and Coherence.   It is clear that some types of inferences are involved in maintaining local coherence. People retrieve information from memory as needed in order to make connections among different sentence concepts. In the examples examined so far, the inferences were necessary in that local coherence would break down without them. But do we also make inferences that are not required for local coherence?

According to a minimalist perspective, the answer to this question should generally be "no," given the assumption that we are building a representation of discourse that sticks close to the discourse content. We use a limited amount of information beyond the text, but this information consists only of those concepts that are strongly and easily activated by the text.

According to the constructivist view, on the other hand, we should expect some elaboration of text. The assumption here is that we interpret the text in terms of the situation described, and that some aspects of the situation are filled in with plausible information from general knowledge. As I noted earlier, however, there must be limits on elaboration; otherwise, any given sentence could send us off on a never-ending chain of associations. Graesser and associates (1994) suggested that, at least in the case of narrative (i.e., story-like) materials, we restrict elaboration to those inferences that help us *explain* the events described in a text. According to this version of constructivist theory, elaborations that help us explain the events of the story should be more common than other types of elaborations.

Psycholinguists have examined several different kinds of elaborative inferences in the process of testing various versions of minimalist and constructivist theories. Early in the chapter, I mentioned one type of elaborative inference that has been studied: inferences about the instrument used to perform an action. As I noted then, the minimalist view predicts that people are conservative about making **instrument inferences** in passages, like the following one, where the instrument is not explicitly named:

(21) Bill dug a deep hole. He put in the young tree and covered the hole.

You could guess that the instrument Bill used was a shovel, but the research on instrument inferences shows that people typically do not infer unnamed instruments (e.g., Dosher & Corbett, 1982; Singer, 1979). For example, Dosher and Corbett (1982) found no priming of the likely instrument when participants read stimuli similar to (21). However, if the context is very constraining about what instrument could be used, or if a possible instrument is mentioned earlier in the text, then people are likely to make such inferences (e.g., Lucas, Tanenhaus & Carlson, 1990; McKoon & Ratcliff, 1981).

These data are consistent with the minimalist view in suggesting that only information that is strongly primed by the context is used to elaborate discourse. But note that the constructivist view does not contend that people make all possible elaborations. Instead, it claims that people make those elaborations that aid coherence, particularly inferences that help the listener or reader form *causal* connections between events.

Another type of inference that has been used to test for elaboration involves **instantiation,** whereby people infer a more concrete concept than the text actually states. Consider the passage below, for example. A category term is used here, but you might infer a specific instance of the category that fits the context:

All the mugger wanted was to steal the woman's money. But when she screamed, he stabbed her with his weapon in an attempt to quiet her.

O'Brien, Shank, Myers, and Rayner (1988) monitored participants' eye movements as they read either this passage or the same passage with *knife* used in place of *weapon*. The investigators were interested in determining gaze times for the word *knife* in the following sentence, which appeared later in the paragraph:

(22) He threw the knife into the bushes and ran away.

If, earlier in the passage, subjects inferred that the weapon was a knife, then their gaze times upon reading the word *knife* in sentence (22) should have been as brief as if *knife* rather than *weapon* was presented earlier in the text. And, indeed, this is the result that O'Brien and associates obtained. The participants instantiated a specific example, *knife*, in place of the general term *weapon*.

Apparently, however, people instantiate only when the context strongly primes a particular instance of the general term. When O'Brien and associates made their passages slightly weaker—for example, by using "he *assaulted* her with his weapon" in the passage above—the subjects did not show evidence of instantiation (cf., Whitney, 1986). Again, these data support both the minimalist view and the restricted constructivist view advocated by Graesser and associates (1994), in that both views predict that people will be conservative in their inference use in these circumstances.

Likewise, both views are consistent with data on inferences that involve cause-effect relationships. Several studies have shown that readers elaborate text representations in order to find the **causal antecedent** for an event (Keenan, Baillet & Brown, 1984; Myers & Duffy, 1990; Myers, Shinjo & Duffy, 1987). In other words, people search for the cause of each event that is described in a text. Table 8.2 shows three pairs of sentences that vary in terms of how easily a reader can determine the cause of the event described in the second sentence. As you would expect, reading times for the second sentence of each pair become increasingly longer with decreasing causal relatedness. Now, however, look at Figure 8.1, which shows the data on memory for the second sentence with the first sentence used as a recall cue. How can we account for the finding that the medium-related sentence pair is associated with the best recall?

Turn to Table 8.2 once again and note that, in the highly related pair of sentences, the causal connection is easy to infer because the first sentence mentions a sufficient cause for the second sentence. Here, all we have to do to bridge the sentences is retrieve the information that beatings cause bruises. In the medium-related pair, we must elaborate on the action to explain the second sentence. That is, to causally connect the medium-related pair, we have to infer that Jimmy's mother acted on her anger by striking him. As we saw in Chapter 3, the use of elaborations to interconnect propositions leads to especially good memory performance (cf., Stein & Bransford, 1979). Finally, in the low-related pair, there is not enough text information to generate an inference that we can be confident will explain the action, so we do not strongly connect the two sentences in memory. Overall, then, the data in Figure 8.1 can be interpreted either in terms of causal elaboration, as predicted by Graesser and associates (1994), or in terms of the inferences needed to support local coherence, as predicted by McKoon and Ratcliff (1992).

As a final example of elaborative inferences that people might make, we'll consider the case of **predictive inferences.** These are inferences in which we anticipate the consequence of some action. A number of studies have presented passages describing actions that could lead to predictions and tested for activation of the possible inference

TABLE 8.2	Varying Causal Relatedness Between Sentences
High Relatedness	*Jimmy's big brother beat him up. The next day he was covered with bruises.*
Medium Relatedness	*Jimmy's mother was furious with him. The next day he was covered with bruises.*
Low Relatedness	*Jimmy went to his friend's house. The next day he was covered with bruises.*

| **FIGURE 8.1** | **Sentence Recall** |

In a study by Myers, Shinjo, and Duffy (1987), participants read sentence pairs like those in Table 8.2. Then they were given the first sentence as a recall cue for the second sentence. The researchers found that the best performance was for sentence pairs with moderate causal connectedness.

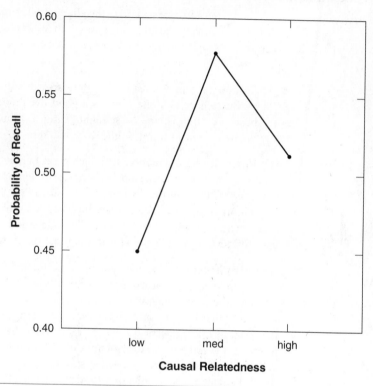

(e.g., Fincher-Kiefer, 1993; McKoon & Ratcliff, 1986; Murray, Klin, & Myers, 1993; Whitney, Ritchie & Crane, 1992). For example, after a passage about someone falling from a twenty-story building, researchers might assess whether the concept "dead" is primed. The findings suggest that, although readers do not routinely make predictive inferences, they will make them if the relevant action is the main focus of the passage and if the context is sufficiently constraining to allow a confident prediction (van den Broek, 1994).

In summary, the data from studies of elaboration could be interpreted as generally supportive of the minimalist framework, inasmuch as elaboration is usually obtained only when the elaborating concepts are easily activated by the discourse and when they are needed for local coherence. On the other hand, the data are also consistent with a somewhat restricted version of the constructivist framework in which elaboration is used to promote coherence by assisting in the formation of a causal model of discourse (Graesser, Millis & Zwaan, 1997; Graesser, Singer & Trabasso, 1994). However, explaining local coherence is only half the battle. We need to be able to explain global coherence, and our explanations of coherence need to extend beyond the story-type materials that are typical in research on local coherence in general and elaborative inferences in particular.

Establishing Global Coherence

Although tying adjacent sentences together is clearly important for coherence, it is not the whole picture. In the following passage, for example, there are cohesive ties between each of the sentences, yet the succession of sentences does not constitute coherent discourse:

> Jill bought a new sweater. Sweaters are sometimes made of wool. Wool production gives some farmers a good livelihood. Farming is a high-risk business. On the news last night, I saw a group of business executives discussing recent trends in the stock market.

What prevents these sentences from being a coherent paragraph is the lack of global coherence. At a minimum, global coherence would imply that each sentence is relevant to the overall topic of the discourse (Reinhart, 1980). However, discourse often has a much more complex structure than this basic definition of global coherence suggests. The structure of discourse is most easily understood in terms of the organization of narrative text, so we'll begin with an examination of that topic.

Narrative Structure.   We have already encountered the idea that schemas influence text comprehension. For example, as noted in Chapter 3, we have a kind of mental script for the events that take place in a restaurant. This script can affect our memory for a story that includes a restaurant scene: As long as a statement is consistent with the restaurant script, it will often be reported as having been in the story about a restaurant—even when it did not appear in the story (Bower, Black & Turner, 1979). We have similar general-knowledge schemas for many common social situations. These schemas affect our memory for text, and, as noted in previous chapters, there is some evidence that they also influence comprehension, perhaps even lexical access processes (e.g., Morris, 1994). As the "Washing Clothes" story illustrated, we have an easier time understanding what each sentence means when we can relate it to a discourse topic.

Let us now consider another kind of general-knowledge schema that is important to narrative comprehension. According to several investigators, people have schemas that specify how stories are organized (e.g., Mandler, 1984; Stein & Glenn, 1979). For example, Mandler (1984) proposed that people have knowledge of the internal organization of folktales and other stories and that such knowledge takes the form of a **story grammar**. This concept is an extension of the idea that grammatical rules specify the organization of the elements in a sentence. In short, a story grammar specifies the abstract organization of the components of a story. As with sentence structure, we can depict a story's organization by means of a tree diagram that captures the hierarchical structure of the story (see Figure 8.2).

There is evidence that readers make use of these hierarchical relationships among story elements when they comprehend discourse. Specifically, a **levels effect** has been found in tests of both comprehension time and memory. Statements from a story that

FIGURE 8.2	An Example of a Story Grammar

Almost all stories have the same basic structure, consisting of a setting and one or more episodes. In turn, an episode consists of an event that, typically, results in an obstacle for someone who then has the goal of overcoming the obstacle. *(Adapted from Just & Carpenter, 1987.)*

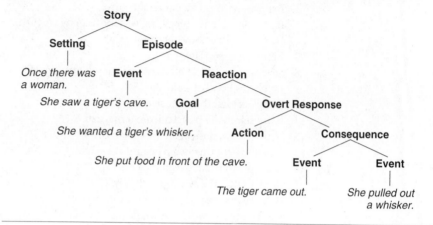

are higher in the hierarchy are read more slowly and are better remembered than statements that are lower in the hierarchy, even after differences in sentence length are taken into account (Cirilo & Foss, 1980; Thorndyke, 1977). In the simple story in Figure 8.2, for example, the goal statement *She wanted a tiger's whisker* is higher in the hierarchy than the event statement *The tiger came out.*

Of course, most stories consist of more than one episode. Sometimes the episodes are embedded, as when a subgoal is developed that is one step toward a main goal. At other times, one episode simply follows another in a sequential fashion. As with complex sentences, it is possible to extend the tree structures for discourse to capture these relationships.

A particularly useful extension of the story grammar concept that can be used to depict the relationships among story events has been developed by Trabasso and colleagues (Suh & Trabasso, 1993; Trabasso & Suh, 1993; Trabasso & van den Broek, 1985). To understand their approach, read the parallel versions of the story shown in Table 8.3; then consult Figure 8.3 for the causal network representations of the relationships among the statements in each version.

The important difference between the two versions is the difference in connections between the goal statement, *Betty really wanted to give her mother a present,* and other statements in each story. In the hierarchical version, this is a superordinate goal that motivates the subgoal in the next episode, *Betty decided to knit a sweater.* But in the sequential version, the goal of coming up with a present is already fulfilled, so knitting a sweater is a new goal, unrelated to the earlier goal.

Trabasso and Suh (1993) used this difference between the two story versions to test whether readers infer the connections depicted in Figure 8.3. Specifically, they wanted to know if readers would show a greater tendency to retrieve the earlier

TABLE 8.3	An Example of the Story Versions Presented by Trabasso and Suh (1993)

Hierarchical Version

1. Once there was a girl named Betty. (S)
2. One day, Betty found that her mother's birthday was coming soon. (E)
3. Betty really wanted to give her mother a present. (G)
4. Betty went to the department store. (A)
5. Betty found that everything was too expensive. (O)
6. Betty could not buy anything. (O)
7. Betty felt sorry. (R)
8. Several days later, Betty saw her friend knitting. (E)
9. Betty was good at knitting. (S)
10. Betty decided to knit a sweater. (G)
11. Betty selected a pattern from a magazine. (A)
12. Betty followed the instructions in the article. (A)
13. Finally, Betty finished a beautiful sweater. (O)
14. Betty pressed the sweater. (A)
15. Betty folded the sweater carefully. (A)
16. Betty gave the sweater to her mother. (O)
17. Her mother was excited when she saw the present. (R)

Sequential Version

1. Once there was a girl named Betty. (S)
2. One day, Betty found that her mother's birthday was coming soon. (E)
3. Betty really wanted to give her mother a present. (G)
4. Betty went to the department store. (A)
5. Betty found a pretty purse. (O)
6. Betty bought the purse. (O)
7. Her mother was very happy. (R)
8. Several days later, Betty saw her friend knitting. (E)
9. Betty was good at knitting. (S)
10. Betty decided to knit a sweater. (G)
11. Betty selected a pattern from a magazine. (A)
12. Betty followed the instructions in the article. (A)
13. Finally, Betty finished a beautiful sweater. (O)
14. Betty pressed the sweater. (A)
15. Betty folded the sweater carefully. (A)
16. Betty put it in the closet for the next time she was going out. (O)
17. Betty was very happy. (R)

Note: The capital letters in this table, as well as in Figure 8.3, refer to the following story elements: (A) action, (E) event, (G) goal, (O) overt response, (R) reaction, and (S) setting.

superordinate goal from memory and connect it to statements 14 and 15 in the hierarchical version as compared to the sequential version. Note that the connections among these statements are logical ones; they are not explicitly signaled by the text. In

FIGURE 8.3	A Causal Network for the Story Versions Presented by Trabasso & Suh (1993)

Arrows are used here to show the causal connections among the sentences in these story versions. Note that in the hierarchical version the goal expressed in sentence 3 is causally related to goals and actions in later episodes, but that this is not the case in the sequential version.

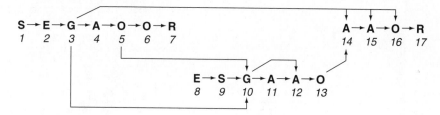

HIERARCHICAL VERSION

SEQUENTIAL VERSION

addition, it is not necessary for the readers to make these connections, because local coherence is maintained even without them. Thus, the connections should be made only if the readers are creating a causal model of the text that is designed to capture global coherence connections among the events. Evidence in favor of the idea that readers naturally form these connections would thus support the constructivist view that readers use general knowledge of cause and effect relations to monitor the global coherence of a passage. In contrast, the minimalist view would suggest that these global connections are not made during reading because they are not needed for local coherence. If the readers had to decide why certain events occurred, they could retrieve the text representation from memory and make these inferences. However, according to the minimalist view, this process of retrieval of superordinate goals is not a natural part of initial comprehension of the text.

The data collected by Trabasso and Suh (1993; Suh & Trabasso, 1993) strongly support the hypothesis that readers *do* make global causal connections during reading. In one experiment, readers talked aloud as they comprehended each sentence. That is, they described whatever came to mind as each sentence was read.* Meanwhile, their

---

* The "talk-aloud method" may remind you of the discredited technique of introspection that was mentioned in Chapter 3. However, unlike introspection, the talk-aloud method requires that people merely verbalize whatever they are thinking. They are not asked to attempt to interpret the nature of the mental processes involved.

| FIGURE 8.4 | **Priming of Sentence Recognition in Trabasso and Suh (1993)** |

Shown here is the mean priming effect at various test points in the two story versions presented in Table 8.3. (The numerals in parentheses refer to the sentence numbers in the table.) The priming effect is defined in terms of how much more quickly subjects verified that goal sentence (3) was presented earlier in the passage when they read the hierarchical version rather than the sequential version. Thus, higher values reflect *faster* processing in the hierarchical condition. The data suggest that the earlier, superordinate goal is reactivated in memory when an action related to that goal is performed.

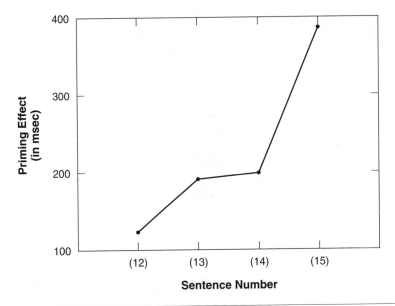

statements were recorded, so that the content could be scored later. The investigators were interested in determining whether subjects were more likely to make explicit references back to the superordinate goal when they read statements 14 and 15 in the hierarchical version than when they read the same statements in the sequential version. As it turns out, most of the participants mentioned the superordinate goal when reading statements 14 and 15 in the hierarchical version, but very few of them made any reference to the goal of getting a present when they read the same sentences in the sequential version.

In a separate experiment, Trabasso and Suh (1993) obtained converging evidence that global connections were being made by readers, specifically by measuring the amount of time needed to recognize that the superordinate goal statement had been previously read. Participants were asked to make this judgment after reading statements 12, 13, 14, or 15 in each version of the passage. As Figure 8.4 shows, participants found it much easier to verify that the goal of getting a present had been mentioned in the story when they were reading the outcomes of the subgoal attempts in the hierarchical version. These data suggest that superordinate goal information is retrieved from memory and connected to subgoal attempts. Other studies, too, have obtained evidence that readers make causal inferences in order to grasp the global coherence of a text (e.g., Long, Golding & Graesser, 1992).

Expository Structure.   Most of the psycholinguistic research on discourse has used story-like materials, yet much of the discourse we comprehend is of an expository nature. This is especially true of college students, who spend a great deal of time reading and listening to discourse that is meant to explain or describe something. One of the main differences between narratives and expositions is that the structure of narratives is much more predictable than that of expositions. In this connection, note that not just the majority of narratives in *our* culture but also most of those in other languages and cultures follow the general story grammar I outlined above (Mandler, Scribner, Cole & DeForest, 1980). In contrast, expositions are organized in numerous different ways. So, in terms of textual structure and the connections needed to maintain global coherence, expositions are much less predictable than narratives (Fletcher, 1986). Investigators have proposed a number of different classification schemes for the logical relations among parts of an expository passage (e.g., Graesser, 1981; Grimes, 1975; Meyer, 1985). A representative scheme is shown in Table 8.4.

Like narratives, expositions can be conceptualized as having a tree structure. However, a difference between the two categories is that, among expositions but not narratives, any of the relationships listed in Table 8.4 can serve as the top-level relationship. The other relationships can then be embedded within this structure. For example, each of the chapters in this textbook has an overall *response* structure because each chapter is organized around a problem (determination of whether a particular hypothesis is correct or not) and a solution (examination of evidence in order to evaluate the hypothesis). In turn, any given subsection of a chapter might involve one of the other relationships listed in the table. For example, some sections contain *descriptions* of theories or particular experiments, whereas other sections provide *comparisons* of two different theories.

The evidence we have examined regarding global coherence of narratives suggests that people do make the necessary inferences to form global connections among the

TABLE 8.4	Relationships Among Expository Text Units
Collection	Ideas or events are related on the basis of some commonality.
Causation	Ideas are joined causally so that one idea is identified as the antecedent and another as the consequence.
Response	Ideas are joined in a problem/solution or question/answer relationship.
Comparison	Ideas are related by pointing out similarities and differences.
Description	General ideas are explained by giving attributes or other specific details.

ideas. So, it seems reasonable to expect that people also try to maintain global coherence when processing expositions. This effort may be complicated by the variability of organization among expositions, however. It follows that we should find evidence that readers track the structure of expository text as long as the texts are of simple to moderate complexity. Faced with texts of greater and greater complexity, readers would presumably need increasingly explicit cues from the texts in order to keep track of the global relationships therein. A number of studies support this idea.

Perhaps the most important part of comprehending an expository passage is understanding the theme. Sometimes an explicit statement, such as "The most important point is . . .," signals the main idea of a passage. Most often, however, readers use sentence position as an indicator of thematic statements. Readers generally assume that the first sentence of an expository passage will be a thematic statement (Kieras, 1984). They then try to connect this statement with the other sentences in the text to confirm that the statement serves as a theme. However, if new information introduced in a later sentence suggests that some other idea serves as the theme of the passage, the readers tend to construct a new theme. This process of evaluating or constructing the main idea of a passage is known as **macroprocessing** (van Dijk & Kintsch, 1983). Macroprocessing is to be distinguished from **microprocessing,** which refers to understanding sentences and establishing local coherence.

Kieras (1982, 1984) observed macroprocessing in action by measuring sentence reading times. An example passage about "metals" is shown in Table 8.5. The average reading time per sentence for a group of participants who read this passage is shown in Figure 8.5.

Of course, the sentences vary in reading time for a number of reasons, including differences in length. Despite this variation, two things are clear from the figure. First,

TABLE 8.5	The "Metals" Passage Presented by Kieras (1982)

1. Different cultures have used metals for different purposes.
2. The ancient Hellenes used bronze swords.
3. The ancient Greeks used copper shields.
4. The Hellenes invaded ancient Greece before the Trojan war.
5. The bronze weapons that were used by the Hellenes could cut through the copper shields that were used by the Greeks.
6. Because the color of gold is beautiful, the Incas used gold in religious ceremonies.
7. The Incas lived in South America.
8. However, the Spaniards craved the monetary value of gold.
9. Therefore, the Spaniards conquered the Incas.
10. Because aluminum does not rust and is light, modern Western culture values aluminum.
11. Aluminum is used in camping equipment.
12. Titanium is used in warplanes and is essential for spacecraft.
13. Warplanes are extremely expensive.
14. Titanium is the brilliant white pigment in oil paints that are used by artists.

| FIGURE 8.5 | **Reading Times for the "Metals" Passage** |

The "good" version of the metals passage is the one shown in Table 8.5. The "poor" version is the same passage except that the first sentence, which is the topic sentence, has been omitted. Without the topic sentence, the reader must infer the topic, resulting in increased reading times for the first several sentences of the passage.

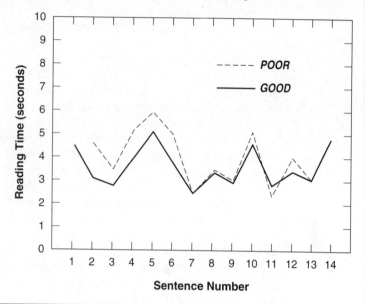

note that the first several sentences took more time to read in the "poor" version of the passage, in which the thematic sentence was not presented. This extra time suggests that the readers' macroprocessing of the "poor" passage was more difficult because they had to infer the theme from the text. Yet once the theme was established, the reading times for this passage were virtually the same as those for corresponding sentences in the "good" version. Second, note that in the "good" version of the passage, sentences 1, 4, and 8 are comparable in length, but reading times for these sentences become shorter as the reader gets farther into the passage. The extra processing time taken on the first sentence of a passage is a very reliable finding across many studies (e.g., Kieras, 1984). It results from the increased attention that the reader gives to this sentence so that the theme becomes well represented in memory.

Kieras's (1981, 1984) data strongly support the idea that readers keep track of global coherence, even when the theme must be inferred. But what happens to macroprocessing when texts with a more complex thematic structure are presented? To answer this question, Lorch, Lorch, and Matthews (1985) measured sentence reading times in texts that discussed twelve related subtopics apiece. They then compared reading times for sentences that represented topic shifts with reading times for matched control sentences that did not shift the topic. As expected, the sentences that shifted the topic were read more slowly. However, when macroprocessing was made easier by the presence of an introductory paragraph that described the topic structure of the passage, topic-change sentences also became easier to process. These data suggest that readers do try to represent the topic structure of a text in memory.

As we saw in the case of narrative texts, the links between ideas that are important to global coherence are usually logical links that must be inferred. This finding strengthens the case for the hypothesis that general cognitive mechanisms are deeply involved in discourse processing. However, texts are not always read in the same way, and readers do not always perform careful macroprocessing. You may have noticed this phenomenon yourself. Have you ever suddenly realized, after reading for a while, that your mind has been on something else? In such instances, your reading involved the scanning of words but only a vague awareness of the meaning of the text. This "shallow reading" is an extreme example of how comprehension processes vary with the circumstances of reading.

Sometimes our reading process seems shallow because of the difficulty of the text. A text with a lot of new vocabulary or densely packed information (as in most college textbooks!) can require so much attention at the *microprocessing* level that the reader may be unable to perform macroprocessing. However, as a variety of studies have shown, **advance organizers** can aid comprehension by improving macroprocessing (e.g., Mannes & Kintsch, 1987; Mayer, 1979; Reder, 1985). By presenting information before the main body of a text is read, advance organizers make it easier for a reader to follow the topic structure of the text. Perhaps the most common advance organizers are outlines and introductory paragraphs that provide an overview of the material to come. These aids, along with instruction on how a particular text is organized (Meyer, 1975), can improve learning from texts.*

In a related vein, Britton and colleagues (Britton, 1994; Britton & Gulgoz, 1991; Britton, Van Dusen, Glynn & Hemphill, 1990) have manipulated text characteristics, such as the number of local and global links that are made explicit in a text, to see if comprehension could be improved. Their findings, along with the other data on global coherence processing we have reviewed, suggest that, in some texts, local and global coherence processes compete for the same limited-capacity attentional or working-memory resources. Thus, manipulations that make one kind of processing easier may improve a reader's ability to perform the other type of processing. As we will see later in the chapter, this idea—that local and global coherence processes may have to compete for general cognitive resources—is a common feature of current models of discourse processing.

Let's briefly take stock here before moving on. It is clear, I hope, that discourse cannot be comprehended using only language-specific processes. There is at least some involvement of the memory system and of general knowledge. But how extensively is our general knowledge used to help us process discourse? Among the studies we have reviewed, there is some support for both the minimalist and constructivist positions.

---

* Indeed, all of the chapters in this textbook are organized around the same "problem-solution" structure so that you, as the reader, can come to expect a certain framework to use for organizing the material, thereby making your macroprocessing job a little easier.

And given that both positions have reasonable support, we can presume there is some truth to each of them. In the next section, I will outline a resolution of the discrepancy between the two views—a resolution that depends on the idea that, in a sense, both views are correct.

Memory for Discourse: The Products of Comprehension

The Nature of Discourse Memory

Even with all the advances made by cognitive psychology toward an understanding of human memory, the popular view of memory is that we have something like a recording device whirring away in our heads. Unlike tape recorders, however, we feel limited in terms of how much we can record at a time—and the older a particular section of our "tape" is, the more information we tend to lose. This "common-sense" view seems to square with our experience of memory and memory failures. For example, if asked to recall the plain-English version of the story about the medical resident, Angie, immediately after reading it, you would have been able to write down most of the passage in wording that was pretty close to the original. But how close can you come right now? What if you tried to recall the passage two weeks from now?

It is when we focus on the apparent loss of detail in memory over time that our memory seems a frail and unreliable record. That is why we are so impressed when we observe "memory experts" performing feats like hearing a long list of unrelated words and repeating it back without error. However, there is a lot more to memory than the rote memorization suggested by the popular view. To see what I mean, consider the case of "S.," a Russian man studied by the pioneering psychologist A. R. Luria. In his book about S., Luria (1965) carefully documented one of the most remarkable cases of "photographic" memory ever observed. You can get a sense of S.'s special nature by trying Activity 8.2, which presents two of the memory tasks that Luria asked S. to perform.

Even without knowing exactly how well you did, I can say with complete confidence that S. beat you hands down on the first task in the activity. Not only was S. able to reproduce the matrix perfectly after a few minutes of study, but, if asked, he could also easily list any particular row, column, or diagonal. What's more, he repeated this performance *months later* without any additional study of the matrix!

I can say with equal confidence that on the second task, you beat S. as thoroughly as he beat you on the first one. S. remembered on the basis of extremely vivid mental images that he formed as material was presented to him. Thus, with prose or poetry he became so caught up in the first few images, such as the exact look of the "old man" in the poem, that he lost track of the meaning of the material. What you find easy, recalling the gist of a passage, S. found extremely difficult.

The point of this story is that "accurate memory" means different things on different occasions. In the context of discourse, accurate memory usually means effective recall of the ideas in the material rather than of how the ideas were stated. Viewed in this way, the "recording device" concept of memory is plainly misleading: With discourse, we can fail to correctly recall a particular sentence in a text, yet still be able to describe the underlying gist of the text in a completely accurate way. Of course,

ACTIVITY 8.2   Two Memory Tasks

Try to perform each of the following memory tasks yourself. Then, for an even more educational experience, put a few friends to the challenge and vary the time interval between study and test in each memory task. How is their performance affected by a delay of twenty minutes? Twenty-four hours? Both of these tasks are based on memory tests that Luria asked S. to perform.

Task 1

Study the following matrix for three minutes. Next, for about one minute, read out loud from a book so that you cannot rehearse the matrix. Finally, try to remember as much of the matrix as you can. How many numbers can you put in the correct place?

```
6 6 8 0
5 4 3 2
1 6 8 4
7 9 3 5
4 2 3 7
3 8 9 1
1 0 0 2
3 4 5 1
2 7 6 8
1 9 2 6
2 9 6 7
5 5 2 0
x 0 1 x
```

it was this kind of text memory performance that led cognitive researchers to conclude that *memory* is a constructive process (e.g., Bartlett, 1932; Bransford & Franks, 1971). But in the previous section, we saw evidence both for and against the hypothesis that *comprehension* is also a constructive process. Our next step, then, is to look at the relationship between the data on comprehension for discourse and the data on memory for discourse. The key discovery in recent research on memory for discourse is that we do not form just one mental representation of discourse; we form several.

The Construction-Integration Model

The idea that we form multiple memories of discourse was proposed by van Dijk and Kintsch (1983). Indeed, this concept is important in several models of discourse comprehension, including the model now being evaluated by Kintsch (1988, 1992). Kintsch's (1988) model, known as **construction-integration theory**, is based on three principles:

- *Discourse processing occurs in a series of cycles.* As each new sentence is input, it must be integrated with parts of the previous information. Therefore, the most

Activity 8.2 *continued*

Task 2

Read the following poem just once at your normal rate of reading. Next, distract yourself for one minute by counting backward from 200 by threes. Finally, in your own words, describe what was happening in the poem. Write out your description so that you can check it against the major elements of the poem. How many of the events and scenes did you recall?

An old man was standing in a grape trough,
Clutching a pole, stamping grapes with his feet.
But the worker in him, grown fierce with greed,
Eyed that river of wine he so revered.

Sunset came as usual, gigantic it rumbled,
Rocking the grass, the wind pounded the old man's hut.
He stepped out of that low wooded trough,
Barefoot entering his hut, now such a jumble.
(Poem by N. Tikhonov; cited in Luria, 1965, p. 121.)

important elements from the previous sentence are kept in working memory so that they can be connected with information in the new sentence. In addition, thematically important parts of the discourse are retained in working memory (or are retrieved from long-term memory) so that global connections can be made.

- *In each cycle there is a construction phase and an integration phase.* In the construction phase, numerous potentially relevant concepts are activated in a bottom-up fashion. In the integration phase, only the most relevant elaborations remain connected to the sentence information.

- *Multiple mental representations are formed during comprehension.* Specifically, construction-integration theory proposes that we form three representations that differ in terms of the kind of information they preserve. The **surface form** preserves the exact wording of each statement. This representation is very short-lived. The other two representations, the **textbase** and the **situational model,** are more lasting. The textbase preserves the meaning of each sentence as an interconnected network of propositions. And the situational model is an elaborated representation. It captures the situation described by the discourse. You can think of the situational model as being more like the sort of memory you'd have if you *experienced* the events in a text rather than read them.

The idea of processing cycles is uncontroversial and has been included in models of discourse comprehension other than Kintsch's model (cf., Just & Carpenter, 1992). As we have already seen in several chapters, the idea that information activation is initially completely bottom-up *is* controversial, but that need not concern us here. The important part of Kintsch's model for reconciling the data from the minimalist and constructivist views is the idea that multiple representations are produced during comprehension.

Evidence for Multiple Discourse Representations

As you probably noticed when you tried Activity 8.2, it isn't that you just forget more and more text as time goes by. Rather, different kinds of information about a text are lost at different rates. Psychologists can get a more precise look at this process by testing recognition memory for sentences that occurred in a discourse context (e.g., Fletcher, 1994; Fletcher & Chrysler, 1990; Kintsch, Welsch, Schmalhofer & Zimny, 1990).

In the study conducted by Kintsch and associates (1990), participants read stories about familiar activities. Let's say that you are one of these participants and you are asked to read a story about going to the movies:

It was Friday night and Jack and Melissa were bored, so they decided to catch a movie. Jack scanned the newspaper. He saw that they could just make the nine o'clock showing of the hot new romantic comedy. Off they went.

The key sentence for your memory test is the second sentence of the paragraph. Figure 8.6 depicts the three different memory representations of this sentence that you might form. Now imagine that you are presented with one of the following sentences and you are asked whether that sentence is one that occurred in the paragraph:

(23) Jack scanned the newspaper.

(24) Jack looked through the newspaper.

(25) Jack looked through the movie ads.

(26) Jack looked over some editorials.

Sentence (23) is the only one you actually read before; but unless you have an especially good surface form representation, you are unlikely to be able to say whether you saw sentence (23) or sentence (24) because sentence (24) is consistent with both the textbase representation and the situational model. Sentence (25) is more than a paraphrase; it adds the inference that what Jack examined in the paper was the movie ads. If you think you previously saw sentence (24) but not sentence (25), then you have a strong textbase representation. Sentence (25) is consistent with the situational model, but sentence (26) is not. If you think you previously read sentence (25) but not (26), you have a good situational model. In short, thinking that you previously saw sentence (24) or (25) is wrong from the standpoint of remembering exactly what the text said, but not from the standpoint of remembering ideas expressed in the text.

Kintsch and associates (1990) reported data on recognition tests like the ones described here. People were tested either immediately after reading a set of passages or after one of several delays of varying lengths. By examining what types of sentences people thought they had seen before, the researchers derived a measure of the strength of each kind of memory representation. These data are shown in Figure 8.7.

At first, memory for the surface form of the text was moderately high, but this memory representation was soon completely lost. The textbase representation became

FIGURE 8.6   **Different Types of Representations for the Same Sentence**

Often, we store not one but three representations of text in memory. The surface form preserves the wording; the textbase preserves the ideas stated in the text, independent of wording; and the situational model depicts the events described, including both text-based information and inferences from general knowledge.

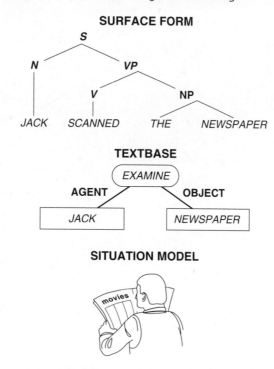

SURFACE FORM

S
N   VP
JACK   V   NP
     SCANNED   THE   NEWSPAPER

TEXTBASE

EXAMINE
AGENT   OBJECT
JACK   NEWSPAPER

SITUATION MODEL

less available more gradually. However, the situational model remained quite strong even after four days. Thus, at least among texts about familiar activities, the memory for the text that is most available to us after a long delay is a model of the situation described. This finding supports the constructivist view that comprehension results in a somewhat elaborated model of discourse. However, we also seem to form a representation of discourse that sticks close to what the text explicitly says. This representation, which is less durable than the situational model, is similar to the one that the minimalist view would say we form.

As Kintsch (1993) has noted, depending on the text or the goals of the reader, more attention could be directed to forming either the textbase or the situational model. Thus, in some circumstances we would expect a weak model and a strong textbase, in accordance with the minimalist view. In other circumstances, however, the situational model could be quite strong and elaborate, in accordance with the constructivist view. (See Just & Carpenter, 1992, for a similar proposal.)

| FIGURE 8.7 | **Forgetting of Discourse Representations** |

Recognition-memory performance can be used to calculate the memory trace strength of each kind of discourse representation over time. As shown in this graph, the situational model remains strong in memory even after a relatively long delay, but the textbase, and especially the surface representation, may be lost quickly.

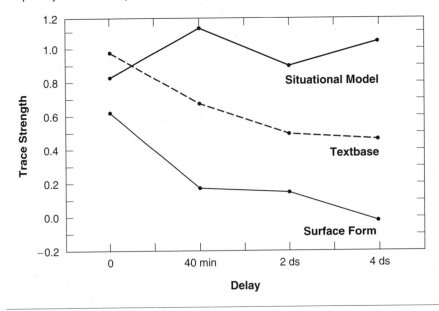

For example, Perrig and Kintsch (1985) found that the way a text is organized can influence the way it is represented in memory. Their participants read one of two versions of a text that described a fictitious town. The information was the same in each version, but it was described differently. The *route version* described the town from the perspective of someone driving through it, so landmarks were mentioned step-by-step as the person moved through the town. The *survey version* gave the perspective of someone looking down on the town from above, so readers could more easily imagine the whole layout at once. The participants who read the route version could paraphrase the text more accurately, but those who read the survey version were better able to draw an accurate map of the town. Perrig and Kintsch's (1985) data thus suggest that the route version led to a better textbase and that the survey version led to a better model of the scene.

These data also suggest that not just the text itself but the reader's goal can influence what kind of representation is formed. The same idea was advanced by Schmalhofer and Glavanov (1986), who examined discourse memory among people who studied a computer programming manual. When the people were told that they would be asked to summarize the text, they formed a strong textbase representation. However, when told that they would be asked to solve some programming problems, they formed a strong situational model but a weak textbase.

Memory and Discourse Reviewed

Overall, the data that we have reviewed on discourse memory, as well as the data on local and global coherence, lead to two important conclusions:

- *Discourse processing is both complex and flexible.* A variety of processes is used to establish local and global coherence and to form the three types of text representations. Moreover, processing varies with context. For example, the degree of involvement of general knowledge in guiding processing depends greatly on the nature of the discourse and the goals of the comprehender.

- *Working memory plays a key role in comprehension.* Although discourse processing varies greatly with context, a consistent feature of understanding discourse—as we have seen throughout this chapter—is that working memory has a key role to play. If sets of information are to be connected for either local coherence or global coherence, concepts must be maintained in working memory or retrieved into it from long-term memory. But because working memory is very limited in capacity, the maintenance of one set of information may mean that less working-memory capacity is available for other needs. Therefore, discourse processing can involve trade-offs. Recall, for example, the evidence that readers sometimes concentrate on forming a situational model to the detriment of a textbase representation (and vice versa).

These two conclusions have important implications for the final topic of this chapter: individual differences in comprehension. There are two main reasons to study individual differences in discourse comprehension, one obvious and one not so obvious. The obvious reason is that the more we know about why some people have good comprehension and others have poor comprehension, the more we can help the poor comprehenders. The less obvious reason is that studying individual differences can play a key role in testing ideas about how discourse comprehension works in general. In fact, as you will soon see, studies of individual differences have recently made major contributions to the testing of the hypothesis that is the focus of this chapter.

Individual Differences in Discourse Comprehension

The first thing to note about differences in comprehension among literate adults is that reading comprehension and listening comprehension amount to virtually the *same* skill in this group. In fact, after about fifth grade, listening and reading comprehension tests correlate highly with each other (Daneman & Carpenter, 1980; Sticht & James, 1984).

The second thing to note is that literate adults exhibit large individual differences in comprehension performance. This is the case even among college students, who, as a group, are generally above average in comprehension performance. In most of the studies we will examine here, college students constituted the participants. The generalizability of the findings may thus be limited in some ways (Perfetti, 1994), but there is no doubt that even within this "select" group a wide gulf separates the better comprehenders from the poorer ones. The question is, What causes all this variation?

The Sources of Individual Differences

To understand why some people comprehend language well while others do not, we need to consider the implications of the conclusion that discourse processing is both complex and flexible. One important implication is that there are a number of potential ways in which comprehension could break down. Therefore, we should be skeptical of "single-factor" explanations for individual differences. If there are many ways in which the system could break down, then we should not expect to find any one deficit that is at the root of all comprehension problems. As you may recall from Chapter 6, the data on dyslexia support this general idea as well.

In addition, given that discourse comprehension is flexible and varies with context, people may use particular strategies to help them cope with a deficit in processing ability. Accordingly, we need to be careful about distinguishing the causes of individual differences from the effects. Just because good and poor comprehenders differ on some process "X," it does not follow that we can assume that the ability for "X" causes the difference in comprehension skill between the two groups. For example, suppose we found that people with poor comprehension tend to be slower at processing anaphoric referents. This does not necessarily mean that their comprehension is poor *because* they are slower at processing anaphoric referents. After all, their deficit in processing could just be one of several "symptoms" of poor comprehension. With these warnings in mind, let's consider some of the proposals that have been advanced for explaining sources of variability in comprehension.

As you saw at the beginning of this chapter, it is possible for your comprehension to be poor, not because of a deficit in your language ability, but because you do not have the relevant knowledge to understand some piece of discourse. The first version of the "Medical Resident" passage was one case in point. However, though lack of knowledge can hinder comprehension, it is uncommon for lack of knowledge to be the primary source of generally poor comprehension.

Of course, people who have trouble reading or comprehending spoken language are more likely to avoid the kinds of activities that help build an extensive knowledge base, thereby further hindering their comprehension. This situation is an example of a **Matthew effect** (Stanovich, 1986).* Perhaps the most familiar context involving a Matthew effect is one in which the "rich get richer and the poor get poorer." In the case of comprehension, an initial disadvantage due to a deficit in processing ability can be compounded because frustration over the deficit leads to lack of practice of comprehension skills, causing the person to fall even further behind.

It is generally accepted that a lack of relevant knowledge plays a supporting rather than leading role in comprehension problems. Indeed, the consensus among language researchers is that comprehension problems arise from deficits in one or more processing abilities (Perfetti, 1994). For example, according to Perfetti's (1985) **verbal efficiency theory**, many comprehension problems are the result of inefficient lexical processing. In cases where "lower-level" processes such as getting access to meanings

---

* The term *Matthew effect* comes from a statement in Matthew's gospel: "For unto every one that hath shall be given, and he shall have an abundance: but from him that hath not shall be taken away even that which he hath."

or phonological codes are not efficient and automatic, these processes drain attentional resources, thus leaving fewer attentional resources for "higher-level" processes such as tracking local and global coherence.

Tests of verbal efficiency theory have generally relied on correlations between lexical processing abilities (such as word naming) and comprehension skill. These lower-level language abilities are more predictive of comprehension skill in children than in adults, but there is some evidence that lexical efficiency can predict adult verbal ability levels (e.g., Bell & Perfetti, 1994; Jackson & McClelland, 1979; Perfetti, 1985).

Another proposal concerning sources of individual differences comes from Gernsbacher (1990), whose view of comprehension is known as the **structure building framework (SBF)**. Consistent with the data we reviewed earlier on local and global coherence, Gernsbacher (1990) believes that comprehension consists of building a mental structure based both on information in the text and on information in memory. The first part of a given piece of discourse lays a foundation, and subsequent sentences are mapped onto the foundation to reflect both local relations and the topic structure. So, we shift from one substructure to another as the story or text shifts from one episode or subtopic to another.

According to the SBF, poor comprehenders develop too many unconnected substructures rather than a fully integrated mental representation. Consistent with this idea, Gernsbacher, Varner, and Faust (1990) found that scrambling the order of sentences in a story disrupted the comprehension of people pretested for high comprehension ability. In contrast, people whose pretests revealed weak comprehension ability scored poorly on tests of story comprehension regardless of whether sentence order was scrambled or not (see Figure 8.8).

Gernsbacher and associates' (1990) finding that story understanding by poor comprehenders is not affected when the sentences of a story occur out of order suggests that these subjects may not be forming well-connected representations for the normal stories either. Why would this be so? The problem is apparently not language-specific, given that Gernsbacher and associates (1990) found the same results regardless of whether the stories were presented in written form, were read aloud, or were presented as a sequence of pictures. Indeed, Gernsbacher (1990; Gernsbacher & Faust, 1991) believes that poor comprehenders are deficient in the basic cognitive process of suppressing the activation of irrelevant information. Like Kintsch's construction-integration theory, Gernsbacher's (1990) SBF maintains that, as a mental representation of discourse is constructed, some of the information activated in memory turns out to be irrelevant to the proper discourse interpretation. And if this irrelevant information is not inhibited, and remains active, it will interfere with the formation of appropriate coherence relations among sentences. In the terms of the SBF, then, too many substructures are built that do not really connect to the real structure of the text.

Consistent with the hypothesis that comprehension problems can be due to a failure to suppress irrelevant information, Gernsbacher (1990; Gernsbacher & Faust, 1991) found that poor comprehenders have difficulty inhibiting the irrelevant meaning of ambiguous words that appear in contexts that bias a particular meaning. According to her studies, the irrelevant meaning of a homograph could be activated in the memory of poor comprehenders as long as 1,000 milliseconds after the proper meaning of the word was made clear from the context.

| FIGURE 8.8 | Comprehension Ability and Memory for Stories |

Scrambling the order of the sentences in a story decreases comprehension for readers with high comprehension ability. However, readers with low comprehension ability are relatively unaffected by scrambled sentences. These data suggest that poor readers may not be constructing a globally coherent representation as they read.

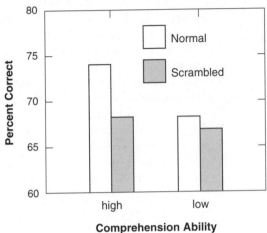

As a final example of a possible source of comprehension deficits, consider the implications of the fundamental role that working memory plays in comprehension. If working memory maintains the information needed to make both local and global coherence connections, what outcome would we expect among people who are unusually limited in terms of how much information they can store and manipulate in working memory? Clearly, if the working memory of such people is overloaded during comprehension, critical information needed to form local or global coherence connections may be lost.

Consistent with the claim that working memory is central to comprehension, a number of investigators have found that measures of working-memory capacity correlate with both reading and listening comprehension skill (Daneman & Carpenter, 1980; Engle, Cantor & Carullo, 1992). For example, people differ in terms of how many words they can hold in memory while simultaneously performing simple arithmetic problems. This task requires that they both store information and manipulate it in their working-memory system. Even though the task is quite different from discourse processing, it predicts overall comprehension ability rather well (Engle, Cantor & Carullo, 1992).

The relationship between working-memory capacity and comprehension is particularly strong if the comprehension task requires language processing that places great demands on working memory, as when people are locating distant anaphoric referents or recovering from garden-path interpretations (Daneman & Carpenter,

1983; Just & Carpenter, 1992). Thus, as the discourse being processed becomes more demanding, poor comprehenders may be less able to use certain comprehension strategies because the attentional demands exceed the resources available. For example, Budd, Whitney, and Turley (1995) found that readers with low working-memory capacity read carefully for details but failed to perform adequate thematic processing when they expected to receive questions about specific details in the passages. In contrast, readers with high working-memory capacity maintained high levels of thematic processing even when they expected questions about details, and their learning of the information in the texts improved accordingly. Apparently, the readers with low working-memory capacity were unable to perform both careful sentence-by-sentence processing and global coherence processing, so they used a reading strategy that de-emphasized global coherence.

Individual Differences and the Language/Cognition Debate

You should not think of the different proposals concerning sources of individual differences in comprehension as mutually exclusive possibilities. For one thing, the various problems outlined above could be partially related. In addition, different subgroups of poor readers may have different deficits. For example, some people may have limited working-memory spans because of the attentional effort that lexical access requires or because their working memory becomes cluttered with irrelevant information, whereas other people may have low working-memory capacity even without lexical access or suppression deficits.

An example of how these various factors may be related comes from studies of language comprehension among the elderly. Some elderly people have normal comprehension for simple sentences, but experience great difficulty understanding discourse that contains long, complex sentences that strain working memory (e.g., Kemper, 1992). This age-related problem in comprehension is attributable in part to declines in working-memory capacity (Carpenter, Miyake, & Just, 1994). In turn, some of this age-related decline in working-memory capacity may be due to increased difficulties in performing the basic microprocesses of language and cognition, such as semantic activation and inhibition (e.g., Hasher & Zacks, 1988; Salthouse, 1994).

Obviously, we are a long way from fully explaining individual differences in discourse comprehension. Nevertheless, the important role that general cognitive mechanisms like working memory play in accounting for individual differences in comprehension supports the hypothesis for this chapter.

C O N C L U S I O N S

The Limits of the "Language Is Special" View

At several points in this text, we have examined the extent to which language processes are "special" and questioned whether they are fundamentally different from other cognitive processes. And in previous chapters, we saw evidence for the special nature of language. However, our study of discourse processing in the present chapter has provided an opportunity to flesh out some of the connections between language abilities and the more general aspects of our cognitive system, particularly world knowledge and working memory.

Overall, the data on discourse processing show that people use both language-specific information and general world knowledge to make the local and global connections that are necessary to understanding discourse. On the one hand, people use explicit text signals and syntactic factors (such as the gender of pronouns) to maintain coherence, and people are conservative about making some kinds of elaborative inferences. And, as we have seen, these findings are in accord with the minimalist view of discourse comprehension, which claims minimal use of general cognitive mechanisms in language. On the other hand, people also make global and local connections based on a discourse model that is constructed, in part, from general knowledge. Moreover, our tracking of causal relationships in narratives and thematic connections in expository text are important examples of our use of general memory and reasoning abilities to understand discourse. These latter findings, of course, are consistent with the constructivist view.

It is when we examine the nature of memory for discourse that we most clearly see why the data support *both* the minimalist view and the constructivist view. People often form both a textbase representation that sticks close to the text itself and a situational model that includes inferences based on background knowledge. So, depending on the nature of the text, and on how memory for the text is tested, a given discourse comprehension experiment could selectively reveal the effects of the minimally elaborated textbase or those of the more elaborated situational model.

The idea that language processing is very dependent on general cognitive mechanisms is further supported by research on individual differences in discourse comprehension. Although some deficits in comprehension appear to involve language-specific processing abilities, the data from Gernsbacher (1990), Just and Carpenter (1992), and others (e.g., Yuill & Oakhill, 1991) suggest that deficits in comprehension also stem from mechanisms that are quite general. In particular, various problems in the activation, maintenance, and suppression of information in memory are important to individual differences in comprehension. Perfetti (1994) has provided a succinct summary of this issue:

> It is quite clear that comprehension requires a massive dose of general cognitive processing. Applying knowledge, making inferences, and solving problems are all patently nonlanguage tasks and are well served by the general cognitive machinery.... This does not mean, however, that there are not some language-particular processes lying at the heart of the story about individual differences. *(p. 884)*

Thus, comprehension as well as comprehension failures are traceable to both language-specific and general cognitive mechanisms. We will build on this theme of the interrelations between language-specific and general cognitive mechanisms in the next several chapters.

CHAPTER REVIEW

Checking Your Understanding

Key Terms

advance organizers (256)
anaphor (239)
anaphoric reference (239)
antecedent (239)
bridging inference (240)
causal antecedent (246)
coherence (235)
cohesion devices (239)
construction-integration theory (258)
constructivist view (237)
discourse (235)
distance effect (242)
foregrounding (243)
given information (240)
given/new strategy (240)
global coherence (237)
instantiation (245)

instrument inferences (245)
levels effect (249)
local coherence (237)
macroprocessing (254)
Matthew effect (264)
microprocessing (254)
minimalist view (238)
new information (240)
predictive inference (246)
pronominal reference (242)
situational model (259)
story grammar (248)
structure building framework (SBF) (265)
surface form (259)
textbase (259)
verbal efficiency theory (264)

Review Questions

1. Distinguish between local coherence and global coherence. According to the minimalist view, in which type of coherence are breaks most likely to be noticed by the reader?

2. Try to identify each of the cohesion devices used in the following passage: *The king's disposition was naturally a kind and generous one. Nevertheless, a king's duties are too varied to be guided by these traits alone. Because of this, the ruler saw that he must also appear strong and resolute.*

3. What role do bridging inferences play in the given/new strategy?

4. What evidence suggests that anaphoric reference involves a search for the antecedent?

5. What types of elaborative inferences seem to be made most reliably during compre-

hension? What does your answer suggest about the basis for connecting narrative propositions together in memory?

6. How does the "levels effect" provide support for the concept of a story grammar?

7. Describe evidence that people form global connections, not just local connections, among elements of a passage as they read.

8. If you know that a poor reader has a specific problem with tracking global connections in a passage, would you expect this reader to have more difficulty, in general, with narrative text or expository text? Explain.

9. Describe at least two studies that show that people can form both a textbase representation and a situational model as they comprehend discourse.

10. How does research on individual differences in comprehension help to support the idea that working memory plays a key role in comprehension?

On Further Reflection . . .

1. Though bright in some respects, Charles has never done well in any language-related subjects in school and always scores on the low end of tests of reading ability. One day he finds himself on jury duty for a rather complicated case. When the jury begins its deliberations, some of the other jurors notice that Charles's opinion seems to be based on several dubious "facts" that surfaced during the trial. Several of these "facts" are mutually inconsistent, and some that came up early in the trial were disproved late in the trial. Strangely, Charles does not see the contradictions and cannot seem to disregard some of the questionable details that were clearly disproved. Explain Charles's behavior from the standpoint of Gernsbacher's structure building framework. Is the SBF consistent or inconsistent with the theory that Charles's comprehension problems are apparently quite general across reading, listening, and event comprehension? Explain.

2. Martha, who, as you'll recall, dumped Jack earlier in this book, is called to jury duty for a sensational murder trial that has already been covered extensively in the newspapers. Martha thinks it will be terribly exciting to be on the jury, so she lies when asked if she has been following the case in the news. She is selected for the jury and hears the case, which lasts several months. Earlier, she believed she could be fair even though she had heard a lot about the case before the trial. During deliberations, however, she can no longer distinguish the information she saw in the newspapers from the information that came out at the trial. It is all hopelessly intertwined in a scenario that she feels is indicative of what really happened. Explain Martha's behavior from the standpoint of Kintsch's construction-integration theory. How important is the passage of time to the problem that Martha is experiencing?

CHAPTER 9

Language Production
and Conversation

sychologists, neuroscientists, and linguists from many different orientations have studied slips of the tongue and of the pen. For example, Wundt (1900) noted that speakers sometimes interchange the initial sounds of words in a way that suggests that the production of a particular sound was anticipated and produced prematurely. Likewise, Lashley (quoted in Jeffress, 1951) cited errors in speech and in typing as evidence that language production is centrally planned, inasmuch as many of the errors involve anticipation of sounds to be produced later in the sentence. Lashley gave the example of the classic old spoonerism:* "Our queer old dean" instead of "Our dear old queen."

Of course, the view of production errors that is best known outside of psychology and linguistics is the Freudian view (e.g., Freud, 1901). Freud believed that most speech errors are not simple confusions of sounds but, rather, the product of unconscious thoughts intruding upon the mechanisms of speech. Thus, in a Freudian slip, the speaker or writer reveals a hidden thought behind the error:

> Among the examples of the mistakes in speech collected by me, I can scarcely find one in which I would be obliged to attribute the speech disturbance to what Wundt calls "contact effect of sound." Almost invariably I discover besides this [sound confusion] a disturbing influence of something *outside* of the intended speech. (p. 73; original emphasis)

One example that Freud cites is the case of a man who wrote a letter to a therapist and complained that he was experiencing anxiety because of business problems caused by freezing temperatures, which destroyed the cotton crop. Intending to complain about the frigid *wave* of cold weather, the man instead wrote, "My trouble is all due to that damned frigid *wife*." According to Freud, this error was caused by the man's repressed anger at his wife over their less-than-satisfactory sexual relationship.

The problem with Freud's view is that it is based on post hoc speculation about a few cases rather than on systematic evaluation of evidence. In recent years, linguists and psycholinguists have taken a systematic look at the basis for speech errors. These investigations have led to conclusions quite different from Freud's ideas. Freud stressed the intrusion of thoughts from *outside* the language system in the creation of speech errors, but the standard linguistic explanations for speech errors emphasize the modular view of language organization. In other words, they maintain that *speech errors reflect the organization of the language system, with earlier stages of production operating autonomously from the later stages* (e.g., Bock & Levelt, 1994; Garrett, 1975, 1980, 1988). This modular view of language production serves as the hypothesis that we will evaluate in the present chapter.

Along the way, we'll look at explanations for speech errors from the linguistic tradition, and consider how the modular view of language production has been bolstered by recent experimental evidence that goes beyond an analysis of speech errors. First, however, we should note that in speech production, as in language

---

* The Reverend William Spooner, head of New College in Oxford in the early 1900s, was so famous for his slips of the tongue that such slips are often called spoonerisms. Another slip attributed to the Reverend was the statement "You have tasted the whole worm" instead of "You have wasted the whole term."

comprehension, there is a major debate over the kind of communication that exists among different stages in the process. Some psychologists believe that the different levels of the language system that are involved in production "communicate" in an interactive rather than modular fashion.

After examining the evidence for and against a modular view of speech production, we will try to get a better understanding of how the language production system interacts with more general cognitive mechanisms by looking at production in naturalistic contexts. Specifically, we will examine the role of language-specific and general cognitive factors in conversation and in the production of written language.

Speech Production and Speech Errors

Why has there been such a long-term interest in production errors? The study of production errors is a specific example of a very general research strategy. Scientists from many different disciplines have noted that one way to understand a very complex system is to observe the ways in which the system breaks down. For example, long before the development of today's sophisticated technology for observing the brain in action, physicians and neuroscientists gained key insights into the workings of the brain by noting the errors in performance made by people who have suffered brain injury.

The study of slips in language production is an example of the same research strategy, but at a representational level of analysis. That is, by studying patterns of errors in production, we gain insight into the normal workings of the language production system. As Fromkin (1973) put it, slips of the tongue and of the pen "provide us with a window into linguistic processes" (pp. 43–44). To see what these errors can tell us about normal production, we first need to survey the most common types of slips that people make. Here are some examples (taken from Dell, 1986):

(1) *sky is in the sky* [anticipation error while attempting *sun is in the sky*]

(2) *writing a mother to my letter* [exchange error while attempting *writing a letter to my mother*]

(3) *pass the salt* [substitution error in which *pass the pepper* was intended]

(4) *slicely thinned* [exchange error while attempting *thinly sliced*]

(5) *to strained it* [addition error in which *to strain it* was intended]

(6) *get its* [shift error while attempting *gets it*]

(7) *leading list* [anticipation error while attempting *reading list*]

(8) *beef needle* [perseveration error while attempting *beef noodle*]

(9) *same sate* [deletion error while attempting *same state*]

The first thing to note about these slips is that they do not involve just a random intermixing of sounds. The mistakes are very orderly in the sense that we can often discern the linguistic unit that is affected. In these examples, errors (1) through (3) involve words, (4) through (6) involve morphemic units within words, and (7) through (9) involve phonemes. Be aware, however, that this list represents only a small sample of the kinds of errors associated with each linguistic unit. You should not infer that, say, phoneme exchanges or morpheme deletions do not occur. Indeed, each category

ACTIVITY 9.1   Observing and Classifying Speech Errors

Try to be very vigilant for a couple of days in noting speech errors made by yourself or others. Write each slip down. Then, when you have accumulated a sample of six or so, try to classify each slip in terms of both the unit involved and the type of error.

While I was writing this chapter, I found myself automatically noting speech errors. To get you started, here is an error I heard recently when a colleague of mine was standing in line at a local bakery. The clerk was both inefficient and rude, so the customers were annoyed by the time they were able to place their orders. When my colleague got to the front of the line, he meant to ask for a cheese twist but instead said:

"Give me a cheese twit."

How would you classify this error? It could be taken a couple of different ways, so see if you can come up with more than one possibility.

of error, substitutions, exchanges, additions, and so on, may occur in relation to each linguistic unit.

A useful way to view these slips is as unintended consequences of the productivity of language. As you learned in Chapter 2, language productivity exists on several levels. Linguists have traditionally explained this productivity in terms of the application of rules for combining units at phonological, morphemic, and syntactic levels. From this perspective, you can think of slips as the misapplication of the generative rules for combining one type of unit or another. If a slip is caused by the misapplication of a rule at a given level, then it makes sense to suggest that in exchanges, for example, similar units are exchanged. Notice how in error (2) one noun is exchanged for another noun. Similarly, in error (4) two word stems are exchanged, even though the suffixes (-ly and -ed) are produced in their proper positions.

The second thing to note about the speech errors shown above is that they demonstrate that an utterance is planned before it is spoken. During the production of a particular phrase, then, many different units and concepts may be available for production. Consequently, various units may "compete" to be produced. This interpretation is all the more credible in light of the two anticipation errors. In each case, a linguistic unit—a word in (1) and a phoneme in (7)—is activated as the utterance is being planned, and the unit is produced earlier than it is intended. The same process may be at work when we produce a word that is not intended to be in the utterance, as in error (3). Apparently, if a close semantic associate of the intended word is activated during planning, it may be produced by mistake.

Of course, I selected these errors because they are clear examples of different kinds of slips. Bear in mind, however, that classification of slips is not always so easy. You can get a feel for the nature of slips and their classification by doing Activity 9.1. Please read the instructions for this activity before you move on.

One way to think of the slip described in Activity 9.1 is to say that it represents a word substitution error. Another possibility is that it represents a phoneme deletion.

Thus, speech errors are not always unambiguous examples of one type or another. However, despite the complexities involved in collecting and classifying slips, language researchers concur that an analysis of the different types of slips, along with an analysis of what a language production system needs to accomplish, yields important information concerning the arrangement of the system's different components, or levels. Based on such analyses (Fromkin, 1971, 1973; Garrett, 1975; Levelt, 1989), there is broad agreement regarding the general outline of the language production system. Its various levels are summarized in Figure 9.1.

FIGURE 9.1   **The Levels of the Speech Production System**

Four levels of speech production mechanisms come into play when we proceed from the message to be communicated to the actual articulation of speech. Researchers agree that the analysis of speech errors shows that slips are often associated with particular levels. However, researchers are divided over whether information flows from the top down only or can also flow from the bottom up.

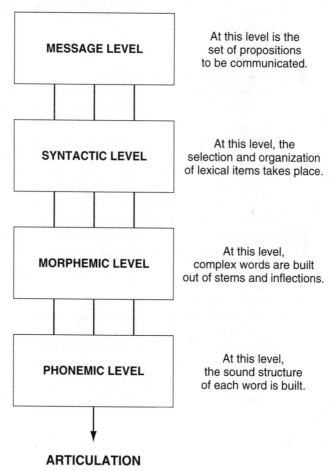

MESSAGE LEVEL

At this level is the set of propositions to be communicated.

SYNTACTIC LEVEL

At this level, the selection and organization of lexical items takes place.

MORPHEMIC LEVEL

At this level, complex words are built out of stems and inflections.

PHONEMIC LEVEL

At this level, the sound structure of each word is built.

ARTICULATION

We start with a message to be communicated. Later, we will examine data on how far ahead we plan utterances while speaking. For the present, however, let's just say the message is a clause or simple sentence that can be represented as a set of propositions. The job of the speech production system is to convert this set of propositions into the appropriate sound sequences. But before that can happen, several intermediate tasks must be accomplished.

First, we have to build a syntactic structure. This structure combines words in a way that conforms to the syntactic rules of the language. Next, we flesh out this basic skeleton of the utterance by building complex words out of morphemic units. Then, we fill in more details of the plan by building the sound structure of each word out of the phonemic units of the language.

Investigators agree that building an utterance occurs in a series of steps at the syntactic, morphemic, and phonological levels. Where they disagree is in trying to specify the nature of the connections among the different levels. Is the syntactic plan built independent of the activation of units at the morphemic and phonological levels, as the modular view suggests? Or is there a flow of information back to the earlier levels from the phonemic level, as the interactive view suggests? Before we address these points of disagreement, let's take a closer look at how the processes within each level operate.

The Syntactic Level

One of the most reliable observations about the slips that involve whole words is that the two words involved in exchanges or substitutions tend to be from the same syntactic category (Fay & Cutler, 1977; Garrett, 1975). This phenomenon is known as the **syntactic category rule.*** For example, in errors (1) through (3) a noun is produced erroneously in place of another noun.

Given that word slips nearly always obey the syntactic category rule, it seems likely that these errors arise as we build a syntactic representation of the intended message (Bock, 1995; Dell, 1995). But how does this process work? Imagine that you have just attended the wedding of Bill and Cheri, and that Cheri's long-time best friend Mandi was the maid of honor. You intend to make an innocent remark to the effect that "Bill kissed Cheri," but instead you say "Bill kissed Mandi." Let's examine how this (possibly embarrassing) speech error could occur.

It is pretty easy to come up with a Freudian interpretation. Obviously, you have long suspected (unconsciously) that Bill is a lecherous cad, so when you said, "Bill kissed Mandi," you were expressing what you think Bill really intends to do at some point, which is to seduce his wife's best friend. How scandalous! How post hoc!

Note that the Freudian explanation, though fun to construct, is neither necessary nor sufficient to account for your slip of the tongue. How, then, can this slip be explained in terms of the language processes that take place? Given the message that you wished to communicate, the obvious starting point is that you must retrieve the words *Bill, kiss,* and *Cheri* from your lexicon. Of course, these words cannot be

---

* Note that the term *rule* is used here in a different sense than usual. The reference is not to a rule that describes the grammar of a language but, rather, to a regular pattern that errors seem to follow.

| FIGURE 9.2 | **Word Substitution in a Syntactic Frame** |

A speaker who intends to say "Bill kissed Cheri" has constructed a syntactic frame that serves as the basic blueprint for the sentence. Slots in the frame must be filled with words that are activated in the lexicon. If the name of Cheri's friend, Mandi, is also activated, the confusion over which item to insert may cause a substitution error.

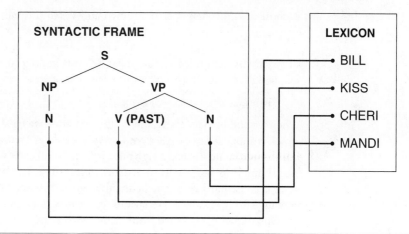

produced in just any order, so you must also build a **syntactic frame,** which provides a structure for the sentence. The syntactic frame contains slots, or placeholders, for the words (see Figure 9.2). Words are placed into the slots according to the syntactic rules of the language. The verb *kiss* (marked for past tense) is placed in the verb slot. And because, in English, the agent of an action is produced first, *Bill* is placed in the initial noun slot.

In this example, the substitution error could have arisen when you tried to fill the final noun slot in the frame. Because your concept of Cheri is closely associated with your concept of her good friend, Mandi, spreading activation has caused both names to become highly activated in your lexicon. Indeed, when two possible words are highly activated, then you are more likely to mistakenly insert an unintended word into the slot in the syntactic frame. An important advantage of this explanation over the Freudian one is that it is easily extended to the other errors, such as (1) through (3) above. Each of these could arise when a term that is highly activated in the lexicon is inserted into the syntactic frame by mistake. In some cases, the activation is due simply to the fact that the word is being used in another part of the utterance, as in errors (1) and (2). However, error (3) is an obvious case in which a close semantic associate is being produced mistakenly. Even Freud would have had difficulty coming up with a sexy explanation for saying *pass the salt* when you mean *pass the pepper.*

Finally, the notion that errors can arise through activation of competing lexical items has received support from experiments on picture naming (e.g., Glaser & Düngelhoff, 1984). As it turns out, people have more difficulty naming a picture if a word with a similar meaning is flashed on the screen at the same time as the picture.

The activation of a word with a meaning similar to that of the picture name causes momentary confusion over which word to produce (Schriefers, Meyer & Levelt, 1990). Furthermore, this may be the same kind of momentary confusion that leads to errors in which the wrong word is produced in the sentence.

The Morphemic Level

Each of the morphemic errors shown above, (4) through (6), involves an incorrect association between a stem and an inflection—in these cases, a suffix. Because stems (e.g., *slice*) and inflections (e.g., *-d*) can be assembled incorrectly, it would seem that stems and inflections constitute separate units in the planning process. Consider the following error, in which *I hoped he would like you* was intended:

(10) *I liked he would hope you.*

When we build a syntactic frame for this sentence, we need a frame for the main verb, which is supposed to be the stem *hope*. However, as Figure 9.2 illustrates, a syntactic frame can contain not just a verb but a layer that indicates that a verb *and* an inflection are required. So, in (10), the past-tense inflection is inserted into the proper slot, but there is an exchange error involving the two verb stems in the sentence. This type of exchange error is known as a **stranding error** because the inflection gets stranded in the sense of being separated from its intended stem.

Note that in error (4), two inflections are stranded when the stem exchange occurs. This example illustrates an important phenomenon in morpheme assembly. Although stems are commonly exchanged in such errors, the inflections tend to remain in their proper place. So, we don't often see errors like *the beeing are buzzes* in place of *the bees are buzzing.*

Like inflections (e.g., *-d* or *-s*), function words from the **closed-class category**—articles such as *a, an,* and *the,* as well as prepositions and pronouns—are only very rarely involved in substitutions or exchanges (Garrett, 1982, 1988). The closed-class category is so called because it tends not to change over time. In contrast, the **open-class category**—which includes content words like adjectives, nouns, and verbs—is always changing. New nouns, verbs, and adjectives are constantly coming into the language.

Why are we unlikely to exchange inflections or words from the closed-class category? Garrett (1982) has suggested that closed-class elements and inflections are unlikely to be exchanged because they are part of the syntactic frame itself and, hence, do not have to be inserted. A mistake might be made in constructing the frame such that an inflection is shifted to the wrong position, but we don't exchange inflections or closed-class words because exchanges are errors of inserting items into slots.

Alternatively, it may be that closed-class items and inflections are inserted into the frame just as morphemes from the open-class category are, but we are less likely to make an error because closed-class items and inflections occur so frequently in the language (MacKay, 1987). In a typical sample of English text, the word *the* occurs about 70,000 times per million words. In contrast, the most frequently occurring open-class word, *time,* occurs about 1,800 times per million words (Burnage, 1990). And, of course, the more frequently an item occurs, the more practice we have had at inserting it into the proper place in a syntactic frame, so the less likely we are to exchange it for another item.

The Phonemic Level

Just as we saw at the syntactic and morphemic levels, there are a number of regularities in the pattern of phonemic errors that give us clues as to how the building of the sound representation of a word proceeds. One of the most important regularities is known as the **consonant-vowel rule:** Consonants replace consonants and vowels replace vowels. The implication is that vowels and consonants represent separate kinds of units in the planning of the phonological form of an utterance (Fromkin, 1973; Garrett, 1975). This is quite similar to the idea that differences between syntactic categories are represented at the word level because errors tend to involve words from the same syntactic category.

Another important regularity in phonemic errors reflects the fact that we use phonological rules when compiling the sounds of words. Even when we produce a slip, the resulting string of sounds obeys the phonological rules of the language. That is, we produce either the wrong word or a nonword with sound combinations that are "legal" for the language. Combinations of sounds that speakers could physically produce, but that do not occur in their language, are not observed among slips of the tongue.

A third regularity in phonemic errors suggests that planning the phonological form of the utterance must include a mechanism that is good at keeping track of the positions of the phonemes within a word. Indeed, people almost never make speech errors in which the initial and final sounds of the word are exchanged, as in saying "dear" when they mean "read" (Dell, 1995).

To account for the systematic nature of phonological errors, investigators have proposed that the sounds for a word are assembled using a mechanism, called a *phonological frame*, that is analogous to the syntactic frame (e.g., Sevald & Dell, 1994; Shattuck-Hufnagel, 1979). A phonological frame specifies the sequence of consonants and vowels needed to form a word, and we assemble the word to be produced by inserting phonemes into the proper slots in the frame (see Figure 9.3).

Imagine that you intend to say "The dog sat on the log pile" but instead say "The log sat on the log pile." As you planned the sentence at the word level, both *dog* and *log* were activated in the lexicon. Thus, both /d/ and /l/ were active enough at the same time to compete for insertion into the initial consonant slot of the C-V-C phonological frame used to assemble the sounds for *dog*.

Consistent with this interpretation, Sevald and Dell (1994) found that they could generate phoneme errors in the laboratory by having people repeat word pairs that were similar but had different initial phonemes. So, for example, in trying to say *pick-tick*, they were prone to say *pick-pick*. The effect was strongest when the two words had similar sounds in the initial position, suggesting that phonemes "compete" to occupy a particular position in a phonological frame.

Communication Among Levels During Production

We have taken a look at how syntactic, morphemic, and phonological planning operate during production. The question now is whether we work through each level from syntactic to phonological in a modular fashion, or whether there is feedback from later levels to earlier levels as we would find in a connectionist network. For example, can the set of phonemes that are activated influence not only the insertion of phonemes

FIGURE 9.3	**Filling a Phonological Frame**

The phonological frame for the word *dog* indicates that it has one syllable, that the onset is a consonant, and that the rhyme portion of the syllable is a vowel-consonant sequence. When slots in this frame are filled by activated phonemes, the intended word is ready for articulation.

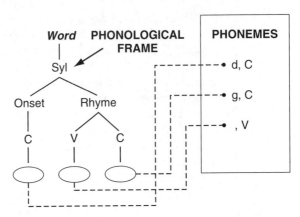

into phonological frames but also the insertion of lexical items into the syntactic frame? This question is important because it speaks to the specific way in which the production system is organized. However, unlike the basic facts of production at each level, the question of how the different levels interact has provoked considerable disagreement.

To test how the speech production system is organized, Levelt and colleagues (Levelt et al., 1991) gave people pictures to name and, on some trials, also presented a spoken word. On these trials the participants made a lexical decision about the spoken words before they named the picture. Some of the spoken words were unrelated to the picture they accompanied, whereas others were semantically or phonologically related to the picture. When the spoken words were presented less than 100 milliseconds after the picture, semantically similar words made it more difficult for subjects to name the picture. Apparently, the spoken words led to semantic activation and lexical access that interfered with selecting the name for the picture. However, when the spoken words were presented more than 600 milliseconds after the picture, only phonologically related words interfered with picture naming.

These data suggest that lexical selection, which is affected by competing sources of semantic activation, occurs early in production, and that phonological selection occurs later as a separate stage. They also suggest that only the phonological selection process was affected by competing sources of phonological activation. This is the pattern of evidence we would expect if the speech production system has a modular organization.

Not so fast, say those who view the production system as an interactive one (e.g., Dell & O'Seaghdha, 1992). Just as we saw in the data on word *recognition*, a system may appear modular in some experiments because the predominant flow of information is in a particular direction. So, for example, there is evidence that visual word recognition appears modular to the extent that information is analyzed at a visual feature level, a phonological level, and a semantic level. Nevertheless, evidence for activation from the semantic level to the early stages of word recognition can be obtained in strongly biasing contexts. The same idea may hold for speech production in which the predominant flow of information is from the semantic to the phonological, but with some activation in the other direction.

According to Dell (1995; Dell & O'Seaghdha, 1992), some of the data on speech errors are better explained by an interactive model. In particular, some slips seem to reflect a mixture of semantic and phonological factors, as in the following error noted by Fromkin (1973):

(11) The competition is a little strougher.

In this sentence, a nonword was produced that is apparently a combination of *stiffer* and *tougher*, two words that are semantically and phonologically similar. This slip is known as a **mixed error** because it seems to have both semantic and phonological sources. Mixed errors are fairly common, as speech errors go (Dell & Reich, 1981; Harley, 1984). This kind of error would be expected as a natural consequence of simultaneous activation of lexical and phonological competitors, as is suggested by connectionist models of speech production (Dell, 1986; Stemberger, 1985).

However, it may also be possible to account for mixed errors in a modular speech production system. For example, error (11) could result from a situation in which two different utterances are planned in parallel (Garrett, 1980). The intended message of the speaker who produced error (11) could be stated as either "The competition is a little tougher" or "The competition is a little stiffer." Perhaps in this case both frames are constructed, so the speaker tries to fill out each frame phonologically; but of course only one of the sentences can be produced at a time. Thus, the fusion of two words into *strougher* may occur late in the production process.

Given what we know about language production at this point in time, we cannot rule out either the modular or the interactive view. Indeed, it may be some time before this issue is completely resolved. Nevertheless, a consideration of the two types of models leads to an interesting question: Would there be any advantages to having one system over the other? It is easy to conjecture that a modular organization helps us make fewer errors by cutting down on interference caused by multiple sources of activation. But why might the system be interactive instead of modular? Dell (1988) noted that activation would have to flow in both directions, from lexical to phonological and from phonological to lexical, if the same network is being used for comprehension and production. According to this view, the phonological-to-lexical connections represent the dominant direction of activation for comprehension, but they also come into play in production.

Another view of the relationship between comprehension and production was taken by Levelt (1992), who noted that speakers often correct their own errors. This observation suggests that we monitor our production system. Earlier, Levelt (1989) proposed that the comprehension system is separate from, but interactive with, the production system. And in his view, the comprehension system is used to monitor our speech outputs. In a sense, then, we are listening to ourselves, and when the phonological plan fails to provide an utterance that matches the intended message, the production system gets feedback about the error. Levelt provided the following "partial error" as an example of the monitoring system in action:

(12) To the left side of the purple disk is a v-, a horizontal line.

In this case, the speaker was describing the layout of several objects and started to say the word *vertical* but then changed it to *horizontal*. The monitor noted that *vertical* was incorrect even before that word had been completely spoken. Quick feedback to the speech production system allowed for a correction.

This monitoring mechanism could be one reason that phonological errors often result in words rather than nonwords. If a person intends to say "I saw that pesky *cat*," but /r/ is mistakenly inserted to produce *rat*, the monitor may be more likely to fail to catch the error in time because the slip still forms a word. However, if /l/ is erroneously inserted, the monitor may catch the error before *lat* is actually spoken.

The question of whether or not there are separate lexical systems for comprehension and production is an interesting one to consider, because it has important implications for how language is implemented in the brain. Do production and comprehension rely on separate physical mechanisms in the brain? We will tackle this question in Chapter 12. For now, however, let's consider a different, but related, question: How is the speech production system integrated into the rest of the general cognitive system?

Speech Production and General Cognitive Mechanisms

Thus far, we have assumed the existence of a message to be communicated and focused our inquiry on the issue of how a message gets translated into a phonological representation that can be articulated. Of course, the message itself must be planned as well. An important difference between the planning of the message and the construction of syntactic, morphemic, and phonological plans is that message planning is typically a much more attention-demanding process (Levelt, 1989). Construction of the linguistic plans is relatively automatic, which is one reason some theorists have suggested they can operate in a modular fashion. However, the operation of these relatively automatic processes must be carefully coordinated with message planning, so that the right information is expressed at the right time. This coordination process is an important point of contact between the language production system and more general cognitive mechanisms.

Based on the range over which word exchanges and sound exchanges occur, Garrett (1988) suggested that syntactic frames are planned ahead about two clauses and that phonological frames are constructed approximately one clause ahead (see also Bock & Cutting, 1992). Clearly, planning at these levels is limited by how far ahead we can plan the message. When the construction of the message is not properly coordinated with the linguistic planning processes, we can get errors in speech or, more frequently, hesitations. These hesitations include both silent pauses and filled pauses in which the speaker says things like "er" or "uhm" to buy some time.

Garrett (1982) noted three principal reasons for hesitations in speech:

- *"Wait till the boat's loaded."* Because message construction takes attentional resources, we often need time before initiating an utterance to select the information that will fulfill the goal of our attempt at communication.

- *"It's in the mail."* Sometimes we experience delays caused by the momentary inaccessibility of some concept or word. We are most likely to notice this block when it is strong enough that we find ourselves in the "tip of the tongue" state. This state, in turn, may set off an attention-demanding search for the inaccessible information.

- *"Don't bother me, I'm busy."* Again, because of the attentional demands of constructing the message itself, other factors that use up attentional resources can cause us to speak more hesitantly. Perhaps the clearest example is public speaking. For someone who is nervous and hasn't rehearsed a speech, the anxiety of speaking in public can greatly increase message planning times, resulting in an awkward, "uhm"-filled delivery.

Where is the bottleneck in processing that limits our ability to construct a message and coordinate its construction with the linguistic production mechanisms? An important clue to answering this question comes from research on the relationship between the duration of short-term memory traces and the rate of articulation of speech. If you give people a list of words and ask them to recall the words immediately, they generally recall as many words or digits as they can pronounce in about two seconds (Baddeley, Thomson & Buchanan, 1975). This finding applies not only to the issue of why some people seem to have a greater short-term memory capacity than others, but also to the issue of why the apparent span of short-term memory varies by language. On the one hand, for example, Welsh digits take longer to articulate than English digits, and speakers of Welsh have a correspondingly lower digit memory span. On the other hand, articulation of digits and simple words is faster in Chinese than in English, and Chinese speakers show a correspondingly higher short-term span (e.g., Cheung & Kemper, 1993).

These data suggest that articulation rate and the verbal short-term store—or the phonological loop, as Baddeley (1986) calls it—are closely associated. We already know that all aspects of working memory, including the phonological loop, are very constrained in terms of how much information can be retained. But do these working-memory constraints affect our message construction and our management of the speaking process? According to Levelt (1989), the answer is "yes." Indeed, the influence of working-memory constraints is important in two different respects.

First, the propositions that we want to express must be actively maintained in working memory while we formulate the language representations needed to express the message. Any attention-demanding distractions that use up some of this working-memory capacity ("Oh no, the people in the audience are falling asleep!") can interfere with our ability to keep track of what we want to say, thus affecting our verbal fluency. Second, as Levelt (1989) suggested, the phonological loop maintains the phonological representation of an utterance before we actually articulate it. This arrangement allows the monitoring system to check for errors. We can then interrupt our speech and correct it—as in error (12)—or pause until we have solved the problem by generating a new linguistic plan.

Consistent with the view that message planning is capacity demanding, Daneman and Green (1986) showed that working-memory capacity is related to fluency in generating speech. They found that a test of working-memory capacity was a good predictor of people's ability to complete a sentence differently from the way it was read to them. In addition, people seem to adjust how far ahead they plan their utterances on the basis of how difficult their descriptive task is (e.g., Schriefers, 1992).

Although psycholinguists have much to learn yet about how we control speech production processes, one point is clear. Despite the speed and efficiency of the production processes at the syntactic, morphemic, and phonemic levels, the production system must interact with a limited-capacity working-memory system. This fact has important implications for understanding communication, as will become clear when we consider issues of production in the more naturalistic, social context of conversation.

Speech Production in Its Social Context: Conversation

As complex a process as uttering a single sentence seems to be, it is important to remember that speech production generally occurs in a context that makes things even more complex. Usually, we aren't just speaking; we are speaking with someone else in a conversation. And like other joint activities, conversations require a great deal of coordination between the participants if the goals are to be accomplished. As an analogy, think about the difference between moving in rhythm with music and ballroom-style dancing with a partner. Dancing as part of a pair entails more than just a sense of rhythm: It requires coordinated activity, subtle reactions to the moves of your partner, and the ability to smoothly improvise changes of direction.

Conversation requires analogous abilities, but they are talents involving mental rather than physical coordination. This was the basic idea behind Grice's four conversational maxims, which we studied in an earlier chapter (see Table 7.2 on page 225). Because speakers and listeners have to coordinate their activities, they follow certain guidelines that aid this coordination. For example, by following the maxim of relation, which says that speakers should make each utterance relevant to the context, the speaker makes the job of the comprehender easier by limiting the number of memory searches needed to make the conversation coherent. However, following Grice's maxims are just the starting point. In conversations, the role of speaker and listener keeps shifting, so it is as though two people are dancing, yet taking turns at leading. Table 9.1 provides an example of a brief conversation so that we can see how this coordination is achieved.

The conversation presented in the table is quite typical and ordinary. Ann has a very straightforward communication goal: to find out if Betty would like a particular bauble that Ann noticed in a store. Ann asks Betty if she'd like one and gets a positive response. You'll notice, however, that matters are not nearly so simple as this summary suggests. The actual conversation sounds nothing like the typical dialogue in a novel. There are periods when the speakers are hesitating, when both are speaking at once, and when Ann is being less than completely clear. Yet, the goal of communication gets accomplished.

TABLE 9.1	A Conversation Fragment	
(1)	ANN	Oh there's one thing I wanted to ask you
(2)	BETTY	mhm-
(3)	ANN	in the village, they've got some of those. I- you're to get to know,. what it is, but it doesn't matter really
(4)	BETTY	mhm
(5)	ANN	u:m. those rings, that er buckles-
(6)	BETTY	that are buckles
(7)	ANN	yes, tha- they they're flat,
(8)	BETTY	mhm
(9)	ANN	and you wrap them around,
(10)	BETTY	Oh yes I know
(11)	ANN	and,. you know,. *they're* a little belt.
(12)	BETTY	*m*m
(13)	ANN	would you like one.
(14)	BETTY	Oh I'd love one Ann-

Note: A period (.) denotes a brief pause; a hyphen (-) denotes a longer pause; *x* *y* means that x and y were produced at the same time; a colon (:) means that the vowel sound was drawn out over time; and a comma (,) indicates the end of an intonation unit.
Source: Svartvik & Quirk, 1980; cited in Clark, 1994.

We shouldn't be surprised that real conversations are not the smooth-flowing exchanges found in literary dialogue. Conversation seems simple or mundane only because it is so familiar; but this apparent simplicity is deceiving. Obviously, conversation involves taking turns, but how do we know when to start or stop our turn? How do we know how much "given" information to provide as a starting point and how much "new" information to provide at other points during the conversation? How do we know whether we have been understood or misunderstood? All of these issues are added to the basic requirements of speaking that we examined in the last section. And, indeed, this observation raises a very basic question for us to answer: How do our language and general cognitive mechanisms coordinate these activities all at once? To address this question, I'll first outline the basic features of conversation and then discuss evidence as to how the necessary processes are accomplished.

Features of Conversations

Perhaps the most basic element of a conversation is that it must have **personnel.** In any conversation there is, at a minimum, a speaker and an addressee. The interactions and role changes of the personnel can be complicated enough when only two participants are involved, as in the conversation between Ann and Betty. However, things often become even more complicated than that. Group conversations require the coordination of multiple participants. And public conversations, whether between two people or among a group of people, may also have eavesdroppers. In such instances, the principal participants are faced with the added problem of limiting the information that eavesdroppers receive (Goffman, 1976). Another thing to keep track of!

As the personnel interact in conversation, they accumulate **common ground.** Common ground refers to the knowledge and beliefs shared by the personnel. People need to make assumptions about what the other person knows or believes in order to coordinate their interaction. Such assumptions involve both the knowledge that the people can be expected to have as members of a particular society or community *and* the knowledge that the people have gained from their personal interaction (Clark, 1994, 1996). For example, in Table 9.1, Ann refers in line (3) to "the village" and assumes, apparently correctly, that Betty understands the specific referent for this expression. Therefore, Ann does not further explain where the object can be found. In contrast to Ann and Betty's conversation, there is little common ground (at least initially) when you strike up a conversation with a stranger. One of the first things you do in such situations is try to establish more common ground by asking questions like the basic "Where are you from?" or, at college parties, the ubiquitous "What is your major?" As a conversation proceeds, you expect that the person will remember (at least for a while) the information exchanged, so the contents of the conversation itself become part of the accumulating common ground.

As I have already noted, any given conversation is a joint activity that fulfills a goal. Yet within a conversation there is also a nested set of smaller joint projects, or **action sequences.** At the most general level, the action sequences in a conversation typically consist of an opening, an exchange of information, and a closing. For instance, the conversational sample in Table 9.1 represents an exchange of information. You can well imagine that this interaction was preceded by a greeting between Ann and Betty, in order to open the conversation, and that it ended perhaps with a plan for meeting again, in order to close the conversation. These actions have to occur in the right sequence for the conversation to work, and within each of the action sequences, in turn, there are often smaller joint projects that must be accomplished. For example, Ann doesn't just come out and ask her question; rather, in line (1) she points out that she has the goal of asking a question, and in line (2) she gets Betty's agreement. Then, Ann has a subgoal of making sure that the item she wants to ask about is part of their common ground. The exchange of information over this issue takes up lines (3) through (12).

The conversational device that allows this sequencing pattern to occur is known as an **adjacency pair** (Clark, 1996; Schegloff & Sacks, 1973). In an adjacency pair, each person contributes something to the completion of a small joint project. For example, in Table 9.1, lines (1) and (2) are an adjacency pair in which Ann proposes an agenda for the conversation and Betty gives her assent. Another example is the question-and-answer sequence in lines (13) and (14).

Finally, for a conversation to be successful, it must result in contributions (Clark & Schaefer, 1989). A **contribution** occurs when the personnel achieve the mutual belief that the addressee has understood the speaker well enough to continue to the next joint project or to end the conversation. The very simple "mhm" that Betty gives several times in the conversation plays the important role of signaling to Ann that a contribution has been completed.

In summary, we have seen that a conversation consists of a series of adjacency pairs that represent a joint communication project. Toward this end, the personnel rely heavily on shared knowledge, which comprises not only their background knowledge before the conversation but also the contributions to common ground established during the conversation. In short, each participant must have a great deal of knowledge readily available during the conversation in order for the goals and subgoals to be accomplished. How do we manage all this information and guide the conversation to its conclusion?

Managing the Demands of Conversation

Engaging in a conversation places two different kinds of demands on a participant. One type of demand is informational: There is a lot of declarative knowledge to keep track of in a conversation. As outlined above, while planning our utterances we must be aware of the existing common ground between participants *and* keep track of what new common ground is accumulating over the course of the conversation. The other type of demand is procedural: We have to do our part in guiding the conversation, though we do not have complete control. We have to know when to take a turn as speaker and when to give it up. We have to determine when to shift to a new action sequence and when not to. How each set of demands is handled will be discussed in turn.

Managing the Informational Demands.   Each person in a conversation engages in both production and comprehension. The comprehension processes are, by and large, the same ones I discussed in the last chapter. As we listen to the other person, and to ourselves, we create a textbase representation of what has been said as well as a mental model that represents the situations that have been described. The sum total of the knowledge that directly reflects the information stored in memory about a conversation is known as the **discourse record** (Clark, 1994; Levelt, 1989). At any given moment in a conversation, we are building up a discourse record in long-term memory that is kept coherent not only by linking the most recent propositions together but also by linking current propositions with the overall themes of the conversation in working memory.

As we saw previously, models of text comprehension are based on the idea that the reader inputs and analyzes information in a series of cycles (e.g., Kintsch, 1988; Kintsch & van Dijk, 1978). In reading, the information receiver has complete control over how much information is input and at what rate. However, in conversations, the addressee has less control over these factors. Fortunately, the way that speakers naturally produce speech in conversations allows listeners to understand the information in a series of input cycles similar to those in text comprehension. Specifically, speakers tend to produce streams of speech in bursts of words that are each about one clause long (Chafe, 1992; Clark, 1994; Grimes, 1975). These bursts of speech are sometimes called **intonation units** because changes in intonation distinguish one unit from another.

As an example of intonation units, note how each speaker in Table 9.1 tends to produce about one clause before either a pause occurs or the other party begins to speak. But as you may notice the next time you overhear a conversation, these short bursts are marked not just by pauses but also by several other features of prosody

(Chafe, 1979, 1992). For example, there tends to be a single point in each intonation unit where the loudness or pitch peaks so as to draw the attention of the listener. In addition, speakers often raise or lower their pitch toward the end of the unit. They may also lengthen the last word of the unit, giving it a distinct boundary, with or without a pause. Intonation units thus reflect the planning units of speakers, as they attend to one aspect of the situational model of their intended message at a time. Conveniently, this arrangement also allows listeners to assimilate one new piece of information at a time into their mental models.

So, much of the problem of managing information during conversations can be solved by drawing upon the comprehension abilities and strategies for which we have seen evidence in studies of text comprehension. In both text comprehension and conversation, the idea of creating a mental model of the situation is fundamental. Note, however, that during a conversation we also need to have, and to update, a mental model of the other participant (Clark & Marshall, 1981; Dell & Brown, 1991). Our use of such a model is revealed in the way that, as speakers, we adapt our production to the specific needs of listeners. For example, we adjust our presentation of given and new information to suit what we know about a particular listener (Clark, 1996). And we adjust the complexity of syntax and the lexical choices we make to fit the listener's age and language skill level (e.g., Newport, Gleitman & Gleitman, 1977).

Adjusting production to the listener is also a factor in **code switching,** a phenomenon in which bilinguals switch from one language to another and back again while conversing (e.g., Gumperz, 1982). Code switching usually occurs at major linguistic boundaries, and it can serve many purposes (including limiting the information flow to eavesdroppers, as when my mother and aunt would switch to French when discussing Christmas presents). Especially when a conversation involves a difficult-to-explain topic, bilinguals will often switch to the more proficient tongue to ease the processing burden. These adjustments need not involve controlled, strategic decisions, but they clearly depend on maintaining access to knowledge of the other participants in a conversation.

Managing the Procedural Demands.   Have you ever had to discuss a very difficult or sensitive issue with someone, so you planned out exactly what you would say and how the conversation would proceed? Chances are that most of your plans went out the window within a few minutes. Indeed, conversations seldom go exactly as planned, because they are **locally managed** (Clark, 1994). In other words, the sequence of events in a conversation is adjusted flexibly as we move through it.

The common-sense interpretation of how we manage conversations is that we simply take turns. But this idea begs several questions. For one, how do speakers know when to take their turn? It is not as though they give up their turn and ask explicitly that the other party take over. In fact, speaker changes are often very fast. For example, Beattie and Barnard (1979) studied telephone conversations and found that a third of such changes were initiated less than 200 milliseconds from the end of an intonation unit. Clearly, speech could be initiated that quickly only because the speakers were anticipating the end of the other person's turn.

What seems to guide turn taking is whether or not the goals of communication are being accomplished. In many conversations, including the example in Table 9.1 that we have been working from, many of the alternations between speakers consist of acknowledgments like "yes" or "I see" or "mhm." We also see many examples of strategic interruptions in which there is overlap in the speech between the two participants. These interruptions are not necessarily impolite, nor do they violate a "take turns" rule. Rather, they can serve as useful signals that the speaker has accomplished a goal and the listener wants to move on, as in line (12) in Table 9.1, or that there has been a breakdown in communication that must be repaired.

Thus, conversation is not just a matter of politely taking turns. More fundamentally, it is a matter of cooperative action toward a goal. This raises another question about conversation that moves us beyond the simple idea of taking turns: How do we accomplish goals that transcend a single joint project? A key to managing the goals of conversation is the use of **pre-sequences** (Clark, 1996; Schegloff, 1980). Pre-sequences are techniques used by a speaker to prepare the listener for what is to come. For example, one participant proposes a goal for a portion of the conversation, to which the other party can agree or disagree. Several types of pre-sequences are shown in Table 9.2. The first one, which duplicates line (1) of the conversation in Table 9.1, is a very typical case. If Ann had been sure that Betty knew exactly what the item was that Ann wanted to ask about, then there would have been no need for a pre-question. However, Ann also needs to describe the item before she gets to her question. The pre-question sets up an agenda for the conversation that both parties, A and B, can agree to follow:

1. *A:* Pre-question, *B:* Answer; If Answer is "yes", then:

2. *A* and *B* achieve common ground on information needed to understand the question.

3. *A:* Question, *B:* Answer.

Other types of pre-sequences establish agendas as well. For example, a pre-narrative seeks agreement for one participant to yield the floor for a longer period of time than usual. As Table 9.2 illustrates, pre-sequences are especially important for the openings and closings of conversations.

In the language of cognitive psychology, you can think of pre-sequences and their associated responses as establishing a procedural schema for part of the conversation. That is, they allow us to use a familiar plan of action that guides the conversation and sets the roles of the participants. Just as in comprehension, where use of a familiar text structure can help the reader maintain coherence, a familiar conversational structure eases the processing demands of maintaining the continuity of the conversation. To observe these components of conversation in action, try Activity 9.2 on page 291.

Of course, conversations do not always go smoothly. When misunderstandings occur, we have to be able to adjust our plan of action based on feedback from the other party. Typically we try again, or explain things another way, and then proceed to a new topic. However, some kinds of communication failures are so persistent and common that we should examine why our usual correction mechanisms are sometimes unsuccessful in dealing with them.

TABLE 9.2	Some Common Pre-Sequences	
	Type of Pre-Sequence	**Example**
	1. Pre-question	*Oh there's one thing I wanted to ask you*
	Response	*mhm*
	2. Pre-announcement	*well, d'you know what they've got*
	Response	*what-*
	3. Pre-invitation	*are you doing anything tonight*
	Response	*no*
	4. Pre-request	*do you have hot chocolate*
	Response	*yes we do*
	5. Pre-closing	*well okay*
	Response	*okay*
	6. Pre-narrative	*I acquired an absolutely magnificent sewing machine, by foul means, did I tell you about that?*
	Response	*no*

Source: Adapted from Clark, 1994.

Communication Problems: The Case of Gender Differences

One main lesson from our study of conversation has been that, because the participants have a great deal of information to manage, it is important that they mutually understand the speech signals for turn taking and agenda setting. Conversely, if two people in a conversation view some signals or communication strategies differently, then the likelihood of a failure to communicate is increased.

Such misunderstandings are common in conversations between two people from different cultures. For example, in the United States business executives are often praised for being direct, clear, and aggressive in their conversational style, whereas in Japan subtlety and indirectness in conversations are more highly valued (Tannen, 1994). As a result, the direct, aggressive approach of an American in negotiations may be viewed as immature and off-putting by a Japanese counterpart; and, in turn, the indirect style of the Japanese executive might be misinterpreted by the American as a sign of submissiveness or subordination.

A less obvious, yet perhaps more pervasive form of miscommunication can occur in conversations between men and women. Consider Robin Lakoff's extensive studies of differences in conversational styles between men and women (Lakoff, 1975, 1990). Lakoff has stressed the idea that, rather than thinking of one style as better than another, we should try to understand how each style emerges from differences in the expectations of men and women's behavior that are imposed by the culture. Some of the differences that she, and others, have observed are as follows:

- Men are less likely to ask questions that make them appear unknowledgeable, such as asking for directions.

- Women tend to use more expressive terms, such as adjectives.

ACTIVITY 9.2   Conversational Analysis

See if you can get permission from a few pairs of friends or family members to record a conversation on tape. You will probably have to let the tape run for a while until your volunteers have relaxed into a normal discussion. For that matter, you might need to use a few questions to prompt them into talking. Make sure, however, that you get each pair of people talking *to each other*. The important thing is to record them conversing in as natural a manner as possible. When you have some exchanges on tape that you believe are pretty natural, transcribe these exchanges. Then see if you can identify some of the pre-sequences defined in Table 9.2.

- Men use fewer hedges ("It could be that . . ."; "I could be wrong, but I think that . . .").

- Women display a more collaborative style of communication in which each party is drawn out. Men are more likely to use a competitive style in which the goal is to prove a point.

- Men are more likely to interrupt and more likely to introduce new topics.

As an example of the empirical research in this area, let's consider a study on the last point given above: gender differences in interruption and topic setting. West and Garcia (1988) studied the conversations of pairs of students, one female and one male in each pair, who were asked to get to know each other before they were given a topic to discuss. West and Garcia found that in their introductory discussions, both women and men initiated topic changes about equally often when the shifts were warranted by the progress made on the prior topic. So, for example, when there had been several contributions from each party on one topic, and then a long pause, the next topic was equally likely to be introduced by the man or the woman. However, in the conversations of the five pairs of students who were studied, there were nine instances in which a topic change was unilateral. That is, one party introduced a new topic before the other person could complete his or her contribution to the previous topic. *All* of these unwarranted topic shifts were made by the men. For example, in one conversation, a woman started to explain why she was thinking of changing colleges, but the man cut off this "complaint" and asked her about her major area of study.

Keep in mind that the differences noted in men's and women's conversational styles are general trends and that there are large individual differences within each sex in conversational style (Carli, 1990; Roger & Nesshoever, 1987). In addition, differences in men's and women's conversational styles are linked to differences in the status of men and women in most societies (e.g., Carli, 1990; Carli, LaFleur & Loeber, 1995; Henley & Kramarae, 1991; Tannen, 1994). In short, if men are thought of as being typically "in charge," then it follows that men will take more control over topic setting and state their positions in a more direct and unqualified manner. For women, on the other hand, problems arise because the kind of speech patterns they are taught to use may be misinterpreted. A woman in a position of responsibility who uses the "typical female style" may be viewed as weak or indecisive. But if she adopts the "male style" of conversation she may be viewed as overly aggressive or "bitchy." Thus, the characteristically "female style" of communication may be more a reflection of the style that lower-status participants are expected to use. Consistent with this idea, Carli (1990) found that women were more tentative about voicing disagreement than men, but only when the women were in mixed-sex pairs. When talking to other women, the female speakers were as forceful as male speakers tend to be.

Although we should be sensitive to variations among people in their approaches to conversation, it is important to recognize that much of our communication is quite effective. Despite our differences, conversations are often successful because of the feedback we can give each other about whether a point has been understood. In written language, the final topic of the chapter, the immediate feedback is lacking. As you will see, this factor presents a serious challenge to writers and, at least in part, helps explain why writing is an especially demanding cognitive process.

The Production of Written Language

I was in the library a couple of nights ago, doing some background research, when a student in an out-of-the-way corner of the library caught my eye. He was muttering to himself and twirling his hair round and round with his finger. Occasionally, he would get up and walk around his table in a circle, sometimes rapping a pencil on his forehead. In other settings, this kind of behavior might result in the administration of psychoactive medication. However, after watching the young man for a few moments, I had no doubt that his "abnormal behavior" was caused by having to write an essay.

Not everyone finds writing as painful as this poor fellow did, but it's equally true that no one who writes often or well finds it easy. In many ways, writing seems much harder than speaking, even though there is overlap among many of the processes involved in both. The main difference has to do with the social nature of each activity. Like speaking, writing involves communicating with other people; but in contrast to speaking, the "social interaction" in writing is displaced in time and space. To see why this displacement makes writing such a challenge, examine Figure 9.4, which presents a schematic diagram of the writing process.

An Overview of the Writing Process

By observing writers' pauses and bursts of writing, and by having writers "think aloud" as they composed, Hayes and Flower (1980; Flower & Hayes, 1984) identified three phases of the writing process: planning, translating, and reviewing. **Planning** consists of setting goals, formulating ideas, and organizing the ideas. **Translating** is their term for the sentence-generation process. And **reviewing** refers to the process of evaluating and editing the text.

These are not three linear stages of writing. Rather, during the composing process, writers shift between these different activities. Each of these activities overlaps with analogous processes in speaking, but there are important differences between writing and speaking, especially in the planning and reviewing phases. In particular, because there is no feedback from the other "participants" in the written-communication

| FIGURE 9.4 | An Overview of the Writing Process |

The basic processes of planning the essay, translating the ideas into sentences, and reviewing the sentences are monitored so that the written product will meet the goals of the assignment and will be appropriate for the audience.

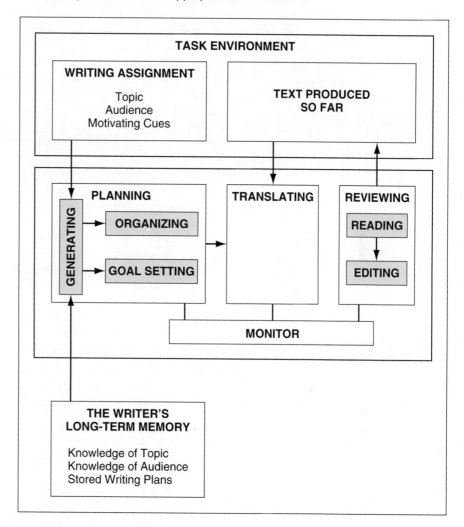

process, the writer must be more vigilant about keeping the audience in mind during the planning stage and more closely review and edit the output to see that it fits both the audience and the goals of the writing assignment or task.

Clearly, if conversing leads to serious demands on attention and working memory, then the demands are even higher for writing. To study the attentional demands involved in different phases of writing, Kellogg (1987) used a dual-task paradigm. Participants were given a writing assignment as their primary task, and as a secondary task they had to respond as quickly as possible to a tone that sounded at random intervals. The longer it took for participants to respond to the tone, the more attentional capacity was being used by the primary task. In addition, the participants were trained to report their activities at any given point as falling into the categories of planning, translating, or reviewing. As illustrated in Figure 9.5, both planning and reviewing were shown to be more demanding than translating. However, you can also see from the figure that *every* phase of the writing process was relatively demanding. Because numerous experiments have used reaction time to a tone as an index of how much attentional capacity is used by a primary task (e.g., Britton, Glynn, Meyer & Penland, 1982; Kahneman, 1973), we can compare tone reaction times in writing with tone reaction times in other primary tasks. Although we should be careful about such cross-experiment comparisons, it seems safe to conclude that writing is among the most demanding cognitive activities.

Given the nature of the connection between working memory and the planning and monitoring processes in speaking that we examined earlier, it seems likely that the attentional demands of writing measured by Kellogg (1987) stem from the burdens placed on working memory. Some direct experimental evidence for the relationship between working memory and writing was obtained recently by Fayol, Largy, and Lemaire (1994). They asked a group of well-educated and fluent French adults to listen to sentences in their native language and then to write them down. In French, when a sentence is written, several marks may be added to indicate that the subject and verb

---

FIGURE 9.5   **A Comparison of the Difficulty of Cognitive Tasks**

By measuring how much a task, like writing, interferes with another task, such as tone detection, psychologists can assess how much attentional capacity is used by a mental activity. The demands of the processes used in writing are comparable to the effort needed to play chess.

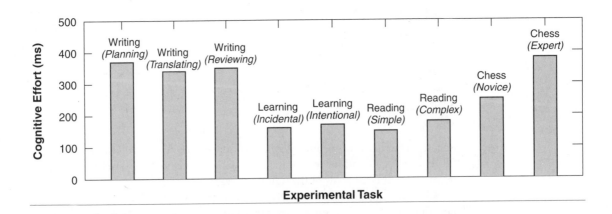

are plural; yet many of these marks are not pronounced in spoken French. In general, both writers and speakers know that subjects and verbs must agree in number, so it is usually not a problem to produce the correct written version. However, Fayol and associates (1994) found that if they loaded working memory by making the participants perform the task while also maintaining five words actively in working memory, the number of subject-verb agreement errors increased substantially. Thus, even the translation process in writing is quite dependent on working memory for correct execution.

Individual Differences in Writing Performance

Given that writing is such a cognitively demanding process, it is not surprising that people vary widely in terms of how well they write. The interesting challenge is to try to understand the differences between good and poor writers. Bereiter and Scardamalia (1987) studied both developmental and individual differences among writers by analyzing the verbal protocols of people thinking aloud as they performed a writing assignment. They found that young writers, and poor writers of adult age, differed from more mature and proficient writers mainly in their planning and revision strategies. In fact, until adolescence there is very little evidence of either planning or revising in writing. Adult writers tend to be more planful but are not always effectively so, and their plans are not always coupled with appropriate revision.

Some writers spend so much time in the beginning stages of planning, and become so frustrated, that they end up doing very little writing (Rose, 1984). Others plan and write in a series of cycles that lead to what Bereiter and Scardamalia (1987) called **knowledge telling.** Writers who engage in knowledge telling plan a single idea and then translate it into a sentence. Then they plan another idea and translate that one into a sentence. If they revise, it is only to see that each sentence reflects the thought they wanted to express. Because little consideration is given to the overall structure or flow of the written product, there may be local coherence but little global coherence.

More mature and proficient writers tend to use a **knowledge transforming** strategy (Bereiter & Scardamalia, 1987; Kellogg, 1994). This strategy allows them to view writing as a problem-solving process in which they plan what sorts of text organization options best fit the ideas that must be expressed. By testing out various ways of expressing their ideas to accomplish the overall goals of the writing task, the writers come to actively transform their knowledge. Thus, the act of writing itself, particularly the act of reviewing and altering a piece of writing, often results in new insights on the part of the person doing the writing.

To accomplish knowledge transforming, as opposed to knowledge telling, writers have to plan at a global level and then be willing to do a kind of revising that is very different from the revision process in knowledge telling. As an example, consider a study by Hayes, Flower, Schriver, Stratman, and Carey (1987) in which they found that first-year college students and more advanced students tended to take very different approaches to revision. When given a poorly written essay to revise, the first-year students dealt with one sentence at a time, polishing errors in grammar or word usage. In contrast, the advanced students focused on a more global level, including problems of organization or clarity of purpose. Likewise, when you are going over your own first draft, it makes more sense to attend to global aspects than to spend time polishing sentences that may need to be omitted altogether. Of course, the revision problems common among first-year students may be related in part to the type of feedback they often receive from teachers. Some instructors hand back first drafts of essays covered with red marks that show all the errors at a local, sentence-by-sentence level. Compared to this profusion of red marks, the instructors' comments in the margins about reorganization or rethinking an issue may seem unimportant to the students.

CONCLUSIONS

Language Production and Modular Organization

Researchers have long tried to understand the processing stages in language production by examining the nature of the errors that people make. An examination of the kinds of errors that people do—and do not—make leads us to the conclusion that there are separable syntactic, morphemic, and phonological processes that allow us to build an utterance.

At present, it is not clear whether these different processes function as autonomous units within a modular organization or as layers of an interactive system. What *is* clear from the research on production of language is that the language system works closely with the rest of our cognitive machinery. In particular, a distinct theme emerging from this research is the difficulty posed by all the information that must be managed during language production. Although there are language-specific mechanisms that operate automatically, as when syntactic and phonemic frames are filled, the process of production also depends on our limited-capacity working-memory system. In short, whether we are engaged in an enjoyable conversation or sweating bullets over a school essay, there is a great deal of information that must be managed.

The demands of information management are especially high in writing because we do not get immediate feedback from others as to whether we have been understood. Thus, it sometimes helps to separate the content problems, what we want to get across in writing, from the rhetorical problems, how to express the message. If we stray too far into rhetorical questions before we are somewhat clear about what it is we want to say, we are likely to end up with a disconnected product based on knowledge telling. Indeed, better writers use outlines and multiple drafts to produce an acceptable written product precisely because these techniques ease the processing demands.

Note, however, that in *all* the areas of production we've examined, monitoring and editing, which depend on retrieving information from memory and maintaining information in memory, play an important communication role. Thus, language production is a good example of the central theme of the present unit: Psychological processes in language depend upon an intricate interplay between language-specific and general cognitive mechanisms. In the next unit, we will explore how this interplay works at an implementational level as we examine the physiological basis for language processes.

CHAPTER REVIEW

Checking Your Understanding

Key Terms

action sequences (286)
adjacency pair (286)
closed-class category (278)
code switching (288)
common ground (286)
consonant-vowel rule (279)
contributions (286)
discourse record (287)
intonation units (287)
knowledge telling (295)
knowledge transforming (295)

locally managed (288)
mixed error (281)
open-class category (278)
personnel (285)
planning (292)
pre-sequences (289)
reviewing (292)
stranding error (278)
syntactic category rule (276)
syntactic frame (277)
translating (292)

Review Questions

1. Contrast the basic ideas behind the Freudian and linguistic approaches to explaining speech errors.

2. What evidence suggests that word-exchange errors reflect a syntactic level of processing?

3. What data led Garrett to suggest that inflections and closed-class elements are part of the syntactic frame? Describe a position different from Garrett's.

4. What do you consider the strongest evidence in support of the modularity of the speech production system? What data do you think most strongly support the interactive view?

5. What role does working memory play in speech production?

6. How is "turn taking" in conversation different from taking turns in other joint activities such as playing chess?

7. Why is the local management in conversation less demanding of attentional capacity than the type of planning needed for written language production?

8. Compare and contrast the role of pre-sequences in conversation, on the one hand, and the role of advanced organizers in discourse comprehension, on the other. (Recall that discourse comprehension is discussed in Chapter 8.)

9. Outline the most important differences between women's and men's conversational strategies. How can an understanding of these differences help improve communication between the sexes?

10. Based on the information in this chapter, what recommendations would you make to composition teachers to help them improve student writing?

On Further Reflection ...

There are two projects you can try, using the conversations you taped for Activity 9.2, that will solidify and extend your understanding of the material in this chapter.

1. One useful project is to monitor the tape again, this time listening for speech errors and hesitations so that you can observe the monitoring system in action. If you find any speech errors, try to classify them by type of unit and error. Did the speakers notice the errors? Are there any differences between the errors they noticed and the errors that bypassed the monitoring system?

2. The other project is to transcribe three or four different parts of the conversations and label the two contributors as Person A and Person B. For each conversational segment, ask some additional friends if they can identify which person is male and which is female. Then, whether they are right or wrong, ask what caused them to identify a speaker as male or female. Do your friends notice any style differences, or are their choices based on the subject matter discussed? Of course, the original participants in your "study" knew they were being taped. In what ways might this knowledge have affected whether gender differences in conversational style were revealed? What does your answer say about how the monitoring system affects production?

What Are the Common Elements Among Different Models of Language Processing?

If you take a few minutes to talk to a typical five-year-old about any topic that she finds exciting, you will immediately discover that she is an adept user of language. However, you may also notice some funny gaps in her ability to communicate. When describing a place that you haven't seen, for example, the five-year-old may seem to completely ignore the given-new contract that binds conversations together, apparently assuming that you know everything she knows. Similarly, in the laboratory, you can place two children in a situation where each is facing an identical arrangement of objects—say, two red blocks and one blue car—such that they know the arrangements are the same but cannot see each other's layout. Then one child might say to the other, "Put the red block behind the blue car." Research has shown that the speaker is likely to be unaware of the ambiguity of this description. Moreover, the listener will usually pick up one of the two red blocks and be quite confident that he has selected the same red block as the speaker has instructed (e.g., Markman, 1977). Compared to the data on conversations that we explored in Chapter 9, the data on young children's conversational abilities indicate a relatively poor ability to monitor the progress of communication and avoid ambiguity. As we saw in that chapter, avoiding such ambiguity depends on a complex coordination of activities between the two parties.

In closing Unit Two of the text, I'd like you to take note of how that key concept of ambiguity kept cropping up in our study of language processes. Much of what people do when producing language involves efforts to avoid ambiguity. As we saw, one reason writing is so hard is that, as writers, we don't have the listener's immediate feedback when we have been ambiguous. Moreover, the research described throughout Unit Two shows that the general problem of ambiguity faces us at every level of language comprehension. The problem of speech recognition is largely a problem of dealing with what the speech signal leaves unclear: where the word breaks are, whether some random variation is occurring in the signal, and what the important part of the signal is. Likewise, when reading we have to deal with words that have multiple meanings. We also have to deal with the question of which meaning, or which shade of meaning, is intended in context, and even whether the literal meaning is intended at all. Indeed, much of the data on sentence processing are concerned with the role of syntax and semantics in resolving potential ambiguities over how to attach a particular phrase to the rest of the sentence.

One of the general themes revisited throughout this unit has to do with the two different schemes that have been proposed to account for people's ability to deal with the ambiguity of language. Some researchers claim that we rely on language-specific information, part of which may be inborn, that allows us to deal with ambiguity. Others claim that we use general cognitive mechanisms and world knowledge to augment bottom-up information from the top down. The battle between these two hypotheses was pitched most fervently in relation to the less complex aspects of language processing: speech processing and word recognition. Then, as the debate widened to include more complex aspects of language, such as sentence and discourse processing, it became clear that general cognitive mechanisms must play an important role. Other evidence, however, has supported the contention that some language-specific information processing, such as syntactic parsing, *may* work in a largely bottom-up fashion.

In Unit Three, we will still be concerned with the ways that language-specific and general cognitive mechanisms interact in language processing, but our approach in that unit will rely on relating mental processes to their biological underpinnings. Our first job will be to directly attack a question first raised in Chapters 1 and 2: To what extent is language built-in?

UNIT THREE

Language and the Brain

CHAPTER 10

Language Acquisition: Biological Foundations

I magine that you are studying the language of an obscure people in a foreign land. While you are walking along one day with a villager, a rabbit runs across the path, and the villager points toward the rabbit and says "gavagai." What do you think *gavagai* means? You will probably assume, tentatively, that *gavagai* means "rabbit" and then test your assumption by observing whether *gavagai* is used again the next time a rabbit is seen by a villager.

This seems a pretty safe way to proceed, but, as Quine (1960) pointed out when he proposed this thought experiment, there are a huge number of possibilities for the meaning of *gavagai* in this situation. After all, even if you do hear *gavagai* the next time a rabbit is spotted, how do you know that it doesn't mean "hop" or "long ears" or "Gee, those are wonderful for dinner" or any of numerous other possibilities?

Of course, you are an adult who already knows what rabbits are, and your knowledge of people and of language may increase your confidence that people are likely to instruct you in their language initially by naming objects. But what about infants just starting to acquire a language? They do not know much about their world or the objects in it, and yet they hear numerous unfamiliar combinations of sounds every day. Somehow, despite all the different possibilities as to what these unfamiliar sounds could refer to, children pick out words and learn their meanings.

Learning words and their meanings is just part of the problem of language acquisition, of course. Children also learn how to produce words and to combine them into sentences. Most remarkably, they accomplish all this very rapidly. As an example of how proficient children are at language acquisition, consider just the learning of new words. By the time a child is six years old, he or she has acquired a vocabulary of about 13,000 words (Carey, 1978; Pinker, 1994). Given the amount of time the average child spends sleeping, this amounts to acquisition of a new word every two waking hours!

As I mentioned in Chapter 2, many linguists and psychologists believe that our rapid acquisition of language is possible because *language is founded on a set of innate ideas*. I want you once again to evaluate that hypothesis, but this time consider it in light of what is known about language acquisition.

Another way of expressing the hypothesis for this chapter is that at least some implementation of the language processor in the brain is specified by our genetic inheritance. This nativist hypothesis suggests not that newborns "know" a lot about language but, rather, that as the brain of the infant matures, it is programmed to acquire language and that this programming is not just part of a general learning ability.

Our brains undergo considerable development after birth, not in terms of growing new nerve cells but in terms of forming new connections, or synapses, between neurons, and increasing the speed of transmission of nerve impulses. The period of the most rapid physical changes in the brain, excluding prenatal development, is from birth to five years of age. This is also the period during which almost all of our language abilities are acquired. As Steven Pinker (1994) suggested:

Language development, then, could be on a maturational timetable, like teeth. Perhaps linguistic accomplishments like babbling, first words, and grammar require minimum levels of brain size, long-distance connections, and extra synapses, particularly in the language centers of the brain. *(p. 289)*

At present, we do not know nearly enough about human genetics to evaluate this hypothesis by direct examination of the genetic code. In addition, as a number of investigators have pointed out, just because language is complex and we acquire it rapidly does not prove that it has a specific innate basis (e.g., Piaget, 1980). The first step toward evaluating the validity of the nativist hypothesis, then, is to realize that the question is really more complicated than "Is language the result of nature or nurture?" Since no one is born knowing a particular language, we can conclude that *if* we are specially prepared biologically to acquire language, then what we are born with is the capacity to acquire any language.

At one extreme is the view that we are born knowing everything that is universal across languages and the only things we acquire are the aspects of our particular language that are unique. A "middle-ground" interpretation is that we may be specially designed to learn some aspects of grammar more easily than we learn other things, but this limited "special endowment" for language depends heavily on cognitive and social abilities that are more general. And, finally, there's the view at the other extreme: All we are born with is a general capacity for learning. In other words, children learn a great many things from birth to five years of age; perhaps language is just one of many skills made possible by our general cognitive abilities (cf., Anderson, 1983b).

How can we determine whether some aspects of language are built into our genetic inheritance? For the answer we will have to closely examine the ways that basic aspects of language—including phonology, the lexicon, and syntax—are acquired. Then we can determine whether the data on each of these aspects of language support a nativist position. As we have seen, understanding how language works is tricky enough even when the focus is on adult language users. It is trickier still to determine how language is acquired among infants and children. So, we will start by reviewing some of the special methods used in the study of language acquisition.

How Can We Study Language Acquisition?

As the great New York Yankee baseball player, Yogi Berra, once said, "Sometimes you can observe a lot by watching." Indeed, our knowledge of language acquisition is founded on observations about children's responses to language and their early production of language. One thing these observations make clear is that young children understand more language than they can produce. Children often understand a word several months before they try to produce it (Clark, 1993). For example, they can recognize their bottle and their favorite blanket, and can let you know which they want, long before they are able to say "bottle" or "blanket."

So, if our quest is to understand early language competence, and where it comes from, we cannot rely on measures of language production alone. In addition, if we want to know whether certain abilities are present from the earliest days of language acquisition, we have to test infants. The kinds of behaviors that researchers can measure to understand infants' capacities are very limited, but as you will see, they have devised very clever ways to test the kinds of sound discriminations that even very young infants can make. We will first take a look at these methods for studying infant speech recognition; then we will get an overview of the study of other receptive language capacities. Next we will focus on methods of studying and quantifying children's language production abilities. Finally, we will briefly consider how the study of language acquisition in atypical situations or by atypical children can help address the nature-nurture question in acquisition.

Methods for Studying Receptive Language Ability

We saw in Chapter 5 that the human capacity for speech perception is both a remarkable feat and a genuine intellectual puzzle. We are able to recognize sounds as being the same despite considerable variation in their production across different speakers and contexts. In addition, we segment speech into words even though pauses within words are often greater than breaks between words. To understand how these abilities are acquired, we have to be able to test infants' abilities to discriminate among different speech sounds. Researchers have developed several methods to accomplish this task, all of which make use of infants' tendency to pay more attention to novel stimuli than to stimuli that were presented recently.

For example, Eimas, Siqueland, Jusczyk, and Vigorito (1971) tested one-month-old infants' ability to make basic sound discriminations. There are not a lot of overt behaviors that can be measured in infants this young, but one that does work is rate of sucking on a pacifier. When infants perceive a novel stimulus, their rate of sucking on a pacifier increases, and the difference can be measured with a monitor that is hooked up to the pacifier. The technique of using sucking rate to detect perceptual abilities is known as the **high-amplitude sucking (HAS)** procedure. In their use of the HAS procedure, Eimas and associates (1971) repeatedly presented a /ba/ sound to an infant, with the initial result of an increased rate of sucking on the pacifier. However, in a short time, the infant **habituated** to the sound. In other words, the sound became familiar enough for the infant to ignore it and the rate of sucking on the pacifier returned to normal. The question is what would happen if the sound changed to /pa/. If the infants can perceive this distinction, then the sound should be novel and their sucking rate should increase again. But if the new sound was too similar to the original /ba/ for the infant to notice the difference, then the rate should not change. Eimas and associates found that even one-month-old infants reacted to the change in sound as a novel stimulus. In short, even very young infants can perceive the /ba/ versus /pa/ distinction.

As children get a little older, the types of behaviors they can produce increase the range of methods that can be used to study their language reception ability. For instance, by the time they are four or five months old, infants can be trained to turn their gaze in a particular direction when they hear a particular sound. This ability is the basis of the **conditioned head turn procedure** that is depicted in Figure 10.1. In this procedure, the test participant hears a continuous set of sounds. When a particular sound is produced, the participant is reinforced for turning his or her head in a particular direction. For example, every time a young child makes a head turn response to the appropriate sound, researchers might reinforce that response by revealing a previously hidden toy. In this manner, they could train the child to turn toward the location of a hidden toy whenever the sound in the background is changed. Then, after training, they could repeatedly present a sound—such as /ba/—and subsequently change to /pa/. Children who are able to detect the change would turn toward the location of the hidden toy, expecting to see the toy revealed. One advantage of this

| FIGURE 10.1 | The Conditioned Head Turn Procedure |

This child was trained to turn her head to see a toy displayed whenever she detected a change in the sound being presented.

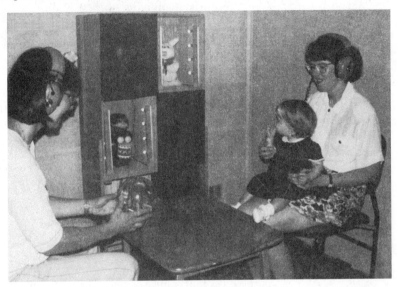

procedure is that, with slight variations, it can be used with adults as well as children, thus permitting researchers to compare speech discrimination abilities across a wide variety of ages (Werker, 1995).*

Another example of a procedure that makes use of children's ability to direct their attention to a particular location was reported by Golinkoff, Hirsh-Pasek, Cauley, and Gordon (1987). In their study, each child was seated in front of two video screens, one on the child's left and one on the right. One of the screens showed Big Bird tickling Cookie Monster and the other showed Cookie Monster tickling Big Bird. In addition, the children heard a tape that described one of the two videos. As it turns out, even seventeen-month-old children looked more at the video that matched the auditory sentence that was played. Golinkoff and associates concluded that the children understood the importance of word order well enough to prefer the video that matched the sentence they had heard.

As children get older, and their capacity for language production increases, it gets easier to test their comprehension in ways that are more similar to the kinds of tasks that psycholinguists use with adults. In these cases, the experimenter can have the

---

* As you might imagine, adults and older children object to participating in the HAS procedure.

children respond verbally to check their comprehension. Bear in mind, however, that this expressive language capability takes time to develop. Accordingly, we turn next to a discussion of methods that are used to study the early development of children's language production skills.

Methods for Studying Expressive Language Ability

As we saw in Chapter 9, much of the data on language production comes from collecting samples of speech production. This is also true of the study of the acquisition of production ability. Records of children's attempts at producing language have been collected for more than a century, usually by parents who wrote down samples of their children's speech at various ages. These so-called **diary studies** can be useful and interesting (Bar-Adon & Leopold, 1971), but they suffer from important shortcomings. For one thing, the diarist is likely to write down only the more unusual or striking utterances of the child, thus yielding a rather biased sample of utterances. In addition, the diarist may not have the objectivity necessary to record utterances accurately and without interpretation by the adult mind.

Nevertheless, it is possible to collect naturalistic samples of children's speech that are representative and objective. One landmark effort in this area was pioneered by Roger Brown of Harvard University during the 1960s. Once a week, Brown's team of researchers went into the homes of three children, known as Adam, Eve, and Sarah, and unobtrusively recorded the speech interactions that took place between the children and their parents. They then transcribed and analyzed the recordings so as to determine when the children went from words to sentences and from simple sentences to complex sentences in their speech (e.g., Brown, 1973). In addition, they examined the feedback that the children received from their parents so that the possible roles of learning and imitation in language acquisition could be determined.

Brown's efforts inspired a number of other projects in which children's speech attempts were recorded and analyzed. Fortunately, a huge database has been created that combines transcripts from Brown's research with findings from many other research efforts (MacWhinney & Snow, 1985). This database is known as the Child Language Data Exchange System (CHILDES). It is maintained and updated by Brian MacWhinney of Carnegie-Mellon University (MacWhinney, 1995). If you have Internet access, you can take a look at the CHILDES database on-line. (The address is <http://poppy.psy.cmu.edu/childes/index.html>.) CHILDES continues to provide extraordinarily detailed information on the language development of hundreds of children.

Yet, as valuable as naturalistic samples of language production can be, we also need other kinds of information to study children's language production abilities. For example, as children get older it becomes easier to make use of **elicited production** techniques. That is, we can present the children with a particular stimulus and record their response to that stimulus. A classic example is Berko's (1958) study of children's mastery of a grammatical rule. The task is depicted in Figure 10.2. By testing how children at various ages respond to a request to form the plural of a novel noun, Berko (1958) could determine when children had mastered the generative application of the rule.

FIGURE 10.2	**The Wug Test**

Drawings like this one, along with experimenters' statements, have been used to test whether children have grasped the general rule for forming plural nouns in English.

THIS IS A WUG.

NOW THERE IS ANOTHER ONE.
THERE ARE TWO OF THEM.
THERE ARE TWO _____.

Studies of Language Development in Atypical Contexts

The techniques we have reviewed so far can give us valuable information about how language skills develop over time. However, studying the typical case of an average child in an average home acquiring his or her first language has some important limitations for answering nature-nurture questions. Given how rapidly children advance in all mental and physical domains from birth to five years of age, it is not easy to distinguish the contributions of biological, cognitive, and social factors to language development. So, to help in answering questions about the nature of language acquisition, we can also look to situations in which either the linguistic environment or the child is atypical in some way. These atypical contexts represent naturalistic experiments that can help us distinguish among different kinds of contributions to language development (e.g., Tager-Flusberg, 1994). But please note that *atypical* means just that—not the typical case. I do not mean to imply that atypical contexts necessarily lead to defective or deficient language ability. For example, a deaf child who grows up in a home where the parents mainly use spoken language can be said to have a language environment that is atypical (though not rare). But this does not mean that the language she develops is an inferior language.

Of course, there are contexts that lead not just to a different path in language acquisition but to very poor development of language skills. Indeed, cases of **feral children** who grow up in the wild with little human contact have long been studied to see if language could be acquired even if exposure to language was delayed until late childhood or adolescence. The "Wild Boy of Aveyron" is one such case. Discovered living like a wild animal in France in 1797, he was brought to civilization and cared for by a young physician. Yet, despite intensive efforts to train him in language, the boy never progressed beyond the ability to name objects (see Lane, 1976).

A more recent case involved a young woman known as Genie (Curtiss, 1981). Though not a feral child, she was nevertheless raised in horrific isolation. Sickly as an infant and diagnosed by a pediatrician as being possibly mentally retarded, she was rejected by her parents and spent every day of her life until age thirteen caged in a crib or tied to a chair. During that time, she was exposed to almost no speech sounds. When she made any vocalizations herself, she was beaten by her father.

Not surprisingly, Genie displayed no language ability at the time she was discovered. With intensive language training, she did learn to produce intelligible sentences, but they remained rudimentary and lacking in grammatical structure. Like the "Wild Boy," she was unable to master language to the degree of even a moderately proficient four-year-old.

According to those theorists who believe that language acquisition is a process of biological maturation, there is a **critical period** for language acquisition (Lenneberg, 1967). In other words, to learn a language naturally and proficiently, we must be exposed to language at a particular period of life, typically proposed to be between eighteen months and middle childhood. Studies of feral and isolated children might be taken as support for the critical-period idea. However, we must be very cautious about drawing conclusions concerning the deficiencies of children who have been so neglected and abused. There is so much damage to the social, emotional, and cognitive abilities of these children that conclusions about language deficits in these cases are risky.

Rather than trying to address the nature-nurture issue through case studies in which language is almost absent, we can examine how language is acquired in contexts that are atypical but not devastating. In fact, one of the most interesting things about the study of atypical contexts is how proficient many children become even when their linguistic environment is not the norm. This type of research will be the focus of the next chapter, in which we examine language acquisition by deaf children, by children in other special circumstances, and by people who are trying to learn a second language later in life. Before we can make use of these atypical situations to understand language acquisition, however, we must examine the developmental progression of language acquisition under more typical circumstances. To prepare for an overview of the typical course of language acquisition, take a look at Activity 10.1 before you read further.

Milestones of Language Acquisition

Most parents, when asked when their child started to learn language, will probably say that the child started around ten or eleven months of age. This is the time when most kids begin to use a few words. The estimate might be a little earlier if the parent is basing it on a generous interpretation of the first time the child seemed to be saying "mama" or "dada." In any case, it is clear that language acquisition begins before the child starts to use a few words. Before any words can be identified *as words*, the child must know something about the sounds and sound combinations of the language. Think back to the "*gavagai* problem." From an infant's perspective, this problem is

ACTIVITY 10.1   **Language Acquisition and Brain Maturation**

Does the development of language follow in step with the maturation of the brain? A close correspondence between brain maturation and specific language attainments would suggest that language acquisition could be, at least in part, a product of maturation. Accordingly, the purpose of this activity is to give you a general picture of the relationship between language acquisition and brain development.

As Figure 10.3 shows, the period during which language is acquired is also a period of remarkable brain development. In addition to the changes depicted in the figure, the brain becomes more efficient at message transmission due to a process called **myelinization.** Myelinization refers to the growth of myelin, a fatty sheath around many nerve fibers that increases the speed of neural transmission.

Copy or trace this figure, and keep it beside you as you continue reading. In the upcoming section, during the discussion of major milestones in language acquisition, write the approximate age associated with each milestone on the timeline in the figure. In this way, by the end of the chapter, you'll have a clearer sense of how language development corresponds to physical changes in the brain.

much more complicated than trying to figure out what a novel word, like *gavagai*, means. For example, given the segmentation problem in speech perception, there is no guarantee that *gavagai* is a single word. From an infant's perspective, there is no guarantee that the sound has any communication value at all! The point is that before children learn to use words and to string them together, they must learn the phonology of their language. Only then are they in a position to build a lexicon and master syntactic rules. Let's take a look at the major developments in each of these areas.

Phonological Development

The most basic ability that a person needs to begin mastering a spoken language is the ability to distinguish among the phonemic contrasts that the language uses. And as I noted above, methods like the HAS procedure allow investigators to test sound discrimination abilities even in very young infants. Of course, being able to discriminate between two sounds played repeatedly under ideal listening conditions is not the same as recognizing phonemes in the naturalistic contexts in which speech occurs. As we examine phonological development, our central focus will be on how early simple discrimination abilities are observed and how infants mature in their ability to deal with the complexity of naturally occurring speech sounds.

Basic Phoneme Distinctions.   By testing infants in their first months of life, numerous researchers have found that the ability to discriminate different speech sounds does *not* appear to be learned (reviewed in Gerken, 1994; Jusczyk, 1995). For example, consider the distinction between /ra/ and /la/. This distinction, which is mastered

FIGURE 10.3   Brain Maturation: Birth to Age Five

This graph shows changes in brain weight and amount of activity in the frontal and temporal (side) areas of the brain. The brain weight data are based on figures obtained by Lemire, Loeser, Leech, and Alvord (1975), whereas the brain activity data are based on electroencephalogram (EEG) readings collected by Fischer and Rose (1995). The EEG is a measure of activity level in broad brain regions taken (painlessly) by electrodes placed on the scalp.

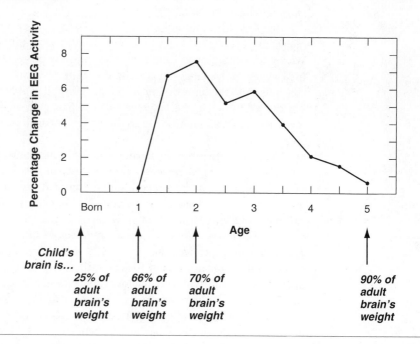

rather late in speech production, presents a continuing source of difficulty for many non-native speakers of English. Yet, Eimas (1975a) found that two-month-old infants were able to perceive the two sounds as different.

These data suggest that the ability to distinguish between two phonemes does *not* depend on an extensive period of exposure to a particular language. To test this idea further, Eimas (1975b) investigated whether American infants who were exposed only to English could perceive a voicing contrast between stop consonants that is found in the Thai language but not in the English language. Eimas found that the infants could perceive the contrast, though the difference in voicing had to be fairly large. Similarly, Streeter (1976) found that Kikuyu infants (from Kenya) could distinguish /ba/ from /pa/, even though that distinction is not used in Kikuyu.

The experiments by Eimas, Streeter, and others (e.g., Best, McRoberts & Sithole, 1988; Werker & Lalonde, 1988) clearly show that infants do not need to have experienced a particular speech contrast in order to perceive the contrast. These data support the view that humans have an inborn capacity to discriminate among the sounds that could be used in *any* language that they will hear. However, psycholinguists continue to disagree over whether this capacity is specific to language or part of our general auditory perception ability (e.g., Best, 1994; Gerkin, 1994; Kluender, 1994).

Whatever the outcome of this debate, our innate ability to discriminate speech sounds is an important foundation for language acquisition. But it is also clear that we have to build extensively on this foundation in order to understand and produce streams of speech in naturalistic contexts. As we deal with more complex stimuli and language contexts, will we see more evidence for an influence from the child's specific language environment?

The first clue to the answer to this question comes from studies of perception of non-native speech contrasts by infants six to twelve months of age. In particular, Werker and Tees (1984) found that the ability to perceive distinctions that are not used in the native language actually *declines* in this age range. Not all non-native contrasts show the same decline in perceptibility (Best, 1993), but the general pattern suggests that, during the latter half of the first year of life, infants are tuning in selectively to those sounds that are important to their particular language environment.

There is another context in which we see evidence that six- to twelve-month-old infants are attending to the speech contrasts used in their language. During this period of life, children are making speech sounds, referred to as *babbling;* but these sounds, for the most part, do not carry meaning. Babbling takes two forms, reduplicated and variegated (Oller, 1980). An infant engaged in **reduplicated babbling** produces the same consonant-vowel sequence over and over, as in [bababababa]. In contrast, **variegated babbling** involves the production of a string of different syllables with a sentence-like intonation, as in [badadomi]. The latter almost sounds as though the infant is conversing with you in a foreign language.

Although early investigators claimed that babbling was independent of the sounds in the child's language environment (e.g., Lenneberg, 1967), later research has shown that infants differ in their babbling depending on the language environment. For example, infants raised in homes where English is spoken produce different vowel sounds from infants raised in homes where Cantonese is spoken (de Boysson-Bardies, Halle, Sagart & Durand, 1989). Moreover, deaf children babble, but the patterns of sound they produce differ from those of hearing children (Gerken, 1994).

Differences in babbling can be observed at nine to 10 months of age, the same period in which we see a loss in children's ability to perceive contrasts that are not used in their native language. Thus, studies of both perception and production converge on the idea that after about six months of age, infants' attention is focused on the phonology of their native language. It is during this stage of development that the innate abilities to discriminate between different sounds are being shaped and guided by the linguistic environment.

Perceiving Sounds in Context.   As discussed in Chapter 4, we can talk in the abstract about making a particular phonemic discrimination, but in practice things are more complicated than that. Depending on the context, the "same" two sounds may be acoustically quite different. And although infants may be able to perceive such a difference between two syllables spoken in isolation, this is a long way from the ability to recognize patterns within a stream of naturally occurring speech. So, how do infants cope with the contextual variability of speech sounds?

As with the perception of basic speech contrasts, some ability to deal with variability in speech sounds is present very early. For example, Jusczyk, Pisoni, and Mullenix (1992) found that two-month-old infants could distinguish between the sound of *bug* and the sound of *dug* regardless of whether the sounds were produced by a male or female speaker. Nevertheless, despite this early ability to deal with variability in speech sounds, the effects of experience show up soon. For example, Kuhl (1991, 1993) has studied infants' discrimination of different vowel sounds. As infants attend more and more to the specific sounds used in their language environment, they seem to represent vowel sounds in terms of a prototype, or best representative, for each vowel category. As long as the particular production of /i/ is close enough to the prototype of /i/, the infants can classify the sound despite variability. With more and more experience, they develop better prototypes for each vowel, and vowel discrimination improves.

Of course, one of the difficulties with vowel sounds is that they vary acoustically depending on the consonant sound with which they are joined. Not surprisingly, then, infants of only a few months of age do not show much evidence of the ability to perceive that the same vowel segment has occurred in two different syllables. For example, Jusczyk and Derrah (1987) found that, in the HAS procedure, young infants responded as though /bi/ and /di/ are as dissimilar as /bi/ and /da/. Over time, however, infants hear enough sound patterns that they can recognize groups of sounds that go together as a unit.

How do infants come to represent the speech sounds, and combinations of sounds, that are used by their native language? At present, we do not have a definitive answer to this question. One possibility, however, is that before their first birthday infants have begun to notice the correspondence between particular sounds and particular objects or events in their environment, and their awareness of these reoccurring strings could draw their attention to the contrasts that are important for their native language (e.g., Studdert-Kennedy, 1986). Initially, infants may recognize the general acoustic pattern of a string of sounds, and only later come to "fine-tune" their representations of these patterns in terms of the precise sounds that compose each string (Gerken, 1994).

Of course, recognizing patterns of sound is the basis for learning words and building a lexicon. But before we turn to a discussion of how the lexicon is built, we must tackle one final question related to phonology: How do children acquiring a language learn to segment different speech strings into the appropriate groupings?

Segmentation and Prosody. Because the speech stream does not always include clear breaks between words, people need ways to segment the stream into meaningful groups. We encountered this problem earlier in our examination of adult speech recognition. However, for adults, the problem is less severe because they have a lexicon. That is, adults can monitor the speech input for sound patterns that match up with patterns for words already stored in memory. Infants, on the other hand, face quite a problem. How do they discover *where* the words are before they know *what* the words are?

An important cue to segmentation that does not require a preexisting lexicon is prosody (see Chapter 5). Indeed, the pattern of stress, pauses, and intonation in spoken language can be used as a cue to the constituents of an utterance (e.g., Cutler, 1996; Gleitman & Wanner, 1982). This idea is known as the **prosodic bootstrapping hypothesis.** For example, the fact that in English most words begin with a syllable that is strongly stressed could serve as a cue that allows children to identify word boundaries within a stream of speech.

For the prosodic bootstrapping hypothesis to be correct, infants would have to be sensitive to the rhythmic pattern of speech. And, indeed, there is considerable evidence that even newborns are sensitive to prosodic variations. For example, four-day-old infants show a listening preference for speech that has the prosodic characteristics of their parents' language (Mehler et al., 1988). Familiar prosody is probably also responsible for newborns' preference for a story that was read to them prenatally (DeCasper & Spence, 1986). Thus, prosody may begin to shape children's speech processing preferences and attention even before they are born!

In their early days, infants are responding to very gross patterns in the rhythm of speech. But with time and experience, they attend to more specific features of prosody. For example, by six to nine months of age, infants exposed to English attend longer to a list of words that show the typical English strong-weak syllable pattern (Jusczyk, Cutler & Redanz, 1993).

During this same period, infants seem to be paying attention to prosodic features that may be a clue to segmentation at the syntactic level (Hirsh-Pasek et al., 1987; Jusczyk et al., 1992). For example, Jusczyk and associates (1992) found that six-month-olds showed a preference for speech in which pauses were inserted at major syntactic boundaries over speech in which pauses were in nonboundary positions. What they concluded is that infants are apparently sensitive to the more natural prosodic pattern of pausing at major boundaries.

The possibility that infants are using prosody to segment speech may help explain why adults speak so differently to infants and young children than they do to other adults. You have probably noticed this distinction yourself. When talking to babies and toddlers, in particular, adults tend to use short sentences with exaggerated intonation and especially clear articulation. This type of speech, known as **child-directed speech (CDS)**, or **motherese,*** may help children use prosody as an aid in segmentation.

A variety of studies have shown that infants attend better to CDS than to adult-directed speech (ADS). For example, Fernald (1985) found that infants of a few months of age will turn toward the source of CDS in preference to ADS. And as verified by research in several different languages, CDS holds infants' attention better (e.g., Werker, Pegg & McLeod, 1994). But the question remains: Does the exaggerated intonation actually help with specific tasks like segmentation? Answering this question has been a matter of controversy (Aslin, Woodward, LaMendola & Bever, 1996).

---

* But just in case Whorf was even partially correct in suggesting that language determines thought, I'll hereafter avoid this term, even though it is commonly found in the developmental literature.

However, according to Hirsh-Pasek and associates (1987), the preference that six-month-olds show for speech with pauses at clause boundaries was found only with CDS, not ADS. The implication is that CDS may play a role in helping infants learn how to segment speech.

It is important to remember that, although prosodic cues may help the infant start to "break the code" of speech, there is undoubtedly more to segmentation into words and clauses than just prosodic bootstrapping. Although pauses and changes in intonation are probably more reliable markers of the structure of an utterance in CDS than in ADS, prosody is far from perfect as a cue for segmenting utterances in general. For example, many pauses do not mark syntactic boundaries (Fernald & McRoberts, 1996; Pinker, 1987). In addition, recent evidence suggests that young children are using cues other than prosody in order to segment speech (Myers et al., 1996). For example, Myers and associates (1996) found that at eleven months of age, but not earlier, children could discriminate between passages in which pauses were inserted at word boundaries and passages in which pauses were inserted within syllable boundaries. Moreover, the children who were able to make this discrimination could do so even when prosodic information was filtered out of the stimuli. This finding certainly supports the contention that the children were using cues besides prosody, but what might these other cues be?

One source of information that children might use to segment speech is their growing knowledge of specific sound combinations. That is, as children start to learn common sound combinations, and then specific words, speech gets easier and easier to segment. In the next section, we will explore how this kind of lexical knowledge could develop. After we examine lexical and then syntactic development, we will be in a position to consider not only different theoretical positions on language acquisition in general but also, more specifically, different views on the sources of the knowledge that guide acquisition. However, before we move on, it may help to review the changes in infant speech processing that we've examined thus far. These changes are summarized in Table 10.1.

TABLE 10.1	**Examples Showing That Language Experience Affects Phonological Processing**
Newborn to 4 months	• Ability to discriminate own from non-native language • Preference for mother's voice • Preference for a story or song heard prenatally
6 months	• Some decline in ability to make non-native sound discriminations • Preference for pauses at clause boundaries in native language only
10 months	• No longer able to discriminate non-native phonemic contrasts • Preference for words with common native stress pattern

Source: Adapted from Werker, Lloyd, Pegg & Polka (1996, p. 435).

Lexical Development

The major lesson from the previous section is that infants, despite the fact that they have tiny attention spans and spend much of their time sleeping, seem to be information sponges when it comes to speech. Indeed, recent evidence suggests that infants are able to pick out specific words in natural speech quite early. Jusczyk and Aslin (1995) familiarized a group of infants with particular words by reading the words in isolation. Then, after this familiarization period, the infants were exposed to a sentence that contained either a familiarized word or a word that differed from the familiarized word by only one or two phonetic features. Remarkably, these infants, who were only seven and a half months old, turned toward, and listened longer to, sentences containing the specific words they had heard before.*

Recently, Saffran, Aslin, and Newport (1996) extended this finding by showing that after only two minutes of familiarization, eight-month-olds can recognize sound combinations that represent nonsense words made up by the experimenters. In this study, the stimuli were strings of sounds that were produced without pauses, stresses, or any other acoustic cues that could signal word boundaries. The only cue that something constituted a "word" was that a particular set of sounds reliably occurred together in sequence amid other randomly paired sounds. Infants' ability to recognize these familiar sequences shows that they have a powerful learning mechanism for segmenting speech and learning words. In essence, infants keep track of which sounds tend to occur together in a specific sequence. This learning mechanism may be part of our general cognitive system, or it may be part of our inherited language ability. Either way, it suggests that, when considering the degree to which knowledge of language is built in, we should be careful not to underestimate the learning abilities of infants.

Early Word Production.   By seven to eight months of age, infants show evidence of noticing specific word patterns in speech. It is only a few months after this that the production side of language takes a great leap forward. Around their first birthday, children start to produce single words. Across different languages and cultures, children's early productions are very similar (Nelson, 1973). Names for things are the most common early words, along with a few action words and expressions like "hi" or "no."

Then, when children are around eighteen months of age, their vocabulary mushrooms and they begin to put word combinations together. By two years of age, children may use anywhere from 50 to 600 different words. Yet even this range underestimates their lexicon, because at two years they can understand many more words than they are able to produce (Clark, 1993).

How can children learn so much so quickly during this period? We don't have all the answers, but we do know that the language stimulation that children receive from their environment greatly influences their rate of progress. For example, when Hart

---

* You may be wondering why the infants in this study attended more to the *familiar* sequences, whereas in habituation paradigms (like the HAS procedure) infants have been shown to attend more to *novel* stimuli. As it turns out, infants attend to familiar stimuli longer when the familiarization phase is relatively brief, as in Jusczyk and Aslin's experiment(1995), but when infants are highly familiar with a stimulus, they prefer novel stimuli over familiar ones.

and Risely (1995) studied parent-child interactions in the homes of both disadvantaged and affluent, educated families, they found huge differences in the extent of verbal interaction that the children received in the first two years of life. On average, the children of professional parents heard 2,100 words per hour, whereas the children from economically and socially disadvantaged homes heard only 600 words per hour. These differences were associated with large differences in the children's later vocabulary size and general level of intellectual ability.

However, just knowing that environmental stimulation is important doesn't tell us how the child's lexicon is built up over time. Some clues about this process come from the pattern of acquisition of early words. When children begin to use a particular word, their use of the word overlaps with the way adults use the word, but it does not match exactly. For instance, a child's usage may start out being very bound to context. He may say "shoe" when shoes are on someone's feet, but fail to use "shoe" to refer to shoes sitting in a closet (Reich, 1976). This is an example of **underextension** of word meaning. At other times, children's early use of a word may reflect **overextension.** In such cases, they use a word to refer to a much wider range of objects than would occur in adult usage. For example, after learning that her pet beagle is a "doggie," a child may soon begin using "doggie" to refer not only to dogs but also to sheep, goats, and cows (Anglin, 1978).

It appears that when children learn a new word, they assign an initial meaning right away. The word becomes part of their lexicon, and they start using the word in various contexts (Carey, 1978; Clark, 1993). By trying to communicate with the word, the children can then refine its meaning over time to more closely match adult usage. However, we have to be careful about assuming that usage in production necessarily reflects a child's understanding of a word. Some overextension, for example, may be due to an inability to produce a more appropriate word. Even when the child is using "doggie" to refer to both dogs and goats, she may be able to correctly select which picture, a dog or a goat, is a "doggie" (Thomson & Chapman, 1977).

In summary, children are practical little communicators. At an age when they cannot yet produce the precisely correct word, they use the best word available that they can produce (Clark, 1995). In addition, they use a new word as soon as they have some idea of its meaning, and they refine its meaning as they try out the word in various contexts.

This practical approach to communication is also evident in the way that children use single words to convey an idea that, for an adult, would be conveyed by a whole sentence. A single word used in context to communicate a more complex idea is known as a **holophrase.** In a sense, the child produces a key word and uses the context as the rest of the "sentence" (Greenfield & Smith, 1976). For example, when a child says "water" while pointing to a glass, it is pretty clear that saying "water" really means "I want some water."

Constraints on Meaning Assignment.   So far, this review of lexical acquisition sounds a lot like the simple hypothesis-testing process in Quine's (1960) "*gavagai* problem." You start out with a reasonable hypothesis about a word's meaning and then you try to use the word to test out its meaning. If you use the word properly, your communication attempts are successful. If not, you adjust your word meaning and try again.

Of course, one- or two-year-old children are not very logical creatures, so it is very unlikely that they consciously entertain hypotheses about what words mean. Nevertheless, you can imagine early ideas of meaning being shaped and refined based on feedback from children's attempts to communicate in a kind of nonconscious hypothesis testing. At the same time, however, this hypothesis-testing notion begs a very important question: Where does the initial idea of a word's meaning come from? The point of the *gavagai* exercise is that, given the arbitrary nature of language, there are limitless possibilities for what a word *might* mean, even if it is heard in several situations. When a parent points to a kitten in a pet-store window and says "kitty," that new word could, in principle, be the name for this particular thing, or it could mean anything with fur, or the fur itself, or just "look at that."

A possible solution to this problem would be to build into the language-acquisition system some innate constraints on the hypotheses that children generate (Fodor, 1981). One constraint that has been proposed is the **whole object assumption.** According to this view, children assume that a new label uttered in the context of an object that has drawn their attention, such as a kitten, refers to the whole object rather than to a part of the object. A related constraint is the **taxonomic assumption,** whereby children assume that verbal labels refer to categories of objects of the same kind. So, whereas a child might initially assume that "kitty" refers to any small fuzzy animal, the child does not assume that "kitty" refers to a description of a scene, such as "a thing in a cage."

Markman (1990) tested children in the eighteen- to twenty-four-month age range to see if their comprehension of novel verbal labels followed these constraints. In one condition, the children were shown a picture of a dog, at which point the experimenter said, "This is a dax. Can you find another dax?" From a set of various pictures, the children chose another picture of a dog—in other words, a taxonomic relative of the whole object. However, in a second condition, the verbal label was omitted. In this case, when the children were just shown a dog and asked if they could find another one, they tended to choose a picture that depicted a thematic relative, such as a bone. According to Markman, these data show that constraints like the taxonomic assumption are specific to language acquisition rather than a part of our general cognitive system.

Of course, these constraints do not tell the entire story. They do not explain how children acquire verbs or names for the parts of objects, for example. One way of addressing this acquisition issue, then, is to suggest that the types of assumptions that the child uses vary depending on the nature of what is being referred to. So, for actions, we might have a whole action assumption that is parallel to the whole object assumption (cf., Clark, 1993; Soja, Carey & Spelke, 1991).

As you might expect, this nativist view of language-specific constraints on word meaning has not gone unchallenged. For example, Nelson (1988) argues that constraints are not necessary because the adult and child work together closely to achieve successful communication. For example, parents tailor their naming of objects to fit the age and mental abilities of their children. Nelson also points out that the constraint approach does not explain the underextensions that young children make when they use a word only in a very specific context. Further, she asserts that it is best to think of these proposed constraints as biases or tendencies, given that children are variable in terms of the degree to which their responses in experiments actually adhere to the assumptions being tested.

Another concern is that some assumptions by their very nature must be only general tendencies, inasmuch as they are occasionally abandoned by the child. For example, Markman and Wachtel (1988) proposed a **mutual exclusivity assumption,** which refers to the tendency of children to assume that an object can have only one label. The mutual exclusivity assumption may help children assign meanings to novel words by considering only those meanings and referents for which they do not already have a label. However, this tendency must be considered just that—a tendency—because it cannot always be followed. Sometimes objects do have more than one label.

So, where do we stand with respect to the acquisition of word meaning? Nelson is probably correct in suggesting that the cooperative nature of conversations helps children narrow down the possibilities for assigning words to concepts. However, it seems unlikely that the context of conversations, by itself, is sufficient to handle the infinite possibilities that a particular naming episode could generate. In addition, Nelson's criticisms of the nativist constraint framework do not strike a lethal blow to this approach. For example, even if the constraints were shown to be innately programmed, we could still expect some variability in performance. One source of this variability could be that the adult and the child are not always in synch about which object or action is being referred to. Unless the child gets this right, the appropriate constraint cannot be applied.

It is important to note that the issue of how the child understands the target of the utterance is not well explained in the constraint view. If it is in this context that the adult-child interaction is important to narrowing down the possibilities, then Nelson (1988) and Markman (1990) may be explaining different aspects of the problem of learning a word's meaning. Given the complexity of the problem, it is likely that a child uses several kinds of information when trying to learn a word's meaning. Note that the word-learning situation is usually quite rich in information. Typically, an adult does not just point to an object and say a word. Rather, the adult speaks to the child in simple sentences. This speech context may facilitate the learning of new words if the children can use their developing knowledge of syntax to assist their lexical acquisition.

Word Meaning and Syntax. In a now classic paper, Brown (1957) summed up the problem we have been considering and even offered a hypothesis toward its solution:

> If there were nothing to suggest to the child the probably relevant features of the nonlinguistic world, discovery of linguistic meanings would be a very laborious affair. However, a new word is ordinarily introduced in a way that makes its part-of-speech membership clear: "Look at the *dog*" or "See him *running.*" . . . A child who had absorbed the semantics of the noun and verb would know, the first time he heard the word *dog*, that it was likely to refer to an object having a characteristic size and shape, whereas *running* would be likely to name some animal motion. *(p. 3)*

The idea that Brown advocated in this paper is called the **syntactic bootstrapping hypothesis** (Gleitman, 1990). It suggests that children may use syntax to infer word meaning. Brown tested this hypothesis by showing children a picture that portrayed an unfamiliar action and then providing a novel word relating to the picture. For example, one picture showed a person performing a task using an unfamiliar tool on a bunch of material. The first trial, in which Brown's preschool subjects were told "In this picture you can see nissing," suggested that *niss* is a verb. When asked to select another picture that showed *nissing,* they chose a picture that depicted the action. However, a second trial, in which the children were told that the picture showed *some niss,* suggested that *niss* is a mass noun. This time, when asked to select a picture for the meaning of *niss,* the children inferred that *niss* was the material. Finally, when told that the picture showed *a niss,* the children inferred that *niss* is a count noun and when asked about the meaning of *niss,* the children selected a picture depicting the tool.

These data provide strong support for the syntactic bootstrapping hypothesis. They have also been extended in a number of ways. For example, even two- to three-year olds can use the mass noun/count noun distinction to determine what a novel label might refer to (Bloom, 1994). And three-year-olds have been observed to focus on objects when the novel word is a noun but on properties of objects when the novel word is an adjective (Gelman & Markman, 1985).

It is important to keep in mind that syntactic bootstrapping cannot serve as a complete explanation of learning word meanings. Nevertheless, syntax, in concert with the other types of cues to word meaning we have reviewed, can greatly narrow down the possibilities of what a particular word could mean. And, of course, syntactic bootstrapping can work only if the young child is parsing the sentences she hears and identifying syntactic relationships among words. We turn now to a discussion of how and when this syntactic processing emerges in language development.

Syntactic Development

In addition to the dramatic increase in children's vocabulary that occurs at eighteen to twenty-four months of age, we see the appearance of utterances that combine words. In the beginning, these are typically two-word combinations like "More milk," "Mommy go," and "No bed." However, even these two-word utterances show evidence of grammatical competence. The words are not combined haphazardly. In more than 95 percent of children's two-word utterances, the words are in their proper order (Brown, 1973). It is as though these utterances are derived from longer sentences, but with only the most important words used in order to make production easier. The early sentences that children produce are sometimes called **telegraphic speech.**[*]

As children grow from two to four years of age, the length and complexity of their sentences increase steadily and rapidly. By the time they are four years old, it is very easy to have a full-fledged conversation with them. In fact, if a child of this age is excited about something, you may wind up on the receiving end of an extended monologue rather than being a participant in the conversation! It is striking that, although they know little about the world at large, have only the most basic understanding of numbers, and believe in most any magical thing they see, four-year-olds have already mastered a great many of the subtleties of language use.

---

[*] In the old days of communication by telegraph, people had to pay by the number of words sent. Thus, messages were short and choppy, giving only the minimum number of words necessary for communication.

The most common way to assess the rapid change in grammatical ability of children is to calculate the **mean length of utterance (MLU)**. This is a measure of the average number of *morphemes* produced per utterance. The extraordinary rate of increase in the MLU of young children can be seen in Figure 10.4, which shows data for the three children studied closely by Roger Brown in his groundbreaking research.

Children's sentences do not just get longer. Indeed, their syntax becomes more and more complex. By four years of age, children display the same kinds of embedding

---

FIGURE 10.4   **Growth in the Mean Length of Utterance**

Shown here are the data on three children studied by Roger Brown and his colleagues (1973). Note that the rate of increase in utterance length surged dramatically whether the children started making two-word utterances early (Eve) or somewhat later (Adam and Sarah). Brown divided the changes he observed into five stages (marked by Roman numerals). Across these stages, syntactic complexity increased along with the length of the utterances.

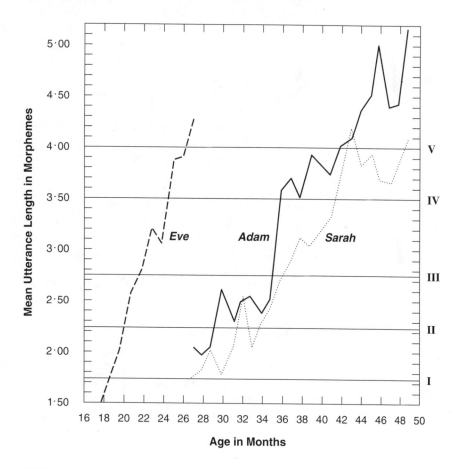

in their sentences as are seen in adult syntax (Slobin, 1985). Here are a few samples of speech from Adam, one of the children whom Brown studied. Adam produced his first word combinations relatively late, at the age of two years and three months ("2;3"), but note the complexity of the grammar he displayed about a year later (Pinker, 1994):

2;3:   Play checkers.
        Big drum.

2;6:   What that egg doing?
        No, I don't want to sit seat.

2;9:   Where Mommy keep her pocket book?
        Show you something funny.

3;0:   I going come in fourteen minutes.
        You dress me up like baby elephant.

3;2:   So, it can't be cleaned?
        Can I keep the screwdriver just like a carpenter keep the screwdriver?

A central problem in trying to understand how this rapid rise in grammatical ability takes place is that children do not receive a great deal of **negative evidence.** In other words, they do not receive much feedback that particular utterances are ungrammatical. They hear others speak grammatically, of course; but how do they come to follow the subtle rules of syntax without being told what forms are incorrect? To put it another way, when Adam said something like "What that egg doing?" and his parents responded to the idea he communicated rather than to the form, how did Adam ever learn that such a sentence is ungrammatical?

The lack of negative evidence in language acquisition has been a particularly unsettling problem for behaviorist views of language. For example, Skinner (1957) proposed that there is nothing special about learning a language. He suggested that parents express approval for grammatical utterances and disapproval for ungrammatical ones. However, when Brown and Hanlon (1970) put this idea to the test by analyzing transcripts of parent-child interactions, they found that feedback to the child depended on whether the utterance was *true*, not whether the utterance was grammatical. Even in studies that have provided evidence for parental feedback on grammar, the feedback is too infrequent and inconsistent to be of value as negative evidence (Marcus, 1993; Penner, 1987).

Somehow, then, children master syntax with little or no negative evidence. There are two general approaches to studying how they accomplish this feat. **Discontinuous theories** assume that children acquire an understanding that sentences consist of different units and from there they learn about syntactic rules and syntactic categories. In contrast, **continuous theories** take a more nativist approach. These latter theories assume that children are born with knowledge of syntactic categories and with constraints on how grammars can work. So, the problem for children, according to continuous theories, is to connect this innate grammatical knowledge with the words and combinations that are found in the particular language being acquired. Let's examine these two types of acquisition theories in more detail.

Discontinuous Acquisition. From this viewpoint, the story of syntactic mastery starts when children are able to carve up sentences into words, perhaps by using prosody. The children note that certain words occur in particular positions within utterances. This initial categorization of words by position is nonsyntactic, but the children may build on this classification scheme as they discover syntactic rules (Braine, 1963). However, it is unlikely that noting regularities in word position yields enough information on which to build a grammar (Pinker, 1987). Accordingly, some theorists have argued that children start with conceptual categories like "object word" and "action word" and that, with experience, these conceptual categories are transformed into syntactic categories like "count noun" or "verb" (e.g., Macnamara, 1982). Unfortunately, this view lacks an explicit proposal for how children go from conceptual categories to syntactic categories.

Continuous Acquisition.   If syntactic categories are built into the maturing language faculty in the brain, then the child does not face the problem of discovering them. Yet the problem of connecting these built-in syntactic categories with the words in a particular language is no easy feat, either. For example, although every language has a syntactic category corresponding to the category *noun,* the nouns across different languages neither sound similar nor occur in the same sentence positions.

A proposal for how the mapping between words and syntax could work is known as the **semantic bootstrapping hypothesis** (Pinker, 1987, 1995). According to this hypothesis, children may use the semantic properties of words (and phrases), inferred from the context surrounding the words, to connect the elements of a specific language with general syntactic categories.

A simple example may help clarify this idea. A piece of syntactic knowledge that might be built in is

NAMES OF OBJECTS ARE COUNT NOUNS.

Now, assuming that children learn from context, let's consider the case of a youngster who, perhaps with the help of constraints on lexical acquisition, discovers that *dog* refers to a particular kind of furry, lively OBJECT. Achieving this semantic insight leads naturally to the child's classification of *dog* as a count noun. Later, when a few words have been assigned to noun and verb categories, it is much easier for the child to discover general syntactic rules. Upon hearing "The dog chased the cat," the child can infer not just that *dog* comes before *chased* but that a noun performing an action comes before the verb that expresses the action.

Semantic bootstrapping makes for a nice story, but I hope that at this point you are jumping up and down with an objection (metaphorically, if not literally). In the section on lexical acquisition, I tried to convince you of the plausibility of *syntactic* bootstrapping, or using syntax to help in the acquisition of word meanings. Now, however, I am talking about *semantic* bootstrapping, in which word meanings are supposed to help in the acquisition of syntax. We can't have it both ways, can we?

We can't have it both ways for the same word. That is, a child cannot use a semantic representation of the word *dog* to assign it to a syntactic category *and* use knowledge that *dog* is a noun to determine its meaning. Nevertheless, it is possible for syntactic bootstrapping and semantic bootstrapping to work together during language acquisition. A child could use context and nonsyntactic constraints such as the whole object assumption to infer the meanings of a few common words and then use semantic bootstrapping to assign those words to syntactic categories. And eventually, once the child has a small working vocabulary that is mapped onto the appropriate lexical categories, syntactic information could start to assist the child in learning new words and accelerate the rate of lexical acquisition (Brown, 1957; Gleitman, 1990). This view certainly favors the hypothesis that language is founded on a set of innate ideas (lexical constraints and syntactic knowledge), but it still leaves a large role for learning syntactic rules from experience. We turn now to an alternative view that assigns an even larger role to innate factors in language acquisition.

Parameter Setting.   In Chapter 2, I introduced you to Chomsky's (1986) "principles and parameters theory." According to this theory, children are born with a universal grammar that has parameters representing the dimensions along which languages can vary. Because principles and parameters theory assumes that much of language grammar is genetically built in, it considers the role of language experience to be rather limited. Specifically, it maintains that acquisition of language is largely a matter of **parameter setting,** such that the role of language experience is to switch the parameters to the right settings for the particular language being acquired.

Word order is a good example of one such parameter (Pinker, 1984, 1995). In some languages, such as English, word order is very important to the question of whether a sentence is grammatical or not. But in other languages—for example, Russian and Swedish—there is more freedom allowed in the ordering of words. If the innate grammar specifies that word order is a parameter, then the "switch" for this parameter could be set to either "fixed word order" or "variable word order."* According to principles and parameters theory, then, children do not have to discover or deduce whether word order matters in the grammar of their language because their language experience triggers the right setting.

The simplest way to ensure that a parameter gets the right setting is to have an initial setting for each parameter. This initial setting could be based on the **subset principle.** That is, a parameter should be set by default at the value that leads to the most restrictive grammar. For example, all languages have subjects (S), verbs (V), and objects (O), but it is a more restricted subset of languages that specifies a particular ordering, as in the SVO ordering of English. Based on the subset principle, children should start out with the word-order parameter on the fixed-order setting. If this setting turns out *not* to be correct, a child will find that out from positive evidence: Many utterances that the child hears will violate a fixed-order rule. This evidence could then trigger a new setting for the parameter.

One reason to think of acquisition in this way is that the parameter-setting idea may explain how children acquire language so quickly, despite the lack of negative evidence. If parents who spoke a "fixed word order" language corrected their children for violating word order and shaped them into using the correct forms, then there would be no need for an initial parameter setting. However, as we have seen, children

---

* It is possible for a parameter to have more than two settings—for example, to allow different degrees of freedom in word order—but, for simplicity, we will stick to the case of just two settings.

actually receive very little negative evidence. By starting out with the parameter set to a more restrictive setting, they can correct the setting, if needed, with only positive evidence.

Parameter setting has been used to explain another phenomenon in children's syntactic development: the omission of subjects. A striking aspect of telegraphic speech is that young children are much more likely to omit subjects than objects, as in these examples from Bowerman (1973) and Bloom, Lightbown, and Hood (1975):

see running

play bed

want go get it

An interesting explanation for the subject-omission phenomenon has been developed based on principles and parameters theory (Hyams, 1986; Hyams & Wexler, 1993). Unlike English, there are some languages, sometimes called **PRO-drop languages,** in which having an explicit subject is optional. For example, in English if we want to express *I go to the movies,* the pronoun is not optional. However, in Italian it is perfectly permissible to say *vado al cinema* (literally, "go to the movies") to mean *I go to the movies.* This distinction among languages may be related to a hypothetical parameter called the **null subject parameter** (Hyams, 1986; Hyams & Wexler, 1993). The setting of this parameter would specify whether or not a sentence could have a null, or missing, subject. Note that there are several other systematic differences between the grammars of PRO-drop languages and those of non-PRO-drop languages, so the parameter is not necessarily related to this single language feature (Bloom, 1994).

Unfortunately, because we don't know the full extent of what the null subject parameter might control, it is not clear which setting should be the initial setting according to the subset principle (Hyams, 1986). However, if the initial setting allows for optional subjects, the phenomenon of subject omission in early speech could be explained. During the stage of telegraphic speech, children may be following a grammar that specifies that subjects are optional. Then, given sufficient experience with a language like English, the children may reset their parameter to the nonoptional subject setting.

It is premature, however, to concede that subject omission supports the nativist view. Let's consider another possibility. Children may omit subjects not because of their level of syntactic competence but, rather, because of the demands of general processing (Pinker, 1984; Valian, 1991). As we saw in the last chapter, language production involves a number of different processing demands, and for children, articulation of sounds is relatively effortful. Thus, young children's omission of subjects may be an adaptation to the general processing demands of language production. In other words, it may be for pragmatic reasons that subjects are more likely to be omitted than objects. Adults, too, may find it easier to infer a topic when the subject is omitted than when other elements are omitted (Greenfield & Smith, 1976). Alternatively, it may be that subject omissions are part of a general tendency among young children to omit weakly stressed syllables (Gerken, 1991). If so, the subject position would be affected more than other positions because pronouns tend to be weakly stressed. In support of this idea, Gerken (1991) found that children drop weakly stressed syllables even when trying to repeat a sentence produced by an adult. This result suggests that the problem may be related to production, not grammatical competence.

You should note that Hyams (1986; Hyams & Wexler, 1993), in proposing a null subject parameter, does not deny that processing load problems play some role in subject omission. However, she argues that the processing explanation does not provide an explicit and formal model for explaining the whole phenomenon. Similarly, Weinberg (1987) proposed that the reason the null subject parameter may be set initially to the optional subject value is that children may need to omit some elements for a while until their processing system becomes more mature.

Psycholinguists continue to disagree over whether a combination of processing load and parameter setting is necessary to explain subject omission. One concern is that the evidence in samples of speech that would trigger a change in the parameter for English-speaking children is less direct than that associated with the word-order parameter. One type of evidence that such children could use, then, is the *absence* of the use of the null subject option by adults. However, it is not clear that lack of evidence for a setting could reset a parameter.

To avoid this problem of relying on absence of use as evidence, Hyams (1986) suggested that the evidence children use is the presence of expletive subjects. No, that doesn't mean parents' use of profanity. In this context, expletive refers to a subject like *It* in the sentence *It is freezing*. PRO-drop languages, such as Italian and Spanish, do not allow expletive subjects. Note, however, that expletive subjects do not just suddenly appear in the child's linguistic environment, after which subject omission stops. Hyams' parameter-setting analysis begs the question as to why it takes time for children to use the triggering evidence that is present. In addition, children would have to be able to set the parameter properly despite exceptional cases in English, which allows the omission of subjects—as in "Close the door!" (Bloom, 1994; Valian, 1990).

Even though the issue of how to explain subject omission is far from settled, there is a general lesson that we can take away from this debate. We have seen considerable evidence throughout this chapter that language acquisition is built on an innate foundation for phonological, lexical, and syntactic processing. Whether this foundation consists of constraints that guide children's hypothesis testing, or whether it includes an entire syntactic framework in the form of a set of parameters, is still an open question. As we try to determine exactly what role innate factors play in language acquisition, we must keep in mind that children are maturing in many ways and learning many things in their first several years of life. If, as I have stressed throughout this book, the language system interacts extensively with the rest of our cognitive system, then general cognitive explanations of some language phenomena, based either on learning and memory or on maturation of general intelligence, may compete with explanations based on language-specific maturation. With respect to other language phenomena, however, the two general types of explanations may be complementary. To explore this notion further, we will now consider one final acquisition phenomenon that helps illuminate the interaction of language-specific and general cognitive factors in explaining the acquisition of language.

A Test Case for Innate Foundations: Overregularization

When you picture some ability improving over time, you probably think in terms of continuous gradual improvements in performance. For instance, when you learned to ride a bike or to skate, at first you were unable to balance yourself at all without assistance. Then, you could wobble along, but only for a short distance before your rear end started imitating Newton's apple. Yet, gradually, you went farther and farther without falling, and then you became proficient.

It would seem strange indeed if you had performed almost perfectly after only a little practice, then you got much worse, only to become proficient again later. Yet, amazingly, children's mastery of the past tense of verbs changes over time in a way that seems similar to the strange developmental progression I just described. Instead of a steady progression toward adult-like use of verb tenses, children perform virtually perfectly early on. That is, they use the regular *-ed* rule when appropriate, as in the verbs *walked* and *stopped;* and they use the correct forms of irregular verbs, as in *found* and *went.* But this phase is followed by a relatively long period, from about two to five years of age, in which children start to make more errors than they made when younger. In particular, they display **overregularization.** That is, they start to apply the regular rule in words that are irregular. So, even though they have never heard others use words like *goed* or *finded,* they start to use these word forms. Later, however, the overregularization errors disappear, and children return to adult-like performance. A phenomenon so counterintuitive to common sense deserves an explanation. By completing Activity 10.2, you will have an opportunity to informally test at least one possible explanation.

An Explanation with a Nativist Component

The phenomenon of overregularization seems obviously related to the learning of a rule. Children say *goed* because they have learned a general rule about forming the past tense in English. For example, in the classic study by Berko (1958) that used the "wug test" (see Figure 10.2), Berko also tested children's use of generative rules that apply to verbs. When the children were shown a picture of a man performing an activity and they were told, "Here is a man who likes to rick. Yesterday he did the same thing. Yesterday he . . .," the children completed the sentence with *ricked.*

Rule acquisition is only part of the story, however. It explains why children might use *goed,* but it doesn't explain why they once used *went,* then used *goed,* and then returned to *went.* Steven Pinker's (1984, 1995) explanation for this puzzling sequence is a good example of how language phenomena may be related to both language-specific and general cognitive mechanisms.

The language-specific part of Pinker's explanation is known as the **blocking principle.** According to this principle, we possess tacit knowledge that we should not use a rule to generate a word, as in *go + ed = goed,* if another word already exists in the lexicon to serve the new word's function. So, as adults, we do not use *goed* in natural speech because it is blocked by *went.* But it is difficult to see how the blocking principle would be learned without negative evidence. Accordingly, Pinker (1995) suggested that this principle exists as part of our innate universal grammar, which serves as the

ACTIVITY **10.2**   **Testing for Overregularization**

When learning about language development, you will find that there's no substitute for talking with children. You may have relatives or friends whose families include a preschool child, or you might visit a daycare in order to interview a few children. *In all cases, make sure you have the permission of the child's parent(s), and that you interview the child with a parent, guardian, or teacher present.*

For this activity, it is best that you interview a child of about three or four years of age. After talking to the child for a few minutes to establish rapport, tell the child that you *goed* to see a movie yesterday and ask if he or she *goed*, too. Does the child seem to notice the error? Try out a few other overregularizations as well. If you want to be a bit more industrious, you can make two puppets and have one say "I *readed* this book" and have the other say the sentence properly. Then ask the child which puppet sounded silly.

The point, of course, is to see if you can get evidence as to whether overregularization reflects a problem of competence or performance. If the children you interview make errors themselves, but can detect errors when made by someone else, then the implication would be that overregularization is based not on limited syntactic knowledge but on a production error. Discuss your results with other members of the class.

foundation for language acquisition. There is disagreement over this interpretation of blocking, however (e.g., Bloom, 1994; Clark, 1987).

Whether the blocking principle is part of an innate grammar or not, it is clear that blocking by itself does not explain overregularization. Young children initially use irregular forms like *went* and *found*. So, why don't these irregular forms block overregularization in the way that we presume they do among adults? This is the part of Pinker's explanation that depends on factors that are not specific to language. In particular, Pinker relates the problem of overregularization to a memory limitation. Both children and adults typically need repeated exposures to an arbitrary association in order to consistently and accurately remember it. This is true regardless of whether the association is between a name and a face or a new word and its referent. But children, of course, will have experienced any given word-referent association far less frequently than adults. Children will occasionally use the irregular form after they've heard it a few times, but their memory trace for an irregular verb is going to be weaker than an adult's memory trace. Soon, the children learn the past-tense rule that applies to many different verbs. What happens then is that they use the rule whenever the retrieval of the irregular past-tense form fails.

For example, until *went* is strongly stored in memory, retrieval of the fact that *went* is the past tense of *go* is going to fail occasionally. When the irregular form cannot be retrieved from memory, that form cannot block the use of the past-tense rule, the use of which gets lots and lots of practice because of its generality.

This "blocking plus memory failure" explanation of overregularization predicts that children should show a mix of using both the correct irregular and the incorrect regular past-tense form of a given verb during the same period of development. It also predicts that the overall rate of overregularization should be fairly low, since memory retrieval failures should happen only occasionally. Both of these predictions receive support from the data on overregularization (Marcus et al., 1992).

As Pinker's (1984, 1995) explanation would suggest, the pattern of overregularization appears haphazard. Children sometimes use both the correct irregular and the incorrect regular form *of the same verb* in the course of one conversation. Moreover, the overall error rate for producing the correct past tense is only about 4 percent between the ages of two and five. Finally, it is worth noting that elderly adults, who have less reliable memory retrieval in general, also show overregularization errors (Ullman et al., 1993). These data are consistent with the hypothesis that blocking can eliminate incorrect verb forms and that retrieval failure occasionally allows errors to be produced.

An Explanation without Nativism

A very different view of this whole process was presented in the form of a computer simulation by Rumelhart and McClelland (1986), who constructed a PDP model of past-tense learning. Recall from Chapter 3 that I discussed how, in a connectionist approach to information representation, information could be stored as a pattern of activation across a set of nodes in a network. In particular, Rumelhart and McClelland tried to determine whether such a network could "learn" how to produce the past tense of English. A simplified view of their model is shown in Figure 10.5.

The model is really just a way of mapping the relationship between root words, such as *play* and *hold*, and their past-tense forms, *played* and *held*. When the model is generating the correct past tense of a word, a rule like "add -*ed* to form the past tense" is not directly stored anywhere in the system's memory; yet the model acts as though it works by this rule because there are strong connections between many root words and the past-tense form -*ed*. Irregular verbs, however, have root forms that are strongly connected to other phonological patterns to represent their past tenses.

The interesting question is whether the model can be trained to perform in this way, and whether the learning phases the model goes through are similar to the course of children's acquisition of past tense. In the beginning, no particular set of connections between word-stem features and past-tense features is more active than other connections. Thus, researchers train the model by presenting it with stems and past tenses. This process is analogous to children hearing the correct forms that their parents produce. As training pairs are presented, the connections between particular sets of features are strengthened. For example, if the model is given *play-played*, then the connections between the stem features representing *play* and the past-tense features representing *played* are strengthened. Based on similarities among words, the model can also generate the past-tense forms of words on which it was not specifically trained. So, having been trained on words like *play*, the model can also produce the correct past-tense of *delay*. Likewise, having been trained on *drink-drank*, the model produces *sank* as the past tense of *sink*, because similar features are activated by the two root words.

FIGURE 10.5   ### A PDP Model of Past-Tense Learning

As word pairs (e.g., *walk-walked*) are presented, the modifiable connections between the features of the root form (*walk*) and the features of the past-tense form (*walked*) are strengthened. After being trained on a number of pairs, the model can generalize the appropriate response to verbs that were not used during the training phase.

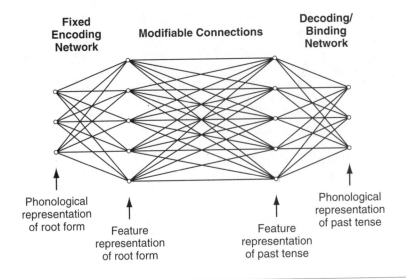

Rumelhart and McClelland (1986) reasoned that children learn high-frequency verbs before low-frequency verbs. Thus, as the most common verbs are irregular, a child should learn a small set of irregular verbs first, then a much larger set of regular verbs. When Rumelhart and McClelland used this order of input to train their model, it went through the same phases as children: correct usage, followed by overregularization, and, finally, back to correct usage. This is the conclusion they offered:

> We chose the study of the acquisition of past tense in part because the phenomenon of regularization is an example often cited in support of the view that children do respond according to general rules of language. Why otherwise, it is sometimes asked, should they generate forms that they have never heard? The answer we offer is that they do so because the past tenses of similar verbs they are learning show such a consistent pattern that the generalization from these similar verbs outweighs the relatively small amount of learning that has occurred on the irregular verb in question. We suspect that essentially similar ideas will prove useful in accounting for other aspects of language acquisition. *(pp. 267–268)*

As you can see, Rumelhart and McClelland's conclusion was distinctly non-nativist. They claimed that the curious developmental course of acquiring past-tense learning could be explained through assumptions about the order of the verbs that children encounter as well as through simple, general learning principles. These ideas, however, are quite controversial. For example, Pinker and colleagues (Marcus et al., 1992; Pinker & Prince, 1988) have identified several problems with Rumelhart and McClelland's PDP model. One of the model's key assumptions is that children start to learn many regular verbs after an initial exposure to mostly irregular verbs. But when Pinker and colleagues checked this assumption against the actual speech samples that Adam, Eve, and Sarah were exposed to, they found that the proportions of regular and irregular verbs remained constant from ages two to five. In addition, Pinker and Prince (1991) argued that it is inaccurate to model past-tense learning as a mapping from one phonological form to another; rather, they claim, it needs to be based on information in the lexicon, which is not part of Rumelhart and McClelland's model. Here's a simple example to consider. When we form the past tense of a verb that is derived from a noun, the past tense is regular even if a similar-sounding irregular verb exists. So, when a person hits a fly ball in a baseball game and the ball is caught, we say that batter *flied out*, not *flew out*.

Given the problems with Rumelhart and McClelland's model, should we conclude that connectionist models, in general, are insufficient for explaining language acquisition? On this question there is no consensus. Some theorists (Pinker & Prince, 1991) argue that the whole approach is fundamentally flawed, but others (e.g., MacWhinney & Leinbach, 1991) believe that PDP models can be constructed that avoid the problems of Rumelhart and McClelland's (1986) pioneering effort. For our present purposes, though, the importance of the PDP approach to overregularization is that it reminds us that we should not assume some aspect of language development depends on innate knowledge just because we have difficulty seeing how the knowledge could be learned. If nothing else, Rumelhart and McClelland's model prompted more traditional psycholinguists to search harder for evidence that would support or refute their alternative model.

CONCLUSIONS

What's in the Foundation?

There is a consensus among psycholinguists that we come into the world ready to distinguish among the phonemes used in any given language. However, there is considerable disagreement over the question of how much additional information must be built in and the extent to which the knowledge we use is specific to language. At the most nativist end of this debate are theories that depend on the triggering of parameter settings—and there is little in the way of what we would normally call learning in this parameter-setting view. At the other extreme are connectionist-style models that build in as little knowledge as possible and try to see how far explanations based on the nature of the input and simple learning principles can take us. And between these extremes are various views that consider acquisition to be a kind of hypothesis-testing procedure in which the possibilities are constrained by innate knowledge. In the next chapter, we will discover further evidence on the question of the role of innate, language-specific knowledge in acquisition by examining how language is acquired in more atypical circumstances.

C H A P T E R   R E V I E W

Checking Your Understanding

Key Terms

blocking principle (327)
child-directed speech (CDS) (314)
conditioned head turn procedure (305)
continuous theories (322)
critical period (309)
diary studies (307)
discontinuous theories (322)
elicited production (307)
feral children (308)
habituated (305)
high-amplitude sucking (HAS) (305)
holophrase (317)
mean length of utterance (MLU) (321)
motherese (314)
mutual exclusivity assumption (319)
myelinization (310)

negative evidence (322)
null subject parameter (325)
overextension (317)
overregularization (327)
parameter setting (324)
PRO-drop languages (325)
prosodic bootstrapping hypothesis (314)
reduplicated babbling (312)
semantic bootstrapping hypothesis (323)
subset principle (324)
syntactic bootstrapping hypothesis (319)
taxonomic assumption (318)
telegraphic speech (320)
underextension (317)
variegated babbling (312)
whole object assumption (318)

Review Questions

1. Describe the nature of Quine's "*gavagai* problem." In what sense is this a phonological problem as well as a lexical one?

2. Review your additions to Figure 10.3, as discussed in the activity. Do these data show a correspondence between language acquisition and the biological maturation of the brain? Do they prove that we have a special biological faculty for language? Why or why not?

3. Describe how the HAS procedure has been used to show that infants lose the ability to distinguish among some sounds that they were able to discriminate shortly after birth.

4. Describe evidence that shows that children's language production ability lags behind their language reception ability.

5. What is the relationship between child-directed speech and the idea of prosodic bootstrapping? What other information might children use to segment speech?

6. If there are innate constraints on the interpretation of new words, why do children still make overextension and underextension errors?

7. As children move from holophrases to telegraphic speech, to what extent is their vocabulary size also increasing? How might changes in syntactic ability be related to both increases in the mean length of utterance and the size of a child's vocabulary?

8. Explain the parameter-setting interpretation of children's adherence to particular word orders in their production. How does this approach explain the fact that children receive little feedback about what forms are not grammatical?

9. How might memory failures be related to children's overregularization errors?

10. Assume, for a moment, that each of the kinds of bootstrapping discussed in the chapter plays a role in language acquisition.

Is there a particular sequence as to when each kind of bootstrapping would be used?

On Further Reflection ...

1. In this chapter, I presented Rumelhart and McClelland's (1986) PDP model of past-tense learning as an example of an approach to syntactic development that does not depend heavily on built-in syntactic knowledge. If we were to extend Rumelhart and McClelland's general approach to other phenomena in language acquisition, would their model necessarily be non-nativist? In what way could innate knowledge be implemented by a PDP-style model?

Discuss the implications of your answer for what may be innate in language acquisition.

2. As we saw in Chapters 5 and 6, lexical ambiguity is quite common in language. What problems, if any, does commonplace lexical ambiguity pose for the proposed constraints on lexical acquisition? What kinds of cues or knowledge could help children acquire word meanings despite lexical ambiguity? Would ambiguities in which both meanings are nouns entail any more difficulty than ambiguities in which one meaning is a noun and the other a verb?

CHAPTER 11

Language Acquisition in Special Circumstances

I t is late in the eighteenth century. You live in a small village along the African coast. One day, while coming back from a hunting expedition, you are ambushed by a group of slave traders. The rest of your party gets away, but you are captured. After a perilous journey by ship to Haiti, you are sold to a plantation owner. There you work closely with a large number of other slaves. Neither the other slaves nor the plantation owners speak your language. In fact, there are so many different languages represented in the group that early attempts at communication produce linguistic chaos. Over time, however, you and the other slaves develop a rudimentary language that is simplified from the language of the plantation overlords.

The rudimentary language that is developed when a group of speakers from different linguistic backgrounds are placed together in close association is called a **pidgin.** The circumstances that have led to pidgins do not always include slavery, but the pattern I described above was typical in the colonial period of the sixteenth to nineteenth centuries. Descriptions of the nature of pidgin languages, and of what happens to these languages in the succeeding generations born to the speakers of pidgin, raise interesting questions about the biological foundation for language. Clearly, the adults who develop the pidgin, as well as the infants who grow up exposed to a pidgin rather than to a full-blown language, are acquiring language under rather atypical circumstances. How is acquisition affected by these circumstances?

This question concerns one of several "natural experiments" that we will consider in this chapter as a means of disentangling maturational and environmental influences on language acquisition. In particular, we will examine whether data on the acquisition of language in atypical environments support or refute the hypothesis that *a major contribution of language experience to acquisition is the triggering of parameter settings within a universal grammar.* The predictions of this strongly nativist hypothesis can be contrasted with views that allow a more central role for learning in language acquisition.

As we saw in the previous chapter, it is possible to combine notions of innate syntactic categories with learning based on bootstrapping to explain the development of syntactic knowledge, as Pinker (1989) did. But other researchers take a less nativist position than Pinker's in suggesting that, although innate linguistic and cognitive competencies guide and constrain language acquisition, the acquisition process itself depends heavily on general principles of learning and memory. In other words, this view maintains that by starting with a set of innate basic abilities, the child uses general memory and mental representation capacities to understand language in much the same way as he or she comes to understand other phenomena in the world (e.g., Braine, 1994; Piaget, 1952).

If the strong nativist position is correct and language does unfold largely on a maturational timetable programmed into our brains, then there are two predictions we can make about studies of atypical circumstances of language acquisition. First, the strong nativist position predicts that there should be relatively little impact of unusual environments on the process of acquisition, because nurture plays a lesser role than nature in this process. Of course, it is possible for there to be some environmental effects on abilities that are hard-wired into the brain because even innate abilities may require a minimum level of environmental stimulation at the right time in order to mature. This is certainly true of the visual system, where cells involved in analyzing certain visual patterns can be lost if visual stimulation is absent early in life (e.g., Riesen & Aarons, 1959). Similarly, some strongly nativist theorists have proposed that there is a **critical period** during which a person must be exposed to language if acquisition is to develop normally (e.g., Lenneberg, 1967).

Second, the most strongly nativist view predicts a *language-specific* genetic endowment, not a general cognitive capacity for inducing rules (Chomsky, 1980; Curtiss, 1988; Fodor, 1983). Therefore, this view predicts that we should expect to find a dissociation between language abilities and other mental abilities. That is, it should be possible to find cases of disturbance to language abilities that leave other cognitive abilities intact, and vice versa. The rest of this chapter is organized into two major sections that review the evidence related to each of these predictions. Then, it ends with a brief summary and some conclusions about the viability of the strong nativist position.

The Effects of Atypical Environments on Acquisition

Beyond Pidgins: A Case of Language Invention

Many linguists over the years have studied the nature of pidgin languages and what happens when adults speak pidgin to their children (e.g., Whinnom, 1965). In general, the development of a pidgin language is characterized by simplifications of full-fledged languages. As shown in Table 11.1, these simplifications occur at several levels.

However, the simplifications do not necessarily extend into the next few generations of speakers. Children who hear mostly pidgin as infants do not grow up to speak pidgin; instead, they speak a more complex language that elaborates upon the pidgin. Such a language is known as a **creole**. The most influential analysis of this process of going from a pidgin to a creole has been provided by Bickerton (1983, 1984). Bickerton's studies have focused on the creoles of Hawaii, where many workers from around the world settled from 1880 to 1930 to work on the sugar plantations. The relatively recent development of Hawaiian creole allowed Bickerton to study not only the

TABLE 11.1	**Examples of Simplifications in a Pidgin Language**	
Characteristics	**Source Language**	**Pidgin Language**
Lexicon:		
Vocabulary	large	small
Compound words	present	absent
Phonology/Morphology:		
Polysyllabic words	present	absent
Inflections	present	absent
Syntax:		
Word order	variable	fixed
Function words	present	absent

original immigrants to the islands who spoke pidgin but also their descendants who spoke creole.

The nature of a pidgin language can be seen in the following example of Pidgin English, which was produced by an immigrant from Korea (Bickerton, 1990):

> Aena tu macha churen, samawl churen, haus mani pei. (And too much children, small children, house money pay.)

Translated into standard English, the speaker's words would be as follows: "And I had too many children, small children, and I had to pay the rent." Note that, despite plenty of content words from which we can infer the sentence meaning, the speech lacks features that show structure. There are no prepositions, no articles, no markers of verb tense.

In contrast, speakers of Hawaiian Creole English mark tense, use prepositions, and produce relative clauses. Consider this example from Bickerton (1983):

> Those days bin [past tense indicated] get no more washing machine, no more pipe water like get inside house nowadays, ah?

In short, the main difference between a pidgin and a creole is a difference in the use of forms that are purely syntactic. According to Bickerton, it is *not* simply that the next generation of people get better at learning an existing language, such as English. After all, their main language input is pidgin, not English. Rather, what happens, Bickerton believes, is that the children use their innate knowledge of grammar to invent a true language, a creole, out of a rudimentary language, a pidgin. Bickerton's view is known as the **language bioprogram hypothesis.** Simply put, this hypothesis attributes a creole's invention by a new generation of speakers to the operation of an innate grammar that elaborates upon and extends the rudimentary pidgin language. Bickerton's language bioprogram hypothesis thus exemplifies a strongly nativist view of acquisition. It also suggests that we can get closer to the content of the innate grammar by studying creoles than by studying languages with a longer history.

The main evidence that Bickerton cites in support of his view is based on the striking similarities among creoles developed in different parts of the world under different circumstances. Bickerton noted that, although most of the content words of Hawaiian Creole English are from standard English, this creole is syntactically more similar to other creoles than to English grammar.

Bickerton's claims are provocative and controversial. Some investigators feel that the similarities among creoles may be explained by numerous other factors, including similar problems of communicating in each of the situations. (See Muysken, 1988, for a review of alternative theories.)

One of several striking similarities among creoles is that almost all of them use a subject-verb-object (SVO) word order. This is not a surprising finding for creoles of English, which is also an SVO language. However, creoles can be SVO even when adapted from a pidgin version of a non-SVO language. For example, creoles of Spanish use an SVO order despite the fact that Spanish makes frequent use of VSO patterns.

Although the similarity among creoles in word order may be imposed by an innate grammar, there are other possible explanations. Perhaps creole languages lack inflections because they are constructed from simpler pidgins. If so, the implication is that word order has a very important syntactic role. Thus, the SVO word order may be very common because it reflects a natural way to express causation: the doer of the action, the action, and the thing being acted upon (cf., Anderson, 1995a). In addition, the SVO word order may be a common word order in the language experiences of the different people who invent pidgins and creoles, in terms of either the original languages of the people or the languages of the slave traders or plantation owners.

Even though historical factors complicate the interpretation of the similarities among creoles, many investigators believe that Bickerton's data are suggestive of the existence of an innate grammar in which default assumptions are used in the absence of adequate language input (e.g., Gleitman & Newport, 1995). To better evaluate this strong nativist position, we need to examine additional circumstances in which the effects of an innate grammar might be seen.

Second-Language Acquisition

Most people around the world speak more than one language with at least some degree of proficiency (Grosjean, 1982; Romaine, 1996). And, indeed, there is an important similarity between the acquisition and use of a second language by bilinguals and the acquisition and use of pidgins and creoles. Just as pidgin speakers had an existing language before they began to use a different language, many bilinguals acquire their second language later in life—that is, after acquiring proficiency in a first language. Other people, however, start to acquire two languages from birth. We can contrast bilingual acquisition in these two different circumstances as a way of looking for evidence of both a critical period for acquisition and an innate language plan.

There is certainly a good deal of evidence suggesting that the earlier people are exposed to a language, the more fluent they become. The old myth that the child exposed to two languages from birth will become confused and not learn either language well has been refuted. One reason people used to believe that early bilingual exposure led to less proficiency in both languages had to do with a phenomenon I mentioned in Chapter 9: code switching. Some people thought that people switched between languages in conversations because they did not know either language very well. In actuality, however, code switching does not indicate a lack of language proficiency (Levelt, 1989; Taeschner, 1983).

Children growing up with two languages will sometimes make a few errors in which one language seems to interfere with the other; but, overall, these children show normal acquisition of both languages. There is evidence from recent studies of both prosody (Mehler, Dupoux, Nazzi & Dehaene-Lambertz, 1996) and syntax (Paradis & Genesee, 1996) that children with early bilingual experience are generally able to avoid confusions between the two languages. In fact, compared to monolingual children, these bilingual youngsters seem to have a better understanding of some of the general ways that languages work (e.g., Reynolds, 1990). Few people end up equally proficient in more than one language; but that is because, as children grow older, whichever language is dominant in their culture tends to get used more.

What about people who are exposed to a second language (L2) after their first language (L1) has been largely mastered? In the early stages of acquiring a second language, adults perform somewhat better than children (Snow & Hoefnagel-Hohle, 1978). If a family moves to a new country with an unfamiliar language, the adults will almost immediately begin to produce rudimentary sentences in L2. Young children, in contrast, may take months to attempt to speak the new language. However, this adult advantage is temporary. Consistent with the critical-period hypothesis, the younger the exposure to L2, the higher the level of mastery that is ultimately achieved (e.g., Johnson & Newport, 1989).

In a study conducted by Johnson and Newport (1989), native speakers of Chinese and Korean were tested on their mastery of English after coming to the United States. The ages of the participants varied, but they'd all had about ten years of exposure to English at the time of testing, and all were motivated to learn English so they could perform well in school and at their jobs. Specifically, the participants were tested on their ability to distinguish between ungrammatical and grammatical versions of English sentences. Figure 11.1 shows the participants' average scores as a function of their age of arrival in the United States. Those people who were immersed in English before age seven performed as well as native speakers of English. But the later the age of exposure, the worse the performance.

One way to explain these results is to assert the existence of an innate grammar that can be fully used only during a specific early period of life (e.g., Long, 1990; Schacter, 1996). According to this view, L2 is acquired without the benefits of guidance from the innate grammar if exposure to L2 occurs after the critical period. Such an interpretation would explain why people whose exposure to L2 occurs in adulthood typically speak with an accent (even after many years of practice with L2) and often

| FIGURE 11.1 | **Age and Second-Language Acquisition** |

Shown here are scores on a test of English grammar (maximum score = 276) as a function of age of arrival in the United States. All of the participants in this study had about ten years of exposure to English prior to testing.

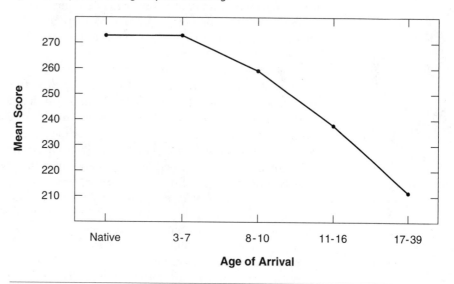

show incomplete mastery of the grammar of L2 (Schacter, 1996). In fact, some investigators have proposed multiple critical periods, given that the upper age for complete mastery varies across different aspects of language. For example, Long (1990) claims that age six marks the end of the critical period for mastery of the phonological characteristics of language, but the critical period for syntactic mastery lasts until about age fifteen.

Although the data concerning age effects on L2 proficiency are consistent with the critical-period interpretation, there are other ways to interpret these findings. It is important to bear in mind that people exposed to L2 when they are older differ in more ways than just age from people exposed to L2 when they are younger. In particular, being older when exposed to L2 also means having had more years of practice using L1. Therefore, L1 would interfere more with L2 in an older person learning a new language. Interestingly, this is a point of agreement between some investigators who take a strong nativist position and some who do not.

A Principles and Parameters Interpretation.   Long's (1990) critical-period interpretation of the data concerning age effects on L2 acquisition is couched in terms of Chomsky's principles and parameters framework. Yet others have used the same framework to argue for an interference interpretation of the L2 acquisition data (e.g., Flynn, 1988, 1996; Lakshmanan, 1995; White, 1989). One way of resolving this apparent paradox is to speculate that the "principles" part of Chomsky's proposed universal grammar is available to the language learner at all ages. Then, the principles that are universal across all languages would still guide L2 acquisition. On the other hand, the "parameters," which specify dimensions along which languages vary, could cause problems in acquiring L2 if its settings need to be different from the L1 settings.

Clearly, if universal principles and parameters are the basis for acquisition of both L1 and L2, people must be able to have different parameter settings for different languages. According to Flynn's (1988) model, what happens is that the L1 settings are used as the initial settings for acquiring L2, and increasing language experience with L2 results in a resetting of the parameters that are different. However, while this resetting is being worked out, we can expect to see errors in L2 performance that reflect the nature of L1.

For example, Flynn (1989) examined whether the setting for the head-parameter in L1 would affect performance in L2. You may recall from our discussion of the head-parameter in Chapter 2 that some languages, such as Spanish and English, are head-first. That is, in a NP or VP, the noun or verb comes before the role players. So, in the VP "walk the dog," the verb comes before the object. Other languages, such as Japanese, are head-last, so that in a NP or a VP, the phrase ends with the noun or verb. Flynn found that Spanish-speaking adults who were learning English assumed that phrases in English were head-first, whereas Japanese speakers trying to learn English showed errors caused by their assumption that English phrases were head-last.

According to Flynn (1996), these interference effects of one language on another reflect problems with working out the application of the universal grammar, not problems with the availability of the universal grammar itself. That is, L2 learners can properly set the parameters for L2, but learning how a parameter maps onto the specific forms of the language may take more time for L2 than for L1.

ACTIVITY 11.1   Who or What Is Performing the Action?

This activity is adapted from a series of experiments reported by Kilborn (1989, 1994). For each of the following "sentences," determine who or what is the one performing the action. The samples may not seem grammatical, but do your best to determine the actor in all of them. When you have made your choices, go back and write down how you arrived at these decisions. What cues did you use to identify the actor?

The waitress pushes the cowboys.

The telephones pushes the cowboys.

Kisses the table the apple.

The baskets the teacher kicks.

Thus, according to the principles and parameters view that Flynn (1996) advocates, the problem with learning L2 after five or six years of age reflects an interference between L1 and L2 rather than a biologically based critical period. Nevertheless, many details of this proposed mechanism for interference still need to be worked out. Exactly how parameters are set, and how the settings for different languages are kept separate, needs to be better specified. Furthermore, the roles of semantic and pragmatic information in acquisition, as well as the possible role of learning strategies, are not well developed in this framework. These issues tend to receive more attention in cognitive-oriented, as opposed to linguistic-oriented, approaches to L2 acquisition.

A Cognitive Processes Interpretation. In contrast to views of L2 acquisition that have grown mainly out of theoretical linguistics, psychologists have more often approached the issue of interference between languages in terms of the congruence of the cognitive processes used within each language. For example, according to the **competition model** (Bates & MacWhinney, 1981; MacWhinney, 1987, 1992), the interference that causes difficulty in L2 acquisition arises because some of the information that a person has learned to use in L1 does not transfer to L2. Before exploring this model in greater detail, however, you will find it helpful to do Activity 11.1.

If you are a native speaker of English, you have learned that position in a sentence is an important cue to which noun is the actor. However, as Activity 11.1 shows, you can use other cues as well. For example, you can also use animacy as a cue, because you assume that animate objects will be actors. And you can use verb agreement. If the verb takes a plural noun, then you assume the actor should be a plural.

So, in the activity, you probably said that the waitress was doing the pushing of the cowboys, even if this seems a little anomalous semantically. Both word order and verb agreement favor that interpretation. However, the second sentence probably seemed very anomalous, because position favors *telephones* as the actor but both verb agreement and animacy suggest that the *cowboys* should be doing the pushing. In the third example most people rely on English word order and assume the object directly follows the verb. And in the last example, you probably used both animacy and agreement cues to say that the *teacher* was the actor.

The use of these particular cues to determine who is doing what to whom is characteristic of English, but the same use of such cues in other languages could interfere with sentence interpretation. Recall my earlier mention of the competition model. According to this model, learners of a second language carry over the strategies they use in processing L1 to their processing of L2. But if there is a mismatch of the processing strategies needed for L1 and L2, the learners will experience problems.

For example, compared to English, German relies less on word order and more on morphological marking of subject-verb agreement to signal which noun is the actor. In Italian, however, animacy plays the most important role of the three cues I have mentioned. In a series of studies, Kilborn (1989, 1994) tested bilingual people, all of whom spoke different native languages but had English as a second language, on tasks like the one you performed in the activity. From these studies Kilborn obtained consistent evidence that bilinguals carry over the dominant processing strategies from their native language to English. So, for example, compared to native English speakers, German speakers, when judging who is the actor in English sentences, place too little emphasis on word order. Note, however, that the more fluent in English that people become the less they carry over processing tendencies from their native language (Kilborn, 1994). The older they are when they take up a second language, the more automatic the processes they use in L1 have become. Thus, the competition model correctly predicts that interference from L1 increases with age of exposure to L2.

A different kind of interference between L1 and L2 is revealed in studies of cross-language lexical processing. A number of researchers have investigated priming effects in bilinguals, particularly in terms of how concepts activated by presenting a word in one language affect accessibility to corresponding words in the other language (e.g., Altarriba & Soltano, 1996; Dufour & Kroll, 1995; Grainger & O'Regan, 1992; Kroll & Stewart, 1994). In general, their data show that bilinguals who are very fluent in L2 are able to go directly from a word in L2 to the meaning of the word. That is, fluent bilinguals need not first translate an L2 word into a corresponding word in their primary language. However, this ability is acquired only gradually. For people who are relatively early in the process of learning a second language, processing words in L2 does activate corresponding words in L1. And this cross-language word priming can be a real hindrance when they are attempting to speak L2. So, when just beginning to learn a second language after having a well-established first language, people have to inhibit the automatic activation of words in L1 in order to produce L2. As we saw in Chapter 9, language production, even in our primary language, requires that a good deal of information be maintained in working memory (cf., Levelt, 1989). The extra effort needed to inhibit words activated in our primary language can rob us of the resources needed to monitor our speech and prevent errors. Thus, it is possible that interference at the lexical level could cause problems "farther downstream"—problems that might show up as grammatical errors.

An Interim Evaluation of the Strong Nativist View.   The data regarding age effects on L2 proficiency are consistent with the hypothesis that language experience sets parameters in an innate universal grammar. The same data are also consistent with the view that this innate grammar is available to guide acquisition only during a critical early period. However, the relative difficulty of learning a second language later in life may be due to interference between L1 and L2. In fact, the competition model explains these data in terms of the transfer of cognitive processing tendencies from one language to another—without invoking either critical periods or innate parameters.

It's possible, of course, for there to be some truth to both of these positions. Indeed, parameter setting, with or without a critical period, could play a major role in the acquisition of syntax. Yet syntax is only part of language learning. As we saw in the last chapter, much of the work of acquisition also involves learning specific lexical items and their roles. White (1989) noted that such properties, which are specific to a particular language, must be learned even if the parameter-setting view is a good description of other aspects of acquisition. Given the role that the three kinds of bootstrapping play in L1 acquisition, it is not surprising that L2 learners would use the same kinds of bootstrapping in going from L1 to L2. The problem with using this strategy to acquire L2, however, is that not all the information used in knowing L1 is relevant to learning L2.

The most we can conclude about the strong nativist hypothesis based on studies of bilingualism is that the data do not refute the hypothesis, though there is still some question as to whether assumptions about innate parameters or universals are necessary to explain the data. We turn now to a related area of investigation, sign-language acquisition among the deaf, in an attempt to find additional evidence, pro or con, relevant to the strong nativist position.

The Acquisition of Sign Language

When a deaf child is born to deaf parents who are fluent in sign, then the child acquires sign language in much the same way that a hearing child acquires a spoken language (Newport & Meier, 1985). However, most deaf children are born into families with hearing parents who have no knowledge of sign language. In many of these cases, the children are not exposed to sign until later in life. In fact, some parents believe that their children will "seem more normal" if, instead of being taught to sign, they learn to read lips and produce spoken language. However, very few totally deaf individuals become truly proficient in the use of spoken language (e.g., Gleitman & Newport, 1995). Unfortunately, what often happens is that many deaf children receive no substantial language experience until after they are four or five years old, the age at which most other children have mastered much of their native language.

Psychologists and linguists have studied the sign-language acquisition of deaf individuals who have experienced such delays in language exposure to see how the delays affect acquisition (e.g., Goldin-Meadow & Mylander, 1984). Potentially, this situation represents a purer test of the critical-period hypothesis because the delay in question pertains to the child's acquisition of a *first* language. Thus, we aren't faced with the confounding effects of interference between languages that complicate the bilingual data. However, before examining such data and drawing conclusions about them for language acquisition in general, we have to address the question of whether it is fair to compare sign languages and spoken languages. Unless the basic principles of both are the same, any data we obtain regarding the acquisition of sign may not be generalizable to the larger issue of innate language abilities.

Is Sign Language a True Language? Until recently, many linguists believed that the sign languages of the deaf were only crude approximations of "real" (i.e., spoken) languages. An influential linguist at the turn of the century, William Dwight Whitney (no relation that I know of), said that sign language "answers for the deaf-mute the same purpose as our speech answers for us, and in the same way, only in an inferior degree, owing to the comparative imperfection of the instrumentality" (Whitney, 1910, p. 411).

Somewhat later, Leonard Bloomfield, one of the most important linguists of the first half of the twentieth century, gave scant attention to sign language in his 1933 text, *Language*. When he did mention it, its status was considered to be something less than that of a full and independent language:

> Linguistic forms, however, result, for the most part, in far more accurate, specific, and delicate co-ordination than could be reached by non-linguistic means. . . . Apparent exceptions, such as elaborate systems of gesture, deaf-and-dumb language, signaling codes, . . . and so on, turn out, upon inspection, to be merely derivatives of language. *(p. 144)*

Many of the issues covered in this book remain controversial and unsettled, but in this case I can tell you, unequivocally, that Whitney, Bloomfield, and others who viewed sign language as a lower form of language were wrong. Extensive research on American Sign Language (ASL) by Bellugi and colleagues (Bellugi & Fischer, 1972; Klima & Bellugi, 1979) has shown that sign language is a fully independent language, not derived from spoken language. Furthermore, sign languages have the major characteristics of all languages.

For example, in spoken language, the morphemes, which carry meaning, can be broken down into a set of basic sounds, or phonemes, which are not meaningful in themselves. Likewise, in sign languages, the signs, which carry meaning, are composed of different sets of **primes**. Primes are the basic parts of a sign, and they play the same role as phonemes in spoken language. As shown in Figure 11.2, the signs of a language differ in terms of the primes that make them up, and these primes fall into three categories of contrasts: hand configuration, place of articulation, and movement (Stokoe, Casterline & Croneberg, 1976).

Thus, sign languages have the same duality of patterning that we see in spoken languages: Simple units without meaning are combined to produce meaningful units. Moreover, the combinations of signs used to form sentences follow syntactic rules that allow for the same level of generativity we see in spoken languages (Poizner, Klima & Bellugi, 1987). In addition, as I discussed in relation to Activity 11.1, languages often use multiple cues to signal the role that different words play in an utterance. This is true of ASL as well. When signing, people use both word order and location of the sign relative to the signer's body to signal grammatical relations like subject or object of the verb (Kegl et al., 1996; Pettito & Bellugi, 1988).

Studies of Delayed Exposure to Sign Language. Given that sign languages are linguistically quite comparable to spoken languages, we can now consider what studies of sign-language acquisition can tell us about the validity of the nativist hypothesis. Interestingly, within the literature on sign-language acquisition, we find converging

FIGURE 11.2   **Three Types of Contrasts in ASL**

In spoken language, the alteration of one feature in producing a sound can change a phoneme, thereby changing what word is produced. Likewise, in sign language, a meaningful difference between two signs can consist of a single featural change in hand configuration, place of articulation, or movement.   *(From Klima & Bellugi, 1979, p. 42.)*

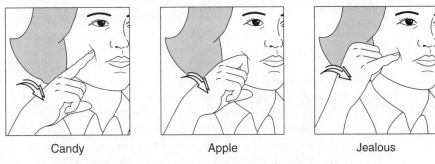

Candy   Apple   Jealous

(a)   **Signs contrasting only in Hand Configuration**

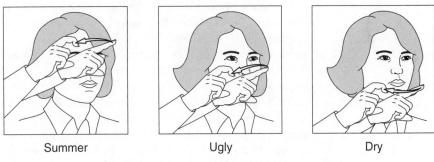

Summer   Ugly   Dry

(b)   **Signs contrasting only in Place of Articulation**

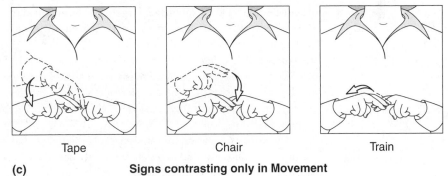

Tape   Chair   Train

(c)   **Signs contrasting only in Movement**

evidence for both of the principal claims of the nativist hypothesis that we have examined so far: (1) Young children show considerable inventiveness when they have impoverished language input, and (2) the longer that exposure to language experience is delayed, the poorer the mastery level achieved.

A series of studies by Goldin-Meadow and her colleagues (Goldin-Meadow & Feldman, 1977; Goldin-Meadow & Mylander, 1984, 1990) has shown that a process resembling Bickerton's description of the development of creoles takes place among deaf children born to hearing parents. These investigators have monitored the gestural language system, called **home-sign,** which is invented by deaf children aged one to four as they try to communicate with their family members.

Just as hearing children start to produce single-word utterances around the time of their first birthday, deaf children at this age start to produce manual signs. These signs are understandable because they resemble the objects they represent. For example, a child might flutter his hand with the fingers spread out as a sign for snow. And similar to hearing children who are acquiring spoken language, deaf children start to put together sentences with two or three signs around age two. Most remarkable is the fact that these early sentences are very systematic. For example, the children use a variety of devices, including position of a sign relative to the body, to denote whether the sign is the subject or object of a sentence.

Of course, the parents of deaf children are also trying to communicate with them, often through various kinds of gestures. In what sense, then, are home-signs a linguistic invention of the children themselves? As it turns out, there is overlap between the spontaneous gestures of the parents and the individual signs used by the children. Thus, the lexicon of each child is affected by input from the parents. However, the children greatly exceed their parents in their ability to take isolated gestures and turn them into a productive linguistic system with a morphology and syntax. Given their lack of understandable language models to display morphological and syntactic rules, these children provide impressive evidence that we have a biological predisposition for language that allows us to structure our communication.

Unfortunately, however, relatively complete language mastery is not something that we can acquire on our own. To look for evidence for a critical period in language acquisition, Newport (1990) examined the mastery level of users of ASL as a function of age of exposure to the language. The effects she obtained resemble the data in Figure 11.1: Whereas the deaf children who experienced ASL only a few years late mastered the language nearly as well as those who had no delay in ASL experience, those who tried to learn ASL in late childhood or adulthood were clearly deficient in their mastery of ASL's grammar. To say that there is a fixed critical period for language acquisition may be too strong a statement, but Newport's (1990) data do suggest that infancy and early childhood are a sensitive period in which the ability to acquire the grammar of a language is at its peak.

Newport's explanation for this apparent sensitive period is an interesting twist on the more typical claim that access to an innate grammar declines over time. Indeed, Newport believes that language-acquisition abilities decline *because of the development of nonlinguistic cognitive abilities.* She calls this the **less-is-more hypothesis.** Briefly, the idea is that, because of their greater short-term and long-term memory abilities, older children and adults store complex verbal utterances and sequences of signs as wholes.

In contrast, given their information-processing limitations, younger children store these complex stimuli in terms of parts or features. This partial storage actually makes it easier for children to catch on to the morphology of an unfamiliar language, whereas adults' perception and storage of language stimuli in terms of larger units may make it harder for them to discover the morphological and syntactic patterns that constitute those units. It is the flip side of the old saying "You can't see the forest for the trees." Adults can see the utterance as one whole forest, but they are less able to focus on the pattern of individual pieces that make it up.

Again, it is important to remember that, in explaining language acquisition, a cognitive processes account like Newport's less-is-more hypothesis and a strong nativist account are not mutually exclusive. It is possible that both kinds of factors play a role in the age effects that we see on second-language and sign-language acquisition. Thus, the strong nativist view remains a viable explanation for some of the phenomena that we see in language acquisition. However, both the idea of interference between languages and the less-is-more idea stress that language acquisition depends in part on general cognitive mechanisms like memory. We turn now to the issue of just how closely language and other cognitive abilities are intertwined in the process of language acquisition.

The Dissociation of Language and Cognition in Acquisition

In Chapter 3, I introduced you to Fodor's (1983) notion of modularity. As you may recall, he argued that input systems like visual perception and language are separate from the central cognitive processes of memory and reasoning. Furthermore, Fodor (1983) argued that an input system like language is composed of modules. These modules have several characteristics, but the most important ones, according to Fodor's claims, are that they (1) deal only with a particular kind of information, (2) receive only bottom-up rather than top-down information, and (3) are localized in a particular brain region. This book has thus far mainly addressed the first two of these three claims. In particular, we have looked at data, pro and con, testing the hypothesis that syntactic processing represents a distinct module, in Fodor's sense of module. In the last chapter of the book, we will explore detailed evidence on how language processes are localized in the brain—a topic in which modularity has been both an influential and controversial hypothesis (cf., Caplan, 1994; Farah, 1994; Shallice, 1988). In the balance of the present chapter, however, we will examine the implications of the language-as-modular idea for explaining acquisition. Both Fodor's (1983) claim about the modularity of language and Chomsky's (1965, 1988) more restricted, but similar, claim for the "autonomy of syntax" are tied to the notion that acquisition is guided by an innate program. If we observe evidence in the acquisition data that language acquisition and the development of other cognitive abilities are not closely associated, then the case for the strong nativist hypothesis would be strengthened. However, if we find close ties between the development of general cognitive abilities and acquisition of language abilities, then the strong nativist views of Fodor and Chomsky would be weakened.

Therefore, one approach to testing the nativist hypothesis is to look for dissociations between cognition and language. In particular, according to the modular view, we should be able to find individuals who have deficits in one domain but not the other. The best evidence of this sort is known as a **double dissociation**. It would mean that we can find cases in which children have language deficits but good cognitive abilities *and* cases in which children have cognitive deficits but good language abilities. Let's review the search for a double dissociation of cognition and language.

Language Deficits with Preserved Cognitive Abilities?

Researchers have studied a number of people with a disorder known as **specific language impairment (SLI)**. These individuals show early and lasting language impairment, even though they perform normally on nonverbal tests of general intelligence and display no evidence of hearing loss (Bishop, 1992; Gopnik, 1990). The most obvious problem affecting people with SLI is their considerable difficulty with mastering a number of grammatical forms (e.g., Rice, Wexler & Cleave, 1995). As Pinker (1994) notes, people with SLI speak slowly and deliberately and produce sentences with high rates of grammatical errors such as these:

The boys eat four cookie.

Carol is cry in the church.

No one has completely determined the cause or causes of SLI, but there is evidence that the disorder runs in families and that it may be controlled by a single dominant gene (Gopnik & Crago, 1991). This genetic evidence, coupled with the poor grammar of such individuals despite normal intelligence, has led some investigators to conclude that SLI comes from a genetic flaw in the instructions for a grammar module (e.g., Pinker, 1994; Van der Lely, 1994). Pinker (1994) summarized the data on SLI in this way:

> So, the syndrome shows that there must be some pattern of genetically guided events in the development of the brain (namely, the events disrupted in this syndrome) that is specialized for the wiring in of linguistic computation. *(p. 324)*

If Pinker's interpretation is correct, then SLI fulfills the first half of our quest for double dissociation: language impairment in the face of intact cognitive ability. However, we need to take a deeper look at the claim that SLI is fundamentally a deficit in syntactic ability that leaves other cognitive abilities unimpaired. Considerable data now suggest that children with SLI have nonlinguistic problems that could be a source, rather than a result, of problems in mastery of syntax. For example, Visto, Cranford, and Scudder (1996) demonstrated that children with SLI have difficulties with the tracking of moving auditory signals. The stimuli in this study were clicks rather than speech forms, so Visto and colleagues did not show the deficit to be associated with speech processing per se. Nevertheless, basic problems with processing auditory signals over time and space could inhibit these children's mastery of phonology, which, in turn, could disrupt their syntactic development. After all, early phonological processing abilities are, themselves, related to syntactic abilities (Tunmer, Herriman & Nesdale, 1988).

Other investigators have found that the speed of processing both linguistic and nonlinguistic information is slower in SLI children than in age-matched controls (e.g., Kail, 1994; Lahey & Edwards, 1996). This slower information-processing speed could have serious consequences for the processing of information, such as speech, that unfolds rapidly over time. It could also account for reports that speed of spatial processing, such as mental rotation of visual images, is disrupted in SLI individuals (Johnston, 1992).

Thus, specific language impairment may be somewhat misnamed. There is growing evidence that the impairment is not language specific, and certainly not syntax specific. Ironically, rather than shedding light on the existence of a grammar module, future SLI research may tell us how basic information-processing skills are related to the development of linguistic abilities.

Cognitive Deficits with Preserved Language Ability?

Let's look at evidence relevant to the other half of the potential double dissociation between language and cognition. A logical approach to searching for good language skills despite general cognitive deficiencies is to test the language skills of children with mental retardation. Before exploring this research literature, however, you should examine the language samples in Activity 11.2. These are actual speech samples taken from case studies in the literature. Some of the samples are from people with mental retardation. See if you can pick out which ones they are before you read any further.

As you could easily tell, some of the samples in this activity showed limited language skills whereas others displayed rather high levels of language proficiency. Which ones are from people with mental retardation? All of them are!

Rebecca is a child with Down syndrome, a genetic disorder that results in mental retardation that can be mild, moderate, or rather severe. Rebecca's IQ is 57. This score, along with her level of everyday functioning, places her in the upper end of the moderate range of mental retardation. Rebecca's speech is typical for a child with Down syndrome. That is, she is clearly behind schedule in language development, but her speech is otherwise normal. In terms of both mean length of utterance (MLU) and syntactic complexity, her speech resembles that of an average three-year-old. Thus, Rebecca, like other children with Down syndrome, gives us mixed evidence on the question of the relationship between cognition and language. On the one hand, mental retardation does not seem to result in a major disturbance of the grammatical acquisition abilities of such children, given that their development seems delayed but not fundamentally altered. On the other hand, the delay is rather significant, and these children tend not to reach normal levels of language proficiency, even as adults (Rondal, 1988). So, in most cases of Down syndrome, general cognitive deficits are associated with problems in language acquisition, although there are reports of very high proficiency in syntactic abilities among some adults with Down syndrome (e.g., Rondal, 1995).

In contrast to Rebecca, D.H. shows a more clear dissociation between cognitive abilities and language proficiency. D.H. displays what is sometimes called the **chatterbox syndrome.** She not only speaks fluently and with proper grammar, but she also performs well on tests of judging the grammaticality of complex sentences (Cromer, 1994). Yet her general intellectual functioning is impaired. D.H. has an IQ of 44. The

ACTIVITY 11.2   Does Speech Reflect Intellectual Functioning?

Can you determine general intellectual level from samples of speech? Three sets of speech samples appear below. Taking into account the age of each person, see if you can figure out which samples came from people with significant levels of impairment in general intelligence.

Rebecca

These samples were collected by Fowler, Gelman, and Gleitman (1994) when Rebecca was between six and seven years old.

Where small trailer he should pull?

What you have in your mouth?

Ann, this thing won't work.

I not get these at store.

D.H.

These speech samples were collected by Cromer (1994) during conversations with D.H., an adolescent.

And Dad's getting fed up with moving around. He thinks it's time that I settle down—to school, which is fair enough.

My Dad's got a canoe and we go canoeing. I threw my Dad in once.

Ben

Ben was sixteen when these samples were collected by Bellugi, Marks, Bihrle, and Sabo (1988).

After it stopped hurting, I was told I could go to school again and do whatever I feel like doing.

They had to give me ether so I wouldn't feel the pain.

level of her ability to answer general information questions or logical reasoning questions is about that of a five-year-old. Despite years of intensive instruction, she has not learned to read and write but her spoken language ability seems normal!

Ben's case represents an equally stark contrast between intellectual functioning and language functioning. Ben has a rare disorder known as **Williams syndrome.** Initially observed in infancy, Williams syndrome is marked by problems with metabolizing calcium (Bellugi, Marks, Bihrle & Sabo, 1988). This metabolic dysfunction in turn affects the child's growth and development, and also results in profound cognitive deficits coupled with generally well-preserved language abilities.

Ben's IQ is 54, and, like others with Williams syndrome, he has difficulties with many everyday tasks. Typically, such individuals need lifelong supervision, have a great deal of trouble handling money, and forget how to do commonplace routines. The cognitive problems associated with Williams syndrome are especially evident on tasks that require logical reasoning or visual-spatial ability.

For example, Bellugi and associates (1988) studied the performance of Ben and two other adolescents with Williams syndrome on basic tests of logical reasoning ability that were devised by the famous developmental psychologist Jean Piaget (Piaget & Inhelder, 1959). According to Piaget (e.g., Piaget & Inhelder, 1969), cognitive development occurs in a series of stages that represent steps toward being able to engage in hypothetical and deductive reasoning. Moreover, Piaget and others (e.g., Piaget, 1963; Sinclair-De Zwart, 1973) have claimed that specific language abilities are tied to mastery of particular cognitive advances that serve as prerequisites.

For example, one major step in children's cognitive development is the ability to reason logically about concrete objects and events. A hallmark of this step is the ability to solve **conservation problems** like the ones depicted in Figure 11.3. What these tasks measure is a child's understanding that a perceptual change in a substance doesn't necessarily mean that the amount of the substance has changed. Some investigators have proposed that children must understand conservation in order to use comparison constructions and passives (e.g., Beilin, 1975). However, although Ben and the other adolescents tested by Bellugi and associates (1988) were easily fooled on tests of conservation, they had no problem correctly using passives, comparisons, or other sophisticated aspects of grammar.

An interesting example of the dissociation between language and visual-spatial ability in Williams syndrome can be seen in a drawing produced by Ben. Figure 11.4 shows Ben's attempt at drawing and labeling the parts of a bicycle. Ben's ability to depict a bicycle is clearly far below his knowledge of its parts and his ability to use the appropriate terms for the parts. In fact, one of the remarkable things about Ben is the nature of his vocabulary. His lexical knowledge is much more extensive than you'd expect on the basis of his general intelligence. For example, on a standard test of vocabulary he showed mastery of such terms as *cornea, spherical,* and *tranquil.* However, it is important to keep in mind that, although Ben and others with Williams syndrome have better than expected vocabularies, their lexical knowledge is still below average compared to their same-age peers (Wang & Bellugi, 1994).

An Evaluation of the Dissociation Evidence

The most consistent pattern running through the data on SLI and various forms of mental retardation is that an individual's grammatical abilities and general intelligence are sometimes quite disparate. However, when we look at the connections between language and more specific cognitive abilities (as opposed to measures of general intelligence), it is more difficult to support the strongly modular and nativist view of grammar. In addition, there is an aspect of these cases that is puzzling from a syntactic module standpoint. What does it mean that individuals with Williams syndrome, and sometimes also those with chatterbox syndrome (Fowler, Gelman & Gleitman, 1994), can have much better than expected vocabularies? Does this mean that aspects of the lexicon may be innate as well?

We might suppose that there are innate constraints that limit the hypotheses considered for learning new words, and that these constraints are undisturbed in some cases of mental retardation. However, it is a great leap of faith to suppose that innate

| FIGURE 11.3 | Examples of Conservation Problems |

Piaget believed that the ability to understand conservation was a major landmark of cognitive development. Before seven or eight years of age, children interpret a change in appearance as a change in amount. Older children do not make this error.

Conservation of Liquid

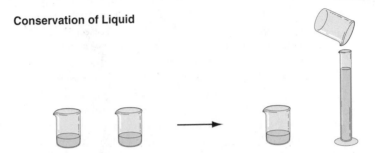

The child sees two glasses of water and says that both contain the same amount. The water from one is then poured into a tall, thin glass. The child is asked, "Which glass has more water?"

Conservation of Substance

The child sees two identical balls of clay and says that both have the same amount. One ball is rolled out, making it longer. "Do the two pieces have the same amount of clay?"

Conservation of Number

The child sees two identical rows of pennies and says there is the same number in each. Then, in one row, they are spread apart. "Do the two rows have the same number of pennies?"

constraints alone could ensure good vocabulary development in the face of serious deficits in general cognitive ability. Cromer (1994) speculated that these cases of individuals with good vocabulary knowledge despite mental retardation represent a kind of syntactic bootstrapping:

FIGURE 11.4   **Ben's Drawing of a Bicycle**

Ben, who has Williams syndrome, produced this drawing of a bicycle (left panel) at age sixteen. Although his drawing shows poor visual-spatial ability, his use of verbal labels for the parts of the bicycle (right panel) demonstrates a surprisingly good vocabulary.

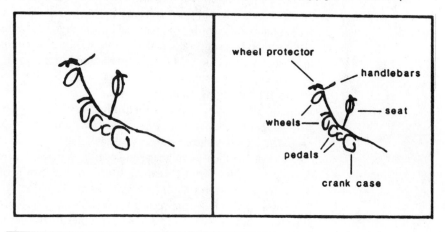

> It could be that they have a well-developed modular core grammar and, through very high motivation, subsequently elaborate that ability into the skillful use of all aspects of language that we see in cases like D.H. *(pp. 151–152)*

This interpretation of cases like D.H. and Ben suggests that preserved core-language abilities can be used to compensate for cognitive problems that would otherwise be expected to limit the acquisition of lexical knowledge. However, another interpretation of the data is also possible. From an interactive view of language and cognition, it might be argued that the existing studies of language-cognition dissociation are not fine-grained enough to detect specific dependencies between language processes and cognitive processes. In other words, the very general nature of IQ tests and logical reasoning tests may give a false impression of the dissociation of cognitive abilities and language. The data on SLI seem to support this hypothesis.

From Fodor's modularity standpoint, it makes sense to look for dissociations between language processes and the kind of general cognitive abilities tapped by IQ tests. After all, Fodor makes a distinction between language as an input system and cognitive abilities as the all-purpose central system. However, throughout this book, we have also seen evidence that is consistent with a more interactive view. According to this view, there are different subprocessors for the different jobs needed in cognitive and linguistic tasks, but these subprocessors can use both top-down and bottom-up information. In such an interactive system, deficits affecting one type of process can cause problems for other interlinked processes, yet it is also possible for one process to somewhat compensate for another process that is not functioning efficiently.

As Shallice (1988) noted, and as we'll explore more fully in the last chapter, the interactive subprocessors view has important implications for understanding dissociations between abilities that are observed in brain-damaged patients. It seems clear that the so-called central cognitive system in Fodor's scheme is itself composed of different subprocessors for different forms of memory and kinds of knowledge. Even though a particular subprocessor may be very specific in terms of what it does (e.g., such as maintaining only visual-spatial information in a buffer), if it is linked interactively with other subprocessors, then we have to be careful about making overly simplistic interpretations of data on dissociations (cf., Farah, 1994). Abnormal brain functioning in one subprocessor affects that process most, but it also affects the pattern of interactions among other areas. The implication for studying the language-cognition relationship, then, is that only by examining specific cognitive-language processing connections could we see whether dissociations are language-specific.

Is there evidence from studies of exceptional language acquisition that suggests a more interactive view of language and cognition may be correct? Let's again consider the case of children with Down syndrome. In their study of Rebecca, for example, Fowler and associates (1994) noted that, like most children with Down syndrome, she showed delayed onset of speech, but then had a period of normal developmental progress in terms of MLU and syntactic complexity. However, as is typical of children with Down syndrome, Rebecca's progress in mastering grammar then stalled and she did not advance normally after that point (see Figure 11.5).

Fowler and associates (1994) noted that Rebecca and other children with Down syndrome seem to get stuck at about the same stage, specifically what Brown (1973) called Stage III. These children are clearly using grammatical rules. In fact, they show the same kinds of overregularizations that we see in normal development, but they fail to continue their progress at a normal rate. Fowler and associates concluded that these children have cognitive limitations that place a ceiling on their level of grammatical development:

> Finally, and most interestingly, the story of language learning in children with Down syndrome raises the possibility that cognitive factors may play a role in advancing, or even reorganizing, the grammatical system. A slowdown at Stage III adds credence to the sense that there is a major stumbling block in language acquisition that needs to be addressed in syntactic theory and in theories of normal language development. *(p. 137)*

What specific cognitive factors might play such an important role in grammatical development? One of the leading candidates for this role is auditory working memory. Indeed, the size of auditory memory span is a good predictor of both vocabulary size and level of grammatical development in first- and second-language acquisition (e.g., Adams & Gathercole, 1996; Ellis, 1996; Gathercole & Baddeley, 1990). This finding makes sense given that, early in language acquisition, the learner must hold strings of (what are at the time) mostly meaningless sounds in working memory (Thal, Bates, Zappia & Oroz, 1996).

The connection between auditory working memory and language acquisition may also explain the relatively good linguistic performance by people with Williams syndrome. Compared to people with Down syndrome, those with Williams syndrome

| FIGURE 11.5 | **Syntactic Development in a Child with Down Syndrome** |

Although Rebecca, who has Down syndrome, started her syntactic development late compared to Sarah (one of the children studied by Brown, 1973), her rate of progress was normal for a time. Then, Rebecca stopped making rapid progress and her rate of MLU increases leveled off. At 90 months of age, she was still producing utterances at an MLU rate of about 3.0.

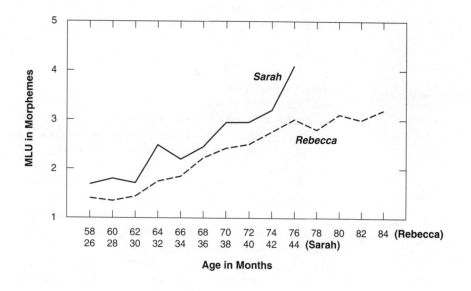

score better on tests of auditory working memory but worse on tests of visual-spatial working memory (Wang & Bellugi, 1994). Indeed, good auditory working memory would help those with Williams syndrome learn language, but it would not prevent them from scoring poorly on many other types of cognitive tasks. And as data from Baddeley (e.g., Baddeley & Hitch, 1974) have shown, there are many complex cognitive tasks, such as reasoning problems, that do not involve much use of auditory working memory. Succinctly put, the cases we have reviewed here reveal dissociations between *some* language processes and *some* cognitive processes, but they do not demonstrate that language is an input system that operates autonomously from the workings of all aspects of the memory system.

CONCLUSIONS

The Nativist Hypothesis and Language

At least one thing is certain about language acquisition: It is very robust, particularly in the sense of a child using syntactic principles to structure language inputs and outputs. Throughout the last two chapters, we have seen evidence that children come to use syntactic structures even if the language input they receive is impoverished. The ability to provide and use language structure survives the haphazard input of a pidgin language, simultaneous exposure to two languages with very different grammars, and even, to a significant degree, profound levels of general mental retardation. One can't help but be amazed at what seems to be a very natural human ability to exploit syntax in order to generate and understand novel utterances.

To Chomsky and others who take a strongly nativist stance, the robust nature of our language-acquisition abilities suggests that language is not so much learned as "grown." That is, Chomsky sees the grammatical basis of language as developing as a kind of mental organ, much like physical organs grow and mature according to a set genetic plan (e.g., Chomsky, 1975). Of course, physical growth can be influenced by environmental events, as when nutritional deprivation or toxic substances cause malformation of organs in the developing fetus. Likewise, Chomsky argues, there is a minimal level of proper environmental stimulation that is necessary for normal development of the language organ. However, as long as the environment provides enough information to set the necessary parameters, the language organ will mature according to plan.

Of course, we have seen evidence that our robust language-acquisition abilities decline with age. But this evidence, too, can be seen as consistent with the language-as-mental-organ metaphor. There are critical periods during which the right factors, whether nutritional or environmental in nature, must be present for normal maturation to occur. (Recall the example I used previously concerning the necessity of early visual stimulation for normal maturation of the visual system.) As we have seen, evidence on the timing of language exposure suggests that the language organ could have a such critical period.

Does Chomsky's metaphor of language as a mental organ have validity as a psycholinguistic theory? We could assume that his principles and parameters framework provides the basic plan of the language organ, and that this organ then matures with minimal environmental input. However, although much of the data we have reviewed can be interpreted within Chomsky's principles and parameters framework, we should be cautious about acceptance of this strong nativist view. The process of parameter setting, in general, and its application to exceptional cases of language acquisition, in particular, are still vague in many respects. There may indeed be innate factors that assist the learning of a grammar, but this is not to say that the role for learning and other cognitive abilities is as limited as the strong nativist view claims. For example, at least some of our difficulty with acquiring a language after early childhood could be due to the specific language experiences we have had (MacWhinney, 1987) or to the cognitive strategies we have learned (Newport, 1990).

Finally, we can also evaluate the strong nativist view in terms of Chomsky's claim, similar to Fodor's idea, that the growth of our language abilities is not very dependent on the growth of other mental faculties. The patterns of deficits we have examined do show that there are intriguing dissociations among the many processes involved in language and cognition. However, the data do not lead inevitably to the view that the language system is composed of modules that function autonomously from the rest of the cognitive system. In fact, the evidence on dissociations in language and cognition is something of a mixed bag. On the one hand, we have seen evidence that syntactic abilities can be worse than expected given a person's overall level of cognitive functioning, as in cases of SLI, or better than expected given rather severe cognitive deficits, as in cases of Williams syndrome. On the other hand, when we look at specific ways that different language and memory processes may interact, we see evidence of important connections, as in cases of stalled syntactic development among people with Down syndrome. Overall, then, this pattern of data suggests a cognitive system with functionally distinct subprocessors that perform both cognitive and language tasks. These subprocessors are more interactive than Fodor's or Chomsky's proposals would predict. In the final chapter, we'll review another source of evidence that addresses the relationship between language and cognition: research that attempts to trace the circuitry of language and other cognitive processes in the brain.

CHAPTER REVIEW

Checking Your Understanding

Key Terms

chatterbox syndrome (349)
competition model (341)
conservation problems (351)
creole (336)
critical period (336)
double dissociation (348)
home-sign (346)

language bioprogram hypothesis (337)
less-is-more hypothesis (346)
pidgin (335)
primes (344)
specific language impairment (SLI) (348)
Williams syndrome (350)

Review Questions

1. Summarize the forms of evidence that favor the idea of a critical period for language acquisition. What are the limitations of each form of evidence?

2. Compare Bickerton's language bioprogram hypothesis with Chomsky's principles and parameters theory.

3. How can a principles and parameters approach be used to explain the problems many people have in acquiring a second language later in life? Describe an alternative to the principles and parameters approach.

4. Compare the syntax in sign languages with the syntax in spoken languages.

5. Do sign languages show duality of patterning? Justify your conclusion.

6. Explain how cases of SLI and Williams syndrome can be interpreted as demonstrating double dissociation.

7. Let's say that some future researchers map out the exact genetic basis for SLI. Would such a finding prove that syntax is autonomous with respect to cognitive processes like memory?

8. What evidence suggests that auditory working memory plays a role in language acquisition? What are the implications of this evidence for the less-is-more hypothesis?

On Further Reflection . . .

1. As I mentioned in this chapter, home-signs often closely resemble the objects they are meant to represent. But what about the signs of ASL and other sign languages? Do they show arbitrariness in the way that spoken words do? Is arbitrariness an absolute feature of language, or are there degrees of arbitrariness in language symbols? To answer these questions, consult a reference text on signs or consult a person who is fluent in a sign language. To what extent do the signs resemble the objects or actions being represented? If possible, compare the signs for the same concept in two different sign languages.

2. Interview one or two people who learned your native language later in life (after age seven). Discuss with them the problems they experienced in learning the language, and ask them how it differs from *their* native tongue. What were the sources of interference? What aspects of the language were, or still are, most difficult for the person: phonology, morphology, or syntax? Why might phonology remain problematic for these people even if they are very fluent otherwise? (Hint: Review the material in the previous chapter on phonological development in infancy.)

CHAPTER 12

Language and the Localization of Function

ur ability to speak and comprehend language during our everyday affairs is typically so automatic and, seemingly, effortless that we take it for granted. A sudden loss of language function, however, can be a swift and effective teacher. Anyone familiar with such a loss truly appreciates that language is an ability of great intricacy and importance. A disturbance or loss of language ability due to brain damage is known as **aphasia.** Howard Kirshner, a neurologist who works with aphasic patients, put it this way: "Patients who have been rendered deficient in verbal communication suffer a disability that strikes at the heart of the human condition" (Kirshner, 1995, p. 1).

Most cases of aphasia are caused by strokes in which a blood vessel in the brain either hemorrhages or closes off, killing the neurons in the nearby region. However, aphasia can also result from other factors that cause brain damage such as traumatic head injuries or infections. Although aphasia can be relatively mild or quite severe, temporary or permanent, any case of language disturbance makes a profound impact on the person who experiences it. Let's consider two cases of language disturbance that were temporary, so that the persons involved could later describe what they experienced.

One March evening, Jean-Paul Grandjean de Fouchy, a prominent scientist of his era, was walking home through an area of road construction. The year was 1784. He tripped on a paving block and fell, face-first, onto a heap of sandstone. The blow cut a gash above his right eye, but he was able to make it home without help. By the next day, de Fouchy was convinced that he had suffered no serious ill effects from his fall except for pain above both the right and left eyes. However, that evening, de Fouchy experienced something quite strange:

> Toward the end of dinner, I felt a little increase in pain above the left eye, and in that very instant I became unable to pronounce the words that I wanted. I heard what was said, and I thought of what I ought to reply, but I spoke other words than those which would express my thoughts. . . . This sort of paroxysm lasted about a minute, and during its course my mind was clear enough to notice this singular distinction in the sensorium, which had only one of its parts affected, without any of the others experiencing the least derangement. *(Excerpted in Hoff, Guillemin & Geddes, 1958, p. 447).*

A particularly interesting feature of de Fouchy's experience with **anomia,** or word-finding difficulty, is that it is one of the few cases in which a scientist, trained in objective observation, could describe his own language disturbance. This case is strikingly similar to another one involving temporary anomia, reported more than two hundred years after de Fouchy's experience. Mark Ashcraft, a cognitive psychologist, experienced a sudden case of anomia caused by a temporary restriction of blood flow in a part of his brain (Ashcraft, 1993). The problem was very transient, and the underlying cause was corrected with surgery. That happy ending gave Ashcraft the opportunity to describe his experience from the vantage point of someone trained in the study of cognition and language.

Ashcraft had been working in his office late one afternoon when suddenly he was unable to understand what should have been familiar labels on computer printouts.

He found that virtually none of the terms used in his profession, words like *data* or *experiment,* were available for retrieval from his memory. In a phone call to his wife, he was able to explain that he was confused, but he had difficulty explaining the nature of the confusion because of his word-retrieval problems. Like de Fouchy, Ashcraft knew the ideas he wanted to express, but the words simply would not come to him:

> The most powerful realization I had during the episode, and the most intriguing aspect to me since then, was the dissociation between a thought and the word or phrase that expresses the thought. The subjective experience consisted of knowing with complete certainty the idea or concept I was trying to express and being completely unable to find and utter the word that expresses the idea or concept. *(Ashcraft, 1993, p. 49)*

Both cases of anomia suggest that access to word forms can be impaired without disturbance of access to semantic concepts. More generally, these cases suggest that there is a distinction between the language system and other aspects of cognition. Anomia, like that experienced by de Fouchy and Ashcraft, is quite common in all kinds of aphasia; but, as we will soon discover, many language disturbances in aphasia extend well beyond word-finding problems. A major issue that we will address in this chapter concerns the implications of language disturbances like these for how language is implemented in the brain.

At several points throughout this text, we have seen evidence for distinctions among different parts of the language system and between the language system and other cognitive abilities. For example, we have distinguished phonological processes from syntactic ones and syntactic processes from semantic ones. These distinctions raise the fundamental question of how language is processed by the brain. Accordingly, throughout this chapter, we will evaluate the hypothesis that *each of the major components of the language system is localized in a particular part of the brain.*

Of course, in order to do so, we must have an idea of what constitutes a major component of language, and we must try to specify how the proposed components coordinate their activities. Thus, to evaluate this hypothesis we must again consider the issue of whether the language system is modular or interactive. Recall Fodor's (1983) argument that language is an input system with modular organization and that language is separate from the "central system" that performs general (nonlinguistic) cognitive processes. One reason Fodor made this claim was that some neurological evidence suggests that language processes are strictly localized to particular brain regions. Other investigators agree that some areas of the brain are dominant in particular kinds of processing, but they have argued that these different areas are highly interactive (e.g., Farah, 1994). Whether the neurological evidence supports Fodor's idea of modularity or the more interactive view is, as we will see in this chapter, an active subject of debate (e.g., Just, Carpenter & Keller, 1996; Waters & Caplan, 1996a).

Bear in mind, though, that the hypothesis for this chapter is not just of theoretical interest. There is intense interest in understanding how the brain processes language so that we can better understand and treat language disorders that arise from brain damage. The more we know about the specific linguistic and cognitive disruptions that a brain lesion causes, the better our chances of designing effective treatment programs (e.g., Benson & Ardila, 1996). To begin the process of evaluating the localization

---

ACTIVITY 12.1 **A Look at Brain Anatomy**

As you probably know, the human brain consists of two fairly symmetrical hemi-spheres. The purpose of this activity is to familiarize you with the areas of the *left* hemisphere that are particularly important for language. First, study panel (a) in Figure 12.1 (opposite). Then cover it and see if you can correctly label each of the four areas indicated in panel (b).

---

hypothesis, we'll take a look at the history of studies of brain-language relations. But to follow this discussion coherently, you need to have some familiarity with the "geography" of the brain, so work through Activity 12.1 before proceeding further.

Aphasia Studies in Historical Perspective: The Classic Language Circuit

Until very recently, the only means for determining brain-language relations was to study the pattern of breakdowns in language as a function of brain damage. The earliest writings that mention disturbances of language (e.g., Hippocrates, c. 380 B.C.) focused on loss of speech rather than on loss of language in general. In fact, as Doody (1993) pointed out, it wasn't until the 1500s that physicians recognized a distinction between loss of speech due to paralysis of the organs of articulation and speechlessness due to a central, brain-related problem. It took longer still to recognize that problems in the comprehension of language could be separated from dementia, or general intellectual decline.

The nineteenth century was the key historical period for genesis of the idea that language is a separate mental ability localized in particular brain areas. Early in that century, data from autopsies led Gall and Spurzheim (1810–1819) to propose that our speech abilities were localized in the frontal lobes (Young, 1970). However, because knowledge of brain anatomy was so sparse, it was difficult to conclusively test this idea. A breakthrough came in 1861 with the publication of a paper by Paul Broca, a French surgeon and anthropologist. Broca's paper described the results of an autopsy on a man who had experienced severe language disturbance for more than twenty years. The man's name was Leborgne, but he is often referred to in the literature by the nickname "Tan" because of the peculiar nature of his language disturbance. Leborgne could answer some questions with gestures, but all he could say was a few curse words and the syllable "tan." Broca carefully examined Leborgne's brain during the autopsy, hoping to *disprove* the idea that speech was localized in the frontal lobes.*

What Broca found was that a chronic infection had left Leborgne's brain with an abscess "the size of a hen's egg." The damaged tissue was in Leborgne's left frontal lobe, in the region now known as **Broca's area**. Broca knew that the question of whether

---

* Broca had recently gotten into an argument at a scientific meeting over whether general intelligence is related to overall brain size, as Broca believed, or whether the size and configuration of specific areas were more important in predicting specific abilities, as others believed.

FIGURE 12.1   **Some Brain Areas Relevant to Language**

Shown here is a side view of the left hemisphere of the brain. After studying panel (a), see if you can identify the areas indicated in panel (b).

Lateral Surface of the Left Hemisphere

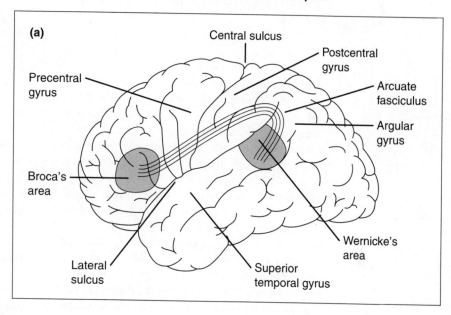

(a)

Central sulcus

Postcentral gyrus

Precentral gyrus

Arcuate fasciculus

Argular gyrus

Broca's area

Wernicke's area

Lateral sulcus

Superior temporal gyrus

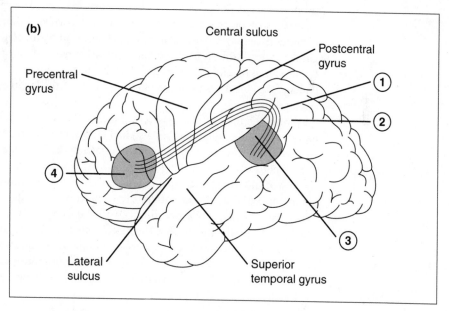

(b)

Central sulcus

Postcentral gyrus

Precentral gyrus

1

2

4

3

Lateral sulcus

Superior temporal gyrus

speech was located in a specific region could not be determined from a single case. So, over the next several years, he studied the brains of many more patients who had lost expressive language ability. In 1865 he published a landmark paper that went against the prevailing view that the two hemispheres of the brain are functionally identical. Broca had found that loss of speech was localized, not just in the frontal lobes, but specifically in the left frontal lobe. Patients with frontal lobe lesions in the right hemisphere did not show the symptoms of aphasia that were observed in Leborgne and others.

A few years later, another physician, Carl Wernicke, noted that not all cases of language disturbance involve a loss of speech, and not all involve Broca's area. After examining the brains of people with several different language problems, Wernicke (1874) proposed that there are two types of aphasia besides the type described by Broca. He noted that damage in the left temporal lobe, in what is now called **Wernicke's area**, tends to result in a loss of the ability to comprehend spoken words, even though speech remains fluent. In addition, Wernicke described a type of aphasia that is due to a lesion in the pathway between Broca's area and Wernicke's area. Today, this disorder is called **conduction aphasia**. Although both comprehension and fluent speech are preserved in patients with conduction aphasia, these individuals lose some ability to monitor their speech and have trouble repeating a sentence that has been spoken.

Wernicke's model was further elaborated by Lichtheim (1885), whose classic "language circuit" remains influential even today. Lichtheim argued that there are three centers for language processing: (1) Wernicke's area stores the sound representations of words, (2) Broca's area is responsible for the planning and organization of speech, and (3) another area stores the representation of concepts. The location of the third center was not clearly identified in Lichtheim's model. But more recently, Geschwind (1970) elaborated on Lichtheim's model by establishing an area in the parietal lobe (around the angular gyrus) as being the portion of the concept center where sensory properties of objects are associated with the corresponding words. The resulting Lichtheim-Geschwind model of how language is implemented in the brain serves as a guide to the classification of different types of aphasia. As suggested in Table 12.1, this classic view is based on the idea that the type of language disturbance we see with brain damage is a direct result of the particular part of the language circuit that has been damaged.

Although the Lichtheim-Geschwind model has had a major impact on the study and treatment of aphasia, it has also had critics. Even at the time of its origins in the work of Broca and Wernicke there were questions about language centers in the brain (e.g., Freud, 1891; Head, 1926; Jackson, 1878). For example, Sigmund Freud rejected the idea of language centers that function relatively autonomously. He noted that many clinical cases did not fit the pattern expected from the models proposed by Broca and Wernicke. Further, while pointing out that different areas of the brain are richly interconnected, he argued that the deficits seen in Broca's and Wernicke's aphasics might be the result not of damage to a "command and control center" but, rather, of damage to a region where several lines of communication cross. If so, damage to a specific area could have a devastating effect even if the language processes are distributed widely throughout the cortex.

Somewhat later, Henry Head (1926) studied language disturbances resulting from gunshot wounds to the brain. Like Freud, Head was impressed with the variability in

TABLE 12.1	The Classic View of Some Major Aphasic Syndromes		
Syndrome	Symptoms	Nature of Deficit	Lesion Site
Broca's aphasia	Speech not fluent; function words often omitted	Disturbance of speech planning and production	Posterior portion of lower frontal lobe
Wernicke's aphasia	Poor auditory comprehension with fluent speech	Disturbance of word sound patterns	Posterior half of temporal area
Conduction aphasia	Disturbance of speech repetition	Disconnection between sound patterns and production area	Arcuate fasciculus
Global aphasia	Disturbance of all language functions	Damage to all language processing components	Large portion of the frontal and temporal lobes

aphasia symptoms across people with similar injuries. He noted that this variability made classifying specific cases into the categories used by Lichtheim much less clear-cut than expected. The data suggested to Head that the language system works as an integrated whole, and that the pattern of symptoms seen in a particular patient are the result both of problems caused by the brain damage *and* of attempts by the patient to compensate for the deficits.

In summary, the current debate between adherents of the modularity view and the interactive view was presaged by a debate between those who believed that different language processes are strictly localized (e.g., Lichtheim) and those who believed that the brain functions holistically with regard to language (e.g., Head). Of course, there is a middle ground between the extremes of localization versus holism. The trick is to specify exactly how much interaction occurs, and where it takes place in the brain. Fortunately, the methods we have now to help us understand these issues are much more precise and sophisticated than the methods available to researchers like Broca and Head. First we will review the methods currently being used to localize language functions in the brain; then we will turn to a discussion of the recent research in this area and explore whether it supports or qualifies the classic view as depicted in Table 12.1.

Modern Methods Used to Study Localization of Function

For the pioneers in aphasia research, the only available technique for the study of brain-language relations was the postmortem examination of the brains of aphasic patients. This technique can provide very precise information on the location and extent of brain injury, so it is still used today. However, it also suffers from some limitations, including, of course, the fact that it doesn't tell us anything about the extent of a particular patient's lesion while the patient is still alive, which could be useful in planning treatment. It is also difficult to match symptoms and damage across various patients using only postmortem examination because of the large differences among patients in the time interval between language disturbance and death. In addition, the usefulness of a particular case can be severely compromised when additional brain disease or damage occurs between the onset of aphasia and the death of the patient. Fortunately, technological advances have now made **neuroimaging** possible. In short, we are able to get images of living brains.

Techniques for Studying Brain-Language Relations

Two relatively recent and important methodological advances have revolutionized the study of brain-language relations:

- In working with brain-damaged patients, those who study aphasia can now get reasonably accurate information on the site and extent of a lesion very soon after the damage occurs. This is possible because the neuroimaging techniques are noninvasive. That is, we can get an image of brain structures without doing surgery on the patient or waiting for an autopsy.

- Several techniques are now available that allow investigators to examine the activation of different brain regions in people with brain damage *and in people without brain damage.* The opportunity to compare abnormal and normal brains has allowed us to observe not just brain *structures* but brain *functions* as well.

Comparative views of some of the techniques that we will discuss are presented in Figure 12.2. After looking more closely at the nature of these techniques, we will consider the logic behind the use of these new techniques to study how language is implemented in the brain.

Locating Brain Lesions. The first of the new techniques for noninvasive imaging of the brain was **computerized tomography (CT) scanning.** CT scanning is a refinement of X-ray technology whereby multiple X-ray scans are computer-enhanced to form a three-dimensional image of the brain. Figure 12.3 shows a series of CT scans of Broca's patient, Leborgne, whose brain was preserved after autopsy. Each "slice" shown in the figure depicts a scan taken at a different depth.

A more recent and refined noninvasive technique is **magnetic resonance imaging (MRI).** This technique creates an image of the brain by exposing it to powerful magnetic fields. When the magnetic fields are turned off, the atoms in the brain briefly produce a voltage reaction—the "resonance" in magnetic resonance—that is monitored by the MRI scanner. The machine uses this resonance to create an image of the brain. MRI scans are safe and painless, and, as you can see in Figure 12.2, they produce more detailed images than CT scans. However, they are also costly, so they are not used as widely as CT scans. Both techniques have greatly aided research on the relationship between language disturbances, on the one hand, and the size and location of a brain lesion, on the other (e.g., Benson & Ardila, 1996).

Examining the Activation of Brain Areas. One technique for studying language processes in the intact brain is based on **electroencephalogram (EEG) technology.** An EEG is a record of the electrical activity of the brain, obtained by placing electrodes on

| FIGURE 12.2 | A Comparison of Brain Imaging Techniques |

This figure illustrates four different ways of getting an image of a "slice" of brain tissue. Image (a) is a photograph of an actual slice of the brain. Image (b) is taken from a CT scan at a particular depth. And images (c) and (d), respectively, show a PET scan and an MRI scan of the same area.

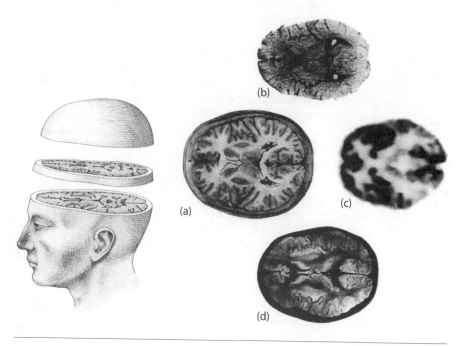

| FIGURE 12.3 | Leborgne's Brain |

Here we see four pictures from a CT scan of the brain of Leborgne, Broca's famous case that helped establish the localization of speech abilities. The frontal lobes appear at the top. Each picture is at a slightly different depth of the midbrain region. The picture on the far left shows a slice that passes through Broca's area. The other pictures show progressively higher regions.

the scalp. This technology provides useful measures of brain activity that can be collected during virtually any kind of language task. In studies based on such tasks, brain activity is recorded in response to stimuli presented over a large number of trials, and the recordings are averaged to yield a record of the consistent changes in activity that occurred in response to the stimuli (e.g., Kutas & Van Petten, 1994). The voltage potentials obtained through this averaging process are known as **event-related potentials, or ERPs.**

The logic of this technique is simple: The processing of a stimulus occurs over time and involves different areas of the brain. An ERP, then, is a record of this processing as it unfolds over time. For example, in an experiment by Kutas and Hillyard (1983), EEGs were recorded as the participants heard sentences that ended in an expected or unexpected fashion. Figure 12.4 shows the ERPs elicited by the final words of the test sentences. Note how differently the participant's brain reacted to the expected ending versus the unexpected ending. In particular, during a trial in which the final word was both semantically and syntactically anomalous, a large negative change in the voltage potential (an "upward" direction in this figure) was observed at about 400 milliseconds after the word was presented. This negative variation occurring about 400 milliseconds after a stimulus, known as the N400 component, is a reliable index of detection of an incongruent stimulus (e.g., Bentin, 1987; Kutas, Lindamood & Hillyard, 1984). So, for example, we can have an anomalous word occur at different points in a sentence and observe whether the N400 component is found shortly after the anomalous word or at the end of the sentence or phrase boundary. Several studies using this approach have found support for the principle of immediacy of interpretation that we studied in Chapter 7 on sentence processing (see Just & Carpenter, 1987; Kutas & Van Petten, 1994). In short, people try to integrate the word with the overall sentence meaning as soon as possible.

Psycholinguists and neuroscientists generally look for N400s, as well as other components of ERPs (e.g., Kluender & Kutas, 1993; Osterhout, Bersick & McLaughlin, 1997), in order to determine when particular mental activities occur during the time course of processing a stimulus. They can also get some idea of localization of function by recording the ERPs at different sites on the scalp. For example, N400 tends to be stronger at parietal and occipital sites than at frontal sites (Kutas & Van Petten, 1994). However, because such measurements are taken from the scalp, EEGs provide a fairly rough index of activity over broad groups of neurons. Consequently, ERPs represent a relatively imprecise way of determining the area of the brain producing the activity. Researchers are thus increasingly turning to some newer techniques to answer questions about localization of function.

Of the new techniques for determining which parts of the brain are most active while a person performs a mental task, the most widely used is **positron emission tomography (PET) scanning.** In this procedure, the individual is injected with a solution of glucose that also contains a harmless radioactive isotope. Glucose is the fuel that the brain uses for energy. So, the more active a particular brain area, the more glucose is being used there. Because the glucose has been tagged with a radioactive isotope, the PET scanner can detect how much activity is occurring in a brain region based on how much of the isotope has collected in that region.

More recently, MRI technology has been refined to allow for faster scans, so it can also be used to monitor changes in blood flow within the brain. This use of MRI

| **FIGURE 12.4** | **ERPs and Incongruity** |

The ERPs evoked in response to the last word of a sentence vary depending on whether the word is a sensible completion of the sentence. An especially large negative peak has been observed to occur about 400 milliseconds after the word when the sentence completion is very incongruent, as in the example sentence shown here ("The pizza was too hot to *cry*").

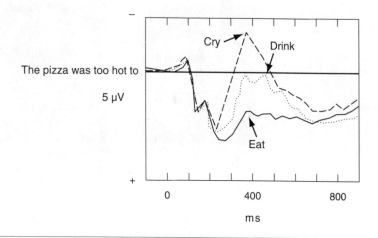

technology, known as **functional magnetic resonance imaging (fMRI)**, provides a functional view of what is happening in the brain along with good visual resolution of the brain structures themselves (Moonen, 1995).

The logic underlying studies of localization of function is the same regardless of whether the researcher employs fMRI or PET. Let's imagine that you want to know which part of the brain is more active when a person is listening to speech as compared to the nonspeech sounds in, say, a symphony. One way to address this issue would be to get PET or fMRI scans under each listening condition and then to compare each listening condition with a control condition in which the person is resting without hearing any sound. By comparing all three scans, you could determine which areas are more active in one condition than in the other. Specifically, if one area is active in the speech condition but not in the other conditions, then you would suspect that this area is important to speech processing.

As the foregoing example illustrates, PET and fMRI scans can provide information about activity levels in brain regions in individuals who have normal brains. But PET and fMRI can also be used with brain-injured patients to see how the damage has affected the activation of different brain regions. This use of brain activation techniques is illustrated in Figure 12.5.

The Logic Behind Localization Studies

An important conclusion we can draw from an examination of Figure 12.5 is that we must be cautious about concluding that a particular area controls a particular language function. If we find that a lesion in a particular location tends to be associated with a

| FIGURE 12.5 | A Comparison of Lesion Site and Site of Abnormal Activity |

A photo of the brain is shown in (a), and the same slice in a CT scan is shown in (b). Note that the left frontal lobe is structurally normal. Nevertheless, a PET scan (c) taken when the patient was still living shows abnormally low activity in the left frontal lobe. Thus, a part of the brain can be intact, yet function abnormally due to lesions elsewhere.

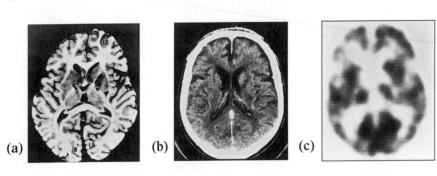

(a)   (b)   (c)

particular language function, then the temptation is to say that the area controls the language function. However, because of the brain's many interconnected pathways, one brain area can influence the activity of another brain area quite distant from the first. In the case depicted in Figure 12.5, the patient's aphasic symptoms were due not to lesions directly located in a language center but, rather, to abnormal activity in the frontal lobes, even though the frontal lobes were structurally normal. Apparently, the lesions affected the communication lines between the frontal lobes and other brain areas.

So, localizing language processes in the brain is more complex than simply noting correspondences between lesions and deficits. Indeed, we must use both studies of deficits and studies of functional activation in the brain to distinguish between two kinds of localization of function. A particular brain area may be *related* to a particular language function, so that the area participates in activities involving that function. We can make this inference if damage to the area disturbs some language tasks but not others, and if the activity in that area is increased for some language tasks but not others. However, this is not the same as saying that a particular brain area is *exclusively related* to a particular language function. An area is exclusively related to a function only if no other brain area participates in the function.

Furthermore, it is important to keep in mind that any theory of localization of language function is, in effect, also proposing a theory of the major subcomponents of the language system. For example, the classic view depicted in Table 12.1 implies a division of the language processor into separate centers for conceptual processing, activation of word sounds, and language production. We might agree that, for example, Broca's area and Wernicke's area are specialized language centers, but disagree with the classic view regarding what language functions are taking place in each area. So, we really have two interrelated questions to answer when considering how language is implemented in the brain: (1) Are there language processes that are exclusively localized to a particular area? and (2) What is the best way to describe the type of processing that takes place in each area?

To answer these questions, we have to combine theories of language functioning with data on the brain regions that participate in various language tasks. And we can be most confident that language theory and brain data have been appropriately synthesized when the study of brain lesions leads to the same conclusions as the study of processing in the intact brain. In short, it is very important to get converging evidence from different techniques, because each of the available methods of studying brain-language relations has both strengths and weaknesses.

Another reason for getting converging evidence is that there is bound to be some variation among people in the ways that processing is localized in the brain. For example, even the well-established principle that expressive language is localized in the left hemisphere has its exceptions. Although around 70 percent of left- and right-handed people have expressive language dominance in the left hemisphere, a substantial minority of left-handers show right-hemisphere or mixed dominance (e.g., Kolb & Whishaw, 1990). Thus, we should keep in mind that there are risks involved in drawing conclusions from only a few cases or from data that rely on only one particular technique. Rather, what we are looking for are patterns that emerge across a variety of studies using different people and different techniques.

The Organization of Language Processes in the Brain

The classic view of brain-language relations based on studies of aphasia is a useful starting point for examining such relations, but researchers have noted two concerns about it. First, the deficits associated with particular brain lesion sites, as described in the model, are actually only general tendencies. There is a great deal of variation in lesion sites that produce a particular set of deficits (Caplan, 1994; Kertesz, 1979; Kirshner, 1995). For example, lesions in Broca's area do not produce Broca's aphasia in all patients (Mohr et al., 1978), and a variety of different lesions can produce the symptoms of Wernicke's aphasia (Kertesz, Lau & Polk, 1993).

A similar conclusion can be derived from data on electrical stimulation of the brain during neurosurgery. Some patients with severe epilepsy have had to undergo surgical removal of small areas of brain tissue to control their seizures. In such surgery, the patients receive local anesthesia but they are kept awake for the operation. The reason for this practice is that the surgeons need to be able to electrically stimulate brain areas around the suspected abnormal brain tissue, so that they can determine the side effects of operating on that area of the brain. At the same time, they have the opportunity to test which functions are controlled by the areas that are being electrically stimulated.

Using this procedure, Ojemann (1983, 1991) has found very large differences among individuals in the exact location of the supposed language centers of the left hemisphere. Such variability in localization further complicates our ability to distinguish between language centers that represent autonomous processing modules and pathways in which interactive information related to language processes is being transmitted around the brain.

A second concern that has been raised about the classic view of brain-language relations is that the aphasia studies on which it is based connect brain damage sites with the ability to perform fairly complex language tasks. Yet each of these language tasks requires a variety of different processes. As an illustration of the problem that is presented by this view, consider Broca's aphasia, which, classically, has been described as involving a deficit of speech planning and production.

Should we consider Broca's area the speech center? If so, it would have to be a very complicated center. Think back for a moment to the discussion of speech production in Chapter 7. We saw evidence that speech production entails a complex collection of processes at the phonological, morphological, syntactic, and semantic levels. In addition, the speech production mechanism makes use of the general cognitive working-memory system. So, in any given case where speech production is said to be disturbed, there are a lot of different mental processes that could be affected. But are all of these aspects of speech affected, or only some of them? Alternatively, is the disturbance really one of speech, or is articulate speech just the most obvious area of difficulty to consider when some particular linguistic ability is lost?

What we really want to know is whether particular psycholinguistic processes are strongly localized. Toward this end, we will review both the activation data and the lesion data that are relevant to three kinds of language processes representing major distinctions used throughout this book: lexical access, syntactic parsing, and semantic integration in sentence and discourse processing.

Is There Localization of Lexical Processing?

As we know, lexical access is itself a complex process. For example, in Chapters 5 and 6 we saw that orthographic visual form processing, phonological processing, and semantic processing can be functionally separated. We also saw that separable meaning-based and sound-based activities are involved in producing words. Therefore, if language processes are strongly localized, we would expect that these different lexical processes might take place in different brain areas. One of the first studies to use PET technology to test this idea was carried out by Posner, Petersen, Fox, and Raichle (1988). Posner and associates had normal volunteers perform several different kinds of tasks on isolated words while their brain activity was monitored using PET scans. The data indicated that processing of the visual forms of words took place entirely within the occipital lobe, whereas listening to words led to activation of auditory processing areas in the temporal lobes and in Wernicke's area.

Indeed, these data on viewing and listening to words were generally supportive of the classic view when the tasks required simple visual or phonological processing. However, in another condition of Posner and associates' (1988) study, a noun was presented on a screen and participants were asked to name a use for the object represented by the noun. For example, when shown the noun *oven*, a person might have responded with the verb *bake*. By comparing the verb-generation condition with a condition in which the person merely had to repeat the word that was presented, the researchers were able to subtract out the activation that was due simply to sensory and motor processes. As it turns out, the brain area that was activated when participants named the use of an object, but not when they repeated a word, was a region to the front of, and below, Broca's area. Most surprising was the finding that Wernicke's area was not activated in either the repeat condition or the verb-generation condition. Indeed, this result seems to go against the idea in the classic language circuit view that Wernicke's area processes the phonological form of a word and, therefore, is necessary to comprehension of the word.

However, before we decide that the classic language circuit is incorrect, there are other data to consider. Recall that most investigators in this field believe there are two routes to lexical access: a direct visual-to-semantic route for very common words and a visual-to-phonological-to-semantic route for other words (e.g., Coltheart, Curtis, Atkins & Haller, 1993). In addition, note that the nouns in Posner's study were very common nouns, and that the participants in the study were highly skilled readers. The implication, then, is that Posner and associates' data may reflect processing in only the more direct route to lexical access. Other studies *have* shown activation in Wernicke's area—specifically, when people perform rhyming or semantic judgment tasks on words. For example, Wise and associates (1991) found activation of Wernicke's area when activation caused by listening to nonwords was subtracted out from activation in the verb-generation task.

The general conclusion from the imaging studies we have reviewed is that the more elementary the mental operation, the more strictly localized the operation is likely to be. In terms of processing single words, the elementary operations are those that involve a single kind of representation, such as access of a phonological code. However, the more complex the process being examined, the harder it becomes to specifically localize the activation. For example, the verb-generation task may involve phonological and semantic processing or a direct visual-to-semantic route, depending on the skill of the participants and the familiarity of the words that are presented. Thus, when even a moderately complex task is performed on an individual word, that performance is likely to depend on interacting pathways in multiple brain regions (Habib & Démonet, 1996).

This general conclusion is also supported by recent data on the effects of brain lesions on lexical processes. Some aspects of these data are in accord with the classic Lichtheim-Geschwind view. For example, patients with Wernicke's aphasia typically have difficulty with both auditory and reading comprehension. This finding is to be expected from the classic view, given that reading words often involves the kind of phonological access presumed to be localized in Wernicke's area. Other data, however, present a more complex picture than we would expect from the classic view. For example, Broca's area is the speech center according to the classic view, but patients with Broca's aphasia often have considerable difficulty with reading as well, even when their spoken language comprehension is relatively normal (Henderson, 1985).

In fact, a variety of different brain lesions can cause problems in reading. People who have lost some aspect of their reading ability due to brain damage are said to have **acquired dyslexia.** This disorder can take any of several different forms, but two of them, **surface dyslexia** and **deep dyslexia,** are of particular interest to us here. Surface dyslexia tends to be associated with temporal lobe damage (e.g., Deloche, Andreewsky & Desi, 1982), whereas deep dyslexia, with or without the expressive difficulties seen in classic Broca's aphasia, is typically observed in patients with damage to Broca's area

TABLE 12.2	Two Forms of Acquired Dyslexia		
Type	**Typical Signs**		**Example of Error**
Surface dyslexia	• Difficulty with irregular spellings • No semantic access until the word is pronounced		• Inability to read *yacht* • Pronunciation of *pint* as if it rhymed with *tint*
Deep dyslexia	• Difficulty reading less familiar words and function words • Inability to read pronounceable nonwords		• Semantic substitutions, such as reading *sword* for *duel* • Substitution of *and* for *was*

and the left parietal area (Kirshner, 1995; Marin, 1980). The features of each of these disorders are summarized in Table 12.2.

In cases of surface dyslexia, what the patients appear to be doing is laboriously sounding out each word. Only when they have pronounced the word do these patients seem to know the word's meaning. Therefore, words with irregular spellings cause great difficulty, and the patients often draw incorrect conclusions about the meaning of a word if they cannot pronounce it correctly. Marshall and Newcombe (1973) give the example of a patient who, when presented with the written word *listen*, pronounced it as "Liston." And when asked to define the word, the patient said it was the name of a famous boxer, apparently thinking it referred to Sonny Liston, once the heavyweight boxing champion. One interpretation of surface dyslexia is that the temporal lobe damage has cut off the connections between visual word forms and the semantic network (Coltheart, Curtis, Atkins & Haller, 1993). This idea fits nicely with Posner and associates' (1988) finding that visual word forms are processed in the occipital lobe and that at least some aspects of semantic processing are handled by the frontal lobes. If so, then temporal damage would occur directly in the pathway between visual and semantic processing.

In a sense, deep dyslexia is the opposite of surface dyslexia. In the terms of the dual-route model of reading, patients with deep dyslexia seem to have lost the spelling-to-sound route for recognizing words. They can recognize very familiar words because the visual-to-semantic route is still available. However, it seems that more is going on in deep dyslexia than just the loss of spelling-to-sound correspondence. Patients with deep dyslexia also have trouble reading function words, such as articles and prepositions, even though these words are very familiar.

As we saw in earlier chapters, there are several differences between the processing of function words and the processing of content words. These differences, in turn, are bolstered by ERP data, which show that the two word classes elicit very different ERP components (e.g., Kluender & Kutas, 1993). A long-standing claim is that function words are more accurately construed as parts of our syntactic processing system (e.g.,

Garrett, 1982). According to this interpretation, then, the reason that patients with deep dyslexia have more trouble with function words is that their syntactic processing ability has been disrupted. Another theory is that deep dyslexia represents a rather extensive deficit in which both semantic access and syntactic processing are disrupted, but for familiar content words the intact *right* hemisphere of the patient is able to provide the words' meanings (e.g., Coltheart, 1987; Parkin, 1996). This latter view thus represents a sharp contrast to the concept of strict localization of lexical access, since it suggests that semantic processing is not exclusively localized in the left hemisphere.

The idea that the right hemisphere may play a role in word recognition would have been considered quite controversial when Geschwind (1965) was summarizing and elaborating upon the classic lesion studies of the nineteenth century. Today, however, there is strong evidence that the right hemisphere can read, even though it cannot speak. One of the most dramatic forms of evidence for right-hemisphere language processing came from studies of so-called **split-brain patients.** In the brains of these patients, the band of fibers that connects the two hemispheres—the **corpus callosum**—was surgically cut in order to help control epileptic seizures (Bogen & Vogel, 1962). This technique was used on patients who were not responding well to other treatments. The hope was that they would benefit from preventing the spread of the seizure activity from one hemisphere to the other.

Roger Sperry and colleagues (e.g., Sperry & Gazzaniga, 1975) studied split-brain patients in order to see what kinds of information were processed by each hemisphere. Given the nature of the pathways from the eyes to the occipital lobes (see Figure 12.6), it is possible to present visual information to someone so that it is initially sent to one hemisphere or the other. In a person whose corpus callosum is intact, the information can be transferred to the opposite hemisphere across the corpus callosum. However, in a split-brain patient, such transfer is not possible.

Sperry and colleagues found that when a word was flashed in the left visual field, and therefore sent to the right hemisphere, some split-brain patients could pick out the object that the word represented, indicating that they had comprehended the word (e.g., Gazzaniga, 1970; Sperry, 1968; Zaidel, 1990). For example, when Sperry utilized a screen to prevent the objects from being seen, a patient whose right hemisphere saw a word was able to select the corresponding object by feel; but when asked what the object was, the person said, "I don't know." It was the person's left hemisphere talking, because only the right hemisphere knew which word had been presented!

A number of studies have been conducted in which words are presented briefly to either the right or the left visual field in people with an intact corpus callosum. The logic is that there should be an advantage in responding to the word if the hemisphere that receives the word first can do the relevant processing; otherwise, the response should be delayed because the information has to be transferred to the other hemisphere. For example, some studies indicate that the right hemisphere is relatively good at processing very concrete, imageable words and relatively poor at processing other types of words (e.g., Coltheart, 1987). However, this conclusion is controversial (Parkin, 1996). Based on a study of semantic priming from each visual field, Beeman and colleagues (1994) have suggested that words presented to the right hemisphere result in weak activation of a wide range of semantic associates, whereas semantic

| FIGURE 12.6 | Pathways from the Eyes to the Brain |

Visual information to the left of fixation (the location where the eyes are fixated) is sent initially to the right hemisphere, and visual information to the right of fixation is sent initially to the left hemisphere. Normally, information can then be sent to the opposite hemisphere across the corpus callosum, which connects the two hemispheres. However, in split-brain patients, whose corpus callosum has been severed to treat epilepsy, an image briefly flashed in one visual field is processed in one hemisphere only.

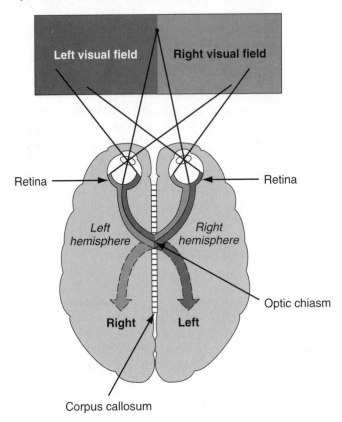

activation in the left hemisphere is stronger and more restricted to closely associated concepts. This conclusion needs further study too, but it certainly fits with the hypothesis that people with deep dyslexia come to rely on the language abilities of their undamaged hemisphere to aid their comprehension of words.

Although there is much about lexical processing in the brain that we still do not understand, the evidence both from lesion studies and from studies of processing in the normal brain appear to be converging on the idea that there are fairly localized regions in which visual processing and phonological processing take place. However, semantic processing seems to be more distributed. Perhaps it is safest to conclude that evidence exists for specialization of different aspects of lexical processing in different brain areas, but the data do not support the idea that each aspect of lexical processing is exclusively related to a particular brain area.

Is There Localization of Syntactic Processing?

The classic description of Broca's aphasia, still repeated in some texts, is that it is a disorder of speech production with relatively normal comprehension. However, as I noted in the discussion of deep dyslexia, a growing body of research suggests that Broca's area is involved in syntactic processing, and that lesions in this area typically affect both production *and* comprehension (e.g., Caramazza & Zurif, 1976). The importance of this insight, gained by integrating neurological and psycholinguistic data, is well illustrated in a case study reported by Byng (1988).

The focus of this case study was a patient with Broca's aphasia, B.R.B., who had made only limited progress in five years of speech therapy. Byng noted that B.R.B's problems were not limited to speech. He also had difficulty comprehending certain kinds of sentences. Consider the following two sentences:

(1) The butcher weighed the meat.

(2) The fireman weighed the policeman.

B.R.B. could pick out a picture that represented the meaning of the first sentence, but he was not able to tell who did the weighing and who was weighed in the second sentence. What does this suggest about B.R.B.'s underlying problem? Byng (1988) believed B.R.B had a deficit that resulted in difficulty assigning sentence elements to their proper syntactic roles, as when determining which noun phrase (NP) is the agent. This deficit was not revealed by sentence (1) because B.R.B. could have used semantics to determine that the butcher has to be the agent. However, in sentence (2), either NP is a possible agent, so B.R.B. had to have guessed. Accordingly, Byng changed B.R.B's therapy so that he started receiving extensive practice at assigning NPs to their proper syntactic roles. Despite little progress in five years of speech therapy, B.R.B showed a marked improvement in sentence comprehension after only two weeks of the new therapy.

Byng's (1988) study is just one of numerous investigations showing that Broca's aphasia often includes **agrammatism,** or disordered syntactic processing. Initially, researchers claimed that Broca's aphasia resulted in virtually complete loss of syntactic ability (e.g., Caramazza & Zurif, 1976). As we have seen, however, this deficit resulted in more obvious problems in production than comprehension because many patients could use general knowledge to compensate for their syntactic problems in comprehension. They could guess a sentence interpretation based only on semantics (as illustrated by B.R.B's case), or they could use a default strategy of assuming that the agent is the first NP in the sentence. (Of course, this strategy works best on sentences that are syntactically simple.)

This view of agrammatism implies that Broca's area is the syntactic module, and that damage to the area knocks the module out of commission. However, we now know that such a view is too simplistic. The syntactic abilities of Broca's aphasics appear to be at least partially preserved: Although these patients do tend to omit inflections and function words from their speech, not all such elements are equally affected (Howard, 1985; Parkin, 1996). For example, the plural inflection *-s* is much less likely to be omitted than the possessive *'s*. And in tests of comprehension, these patients' performance on syntactically complex sentences is below normal, but not as poor as we would expect if the patients relied completely on semantics and on rules like "The first NP is the agent." In addition, some patients show symptoms of agrammatism even though they have lesions outside of Broca's area (Caplan & Hildebrandt, 1988). Thus, it now appears doubtful that all syntactic processing takes place in Broca's area and that extensive damage to the area knocks out all syntactic competence.

The trend in research on agrammatism has been toward explaining the deficit in terms of a disruption, not a complete loss, of the left hemisphere's syntactic processing ability. Many theories in this field are currently being tested, but the different views tend to fall into either of two types of explanations. Some investigators believe that damage to Broca's area causes a loss of a particular aspect of syntactic competence (e.g., Grodzinsky, 1991), whereas other investigators argue that agrammatism results from a lowering of processing capacity that makes syntactic processing more difficult (e.g., Carpenter, Miyake & Just, 1994; Waters & Caplan, 1996b).

As an example of a competence-based view, I will briefly outline Grodzinky's (1990) view of agrammatism, which is known as the **trace deletion hypothesis.** This hypothesis interprets problems in syntactic processing in terms of Chomsky's (1981a) principles and parameters theory. As you may recall, in Chomsky's theory the surface structure (now called "s-structure") of a sentence is said to contain traces that reflect the movements of sentence elements from their position in the deep structure (now called the "d-structure"). For example, if you had several pets and your neighbor's dog chased one of them, you might say:

(3) It was the rabbit($_i$) that the dog chased (t_i).

This way of depicting the s-structure shows that the NP *the rabbit,* which is the object of the verb *chased,* has been moved from its "normal" position following the verb. The NP that was moved is indexed ($_i$) to a trace (t) indicating the role that the NP plays in the sentence.

Now, with that in mind, imagine what would happen if damage to Broca's area left you unable to represent traces in the s-structure. The result would be that whenever a sentence differed from the typical structure of the initial NP in the sentence serving as the agent, you would have a great deal of difficulty assigning NPs to their roles in the sentence. For example, there would be no trace to indicate in sentence (3) that *rabbit* is the thing being chased, even though the word *rabbit* comes before the verb. Grodzinsky (1990) suggested that agrammatic aphasics experience just such a problem, and they try to cope by guessing that the initial NP is always the agent.

According to capacity theories, there is no loss of syntactic knowledge or competence in agrammatism, as Grodzinky's view maintains. Instead, patients perform poorly when production or comprehension places high demands on their capacity to perform syntactic operations. In Waters and Caplan's (1996b; Waters, Caplan & Hildebrandt, 1991) version of the capacity hypothesis, damage to Broca's area causes a lowering of processing capacity that is specifically dedicated to syntactic processes. It's as if there is a separate working-memory buffer for the syntactic module and this syntactic working memory is disrupted by damage to Broca's area. Alternatively, Carpenter and associates (1994) believe that one general capacity is used by the different language processes and this capacity is lessened when Broca's area is damaged. So, as the syntax of sentences becomes more complex, capacity limits are exceeded and the aphasic person is unable to fully parse the complex sentences. To get a sense of how capacity limitations might affect syntactic parsing, try Activity 12.2.

As yet, it is not clear whether a particular version of a competence-based or capacity-based view will prove to be the most useful explanation for agrammatism. What is clear, however, is that Broca's area plays an important role in syntactic processing. Further evidence for this conclusion was obtained in a recent study by Stromswold, Caplan, Alpert, and Rauch (1996). These investigators used PET to measure the regional cerebral blood flow in normal, rather than aphasic, individuals. The participants read and judged the acceptability of sentences that had either center-embedded relative clauses (like those in Sentence List A in Activity 12.2) or right-branching relative clauses (like those in Sentence List B).

The interesting question is whether the extra syntactic processing required for the center-embedded clauses would cause a particular brain area to become more activated than it was for the right-branching clauses. Stromswold and associates (1996) found that the only area with increased activation for the center-embedded condition was Broca's area in the left hemisphere.

Here we need to be careful not to stray too far beyond the data. Although it is tempting to conclude from Stromswold and associates' findings that Broca's area is the site where specific syntactic operations are performed, there are other plausible explanations. For example, it could be that the increased activation in Broca's area reflects increased demands on the working-memory system in general rather than activity specifically related to syntax. In other words, nonsyntactic activities that place demands on temporary storage of information may also increase the activation in this area. A related idea comes from the finding that Broca's area is activated by tasks in which a person uses rehearsal to maintain information in memory (e.g., Zatorre, Meyer, Gjedde & Evans, 1996). Perhaps people thus use rehearsal to aid their comprehension of the more complex center-embedded clauses.

Although we do not know precisely why Broca's area is more active for more syntactically complex sentences, the PET data from Stromswold and associates (1996), together with the data on Broca's aphasia, clearly show that Broca's area is *related* to syntactic processing. However, it is premature to conclude that Broca's area is *exclusively related* to syntactic processing.

One question that you might raise at this point is whether agrammatic aphasics might retain some syntactic abilities due to a right-hemisphere syntactic ability. After all, you saw that people with deep dyslexia may come to rely on the limited semantic processing ability of the right hemisphere. Could an analogous process be at work in agrammatism? In a fascinating series of studies, Bellugi and colleagues (e.g., Bellugi, Poizner & Klima, 1990; Hickok, Say, Bellugi & Klima, 1995) have explored the question of just how strong is the tendency for syntactic processes to be localized in the left hemisphere. In particular, they examined the effects of both left-hemisphere and right-hemisphere lesions on the language processes of native speakers of ASL. What is especially interesting about aphasic disruption of sign languages is that these

ACTIVITY 12.2   **Do Syntactic Structures Vary in Their Processing Demands?**

For this activity, it is best if you work with a partner. One person should be the "experimenter" and the other the "participant." The experimenter should time the participant while he or she reads through Sentence List A below and writes down a one-word answer to each question. The participant should work through the list as quickly as possible, while still comprehending each sentence and giving the correct answers. Next, the experimenter should time the participant on Sentence List B. Finally, switch experimenter and participant roles. The second participant should do Sentence List B, then Sentence List A. Record how long each person takes to complete each list, using a stopwatch if possible. Check the accuracy of all answers to the questions.

Sentence List A

1. The poem that the boy recited angered the minister. (Who recited the poem?)
2. The merchant that the sailor knew carried the boxes. (Who carried the boxes?)
3. The pet that the boy loved played in the sandbox. (What did the boy love?)
4. The player that the coach benched made a huge salary. (Who made a huge salary?)
5. The lightning that the people saw scared the children. (Who saw the lightning?)
6. The accident that the teacher caused alarmed the parents. (Who caused the accident?)
7. The water that the mother spilled surprised the young child. (Who spilled the water?)
8. The woman that the policeman saw sped from the scene. (Who saw the woman?)

Stop! Record the time taken for Sentence List A.

languages, unlike spoken languages, rely heavily on visual-spatial information to convey syntactic relationships. Moreover, a variety of studies have shown that the right hemisphere tends to be dominant in tasks that require visual-spatial ability, such as copying a drawing (e.g., Poizner, Klima & Bellugi, 1989). So, a natural question to ask is whether native users of ASL use the right hemisphere for syntactic processing instead of the left.

To answer this question, Hickok and associates (1996) studied a native signer with an extensive right-hemisphere lesion (patient S.J.) as well as a native signer with a left-hemisphere lesion that included Broca's area (patient R.S.). Both patients were

Activity 12.2 *continued*

Sentence List B

1. The child gave the present that the father loved. (Who gave the present?)
2. The farmer planted the crops that grew on the hill. (What grew on the hill?)
3. The clerk sold the umbrella that the woman used. (Who used the umbrella?)
4. The car had the wheels that the thieves wanted. (What did the thieves want?)
5. The moss grew in the valley where the explorers roamed. (Who roamed in the valley?)
6. The bird rested in the tree that the boy planted. (What rested in the tree?)
7. The politician released the report that the committee wanted. (Who released the report?)
8. The board voted on the plan that the parents devised. (Who devised the plan?)

Stop! Record the time taken for Sentence List B.

Was one of the lists more difficult to work through, in terms of either the time taken or the number of errors made in answering the questions? Note that the average length of the sentences is the same for the two lists and that all the sentences use familiar terms. The only important difference between the lists is that in Sentence List A the sentences all have center-embedded relative clauses (i.e., clauses that come between subject and verb), whereas those in Sentence List B all have right-branching relative clauses (i.e., clauses to the right of the object). Sentences with center-embedded clauses are generally more difficult to process than sentences with right-branching clauses, perhaps because it requires more capacity to buffer the embedded clause while trying to link the subject and main verb. The implication is that if a particular lesion decreases the capacity for syntactic processing, then the sentences with center-embedded clauses should be more difficult to parse than those with right-branching clauses.

tested on their ability to comprehend sentences that are reversible. For example, to produce the ASL equivalent of "The dog bit the cat," a signer would typically give the sign for *dog* and indicate a position in space, give the sign for *cat* and indicate another position in space, and then move the sign for *bit* from the position for *dog* to the position for *cat*. To produce "The cat bit the dog," the signer would proceed in the same way, except that the *bit* sign would be moved from the position for *cat* to the position for *dog*. Thus, in ASL, the assignment of nouns to their roles in a sentence is indicated by location and movement in space—in short, by a visual-spatial form of information.

The study of Hickok and associates (1996) compared both patients' performance on the sentence-comprehension test with their performance on another task that required visual-spatial processing but did not involve sentences. In the nonsentence task, signs for different objects were given in various spatial locations that showed how the objects were arranged in a room. The two patients were then asked to verify whether the set of signs accurately described the arrangement of objects shown in a picture. The performance of each patient on each task is illustrated in Figure 12.7.

The most interesting result was that R.S., who has left-hemisphere damage (LHD), was severely limited in her ability to use visual-spatial information *for syntactic processing*. However, her performance was fine when the visual-spatial processing did not involve syntax. S.J., who has right-hemisphere damage (RHD), displayed exactly the opposite pattern of results. These data, along with similar findings on other native signers with aphasia (see Poizner, Klima & Bellugi, 1989), show that syntactic processes

FIGURE 12.7 **Language and Spatial Abilities in ASL Users with Brain Damage**

A patient with damage to the left hemisphere (R.S.) and a patient with damage to the right hemisphere (S.J.) performed two tasks. One task involved using spatial information to understand the syntax of a sentence, and the other task involved comprehending spatial information about the layout of objects in a room. Even though both tasks involved spatial information, performance on the two tasks was affected differently by the location of the brain damage. In particular, a disturbance of the ability to use spatial information syntactically was observed only in cases of damage to the left hemisphere.

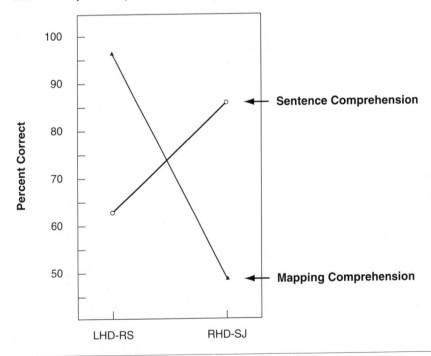

are strongly localized in the left hemisphere even when the syntactic cues are conveyed by the type of information for which the right hemisphere usually has processing dominance. We can also argue that, if the right hemisphere does not contribute to syntactic processing in ASL, it is unlikely to play a role in syntactic processing in spoken languages. This conclusion is bolstered by recent studies examining whether right-hemisphere damage affects language processing (e.g., Brownell, Gardner, Prather & Martino, 1995). As we will see in the next section, right-hemisphere damage does affect some language abilities, but syntactic processing is not one of them.

Is There Localization of Integrative Processing?

When we are comprehending or producing sentences or discourse, the lexical and syntactic information in them must be integrated into a coherent whole. And, as we saw in Chapters 7 through 9, this integration is achieved through a variety of processing mechanisms. In comprehension, we use both sentence-based and knowledge-based information to make inferences, and we sometimes go beyond literal meanings when attempting to understand metaphor and analogy. In production, we use intonation, knowledge of the listener, and social conventions, as well as lexical, syntactic, and semantic mechanisms, to communicate with another person. Moreover, if it is true that strict localization holds only for the most elementary processes, then we would not expect integrative processes to be exclusively related to one particular brain area. Even so, we can still determine what areas are involved in the more complex aspects of comprehension and production.

Of course, the kind of left-hemisphere damage that we have considered so far in this chapter can have major consequences for global aspects of comprehension and production. If the bottom-up flow of information is disrupted at the lexical or syntactic level, then integrative processing cannot proceed normally because it depends on this bottom-up information. The question we want to answer, though, is what brain areas are directly involved in performing the higher-level integrative processes themselves. Much of the research on this question has focused on the role of the right hemisphere (e.g., Joanette & Brownell, 1990).

Compared to research on the effects of LHD, studies of RHD have paid less attention to the exact site and extent of the lesions involved. And one reason for this lesser concern with lesion sites in RHD is the general belief that the right hemisphere operates in a more holistic fashion than the left hemisphere (e.g., Semmes, 1968). It is certainly possible that researchers have underestimated the degree to which the right hemisphere has specialized areas (Brownell, Gardner, Prather & Martino, 1995). Nevertheless, despite the relative lack of precision in specifying the nature of RHD in many studies, there is a fair amount of consistency among the kinds of language deficits reported.

A study by Hough (1990) provides a representative example of the language problems experienced by patients with RHD. Take a look at the two versions of the story in Table 12.3. What is different about the two versions is the placement of the central theme of the story—in this case, that Pete was supposed to be watching his little brother. When the theme is delayed as opposed to stated at the outset, the comprehender must integrate the early sentences into a coherent idea without as much help from the discourse itself. Hough (1990) presented story versions like these to three groups:

TABLE 12.3	An Example of the Stimuli Used by Hough (1990)

Normal Theme Presentation

Pete was in the front yard with his little brother, Glen. Their parents went shopping and Pete had to watch Glen until they returned. Glen always seemed to be getting into some kind of trouble. One of Pete's friends came by on his bicycle and stopped to talk to Pete. Glen headed for the street but Pete caught him in time. Then Glen started running up the concrete stairs to their house. Before Pete could get to him, Glen fell and scraped his knee. Glen was screaming as their parents pulled in the driveway.

Delayed Theme Presentation

Glen always seemed to be getting into some kind of trouble. One of Pete's friends came by on his bicycle and stopped to talk to Pete. Glen headed for the street but Pete caught him in time. Then Glen started running up the concrete stairs to their house. Before Pete could get to him, Glen fell and scraped his knee. Glen was screaming as their parents pulled in the driveway. Pete had been watching his little brother in the front yard while his parents went shopping.

patients with RHD, patients with aphasia due to LHD, and normal controls. The participants later had to answer questions about the central ideas in each version of the story. In the normal theme condition, the RHD patients and the aphasic patients answered about 80 percent of the questions correctly whereas the normal controls answered about 95 percent of the questions correctly. Most interesting, though, was the performance in the delayed theme condition. In this condition, the RHD patients answered only 52 percent of the questions correctly. Their performance was worse than that of either the normal controls (94 percent correct) *or the aphasic patients* (74 percent correct). These data suggest that people with RHD are especially deficient at integrating the information in separate sentences into a coherent theme.

The same general type of problem is often observed in the conversations of RHD patients. These patients have difficulty detecting that a statement marks a change in topic (Rehak, Kaplan & Gardner, 1992). Likewise, when describing a scene to someone else, they often mention a lot of concrete details without giving the setting or theme of what they are describing (Myers, 1993). In their conversations, RHD patients are also noticeably lacking in variations in intonation, and they seem deficient in picking up on the stress patterns that other speakers use to emphasize a particular point (Knapp & Hall, 1992). Because their own intonations are so flat and they are so deficient in picking up on the mood of the other person in a conversation, people with RHD are sometimes misclassified as having depression, even when they are not truly depressed (Brownell, Gardner, Prather & Martino, 1995).

All of the deficiencies that I have mentioned thus far occur in situations where a great deal of information must be managed at once, as in extended discourse and conversation. However, RHD patients also experience some comprehension problems in situations that seem less complex. These problems are particularly evident when the patients are asked if they understand something ambiguous, metaphorical, or ironic.

They have difficulty even with familiar idioms like "turning over a new leaf." RHD patients tend to take such phrases very literally. Consequently, on tests of comprehension that involve metaphoric stimuli, patients with RHD may perform worse than patients with Wernicke's aphasia (Winner & Gardner, 1977).

Taken together, these symptoms—discourse comprehension problems, excessive literalness, flat intonation, and wandering conversation style—constitute the **right-hemisphere syndrome**. But are these symptoms multiple separate problems, or is there one particular deficit that underlies all of the symptoms? At present, we do not know the answer to this question, but there do appear to be connections among at least some of the different symptoms associated with the right-hemisphere syndrome. According to Chiarello (1988), the right hemisphere plays the important role of holding onto alternative meanings until a final interpretation can be resolved. Thus, the problems that RHD patients have with integrating information around a theme and with processing metaphor or ambiguity may reflect a loss of the ability to maintain alternate interpretations.

CONCLUSIONS

What's Become of the Classic Language Circuit?

Now that we've reviewed a considerable amount of research on language functioning in both normal and lesioned brains, what can we say about the hypothesis for this chapter? Is it true that each of the major components of the language system is localized in a particular part of the brain? The classic view, which grew out of autopsy data from patients with aphasia, certainly supported this hypothesis. However, an assumption of the classic view was that the major components of language could be separated into sensory and motor aspects. Thus, there were two areas of primary concern: Wernicke's area, devoted to the analysis of the sensory input of language, and Broca's area, devoted to the motor output of language.

Over the last few decades a fundamental change has occurred in terms of what investigators consider to be the major components of the language system, thus altering the way we view localization of language functions. Rather than asking where the sensory functions are localized, or where the speech output functions are localized, investigators now seek evidence for the localization of processing constructs developed in psycholinguistics. For example, we now see studies focused on determining where phonological or syntactic processing takes place. As we have come to ask questions about the implementation of these psycholinguistic processes in the brain, the dominant view of localization has shifted to a middle ground between the classic view of strict localization and the holistic view espoused by Freud, and, to some extent, by Head.

As we now know, and as the classic view claimed, the basic circuitry studied by Broca, Wernicke, and Lichtheim *is* especially important in language tasks. This conclusion has been confirmed not only by additional studies of aphasia but also by PET and fMRI studies, which consistently show activation of Broca's and Wernicke's areas in many language tasks. Broca's area participates not only in syntactic processing

(Stromswold, Caplan, Alpert & Rauch, 1996) but also in tasks in which the person is rehearsing information with internal speech (Poeppel, 1996; Zatorre, Meyer, Gjedde & Evans, 1992). Damasio (1992) succinctly expressed the general nature of the functions handled by Broca's area when he said that it is involved in "the ordering of linguistic components in time and space" (p. 534). Meanwhile, studies of activation in Wernicke's area have invariably shown that it participates in processing auditory verbal stimuli. Habib and Démonet (1996) characterized the nature of this area of the brain by saying that it connects phonological and semantic information. As such, it may also be involved in reading when a phonological route to semantics is used.

At the same time, we have learned more about the language-relevant processing that takes place outside of the areas that were emphasized in the classic view. For example, data suggest that areas more frontal than Broca's area may be important to semantic processing (Posner, Peterson, Fox & Raichle, 1988). And there is growing evidence that the right hemisphere plays an important role both in the semantic processing of individual words (Beeman et al., 1994) and in the integration and maintenance of separate ideas in processing discourse (Brownell, Gardner, Prather & Martino, 1995).

Today, the dominant view of how language is implemented in the brain holds that there are multiple networks of neurons in different brain regions, and that these networks carry out a variety of basic functions. In addition, according to this view, each of the processing areas is richly interconnected with networks in other areas (Habib & Démonet, 1996; Mesulam, 1990). It is possible that some of these networks could function in a modular fashion—that is, rather autonomously—but at present the neurological data do not support a modular view over an interactive one. Moreover, the sheer variety of brain regions involved in language tasks indicates that language-specific processing areas are richly interconnected with areas that seem to be involved with more general cognitive processes like attention and working memory (Brownell et al., 1995; Just, Carpenter & Keller, 1996). For example, the evidence that right-hemisphere damage can seriously affect a person's ability to communicate, even when the language-specific processes of the left hemisphere are undisturbed, is an excellent demonstration of a major theme of this text: Language processes and other cognitive processes are closely intertwined. So, go ahead and keep talking to yourself. You're not crazy; you're just helping yourself think.

CHAPTER REVIEW

Checking Your Understanding

Key Terms

acquired dyslexia (373)
agrammatism (377)
anomia (360)
aphasia (360)
Broca's area (362)

conduction aphasia (364)
corpus callosum (375)
computerized tomography (CT) scanning (366)
deep dyslexia (373)
electroencephalogram (EEG) (366)

event-related potentials (ERPs) (368)
functional magnetic resonance imaging
  (fMRI) (369)
magnetic resonance imaging (MRI) (366)
neuroimaging (366)
positron emission tomography (PET)
  scanning (368)

right-hemisphere syndrome (385)
split-brain patients (375)
surface dyslexia (373)
trace deletion hypothesis (378)
Wernicke's area (364)

Review Questions

1. Explain how cases of anomia lend support to the idea that there is a distinction between conceptual representations and the words we use to express concepts.

2. Along the way to establishing our modern understanding of aphasia, investigators had to learn to distinguish between speech and language, and between language and other intellectual abilities. What role did Paul Broca and Carl Wernicke play in validating each of these two distinctions?

3. Both lesion data and functional imaging data play roles in helping us understand brain-language relations. What are the strengths and weaknesses of each of these types of data?

4. Draw a sketch of the left hemisphere of the brain and indicate the classic language circuit described by Lichtheim and Geschwind.

5. Describe how the classic language circuit view explains the symptoms seen in Broca's, Wernicke's, and conduction aphasias.

6. Imagine that you are undergoing a fMRI. If functional images are observed during your semantic processing of words, what factors would determine whether activation is found in Wernicke's area?

7. How are surface dyslexia and deep dyslexia explained by the dual-route model of reading?

8. Charles is a stroke victim. His nonfluent speech resembles the telegraphic speech of young children, but with many hesitations. He has difficulty understanding sentences with complex syntax, but otherwise shows relatively good comprehension.

   (a) If Charles undergoes a CT scan, where would you expect a lesion to be found?
   (b) How would the trace deletion hypothesis explain Charles's deficits?
   (c) How could you explain Charles's deficits from a capacity view?
   (d) Can a general capacity view like that of Just, Carpenter & Keller (1996) explain both comprehension and production problems in a case like Charles's?

9. Why are data from aphasic users of sign language especially valuable for testing hemispheric localization of syntactic processes?

10. Describe two different sources of evidence that the right hemisphere is involved in some aspects of semantic processing. (Note: You may wish to think about semantic processing at both the lexical level and the discourse level.)

On Further Reflection ...

1. The case study by Byng (1988) that I discussed in the chapter was a good illustration of how a better understanding of aphasia can help lead to better treatment.

Several journals (e.g., *Aphasiology, Brain and Language, Brain, Journal of Psycholinguistic Research*) publish reports of case studies involving treatments for aphasia.

Find a description of a language rehabilitation program in one of these reports. What basic assumptions does the program make about the cause or causes of the type of aphasia being treated? Does the potential effectiveness of the treatment depend on whether linguistic competence or processing capacity is lost? Alternatively, you can use the Internet to access the homepage of the National Aphasia Association. This association provides links to descriptions of numerous rehabilitation efforts. Analyze some of these efforts in terms of the basic assumptions they reflect about the nature of the language deficits being treated.

2. Imagine that you are in charge of a well-funded research team that has access to normal volunteers and aphasic patients as well as to fMRI or PET scanners. Your objective is to test whether semantic knowledge can affect the initial syntactic parsing of a sentence. In other words, you want to design a study that uses language stimuli and physiological measures to test for syntactic modularity. Can ERP data contribute to this issue beyond the information that can be gained through the use of neuro-imaging data? To address this question, you may wish to review some of the research discussed in Chapter 7. Also, ask a classmate to critique your research idea. Will you be able to definitively test the modularity question with this experimental design?

What Has the Psychology of Language Explained?

What first captivated me about psychology, going all the way back to my introductory psychology class as an undergraduate, was what psychologists did *not* know. In short, it was the frontiers of knowledge, the still-open questions, that I found to be the most fascinating aspects of the field. Like other people who do psychological research, I still consider the frontiers of knowledge most interesting to think about, and to communicate to students. However, I realize that students sometimes find the lack of definite answers to fundamental questions to be frustrating. Therefore, it is worth taking stock, every now and then, of what we do know for certain. In science, paradoxically, what we know for certain are usually what claims are *not* true. So, now that we have completed Unit Three, let's consider what we know is not true about the implementation of language processes in the brain.

Take a look at the figure shown on the next page. It represents some early ideas about localization of function in the brain. In the last century, Franz Gall theorized that the brain was divided into a series of "faculties," or mental organs like those depicted in the figure, and that the degree to which a person possessed one of these faculties was determined by the relative size of the corresponding brain area for that individual. Further, Gall claimed that the size of each brain area could be determined by measurements of the skull. Note where the language area is positioned in the figure. Gall believed that people with protruding eyes had a large forebrain, which gave them above-average language ability. He arrived at this idea when he studied the case of a man with anomia that had resulted from a fencing accident in which the blade pierced the man's face next to the left nostril and traveled upward into the left frontal lobe (Young, 1970).

My point here is not just that the ideas embodied in the figure are incorrect, but that they are incorrect in some interesting ways that reflect the general ideas we studied in this final unit. You'll note that the figure makes an assumption that is still with us: that there are specialized regions of the cortex. However, it shows nothing that resembles the classic language circuit. This observation serves as a reminder that a good functional, representational theory of what kinds of processes we need to look for in the brain is essential to locating the "right" functions in the right places. Indeed, we can draw the same conclusion from the downfall of the classic language circuit, which looked at language in terms of receptive and expressive abilities rather than in terms of psycholinguistic processes.

It does seem to be the case that some brain areas are especially active during particular types of processing. But the more we examine the localization of function in the brain, the more we see that strict localization is likely to be realized only for rather elementary processes. Even moderately complex activities, like accessing the meaning of a word, do not appear to be assigned to one specific region.

So, the brain is both specialized *and* interactive when it comes to language—but sorting out exactly how this works will probably take quite some time. Likewise, when we explore how language becomes implemented in the brain, we see strong evidence for both innate and learned aspects. Yet we now know for certain that both the extreme nature view and the extreme nurture view are false.

One final falsehood I would like to address is the misconception about how scientists answer questions about language and other phenomena. Many people have the impression that science always starts with

Shown is the cover of a nineteenth-century journal of phrenology, which depicts the brain areas believed to be associated with mental attributes.

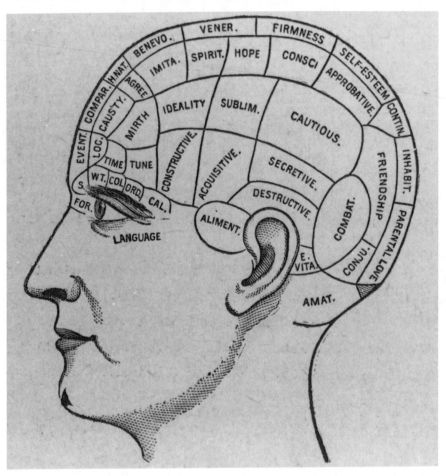

basic research that ignores individual differences and then conducts applied research that uses general principles to explain individual behavior. But as I hope this unit has made clear, the study of individual differences can be quite informative about general theory. Much of what we know about the genetic endowment for language, and about localization of function in the brain, comes from the study of individual differences and language disturbances across specific cases. That, at least, Gall had observed correctly. We *can* learn a lot about the general nature of things from the study of individual differences.

GLOSSARY

acquired dyslexia A loss of reading ability due to brain damage.

action sequences The basic units of which conversations are composed. The actions typically occur in a particular order, as when a conversation is opened, information is exchanged, and the conversation is closed.

adjacency pair A set of two ordered utterances in a conversation, such as a question followed by an answer.

advance organizers Previews, outlines, and other devices that help a reader anticipate the connections among the ideas in a passage.

affricates Consonant sounds that start with a complete closure of the vocal tract, followed by a gradual release of air. The beginning and ending sound of *church* is an example.

agrammatism An aspect of aphasia, usually Broca's aphasia, in which the affected persons lose some of their syntactic processing ability. This dysfunction is most evident in the lack of grammatical structure in their speech.

algorithms Step-by-step procedures used to perform an activity.

allophone One of possibly several variations in the pronunciation of a particular phoneme. For example, the [t] in *type* and *bet* are different allophones.

alphabetic system A writing system in which the characters correspond, approximately, to the phonemes of the language.

amplitude The height of a wave, from its highest point to its lowest. In sound waves, differences in amplitude are associated with differences in loudness.

anaphor A term that gets its meaning from another expression, typically one that precedes it in the text.

anaphoric reference The process of using an expression that refers back to prior information in the discourse.

anomia A brain dysfunction involving great difficulty in retrieving words.

antecedent The earlier term to which a later term refers in an anaphoric reference.

anthropologists Scientists who study human cultures, societies, and their origins.

antonymy A semantic relationship in which two words have opposite meanings.

aphasia Loss of one or more aspects of language ability due to brain damage.

arbitrariness A universal feature of language dictating that language symbols do not bear any resemblance to the things that they represent.

articulatory suppression task A task in which a subject repeats a familiar word or set of numbers over and over in order to use the phonological loop without consuming attentional resources.

assembled route Referring to the hypothesis that we access the meaning of a written word by first processing the sound of the word.

assimilation A process in which the pronunciation of a sound is altered to make it similar to an adjacent sound in the utterance.

associative stage The second stage of skill acquisition in which the different parts of performing the skill become more closely linked as a single unit.

automatic process A mental process that requires little in the way of attentional resources.

autonomous stage The final stage of skill acquisition in which performance of the skill becomes increasingly automatic and error free.

basic-level concepts The level of abstraction at which we most often categorize objects.

bigram frequency The frequency of occurrence of a two-letter combination.

blocking principle The principle whereby tacit knowledge used in language acquisition specifies that we should not apply a grammatical rule to generate a word form if a lexical entry that fulfills the same role already exists.

bridging inference An inference based on information that we retrieve from memory in order to make a connection between two sentences.

Broca's area A region of the left frontal lobe of the brain that plays an important role in grammatical processing.

case role grammar A grammar based on the idea that lexical entries for verbs include information about what roles (e.g., doer of the action, object acted upon) need to be filled when those verbs appear in a sentence.

categorical perception In speech perception, the phenomenon whereby listeners are much better able to discriminate between two sounds in different phonemic categories than between two sounds in the same phonemic category.

causal antecedent An event or circumstance that produces an effect.

central executive According to Baddeley's model, the working memory structure that allocates attentional resources to the phonological and visual-spatial buffers of working memory.

chatterbox syndrome A disorder in which mental retardation is coupled with better than expected language abilities. Individuals with this disorder not only talk excessively but also use correct grammatical forms.

child-directed speech (CDS) Speech directed at young children. CDS is characterized by short sentences, exaggerated intonation, and very clear articulation.

class inclusion assertions Sentences that entail decisions about whether a particular item is a member of a given category.

closed-class category A syntactic category consisting of function words (e.g., the, an, or of), which, unlike content words, tend to remain constant over time within a language.

coarticulation The influence on a given sound by an adjacent sound. Coarticulation occurs because the motor movements that produce each phoneme are overlapping.

codability The ease with which a concept can be described.

code switching Changing which language is being spoken during an utterance.

cognitive grammar A grammar based on the idea that the rules of language can be reduced to semantic and phonological information, without a separate syntactic level of knowledge. The theory of cognitive grammar maintains that both word meanings and sentence meanings are understood in terms of idealized models that represent objects and situations.

cognitive psychology The branch of psychology that studies mental processes such as attention, memory, language, and problem solving.

cognitive stage The initial stage of skill acquisition in which a person encodes the different parts of performing the skill as a set of declarative rules.

coherence The relationships among the sentences in discourse.

cohesion devices Signals within a text that indicate connections among sentences.

common ground The knowledge and beliefs shared by the people in a conversation.

competence The object of linguistic inquiry, according to Chomsky. In other words, linguists should try to describe the knowledge that any user of a language must have.

competition model The idea that second-language acquisition may be inhibited because some of the linguistic principles learned during acquisition of the first language do not transfer to the second language.

compositional semantics Referring to the study of phrase or sentence meanings, based on combined word meanings.

computational level The level of analyzing any information-processing system at which we consider what kinds of problems that system was designed to solve.

computerized tomography (CT) scanning A technique that uses computer enhancement of a series of X-rays to produce a three-dimensional view of the brain.

conceptual semantics Referring to a theory proposed by Jackendoff, who argued that semantics is a matter of mapping between a syntactic structure and a mental representation of sentence meaning.

conditioned head turn procedure A procedure used to test the speech recognition abilities of infants. The infants are rewarded for turning their heads to look in a particular location whenever they notice a change in the speech sound that is being presented.

conduction aphasia A language disturbance in which the most obvious symptom is an inability to repeat what was just heard.

connectionism An approach to cognitive modeling that is based on interactions among simple processing units.

conservation problems Tasks that measure a child's ability to recognize that the properties of a substance, such as volume or number, remain constant despite changes in shape, length, or position.

consonant-vowel rule The pattern whereby, in speech errors, consonants replace consonants and vowels replace vowels.

construction-integration theory A model of text comprehension claiming that we build different mental representations of text during processing cycles that consist of widespread activation of concepts followed by narrowing of activation based on contextual constraints.

constructivist view The idea that comprehension is based on building a mental model by using both text-based information and information from the general knowledge base.

continuity view Among theories of language evolution, the view that language evolved gradually from the gestures and calls used by other primates.

continuous theories Theories of syntactic development that assume children have some innate syntactic knowledge, which they connect with the words and combinations that are found in their native language.

contribution The fulfillment of a conversational goal, which occurs when both people in a conversation conclude that they can move on to another goal.

controlled process A mental process that requires conscious attention.

corpus callosum A band of neural fibers that connects the two hemispheres of the brain.

counterfactual reasoning Thinking hypothetically about a situation that is contrary to fact.

creole A type of language that develops among children whose language exposure consists of a rudimentary language, or pidgin.

critical period A period of life in which a particular behavior or skill, such as internalizing the rules of grammar, must be acquired if acquisition is to proceed normally.

CT scanning *See* computerized tomography scanning.

decay theory A theory that attributes forgetting to loss of information from memory due to the passage of time.

declarative memory Memory for facts and personal experiences. The information in declarative memory is available to consciousness.

deep dyslexia A reading disorder, caused by brain damage, in which the affected person is unable to use spelling-to-sound correspondence to recognize words.

deep orthography An alphabetic writing system in which there is relatively little correspondence between spelling and pronunciation.

deep structure The phrase structure that expresses the relationships among sentence elements, independent of how the sentence is actually stated.

derivational theory of complexity (DTC) An early application of Chomsky's transformational grammar to the problem of developing a psychological model of sentence comprehension. According to the DTC, comprehension time increases with the complexity of the transformations between surface structure and deep structure.

descriptive adequacy One criterion for evaluating a linguistic description of grammar. According to this criterion, a grammar should specify what sentences are permissible and how different sentence structures are related to each other.

diary studies Studies of language acquisition in which someone records language samples from a particular child at different ages.

direct route Referring to the hypothesis that we access the meaning of a written word by going from print to meaning without processing the sound of the word.

discontinuity view Among theories of language evolution, the view that language evolved from mental abilities that are uniquely human and of recent evolutionary origin.

discontinuous theories Theories of syntactic development that stress the role of learned rather than innate factors.

discourse A set of sentences that are related to one another in a meaningful way.

discourse record The sum total of the knowledge that directly reflects the information stored in memory about a conversation.

discreteness A universal feature of language dictating that all languages are composed of separate symbols, either distinct words or distinct signs.

displacement A universal feature of language dictating that all languages allow us to communicate about things that are not present physically.

distance effect In discourse, the phenomenon whereby the farther back in a text the antecedent for an anaphor appeared, the more time is required to find it.

domain-specific Referring to one of the defining characteristics of a module, in Fodor's use of the term. A module is domain-specific in that it works with only one type of information.

double dissociation The most convincing type of evidence for concluding that two abilities are differentiated in the brain. For example, there is a double dissociation between ability A and ability B if we find cases of good ability on A and poor ability on B *and* cases of poor ability on A and good ability on B.

dual-route model The idea that visual word recognition can be accomplished in either of two ways: from print to meaning (the direct route) or from print to sound to meaning (the assembled route).

duality of patterning A universal feature of language dictating that each meaningful symbol in a language can be broken down into separate units that do not have meaning by themselves. For example, a spoken word can be broken down into its component sounds.

duplex perception Referring to a technique in which the different parts of a sound are separated so that formant transitions are presented to one ear and steady states are presented to the other ear.

dyslexia Severe impairment of the ability to recognize words, either as a child tries to learn to read (developmental dyslexia) or because brain damage disrupts the abilities of a previously normal reader (acquired dyslexia).

EEG *See* electroencephalogram.

electroencephalogram (EEG) A graphic record of the electrical activity of the brain, measured by means of electrodes placed on the scalp.

elicited production Referring to techniques in which experimenters obtain language data from children by having them respond to a particular stimulus that is under the control of the experimenters.

emergent features Properties of a combination of concepts that are not characteristic of either concept in isolation.

encoding specificity principle The idea that the memorability of a stimulus depends on the overlap between the conditions at encoding and the conditions at retrieval.

entailment A logical implication of the meaning of a sentence.

episodic memory Memory for events and personal experiences that are tied to a specific context.

ERPs *See* event-related potentials.

event-related potentials (ERPs) Voltage potentials that, when averaged, indicate the consistent pattern of brain activity that occurs in response to a particular type of stimulus.

explanatory adequacy One criterion for evaluating a linguistic description of grammar. According to this criterion, a grammar should be consistent with the facts of language acquisition by children.

fan effect A phenomenon in which retrieval is slowed as the number of facts associated with a concept is increased.

feral children Children reared in conditions that isolated them from human contact.

finite-state grammar (FSG) A grammar based on the idea that a sentence is a chain of words, with each word determined by the immediately preceding word.

fixations In reading, the times during which the eyes pause on particular words.

fMRI *See* functional magnetic resonance imaging.

foregrounding Putting particular discourse concepts into the focus of attention by mentioning them first, repeating them, or using other attention-capturing devices.

formant transition A shift in formant frequency over time.

formants Dark bands on a speech spectrogram that indicate the frequencies of greatest intensity.

framing effect The tendency for people to choose different alternatives depending on how the alternatives are worded.

frequency The number of times a wave cycles from peak to valley and back in a given unit of time. In sound waves, differences in frequency are associated with differences in pitch.

fricatives Consonant sounds that are produced by constricting the vocal tract before air is forced through it. The [f] in *fan* is an example.

functional magnetic resonance imaging (fMRI) A technique that uses powerful magnetic fields to obtain a record of the parts of the brain most active during performance of a particular cognitive task.

fuzzy logic model of perception (FLMP) Massaro's proposal that we process speech by classifying the sounds based on their similarity to typical examples of each syllable.

garden-path sentence A sentence that initially leads to an incorrect parsing or an incorrect interpretation of its meaning.

given information Information that the speaker or writer assumes the listener or reader already knows.

given/new strategy A comprehension strategy in which we determine what information in a sentence is already in memory and associate that given information with the new information in the sentence.

glides Sounds produced with little obstruction of the air flow in the vocal tract—for example, the /y/ sound.

global coherence In discourse, coherence based on the relationship between all of the sentences and the overall theme.

government and binding theory Another name for Chomsky's *principles and parameters theory*.

ground The basis for comparing the two concepts in a metaphor.

habituated Decreased or eliminated a response to a stimulus due to repeated presentation of the stimulus.

head The constituent of a phrase that determines what kind of phrase it is. For example, a noun is the head of a noun phrase.

head-parameter A principle of grammar in which a language takes either of two values—namely, that the head of a phrase comes at the beginning of the phrase or at the end of the phrase.

Hertz (Hz) A unit of measure for sound frequencies, referring to the number of cycles per second.

high-amplitude sucking (HAS) A technique for investigating speech recognition in infants. The rate of sucking on a pacifier is the criterion used to determine whether the infant perceives a stimulus as familiar or novel.

holophrase A single word utterance that a child uses to express an entire proposition.

home-sign The gestural system invented by young deaf children as they try to communicate with their hearing parents.

homographs Words in which the same spelling pattern is associated with multiple meanings (e.g., *bug*, an insect, and *bug*, a secret listening device).

illocutionary force The action that is performed in the act of uttering a particular sentence.

illusory conjunction A visual illusion in which a particular feature, such as color, is perceptually attached to the wrong pattern.

image schema A simple mental model that represents a basic aspect of objects and situations in the world. For example, the PART-WHOLE image schema represents the idea that many objects are composed of different parts.

immediacy of interpretation Referring to the hypothesis that, as each word in a sentence is received, it is integrated as fully as possible into the developing sentence interpretation.

implementational level The level of analyzing any information-processing system at which we consider how the processes are performed physically. Regarding human cognition, for example, at this level of analysis we might ask how and where mental processes are performed in the brain.

indirect speech act An utterance that makes a command or otherwise performs some action through its nonliteral interpretation. For example, "Do you have the time?" is really a request for the time of day.

informationally encapsulated Referring to one of the defining characteristics of a module, in Fodor's use of the term. A module is informationally encapsulated if it does not receive top-down information about context or expectations.

insight problems Problems that are solved all at once with one key idea.

instantiation An inference process in which the comprehender uses background knowledge to make a general term more concrete. For example, an instantiation for *The fish attacked the swimmer* might be "shark."

instrument inferences Inferences about the instrument used to perform an action. For example, an instrument inference related to *Tom sliced the tomato* might be "knife."

interactive compensatory processing The tendency of poor readers to try to identify a word by guessing based on context rather than by sounding out the word.

interactive view The idea that language and other cognitive processes influence each other through all stages of processing. For example, in a case where we use word or sentence meaning to help determine sentence structure *and* we use sentence structure to help determine meaning, meaning and structure are being processed interactively.

interference theory A theory that attributes forgetting to retrieval failure caused by memories other than the one a person is attempting to retrieve.

intonation units Bursts of speech set off by variations in prosody. Each intonation unit is typically about one clause long.

introspection The method of analyzing one's own mental processes in order to discover the basic elements of conscious experience. Introspection was used by Wundt in the late 1800s and early 1900s.

iteration A feature of the productivity of all languages whereby, in principle, we can always add a new phrase onto the end of a sentence.

knowledge telling A writing style in which each idea is translated into a sentence as it occurs to the writer, such that little attention is given to the global structure of the text.

knowledge transforming A writing style in which the writer plans the organization of information so that it can best be understood by the reader.

lack of invariance problem In speech perception, the problem of identifying phonemic cues that do not change with context.

language bioprogram hypothesis The idea, advanced by Bickerton, that an innate grammar allows children to invent a true language when their early language experience is limited to exposure to a rudimentary language, or pidgin.

late closure A syntactic parsing strategy in which we try to attach new sentence elements to the most recently processed phrase.

less-is-more hypothesis The idea that adults may have a more difficult time than children in acquiring a second language because the adults' more advanced memory abilities cause them to store utterances as holistic patterns that are harder to analyze into their component parts.

levels effect The finding that memory for information increases with height in the hierarchical network of relations among the propositions in a discourse.

levels of analysis The three interdependent levels at which any complex information-processing system can be understood, conceptualized as questions asked about that system: What problems does it solve (computational level), what steps does it use to perform its functions (representational level), and how are these steps accomplished physically (implementational level)?

levels of processing theory A memory theory maintaining that memories are by-products of the way stimuli are analyzed. The more deeply analyzed the stimulus, the stronger the memory.

lexical ambiguity A word that has more than one meaning.

lexical decision task A technique used in many language and priming experiments in which a person is presented with a string of letters and must quickly decide if the string represents a word or a nonword.

lexical decomposition Referring to the principle that word meanings (such as the meaning of *robin*) can be broken down into primitive elements (such as *animate, lays eggs, sings,* and *red-breasted).*

Lexical functionalist grammar (LFG) A grammar in which the possible relationships among words in a sentence are specified in the lexicon rather than by a set of transformational rules.

lexical semantics Referring to the study of the meanings of individual words.

linguistic category model A theory that posits four different levels of abstraction at which the same behavior can be described.

linguistic determinism The idea that we can think only in terms of concepts for which there are words in our language. Thus, language determines how we think.

linguistic intergroup bias (LIB) Referring to the tendency of people to describe the behavior of others in a way that reflects more positively on those they like and less positively on those they do not like.

linguistic relativity Referring to the idea that cross-cultural variations in cognition are associated with differences in languages.

linguists Scientists who study the nature of the rules and other components that underlie all languages.

liquids Consonant sounds, including /l/ and /r/, that are produced with a slight obstruction of the airway.

local coherence In discourse, coherence based on the relationship between adjacent pairs of sentences.

localization of function The degree to which a given mental process is confined to a particular region of the brain.

locally managed Referring to the fact that conversations tend to be coordinated in an ongoing fashion through the cooperation of both parties rather than completely planned in advance.

locutionary meaning Meaning in the ordinary sense, involving the combined meanings of the words in a sentence rather than the actions or implications that the sentence entails.

logogen An entry in the lexicon, corresponding to a word, that becomes activated when it can be matched with orthographic, phonological, syntactic, or semantic information in the visual or auditory input.

logographic system A writing system in which the characters correspond to words or morphemes.

long-term store (LTS) According to the multistore model, the memory structure that contains information that is stored relatively permanently.

macroprocessing The processing involved in understanding the gist of discourse.

magnetic resonance imaging (MRI) A technique that uses powerful magnetic fields to obtain a high-resolution image of the brain.

manner of articulation One characteristic of the production of speech sounds. Manner of articulation refers to the way that the air flow is altered (e.g., by stopping and then releasing or by channeling some air through the nose) in order to produce a particular sound.

Matthew effect The phenomenon whereby, without intervention, children who have difficulty learning to read tend to fall further and further behind their peers in reading because they do not read enough to develop additional comprehension skills.

McGurk effect The phenomenon whereby a percept is based on a combination of sight and sound when the listener hears one sound being produced but simultaneously sees a different sound being produced.

mean length of utterance (MLU) The most common way of measuring the grammatical ability of children. The MLU is the average number of *morphemes* produced per utterance.

mental model A representation in the mind that depicts a situation or a possible state of affairs in the world.

microprocessing The processing involved in understanding a sentence and its connection to the preceding sentence in discourse.

minimal attachment A syntactic parsing strategy in which we try to construct the simplest phrase structure tree possible for a sentence.

minimalist view The idea that comprehension of discourse involves forming a mental representation that sticks close to information that is stated directly, with minimal elaboration based on general knowledge.

mixed error A speech error that appears to be based on confusion at two different levels, as when a slip has both phonological and semantic sources.

module A specialized system for performing a specific mental task, involving a particular type of information. For example, some theorists believe humans have a module that analyzes only the syntax of a sentence, independent of sentence meaning.

morpheme The smallest unit of language that has meaning. Root words, prefixes, and suffixes are all morphemes. For example, *untreated* consists of three morphemes: *un + treat + ed*.

motherese *See* child-directed speech (CDS).

motor theory The proposal that we perceive speech by relating the sound produced to the articulatory movements or commands that would be needed to produce the sound.

MRI *See* magnetic resonance imaging.

multistore model A theory of memory that claims that temporary holding of information is handled by a short-term store and that more permanent storage is handled by a long-term store.

mutual exclusivity assumption The idea that children assume that an object can have only one label. The mutual exclusivity assumption may help children assign meanings to novel words.

myelinization The development of a fatty sheath, myelin, which covers certain nerve fibers and speeds the rate of conduction of nerve impulses.

nasals Consonant sounds in which air is channeled through the nasal cavity. An example is the initial sound of the words *naughty* and *nasal*.

nativist hypothesis The proposal that much of the knowledge required to use language is innate.

negative evidence Feedback that an utterance was not grammatical. Children acquire syntactic knowledge even though they receive very little negative evidence.

neighborhood effect The influence of similar-sounding or similar-looking words on the recognition of a particular word.

neuroimaging A general term for a set of techniques, such as CT scans and MRIs, that are used to reveal brain structure and the locations of brain lesions.

new information The information in a sentence that the speaker or writer believes is unknown to the person comprehending the sentence.

null subject parameter A parameter, in Chomsky's sense of the term, that specifies whether or not a sentence can have a missing subject.

open-class category A syntactic category consisting of the content words of a language (e.g., nouns and verbs), which, as a set, keep changing as new words are added and old words fall into disuse.

overextension A child's usage of a word to refer to a wider set of referents than the word's real meaning allows.

overregularization An error in which a valid linguistic rule is applied to an exception word, as when a child says "Somebody *taked* my candy."

paired associate learning Referring to a learning task in which a person studies items that come in pairs. Upon being tested, the person is provided one item from each pair and asked to supply the other.

parallel distributed processing (PDP) An approach to cognitive modeling that is based on interconnections among simple neuron-like units. A type of connectionist modeling.

parameter setting An important mechanism of language acquisition in Chomsky's (1986) "principles and parameters theory." According to this theory, children are born with a universal grammar that has parameters representing the dimensions along which languages can vary. The role of language experience, then, is to determine which of the possible values for a parameter is used in a particular language.

performance   The mental processes involved in language use. Performance is what psychologists study, as opposed to competence, which linguists study.

personnel   The people involved in a conversation.

PET scanning   *See* positron emission tomography scanning.

phoneme   The smallest unit of sound that makes a difference to meaning. For example, *cat* and *bat* differ only in their initial phoneme.

phonemic restoration effect   The illusion that a phoneme deleted from a stream of speech is actually present.

phonological loop   One of the buffers in Baddeley's model of working memory. The phonological loop temporarily maintains a limited amount of sound-based information. For example, a person who rehearses a phone number before dialing it makes use of the phonological loop.

phonology   The sound system of a language. Phonology concerns both the individual sounds that are used and the rules for how these sounds can be combined into words.

phrase structure rules   Rules that describe the permissible arrangements of sentence elements.

pidgin   A simplified, rudimentary communication system that is developed when speakers of different languages must cooperate.

planning   In writing, the stage in which communication goals are set and the writer devises a way to accomplish these goals.

point of articulation   A feature of consonant production that describes where in the vocal tract the air flow is constricted—at the teeth versus at the lips, for example.

polysemous.   Having more than one meaning.

positron emission tomography (PET) scanning   A technique for observing brain activity during performance of cognitive tasks, based on tracking the areas in which glucose is being most utilized in the brain.

pre-sequences   In conversation, the techniques used by a speaker to prepare the listener for what is to come. For example, "Oh, I wanted to ask you something" is a pre-sequence that leads to a question.

predictive inferences   Inference about the likely outcome of an event.

primatologists   Scientists who study and compare the behavior and mental abilities of apes, monkeys, and humans.

primes   The basic parts of a sign. Primes play the same role as phonemes in spoken language. Examples include particular hand configurations, places of articulation, and movements that are combined to form a given set of signs in a sign language.

principles and parameters theory   Chomsky's most recent theory of grammar, which specifies not only the nature of grammatical relations but also the kinds of innate knowledge that may explain language acquisition.

PRO-drop languages   Languages in which it is permissible to omit a personal pronoun used as the subject of a sentence. Italian is an example of a PRO-drop language; English is not.

problem of speaker variability   In speech perception, the problem of identifying phonemes or syllables that are physically quite different when compared across different speakers or in the same person across different occasions.

procedural memory   Your memory for information about how to perform a task.

productivity   A universal feature of language dictating that sounds and words (or movement features and signs) can be combined to form an infinite variety of sentences.

pronominal reference   The process of using a pronoun to refer to a noun stated earlier in the discourse.

proposition   A unit of meaning that is composed of a predicate (a relational term such as a verb) and at least one argument (a noun or pronoun).

prosodic bootstrapping hypothesis   The idea that the pattern of stresses, pauses, and intonation in spoken language can be used as a cue to the segmentation of an utterance.

prosody   Patterns such as intonation, syllable stress, and rate of production that occur as sentences are spoken.

psycholinguistics   The scientific study of the mental processes involved in understanding and producing language.

recursion   A feature of the productivity of all languages whereby, in principle, we can always add to a sentence by embedding new phrases inside it.

reduplicated babbling   Babbling in which an infant produces the same consonant-vowel sequence over and over, as in /babababa/.

reference   The object or situation in the world to which a linguistic expression corresponds.

representational level   The level of analyzing any information-processing system at which we consider the steps that must be performed in order to complete an activity. Regarding human cognition, for example, at this level of analysis we might ask what mental steps and strategies are used to perform language and memory tasks.

reviewing In writing, the stage in which the writer evaluates whether some part of the written product fulfills the intended goals.

right-hemisphere syndrome A set of language problems associated with damage to the right hemisphere. These problems include discourse comprehension difficulty, excessive literalness, flat intonation, and a wandering style of conversation.

role players Participants that help define the thing or the action specified by a phrase.

saccades In reading, the movements of the eyes that allow us to gaze at the next word.

Sapir-Whorf hypothesis The idea that language and thought are highly related, even to the point that language differences cause differences among cultures in ways of thinking.

schema A structured unit of generalized knowledge that specifies the parts of a concept, activity, or event as well as the ways those parts relate to each other.

segmentation problem In speech perception, the problem posed by the lack of clear separations between spoken words.

semantic bootstrapping hypothesis The idea that children may use context to infer the semantic properties of words and to connect the specific words with general syntactic categories.

semantic memory Memory for generalized knowledge about the world, including word meanings and their interrelations.

semantic priming The effect of a prior stimulus on the response to a subsequent stimulus that is caused by a meaning-based relationship between the two stimuli.

semantic primitives Meaning features that represent basic, perhaps innate, contrasts among things in the world (e.g., *animate* versus *inanimate*).

semanticity A universal feature of language dictating that all languages use symbols that have meaning.

sense The meaning of an expression, in terms of the composite meaning of its individual words.

shallow orthography An alphabetic writing system in which there is a relatively close correspondence between spelling and pronunciation.

short-term store (STS) According to the multistore model, the memory structure that maintains information for a brief period of time.

situational model In discourse processing, a mental representation of the events described rather than a representation of the discourse itself.

specific language impairment (SLI) A disorder in which a person has very poor language skills, particularly in terms of syntactic ability, yet performs normally on nonverbal tests of intelligence.

speech act An utterance that has illocutionary force—that is, performs an action. For example, the statement "I now pronounce you husband and wife" initiates a legal arrangement.

speech spectrogram A visual record of a speech sound. Speech spectrograms show the frequencies of sound that were produced over time.

speech spectrograph An instrument for speech analysis. Speech spectographs produce a visual record of speech by displaying sound frequencies over time.

split-brain patients People whose corpus callosum has been surgically cut in an attempt to control seizures.

steady-state formant A formant, or segment of a formant, that does not change much in frequency over time.

stimulus onset asynchrony (SOA) The time interval between the appearance of one stimulus and the appearance of another stimulus.

stops Consonant sounds in which air in the vocal tract is completely blocked and then released. The [b] in *ball* is an example.

story grammar A mental representation of the general sequence of events in a story.

stranding error A speech error in which an inflection, such as the past-tense signifier -*ed*, is attached to the wrong stem.

structure building framework (SBF) A theory of text comprehension claiming that we understand discourse by laying a foundation based on the initial ideas in the discourse, and by using world knowledge and new text information to attach additional information to the developing structure.

subset principle The idea that language acquisition may be facilitated by having the parameters of universal grammar set by default at the value that leads to the most restrictive grammar.

surface dyslexia A reading disorder, caused by brain damage, in which the affected person must carefully sound out each word. Surface dyslexia results in slow, nonfluent reading and great difficulty in recognizing words with irregular spelling.

surface form In discourse processing, a mental representation that captures not just the ideas stated but also the precise way in which they were phrased.

surface structure The syntactic structure of a sentence that is mapped onto the phonemic structure of the sentence. That is, the surface structure specifies the organization of the elements of the sentence in a form closest to what is actually uttered.

syllabic system A writing system in which the characters correspond to syllables.

syllogisms Reasoning problems in which a conclusion is evaluated as to whether it follows logically from two premises.

synonymy Equivalence of meaning between words or phrases.

syntactic ambiguity A sentence or phrase that is ambiguous because it can be parsed in a couple of different ways, at least until further information is provided.

syntactic bootstrapping hypothesis The idea that children may use syntactic knowledge to help them infer the meaning of a word.

syntactic category rule A pattern among slips of the tongue and of the pen whereby two words involved in an exchange error tend to be from the same syntactic class. Thus, the initial sounds of two nouns are more likely to be exchanged than the initial sounds of a noun and a verb.

syntactic frame A mental structure for ordering words when producing an utterance.

syntax The component of grammar that specifies the ordering of words and phrases in sentences.

tacit knowledge Knowledge that we are not consciously aware of or cannot easily describe.

taxonomic assumption The idea that children assume that verbal labels refer to categories of objects. For example, a child might assume that "kitty" refers to any small furry animal.

telegraphic speech A stage of language production in which children use simple two- or three-word utterances that omit the function words.

templates Stored images used in pattern recognition to identify a visual pattern without breaking the pattern up into its component features. Templates are often involved in pattern recognition by machines, but they are not a realistic construct for pattern recognition by people.

textbase In discourse processing, a mental representation that captures the ideas that were stated but not the exact phrasing of those ideas.

tonal language A language in which variations in vocal pitch signify different phonemes.

topic The subject of a metaphorical statement. For example, in the sentence "That politician is a cobra," *politician* is the topic.

trace deletion hypothesis A possible explanation for the nature of grammatical problems that are associated with damage to Broca's area. According to this hypothesis, some aphasics lose the ability to keep track of the movements of sentence elements based on the position of these elements in the deep structure.

transfer-appropriate processing The idea that memory performance improves when the way that information is encoded matches the way that memory is tested.

transformation A syntactic rule for moving, deleting, or adding elements within a phrase structure.

translating In writing, the stage in which a writer converts the propositions to be expressed into sentences.

truth-conditional semantics Referring to the philosophical view that explains meaning as a relationship between symbols and a model of objects in the world.

typicality The degree to which a category member is representative of other members of the category.

typicality effect The influence of the representativeness of a category member on the time it takes to classify the member as belonging to the category.

underextension A child's usage of a word to refer to a smaller set of referents than the word's real meaning allows.

uniqueness principle A possibly innate principle that helps us acquire language. According to this principle, we accept only one word as the proper derivational form. For example, once we learn that *took* is the past tense of *take*, the word *taked* drops out of our lexicon.

Universal Grammar (UG) The design features common to all languages, which Chomsky believes are built in to our genetic code.

variegated babbling Babbling in which an infant produces a string of different syllables, as in /dadudomimu/, with a sentence-like intonation.

vehicle The concept to which the topic of a metaphorical statement is compared. For example, in the sentence "That politician is a cobra," *cobra* is the vehicle.

verbal efficiency theory A theory of individual differences in comprehension stating that many comprehension problems arise from inefficient lexical access.

visual-spatial sketch pad One of the buffers in Baddeley's model of working memory. The visual-spatial sketch pad temporarily maintains a limited amount of imagery-based information.

voice-onset time (VOT) The time interval between the release of air in stop consonants and the vibration of the vocal folds that marks the beginning of the adjacent vowel.

voicing A feature of consonant production describing whether the vocal folds vibrate when air is released to make a sound.

Wernicke's area A region of the left temporal lobe of the brain that plays a key role in language comprehension.

whole object assumption The idea that children assume that a new label uttered in the context of an object refers to the whole object rather than to a part of the object.

Williams syndrome A rare metabolic disorder that results in profound cognitive deficits coupled with generally well-preserved language abilities.

word superiority effect A phenomenon whereby, during a brief visual presentation, identification of a word is easier than identification of a single letter or nonword.

working memory (WM) A term referring to the limited-capacity mental workbench where information is consciously manipulated.

Zipf's law The tendency for the most frequent words to be shorter words.

REFERENCES

Abbott, V., Black, J. B., & Smith, E. E. (1985). The representation of scripts in memory. *Journal of Memory and Language, 24*, 179–199.

Adams, A., & Gathercole, S. E. (1996). Phonological working memory and spoken language development in young children. *Quarterly Journal of Experimental Psychology: Human Experimental Psychology, 49A*, 216–233.

Ahlum-Heath, M. E., & diVesta, F. J. (1986). The effect of conscious controlled verbalization of a cognitive strategy on transfer in problem solving. *Memory and Cognition, 14*, 281–285.

Alba, J. W., & Hasher, L. (1983). Is memory schematic? *Psychological Bulletin, 93*, 203–231.

Allbritton, D. W., McKoon, G., & Gerrig, R. J. (1995). Metaphor-based schemas and text representations: Making connections through conceptual metaphors. *Journal of Experimental Psychology: Learning, Memory, and Cognition, 21*, 612–625.

Allport, G. (1954). *The nature of prejudice.* Reading, MA: Addison-Wesley.

Altarriba, J., & Soltano, E. G. (1996). Repetition blindness and bilingual memory: Token individuation for translation equivalents. *Memory and Cognition, 24*, 700–711.

Altmann, G., & Steedman, M. (1988). Interaction with context during human sentence processing. *Cognition, 30*, 191–238.

American Psychiatric Association. (1994). Diagnostic and statistical manual of mental disorders: DSM-IV. Washington DC: APA.

Anderson, A., Garrod, S. C., & Sanford, A. J. (1983). The accessibility of pronominal antecedents as a function of episode shifts in narrative text. *Quarterly Journal of Experimental Psychology, 35*, 427–440.

Anderson, J. R. (1983a). A spreading activation theory of memory. *Journal of Verbal Learning and Verbal Behavior, 22*, 261–295.

Anderson, J. R. (1983b). *The architecture of cognition.* Cambridge, MA: Harvard University Press.

Anderson, J. R. (1995a). *Cognitive psychology and its implications.* New York: W. H. Freeman.

Anderson, J. R. (1995b). *Learning and memory.* New York: Wiley.

Anderson, R. C., Hiebert, E. H., Scott, J. A., & Wilkinson, I. A. G. (1985). *On becoming a nation of readers: The report of the commission on reading* (Contract No. 400-83-0057). Washington, DC: NIE.

Anderson, R. C., Reynolds, R. E., Schallert, D. L., & Goetz, E. T. (1977). Frameworks for comprehending discourse. *American Education Research Journal, 14*, 367–381.

Anderson, S. A. (1988). Morphological change. In F. J. Newmeyer (Ed.) *Linguistics: The Cambridge Survey. Vol. I, Linguistic theory: Foundations.* Cambridge: Cambridge University Press.

Andrews, S. (1989). Frequency and neighborhood size effects on lexical access: Activation or search? *Journal of Experimental Psychology: Learning, Memory, and Cognition, 15*, 802–814.

Andrews, S. (1992). Frequency and neighborhood effects on lexical access: Lexical similarity or orthographic redundancy? *Journal of Experimental Psychology: Learning, Memory, and Cognition, 18*, 234–254.

Anglin, J. M. (1978). From reference to meaning. *Child Development, 49*, 969–976.

Ashcraft, M. H. (1992). Cognitive arithmetic: A review of data and a theory. *Cognition, 44*, 75–106.

Ashcraft, M. H. (1993). A personal case history of transient anomia. *Brain and Language, 44*, 47–57.

Aslin, R. N., Woodward, J. Z., LaMendola, N. P., & Bever, T. G. (1996). Models of word segmentation in fluent maternal speech to infants. In J. L. Morgan & K. Demuth (Eds.), *Signal to syntax: Bootstrapping from speech to grammar in early acquisition* (pp. 117–137). Mahwah, NJ: Lawrence Erlbaum Associates.

Atkinson, R. C., & Shiffrin, R. M. (1968). Human memory: A proposed system and its control processes. In K. W. Spence & J. T. Spence (Eds.), *The psychology of learning and motivation,* Vol. 2 (pp. 89–195). New York/Orlando: Academic Press.

Au, T. K. (1983). Chinese and English counterfactuals: The Sapir-Whorf hypothesis revisited. *Cognition, 15*, 155–187.

Au, T. K. (1992). Counterfactual reasoning. In G. R. Semin & K. Fiedler (Eds.), *Language, interaction and social cognition.* London: Sage.

Austin, J. (1962). *How to do things with words.* Cambridge, MA: Harvard University Press.

Bach, K., & Harnish, R. (1979). *Linguistic communication and speech acts.* Cambridge, MA: MIT Press.

Baddeley, A. (1986). *Working memory.* Oxford: Clarendon Press/Oxford University Press.

Baddeley, A. (1992). Working memory. *Science, 255*, 556–559.

Baddeley, A. D., & Hitch, G. (1974). Working memory. In G. H. Bower (Ed.), *The psychology of learning and motivation,* Vol. 8 (pp. 47–89). New York: Academic Press.

Baddeley, A. D., & Lieberman, K. (1980). Spatial working memory. In R. Nickerson (Ed.), *Attention and performance VIII* (pp. 521–539). Hillsdale, NJ: Lawrence Erlbaum Associates.

Baddeley, A. D., Thomson, N., & Buchanan, M. (1975). Word length and the structure of short-term memory. *Journal of Verbal Learning and Verbal Behavior, 14*, 575–589.

Balota, D. A. (1994). Visual word recognition: The journey from features to meaning. In M. A. Gernsbacher (Ed.), *Handbook of psycholinguistics* (pp. 303–358). San Diego: Academic Press.

Balota, D. A., & Chumbley, J. I. (1984). Are lexical decisions a good measure of lexical access? The role of word frequency in the neglected decision stage. *Journal of Experimental Psychology: Human Perception and Performance, 10*, 340–357.

Balota, D. A., & Lorch, R. F. (1986). Depth of automatic spreading activation: Mediated priming effects in pronunciation but not in lexical decision. *Journal of Experimental Psychology: Learning, Memory, and Cognition, 12*, 336–345.

Bar-Adon, A., & Leopold, W. F. (Eds.). (1971). *Child language: A book of readings.* Englewood Cliffs, NJ: Prentice Hall.

Bartlett, F. C. (1932). *Remembering.* Cambridge: Cambridge University Press.

Barton, D. (1994). *Literacy: An introduction to the ecology of written language.* Cambridge, MA: Blackwell.

Bates, E., & MacWhinney, B. (1981). Second-language acquisition from a functionalist perspective: Pragmatic, semantic, and perceptual strategies. *Annals of the New York Academy of Sciences, 379*, 190–214.

Beattie, G. W., & Barnard, P. J. (1979). The temporal structure of natural telephone conversations (direct enquiry calls). *Linguistics, 17*, 213–229.

Becker, C. A. (1979). Semantic context and word frequency effects in visual word recognition. *Journal of Experimental Psychology: Human Perception and Performance, 5*, 252–259.

Beeman, M., Friedman, R. B., Grafman, J., Perez, E., Diamond, S., & Beadle Lindsay, M. B. (1994). Summation priming and coarse semantic coding in the right hemisphere. *Journal of Cognitive Neuroscience, 6*, 26–45.

Beilin, H. (1975). *Studies in the cognitive basis of language development.* New York: Academic Press.

Bell, L. C., & Perfetti, C. A. (1994). Reading skill: Some adult comparisons. *Journal of Educational Psychology, 86*, 244–255.

Bellugi, U., & Fischer, S. (1972). A comparison of sign language and spoken language. *Cognition, 1*, 173–200.

Bellugi, U., Marks, S., Bihrle, A., & Sabo, H. (1988). Dissociation between language and cognitive functions in Williams syndrome. In D. Bishop & K. Mogford (Eds.), *Language development in exceptional circumstances* (pp. 177–189). Edinburgh: Churchill Livingstone.

Bellugi, U., Poizner, H., & Klima, E. (1990). Mapping brain functions for language: Evidence from sign language. In G. M. Edelman, W. E. Gall, & W. M. Cowan (Eds.), *Signal and sense: Local and global order in perceptual maps* (pp. 521–543). New York: Wiley-Liss.

Benson, D. F., & Ardila, A. (1996). *Aphasia: A clinical perspective.* New York: Oxford University Press.

Bentin, S. (1987). Event-related potentials, semantic processes, and expectancy factors in word recognition. *Brain and Language, 31*, 308–327.

Bereiter, C., & Scardamalia, M. (1987). *The psychology of written composition.* Hillsdale, NJ: Lawrence Erlbaum Associates.

Berko, J. (1958). The child's learning of English morphology. *Word, 14*, 150–177.

Berlin, B., & Kay, P. (1969). *Basic color terms: Their universalty and evolution.* Berkeley: University of California Press.

Besner, D., Twilley, L. McCann, R. S., & Seergobin, K. (1990). On the association between connectionism and data: Are a few words necessary? *Psychological Review, 97*, 432–446.

Best, C. T. (1993). Emergence of language-specific constraints in perception of non-native speech: A window on early phonological development. In B. de Boysson-Bardies, S. de Schonen, P.W. Jusczyk, P. McNeilage, & J. Morton (Eds.), *Developmental neurocognition: Speech and face processing in the first year of life* (pp. 289–304). Dordrecht, Netherlands: Kluwer Academic Publishers.

Best, C. T. (1994). The emergence of native-language phonological influences in infants: A perceptual assimilation model. In J. C. Goodman & H. C. Nusbaum (Eds.), *The development of speech perception: The transition from speech sounds to spoken words* (pp. 167–224). Cambridge, MA: MIT Press.

Best, C. T., McRoberts, G. W., & Sithole, N. M. (1988). Examination of perceptual reorganization for non-native speech contrasts: Zulu click discrimination by English-speaking adults and infants. *Journal of Experimental Psychology: Human Perception and Performance, 14*, 345–360.

Bickerton, D. (1983). Creole languages. *Scientific American, 249*, 116–122.

Bickerton, D. (1984). The language biprogram hypothesis. *Behavioral and Brain Sciences, 7*, 173–221.

Bickerton, D. (1990). *Language and species.* Chicago: University of Chicago Press.

Bishop, D. V. (1992). The underlying nature of specific language impairment. *Journal of Child Psychology and Psychiatry and Allied Disciplines, 33*, 3–66.

Blasko, D. G., & Connine, C. M. (1993). Effects of familiarity and aptness on metaphor processing. *Cognition, 19*, 295–308.

Bloom, A. H. (1984). Caution—The words you use may affect what you say: A response to Au. *Cognition, 17*, 275–287.

Bloom, L. (1981). *The linguistic shaping of thought.* Hillsdale, NJ: Lawrence Erlbaum Associates.

Bloom, L., Lightbown, P., & Hood, L. (1975). Structure and variation in child language. *Monographs of the Society for Research in Child Development, 40* (2, Serial No. 160).

Bloom, P. (1994). Recent controversies in the study of language acquisition. In M. A. Gernsbacher (Ed.), *Handbook of psycholinguistics* (pp. 741–779). San Diego: Academic Press.

Bloomfield, L. (1933). *Language.* New York: Henry Holt. (Reprinted in 1961 by Holt, Rinehart & Winston.)

Blumenthal, A. L. (1970). *Language and psychology: Historical aspects of psycholinguistics.* New York: Wiley.

Blumenthal, A. L., & Boakes, R. (1967). Prompted recall of sentences. *Journal of Verbal Learning and Verbal Behavior, 6*, 674–676.

Boas, F. (1911). *Handbook of American Indian Languages.* Washington, DC: Government Printing Office.

Boas, F. (Ed.). (1938). *General anthropology.* Boston: D. C. Heath.

Bock, K. (1995). Sentence production: From mind to mouth. In J. L. Miller & P. D. Eimas (Eds.), *Speech, language, and communication: Handbook of perception and cognition*, Vol. II, 2nd ed. (pp. 181–216). San Diego: Academic Press.

Bock, K., & Cutting, J. C. (1992). Regulating mental energy: Performance units in language production. *Journal of Memory and Language, 31*, 99–127.

Bock, K., & Levelt, W. (1994). Language production: Grammatical encoding. In M. A. Gernsbacher (Ed.), *Handbook of psycholinguistics* (pp. 945–984). San Diego: Academic Press.

Boder, E. (1973). Developmental dyslexia: A diagnostic approach based on three atypical reading-spelling patterns. *Development Medicine and Child Neurology, 15,* 663–687.

Bogen, J. E., & Vogel, P. J. (1962). Cerebral commissurotomy in man. *Bulletin of the Los Angeles Neurological Society, 27,* 169–172.

Bousfield, W. A. (1953). The occurrence of clustering in the recall of randomly arranged associates. *Journal of General Psychology, 49,* 229–240.

Bower, G. H., Black, J. B., & Turner, T. J. (1979). Scripts for memory in text. *Cognitive Psychology, 11,* 177–220.

Bowerman, M. (1973). Structural relationships in children's utterances: Syntactic or semantic? In T. E. Moore (Ed.), *Cognitive development and the acquisition of language* (pp. 197–213). New York: Academic Press.

Bradley, D. C., & Forster, K. I. (1987). A reader's view of listening. *Cognition, 25,* 103–134.

Braine, M. D. S. (1963). The ontogeny of English phrase structure: The first phase. *Language, 39,* 3–13.

Braine, M. D. S. (1994). Is nativism sufficient? *Journal of Child Language, 21,* 9–31.

Bransford, J. D., Barclay, J. R., & Franks, J. J. (1972). Sentence memory: A constructive versus interpretive approach. *Cognitive Psychology, 3,* 193–209.

Bransford, J. D., & Franks, J. J. (1971). The abstraction of linguistic ideas. *Cognitive Psychology, 2,* 331–350.

Bransford, J. D., Franks, J. J., Morris, C. D., & Stein, B. S. (1979). Some general constraints on learning and memory research. In C. S. Cermak & F. I. M. Craik (Eds.), *Levels of processing in human memory* (pp. 331–354). Hillsdale, NJ: Lawrence Erlbaum Associates.

Bransford, J. D., & Johnson, M. K. (1972). Contextual prerequisites for understanding: Some investigations of comprehension and recall. *Journal of Verbal Learning and Verbal Behavior, 11,* 717–726.

Bréal, M. (1900). *Essai de semantique. English semantics: Studies in the science of meaning.* (Mrs. Henry Cust, Trans.). New York: Dover Publications. (Reprinted in 1964.)

Bresnan, J. (1981). An approach to Universal Grammar and the mental representation of language. *Cognition, 10,* 39–52.

Bresnan, J. W. (1978). A realistic transformational grammar. In J. Bresnan, M. Halle, & G. Miller (Eds.), *Linguistic theory and psychological reality* (pp. 1–59). Cambridge, MA: MIT Press.

Briere, J., & Lanktree, C. (1983). Sex-role-related effects of sex bias in language. *Sex Roles, 9,* 625–632.

Britton, B. K. (1994). Understanding expository text: Building mental structures to induce insights. In M. A. Gernsbacher (Ed.), *Handbook of psycholinguistics* (pp. 641–674). San Diego: Academic Press.

Britton, B. K., Glynn, S. M., Meyer, B. J., & Penland, M. J. (1982). Effects of text structure on use of cognitive capacity during reading. *Journal of Educational Psychology, 74,* 51–61.

Britton, B. K., & Gulgoz, S. (1991). Using Kintsch's computational model to improve instructional text: Effects of repairing inference calls on recall and cognitive structures. *Journal of Educational Psychology, 83,* 329–345.

Britton, B. K., Van Dusen, L., Glynn, S. M., & Hemphill, D. (1990). The impact of inferences on instructional text. In A. C. Graesser & G. H. Bower (Eds.), *The psychology of learning and motivation,* Vol. 25 (pp. 53–70). New York: Academic Press.

Broca, P. (1861). *Some papers on the cerebral cortex.* Springfield, FL: Charles Thomas. (G. von Bonim, Trans.) (Reprinted in 1960.)

Bronkhorst, A. W., Bosman, A. J., & Smoorenburg, G. F. (1993). A model for context effects in speech recognition. *Journal of the Acoustical Society of America, 93,* 499–509.

Brooks, L. R. (1968). Spatial and verbal components of the act of recall. *Canadian Journal of Psychology, 22,* 349–368.

Brown, R. (1957). Linguistic determinism and the parts of speech. *Journal of Abnormal and Social Psychology, 55,* 1–5.

Brown, R. (1958). *Words and things.* Glencoe, IL: The Free Press.

Brown, R. (1973). *A first language: The early stages.* Cambridge, MA: Harvard University Press.

Brown, R. (1976). Reference: In memorial tribute to Eric Lenneberg. *Cognition, 4,* 125–153.

Brown, R., & Hanlon, C. (1970). Deviational complexity and order of acquisition in child speech. In J. R. Hayes (Ed.), *Cognition and the development of language* (pp. 11–53). New York: Wiley.

Brownell, H., Gardner, H. Prather, P., & Martino, G. (1995). Language, communication, and the right hemisphere. In H. S. Kirshner (Ed.), *Handbook of neurological speech and language disorders: Neurological disease and therapy,* Vol. 33 (pp. 325–350). New York: Marcel Dekker.

Bryan, W. L., & Harter, N. (1899). Studies of the telegraphic language: The acquisition of a hierarchy of habits. *Psychological Review, 6,* 345–375.

Budd, D., Whitney, P., & Turley, K. J. (1995). Individual differences in working memory strategies for reading expository text. *Memory and Cognition, 23,* 735–748.

Burling, R. (1993). Primate calls, human language, and nonverbal communication. *Current Anthropology, 34,* 25–53.

Burnage, A. G. (1990). *Celex: A guide for users.* Nijmegen, Netherlands: University of Nijmegen Press.

Byng, S. (1988). Sentence processing deficits: Theory and therapy. *Cognitive Neuropsychology, 5,* 629–676.

Cacciari, C., & Glucksberg, S. (1994). Understanding figurative language. In M. A. Gernsbacher (Ed.), *Handbook of psycholinguistics* (pp. 447–478). San Diego: Academic Press.

Callary, E. (1985). Phonetics. In V. P. Clark, P. A. Eschholz, & A. F. Rosa (Eds.), *Language: Introductory readings.* (pp. 203–235). New York: St. Martin's Press.

Cameron, D. (Ed.). (1990). *The feminist critique of language: A reader.* London/New York: Routledge.

Caplan, D. (1992). *Language: Structure, processing, and disorders.* Cambridge, MA: MIT Press.

Caplan, D. (1994). Language and the brain. In M. A. Gernsbacher (Ed.), *Handbook of psycholinguistics* (pp. 1023–1053). San Diego: Academic Press.

Caplan, D., & Hildebrandt, N. (1988). *Disorders of syntactic comprehension.* Cambridge, MA: MIT Press.

Caramazza, A., & Zurif, E. B. (1976). Dissociation of algorithmic and heuristic processes in language comprehension: Evidence from aphasia. *Brain and Language, 3,* 572–582.

Carey, S. (1978). The child as word learner. In M. Halle, J. Bresnan, & G. Miller (Eds.), *Linguistic theory and psychological reality* (pp. 264–293). Cambridge, MA: MIT Press.

Carli, L. L. (1990). Gender, language, and influence. *Journal of Personality and Social Psychology, 59,* 941–951.

Carli, L. L., LaFleur, S. J., & Loeber, C. C. (1995). Nonverbal behavior, gender, and influence. *Journal of Personality and Social Psychology, 68*, 1030–1041.

Carmichael, L., Hogan, H. P., & Walter, A. A. (1932). An experimental study of the effect of language on the reproduction of visually perceived form. *Journal of Experimental Psychology, 15*, 73–86.

Carpenter, P. A., Miyake, A., & Just, M. A. (1994). Working memory constraints in comprehension: Evidence from individual differences, aphasia, and aging. In M. A. Gernsbacher (Ed.), *Handbook of psycholinguistics* (pp. 1075–1122). San Diego: Academic Press.

Cartmill, M. (1990). Human uniqueness and theoretical content in paleoanthropology. *International Journal of Primatology, 11*, 173–192.

Casey, P. J. (1993). That man's father is my father's son: The roles of structure, strategy, and working memory in solving convoluted verbal problems. *Memory and Cognition, 21*, 506–518.

Castles, A., & Coltheart, M. (1993). Varieties of developmental dyslexia. Experimental Psychology Conference (1992, Sydney, Australia). *Cognition, 47*, 149–180.

Cattell, J. M. (1886). The time taken up by cerebral operations. *Mind, 11*, 220–242, 377–392, 524–538.

Chafe, W. (1992). *Intonation units and prominences in English natural discourse.* Proceedings of the University of Pennsylvania Prosodic Workshop, Philadelphia.

Chafe, W. L. (1976). Givenness, contrastiveness, definiteness, subjects, topics, and point of view. In C. N. Li (Ed.), *Subject and topic* (pp. 25–55). New York: Academic Press.

Chafe, W. L. (1979). The flow of thought and the flow of language. In T. Givon (Ed.), *Syntax and semantics: 12. Discourse and syntax.* New York: Academic Press.

Chang, F. R. (1980). Active memory processes in visual sentence comprehension: Clause effects and pronominal reference. *Memory and Cognition, 8*, 58–64.

Cheung, H., & Kemper, S. (1993). Recall and articulation of English and Chinese words by Chinese-English bilinguals. *Memory and Cognition, 21*, 666–670.

Chiarello, C. (1988). More on words, hemifields, and hemispheres: A reply to Schwartz and Kirshner. *Brain and Cognition, 7*, 394–401.

Chomsky, N. (1957). *Syntactic structures.* The Hague: Mouton.

Chomsky, N. (1959). Review of Skinner's *Verbal Behavior. Language, 35*, 26–58.

Chomsky, N. (1965). *Aspects of the theory of syntax.* Cambridge, MA: MIT Press.

Chomsky, N. (1970, December 30). The case against B. F. Skinner. *New York Review of Books*, 18–24.

Chomsky, N. (1975). *The logical structure of linguistic theory (with a new introduction).* New York: Plenum.

Chomsky, N. (1980). *Rules and representations.* New York: Columbia University Press.

Chomsky, N. (1981a). Knowledge of language: Its elements and origins. *Philosophical Transactions of the Royal Society of London, 295*, 223–234.

Chomsky, N. (1981b). *Lectures on government and binding: The Pisa lectures.* Dordrecht, Netherlands: Foris.

Chomsky, N. (1982). *Some concepts and consequences of the theory of government and binding.* Cambridge, MA: MIT Press.

Chomsky, N. (1986). *Knowledge of language: Its nature, origin, and use.* New York: Praeger.

Chomsky, N. (1988). *Language and problems of knowledge: The Managua lectures.* Cambridge, MA: MIT Press.

Cirilo, R. K., & Foss, D. J. (1980). Text structure and reading time for sentences. *Journal of Verbal Learning and Verbal Behavior, 19*, 96–109.

Clark, E. V. (1987). The principle of contrast: A constraint on language acquisition. In B. MacWhinney (Ed.), *Mechanisms of language acquisition.* Hillsdale, NJ: Lawrence Erlbaum Associates.

Clark, E. V. (1993). *The lexicon in acquisition.* Cambridge: Cambridge University Press.

Clark, E. V. (1995). Language acquisition: The lexicon and syntax. In J. L. Miller & P. D. Eimas (Eds.), *Speech, language, and communication* (pp. 303–338). San Diego: Academic Press.

Clark, H., & Schaefer, E. F. (1989). Contributing to discourse. *Cognitive Science, 13*, 259–294.

Clark, H. H. (1994). Discourse in production. In M. A. Gernsbacher (Ed.), *Handbook of psycholinguistics* (pp. 985–1021). San Diego: Academic Press

Clark, H. H. (1996). *Using language.* Cambridge: Cambridge University Press.

Clark, H. H., & Clark, E. V. (1977). *Psychology and language.* New York: Harcourt Brace Jovanovich.

Clark, H. H., & Haviland, S. (1977). Comprehension and the Given-New Contract. In R. Freedle (Ed.), *Discourse processes: Advances in research and theory* (pp. 1–40). Norwood, NJ: Ablex.

Clark, H. H., & Lucy, P. (1975). Understanding what is meant by what is said: A study in conversationally conveyed requests. *Journal of Verbal Learning and Verbal Behavior, 14*, 56–72.

Clark, H. H., & Marshall, C. R. (1981). Definite reference and mutual knowledge. In A. K. Joshi, B. L. Webber, & I. A. Sag (Eds.), *Elements of discourse understanding.* Cambridge: Cambridge University Press.

Clifton, C., Kurtz, J., & Jenkins, J. J. (1965). Grammatical relations as determinants of sentence similarity. *Journal of Verbal Learning and Verbal Behavior, 4*, 112–117.

Cole, C. M., Hill, F. A., & Dayley, L. J. (1983). Do masculine pronouns used generically lead to thoughts of men? *Sex Roles, 9*, 737–750.

Cole, R. A., & Jakimik, J. (1978). Understanding speech: How words are heard. In G. Underwood (Ed.), *Strategies of information processing* (pp. 67–116). London: Academic Press.

Cole, R. A., Yan, Y., & Bailey, T. (1996). The influence of bigram constraints on word recognition by humans: Implications for computer speech recognition. In *Proceedings of the International Conference on Spoken Language Processing*, Philadelphia.

Collins, A. M., & Loftus, E. F. (1975). A spreading-activation theory of semantic processing. *Psychological Review, 82*, 407–428.

Collins, D. R. F. (1990). *Arctic languages: An awakening.* Paris: UNESCO.

Coltheart, M. (1978). Lexical access in simple reading tasks. In G. Underwood (Ed.), *Strategies of information processing* (pp. 151–216). London/New York: Academic Press.

Coltheart, M. (1987). Varieties of developmental dyslexia: A comment on Bryant and Impey. *Cognition, 27*, 97–101.

Coltheart, M., Curtis, B., Atkins, P., & Haller, M. (1993). Models of reading aloud: Dual-route and parallel-distributed-processing approaches. *Psychological Review, 100*, 589–608.

Coltheart, M., Davelaar, E., Jonasson, J. T., & Besner, D. (1977). Access to the internal lexicon. In S. Dornic (Ed.), *Attention and performance*, Vol. VI (pp. 535–555). Hillsdale, NJ: Lawrence Erlbaum Associates.

Connine, C. M. (1987). Constraints on interactive processes in auditory word recognition: The role of sentence context. *Journal of Memory and Language, 26*, 527–538.

Connine, C. M., & Blasko, D. G. (1993). Effects of familiarity and aptness in the processing of metaphor. *Journal of Experimental Psychology: Learning, Memory, and Cognition, 19*, 295–308.

Connine, C. M., & Clifton, C. E. (1987). Interactive use of lexical information in speech perception. *Journal of Experimental Psychology: Human Perception and Performance, 13*, 291–299.

Cook, V. J. (1988). *Chomsky's universal grammar: An introduction.* Cambridge, MA: Blackwell.

Cooper, F. S. (1950). Research on reading machines for the blind. In P. A. Zahl (Ed.), *Blindness: Modern approaches to the unseen environment* (pp. 512–543). Princeton, NJ: Princeton University Press.

Cooper, F. S., Delattre, P. C., Liberman, A. M., Borst, J. M., & Gerstman, L. J. (1952). Some experiments on the perception of synthetic speech sounds. *Journal of the Acoustical Society of America, 24*, 597–606.

Cooper, F. S., Liberman, A. M., & Borst, J. M. (1951). The interconversion of audible and visible patterns as a basis for research on the perception of speech. *Proceedings of the National Academy of Sciences, 37*, 318–327.

Corbett, A. T., & Chang, F. R. (1983). Pronoun disambiguation: Accessing potential antecedents. *Memory and Cognition, 11*, 283–294.

Craik, F. I., & Lockhart, R. S. (1972). Levels of processing: A framework for memory research. *Journal of Verbal Learning and Verbal Behavior, 11*, 671–684.

Cromer, R. (1994). A case study of dissociations between language and cognition. In H. Tager-Flusberg (Ed.), *Constraints on language acquisition: Studies of atypical children* (pp. 141–153). Hillsdale, NJ: Lawrence Erlbaum Associates.

Cuetos, F., & Mitchell, D. C. (1988). Cross-linguistic differences in parsing: Restrictions on the use of the Late Closure strategy in Spanish. *Cognition, 30*, 73–105.

Curtiss, S. (1981). Dissociations between language and cognition: Cases and implications. *Journal of Autism and Developmental Disorders, 11*, 15–30.

Curtiss, S. (1988). Abnormal language acquisition and the modularity of language. In F. J. Newmeyer (Ed.), *Linguistics: The Cambridge Survey. Vol. II, Linguistic Theory: Extensions and implications* (pp. 96–116). Cambridge: Cambridge University Press.

Cutler, A. (1995). Spoken word recognition and production. In J. L. Miller & P. D. Eimas (Eds.), *Speech, language, and communication* (pp. 97–136). San Diego: Academic Press.

Cutler, A. (1996). Prosody and the word boundary problem. In J. L. Morgan & K. Demuth (Eds.), *Signal to syntax: Bootstrapping from speech to grammar in early acquisition* (pp. 87–99). Mahwah, NJ: Lawrence Erlbaum Associates.

Damasio, A. R. (1992). Aphasia. *New England Journal of Medicine, 326*, 531–539.

Daneman, M., & Carpenter, P. A. (1980). Individual differences in working memory and reading. *Journal of Verbal Learning and Verbal Behavior, 19*, 450–466.

Daneman, M., & Carpenter, P. A. (1983). Individual differences in integrating information between and within sentences. *Journal of Experimental Psychology: Learning, Memory, and Cognition, 9*, 561–584.

Daneman, M., & Green, I. (1986). Individual differences in comprehending and producing words in context. *Journal of Memory and Language, 25*, 1–18.

Darwin, C. J., Turvey, M. T., & Crowder, R. C. (1972). An auditory analogue of the Sperling partial report procedure: Evidence for brief and partial storage. *Cognitive Psychology, 3*, 255–267.

Davidson, I., & Noble, W. (1993). On the evolution of language. *Current Anthropology, 34*, 165–166.

de Boysson-Bardies, B., Halle, P., Sagart, L., & Durand, C. (1989). A crosslinguistic investigation of vowel formants in babbling. *Journal of Child Language, 16*, 1–17.

Deacon, T. W. (1992). Brain-language coevolution. In J. A. Hawkins & M. Gell-Mann, *Proceedings, Sante Fe Institute Studies in the Sciences of Complexity*, Vol. II (pp. 49–83). Redwood City, CA: Addison-Wesley.

DeCasper, A. J., & Spence, M. J. (1986). Prenatal maternal speech influences newborns' perception of speech sounds. *Infant Behavior and Development, 9*, 133–150.

DeFrancis, J. (1989). *Visible speech: The diverse oneness of writing systems.* Honolulu: University of Hawaii Press.

Delattre, P., Liberman, A. M., Cooper, F. S., & Gerstman, L. J. (1952). An experimental study of the acoustic determinants of vowel color: Observations on one- and two-format vowels synthesized from spectrographic patterns. *Word, 8*, 195–210.

Dell, G. S. (1986). A spreading activation theory of retrieval in sentence production. *Psychological Review, 93*, 283–321.

Dell, G. S. (1988). The retrieval of phonological forms in production: Tests of predictions from a connectionist model. *Journal of Memory and Language, 27*, 124–142.

Dell, G. S. (1995). Speaking and misspeaking. In L. R. Gleitman & M. Liberman (Eds.), *Language: An invitation to cognitive science*, Vol. 1, 2nd ed. (pp. 183–208). Cambridge, MA: MIT Press.

Dell, G. S., & Brown, P. M. (1991). Mechanisms for listener-adaptation in language production: Limiting the role of the "model of the listener." In D. J. Napoli & J. A. Kegl (Eds.), *Bridges between psychology and linguistics: A Swarthmore festschrift for Lila Gleitman* (pp. 105–130). Hillsdale, NJ: Lawrence Erlbaum Associates.

Dell, G. S., McKoon, G., & Ratcliff, R. (1983). The activation of antecedent information during the processing of anaphoric reference in reading. *Journal of Verbal Learning and Verbal Behavior, 22*, 121–132.

Dell, G. S., & O'Seaghdha, P. G. (1992). Stages of lexical access in language production. *Cognition, 42*, 287–314.

Dell, G. S., & Reich, P. A. (1981). Stages in sentence production: An analysis of speech error data. *Journal of Verbal Learning and Verbal Behavior, 20*, 611–629.

Deloche, G., Andreewsky, E., & Desi, M. (1982). Surface dyslexia: A case report and some theoretical implications to reading models. *Brain and Language, 15*, 12–31.

Dodd, B., & Campbell, R. (Eds.). (1987). *Hearing by eye: The psychology of lip reading.* London: Lawrence Erlbaum Associates.

Dodge, R. (1900). Visual perception during eye movement. *Psychological Review, 7*, 454–465.

Doody, R. S. (1993). A reappraisal of localization theory with reference to aphasia. Part 1: Historical considerations. *Brain and Language, 44,* 296–326.

Dosher, B. A., & Corbett, A. T. Instrument inferences and verb schemata. *Memory & Cognition, 10,* 531–539.

Drews, E., & Zwitserlood, P. (1995). Morphological and orthographic similarity in visual word recognition. *Journal of Experimental Psychology: Human Perception and Performance, 21,* 1098–1116.

Duffy, S. A., Morris, R. K., & Rayner, K. (1988). Lexical ambiguity and fixation times in reading. *Journal of Memory and Language, 27,* 429–446.

Dufour, R., & Kroll, J. F. (1995). Matching words to concepts in two languages: A test of the concept mediation model of bilingual representation. *Memory and Cognition, 23,* 166–180.

Eberhard, K. M., Spivey-Knowlton, M. J., Sedivy, J. C., & Tanenhaus, M. K. (1995). Eye movements as a window into real-time spoken language comprehension in natural contexts. *Journal of Psycholinguistic Research, 24,* 409–434.

Ehrlich, K., & Rayner, K. (1983). Pronoun assignment and semantic integration during reading: Eye movements and immediacy of processing. *Journal of Verbal Learning and Verbal Behavior, 22,* 75–87.

Eimas, P. D. (1975a). Auditory and phonetic coding of the cues for speech: Discrimination of the [r-1] distinction by young infants. *Perception and Psychophysics, 18,* 341–347.

Eimas, P. D. (1975b). Speech perception in early infancy. In L. B. Cohen & P. Salapatek (Eds.), *Infant perception: From sensation to cognition.* New York: Academic Press.

Eimas, P. D. (1985). The equivalence of cues in the perception of speech by infants. *Infant Behavior and Development, 8,* 125–138.

Eimas, P. D., Siqueland, E. R., Jusczyk, P., & Vigorito, J. (1971). Speech perception in infants. *Science, 171,* 303–306.

Einstein, A. (1954). *Ideas and opinions.* New York: Crown.

Ellis, N. C. (1996). Sequencing in SLA: Phonological memory, chunking, and points of order. *Studies in Second Language Acquisition, 18,* 91–126.

Elman, J. L., & McClelland, J. L. (1988). Cognitive penetration of the mechanisms of perception: Compensation for coarticulation of lexically restored phonemes. *Journal of Memory and Language, 27,* 143–165.

Engle, R. W., Cantor, J., & Carullo, J. J. (1992). Individual differences in working memory and comprehension: A test of four hypotheses. *Journal of Experimental Psychology: Learning, Memory, and Cognition, 18,* 972–992.

Ericsson, K. A., & Simon, H. A. (1984). *Protocol analysis: Verbal reports as data.* Cambridge, MA: MIT Press.

Ericsson, K. A., & Smith, J. (1991). *Toward a general theory of expertise: Prospects and limits.* Cambridge: Cambridge University Press.

Fahey, T. (1990). *The joys of jargon.* New York: Barron's Educational Series.

Fainsilber, L., & Ortony, A. (1987). Metaphorical uses of language in the expression of emotions. *Metaphor and Symbolic Activity, 2,* 239–250.

Farah, M. J. (1994). Neuropsychological inference with an interactive brain: A critique of the "locality" assumption. *Behavioral and Brain Sciences, 17,* 43–104.

Fauconnier, G. (1985). *Mental spaces: Aspects of meaning construction in natural language.* Cambridge, MA: MIT Press/Bradford Books.

Fay, D., & Cutler, A. (1977). Malapropisms and the structure of the mental lexicon. *Linguistic Inquiry, 8,* 505–520.

Fayol, M., Largy, P., & Lemaire, P. (1994). Cognitive overload and orthographic errors: When cognitive overload enhances subject-verb agreement errors: A study in French written language. *Quarterly Journal of Experimental Psychology: Human Experimental Psychology, 47A,* 437–464.

Feldman, L. B. (1994). Beyond orthography and phonology: Differences between inflections and derivations. *Journal of Memory and Language, 33,* 442–470.

Feldman, L. B., & Andjelkovic, D. (1992). Morphological analysis in word recognition. In R. Frost & L. Katz (Eds.), *Orthography, phonology, morphology, and meaning: Advances in psychology,* Vol. 94. Amsterdam: North-Holland.

Feldman, L. B., Frost, R., & Pnini, T. (1995). Decomposing words into their constituent morphemes: Evidence from Hebrew and English. *Journal of Experimental Psychology: Learning, Memory, and Cognition, 21,* 947–960.

Fernald, A. (1985). Four-month-old infants prefer to listen to motherese. *Infant Behavior and Development, 8,* 181–195.

Fernald, A., & McRoberts, G. (1996). Prosodic bootstrapping: A critical analysis of the argument and the evidence. In J. L. Morgan & K. Demuth (Eds.), *Signal to syntax: Bootstrapping from speech to grammar in early acquisition* (pp. 365–388). Mahwah, NJ: Lawrence Erlbaum Associates.

Ferreira, F., Anes, M. D., & Horine, M. (1996). Exploring the use of prosody during language comprehension using the auditory moving window technique. *Journal of Psycholinguistic Research, 25,* 273–290.

Fillenbaum, S. (1974). Pragmatic normalization: Further results for some conjunctive and disjunctive sentences. *Journal of Experimental Psychology, 102,* 574–578.

Fillmore, C. J. (1968). The case for case. In E. Bach & R. T. Harms (Eds.), *Universals in linguistic theory* (pp. 1–90). New York: Holt, Rinehart and Winston.

Fillmore, C. J. (1971). Some problems for case grammar. In R. J. O'Brien (Ed.), *22nd annual round table meeting on linguistics and language studies* (pp. 35–56). Washington, DC: Georgetown University Press.

Fincher-Kiefer, R. (1993). The role of predictive inferences in situation model construction. *Discourse Processes, 16,* 99–124.

Fischer, K. W., & Rose, S. P. (1995, Fall). Concurrent cycles in the dynamic development of brain and behavior. *SRCD Newsletter,* pp. 3–4, 15–16.

Fitts, P. M., & Posner, M. I. (1967). *Human performance.* Belmont, CA: Brooks/Cole.

Fletcher, C. R. (1984). Markedness and topic continuity in discourse processing. *Journal of Verbal Learning and Verbal Behavior, 23,* 487–493.

Fletcher, C. R. (1986). Strategies for the allocation of short-term memory during comprehension. *Journal of Memory and Language, 25,* 43–58.

Fletcher, C. R. (1994). Levels of representation in memory for discourse. In M. A. Gernsbacher (Ed.), *Handbook of psycholinguistics* (pp. 589–608). San Diego: Academic Press.

Fletcher, C. R., & Chrysler, S. T. (1990). Surface forms, textbases, and situation models: Recognition memory for three types of textual information. *Discourse Processes, 13*, 175–190.

Flower, L. S., & Hayes, J. R. (1984). Images, plans, and prose: The representation of meaning in writing. *Written Communication, 1*, 120–160.

Flynn, S. (1988). Second language acquisition and grammatical theory. In F. J. Newmeyer (Ed.), *Linguistics: The Cambridge survey. Vol. 2, Linguistic theory: Extensions and implications* (pp. 53–73). Cambridge: Cambridge University Press.

Flynn, S. (1989). The role of the head-initial/head-final parameter in the acquisition of English clauses by adult Spanish and Japanese speakers. In S. Gass & J. Schachter (Eds.), *Linguistic perspectives on second language acquisition* (pp. 89–108). Cambridge: Cambridge University Press.

Flynn, S. (1996). A parameter setting approach to second language acquisition. In W. C. Ritchie & T. K. Bhatia (Eds.), *Handbook of second language acquisition* (pp. 121–158). San Diego: Academic Press.

Fodor, J. A. (1970). Three reasons for not deriving *kill* from *cause to die*. *Linguistic Inquiry, 1*, 429–438.

Fodor, J. A. (1980). Methodological solipsism considered as a research strategy in cognitive psychology. *Behavioral and Brain Sciences, 3*, 63–109.

Fodor, J. A. (1981). The present status of the innateness controversy. In J. A. Fodor (Ed.), *Representations: Philosophical essays on the foundations of cognitive science* (pp. 257–316). Cambridge, MA: MIT Press.

Fodor, J. A. (1983). *The modularity of mind: An essay on faculty psychology.* Cambridge, MA: MIT Press.

Fodor, J. A., Bever, T. G., & Garrett, M. F. (1974). *The psychology of language: An introduction to psycholinguistics and generative grammar.* New York: McGraw-Hill.

Fodor, J. D. (1980). *Semantics: Theories of meaning in generative grammar.* Cambridge, MA: Harvard University Press.

Fodor, J. D., Fodor, J. A., & Garrett, M. F. (1975). The psychological unreality of semantic representations. *Linguistic Inquiry, 4*, 515–531.

Forster, K. I. (1976). Accessing the mental lexicon. In R. J. Wales & E. Walker (Eds.), *New approaches to language mechanisms* (pp. 257–287). Amsterdam: North-Holland.

Forster, K. I. (1979). Levels of processing and the structure of the language processes. In W. E. Cooper & E. C. T. Walker (Eds.), *Sentence processing: Psycholinguistic studies presented to Merril Garret* (pp. 27–84). Hillsdale, NJ: Lawrence Erlbaum Associates.

Forster, K. I. (1980). Absence of lexical and orthographic effects of a same-different task. *Memory and Cognition, 8*, 210–215.

Forster, K. I. (1987). Form-priming with masked primes: The best match hypothesis. In M. Coltheart (Ed.), *Attention and performance XII: The psychology of reading* (pp. 127–146). Hove, England: Lawrence Erlbaum Associates.

Forster, K. I. (1989). Basic issues in lexical processing. In W. Marslen-Wilsen (Ed.), *Lexical representation and process* (pp. 75–107). Cambridge, MA: MIT Press.

Forster, K. I. (1990). Lexical processing. In D. Osherson & H. Lasnik (Eds.), *Language* (pp. 94–131). Cambridge, MA: MIT Press.

Forster, K. I., & Shen, D. (1996). No enemies in the neighborhood: Absence of inhibitory neighborhood effects in lexical decision and semantic categorization. *Journal of Experimental Psychology, 22*, 696–713.

Fowler, A. E., Gelman, R., & Gleitman, L. R. (1994). The course of language learning in children with Down syndrome. In H. Tager-Flusberg (Ed.), *Constraints on language acquisition: Studies of atypical children* (pp. 94–140). Hillsdale, NJ: Lawrence Erlbaum Associates.

Frazier, L. (1987). Theories of sentence processing. In J. L. Garfield (Ed.), *Modularity in knowledge representation and natural language understanding* (pp. 291–307). Cambridge, MA: MIT Press.

Frazier, L. (1989). Against lexical generation of syntax. In W. D. Marslen-Wilson (Ed.), *Lexical representation and process* (pp. 505–508). Cambridge, MA: MIT Press.

Frazier, L., & Fodor, J. D. (1978). The sausage machine: A new two-stage parsing model. *Cognition, 6*, 291–326.

Frazier, L., & Rayner, K. (1982). Making and correcting errors during sentence comprehension: Eye movements in the analysis of structurally ambiguous sentences. *Cognitive Psychology, 14*, 178–210.

Frazier, L., & Rayner, K. (1987). Resolution of syntactic category ambiguities: Eye movements in parsing lexically ambiguous sentences. *Journal of Memory and Language, 26*, 505–526.

Frege, G. (1879). *Begriffsschrift, eine der Arithmetischen nachgebildete Formelsprache des reinen Denkens, Halle: Nebert.* Translated by T. W. Bynum, *Conceptual notation and related articles.* Oxford: Clarendon Press, 1972.

Freud, S. (1891). *On aphasia: A critical study.* New York: International Universities Press (E. Stengel, Trans.). (Reprinted in 1953.)

Freud, S. (1901). *Psychopathology of everyday life.* (A. A. Brill, Trans.). New York: New American Library, Mentor. (Reprinted in 1958.)

Fromkin, V. A. (1971). The non-anomalous nature of anomalous utterances. *Language, 47*, 27–52.

Fromkin, V. A. (1973a). Slips of the tongue. *Scientific American, 229*, 110–117.

Fromkin, V. A. (Ed.). (1973b). *Speech errors as linguistic evidence.* The Hague: Mouton.

Frost, R., Katz, L., & Bentin, S. (1987). Strategies for visual word recognition and orthographical depth: A multilingual comparison. *Journal of Experimental Psychology: Human Perception and Performance, 13*, 104–115.

Gagne, R. H., & Smith, E. C. (1962). A study of the effects of verbalization on problem solving. *Journal of Experimental Psychology, 63*, 12–18.

Gall, F., & Spurzheim, G. (1810–1819). *Anatomie et Physiologie du Systéme nerveux en général et du Cerveau en particulier avec des Observations sur la Possibilité de Reconnoître plusiers Dispositions intellectuelles et morales de l'Homme et des Animaux par la Configuration de leurs Têtes* (4 vols.). Paris: F. Schoell.

Gardner, B. T. (1981). Project Nim: Who taught whom? *Contemporary Psychology, 26*, 425–427.

Gardner, H. (1985). *The mind's new science: A history of the cognitive revolution.* New York: Oxford University Press.

Gardner, R. A., & Gardner, B. T. (1969). Teaching sign language to a chimpanzee. *Science, 165*, 664–672.

Gardner, R. A., & Gardner, B. T. (1975). Evidence for sentence constituents in the early utterances of child and chimpanzee. *Journal of Experimental Psychology: General, 104*, 244–267.

Garrett, M. (1975). The analysis of sentence production. In G. Bower (Ed.), *Psychology of learning and motivation,* Vol. 9. New York: Academic Press.

Garrett, M. (1980). Levels of processing in sentence production. In B. Butterworth (Ed.), *Language production,* Vol. 1. New York: Academic Press.

Garrett, M. F. (1982). Production of speech: Observations from normal and pathological language use. In A. Ellis (Ed.), *Normality and pathology in cognitive functions.* London: Academic Press.

Garrett, M. F. (1988). Processes in language production. In F. J. Newmeyer (Ed.), *Language: Psychological and biological aspects. Linguistics: The Cambridge survey,* Vol. 3 (pp. 69–98). Cambridge: Cambridge University Press.

Garrod, S., & Sanford, A. J. (1982). Bridging inferences in the extended domain of reference. In A. Baddeley & J. Long (Eds.), *Attention and performance IX* (pp. 331–346). Hillsdale, NJ: Lawrence Erlbaum Associates.

Garrod, S., & Sanford, A. J. (1983). Topic dependent effects in language processing. In G. B. Flores d'Arcais & R. Jarvella (Eds.), *The process of language comprehension* (pp. 271–295). Chichester: Wiley.

Garrod, S., Freudenthal, D., & Boyle, E. A. (1994). The role of different types of anaphor in the on-line resolution of sentences in a discourse. *Journal of Memory and Language, 33,* 39–68.

Garrod, S. C., & Sanford, A. J. (1994). Resolving sentences in a discourse context: How discourse representation affects language understanding. In M. A. Gernsbacher (Ed.), *Handbook of psycholinguistics* (pp. 675–698). San Diego: Academic Press.

Garry, M., Manning, C. G., Loftus, E., & Sherman, S. J. (1996). Imagination inflation: Imagining a childhood event inflates confidence that it occurred. *Psychonomic Bulletin and Review, 3,* 208–214.

Gastil, J. (1990). Generic pronouns and sexist language: The oxymoronic character of masculine generics. *Sex Roles, 23,* 629–643.

Gathercole, S. E., & Baddeley, A. D. (1990). The role of phonological memory in vocabulary acquisition: A study of young children learning new names. *British Journal of Psychology, 81,* 439–454.

Gazdar, G. (1979). *Pragmatics: Implicature, presupposition and logical form.* New York: Academic Press.

Gazdar, G. (1982). Reviews of Brame (1978, 1979). *Journal of Linguistics, 18,* 464–473.

Gazzaniga, M. S. (1970). *The bisected brain.* New York: Appleton-Century-Crofts.

Geiselman, R. E., & Bellezza, F. S. (1977). Incidental retention of speaker's voice. *Memory and Cognition, 5,* 658–665.

Gelman, S. A., & Markman, E. M. (1985). Implicit contrast in adjectives vs. nouns: Implications for word-learning in preschoolers. *Journal of Child Language, 12,* 125–143.

Gerken, L. (1991). The metrical basis for children's subjectless sentences. *Journal of Memory and Language, 30,* 431–451.

Gerken, L. (1994). Child phonology: Past research, present questions, future directions. In M. A. Gernsbacher (Ed.), *Handbook of psycholinguistics* (pp. 781–820). San Diego: Academic Press.

Gernsbacher, M. A. (1989). Mechanisms that improve referential access. *Cognition, 32,* 99–156.

Gernsbacher, M. A. (1990). *Language comprehension as structure building.* Hillsdale, NJ: Lawrence Erlbaum Associates.

Gernsbacher, M. A., & Faust, M. E. (1991). The mechanism of suppression: A component of general comprehension skill. *Journal of Experimental Psychology: Learning, Memory, and Cognition, 17,* 245–262.

Gernsbacher, M. A., Varner, K. R., & Faust, M. E. (1990). Investigating differences in general comprehension skill. *Journal of Experimental Psychology: Learning, Memory, and Cognition, 16,* 430–445.

Geschwind, N. (1965). Disconnection syndromes in animals and man. *Brain, 88,* 237–294, 585–644.

Geschwind, N. (1970). The organization of language and the brain. *Science, 170,* 940–944.

Gibbs, R. (1979). Contextual effects in understanding indirect requests. *Discourse Processes, 2,* 1–10.

Gibbs, R. W. (1980). Spilling the beans on understanding and memory for idioms in conversation. *Memory and Cognition, 8,* 149–156.

Gibbs, R. W. (1981). Memory for requests in conversation. *Journal of Verbal Learning and Verbal Behavior, 20,* 630–640.

Gibbs, R. W. (1984). Literal meaning and psychological theory. *Cognitive Science, 8,* 275–304.

Gibbs, R. W. (1992a). Categorization and metaphor understanding. *Psychological Review, 99,* 572–577.

Gibbs, R. W. (1992b). What do idioms really mean? *Journal of Memory and Language, 31,* 485–506.

Gibbs, R. W. (1994). Figurative thought and figurative language. In M. A. Gernsbacher (Ed.), *Handbook of psycholinguistics* (pp. 411–466). San Diego: Academic Press.

Gibbs, R. W. (1994). The poetics of mind: Figurative thought, language, and understanding. Cambridge: Cambridge University Press.

Gildea, P., & Glucksberg, S. (1983). On understanding metaphor: The role of context. *Journal of Verbal Learning and Verbal Behavior, 22,* 577–590.

Glaser, W. R., & Dungelhoff, F.-J. (1984). The time course of picture-word interference. *Journal of Experimental Psychology: Human Perception and Performance, 10,* 640–654.

Gleitman, L. (1990). The structural sources of word meanings. *Language Acquisition: A Journal of Developmental Linguistics, 1,* 3–55.

Gleitman, L. R., & Newport, E. L. (1995). The invention of language by children: Environmental and biological influences on the acquisition of language. In L. R. Gleitman & M. Liberman (Eds.), *Language,* 2nd ed. (pp. 1–24). Cambridge, MA: MIT Press.

Gleitman, L. R., & Wanner, E. (1982). Language acquisition: The state of the state of the art. In E. Wanner & L. R. Gleitman (Eds.), *Language acquisition: The state of the art.* Cambridge: Cambridge University Press.

Glenberg, A. M., Kruley, P., & Langston, W. E. (1994). Analogical processes in comprehension: Simulation of a mental model. In M. A. Gernsbacher (Ed.), *Handbook of psycholinguistics* (pp. 609–640). San Diego: Academic Press.

Glucksberg, S. (1991). Beyond literal meaning: The psychology of allusion. *Psychological Science, 2,* 146–152.

Glucksberg, S., & Keysar, B. (1990). Understanding metaphorical comparisons: Beyond similarity. *Psychological Review, 97,* 3–18.

Goffman, E. (1976). Replies and responses. *Language in Society, 5,* 257–313.

Goldin-Meadow, S., & Feldman, H. (1977). The development of language-like communication without a language model. *Science, 197,* 401–403.

Goldin-Meadow, S., & Mylander, C. (1984). Gestural communication in deaf children: The effects and noneffects of parental input on early language development. *Monographs of the Society for Research in Child Development, 49*, 1–121.

Goldin-Meadow, S., & Mylander, C. (1990). The role of parental input in the development of a morphological system. *Journal of Child Language, 17*, 527–563.

Golinkoff, R. M., Hirsh-Pasek, K., Cauley, K. M., & Gordon, L. (1987). The eyes have it: Lexical and syntactic comprehension in a new paradigm. *Journal of Child Language, 14*, 23–45.

Gopnik, M. (1990). Feature blindness: A case study. *Language Acquisition: A Journal of Developmental Linguistics, 1*, 139–164.

Gopnik, M., & Crago, M.B. (1991). Familial aggregation of a developmental language disorder. *Cognition, 39*, 1–50.

Gould, S. J., & Eldridge, N. (1977). Punctuated equilibria: The tempo and mode of evolution reconsidered. *Paleobiology, 3*, 115–151.

Graesser, A., Long, D., & Mio, J. (1989). What are the cognitive and conceptual components of humorous texts? *Poetics, 18*, 143–164.

Graesser, A. C. (1981). *Prose comprehension beyond the word.* New York: Springer-Verlag.

Graesser, A. C., Millis, K., & Zwaan, R. A. (1997). Discourse comprehension. *Annual Review of Psychology, 48*, 163–189.

Graesser, A. C., Singer, M., & Trabasso, T. (1994). Constructing inferences during narrative text comprehension. *Psychological Review, 101*, 371–395.

Grainger, J., & Jacobs, A. M. (1996). Orthographic processing in visual word recognition: A multiple read-out model. *Psychological Review, 103*, 518–565.

Grainger, J., & O'Regan, K. (1992). A psychophysical investigation of language priming effects in two English-French bilinguals. *European Journal of Cognitive Psychology, 23*, 323–339.

Grainger, J., & Segui, J. (1990). Neighborhood frequency effects in visual word recognition: A comparison of lexical decision and masked identification latencies. *Perception and Psychophysics, 47*, 191–198.

Greenberg, J. H. (1978). Generalizations about numeral systems. In J. H. Greenberg (Ed.), *Universals of human language. Vol. 3, Word Structure* (pp. 249–295). Stanford, CA: Academic Press.

Greene, S. B., Gerrig, R. J., McKoon, G., & Ratcliff, R. (1994). Unheralded pronouns and management by common ground. *Journal of Memory and Language, 33*, 511–526.

Greenfield, P. M., & Smith, J. H. (1976). *The structure of communication in early language development.* New York: Academic Press.

Grice, H. P. (1975). Logic and conversation. In P. Cole & J. L. Morgan (Eds.), *Syntax and Semantics. Vol. 3, Speech Acts* (pp. 41–58). New York: Academic Press.

Grimes, J. E. (1975). *The thread of discourse.* The Hague: Mouton.

Grodzinsky, Y. (1990). Theoretical perspectives on language deficits. Cambridge, MA: MIT Press.

Grodzinsky, Y. (1991). There is an entity called agrammatic aphasia. *Brain and Language, 41*, 555–564.

Grosjean, F. (1982). *Life with two languages: An introduction to bilingualism.* Cambridge, MA: Harvard University Press.

Guller, B., Case, P., Sing, M., & Kelson, J. A. (1994). The nonlinear dynamics of speech categorization. *Journal of Experimental Psychology: Human Perception and Performance, 20*, 3–16.

Gumperz, J. J. (1982). *Discourse strategies.* Cambridge: Cambridge University Press.

Habib, M., & Démonet, J.-F. (1996). Cognitive neuroanatomy of language: The contribution of functional neuroimaging. *Aphasiology, 10*, 217–234.

Halle, M. (1990). Phonology. In D. N. Osherson & H. Lasnik (Eds.), *Language: An invitation to cognitive science,* Vol. 1. Cambridge, MA: MIT Press.

Hardin, C., & Banaji, M. R. (1993). The influence of language on thought. *Social Cognition, 11*, 277–308.

Harley, T. A. (1984). A critique of top-down independent levels models of speech production: Evidence from non-plan-internal speech errors. *Cognitive Science, 8*, 191–219.

Harris, R., & Taylor, T. J. (1989). *Landmarks in linguistic thought: The western tradition from Socrates to Saussure.* New York: Routledge.

Harris, R. A. (1993). *The linguistic wars.* New York: Oxford University Press.

Hart, B., & Risely, T. R. (1995). *Meaningful differences in the everyday experience of American children: The everyday experience of two year old American children.* Baltimore: Paul H. Brookes Co.

Hasher, L., & Zacks, R. T. (1988). Working memory, comprehension, and aging: A review and a new view. In G. H. Bower (Ed.), *The psychology of learning and motivation: Advances in research and theory,* Vol. 22 (pp. 193–225). San Diego: Academic Press.

Haviland, S. E., & Clark, H. H. (1974). What's new? Acquiring new information as a process in comprehension. *Journal of Verbal Learning and Verbal Behavior, 13*, 512–521.

Hayes, C. W., Ornstein, J., & Gage, W. W. (1987). *The ABC's of language and linguistics.* Lincolnwood, IL: NTC Publishing Group.

Hayes, J. R., & Flower, L. S. (1980). Identifying the organization of writing processes. In L. W. Gregg & E. R. Steinberg (Eds.), *Cognitive processes in writing* (pp. 3–30). Hillsdale, NJ: Lawrence Erlbaum Associates.

Hayes, J. R., Flower, L., Schriver, K. A., Stratman, J. F., & Carey, L. (1987). Cognitive processes in revision. In S. Rosenberg (Ed.), *Advances in applied psycholinguistics. Vol. 2, Reading, writing, and language learning. Cambridge monographs and texts in applied psycholinguistics.* New York: Cambridge University Press.

Head, H. (1926). *Aphasia and kindred disorders of speech.* Cambridge: Cambridge University Press.

Heider, E. R. (1972). Universals in color naming and memory. *Journal of Experimental Psychology, 93*, 10–20.

Henderson, V. W. (1985). Lesion localization in Broca's aphasia: Implications from Broca's aphasia without hemiparesis. *Archives of Neurology, 42*, 1210–1212.

Henley, N. M., & Kramarae, C. (1991). Gender, power, and miscommunication. In N. Coupland, H. Giles, & J. M. Wiemann (Eds.), *"Miscommunication" and problematic talk.* Newbury Park, CA: Sage.

Hess, D. J., Foss, D. J., & Carroll, P. (1995). Effects of global and local context on lexical processing during language comprehension. *Journal of Experimental Psychology: General, 124*, 62–82.

Hewes, G. W. (1973). Primate communication and the gestural origin of language. *Current Anthropology, 14*, 5–24.

Hickok, G., Say, K., Bellugi, U., & Klima, E. S. (1996). The basis of hemispheric asymmetries for language and spatial cognition: Clues from focal brain damage in two deaf native signers. *Aphasiology, 10*, 577–591.

Hill, J. H. (1988). Language, culture, and world view. In F. J. Newmeyer (Ed.), *Language: The socio-cultural context. Linguis-*

tics: The Cambridge survey, Vol. 4. Cambridge: Cambridge University Press.

Hinton, G. E. (1992). How neural networks learn from experience. *Scientific American, 267,* 105–109.

Hinton, G. E. (1993). How neural networks learn from experience. In *Mind and brain: Readings from Scientific American magazine.* New York: W. H. Freeman.

Hirsh-Pasek, K., Kemler Nelson, D. G., Jusczyk, P. W., Cassidy, K. W., Druss, B., & Kennedy, L. J. (1987). Clauses are perceptual units for young infants. *Cognition, 26,* 269–286.

Hobbs, J. R. (1979). Coherence and coreference. *Cognitive Science, 3,* 67–90.

Hockett, C. (1955). *Manual of phonology* (Publications in Anthropology and Linguistics No. 11). Bloomington: Indiana University Press.

Hockett, C. F. (1954). Two models of grammatical description. *Word, 10,* 210–234.

Hockett, C. F. (1959). Animal "languages" and human languages. In J. N. Spuhler (Ed.), *The evolution of man's capacity for culture* (pp. 32–39). Detroit, MI: Wayne State University Press.

Hockett, C. F. (1960, October). The origin of speech. *Scientific American, 203,* 89–96.

Hockett, C. F. (1961). The problem of universals in language. In J. H. Greenberg (Ed.), *Universals of language* (pp. 1–29). Cambridge, MA: MIT Press.

Hockett, C. F. (1963). The problem of universals in language. In J. H. Greenberg (Ed.), *Universals of language* (pp. 1–22). Cambridge, MA: MIT Press.

Hockett, C. F. (1978). In search of Jove's brow. *American Speech, 53,* 243–319.

Hoff, H. E., Guillemin, R., & Geddes, L. A. (1958). An 18th-century scientist's observation of his own aphasia. *Bulletin of the History of Medicine, 32,* 446–450.

Hoffman, C., Lau, I., & Johnson, D. R. (1986). The linguistic relativity of person cognition: An English-Chinese comparison. *Journal of Personality and Social Psychology, 51,* 1097–1105.

Hoffman, R., & Kemper, S. (1987). What could reaction-times tell us about metaphor comprehension? *Metaphor and Symbolic Activity, 1,* 149–186.

Hough, M. S. (1990). Narrative comprehension in adults with right and left hemisphere brain-damage: Theme organization. *Brain and Language, 38,* 253–277.

Howard, D. (1985). Introduction to "On agrammatism" (Ueber Agrammatismus). *Cognitive Neuropsychology, 2,* 303–307. (Original work published in 1922 by M. Isserlin.)

Huey, E. B. (1908). *The psychology and pedagogy of reading.* Cambridge, MA: MIT Press. (Reprinted in 1968.)

Humboldt, W. F. V. (1836) *Introduction to Kawisprache,* translated in Peter Heath, *On language: The diversity of human language-structure and its influence on the mental development of mankind* (p. 215). Cambridge, MA: Cambridge University Press, 1988.

Humphreys, G. W., & Evett, L. J. (1985). Are there independent lexical and nonlexical routes in word processing? An evaluation of the dual-route theory of reading. *Brain and Behavioral Sciences, 8,* 689–740.

Hunt, E., & Agnoli, F. (1991). The Whorfian hypothesis: A cognitive psychology perspective. *Psychological Review, 98,* 377–389.

Hyams, N. (1986). *Language acquisition and the theory of parameters.* Dordrecht, Netherlands: Reidel.

Hyams, N., & Wexler, K. (1993). On the grammatical basis of null subjects in child language. *Linguistic Inquiry, 24,* 421–459.

Hyde, T. S., & Jenkins, J. J. (1969). Differential effects of incidental tasks on the organization of recall of a list of highly associated words. *Journal of Experimental Psychology, 82,* 472–481.

Hyona, J., & Olson, R. K. (1995). Eye fixation patterns among dyslexic and normal readers: Effects of word length and word frequency. *Journal of Experimental Psychology: Learning, Memory, and Cognition, 21,* 1430–1440.

Jackendoff, R. (1983). *Semantics and cognition.* Cambridge, MA: MIT Press.

Jackendoff, R. S. (1975). Morphological and semantic regularities. *Language, 51,* 639–671.

Jackendoff, R. S. (1992). *Languages of the mind: Essays on mental representation.* Cambridge, MA: MIT Press.

Jackson, J. H. (1878). On affections of speech from disease of the brain. *Brain, 1,* 304–330.

Jackson, M. D., & McClelland, J. L. (1979). Processing determinants of reading speed. *Journal of Experimental Psychology: General, 108,* 151–181.

Jacobson, E. (1932). Electrophysiology of mental activities. *American Journal of Psychology, 44,* 677–694.

James, W. (1890). *The principles of psychology,* Vol. 1. New York: Holt.

Jared, D., & Seidenberg, M. S. (1990). Naming multisyllabic words. *Journal of Experimental Psychology: Human Perception and Performance, 16,* 92–105.

Jared, D., & Seidenberg, M. S. (1991). Does word identification proceed from spelling to sound to meaning? *Journal of Experimental Psychology: General, 120,* 358–394.

Jeffress, L. A. (1951). *Cerebral mechanisms in behavior: The Hixon Symposium.* New York: John Wiley.

Jenkins, J. J., Strange, W., & Edman, T. R. (1983). Identification of vowels in "vowel-less" syllables. *Perception and Psychophysics, 34,* 441–450.

Joanette, Y., & Brownell, H. (Eds.). (1990). *Discourse ability and brain damage.* New York: Springer-Verlag.

Johnson, J. S., & Newport, E. L. (1989). Critical-period effects in second language learning: The influence of maturational state on the acquisition of English as a second language. *Cognitive Psychology, 21,* 60–99.

Johnson-Laird, P. N. (1983). *Mental models: Towards a cognitive science of language, inference, and consciousness.* Cambridge, MA: Harvard University Press.

Johnson-Laird, P. N. (1988). *The computer and the mind: An introduction to cognitive science.* Cambridge, MA: Harvard University Press.

Johnston, J. R. (1992). Cognitive abilities of language-impaired children. In P. Fletcher & D. Hall (Eds.), *Specific speech and language disorders in children* (pp. 105–116). London: Whurr Publishers.

Jou, J., Shanteau, J., & Harris, R. J. (1996). An information processing view of framing effects: The role of causal schemas in decision making. *Memory and Cognition, 24,* 1–15.

Juang, B. H., Perdue, R. J., Jr., & Thompson, D. L. (1995). Deployable automatic speech recognition systems: Advances and challenges. *AT & T Technical Journal, 74,* 45–56.

Jusczyk, P. W. (1995). Language acquisition: Speech sounds and the beginning of phonology. In J. L. Miller & P. D. Eimas (Eds.),

Speech, language, and communication: Handbook of perception and cognition, 2nd ed. (pp. 263–295). San Diego: Academic Press.

Jusczyk, P. W., & Aslin, R. N. (1995). Infants' detection of the sound patterns of words in fluent speech. *Cognitive Psychology, 29,* 1–23.

Jusczyk, P. W., Cutler, A., & Redanz, N. J. (1993). Infants' preference for the predominant stress patterns of English words. *Child Development, 64,* 675–687.

Jusczyk, P. W., & Derrah, C. (1987). Representation of speech sounds by young infants. *Developmental Psychology, 23,* 648–654.

Jusczyk, P. W., Hirsh-Pasek, K., Kemler Nelson, D. G., Kennedy, L. J., Woodward, A., & Piwoz, E. G. (1992). Perception of acoustic correlates of major phrasal units by young infants. *Cognitive Psychology, 24,* 252–293.

Jusczyk, P. W., Pisoni, D. B., & Mullenix, J. (1992). Some consequences of stimulus variability on speech processing by 2-month-old infants. *Cognition, 43,* 253–291.

Jusczyk, P. W., Smith, L. B., & Murphy, C. (1981). The perceptual classification of speech. *Perception and Psychophysics, 30,* 10–23.

Just, M. A., & Carpenter, P. A. (1980). A theory of reading: From eye fixations to comprehension. *Psychological Review, 87,* 329–354.

Just, M. A., & Carpenter, P. A. (1987). *The psychology of reading and language comprehension.* Boston: Allyn & Bacon.

Just, M. A., & Carpenter, P. A. (1992). A capacity theory of comprehension: Individual differences in working memory. *Psychological Review, 99,* 122–149.

Just, M. A., Carpenter, P. A., & Keller, T. A. (1996). The capacity theory of comprehension: New frontiers of evidence and arguments. *Psychological Review, 103,* 773–780.

Kahneman, D. (1973). *Attention and effort.* Englewood Cliffs, NJ: Prentice Hall.

Kahneman, D., & Tversky, A. (1979). On the interpretation of intuitive probability: A reply to Jonathan Cohen. *Cognition, 7,* 409–411.

Kail, R. (1994). A method for studying the generalized slowing hypothesis in children with specific language impairment. *Journal of Speech and Hearning Research, 37,* 418–421.

Kandel, E. R., & Schwartz, J. H. (Eds.). (1985). *Principles of neural science.* New York: Elsevier.

Karpinski, A., & Von Hippel, W. (1996). The role of the linguistic intergroup bias in expectancy maintenance. *Social Cognition, 14,* 141–148.

Kassin, S. (1995). *Psychology.* Boston: Houghton Mifflin Co.

Katz, A. N., & Mio, J. S. (1996). *Metaphor: Implications and applications.* Mahwah, NJ: Lawrence Erlbaum Associates.

Katz, J., & Fodor, J. A. (1963). The structure of a semantic theory. *Language, 39,* 170–210.

Kay, P., & Kempton, W. (1984). What is the Sapir-Whorf hypothesis? *American Anthropologist, 86,* 65–79.

Keenan, J. M., Baillet, S. D., & Brown, P. (1984). The effects of causal cohesion on comprehension and memory. *Journal of Verbal Learning and Verbal Behavior, 23,* 115–126.

Kegl, J., Neidle, C., MacLaughlin, D., Hoza, J., & Bahan, B. (1996). The case for grammar, order and position in ASL: A reply to Bouchard and Dubuisson. *Sign Language Studies, 90,* 1–23.

Kellas, G., Ferraro, F. R., & Simpson, G. B. (1988). Lexical ambiguity and the timecourse of attentional allocation in word recognition. *Journal of Experimental Psychology: Human Perception and Performance, 14,* 601–609.

Kellogg, R. T. (1986). Designing idea processors for document composition. Paper presented at the 15th annual meeting of the Society for Computers in Psychology (1985, Boston). Printed in *Behavior Research Methods, Instruments, and Computers, 18,* 118–128.

Kellogg, R. T. (1987). Effects of topic knowledge on the allocation of processing time and cognitive effort to writing processes. *Memory and Cognition, 15,* 256–266.

Kellogg, R. T. (1994). *The psychology of writing.* New York: Oxford University Press.

Kellogg, W. N., & Kellogg, L. A. (1933). *The ape and the child: A study of environmental influence on early behavior.* New York: Hafner.

Kemper, S. (1992). Language and aging. In F. I. M. Craik & T. A. Salthouse (Eds.), *The handbook of aging and cognition* (pp. 213–270). Hillsdale, NJ: Lawrence Erlbaum Associates.

Kertesz, A. (1979). *Aphasia and associate disorders.* New York: Grune and Stratton.

Kertesz, A., Lau, W. K., & Polk, M. (1993). The structural determinants of recovery in Wernicke's aphasia. *Brain and Language, 44,* 153–164.

Khosroshahi, F. (1989). Penguins don't care, but women do: A social identity analysis of a Whorfian problem. *Language in Society, 18,* 505–525.

Kieras, D. E. (1980). Initial mention as a signal to thematic content in technical passages. *Memory and Cognition, 8,* 345–353.

Kieras, D. E. (1981). Topicalization effects in cued recall of technical prose. *Memory and Cognition, 9,* 541–549.

Kieras, D. E. (1982). A model of reader strategy for abstracting main ideas from simple technical prose. *Text, 2,* 47–81.

Kieras, D. E. (1984). A method for comparing a simulation to reading time data. In D. E. Kieras & M. A. Just (Eds.), *New methods in reading comprehension research* (pp. 299–326). Hillsdale, NJ: Lawrence Erlbaum Associates.

Kilborn, K. (1989). Sentence processing in a second language: The timing of transfer. *Language and Speech, 32,* 1–23.

Kilborn, K. (1994). Learning a language late: Second language acquisition in adults. In M. A. Gernsbacher (Ed.), *Handbook of psycholinguistics* (pp. 917–944). San Diego: Academic Press.

King, B. J. (1994). *The information continuum: Evolution of social information transfer in monkeys, apes, and hominids.* Santa Fe, NM: School of American Research Press.

Kinney, G. C., Marsetta, M., & Showman, D. J. (1966). *Studies in display symbol legibility. Part XII, The legibility of alphanumeric symbols for digitized television* (ESD-TR066-117). Bedford, MA: Mitre Corporation.

Kintsch, W. (1988). The role of knowledge in discourse comprehension: A construction-integration model. *Psychological Review, 95,* 163–182.

Kintsch, W. (1992). A cognitive architecture for comprehension. In H. L. Pick, Jr., P. W. van den Broek, & D. C. Knill (Eds.), *Cognition: Conceptual and methodological issues* (pp. 143–163). Washington, DC: American Psychological Association.

Kintsch, W. (1993). Information accretion and reduction in text processing: Inferences. Special Issue: Inference generation during text comprehension. *Discourse Processes, 16,* 193–202.

Kintsch, W., & Van Dijk, T. A. (1978). Toward a model of text comprehension and production. *Psychological Review, 85,* 363–394.

Kintsch, W., Welsch, D., Schmalhofer, F., & Zimny, S. (1990). Sentence memory: A theoretical analysis. *Journal of Memory and Language, 29,* 133–159.

Kirshner, H. S. (1995). Introduction to aphasia. In H. S. Kirshner (Ed.), *Handbook of neurological speech and language disorders* (pp. 1–22). New York: Marcel Dekker.

Klima, E., & Bellugi, U. (1979). *The signs of language.* Cambridge, MA: Harvard University Press.

Kluender, K. R. (1994). Speech perception as a tractable problem in cognitive science. In M. A. Gernsbacher (Ed.), *Handbook of psycholinguistics* (pp. 173–217). San Diego: Academic Press.

Kluender, R., & Kutas, M. (1993). Bridging the gap: Evidence from ERPs on the processing of unbounded dependencies. *Journal of Cognitive Neuroscience, 5,* 196–214.

Knapp, M. L., & Hall, J. A. (1992). Nonverbal communication in human interaction. Fort Worth, TX: Holt, Rinehart & Winston.

Kolb, B., & Whishaw, I. Q. (Eds.). (1990). *Fundamentals of human neuropsychology.* San Francisco: Freeman.

Kosslyn, S. M., & Koenig, O. (1992). *Wet mind: The new cognitive neuroscience.* New York: The Free Press.

Kozol, J. (1985). *Illiterate America.* Garden City, NY: Anchor.

Kripke, S. (1963). Semantic considerations on modal logic. *Acta Philosophica Fennica, 16,* 83–94.

Kroll, J. F., & Stewart, E. (1994). Category interference in translation and picture naming: Evidence for asymmetric connections between bilingual memory representations. *Journal of Memory and Language, 33,* 149–174.

Kroll, N. E. (1972). Short-term memory and the nature of interference from concurrent shadowing. *Quarterly Journal of Experimental Psychology, 24,* 414–419.

Kucera, H., & Francis, W. N. (1967). *A computational analysis of present-day American English.* Providence, RI: Brown University Press.

Kuhl, P. K. (1981). Discrimination of speech by nonhuman animals: Basic auditory sensitivities conducive to the perception of speech categories. *Journal of the Acoustical Society of America, 70,* 340–349.

Kuhl, P. K. (1987). The special-mechanisms debate in speech research: Categorization tests on animals and infants. In S. Harnad (Ed.), *Categorical perception: The groundwork of cognition* (pp. 355–386). Cambridge: Cambridge University Press.

Kuhl, P. K. (1991). Human adults and human infants show a "perceptual magnet effect" for the prototypes of speech categories; monkeys do not. *Perception and Psychophysics, 50,* 93–107.

Kuhl, P. K. (1993). Infant speech perception: A window on psycholinguistic development. *International Journal of Psycholinguistics, 9,* 33–56.

Kurtzman, H. S., & MacDonald, M. C. (1993). Resolution of quantifier scope ambiguities. *Cognition, 48,* 243–279.

Kutas, M., & Hillyard, S. A. (1983). Event-related potentials to grammatical errors and semantic anomalies. *Memory and Cognition, 11,* 539–550.

Kutas, M., Lindamood, T. E., & Hillyard, S. A. (1984). Word expectancy and event-related brain potentials during sentence processing. In S. Kornblum & J. Requin (Eds.), *Preparatory states and processes* (pp. 217–237). Hillsdale, NJ: Lawrence Erlbaum Associates.

Kutas, M., & Van Petten, C. K. (1994). Psycholinguistics electrified. In M. A. Gernsbacher (Ed.), *Handbook of psycholinguistics* (pp. 83–143). San Diego: Academic Press.

Lachman, R., Lachman, J. L., & Butterfield, E. C. (1979). *Cognitive psychology and information processing: An introduction.* Hillsdale, NJ: Lawrence Erlbaum Associates.

Lahey, M., & Edwards, J. (1996). Why do children with specific language impairment name pictures more slowly than their peers? *Journal of Speech and Hearing Research, 39,* 1081–1098.

Lakoff, G. (1987a). Cognitive models and prototype theory. In U. Neisser (Ed.), *Concepts and conceptual development: Ecological and intellectual factors in categorization. Emory symposia in cognition, 1.* New York: Cambridge University Press.

Lakoff, G. (1987b). *Women, fire, and dangerous things: What categories reveal about the mind.* Chicago: University of Chicago Press.

Lakoff, G., & Johnson, M. (1980). The metaphorical structure of the human conceptual system. *Cognitive Science, 4,* 195–208.

Lakoff, R. (1973). Language and woman's place. *Language in Society, 1,* 45–80.

Lakoff, R. T. (1975). *Language and woman's place.* New York: Harper & Row.

Lakoff, R. T. (1990). *Talking power: The politics of language in our lives.* New York: Basic Books.

Lakshmanan, U. (1995). Child second language acquisition of syntax. *Studies in Second Language Acquisition, 17,* 301–329.

Landar, H. J., Ervin, S. M., & Horowitz, A. E. (1960). Navaho color categories. *Language, 36,* 368–382.

Lane, H. (1976). *The wild boy of Aveyron.* Cambridge, MA: Harvard University Press.

Langacker, R. W. (Ed.). (1977). *Studies in Uto-Aztecan 1: An overview of Uto-Aztecan grammar.* SIL Publications in Linguistics, Vol. 56. Dallas: Summer Institute of Linguistics/Arlington: University of Texas.

Langacker, R. W. (1978). The form and meaning of the English auxiliary. *Language, 54,* 853–882.

Langacker, R. W. (1986). *Foundations of cognitive grammar,* Vol. 1. Stanford, CA: Stanford University Press.

Langacker, R. W. (1987). *Foundations of cognitive grammar 1: Theoretical prerequisites.* Stanford, CA: Stanford University Press.

Langacker, R. W. (1991). *Foundations of cognitive grammar 2: Descriptive application.* Stanford, CA: Stanford University Press.

Larson, R. K. (1990). Semantics. In D. N. Osherson & H. Lasnik (Eds.), *Language: An invitation to cognitive science,* Vol. I. (pp. 5–22). Cambridge, MA: MIT Press.

Leakey, R. (1994). *The origin of humankind.* New York: Basic Books.

Lederer, R. (1979). *Anguished English.* New York: Dell Publishing.

Lederer, R. (1987). *Anguished English.* Charleston: Wyrick.

Lemire, R. J., Loeser, J. D., Leech, R. W., & Alvord, E. C. (1975). *Normal and abnormal development of the human nervous system.* New York: Harper & Row.

Lenneberg, E. (1967). *Biological foundations of language.* New York: Wiley.

Levelt, W. J. (1992). The Perceptual Loop theory not disconfirmed: A reply to MacKay. *Consciousness and Cognition: An International Journal, 1,* 226–230.

Levelt, W. J., Schriefers, H., Vorberg, D., Meyer, A. S., Pechmann, T., & Havinga, J. (1991). Normal and deviant lexical processing:

Reply to Dell and O'Seaghdha. *Psychological Review, 98*, 615–618.

Levelt, W. J. M. (1989). *Speaking: From intention to articulation.* Cambridge, MA: MIT Press.

Liberman, A. M. (1970). The grammars of speech and language. *Cognitive Psychology, 1*, 301–323.

Liberman, A. M. (1982). On finding that speech is special. *American Psychologist, 37*, 148–167.

Liberman, A. M., Cooper, F. S., Shankweiler, D. P., & Studdert-Kennedy, M. (1967). Perception of the speech code. *Psychological Review, 74*, 431–461.

Liberman, A. M., Harris, K. S., Hoffman, H. S., & Griffith, B. C. (1957). The discrimination of speech sounds within and across phoneme boundaries. *Journal of Experimental Psychology, 54*, 358–368.

Liberman, A. M., & Mattingly, I. G. (1985). The motor theory of speech perception revised. *Cognition, 21*, 1–36.

Liberman, M., & Prince, A. (1977). On stress and linguistic rhythm. *Linguistic Inquiry, 8*, 249–336.

Lichtheim, L. (1885). On aphasia. *Brain, 7*, 433–484.

Lieberman, P. (1991). *Uniquely human: The evolution of speech, thought, and selfless behavior.* Cambridge, MA: Harvard University Press.

Lima, S. D. (1987). Morphological analysis in sentence reading. *Journal of Memory and Language, 26*, 84–99.

Liu, L. G. (1985). Reasoning counterfactually in Chinese: Are there any obstacles? *Cognition, 21*, 239–270.

Lively, S. E., & Pisoni, D. B. (1990). *Some lexical effects in phoneme categorization: A first report. Research on speech perception* (Progress Report No. 16). Bloomington: Indiana University, Speech Research Laboratory.

Lively, S. E., Pisoni, D. B., & Goldinger, S. D. (1994). Spoken word recognition. In M. A. Gernsbacher (Ed.), *Handbook of Psycholinguistics* (pp. 265–318). San Diego: Academic Press.

Loftus, E. F., Miller, D. G., & Burns, H. J. (1978). Semantic integration of verbal information into a visual memory. *Journal of Experimental Psychology: Human Learning and Memory, 4*, 19–31.

Loftus, E. F., & Palmer, J. C. (1974). Reconstruction of automobile destruction: An example of the interaction beween language and memory. *Journal of Verbal Learning and Verbal Behavior, 13*, 585–589.

Loftus, E. F., & Zanni, G. (1975). Eyewitness testimony: The influence of the wording of a question. *Bulletin of the Psychonomic Society, 5*, 86–88.

Long, D. L., Golding, J. M., & Graesser, A. C. (1992). A test of the on-line status of goal-related inferences. *Journal of Memory and Language, 31*, 634–647.

Long, M. (1990). Maturational constraints on language development. *Studies in Second Language Acquisition, 12*, 251–286.

Longacre, R. E. (1956). Review of *Language and reality* by Wilbur M. Urban and *Four articles on metalinguistics* by Benjamin Lee Whorf. *Language, 32*, 298–308.

Lorch, R. F. (1982). Priming and search processes in semantic memory: A test of three models of spreading activation. *Journal of Verbal Learning and Verbal Behavior, 21*, 468–492.

Lorch, R. F., Lorch, E. P., & Matthews, P. D. (1985). On-line processing of the topic structure of a text. *Journal of Memory and Language, 24*, 350–362.

Lucas, M. M., Tanenhaus, M. K., & Carlson, G. N. (1990). Levels of representation in the interpretation of anaphoric reference and instrument inference. *Memory and Cognition, 18*, 611–631.

Luce, P. A. (1986). A computational analysis of uniqueness points in auditory word recognition. *Perception and Psychophysics, 39*, 155–158.

Luce, P. A., Pisoni, D. B., & Goldinger, S. D. (1990). Similarity neighborhoods of spoken words. In G. T. M. Altmann (Ed.), *Cognitive models of speech processing* (pp. 122–147). Cambridge, MA: MIT Press.

Lucy, J. A. (1992). *Language diversity and thought: A reformulation of the linguistic relativity hypothesis.* Cambridge: Cambridge University Press.

Lucy, J. A., & Shweder, R. A. (1979). Whorf and his critics: Linguistic and nonlinguistic influences on color memory. *American Anthropologist, 81*, 581–615.

Lucy, J. A., & Wertsch, J. V. (1987). Vygotsky and Whorf: A comparative analysis. In M. Hickmann (Ed.), *Social and functional approaches to language and thought.* Orlando, FL: Academic Press.

Luria, A. R. (1965). Solotaroff, L. (Trans.) The mind of a mnemonist: A little book about a vast memory. Cambridge, MA: Harvard University Press. (Reprinted in 1987.)

Maass, A., Milesi, A., Zabbini, S., & Stahlberg, D. (1995). Linguistic intergroup bias: Differential expectancies or in-group protection? *Journal of Personality and Social Psychology, 68*, 116–126.

Maass, A., Salvi, D., Arcuri, L., & Semin, G. R. (1989). Language use in intergroup contexts: The linguistic intergroup bias. *Journal of Personality and Social Psychology, 57*, 981–993.

MacDonald, M. C. (1993). The interaction of lexical and syntactic ambiguity. *Journal of Memory and Language, 32*, 692–715.

MacKay, D. G. (1987). *The organization of perception and action: A theory for language and other cognitive skills.* New York: Springer-Verlag.

Macnamara, J. (1982). *Names for things: A study of child language.* Cambridge, MA: MIT Press.

MacNeilage, P. F. (1970). Motor control of serial ordering of speech. *Psychological Review, 77*, 182–196

MacNeilage, P. F. (1972). Speech physiology. In J. H. Gilbert (Ed.), *Speech and cortical functioning* (pp. 1–72). New York: Academic Press.

MacNeilage, P. F., Rootes, T. P., & Chase, R. A. (1967). Speech production and perception in a patient with severe impairment of somesthetic perception and motor control. *Journal of Speech and Hearing Research, 10*, 449–467.

MacWhinney, B. (1987). Applying the competition model to bilingualism. *Applied Psycholinguistics, 8*, 315–327.

MacWhinney, B. (1992). Transfer and competition in second language learning. In R. J. Harris (Ed.), *Cognitive processing in bilinguals* (pp. 371–390). Amsterdam: North-Holland.

MacWhinney, B. (1995). *The CHILDES project: Tools for analyzing talk*, 2nd ed. Hillsdale, NJ: Lawrence Erlbaum Associates.

MacWhinney, B., & Leinbach, J. (1991). Implementations are not conceptualizations: Revising the verb learning model. *Cognition, 40*, 121–157.

MacWhinney, B., & Snow, C. (1985). The child language data exchange system. *Journal of Child Language, 12*, 271–295.

Malotki, E. (1983). *Hopi time: A linguistic analysis of the temporal concepts in the Hopi language.* Berlin/New York: Mouton.

Mandler, J. M. (1984). Stories, scripts, and scenes: Aspects of schema theory. Hillsdale, NJ: Lawrence Erlbaum Associates.

Mandler, J. M., Scribner, S., Cole, M., & DeForest, M. (1980). Cross-cultural invariance in story recall. *Child Development, 51,* 19–26.

Mann, V. A. (1993). Phoneme awareness and future reading ability. *Journal of Learning Disabilities, 26,* 259–269.

Mann, V. A., Madden, J., Russell, J. M., & Liberman, A. (1981). Further investigation into the influence of preceding liquids on stop consonant perception. *Journal of the Acoustical Society of America, 69,* S91 (Abstract).

Mann, V. A., & Repp, B. H. (1981). Influence of preceding fricative on stop consonant perception. *Journal of the Acoustical Society of America, 69,* 548–558.

Mannes, S. M., & Kintsch, W. (1987). Knowledge organization and text organization. *Cognition and Instruction, 4,* 91–115.

Marantz, A. (1982). Re reduplication. *Linguisitic Inquiry, 13,* 150–177.

Marcus, G. F. (1993). Negative evidence in language acquisition. *Cognition, 46,* 53–85.

Marcus, G. F., Pinker, S., Ullman, M., Hollander, M., Rosen, T. J., & Xu, F. (1992). Overregulation in language acquisition. *Monographs of the Society for Research in Child Development, 57* (Serial No. 228), i–182.

Marin, O. S. M. (1980). CAT scans of five deep dyslexic patients. In M. Coltheart, K. Patterson, & J. C. Marshall (Eds.), *Deep dyslexia* (pp. 407–409). London: Routledge and Kegan Paul.

Markman, E. M. (1977). Realizing that you don't understand: A preliminary investigation. *Child Development, 48,* 986–992.

Markman, E. M. (1990). Constraints children place on word meanings. *Cognitive Science, 14,* 57–77.

Markman, E. M., & Wachtel, G. F. (1988). Children's use of mutual exclusivity to constrain the meaning of words. *Cognitive Psychology, 20,* 121–157.

Markowitz, J. A. (1995). Talking to computers. *Journal of Systems Management, 46,* 8–13.

Marr, D. (1982). *Vision.* San Francisco: W. H. Freeman.

Marshall, J. C., & Newcombe, F. (1973). Patterns of paralexia: A psycholinguistic approach. *Journal of Psycholinguistic Research, 2,* 175–199.

Marslen-Wilson, W. (1973). Linguistic structure and speech shadowing at very short latencies. *Nature, 244,* 522–523.

Marslen-Wilson, W. D. (1984). Function and process in spoken word recognition. In H. Bouma & D. G. Bouwhius (Eds.), *Attention and performance. Vol. X, Control of language processes* (pp. 125–150). Hillsdale, NJ: Lawrence Erlbaum Associates.

Marslen-Wilson, W. D. (1987). Parallel processing in spoken word recognition. *Cognition, 25,* 71–102.

Marslen-Wilson, W. D. (1990). Activation, competition and frequency in lexical access. In G. T. M. Altmann (Ed.), *Cognitive models of speech processing* (pp. 148–172). Cambridge, MA: MIT Press.

Marslen-Wilson, W., Tyler, L. K., Waksler, R., & Older, L. (1994). Morphology and meaning in the English mental lexicon. *Psychological Review, 101,* 3–33.

Marslen-Wilson, W. D., & Welsh, A. (1978). Processing interactions and lexical access during word recognition in continuous speech. *Cognitive Psychology, 10,* 29–63.

Martell, R. F., Lane, D. M., & Emrich, C. (1996). Male-female differences: A computer simulation. *American Psychologist, 51,* 157–158.

Martijn, C., van der Pligt, J., & Spears, R. (1996). Self-serving bias in attitude agreements: The use of person versus issue-implicated language. *Social Cognition, 14,* 77–91.

Massaro, D. (1994). Psychological aspects of speech perception: Implications for research and theory. In M. A. Gernsbacher (Ed.), *Handbook of psycholinguistics* (pp. 219–263). San Diego: Academic Press.

Massaro, D. M. (1979). Letter information and orthographic context in word perception. *Journal of Experimental Psychology: Human Perception and Performance, 5,* 595–609.

Massaro, D. W. (1987). *Speech perception by ear and eye: A paradigm for psychological inquiry.* Hillsdale, NJ: Lawrence Erlbaum Associates.

Massaro, D. W. (1989). Testing between the TRACE model and the fuzzy logic model of speech perception. *Cognitive Psychology, 21,* 398–421.

Massaro, D. W., & Cohen, M. M. (1983). Evaluation and integration of visual and auditory information in speech perception. *Journal of Experimental Psychology: Human Perception and Performance, 9,* 753–771.

Masson, M. E. J. (1995). A distributed memory model of semantic priming. *Journal of Experimental Psychology: Learning, Memory, and Cognition, 21,* 3–23.

Mayer, R. E. (1979). Twenty years of research on advance organizers: Assimilation theory is still the best predictor of results. *Instructional Science, 8,* 133–167.

Mayr, E. (1991). *One long argument.* Cambridge, MA: Harvard University Press.

McClelland, J. L., & Elman, J. L. (1986). Interactive processes in speech perception: The TRACE model. In J. L. McClelland & D. E. Rumelhart (Eds.), *Parallel distributed processing: Explorations in the microstructure of cognition. Vol. 2, Psychological and biological models* (pp. 58–121). Cambridge, MA: MIT Press.

McClelland, J. L., & Rumelhart, D. E. (1981). An interactive activation model of context effects in letter perception: I. An account of basic findings. *Psychological Review, 88,* 375–407.

McClelland, J. L., & Rumelhart, D. E. (1985). Distributed memory and the representation of general and specific information. *Journal of Experimental Psychology: General, 114,* 159–188.

McClelland, J. L., & Rumelhart, D. E. (1986a). On learning the past tenses of English verbs. In J. L. McClelland & D. E. Rumelhart (Eds.), *Parallel distributed processing: Explorations in the microstructure of cognition. Vol. 2, Psychological and biological models* (pp. 216–271). Cambridge, MA: MIT Press.

McClelland, J. L., & Rumelhart, D. E. (1986b). *Parallel distributed processing: Explorations in the microstructure of cognition. Vol. 1, Foundations.* Cambridge, MA: MIT Press.

McClelland, J. L., & Rumelhart, D. E. (1986c). A distributed model of human learning and memory. In J. L. McClelland & D. E. Rumelhart (Eds.), *Parallel distributed processing: Explorations in the microstructure of cognition. Vol 2, Psychological and biological models* (pp. 216–271). Cambridge, MA: MIT Press.

McCloskey, M., & Cohen, N. J. (1989). Catastrophic interference in connectionist networks: The sequential learning problem. In G. H. Bower (Ed.), *The psychology of learning and motivation: Advances in research and theory,* Vol. 24. New York: Academic Press.

McCloskey, M., & Zaragoza, M. (1985). Misleading postevent information and memory for events: Arguments and evidence against the memory impairment hypothesis. *Journal of Experimental Psychology: General, 114,* 1–16.

McConkie, G. W., & Rayner, K. (1975). The span of the effective stimulus during a fixation in reading. *Perception and Psychophysics, 17,* 578–586.

McConkie, G. W., & Zola, D. (1981). Language constraints and the functional stimulus in reading. In A. M. Lesgold & C. A. Perfetti (Eds.), *Interactive processes in reading.* Hillsdale, NJ: Lawrence Erlbaum Associates.

McConnell, A. R., & Fazio, R. H. (1996). Women as men and people: Effects of gender-marked language. *Personality and Social Psychology Bulletin, 22,* 1004–1013.

McConnell, A. R., & Gavanski, I. (1994, May). Women as men and people: Occupation title suffixes as primes. Paper presented at the 66th annual meeting of the Midwestern Psychological Association, Chicago.

McCormick, S. (1994). A nonreader becomes a reader: A case study of literacy acquisition by a severely disabled reader. *Reading Research Quarterly, 29,* 157–176.

McGurk, H., & MacDonald, J. (1976). Hearing lips and seeing voices. *Nature, 264,* 746–748.

McKoon, G., Gerrig, R. J., & Greene, S. B. (1996). Pronoun resolution without pronouns: Some consequences of memory-based text processing. *Journal of Experimental Psychology: Learning, Memory, and Cognition, 22,* 919–932.

McKoon, G., & Ratcliff, R. (1981). The comprehension processes and memory structures involved in instrumental inference. *Journal of Verbal Learning and Verbal Behavior, 20,* 671–682.

McKoon, G., & Ratcliff, R. (1986). Inferences about predictable events. *Journal of Experimental Psychology: Learning, Memory, and Cognition, 12,* 82–91.

McKoon, G., & Ratcliff, R. (1992). Inference during reading. *Psychological Review, 99,* 440–466.

McNamara, T. P. (1992). Theories of priming: I. Associative distance and lag. *Journal of Experimental Psychology: Learning, Memory, and Cognition, 18,* 1173–1190.

McQueen, J. M., Cutler, A., Briscoe, T., & Novis, D. (1995). Models of continuous speech recognition and the contents of the vocabulary. *Language and Cognitive Processes, 10,* 309–331.

McQueen, J. M., Norris, D. G., & Cutler, A. (1994). Competition in spoken word recognition: Spotting words in other words. *Journal of Experimental Psychology: Learning, Memory, and Cognition, 20,* 621–638.

Medin, D. L., & Shoben, E. J. (1988). Context and structure in conceptual combination. *Cognitive Psychology, 20,* 158–190.

Mehler, J., Dupoux, E., Nazzi, T., & Dehaene-Lambertz, G. (1996). Coping with linguistic diversity: The infant's viewpoint. In J. L. Morgan & K. Demuth (Eds.), *Signal to syntax: Bootstrapping from speech to grammar in early acquisition* (pp. 101–116). Mahwah, NJ: Lawrence Erlbaum Associates.

Mehler, J., Jusczyk, P., Lambertz, G., Halsted, N., Bertoncini, J., & Amiel-Tison, C. (1988). A precursor of language acquisition in young infants. *Cognition, 29,* 143–178.

Mesulam, M.-M. (1990). Large-scale neurocognitive networks and distributed processes for attention, language, and memory. *Annals of Neurology, 28,* 597–613.

Meyer, B. J. (1975). Identification of the structure of prose and its implications for the study of reading and memory. *Journal of Reading Behavior, 7,* 7–47.

Meyer, B. J. F. (1985). Prose analysis: Purposes, procedures, and problems. In B. K. Britton & J. B. Black (Eds.), *Understanding Expository Text* (pp. 11–64). Hillsdale, NJ: Lawrence Erlbaum Associates.

Meyer, D. E., & Schvaneveldt, R. W. (1971). Facilitation in recognizing pairs of words: Evidence of a dependence between retrieval operations. *Journal of Experimental Psychology, 90,* 227–234.

Miles, L. H. (1983). Apes and language: The search for communicative competence. In J. de Luce & H. T. Wilder (Eds.), *Language in primates: Perspectives and implications* (pp. 43–62). New York: Springer-Verlag.

Miller, G. A. (1956). The magical number seven, plus or minus two: Some limits on our capacity for processing information. *Psychological Review, 63,* 81–97.

Miller, G. A. (1962). Some psychological studies of grammar. *American Psychologist, 17,* 748–762.

Miller, G. A. (1978). Semantic relations among words. In M. Halle, J. Bresnan, & G. A. Miller (Eds.), *Linguistic theory and psychological reality.* Cambridge, MA: MIT Press.

Miller, G. A., & Chomsky, N. (1963). Finitary models of language users. In R. D. Luce, R. Bush, & E. Galanter (Eds.), *Handbook of mathematical psychology,* Vol. 2. New York: Wiley.

Miller, G. A., Heise, G., & Lichten, W. (1951). The intelligibility of speech as a function of the context of the test materials. *Journal of Experimental Psychology, 4,* 329–335.

Miller, G., & Johnson-Laird, P. (1976). *Language and perception.* Cambridge, MA: Belknap Press of Harvard University Press.

Miller, J. L. (1987). Rate-dependent processing in speech perception. In I. Ellis (Ed.), *Progress in psychology of language* (pp. 119–157). Hillsdale, NJ: Lawrence Erlbaum Associates.

Miller, K. F., & Stigler, J. W. (1987). Counting in Chinese: Cultural variation in a basic cognitive skill. *Cognitive Development, 2,* 279–305.

Mitchell, D. C. (1989). Verb guidance and other lexical effects in parsing. Special Issue: Parsing and interpretation. *Language and Cognitive Processes, 4,* SI123–SI154.

Mitchell, D. C. (1994a). Sentence parsing. In M. A. Gernsbacher (Ed.), *Handbook of psycholinguistics* (pp. 375–410). San Diego: Academic Press.

Mitchell, D. C. (1994b). Syntactic processing. In M. A. Gernsbacher (Ed.), *Handbook of psycholinguistics.* New York: Academic Press.

Miura, I. T. (1987). Mathematics achievement as a function of language. *Journal of Educational Psychology, 79,* 79–82.

Miura, I. T., & Okamoto, Y. (1989). Comparisons of U.S. and Japanese first graders' cognitive representation of number and understanding of place value. *Journal of Educational Psychology, 81,* 109–114.

Miura, I. T., Okomoto, Y., Kim, C. C., Steere, M., & Fayol, M. (1993). First graders' cognitive representation of number and understanding of place value: Cross-national comparisons: France, Japan, Korea, Sweden, and the United States. *Journal of Educational Psychology, 85,* 24–30.

Mohr, J. P., Pessin, M. S., Finkelstein, S., Funkenstein, H. H., Duncan, G. W., & Davis, K. R. (1978). Broca's aphasia: Pathologic and clinical. *Neurology, 28,* 311–324.

Montague, R. (1974). *Formal philosophy: Selected papers.* New Haven: Yale University Press.

Moonen, C. T. W. (1995). Imaging of human brain activation with functional MRI. *Biological Psychiatry, 37,* 141–143.

Morris, C. D., Bransford, J. D., & Franks, J. J. (1977). Levels of processing versus transfer appropriate processing. *Journal of Verbal Learning and Verbal Behavior, 16*, 519–533.

Morris, R. K. (1994). Lexical and message-level sentence context effects on fixation times in reading. *Journal of Experimental Psychology: Learning, Memory, and Cognition, 20*, 92–113.

Morton, J. (1964). The effects of context on the visual duration threshold for words. *British Journal of Psychology, 55*, 165–180.

Morton, J. (1969). The interaction of information in word recognition. *Psychological Review, 76*, 165–178.

Morton, J. (1982). Disintegrating the lexicon: An information processing approach. In J. Mehler, E. Walker, & M. Garret (Eds.), *On mental representation.* Hillsdale, NJ: Lawrence Erlbaum Associates.

Morton, J., & Broadbent, D. E. (1967). Passive versus active recognition models, or is your homunculus really necessary? In W. Wathen-Dunn (Ed.), *Models for the perception of speech and visual form* (pp. 103–110). Cambridge, MA: MIT Press.

Mullennix, J. W., & Pisoni, D. B. (1990). Stimulus variability and processing dependencies in speech perception. *Perception and Psychophysics, 47*, 379–390.

Murray, J. D., Klin, C. M., & Myers, J. L. (1993). Forward inferences in narrative text. *Journal of Memory and Language, 32*, 464–473.

Muysken, P. (1988). Are Creoles a special type of language? In F. J. Newmeyer (Ed.), *Linguistics: The Cambridge Survey. Vol 2, Linguistic theory: Extensions and applications* (pp. 285–301). Cambridge: Cambridge University Press.

Myers, J., Jusczyk, P. W., Kemler Nelson, D. G., Charles-Luce, J., Woodward, A., & Hirsh-Pasek, K. (1996). Infants' sensitivity to word boundaries in fluent speech. *Journal of Child Language, 23*, 1–30.

Myers, J. L., & Duffy, S. A. (1990). Causal inferences and text memory. In A. C. Graesser & G. H. Bower (Eds.), *The psychology of learning and motivation,* Vol. 25 (pp. 159–174). Orlando, FL: Academic Press.

Myers, J. L., Shinjo, M., & Duffy, S. A. (1987). Degree of causal relatedness and memory. *Journal of Memory and Language, 26*, 453–465.

Myers, P. S. (1993). Narrative expressive deficits associated with right-hemisphere damage. In H. H. Brownell & Y. Joanette (Eds.), *Narrative discourse in neurologically impaired and normal aging adults* (pp. 279–296). San Diego: Singular Publishing.

Neely, J. H. (1977). Semantic priming and retrieval from lexical memory: Roles of inhibitionless spreading activation and limited-capacity attention. *Journal of Experimental Psychology: General, 106*, 226–254.

Nelson, K. (1973). Structure and strategy in learning to talk. *Monographs of the Society for Research in Child Development, 38*, 136.

Nelson, K. (1988). Constraints on word learning? *Cognitive Development, 3*, 221–246.

Newport, E., & Meier, R. (1985). Acquisition of American Sign Language. In D. Slobin (Ed.), *The cross-linguistic study of language acquisition* (pp. 881–938). Hillsdale, NJ: Lawrence Erlbaum Associates.

Newport, E. L. (1990). Maturational constraints on language learning. *Cognitive Science, 14*, 11–28.

Newport, E. L., Gleitman, H., and Gleitman, L. R. (1977). Mother, I'd rather do it myself: Some effects and non-effects of maternal speech style. In C. Snow & C. Ferguson (Eds.), *Talking to children* (pp. 109–149). Cambridge: Cambridge University Press.

Ng, S. H. (1990). Adrenocentric coding of man and his memory by language users. *Journal of Experimental Social Psychology, 26*, 455–464.

Noble, W., & Davidson, I. (1991). The evolutionary emergence of modern human behavior: Language and its archeology. *Man, 26*, 223–253.

Norman, D. A. (1986). Reflections on cognition and parallel distributed processing. In J. L. McClelland and D. E. Rumelhart (Eds.), *Parallel distributed processing: Explorations in the microstructure of cognition. Vol. 2, Psychological and biological models* (pp. 531–546). Cambridge, MA: MIT Press.

Norris, D. (1994). Shortlist: A connectionist model of continuous speech recognition. *Cognition, 52*, 189–234.

Norris, D., McQueen, J. M., & Cutler, A. (1995). Competition and segmentation in spoken word recognition. *Journal of Experimental Psychology: Learning, Memory, and Cognition, 21*, 1209–1228.

Nygaard, L. C., & Pisoni, D. B. (1995). Speech perception: New directions in research and theory. In J. L. Miller & P. D. Eimas (Ed.), *Speech, language and communication* (pp. 63–90). San Diego: Academic Press.

Nygaard, L. C., Sommers, M. S., & Pisoni, D. B. (1994). Speech perception as a talker-contingent process. *Psychological Science, 5*, 42–46.

O'Brien, E. J. (1987). Antecedent search processes and the structure of text. *Journal of Experimental Psychology: Learning, Memory, and Cognition, 13*, 278–290.

O'Brien, E. J., Albrecht, J. E., Hakala, C. M., & Rizzella, M. L. (1995). Activation and suppression of antecedents during restatement. *Journal of Experimental Psychology: Learning, Memory, and Cognition, 21*, 626–634.

O'Brien, E. J., Shank, D. M., Myers, J. L., & Rayner, K. (1988). Elaborative inferences during reading: Do they occur on-line? *Journal of Experimental Psychology: Learning, Memory, and Cognition, 14*, 410–420.

Ojemann, G. A. (1983). Brain organization for language from the perspective of electrical stimulation mapping. *Behavioral and Brain Sciences, 6*, 189–230.

Ojemann, G. A. (1991). Cortical organization of language. *Journal of Neuroscience, 11*, 2281–2287.

Oller, D. K. (1980). The emergence of the sounds of speech in infancy. In G. Yeni-Komoshian, J. F. Kavanaugh, & C. A. Ferguson (Eds.), *Child phonology. Vol 1, Production* (pp. 93–112). New York: Academic Press.

Olson, R. K. (1994). Language deficits in "specific" reading disability. In M. A. Gernsbacher (Ed.), *Handbook of psycholinguistics.* (pp. 895–916) San Diego: Academic Press.

Onifer, W., & Swinney, D. A. (1981). Accessing lexical ambiguities during sentence comprehension: Effects of frequency of meaning and contextual bias. *Memory and Cognition, 9*, 225–236.

Ortony, A. (1975). Why metaphors are necessary and not just nice. *Educational Theory, 25*, 45–53.

Ortony, A., Schallert, D. L., Reynolds, R. E., & Antos, S. J. (1978). Interpreting metaphors and idioms: Some effects of context on comprehension. *Journal of Verbal Learning and Verbal Behavior, 17*, 465–477.

Osgood, C. E. (1971). Where do sentences come from? In D. D. Steinberg & L. A. Jakoborits (Eds.), *Semantics: An interdisciplinary reader in philosophy, linguistics, and psychology* (pp. 497–529). Cambridge: Cambridge University Press.

Osterhout, L., Bersick, M., & McLaughlin, J. (1997). Brain potentials reflect violations of gender stereotypes. *Memory & Cognition, 25,* 273–285.

Paradis, J., & Genesee, F. (1996). Syntactic acquisition in children: Autonomous or independent? *Studies in Second Language Acquisition, 18,* 1–25.

Parker, E. S., Birnbaum, I. M., & Noble, E. P. (1976). Alcohol and memory: Storage and state dependency. *Journal of Verbal Learning and Verbal Behavior, 15,* 691–702.

Parkin, A. J. (1996). *Explorations in cognitive neuropsychology.* Oxford: Blackwell.

Patterson, F. (1978). The gestures of a gorilla: Language acquisition in another pongid. *Brain Language, 5,* 56–71.

Patterson, K. E., & Besner, D. (1984). Is the right hemisphere literate? *Cognitive Neuropsychology, 1,* 315–342.

Pavlov, I. P. (1927). *Conditioned reflexes.* (G. V. Anrep, Trans.). London: Oxford University Press.

Penner, S. G. (1987). Parental responses to grammatical and ungrammatical child utterances. *Child Development, 58,* 376–384.

Perfetti, C. A. (1985). *Reading ability.* New York: Oxford University Press.

Perfetti, C. A. (1992). The representation problem in reading acquisition. In P. B. Gough, L. C. Ehri, & R. Treiman (Eds.), *Reading acquisition.* Hillsdale, NJ: Lawrence Erlbaum Associates.

Perfetti, C. A. (1994). Psycholinguistics and reading ability. In M. A. Gernsbacher (Ed.), *Handbook of psycholinguistics* (pp. 849–894). San Diego: Academic Press.

Perrig, W., & Kintsch, W. (1985). Propositional and situational representations of text. *Journal of Memory and Language, 24,* 503–518.

Petitto, L. A., & Bellugi, U. (1988). Spatial cognition and brain organization: Clues from the acquisition of a language in space. In J. Stiles-Davis, M. Kritchevsky, & U. Bellugi (Eds.), *Spatial cognition: Brain bases and development* (pp. 299–326). Hillsdale, NJ: Lawrence Erlbaum Associates.

Piaget, J. (1952). *The origins of intelligence in children* (M. Cook, Trans.) New York: International Universities Press.

Piaget, J. (1963). Language et opérations intellectuelles [Language and intellectual operations]. In Collectif, *Problems de Psycholinguistique* [Problems of psycholinguistics]. Paris: Presses Universitaires de France.

Piaget, J. (1974). *Biology and knowledge.* Chicago: University of Chicago Press.

Piaget, J. (1980). What is psychology? *Bulletin de Psychologie, 34,* 7–9.

Piaget, J., & Inhelder, B. (1959). *La genése des structures logiques élémentaires: classifications et sériations.* Neuchatel, Switzerland: Delachaux et Niestle.

Piaget, J., & Inhelder, B. (1969). *Psychologie de l'enfant.* (H. Weaver, Trans.). New York: Basic Books.

Piattelli-Palmarini, M. (1989). Evolution, selection, and cognition: From "learning" to parameter setting in biology and in the study of language. *Cognition, 31,* 1–44.

Piattelli-Palmarini, M. (1994). Ever since language and learning: Afterthoughts on the Piaget-Chomsky debate. *Cognition, 50,* 315–346.

Pickett, J. M. (1980). *The sounds of speech communication: A primer of acoustic phonetics and speech perception.* Baltimore: University Park Press.

Pinker, S. (1984). *Language learnability and language development.* Cambridge, MA: Harvard University Press.

Pinker, S. (1987). The bootstrapping problem in language acquisition. In B. MacWhinney (Ed.), *Mechanisms of language acquisition.* Hillsdale, NJ: Lawrence Erlbaum Associates.

Pinker, S. (1989). *Learnability and cognition.* Cambridge, MA: MIT Press.

Pinker, S. (1990). Language acquisition. In D. N. Osherson & H. Lasnik (Eds.), *Language: An invitation to cognitive science,* Vol. 1. Cambridge, MA: MIT Press.

Pinker, S. (1994). *The language instinct: How the mind creates language.* New York: William Morrow & Co..

Pinker, S. (1995). Language acquisition. In L. R. Gleitman & M. Liberman (Eds.), *Language: An invitation to cognitive science,* Vol. 1, 2nd ed. *An invitation to cognitive science* (pp. 135–182). Cambridge, MA: MIT Press.

Pinker, S., & Prince, A. (1988). On language and connectionism: Analysis of a parallel distributed processing model of language acquisition. *Cognition, 28,* 73–193.

Pinker, S., & Prince, A. (1991). *Regular and irregular morphology and the psychological status of rules of grammar.* Proceedings of the 17th annual meeting of the Berkeley Linguistics Society, Berkeley.

Pisoni, D. B., Nusbaum, H. C., Luce, P. A., & Slowiaczek, L. M. (1985). Speech perception, word recognition and the structure of the lexicon. *Speech Communication, 4,* 75–95.

Poeppel, D. (1996). A critical review of PET studies of phonological processing. *Brain and Language.*

Poizner, H., Klima, E. S., & Bellugi, U. (1987). *What the hands reveal about the brain.* Cambridge, MA: MIT Press/Bradford Books.

Pollack, G., & Pickett, J. M. (1964). The intelligibility of excerpts from conversation. *Language and Speech, 6,* 165–171.

Posner, M. I., Peterson, S. E., Fox, P. T., & Raichle, M. E. (1988). Localization of cognitive operations in the human brain. *Science, 240,* 1627–1631.

Posner, M. I., & Raichle, M. E. (1994). *Images of mind.* New York: Scientific American Library/Scientific American Books.

Premack, D. (1971). Language in chimpanzees? *Science, 172,* 808–822.

Premack, D. (1979). *Trivial language in a nontrivial mind.* Paper presented at the annual Western Psychological Association meeting, San Diego, CA.

Premack, D. (1983). The codes of men and beasts. *Behavioral and Brain Sciences, 6,* 125–168.

Prinzmetal, W., Treiman, R., & Rho, S. H. (1986). How to see a reading unit. *Journal of Memory and Language, 25,* 461–475.

Pulleyblank, E. G. (1989). The meaning of duality of patterning and its importance in language evolution. In J. Wind, E. G. Pulleyblank, E. de Grolier, & B. H. Bichakjian (Eds.), *Studies in language origins,* Vol. I (pp. 53–65). Amsterdam: John Benjamin.

Quine, W. V. O. (1960). *Word and object.* Cambridge, MA: MIT Press.

Rabiner, L., & Juang, B. H. (1993). *Fundamentals of speech recognition.* Englewood Cliffs, NJ: Prentice-Hall.

Radvansky, G. A., Zacks, R. T., & Hasher, L. (1996). Fact retrieval in younger and older adults: The role of mental models. *Psychology & Aging, 11,* 258–271.

Rapp, B. C. (1992). The nature of sublexical orthographic organization: The bigram trough hypothesis examined. *Journal of Memory and Language, 31,* 33–53.

Rayner, K., Carlson, M., & Frazier, L. (1983). The interaction of syntax and semantics during sentence processing: Eye movements in the analysis of semantically biased sentences. *Journal of Verbal Learning and Verbal Behavior, 22,* 358–374.

Rayner, K., Pollatsek, A., & Bilsky, A. B. (1995). Can a temporal processing deficit account for dyslexia? *Psychonomic Bulletin and Review, 2,* 501–507.

Redelmeier, D. A., & Tversky, A. (1992). On the framing of multiple prospects. *Psychological Science, 3,* 191–193.

Reder, L. M. (1985). Techniques available to author, teacher, and reader to improve retention of the main ideas of a chapter. In S. F. Chipman, J. W. Segal, & J. R. Glaser (Eds.), *Thinking and learning skills. Vol. 2, Research and open questions* (pp. 37–63). Hillsdale, NJ: Lawrence Erlbaum Associates.

Reder, L. M., & Ross, B. H. (1983). Integrated knowledge in different tasks: The role of retrieval strategy on fan effects. *Journal of Experimental Psychology: Learning, Memory, and Cognition, 9,* 55–72.

Rehak, A., Kaplan, J. A., & Gardner, H. (1992). Sensitivity to conversational deviance in right-hemisphere-damaged patients. *Brain and Language, 42,* 203–217.

Reich, P. A. (1976). The early acquisition of word meaning. *Journal of Child Language, 3,* 117–173.

Reicher, G. M. (1969). Perceptual recognition as a function of meaningfulness of stimulus material. *Journal of Experimental Psychology, 81,* 275–280.

Reinhart, T. (1980). Conditions of coherence. *Poetics Today, 1,* 161–180.

Remez, R. E. (1994). A guide to research on the perception of speech. In M. A. Gernsbacher (Ed.), *Handbook of psycholinguistics* (pp. 145–172). San Diego: Academic Press.

Repp, B. (1984). Categorical perception: Issues, methods, findings. In N. J. Lass (Ed.), *Speech and language: Advances in basic research and practice,* Vol. 10 (pp. 243–335). San Diego: Academic Press.

Reyna, V. F. (1996). Meaning, memory, and the interpretation of metaphors. In J. S. Mio & A. L. Katz (Eds.), *Metaphor: Implications and applications* (pp. 39–57). Mahwah, NJ: Lawrence Erlbaum Associates.

Reynolds, A. (1990). The cognitive consequences of bilingualism. In A. G. Reynolds (Ed.), *Bilingualism, multiculturalism, and second language learning: The McGill conference in honor of Wallace E. Lambert.* Hillsdale, NJ: Lawrence Erlbaum Associates.

Rice, M. L., Wexler, K., & Cleave, P. L. (1995). Specific language impairment as a period of extended optional infinitive. *Journal of Speech and Hearing Research, 38,* 850–863.

Richardson-Klavehn, A., & Bjork, R. A. (1988). Measures of memory. *Annual Review of Psychology, 39,* 475–543.

Ridgeway, C. L., & Smith-Lovin, L. (1996). Gender and social interaction. *Social Psychology Quarterly, 59,* 173–175.

Riesen, A. H., & Aarons, L. (1959). Visual movement and intensity discrimination in cats after early deprivation of pattern-vision. *Journal of Comparative and Physiological Psychology, 52,* 142–149.

Roediger, H. L., III, & Craik, F. I. M. (Eds.). (1989). *Varieties of memory and consciousness: Essays in honor of Endel Tulving.* Hillsdale, NJ: Lawrence Erlbaum Associates.

Roger, D., & Nesshoever, W. (1987). Individual differences in dyadic conversation strategies: A further study. *British Journal of Social Psychology, 26,* 247–255.

Romaine, S. (1996). Bilingualism. In W. C. Ritchie & T. K. Bhatia (Eds.), *Handbook of second language acquisition* (pp. 571–604). San Diego: Academic Press.

Rondal, J. A. (1988). Language development in Down's syndrome: A life-span perspective. *International Journal of Behavioral Development, 11,* 21–36.

Rondal, J. A. (1995). *Exceptional language development in Down's syndrome: Implications for the cognition-language relationship.* New York: Cambridge University Press.

Rosch, E., & Mervis, C. B. (1975). Family resemblances: Studies in the internal structure of categories. *Cognitive Psychology, 7,* 573–605.

Rosch, E., Mervis, C. B., Gray, W. D., Johnson, D. M., & Boyes-Braem, P. (1976). Basic objects in natural categories. *Cognitive Psychology, 8,* 382–439.

Rose, M. (1984). *Writer's block: The cognitive dimension.* Carbondale: Southern Illinois University Press.

Rudnicky, A. J., Hauptmann, A. G., & Lee, K. F. (1994). Survey of current speech technology. *Communications of the ACM, 37,* 52–56.

Rumelhart, D. E., & McClelland, J. L. (1986). On learning the past tenses of English verbs. In J. L. McClelland & D. E. Rumelhart (Eds.), *Parallel distributed processing: Explorations in the microstructure of cognition. Vol. 2, Psychological and biological models* (pp. 216–271). Cambridge, MA: Bradford Books/MIT Press.

Saffran, J. R., Aslin, R. N., & Newport, E. L. (1996). Statistical learning by 8-month-old infants. *Science, 274,* 1926–1928.

Salame, P., & Baddeley, A. D. (1982). Disruption of short-term memory by an attended speech: Implications for the structure of working memory. *Journal of Verbal Learning and Verbal Behavior, 21,* 150–164.

Salthouse, T. A. (1994). The aging of working memory. *Neuropsychology, 8,* 535–543.

Samuel, A. G. (1981). Phonemic restoration: Insights from a new methodology. *Journal of Experimental Psychology: General, 110,* 474–494.

Sanford, A. J., & Garrod, S. C. (1981). *Understanding written language.* Chichester, England: Wiley.

Savage-Rumbaugh, E. S., McDonald, K., Sevcik, R. A., Hopkins, W. D., & Rubert, E. (1986). Spontaneous symbol acquisition and communicative use by pygmy chimpanzees (*Pan paniscus*). *Journal of Experimental Psychology: General, 115,* 211–235.

Savage-Rumbaugh, E. S., Murphy, J., Sevcik, R. A., Brakke, K. E., Williams, S. L., & Rumbaugh, D. M. (1993). Language comprehension in ape and child. *Monographs of the Society for Research in Child Development, 58* (3–4, Serial No. 233).

Savin, H. B. (1963). Word-frequency effect and errors in the perception of speech. *Journal of the Acoustical Society of America, 35,* 200–206.

Schacter, J. (1996). Maturation and the issue of universal grammar in second language acquisition. In W. C. Ritchie & T. K. Bhatia (Eds.), *Handbook of second language acquisition* (pp. 159–193). San Diego: Academic Press.

Schank, R. G., & Abelson, R. P. (1977). *Scripts, plans, goals, and understanding.* Hillsdale, NJ: Lawrence Erlbaum Associates.

Schegloff, E. A. (1980). Preliminaries to preliminaries: "Can I ask you a question?" *Sociological Inquiry, 50,* 104–152.

Schegloff, E. A., & Sacks, H. (1973). Opening up closings. *Semiotica, 8*, 289–327.

Schmalhofer, F., & Glavanov, D. (1986). Three components of understanding a programmer's manual: Verbatim, propositional, and situational representations. *Journal of Memory and Language, 25*, 279–294.

Schneider, W. (1993). Varieties of working memory as seen in biology and in connectionist/control architectures. *Memory and Cognition, 21*, 184–192.

Schneider, W., & Shiffrin, R. M. (1977). Controlled and automatic human information processing: I. Detection, search, and attention. *Psychological Review, 84*, 1–66.

Schooler, J. W., Ohlsson, S., & Brooks, K. (1993). Thoughts beyond words: When language overshadows insight. *Journal of Experimental Psychology: General, 122*, 166–183.

Schriefers, H. (1992). Lexical access in the production of noun phrases. *Cognition, 45*, 33–54.

Schriefers, H., Meyer, L. S., & Levelt, W. J. (1990). Exploring the time course of lexical access in language production: Picture-word interference studies. *Journal of Memory and Language, 29*, 86–102.

Searle, J. R. (1975). Indirect speech acts. In P. Cole & J. L. Morgan (Eds.), *Syntax and semantics. Vol. 3, Speech acts* (pp. 59–82). New York: Seminar Press.

Searle, J. R. (1980). Minds, brains, and programs. *Behavioral and Brain Sciences, 3*, 417–424.

Segui, J., & Grainger, J. (1990). Priming word recognition with orthographic neighbors: Effects of relative prime-target frequency. *Journal of Experimental Psychology: Human Perception and Performance, 16*, 65–74.

Seidenberg, M. S. (1987). Sublexical structures in visual word recognition: Access units or orthographic redundancy? In M. Coltheart (Ed.), *Attention and performance XII: The psychology of reading* (pp. 245–264). Hove, England: Lawrence Erlbaum Associates.

Seidenberg, M. S. (1990). Lexical Access: Another theoretical soupstone? In D. A. Balota, G. B. F. d'Arcais, & K. Rayner (Eds.), *Comprehension processes in reading* (pp. 33–71). Hillsdale, NJ: Lawrence Erlbaum Associates.

Seidenberg, M. S. (1995). Visual word recognition: An overview. In J. L. Miller & P. D. Eimas (Eds.), *Speech, language, and communication* (pp. 137–179). San Diego: Academic Press.

Seidenberg, M. S., & Manis, F. R. (1994, November). On the bases of the "surface" and "phonological" subtypes of developmental dyslexia. Paper presented at the meeting of the Psychonomic Society, St. Louis.

Seidenberg, M. S., & McClelland, J. L. (1989). A distributed developmental model of word recognition and naming. *Psychological Review, 96*, 523–568.

Seidenberg, M. S., & Petitto, L. A. (1979). Signing behavior in apes: A critical review. *Cognition, 1*, 177–215.

Seidenberg, M. S., Tanenhaus, M. K., Leiman, J. M., & Bienkowski, M. (1982). Automatic access of the meanings of ambiguous words in context: Some limitations of knowledge-based processing. *Cognitive Psychology, 14*, 489–537.

Seidenberg, M. S., Waters, G. S., Barnes, M. A., & Tanenhaus, M. (1984). When does irregular spelling or pronunciation influence word recognition? *Journal of Verbal Learning and Verbal Behavior, 23*, 383–404.

Selfridge, O. G. (1959). Pandemonium: A paradigm for learning. In *Proceedings of symposium on the mechanization of thought processes* (pp. 511–526). London: H.M. Stationery Office.

Semin, G. R., & Fiedler, K. (1992). The inferential properties of interpersonal verbs. In G. R. Semin & K. Fiedler (Eds.), *Language, interaction and social cognition*. London: Sage.

Semmes, J. (1968). Hemispheric specialization. *Neuropsychologia, 6*, 11–26.

Sevald, C. A., & Dell, G. S. (1994). The sequential cuing effect in speech production. *Cognition, 53*, 91–127.

Seyfarth, R. M., Cheney, D. L., & Marler, P. (1980). Monkey responses to three different alarm calls: Evidence of predator classification and semantic communication. *Science, 210*, 801–803.

Shallice, T. (1988). *From neuropsychology to mental structure*. New York: Cambridge University Press.

Shallice, T. (1991). From neuropsychology to mental structure (Precis). *Behavioral and Brain Sciences, 14*, 429–469.

Shankweiler, D., & Crain, S. (1986). Language mechanisms and reading disorder: A modular approach. *Cognition, 24*, 139–168.

Shannon, C. E., & Weaver, W. (1949). *The mathematical theory of communication*. Urbana: University of Illinois Press.

Shattuck-Hufnagel, S. (1979). Speech errors as evidence for a serial-order mechanism in sentence production. In W. E. Cooper & E. C. T. Walker (Eds.), *Sentence processing: Psycholinguistic studies presented to Merrill Garrett* (pp. 295–324). Hillsdale, NJ: Lawrence Erlbaum Associates.

Shepard, R. N., & Metzler, J. (1971). Mental rotation of three-dimensional objects. *Science, 171*, 701–703.

Shiffrin, R. M. (1993). Short-term memory: A brief commentary. *Memory and Cognition, 21*, 193–197.

Shiffrin, R. M., & Atkinson, R. C. (1969). Storage and retrieval processes in long-term memory. *Psychological Review, 76*, 179–193.

Shinjo, M., & Myers, J. L. (1987). The role of context in metaphor comprehension. *Journal of Memory and Language, 26*, 226–241.

Shulman, H. G. (1972). Semantic confusion errors in short-term memory. *Journal of Verbal Learning and Verbal Behavior, 11*, 221–227.

Simpson, G. B. (1981). Meaning dominance and semantic context in the processing of lexical ambiguity. *Journal of Verbal Learning and Verbal Behavior, 20*, 120–136.

Simpson, G. B. (1994). Context and the processing of ambiguous words. In M. A. Gernsbacher (Ed.), *Handbook of psycholinguistics* (pp. 359–374). San Diego: Academic Press.

Simpson, G. B., & Kreuger, M. A. (1991). Selective access of homograph meanings in sentence context. *Journal of Memory and Language, 30*, 627–643.

Sinclair-DeZwart, H. (1973). Language acquisition and cognitive development. In T. Moore (Ed.), *Cognitive development and the acquisition of language*. New York: Academic Press.

Singer, M. (1979). Processes of inference during sentence encoding. *Memory and Cognition, 7*, 192–200.

Singer, M., Halldorson, M., Lear, J. C., & Andrusiak, P. (1992). Validation of causal bridging inferences in discourse understanding. *Journal of Memory and Language, 31*, 507–524.

Skinner, B. F. (1938). *The behavior of organisms*. New York: Appleton-Century-Crofts.

Skinner, B. F. (1957). *Verbal behavior*. New York: Appleton-Century-Crofts.

Slobin, D. (1985). Crosslinguistic evidence for the language-making capacity. In D. Slobin (Ed.), *The crosslinguistic study of language acquisition. Vol. 2, Theoretical Issues* (pp. 1157–1249). Hillsdale, NJ: Lawrence Erlbaum Associates.

Smith, E. E., & Medin, D. L. (1981). *Categories and concepts.* Cambridge, MA: Harvard University Press.

Smith, E. E., Shoben, E. J., & Rips, L. J. (1974). Structure and process in semantic memory: A featural model for semantic decisions. *Psychological Review, 81*, 214–241.

Smith, S. M., Brown, H. O., Toman, J. E. P., & Goodman, L. S. (1947). The lack of cerebral effects of d-Tubercurarine. *Anesthesiology, 8*, 1–14.

Smith, S. M., Glenberg, A., & Bjork, R. L. (1978). Environmental context and human memory. *Memory and Cognition, 6*, 342–353.

Snow, C. E., & Hoefnagel-Hohle, M. (1978). The critical period for language acquisition: Evidence from second language learning. *Child Development, 49*, 1114–1128.

Snowling, M., Hulme, C., & Goulandris, N. (1994). Word recognition in developmental dyslexia: A connectionist interpretation. *Quarterly Journal of Experimental Psychology: Human Experimental Psychology, 47A*, 895–916.

Soja, N. N., Carey, S., & Spelke, E. S. (1991). Ontological categories guide young children's inductions of word meaning: Object terms and substance terms. *Cognition, 38*, 179–211.

Sommers, M. S., Nygaard, L. C., & Pisoni, D. B. (1992). The effects of speaking rate and amplitude variability on perceptual identification. *Journal of the Acoustical Society of America, 91*, 2340.

Sommers, M. S., Nygaard, L. C., & Pisoni, D. B. (1994). Stimulus variability and spoken word recognition: I. Effects of variability in speaking rate and overall amplitude. *Journal of the Acoustical Society of America, 96*, 1314–1324.

Sperling, G. (1960). The information available in brief visual presentations. *Psychological Monographs, 74* (Whole No. 498).

Sperry, R. W. (1968). Hemisphere deconnection and unity in conscious awareness. *American Psychologist, 23*, 723–733.

Sperry, R. W., & Gazzaniga, M. S. (1975). Dichotic testing of partial and complete split-brain subjects. *Neuropsychologia, 13*, 341–346.

Spoehr, K. T., & Smith, E. E. (1973). The role of syllables in perceptual processing. *Cognitive Psychology, 5*, 71–89.

Sproat, R. (1992). *Morphology and computation.* Cambridge, MA: MIT Press.

Stanners, R. F., Neiser, J. J., Hernon, W. P., & Hall, R. (1979). Memory representation for morphologically related words. *Journal of Verbal Learning and Verbal Behavior, 18*, 399–412.

Stanovich, K. E. (1986). Matthew effects in reading: Some consequences of individual differences in the acquisition of literacy. *Reading Research Quarterly, 21*, 360–406.

Stanovich, K. E. (1988). Explaining the difference beween the dyslexic and the garden-variety poor reader: The phonological-core variable-difference model. *Journal of Learning Disabilities, 21*, 590–604.

Stanovich, K. E., & West, R. F. (1979). Mechanisms of sentence context effects in reading: Automatic activation and conscious attention. *Memory and Cognition, 7*, 77–85.

Stanovich, K. E., & West, R. F. (1983). On priming by a sentence context. *Journal of Experimental Psychology: General, 112*, 1–36.

Stefflre, V., Castillo Vales, V., & Morley, L. (1966). Language and cognition in Yucatan: A cross-cultural replication. *Journal of Personality and Social Psychology, 4*, 112–115.

Stein, B. S., & Bransford, J. D. (1979). Constraints on effective elaboration: Effects of precision and subject generation. *Journal of Verbal Learning and Verbal Behavior, 16*, 769–777.

Stein, N. L., & Glenn, C. G. (1979). An analysis of story comprehension in elementary school children. In R. O. Freedle (Ed.), *New directions in discourse processing. Vol. 2, Advances in discourse processes* (pp. 53–120). Norwood, NJ: Ablex.

Stemberger, J. P. (1985). Bound morpheme loss errors in normal and agrammatic speech: One mechanism or two? *Brain and Language, 25*, 246–256.

Sternberg, R. J., & Ben-Zeev, T. (1996). *The nature of mathematical thinking.* Mahwah, NJ: Lawrence Erlbaum Associates.

Stevenson, R. J., & Vitkovitch, M. (1986). The comprehension of anaphoric relations. *Language and Speech, 29*, 335–360.

Sticht, T. G., & James, J. H. (1984). Listening and reading. In P. D. Pearson, R. Barr, M. L. Kamil, & P. Mosenthal (Eds.), *Handbook of reading research* (pp. 293–318). New York: Longman.

Stokoe, W. C., Casterline, D. C., & Croneberg, C. G. (1976). *A dictionary of American Sign Language on linguistic principles.* Silver Spring, MD: Linstok Press.

Strange, W. (1989). Evolving theories of vowel perception. *Journal of the Acoustical Society of America, 85*, 2081–2087.

Streeter, L. A. (1976). Language perception of 2-month-old infants shows effects of both innate mechanisms and experience. *Nature, 259*, 39–41.

Stringer, C. B., & Andrews, P. (1988). Genetic and fossil evidence for the origin of modern humans. *Science, 239*, 1263–1268.

Stromswold, K., Caplan, D., Alpert, N., & Rauch, S. (1996). Localization of syntactic comprehension by positron emission tomography. *Brain and Language, 52*, 452–473.

Studdert-Kennedy, M. (1976). Speech perception. In N. J. Lass (Ed.), *Contemporary issues in experimental phonetics* (pp. 243–293). New York: Academic Press.

Studdert-Kennedy, M. (1986). Sources of variability in early speech development. In J. S. Perkell & D. H. Klatt (Eds.), *Invariance and variability in speech processes.* Hillsdale, NJ: Lawrence Erlbaum Associates.

Suh, S., & Trabasso, T. (1993). Inferences during reading: Converging evidence from discourse analysis, talk-aloud protocols, and recognition priming. *Journal of Memory and Language, 32*, 279–300.

Svartvik, J., & Quirk, R. (Eds.). (1980). *A corpus of English conversation.* Lund: CWK Gleerup.

Sweetser, E. (1991). *From etymology to pragmatics: Metaphorical and cultural aspects of semantic structure.* Cambridge: Cambridge University Press.

Swinney, D. A. (1979). Lexical access during sentence comprehension: (Re)consideration of context effects. *Journal of Verbal Learning and Verbal Behavior, 18*, 645–659.

Tabossi, P. (1988). Accessing lexical ambiguity in different types of sentential contexts. *Journal of Memory and Language, 27*, 324–340.

Tabossi, P., Spivey-Knowlton, M., McRae, K., & Tanenhaus, M. K. (1994). Semantic effects on syntactic ambiguity resolution: Evidence for a constraint-based resolution process. In C. Umilta & M. Moscovitch (Eds.), *Attention and performance XV* (pp. 596–615). Hillsdale, NJ: Lawrence Erlbaum Associates.

Tabossi, P., & Zardon, F. (1993). Processing ambiguous words in context. *Journal of Memory and Language, 32*, 359–372.

Taeschner, T. (1983). *The sun is feminine: A study on language acquisition in bilingual children*. Berlin/New York: Springer-Verlag.

Taft, M., & Forster, K. I. (1975). Lexical storage and retrieval of prefixed words. *Journal of Verbal Learning and Verbal Behavior, 14,* 638–647.

Taft, M., & Forster, K. I. (1976). Lexical storage and retrieval of polymorphemic and polysyllabic words. *Journal of Verbal Learning and Verbal Behavior, 15,* 607–620.

Tager-Flusberg, H. (1994). *Constraints on language acquisition: Studies of atypical children*. Hillsdale, NJ: Lawrence Erlbaum Associates.

Tanenhaus, M. K. (1988). Psycholinguistics: An overview. In F. J. Newmeyer (Ed.), *Linguistics: The Cambridge Survey. Vol. III, Language: Psychological and biological aspects* (pp. 1–37). Cambridge, MA: Cambridge University Press.

Tanenhaus, M. K., Spivey-Knowlton, M., Eberhard, K., & Sedivy, J. (1995). The interaction of visual and verbal information in spoken language comprehension. *Science, 268,* 1632–1634.

Tannen, D. (1994). *Talking from 9 to 5: How women's and men's conversational styles affect who gets heard, who gets credit, and what gets done at work*. New York: William Morrow & Co..

Taraban, R., & McClelland, J. L. (1988). Constituent attachment and thematic role assignment in sentence processing: Influences of content-based expectations. *Journal of Memory and Language, 27,* 597–632.

Taraban, R., & McClelland, J. L. (1990). Parsing and comprehension: A multiple-constraint view. In D. A. Balota, G.B. Flores d'Arcais, & K. Rayner (Eds.), *Comprehension processes in reading* (pp. 231–263). Hillsdale, NJ: Lawrence Erlbaum Associates.

Tartter, V. C. (1986). *Language processes*. New York: Holt, Rinehart & Winston.

Taylor, I. (1981). Writing systems and reading. In G. E. MacKinnon & T. G. Waller (Eds.), *Reading research: Advances in theory and practice,* Vol. 2. New York: Academic Press.

Terrace, H. S. (1979). Is problem solving language? *Journal of Experimental Analysis of Behavior, 31,* 161–175.

Terrace, H. S. (1983). Apes who "talk" or projections of language by their teachers? In J. DeLuce & H. T. Valker (Eds.), *Language in primates: Perspectives and implications* (pp. 19–42). New York: Springer-Verlag.

Terrace, H. S., Petitto, L. A., Sanders, D. J., & Bever, T. G. (1980). On the grammatical capacities of apes. In K. Nelson (Ed.), *Children's language,* Vol. 2. New York: Gardner Press.

Thal, D. J., Bates, E., Zappia, M.J., & Oroz, M. (1996). Ties between lexical and grammatical development: Evidence from early-talkers. *Journal of Child Language, 23,* 349–368.

Thomson, D. M., & Tulving, E. (1970). Associative encoding and retrieval: Weak and strong cues. *Journal of Experimental Psychology, 86,* 255–262.

Thomson, J. R., & Chapman, R. S. (1977). "Who is daddy" revisited: The status of two-year-olds' over-extended words in use and comprehension. *Journal of Child Language, 4,* 359–375.

Thorndike, E. (1917). Reading as reasoning: A study of mistakes in paragraph reading. *Journal of Educational Psychology, 8,* 323–332.

Thorndike, E. L., & Lorge, I. (1944). *The teacher's word book of 30,000 words*. New York: Teachers College, Columbia University.

Thorndyke, P. W. (1977). Cognitive structures in comprehension and memory of narrative discourse. *Cognitive Psychology, 9,* 77–110.

Tinker, M. A. (1939). Reliability and validity of eye-movement measures of reading. *Journal of Experimental Psychology, 19,* 732–746.

Tourangeau, R., & Rips, L. (1991). Interpreting and evaluating metaphors. *Journal of Memory and Language, 30,* 452–472.

Tourangeau, R., & Sternberg, R. J. (1982). Understanding and appreciating metaphors. *Cognition, 11,* 203–244.

Trabasso, T., & Suh, S. (1993). Understanding text: Achieving explanatory coherence through on-line inferences and mental operations in working memory. *Discourse Processes, 16,* 3–34.

Trabasso, T., & van den Broek, P. (1985). Causal thinking and the representation of narrative events. *Journal of Memory and Language, 24,* 612–630.

Trueswell, J. C., Tanenhaus, M., & Garnsey, S. (1994). Semantic influences on parsing: Use of thematic role information on syntactic ambiguity resolution. *Journal of Memory and Language, 33,* 285–318.

Tuller, B., Case, P., Mingzhou, D., & Kelso, J. A. S. (1994). The nonlinear dynamics of speech categorization. *Journal of Experimental Psychology: Human Perception and Performance, 20,* 3–16.

Tulving, E. (1983). *Elements of episodic memory*. New York: Oxford University Press.

Tulving, E. (1985). How many memory systems are there? *American Psychologist, 40,* 385–398.

Tulving, E., & Thomson, D. M. (1971). Retrieval processes in recognition memory: Effects of associative context. *Journal of Experimental Psychology, 87,* 116–124.

Tunmer, W. E., Herriman, M. L., & Nesdale, A. R. (1988). Metalinguistic abilities and beginning reading. *Reading Research Quarterly, 23,* 134–158.

Tversky, A., & Kahneman, D. (1981). The framing of decisions and the psychology of choice. *Science, 211,* 453–458.

Tyler, L. K., & Wessels, J. (1983). Quantifying contextual contributions toward recognition processes. *Perception and Psychophysics, 34,* 409–420.

Ullman, M., Corkin, S., Pinker, S., Coppola, M., Locascio, J., & Growdon, J. H. (1993). *Neural modularity in language: Evidence from Alzheimer's and Parkinson's disease*. Paper presented at the 23rd annual meeting of the Society for Neuroscience, Washington, D.C.

Umiker-Sebeok, J., & Sebeok, T. A. (1981). Clever Hans and Smart Simians: The self-fulfilling prophecy and kindred methodological pitfalls. *Anthropos, 76,* 89–165.

Valian, V. (1990). Null subjects: A problem for parameter-setting models of language acquisition. *Cognition, 35,* 105–122.

Valian, V. (1991). Syntactic subjects in the early speech of American and Italian children. *Cognition, 40,* 21–81.

van den Broek, P. (1994). Comprehension and memory of narrative texts: Inferences and coherence. In M. A. Gernsbacher (Ed.), *Handbook of psycholinguistics* (pp. 539–588). San Diego: Academic Press.

Van der Lely, H. K. J. (1994). Canonical linking rules: Forward versus reverse linking in normally developing and specifically language-impaired children. *Cognition, 51,* 29–72.

van Dijk, T. A., & Kintsch, W. (1983). *Strategies of discourse comprehension*. New York: Academic Press.

Van Orden, G. C. (1987). A ROWS is a ROSE: Spelling, sound, and reading. *Memory and Cognition, 15*, 181–198.

Van Orden, G. C., Pennington, B. F., & Stone, G. O. (1990). Word identification in reading and the promise of subsymbolic psycholinguistics. *Psychological Review, 97*, 1–35.

Vellutino, F. R. (1979). The validity of perceptual deficit explanations of reading disability: A reply to Fletcher and Satz. *Journal of Reading Disabilities, 12*, 160–167.

Visto, J. C., Cranford, J. L., & Scudder, R. (1996). Dynamic temporal processing of nonspeech acoustic information by children with specific language impairment. *Journal of Speech and Hearing Research, 39*, 510–517.

von Frisch, K. (1974). *Die Entschlussung der Bienensprache*. Nobel Award Lecture.

Vygotsky, L. (1934). *Thought and language*. Cambridge, MA: The MIT Press. (Revised translation, 1986).

Wallman, J. (1992). *Aping language*. Cambridge, MA: Cambridge University Press.

Wang, P. P., & Bellugi, U. (1994). Evidence from two genetic syndromes for a dissociation between verbal and visual-spatial short-term memory. *Journal of Clinical and Experimental Neuropsychology, 16*, 317–322.

Warren, R. M. (1970). Perceptual restoration of missing speech sounds. *Science, 167*, 392–395.

Warren, R. M., & Warren, R. P. (1970). Auditory illusions and confusions. *Scientific American, 223*, 30–36.

Waters, G. S., & Caplan, D. (1996a). The capacity theory of sentence comprehension: Critique of Just and Carpenter (1992). *Psychological Review, 103*, 761–772.

Waters, G. S., & Caplan, D. (1996b). The measurement of verbal working memory capacity and its relation to reading comprehension. *Quarterly Journal of Experimental Psychology: Human Experimental Psychology, 49A*, 51–79.

Waters, G., Caplan, D., & Hildebrandt, N. (1991). On the structure of verbal short-term memory and its functional role in sentence comprehension: Evidence from neuropsychology. *Cognitive Neuropsychology, 8*, 81–126.

Watson, J. B. (1925). *Behaviorism*. New York: W. W. Norton.

Weinberg, A. (1987). Language processing and linguistic explanation. In M. Coltheart (Ed.), *Attention and performance 12: The psychology of reading*. Hove, England: Lawrence Erlbaum Associates.

Weingardt, K. R., Loftus, E. F., & Lindsay, D. S. (1995). Misinformation revisited: New evidence on the suggestibility of memory. *Memory and Cognition, 23*, 72–82.

Werker, J. (1991). The ontogeny of speech perception. In I. G. Mattingly & M. Studdert-Kennedy (Eds.), *Modularity and the motor theory of speech perception* (pp. 91–109). Hillsdale, NJ: Lawrence Erlbaum Associates.

Werker, J. F. (1995). Exploring developmental changes in cross-language speech perception. In L. R. Gleitman & M. Liberman (Eds.), *Language: An invitation to cognitive science. Vol. 1 (2nd ed.), An invitation to cognitive science* (pp. 87–106). Cambridge, MA: MIT Press.

Werker, J. F., & Lalonde, C. E. (1988). Cross-language speech perception: Initial capabilities and developmental change. *Developmental Psychology, 24*, 672–683.

Werker, J. F., Lloyd, V. L., Pegg, J. E., & Polka, L. (1996). Putting the baby in the bootstraps: Toward a more complete understanding of the role of the input in infant speech processing. In J. L. Morgan & Katherine Demuth (Eds.), *Signal to syntax: Bootstrapping from speech to grammar in early acquisition* (pp. 427–447). Mahwah, NJ: Lawrence Erlbaum Associates.

Werker, J. F., Pegg, J. E., & McLeod, P. J. (1994). A cross-language investigation of infant preference for infant-directed communication. *Infant Behavior and Development, 17*, 323–333.

Werker, J. F., & Tees, R. C. (1984). Cross-language speech perception: Evidence for perceptual organization during the first year of life. *Infant Behavior and Development, 7*, 49–63.

Wernicke, C. (1874). Der Aphasische Symptomen Komplex. Breslau: Cohn & Weigert. Reprinted in G. Eggert (Ed.), *Wernicke's works on aphasia: A source book and review*, Vol. 1. The Hague: Mouton, 1977.

West, C., & Garcia, A. (1988). Conversational shift work: A study of topical transitions between women and men. *Social Problems, 35*, 551–575.

Wheeler, D. D. (1970). Processes in word recognition. *Cognitive Psychology, 1*, 59–85.

Whinnom, K. (1965). The origin of European-based pidgins and creoles. *Orbis, 14*, 509–527.

White, L. (1989). *Universal grammar and second language acquisition*. Amsterdam: John Benjamins.

White, L. (1990). Second language acquisition and universal grammar. *Studies in Second Language Acquisition, 11*, 385–396.

Whitney, P. (1986). Processing category terms in context: Instantiations as inferences. *Memory & Cognition, 14*, 39–48.

Whitney, P., Budd, D., Bramucci, R. S., & Crane, R. S. (1995). On babies, bath water, and schemata: A reconsideration of top-down processes in comprehension. *Discourse Processes, 20*, 135–166.

Whitney, P., & Kellas, G. (1984). Processing category items in context: Instantiation and the structure of semantic categories. *Journal of Experimental Psychology: Learning, Memory, and Cognition, 10*, 95–103.

Whitney, P., Ritchie, B. G., & Crane, R. S. (1992). The effect of foregrounding on readers' use of predictive inferences. *Memory & Cognition, 20*, 424–432.

Whitney, W. D. (1910). *Language and the study of language: Twelve lectures on the principles of linguistic science*. New York: Scribner's.

Whorf, B. L. (1956). *Language, thought, and reality: Selected writings of Benjamin Lee Whorf*. New York: Wiley.

Wierzbicka, A. (1985). A semantic metalanguage for a cross-cultural comparison of speech acts and speech genres. *Language in Society, 14*, 491–513.

Williams-Whitney, D., Mio, J. S., & Whitney, P. (1992). Metaphor production in creative writing. *Journal of Psycholinguistic Research, 21*, 497–509.

Winner, E., & Gardner, H. (1977). The comprehension of metaphor in brain-damaged patients. *Brain, 100*, 717–729.

Wise, B. W., & Olson, R. K. (1992). How poor readers and spellers use interactive speech in a computerized spelling program. *Reading and Writing, 4*, 145–163.

Wise, R. J., Chollet, F., Hudar, U., Friston, K., Hoffner, E., & Frackowiak, R. (1991). Distribution of cortical neural networks involved in word comprehension and word retrieval. *Brain, 114*, 1803–1817.

World Bank (1988). Education in subsaharan Africa. Washington, DC: World Bank.

Wundt, W. (1900). *Die Sprache* (2 vols.). Leipzig: Kröner.

Wundt, W. M. (1907). *Outlines of psychology.* (C. H. Judd, Trans.). Leipzig: W. Engelmann/London: Williams & Norgate/New York: G. E. Stechert and A. Kroner.

Yan, Y., Fanty, M., & Cole, R. (1997). Speech recognition using neural networks with forward-backward probability generated targets. *Proceedings of the International Conference on Acoustics, Speech, and Signal Processing.*

Young, R. M. (1970). *Mind, brain and adaption in the nineteenth century: Cerebral localization and its biological context from Gall to Ferrier.* New York: Oxford University Press. (Reprinted in 1990.)

Yuill, N., & Oakhill, J. (1991). *Children's problems in text comprehension: An experimental investigation.* Cambridge: Cambridge University Press.

Yule, W., Rutter, M., Berger, M., & Thompson, J. (1974). Over- and under-achievement in reading: Distribution in the general population. *British Journal of Educational Psychology, 44,* 1–12.

Zaidel, E. (1990). Language functions in the two hemispheres following complete cerebral commissurotomy and hemispherectomy. In R. D. Nebes & S. Corkin (Eds.), *Handbook of neuropsychology,* Vol. 4 (pp. 115–150). Amsterdam: Elsevier Science Publishing.

Zaragoza, M. S., & Lane, S. M. (1994). Source misattributions and the suggestibility of eyewitness memory. *Journal of Experimental Psychology: Learning, Memory, and Cognition, 20,* 934–945.

Zatorre, R. J., Meyer, E., Gjedde, A., & Evans, A. C. (1996). PET studies of phonetic processes in speech perception: Review, replication, and re-analysis. *Cerebral Cortex, 6,* 21–30.

Zipf, G. K. (1935). *The psycho-biology of language: An introduction to dynamic philology.* Boston: Houghton Mifflin Co.

Zola, D. (1984). Redundancy and word perception during reading. *Perception and Psychophysics, 36,* 277–284.

CREDITS

Chapter 1: **p. 12:** Figure 1.3, © The Nobel Foundation 1974. **p. 16:** Activity 1.1, Courtesy Eric Mose/Scientific American. **p. 19:** Figure 1.4 from H. S. Terrace (1983). "Apes who can 'talk': Language or projections of language by their teachers?" in J. DeLuce & H. T. Wilder (eds.), *Language in primates: Perspectives and implications.* Reprinted by permission of Springer-Verlag New York, Inc.

Chapter 2: **p. 54:** Figure 2.8 from *The Linguistics Wars* by Randy Allen Harris. Copyright © 1993 by Randy Allen Harris. Used by permission of Oxford University Press. **p. 55:** Figure 2.9 from V. J. Cook, *Chomsky's universal grammar: An introduction.* Cambridge, MA: Blackwell. Reprinted by permission. **p. 64:** Figure 2.11 from Ray Jackendoff, *Languages of the Mind,* MIT Press. **p. 67:** Figure 2.13 from George Lakoff, *Women, fire, and dangerous things: What categories reveal about the mind,* University of Chicago Press.

Chapter 3: **p. 81:** Figure 3.1, Copyright © 1969 by the American Psychological Association. Reprinted with permission. **p. 86:** Figure 3.2, Copyright 1968. Canadian Psychological Association. Reprinted by permission. **p. 91:** Figure 3.6, Copyright © 1977 by the American Psychological Association. Adapted with permission. **p. 93:** Figure 3.7, Copyright © 1977 by the American Psychological Association. Adapted with permission. **p. 96:** Figure 3.8 from R. G. Schank & R. P. Abelson, *Scripts, plans, goals, and understanding,* Lawrence Erlbaum Associates. Reprinted by permission. **p. 105:** Figure 3.11 reprinted by permission of the publisher from *The Computer And The Mind* by P. N. Johnson-Laird. Cambridge, MA: Harvard University Press, Copyright © 1988 by the President and Fellows of Harvard College. **p. 106:** Figure 3.12 reprinted by permission of the publisher from *The Computer And The Mind* by P.N. Johnson-Laird. Cambridge, MA: Harvard University Press, Copyright © 1988 by the President and Fellows of Harvard College.

Chapter 4: **p. 132:** Figure 4.3, Copyright © 1993 by the American Psychological Association. Adapted with permission. **p. 134:** Figure 4.4, Copyright © 1993 by the American Psychological Association. Adapted with permission.

Chapter 5: **p. 144:** Figure 5.2 from J. M. Pickett, *The Sounds of Speech Communication: A Primer of Acoustic Phonetics & Speech Perception* (Baltimore: University Park Press, 1980), p. 35. Re-printed by permission of Allyn & Bacon. **p. 145:** Figure 5.3, © Vivien C. Tartter, *Language Processes,* 1986. **p. 145:** Figure 5.4 from J. M. Pickett, *The Sounds of Speech Communication: A Primer of Acoustic Phonetics & Speech Perception* (Baltimore: University Park Press, 1980), p. 116. Reprinted by permission of Allyn & Bacon. **p. 146:** Figure 5.5 from P. W. Jusczyk, et. al. (1981) "The Perceptual Classification of Speech." *Perception & Psychophysics, 30,* 13. Reprinted by permission of Psychonomic Society, Inc. **p. 147:** Figure 5.6 © Vivien C. Tartter, *Language Processes,* 1986. **p. 148:** Figure 5.7 from S. E. Lively, "Spoken Word Recognition." In Gensbacher (Ed.), *Handbook of Psycholinguisitcs,* (San Diego: Academic Press, 1994), p. 267. Reprinted by permission of Academic Press, Inc. **p. 150:** Figure 5.8 from M. Studdert-Kennedy (1976). Speech perception. In N. J. Lass (Ed.), *Contemporary issues in experimental phonetics* (pp. 243–293). New York: Academic Press. Reprinted by permission. **p. 154:** Figure 5.10 from A. M. Liberman (1970), "The grammars of speech and language." *Cognitive Psychology, 1.* Reprinted by permission of Academic Press. **p. 157:** Figure 5.11 from D. Massaro, Psychological aspects of speech perception: Implications for research and theory. In M. A. Gernsbacher (Ed.), Handbook of psycholinguistics (pp. 219–263). Reprinted by permission of Academic Press.

Chapter 6: **p. 174:** Figure 6.1 from J. Defrancis, *Visible Speech: The diverse oneness of writing systems.* (Honolulu: University of Hawaii, 1989), flyleaf page. Reprinted by permission of University of Hawaii Press. **p. 177:** Figure 6.2 from P. H. Lindsay & D. A. Norman, *Human Information Processing: An Introduction to Psychology.* (New York: Academic Press, 1972), p. 121. Reprinted by permission of Academic Press, Inc. **p. 180:** Figure 6.3 From M. A. Just & P. A. Carpenter, *The Psychology of Reading and Language Comprehension.* © 1987 by Allyn and Bacon. Reprinted by permission. **p. 190:** Figure 6.5, Copyright © 1980 by the American Psychological Association. Reprinted with permission. **p. 192:** Figure 6.6, Copyright © 1969 by the American Psychological Association. Reprinted with permission. **p. 194:** Figure 6.7 from K. I. Forster, "Levels of processing and the structure of the language processes." In W. E. Cooper & E. C. T. Walker (Eds.), *Sentence processing: Psycholinguistic studies presented to Merril Garret* (pp. 27–84). Hillsdale, NJ: Lawrence Erlbaum Associates. Reprinted by permission. **p. 196:** Figure 6.8 from M. S. Seidenberg, "Visual word recognition: An overview." In J. L. Miller & P. D. Eimas (Eds.), *Speech, language, and communication* (pp. 137–179). San Diego: Academic Press. Reprinted by permission.

p. 198: Figure 6.9 From M. A. Just & P. A. Carpenter, *The Psychology of Reading and Language Comprehension.* © 1987 by Allyn and Bacon. Reprinted by permission.

Chapter 7: p. 211: Table 7.1 from S. A. Duffy, R. K. Morris, & K. Rayner (1988). "Lexical ambiguity and fixation times in reading." *Journal of Memory and Language, 27,* 429–446. Reprinted by permission. **p. 217:** Figure 7.4 from R. Taraban & J. L. McClelland (1988). "Constituent attachment and thematic role assignment in sentence processing: Influences of content-based expectations." *Journal of Memory and Language, 27,* 597–632. Adapted with permission. **pp. 219, 220, 221:** Figures 7.5–7.8 from K. M. Eberhard, M. J. Spivey-Knowlton, J. C. Sedivy, & M. K. Tanenhaus (1995). "Eye movements as a window into real-time spoken language comprehension in natural contexts." *Journal of Psycholinguistic Research, 24,* 409-434. Reprinted by permission.

Chapter 8: p. 246: Table 8.2 from J. L. Myers & S. A. Duffy (1990). "Causal inferences and text memory." In A. C. Graesser & G. H. Bower (Eds.), *The psychology of learning and motivation,* Vol. 25 (pp. 159–174). Orlando, FL: Academic Press. Reprinted by permission. **p. 249:** Figure 8.2 From M. A. Just & P. A. Carpenter, *The Psychology of Reading and Language Comprehension.* © 1987 by Allyn and Bacon. Reprinted by permission. **p. 250:** Table 8.3 from T. Trabasso & S. Suh (1993). "Understanding text: Achieving explanatory coherence through on-line inferences and mental operations in working memory." *Discourse Processes, 16,* 3–34. Reprinted by permission. **p. 251:** Figure 8.3 from T. Trabasso & S. Suh (1993). "Understanding text: Achieving explanatory coherence through on-line inferences and mental operations in working memory." *Discourse Processes, 16,* 3–34. Reprinted by permission. **p. 254:** Table 8.5 from D. E. Kieras (1980). Initial mention as a signal to thematic content in technical passages. *Memory and Cognition, 8,* 345–353. Reprinted by permission. **p. 262:** Figure 8.7 from W. Kintsch, D. Welsch, F. Schmalhofer, & S. Zimny (1990). Sentence memory: A theoretical analysis. *Journal of Memory and Language, 29,* 133–159. Reprinted by permission.

Chapter 9: p. 280: Figure 9.3 Dell, G. S. (1995). Speaking and misspeaking. In L. R. Gleitman & M. Liberman (Eds.), *Language: An invitation to cognitive science, Vol. 1* (2nd edition). MIT Press. **p. 285:** Table 9.1 from J. Svartvik & R. Quirk (Eds.). (1980). *A corpus of English conversation.* Lund: CWK Gleerup. Reprinted by permission. **p. 290:** Table 9.2 from H. H. Clark (1994). Discourse in production. In M. A. Gernsbacher (Ed.), *Handbook of psycholinguistics* (pp. 985–1021). San Diego: Academic Press. Reprinted by permission. **p. 293:** Figure 9.4 from J. R. Hayes & L. S. Flowers (1980). Identifying the organization of writing processes. In L. W. Gregg & E. R. Steinberg (Eds.), *Cognitive processes in writing* (pp. 3–30). Hillsdale, NJ: Lawrence Erlbaum Associates. Reprinted by permission. **p. 294:** Figure 9.5 from Behavior Research Methods, Instruments, & Computers, 18, 118-128. Reprinted by permission of Psychonomic Society, Inc.

Chapter 10: p. 306: Figure 10.1 from Lila R. Gleitman & Mark Liberman (Eds.), *Language: An Invitation to Cognitive Science,* 2nd ed., vol. 1 (Cambridge, MA: MIT Press, 1995) p. 90. Reprinted by permission of Steve Heine. **p. 315:** Table 10.1 from J. F. Werker, V. L. Lloyd, J. E. Pegg, & L. Polka (1996). Putting the baby in the bootstraps: Toward a more complete understanding of the role of the input in infant speech processing. In J. L. Morgan & Katherine Demuth (Eds.), *Signal to syntax: Bootstrapping from speech to grammar in early acquisition* (pp. 427–447). Mahwah, NJ: Lawrence Erlbaum Associates. Reprinted by permission. **p. 308:** Figure 10.2 from J. Berko (1958). The child's learning of English morphology. *Word, 14,* 150-177. Reprinted by permission. **p. 321:** Figure 10.4 reprinted by permission of the publisher from *A First Language* by R. Brown, Cambridge, MA: Harvard University Press, Copyright © 1973 by the President and Fellows of Harvard College. **p. 330:** Figure 10.5 from D. E. Rumelhart & J. L. McClelland (1986). On learning the past tenses of English verbs. In J. L. McClelland & D. E. Rumelhart (Eds.), *Parallel distributed processing: Explorations in the microstructure of cognition. Vol. 2 .* MIT Press.

Chapter 11: p. 339: Figure 11.1 from J. S. Johnson & E. L. Newport (1989). "Critical-period effects in second language learning: The influence of maturational state on the acquisition of English as a second language." *Cognitive Psychology, 21,* 60–99. Reprinted by permission. **p. 345:** Figure 11.2 reprinted by permission of the publisher from *The Signs of Language* by E. Klima and U. Bellugi. Cambridge, MA: Harvard University Press, Copyright © 1979 by the President and Fellows of Harvard College. **p. 352:** Figure 11.3 from S. Kassin (1995). *Psychology.* Boston: Houghton Mifflin. Reprinted by permission. **p. 353:** Figure 11.4 from D. Bishop and K. Mogford (Eds.), *Language Development in Exceptional Circumstances.* (Edinburgh: Churchill Livingstone), p. 181. Reprinted by permission of Churchill Livingstone. **p. 355:** Figure 11.5 from A. E. Fowler, R. Gelman, & L. R. Gleitman (1994). The course of language learning in children with Down syndrome. In H. Tager-Flusberg (Ed.), *Constraints on language acquisition: Studies of atypical children* (pp. 94–140). Hillsdale, NJ: Lawrence Erlbaum Associates. Adapted with permission.

Chapter 12: p. 363: Figure 12.1 From Kandel, Shwartz, & Jessell (1991). *Principles of Neural Science* (3rd Ed.). © 1991 by Appleton & Lange. **p. 367:** Figure 12.2 from M. I. Posner & M. E. Raichle, *Images of Mind.* (New York: Scientific American Library: Scientific American Books, 1994), p. 19. **p. 367:** Figure 12.3 from J. L. Signoret et. al. (1984). Rediscovery of Leborgne's brain: Anatomical Description with CT scan. *Brain & Language, 22,* pp. 303–319. Reprinted by permission of Academic Press. **p. 369:** Figure 12.4 reprinted from M. Kutas & S. A. Hillyard (1988). "Contextual effects in language comprehension: Studies using event-related brain potentials." In F. Plum (Ed.), *Language, Communication, and the Brain.* (pp. 87–100). New York: Raven Press. **p. 370:** Figure 12.5 from E. J. Metter, et. al. (1985). "Comparison of x-ray CT, glucose metabolism and postmortem data in a patient with multiple infarctions." *Neurology, 35,* pp. 1695–1701. Reprinted by permission of Lippincott Raven Publishers. **p. 376:** Figure 12.6 from S. Kassin (1995). *Psychology.* Boston: Houghton Mifflin. Reprinted by permission. **p. 382:** Figure 12.7 from G. Hickok, K. Say, U. Bellugi & E. S. Klima (1996). "The basis of hemispheric asymmetries for language and spatial cognition: Clues from focal brain damage in two deaf native singers." *Aphasiology, 10,* 577–591. Reprinted by permission. **p. 384:** Table 12.3 from M. S. Hough (1990). "Narrative comprehension in adults with right and left hemisphere brain-damage: Theme organization." *Brain and Language, 38,* 253–277.

NAME INDEX

SUBJECT INDEX